OFFICIAL TOURIST B

C000053642

Days Out For All

Contents

VisitBritain

VisitBritain is the organisation created to market Britain
to the rest of the world, and England to the British.

Formed by the merger of the British Tourist Authority
and the English Tourism Council, its mission is to build
the value of tourism by creating world-class
destination brands and marketing campaigns.

It will also build partnerships with – and provide
insights to – other organisations which have a stake in
British and English tourism.

Eureka! Halifax, West Yorkshire

This Enjoy England guide is packed with information from what to see and do, where to stay, and how to get there. In fact, everything you need to know to enjoy a great day out.

The guide that gives you
more

endless
possibilities
for great
days out
and
fun-filled
holidays

Places to visit

When it comes to having a great time, there's no better place than England! It's brimming with new and interesting attractions, theme-park thrills, natural wonders, fascinating history and colourful culture. There really is something to keep everyone happy whatever their age and interests. Dip into this guide and you'll find more than 2,000 places to visit plus Blue Flag and other beaches in the country. And, if you turn to the back, there's a selection of special offer vouchers for great savings and added extras.

You may also like to tie in your visit with a special event – a selection is featured at the beginning of each county.

Quality accommodation

Choose from quality-assessed hotels, B&B guest accommodation, self-catering properties, and camping & caravan parks to suit all budgets and tastes. Every establishment featured in this guide is a member of an Enjoy England Quality Rose assessment scheme – just look for the Quality Rose, the official marque of Enjoy England quality-assessed accommodation – or The British Graded Holiday Parks Scheme.

Tourist Information Centres

Tourist Information Centres offer a wealth of local information. Phone before you go or call in person. You'll find a useful list of Tourist Information Centre contacts within each regional section, or you can text **TIC LOCATE** to 64118 to find the one nearest to you.

St Michael's Mount, Marazion, Cornwall

How to use
this guide

In this brand-new Days Out For All guide, you'll find a
fantastic selection of activities and attractions, Blue Flag
beaches and a choice of accommodation including hotels,
B&B guest accommodation, self-catering properties, and
camping & caravan parks.

Finding entries is easy

The guide is divided into four regional sections – Northern England, Central England, South West England and South East England – each including attractions, beaches and accommodation in the area. Turn to page 19 to find a map showing the four regions and a list of the counties within each one.

Attractions

Attractions within each region are divided into counties. To help you find a particular type of experience, attractions are listed by category (see page 9) within each county. You can also begin with the maps, starting on page 20, which show all attractions with an enhanced entry, then turn to the index at the back to find the page number.

Look out for entries that include a special offer – vouchers are at the back of the guide – and for the Visitor Attraction Quality Assurance sign that guarantees a first-class experience (see page 8).

If you know the name of the attraction you wish to visit, turn to the index for a complete alphabetical listing.

Beaches

Blue Flag and other beaches are listed alphabetically by name and with over 200 to choose from you can be assured of finding the perfect day by the sea. Blue Flag is a prestigious, international award only given to beaches that have achieved the highest quality in water, facilities, safety, environmental education and management. ENCAMS manages the Blue Flag Award scheme in England. The Blue Flag beaches featured in this guide received their awards in summer 2006. For further information, visit blueflag.org.uk.

Accommodation

Detailed accommodation entries are listed by their marketing location and type of establishment, and include descriptions, prices and facilities (see page 15). You'll also find special offers and themed breaks to suit your interests and budget.

Each property has been assessed by Enjoy England assessors to nationally agreed standards so that you can book with confidence knowing your accommodation has been checked and rated for quality.

Use the maps starting on page 20 to pinpoint the location of all the accommodation featured. Then refer to the place index at the back of the guide to find the page number. If you know the name of the establishment, use the property index.

Quality Assurance Service
The Visitor Attraction

A visitor attraction can range from pure fun to high culture and includes historic houses, castles, farm attractions, country parks, museums and theme parks. **When you are looking for that perfect day out, VisitBritain's Visitor Attraction Quality Assurance Service (VAQAS) can help.**

The Visitor Attraction Quality Assurance Service offers a quality assessment on all areas of the attraction that impact on the visitor experience. The assessment is an annual visit that takes place at any time the attraction is open to the public and is carried out by an experienced quality assurance assessor. Assessors will 'experience' all aspects of an attraction, from initial phone enquiries to departure. They will sample all facilities and activities such as guided tours, rides, or film shows, as well as catering, retail and toilet facilities.

All well-run attractions that meet the required standard receive the accreditation of **Quality Assured Visitor Attraction**. If the VAQAS sign is on display you can be assured of an excellent day out for all the family.

Attraction
entries explained

Each attraction entry contains information provided by the management to help you decide if you wish to visit it. Our aim has been to ensure that it is as objective and factual as possible.

1 Attraction name
2 Address
3 Telephone and website
4 Opening and admission information
5 Attraction category/categories, including VAQAS if applicable
6 Detailed description
7 Facility symbols and map reference
8 Indicates a voucher is available

Attractions are listed under the following categories within each county

 Family fun

 Nature and wildlife

 Historic England

 Outdoor activities

 Entertainment and culture

 Food and drink

 Relaxing and pampering

Look out, too, for the Quality Assured Visitor Attraction sign. This indicates that the attraction is assessed annually and meets the standards required to receive the quality marque.

Key to attraction facilities
Cafe/restaurant .... 🍵
Picnic area .... 🛋
No dogs except service dogs .... 🐕
Partial disabled access .... ♿
Full disabled access .... ♿

(1) **Chelsea Physic Garden** (5)

(2) Swan Walk, (off Royal Hospital Road), London SW3 4HS
(3) **t** (020) 7352 5646
w chelseaphysicgarden.co.uk
open Apr-Oct, Wed 1200-dusk, Thu-Fri 1200-1700, Sun 1200-1800. Last entry 30 mins
(4) before closing.
admission Adult: £7

London's oldest botanic garden and best-kept secret – a magical 300-year-old oasis in the heart of the capital. Discover the myriad uses of plants via free guided tours with entertaining (6) guides, enjoy delicious refreshments at the garden's renowned tearoom, and browse the eclectic selection of garden-related gifts in the shop.

🍵 🐕 ♿ Map ref X00 (7)

V *voucher offer – see back section* (8)

A key to symbols can also be found on the inside back cover.

Accommodation ratings and awards
at a glance

Reliable, rigorous, easy to use – look out for the following ratings and awards to help you choose with confidence:

Ratings made easy

★ Simple, practical, no frills

★★ Well presented and well run

★★★ Good level of quality and comfort

★★★★ Excellent standard throughout

★★★★★ Exceptional with a degree of luxury

For full details of Enjoy England Quality Rose assessment schemes, go online at **enjoyengland.com/quality**

Guest accommodation – Diamond ratings

Establishments with a diamond rating were awaiting re-assessment under the new common standards star-rating scheme at the time of going to press.

rest assured with our official quality ratings

Star ratings

Establishments are awarded a rating of one to five stars based on a combination of quality of facilities and services provided. Put simply, the more stars, the higher the quality and the greater the range of facilities and level of service.

The process to arrive at a star rating is very thorough to ensure that when you book accommodation you can be confident it will meet your expectations. Enjoy England professional assessors visit establishments annually and work to strict criteria to rate the available facilities and service.

A quality score is awarded for every aspect of the experience. For hotels and guest accommodation this includes the comfort of the bed, the quality of the breakfast and dinner and, most importantly, the cleanliness. For self-catering properties the assessors also take into consideration the layout and design of the accommodation, the ease of use of all the appliances, the range and quality of the kitchen equipment, and the variety and presentation of the visitor information provided. Camping and caravan parks are awarded a rating following an assessment of the quality, cleanliness,

maintenance and condition of the various facilities provided. The warmth of welcome and the level of care that each establishment offers its guests are noted, and places that go the extra mile to make every stay a special one will be rewarded with high scores for quality.

All the national assessing bodies (VisitBritain, VisitScotland, Visit Wales and the AA*) now operate to a common set of standards for rating hotels, guest accommodation and self-catering properties, giving holidaymakers and travellers a clear guide on exactly what to expect at each level. An explanation of all star ratings can be found on pages 444-446.

The range of accommodation within this guide differs greatly in style, so to help you make your choice, the rating scheme also includes categories that give an indication of the type of establishment. Descriptions of these can be found on the following pages.

*The AA does not assess self-catering properties.

Gold and Silver Awards

These Enjoy England awards are highly prized by proprietors and are only given to hotels and bed and breakfast accommodation offering the highest levels of quality within their star rating, particularly in areas of housekeeping, service and hospitality, bedrooms, bathrooms and food.

Walkers and Cyclists Welcome

Participants in these Enjoy England schemes actively encourage walking and cycling. Proprietors go out of their way to make special provision for guests who enjoy these activities to ensure they have a comfortable stay.

National Accessible Scheme

Establishments with a National Accessible rating provide access and facilities for guests with special visual, hearing and mobility needs (see page 20).

Caravan Holiday Home Award Scheme

VisitBritain runs an award scheme for individual holiday caravan homes on highly graded caravan parks. In addition to complying with standards for Holiday Parks, these exceptional caravans must have a shower or bath, toilet, mains electricity and water heating (at no extra charge) and a fridge (many also have a colour TV).

Categories explained

The following categories will help you decide which type of accommodation is right for you, whether you are seeking a non-stop, city-buzz holiday; a quiet weekend away; a home-from-home break or camping fun for all the family.

Hotels

Hotel	A minimum of six bedrooms, but more likely to have over 20.
Small Hotel	A maximum of 20 bedrooms and likely to be more personally run.
Country House Hotel	Set in ample grounds or gardens, in a rural or semi-rural location, with the emphasis on peace and quiet.
Town House Hotel	In a city or town-centre location, high quality with a distinctive and individual style. Maximum of 50 bedrooms, with a high ratio of staff to guests. Possibly no dinner served, but room service available. Might not have a dining room, so breakfast may be served in the bedrooms.
Metro Hotel	A city or town-centre hotel offering full hotel services, but no dinner. Located within easy walking distance of a range of places to eat. Can be of any size.
Budget Hotel	Part of a large branded hotel group, offering limited services. A Budget Hotel is not awarded a star rating.

Hotels awaiting re-assessment under the common standards rating scheme may have a category that is not entirely representative of the facilities and services they offer.

Guest Accommodation

Guest Accommodation	Encompassing a wide range of establishments from one-room bed and breakfasts to larger properties, which may offer dinner and hold an alcohol licence.
Bed and Breakfast	Accommodating no more than six people, the owners of these establishments welcome you into their home as a special guest.
Guest House	Generally comprising more than three rooms. Dinner is unlikely to be available (if it is, it will need to be booked in advance). May possibly be licensed.
Farmhouse	Bed and breakfast, and sometimes dinner, but always on a farm.
Restaurant with Rooms	A licensed restaurant is the main business but there will be a small number of bedrooms, with all the facilities you would expect, and breakfast the following morning.
Inn	Pubs with rooms, and many with restaurants as well.

Guest accommodation awaiting re-assessment under the common standards rating scheme may have a category that is not entirely representative of the facilities and services they offer.

Self Catering

Self Catering	Choose from cosy country cottages, smart town-centre apartments, seaside villas, grand country houses for large family gatherings, and even quirky conversions of windmills, railway carriages and lighthouses. Most take bookings by the week, generally from a Friday or Saturday, but short breaks are increasingly offered, particularly outside the main season.
Serviced Apartments	City-centre serviced apartments are an excellent alternative to hotel accommodation, offering hotel services such as daily cleaning, room service, concierge and business centre services, but with a kitchen and lounge area that allow you to eat in and relax when you choose. A telephone and Internet access tend to be standard. Prices are generally based on the property, so they often represent excellent value for money for families and larger groups. Serviced apartments tend to accept bookings for any length of period, and many are operated by agencies whose in-depth knowledge and choice of properties makes searching easier at busy times.

Camping and Caravan Parks

Camping Park   These sites only have pitches available for tents.

Touring Park   If you are planning to travel with your own caravan, motor home or tent, then look for a Touring Park.

Holiday Park   If you want to hire a caravan holiday home for a short break or longer holiday, or are looking to buy your own holiday home, a Holiday Park is the right choice. They range from small, rural sites to larger parks with all the added extras, such as a pool.

Many parks will offer a combination of these categories.

Holiday Village   Holiday Villages usually comprise a variety of types of accommodation, with the majority in custom-built rooms, chalets for example. The option to book on a bed and breakfast, or dinner, bed and breakfast basis is normally available. A range of facilities, entertainment and activities are also provided which may, or may not, be included in the tariff.

Holiday Villages must meet a minimum entry requirement for both the provision and quality of facilities and services, including fixtures, fittings, furnishings, decor and any other extra facilities. Progressively higher levels of quality and customer care are provided at each star level.

Accommodation
entries explained

Each accommodation entry contains detailed information to help you decide if it is right for you. This has been provided by proprietors and our aim is to ensure that it is as objective and factual as possible.

(1) (2) (3) (4)   (5)   (6) (7)

AMBLESIDE, Cumbria   Map ref 2A3   **HOTEL**

★ ★ ★
**COUNTRY HOUSE HOTEL
GOLD AWARD**

Hanover Lodge Hotel
Bury Road, Ambleside LA23 1HO   **t** (015394) 555329   **f** (015394) 555331
e info@hanoverlodge.co.uk   **w** hanoverlodge.co.uk

B&B per room per night
s £80.00-£120.00
d £150.00-£250.00
HB per person per night
£110.00-£160.00

open All year
bedrooms 35 double, 20 twin, 14 single, 2 family
bathrooms All en suite
payment Credit/debit card, euros

In 63 acres of beautiful countryside, the Hanover offers a choice of luxury bedrooms, some featuring jacuzzi bath, four-poster bed and extensive views. Open fires and comfortable sofas abound in spacious lounges. Our award-winning restaurant is open for breakfast, lunch and dinner for residents and non-residents.

⊕ *Follow signs for Ambleside and the A593 Coniston. On A593 go over Rothay Bridge and turn immediately right into Bury Road.*

❤ *Special weekend and mid-week breaks available throughout the year.*

Pets   Room   General   Leisure

Sample enhanced entry

(8) (9)   (10)   (11) (12)

1 Listing under town or village with map reference

2 Enjoy England star rating plus Gold or Silver Award where applicable

3 Category

4 Prices

    Hotels – per room for bed and breakfast (B&B) and per person for half board (HB)

Guest accommodation – per room for bed and breakfast (B&B) and per person for evening meal
Self catering – per unit per week for low and high season
Camping and caravan parks – per pitch per night for touring pitches; per unit per week for caravan holiday homes

5 Establishment name and booking details

6 Indicates when the establishment is open

7 Accommodation details and payment accepted

8 Accessible rating where applicable

9 Walkers/Cyclists Welcome where applicable

10 Travel directions

11 Special promotions and themed breaks

12 At-a-glance facility symbols

**A key to symbols can be found on the back-cover flap.
Keep it open for easy reference.**

National
Accessible Scheme

Finding suitable accommodation is not always easy, especially if you have to seek out ground-floor rooms or large print menus. Use the National Accessible Scheme to help you make your choice.

**accessible
accommodation
for a
comfortable
stay**

Proprietors of accommodation taking part in the National Accessible Scheme have gone out of their way to ensure a comfortable stay for guests with special hearing, visual or mobility needs. These exceptional places are full of extra touches to make everyone's visit trouble-free, from handrails, ramps and step-free entrances (ideal for buggies too) to level-access showers and colour contrast in the bathrooms. Members of the staff or owners may have attended a disability awareness course and will know what assistance will really be appreciated.

Appropriate National Accessible Scheme symbols (shown opposite) are included in the guide entries. If you have additional needs or special requirements we strongly recommend that you make sure these can be met by your chosen establishment before you confirm your reservation.

The National Accessible Scheme forms part of the Tourism for All Campaign that is being promoted by VisitBritain and national/regional tourism organisations. Additional help and guidance on finding suitable holiday accommodation for those with special needs can be obtained from:

Tourism for All
c/o Vitalise, Shap Road Industrial Estate, Kendal LA9 6NZ

information helpline 0845 124 9971
reservations 0845 124 9973
(lines open 9-5 Mon-Fri)

f (01539) 735567

e info@tourismforall.org.uk

w tourismforall.org.uk

The criteria VisitBritain and national/regional tourism organisations have adopted do not necessarily conform to British Standards or to Building Regulations. They reflect what the organisations understand to be acceptable to meet the practical needs of guests with mobility or sensory impairments and encourage the industry to increase access to all.

Mobility Symbols

 Typically suitable for a person with sufficient mobility to climb a flight of steps but who would benefit from fixtures and fittings to aid balance.

 Typically suitable for a person with restricted walking ability and for those who may need to use a wheelchair some of the time and can negotiate a maximum of three steps.

 Typically suitable for a person who depends on the use of a wheelchair and transfers unaided to and from the wheelchair in a seated position. This person may be an independent traveller.

 Typically suitable for a person who depends on the use of a wheelchair in a seated position. This person also requires personal/mechanical assistance to aid transfer (eg carer, hoist).

 Access Exceptional is awarded to establishments that meet the requirements of independent wheelchair users or assisted wheelchair users shown above and also fulfil more demanding requirements with reference to the British Standards BS8300:2001.

Visual Impairment Symbols

 Typically provides key additional services and facilities to meet the needs of visually impaired guests.

 Typically provides a higher level of additional services and facilities to meet the needs of visually impaired guests.

Hearing Impairment Symbols

 Typically provides key additional services and facilities to meet the needs of guests with hearing impairment.

 Typically provides a higher level of additional services and facilities to meet the needs of guests with hearing impairment.

England's counties

Northern England

1 Cheshire
2 County Durham
3 Cumbria
4 East Riding of Yorkshire
5 Greater Manchester
6 Lancashire
7 Merseyside
8 North Yorkshire
9 Northumberland
10 South Yorkshire
11 Tees Valley
12 Tyne and Wear
13 West Yorkshire

Note: All Yorkshire counties can be found under Yorkshire

Central England

14 Bedfordshire
15 Cambridgeshire
16 Derbyshire
17 Essex
18 Herefordshire
19 Hertfordshire
20 Leicestershire
21 Lincolnshire
22 Norfolk
23 Northamptonshire
24 Nottinghamshire
25 Rutland
26 Shropshire
27 Staffordshire
28 Suffolk
29 Warwickshire
30 West Midlands
31 Worcestershire

South East England

32 Berkshire
33 Buckinghamshire
34 East Sussex
35 Hampshire
36 Isle of Wight
37 Kent
38 London
39 Oxfordshire
40 Surrey
41 West Sussex

South West England

42 Bristol
43 Cornwall
44 Devon
45 Dorset
46 Gloucestershire
47 Isles of Scilly
48 Somerset
49 Wiltshire

The map opposite will help you to locate the counties which fall within each region in this guide. To help readers, we do not refer to unitary authorities.

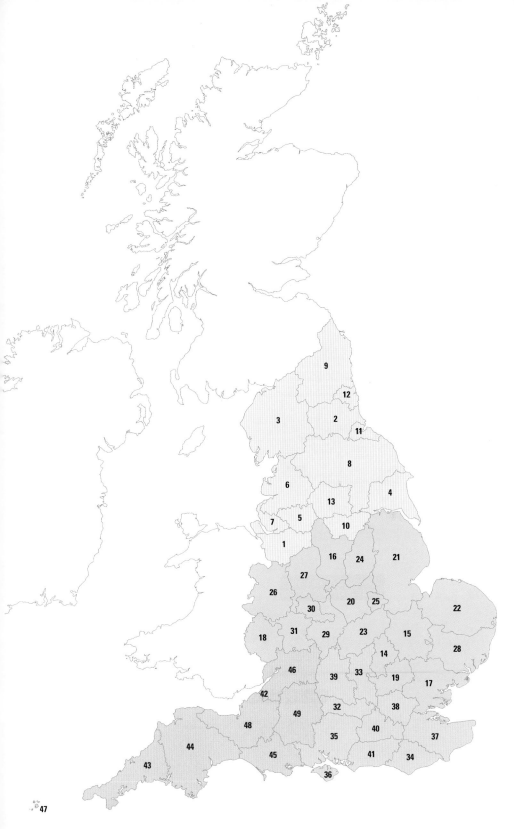

Map 1

A   B

Location
Maps

1

All place names appearing in the accommodation section of this guide are shown in black type on the maps. This enables you to find other places in your chosen area which may have suitable accommodation – the place index (at the back of this guide) gives page numbers.

Places to visit with an enhanced entry in this guide are shown in purple – use the attraction index to find the page number.

MAP 5
Newcastle upon Tyne
Carlisle

MAP 4
York
Manchester
Lincoln

Birmingham
Ipswich

MAP 2
Oxford
MAPS 6&7
Bristol
London
Dover
Southampton
MAP 1
MAP 3
Exeter

2

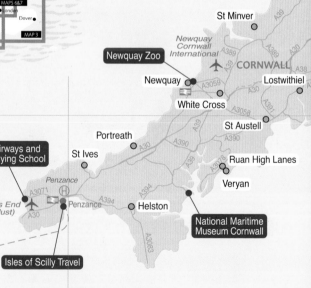

Boscastle

St Minver

A39

Newquay
Cornwall
International

Newquay Zoo

CORNWALL
A38

Newquay
A3059
Lostwithiel

White Cross
A3058

St Austell

A39
A390
A390

Portreath
A30

St Ives
A39

Westward Airways and
Land's End Flying School

Ruan High Lanes

Veryan

Penzance

Land's End
(St Just)
Penzance
A394
Helston

National Maritime
Museum Cornwall

3

Tresco *Isles of Scilly*
St Mary's
Isles of Scilly

Isles of Scilly Travel

Key to regions: South West England

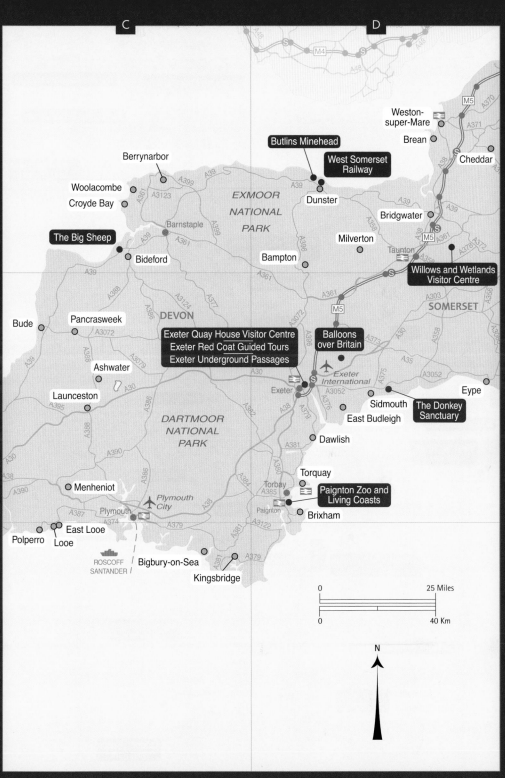

Map 1

Map 2

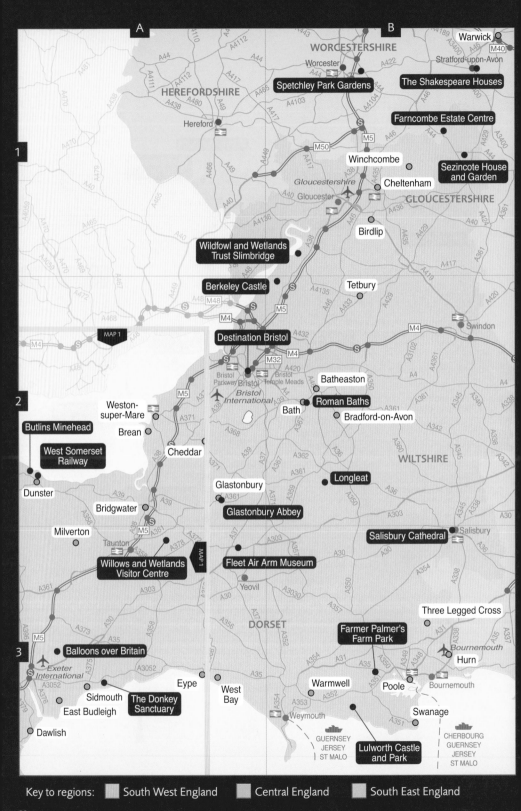

A   B

WORCESTERSHIRE

Warwick

Worcester

Stratford-upon-Avon

Spetchley Park Gardens

The Shakespeare Houses

HEREFORDSHIRE

Farncombe Estate Centre

Hereford

Sezincote House and Garden

1

Winchcombe

Gloucestershire

Cheltenham

GLOUCESTERSHIRE

Gloucester

Birdlip

Wildfowl and Wetlands Trust Slimbridge

Berkeley Castle

Tetbury

Swindon

Destination Bristol

MAP 1

Bristol Parkway

Bristol Temple Meads

Batheaston

2

Bristol International

Roman Baths

Weston-super-Mare

Bath

Bradford-on-Avon

Brean

Butlins Minehead

Cheddar

WILTSHIRE

West Somerset Railway

Dunster

Glastonbury

Longleat

Bridgwater

Glastonbury Abbey

Milverton

Taunton

Salisbury Cathedral

Salisbury

Willows and Wetlands Visitor Centre

MAP 1

Fleet Air Arm Museum

Yeovil

Three Legged Cross

DORSET

Farmer Palmer's Farm Park

Bournemouth

3

Balloons over Britain

Hurn

Exeter International

Bournemouth

Eype

West Bay

Warmwell

Poole

Sidmouth

The Donkey Sanctuary

Swanage

East Budleigh

Dawlish

Weymouth

GUERNSEY JERSEY ST MALO

CHERBOURG GUERNSEY JERSEY ST MALO

Lulworth Castle and Park

Key to regions: South West England   Central England   South East England

Map 2

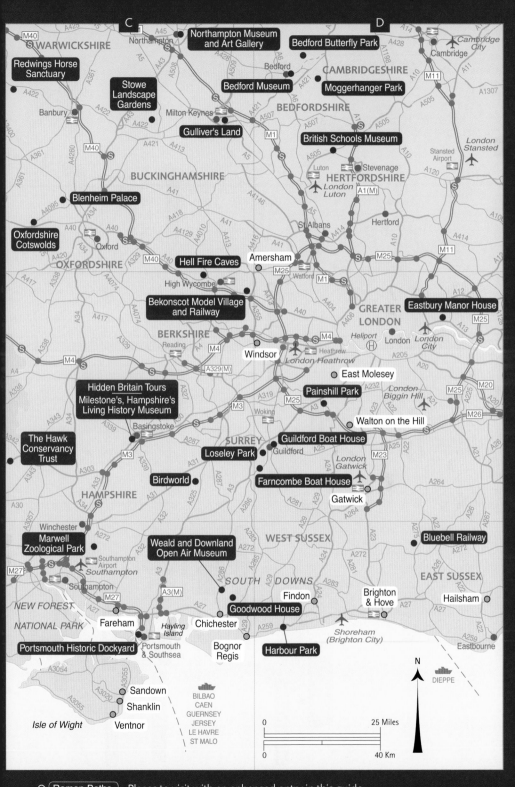

C

D

Redwings Horse Sanctuary

WARWICKSHIRE

Northampton Museum and Art Gallery

Northampton

Bedford Butterfly Park

Cambridge City

Cambridge

Stowe Landscape Gardens

Banbury

Bedford

CAMBRIDGESHIRE

Milton Keynes

Bedford Museum

Moggerhanger Park

BEDFORDSHIRE

Gulliver's Land

British Schools Museum

London Stansted

Blenheim Palace

Luton

Stevenage

Stansted Airport

HERTFORDSHIRE

London Luton

Oxfordshire Cotswolds

Oxford

St Albans

Hertford

OXFORDSHIRE

Hell Fire Caves

Amersham

BUCKINGHAMSHIRE

High Wycombe

Watford

Bekonscot Model Village and Railway

BERKSHIRE

GREATER LONDON

Eastbury Manor House

Reading

Heliport

London

London City

Windsor

London Heathrow

Heathrow

East Molesey

London Biggin Hill

Hidden Britain Tours
Milestone's, Hampshire's Living History Museum

Painshill Park

Basingstoke

Woking

Walton on the Hill

The Hawk Conservancy Trust

SURREY

Guildford Boat House

Loseley Park

Guildford

London Gatwick

Birdworld

HAMPSHIRE

Farncombe Boat House

Gatwick

Winchester

Bluebell Railway

Marwell Zoological Park

Weald and Downland Open Air Museum

WEST SUSSEX

SOUTH DOWNS

EAST SUSSEX

Southampton Airport

Southampton

Findon

Brighton & Hove

Hailsham

NEW FOREST

Fareham

Hayling Island

Goodwood House

Chichester

NATIONAL PARK

Portsmouth & Southsea

Shoreham (Brighton City)

Eastbourne

Portsmouth Historic Dockyard

Bognor Regis

Harbour Park

N

DIEPPE

Sandown

BILBAO
CAEN
GUERNSEY
JERSEY
LE HAVRE
ST MALO

Shanklin

Isle of Wight

Ventnor

0   25 Miles

0   40 Km

○ Roman Baths   Places to visit with an enhanced entry in this guide

● East Molesey   Locations offering accommodation in this guide

Map 3

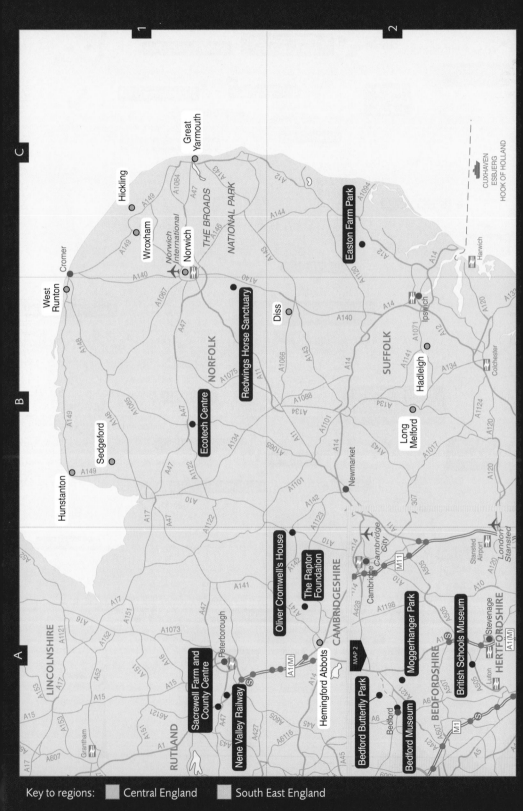

Key to regions: ▮ Central England ▮ South East England

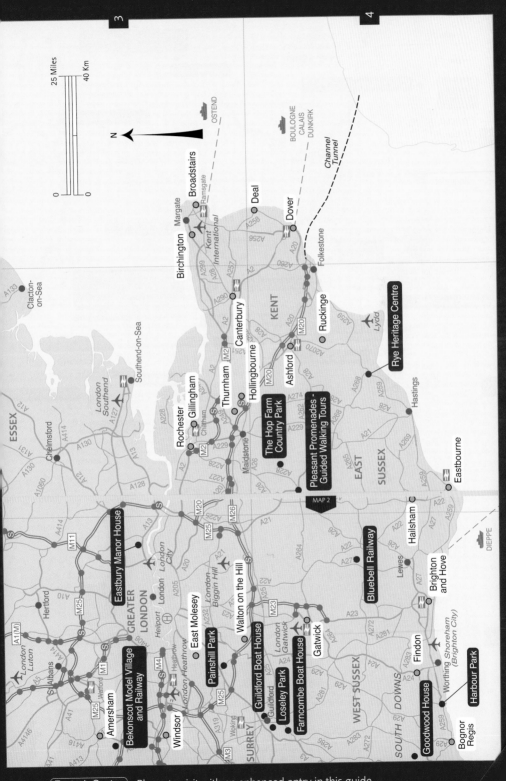

Map 3

25 Miles
40 Km

N

OSTEND

BOULOGNE
CALAIS
DUNKIRK

Channel
Tunnel

Broadstairs
Ramsgate
Margate
Birchington
Kent
International
Deal
Dover
Folkestone

Canterbury
KENT
Ruckinge
Rye Heritage Centre
Lydd
Hastings

A133
Clacton-
on-Sea

ESSEX
Chelmsford
Southend-on-Sea
London
Southend

Rochester
Gillingham
Chatham
Thurnham
Hollingbourne
Ashford
The Hop Farm
Country Park
Pleasant Promenades -
Guided Walking Tours
Maidstone

EAST
SUSSEX
Eastbourne

MAP 2

Eastbury Manor House

Hertford

M11
London
City
GREATER
LONDON
London
Biggin Hill

Bluebell Railway
Hailsham
Lewes
Brighton
and Hove

DIEPPE

A1(M)
London
Luton
St Albans
Watford
Amersham

Bekonscot Model Village
and Railway

Windsor
London
Heathrow
Heliport
London

East Molesey
Painshill Park
Walton on the Hill
London
Gatwick
Gatwick
Guildford Boat House
Loseley Park
Guildford
Farncombe Boat House
Woking

SURREY

WEST SUSSEX
SOUTH DOWNS
Findon
Worthing
Shoreham
(Brighton City)
Harbour Park

Goodwood House
Bognor
Regis

○ (Ecotech Centre)   Places to visit with an enhanced entry in this guide

● (Great Yarmouth)   Locations offering accommodation in this guide

Map 4

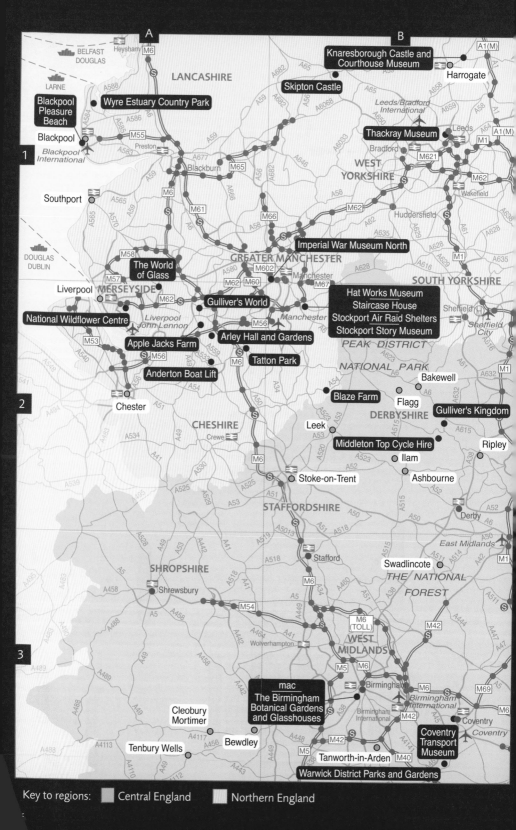

A **B**

BELFAST DOUGLAS · Heysham · M6

LARNE

LANCASHIRE

A588 A682 A65

Knaresborough Castle and Courthouse Museum · Harrogate · A1(M)

Skipton Castle · A65

Wyre Estuary Country Park · A59 A682 A6068

Leeds/Bradford International

Blackpool Pleasure Beach · Blackpool · A584 A585 A586

Blackpool International · M55 · Preston · Blackburn · A677 · A646

Bradford · Leeds · A64 · A1(M)

Thackray Museum · M621 · M1

WEST YORKSHIRE

M62 · Wakefield

Southport · A565 · A570 · M6 · M61 · A6 · A58 · A646

Huddersfield · A635

DOUGLAS DUBLIN · M58 · M57

The World of Glass

Liverpool · MERSEYSIDE · M62

Imperial War Museum North

GREATER MANCHESTER · M602 · Manchester · M62 M60 · M67

SOUTH YORKSHIRE

Gulliver's World

National Wildflower Centre · Liverpool John Lennon

Hat Works Museum Staircase House Stockport Air Raid Shelters Stockport Story Museum

Sheffield · Sheffield City

M53 · **Arley Hall and Gardens** · M56

Apple Jacks Farm · M56 · M55 · A533 · A559 · M6

Tatton Park

PEAK DISTRICT NATIONAL PARK

Anderton Boat Lift · A54 · A49 · A530

Blaze Farm · **Bakewell** · A6

Chester · A51 · CHESHIRE · Crewe · A530 · A500

Flagg

DERBYSHIRE · **Gulliver's Kingdom**

A534 · A41 · A525 · A51 · A53

Leek · A523

Middleton Top Cycle Hire · **Ilam** · **Ashbourne**

Ripley

M6 · **Stoke-on-Trent** · A52

STAFFORDSHIRE · A50 · A515 · Derby

A5013 · A51 · A518

East Midlands · M1

SHROPSHIRE · A518 · Stafford

Swadlincote · THE NATIONAL FOREST

Shrewsbury · M54 · A5 · A449

M6 · A460 · A38

M6 (TOLL) · M42

WEST MIDLANDS

Wolverhampton · A464 · A41

M5 · M6

Birmingham International

mac The Birmingham Botanical Gardens and Glasshouses

Cleobury Mortimer · A4117 · A456 · **Bewdley**

Tenbury Wells · A443

M42 · M5 · **Tanworth-in-Arden** · M40

M6 · M69

Coventry · Coventry

Coventry Transport Museum

Warwick District Parks and Gardens

Key to regions: ▮ Central England ▮ Northern England

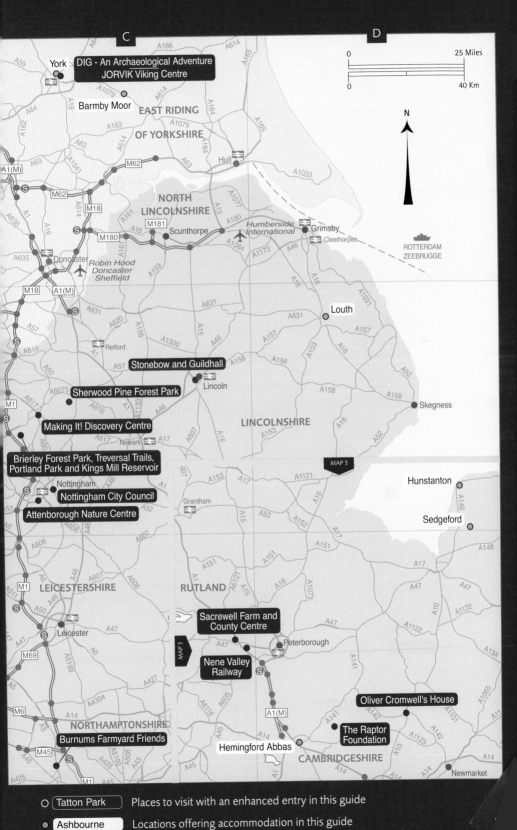

Map 4

25 Miles

40 Km

N

York

DIG - An Archaeological Adventure
JORVIK Viking Centre

Barmby Moor

EAST RIDING
OF YORKSHIRE

Hull

NORTH
LINCOLNSHIRE

Scunthorpe

Humberside
International

Grimsby

Cleethorpes

ROTTERDAM
ZEEBRUGGE

Doncaster

Robin Hood
Doncaster
Sheffield

Louth

Retford

Stonebow and Guildhall

Lincoln

Sherwood Pine Forest Park

LINCOLNSHIRE

Skegness

Making It! Discovery Centre

Newark

MAP 3

Brierley Forest Park, Treversal Trails,
Portland Park and Kings Mill Reservoir

Nottingham

Nottingham City Council

Grantham

Hunstanton

Attenborough Nature Centre

Sedgeford

LEICESTERSHIRE

RUTLAND

Leicester

MAP 3

Sacrewell Farm and
County Centre

Peterborough

Nene Valley
Railway

Oliver Cromwell's House

NORTHAMPTONSHIRE

Burnums Farmyard Friends

Hemingford Abbas

The Raptor
Foundation

CAMBRIDGESHIRE

Newmarket

○ Tatton Park Places to visit with an enhanced entry in this guide

● Ashbourne Locations offering accommodation in this guide

Map 5

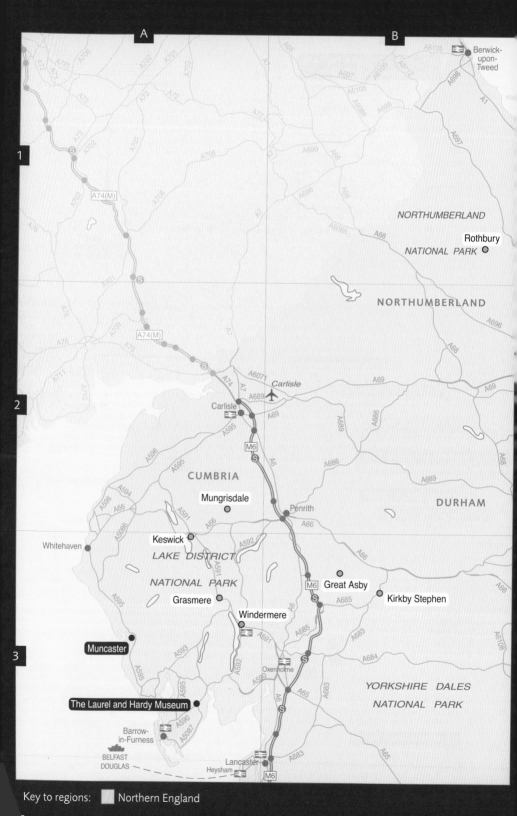

Key to regions: ☐ Northern England

Map 5

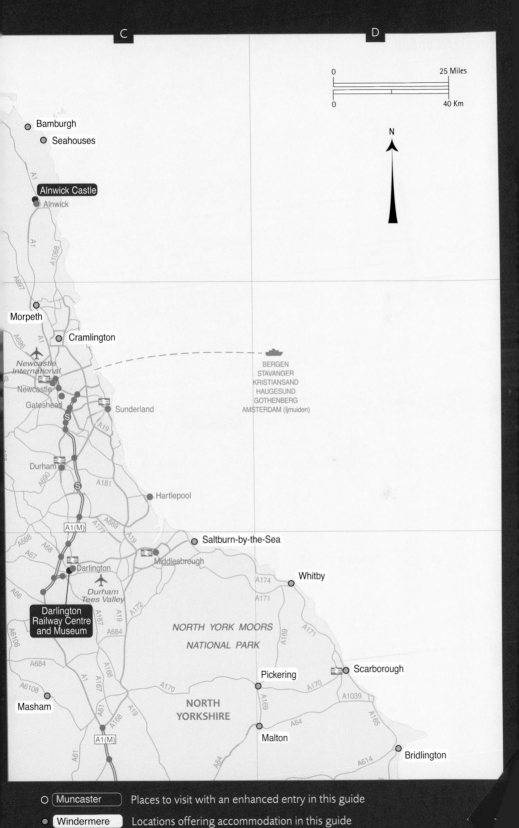

C

D

0   25 Miles

0   40 Km

N

Bamburgh

Seahouses

A1

Alnwick Castle
Alnwick

A1

A1068

A697

Morpeth

A696

Cramlington

Newcastle
International

BERGEN
STAVANGER
KRISTIANSAND
HAUGESUND
GOTHENBERG
AMSTERDAM (Ijmuiden)

Newcastle

Gateshead   Sunderland

S

A19

Durham

A690   A181

S

Hartlepool

A1(M)

A689

A688   A68

A67

A19

Saltburn-by-the-Sea

Middlesbrough

Darlington

A66

Durham
Tees Valley

A174   Whitby

Darlington
Railway Centre
and Museum

A167   A684

A171

A172

A19

NORTH YORK MOORS

NATIONAL PARK

A169   A171

A6108

A684

A168

A167

A1

Scarborough

A684

A170

Pickering

A170

A1039

A6108

A169

A64

Masham

A61

A168

A19

NORTH
YORKSHIRE

Malton

A165

A1(M)

A61

A64

Bridlington

A614

○ Muncaster   Places to visit with an enhanced entry in this guide

● Windermere   Locations offering accommodation in this guide

Map 6

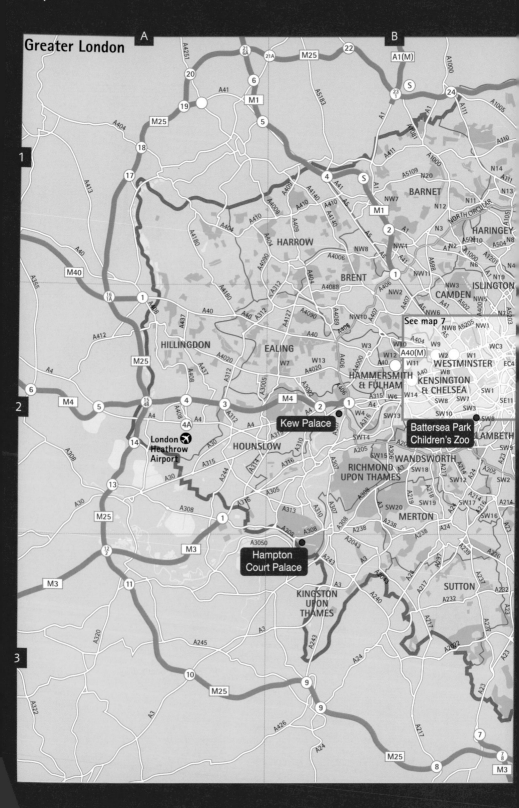

Greater London

Map 6

○ Kew Palace   Places to visit with an enhanced entry in this guide

Map 7

Central London

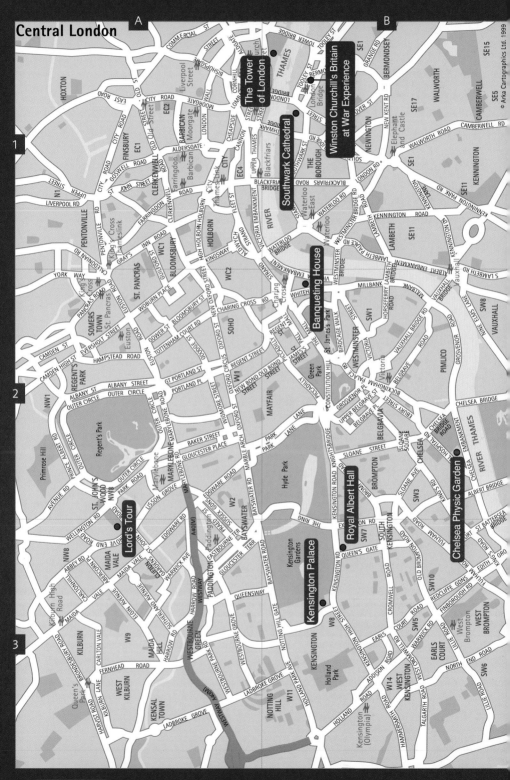

A

B

© Arka Cartographics Ltd. 1999

The Tower of London

Winston Churchill's Britain at War Experience

Southwark Cathedral

Banqueting House

Lord's Tour

Royal Albert Hall

Kensington Palace

Chelsea Physic Garden

○ (Lord's Tour) Places to visit with an enhanced entry in this guide

"It was on this very spot..."

Five of the greatest palaces ever built with centuries of extraordinary tales to tell.

Explore their stories and discover how the people of the palaces helped shape the world we live in today.

**You should have been here
Now you can be**

The Tower of London

Kensington Palace

...ngton Court Palace

Banqueting House

Kew Palace

Northern England

Making musical
connections in Liverpool

**Cheshire, County Durham,
Cumbria, Greater Manchester,
Lancashire, Merseyside,
Northumberland, Tees Valley,
Tyne and Wear, Yorkshire**

Investigate the mysteries
of The Deep, Hull

It's out of this **world...**

Windswept moors and breathtaking coastlines. Mirrored glass lakes and the magnificent cathedrals of York and Durham. The urban wonders of the Gateshead Millennium Bridge and Urbis in Manchester. Not forgetting all-year-round fun and games at Blackpool... **It's all just part of an ordinary day in England's proud and historic North.**

Full steam ahead at The Museum of Science & Industry, Manchester

explore. Wander lonely as a cloud in the Lake District – home to William Wordsworth and Samuel Taylor Coleridge – and then hop, skip and jump straight into Mr McGregor's garden at the charming World of Beatrix Potter Attraction, Windermere. Can you sense mystical goings-on at Alderley Edge, Cheshire, linked to the legends of King Arthur? Build a few castles along miles and miles of sandy beaches, such as Spittal and St Aidans, in the North East, or board a boat to Holy Island to behold the treasured Lindisfarne Gospels. Don't forget the binoculars; the Farne Islands are home to hundreds of thousands of puffins and dewy-eyed Grey Seals.

Hands-on heritage

Where did the Industrial Revolution gather pace? In northern England, of course! Experience its legacy in a multitude of ways. Meet people who once worked in cotton mills with a lifetime of stories to share with you at Quarry Bank Mill in Cheshire, and learn more about early industrialisation at the Armley Mills Leeds Industrial Museum. Get a taste of Victorian times at Saltaire World Heritage Site, a 'model' industrial village. Hear vivid tales at the National Coal Mining Museum in Wakefield, and let the youngsters try their skills at sweet making at the award-winning Beamish, The North of England Open Air Museum – alternatively they could attend lessons at the village school! Drift along a canal, the essential transport system of the period, past breathtaking countryside and urban heartlands. Imagine once more the romantic age of steam on the Settle-Carlisle or East Lancashire Railway (pinch your noses against the smell of clinker!), or watch the children gaze in wonder at the giant locomotives at the National Railway Museum in York and Locomotion in Shildon.

> From fearless Romans to dazzling Bollywood, there's an unbelievable range of attractions in the fantastic North

Run free

Take to the hills and fly a kite from high on the North York Moors, or gawp at the professionals at Sunderland International Kite Festival in June. Wide-open spaces abound in the National Parks – Yorkshire alone has over 1,000 square miles to

Roman Britain

Pace along Hadrian's Wall just as soldiers did nearly two millennia ago. The wall was a huge undertaking – 73 miles long and built in six years. Let the kids explore the many forts, milecastles and turrets that dot its length then bring their history lessons to life with a visit to Housesteads Fort, the most complete remaining outpost. The walled city of Chester is Britain's best-preserved Roman town – complete with partially excavated amphitheatre. The Dewa fortress – buried beneath the town – now lives on through the Dewa Roman Experience: wriggle into a suit of Roman armour and see, touch and smell just how it was!

Step back in time at Segedunum Roman Fort

Built to impress

Northern England has more than its fair share of remarkable buildings. Children will be thrilled to visit Alnwick Castle, magically transformed into a location for the renowned Harry Potter films, and you bet they just won't come down from the world's largest treehouse when it's time to go! A little less in the way of high spirits are required to tiptoe beneath the towering vaulted ceilings of York Minster, the largest medieval Gothic

Main Relax on the Shropshire Union Canal, near Bunbury **Left** Step into a miner's shoes at Killhope: The North of England Lead Mining Museum; capture the moment by the Millennium Bridge, NewcastleGateshead; relive childhood memories at The World of Beatrix Potter Attraction, Bowness-on-Windermere; surf's up at Saltburn-by-the-Sea

cathedral in Northern Europe. Equally impressive is 900-year-old Durham cathedral, which perches in all its glory high above the city. Built on simpler scales, the twin Anglo-Saxon monastery of Wearmouth-Jarrow, home to the Venerable Bede, is the UK's nomination for World Heritage Status in 2009. Fountains Abbey, Britain's largest monastic ruin, and adjacent Studley Royal Water Garden, are must-sees. Are your walls at home a bit bare? This wasn't a problem at Castle Howard where Canalettos, Holbeins and Gainsboroughs are just some of the art treasures on display. How about some nice wallpaper? William Morris did a good line – see for yourself in Liverpool's half-timbered Speke Hall.

Having a blast at Blackpool Pleasure Beach

Young hearts and minds

Candy floss and sticky rock, thrills and spills – head for the Pleasure Beach at Blackpool or Pleasureland Southport. Win Brownie points and book ringside seats at the UK's best circus at the Blackpool Tower! The Forbidden Corner, Leyburn, promises giggles galore as you get lost in the underground labyrinth of chambers and passages. Forget Sudoku, stimulate the brain cells at Rotherham's Magna, a science adventure centre where fun is unavoidable, or test out a fascinating world of hands-on exploration at Eureka! in Halifax. And, at the end of the day, Seven Stories, the Centre for Children's Books in Newcastle will touch their imaginations and put them in the mood for that bedtime tale...

City art and culture

You can't ignore the vibes of northern England's dynamic cities where regeneration is the name of the game. Enjoy the renaissance of Newcastle and Gateshead, highlighted by the stunning architecture of the Gateshead Millennium Bridge, and join in the festivities in Hull, all set to celebrate the 200th anniversary of the abolition

> ## Get with the Mersey beat, study contemporary art or simply build castles on a sandy beach

of slavery. Explore Liverpool and Manchester, both with music beating through their veins. Liverpool, European Capital of Culture 2008, is set to explode with spectacular events as it celebrates its 800th anniversary in 2007. Famed as the birthplace of The Beatles, you can follow in their footsteps, from the world-famous Cavern Club, to John Lennon's childhood home, Mendips, now in the care of the National Trust. Not into golden oldies? Catch some of the best new bands live at the Zanzibar, the Academy or the Royal Court. If contemporary art is your thing, you'll love Tate Liverpool.

In Manchester head for Salford Quays and The Lowry, an inspirational waterfront centre for the visual arts and entertainment. The gallery scene embraces Manchester Art Gallery, the Cornerhouse and The Whiteworth, and there's a choice of 50 free museums, including the Imperial War Museum North designed by Daniel Libeskind. In this region that's so culturally rich, check out new artists at the Baltic in Gateshead, the Centre for Contemporary Art, or listen to a favourite score at Opera North. The razzmatazz of Bollywood comes to the North when the International Indian Film Academy Awards hit Leeds, Bradford, Sheffield, York and Hull in summer 2007. Middlesbrough may not have attained city-status but the newly opened Middlesbrough Institute of Modern Art is a gallery of national importance, housing works by Emin, Hockney and Frink among others.

Further **information**

England's Northwest
t 0845 600 6040
w visitenglandsnorthwest.com

One NorthEast Tourism Team
t 0870 160 1781
w visitnortheastengland.com

Yorkshire Tourist Board
t 0870 609 0000
w yorkshirevisitor.com

Tourist Information Centres

When you arrive at your destination, visit a Tourist Information Centre for help with accommodation and information about local attractions and events, or email your request before you go.

Cheshire

Altrincham	20 Stamford New Road	(0161) 912 5931	tourist.information@trafford.gov.uk
Chester (Town Hall)	Northgate Street	(01244) 402111	tis@chestercc.gov.uk
Chester Visitor Centre	Vicars Lane	(01244) 402111	tis@chestercc.gov.uk
Congleton	High Street	(01260) 271095	tourism@congleton.gov.uk
Ellesmere Port	Kinsey Road	(0151) 356 7879	
Knutsford	Toft Road	(01565) 632611	ktic@macclesfield.gov.uk
Macclesfield	Town Hall	(01625) 504114	Informationcentre@macclesfield.gov.uk
Nantwich	Church Walk	(01270) 610983	touristi@crewe-nantwich.gov.uk
Northwich	1 The Arcade	(01606) 353534	tourism@valeroyal.gov.uk
Warrington	Bus Interchange	(01925) 428585	informationcentre@warrington.gov.uk
Wilmslow	Rectory Fields	(01625) 522275	i.hillaby@macclesfield.gov.uk

County Durham

Barnard Castle	Woodleigh, Flatts Road	(01833) 690909	tourism@teesdale.gov.uk
Bishop Auckland	Market Place	(01388) 604922	bishopauckland.tourisminfo@durham.gov.uk
Durham	2 Millennium Place	(0191) 384 3720	touristinfo@durhamcity.gov.uk
Middleton-in-Teesdale	10 Market Place	(01833) 641001	middletonplus@compuserve.com
Peterlee	4 Upper Yoden Way	(0191) 586 4450	touristinfo@peterlee.gov.uk
Stanhope	Durham Dales Centre	(01388) 527650	durham.dales.centre@durham.gov.uk

Cumbria

Alston Moor	Front Street	(01434) 382244	alston.tic@eden.gov.uk
Ambleside	Market Cross	(015394) 32582	amblesidetic@southlakeland.gov.uk
Appleby-in-Westmorland	Boroughgate	(017683) 51177	tic@applebytown.org.uk
Barrow-in-Furness	Duke Street	(01229) 894784	touristinfo@barrowbc.gov.uk
Bowness	Glebe Road	(015394) 42895	bownesstic@lake-district.gov.uk
Brampton*	Market Place	(016977) 3433	tourism@carlisle.gov.uk
Broughton in Furness	The Square	(01229) 716115	email@broughton-tic.fsnet.co.uk
Carlisle	Greenmarket	(01228) 625600	tourism@carlisle.gov.uk
Cockermouth	Market Street	(01900) 822634	email@cockermouth-tic.fsnet.co.uk
Coniston	Ruskin Avenue	(015394) 41533	mail@conistontic.org
Egremont	12 Main Street	(01946) 820693	email@egremont-tic.fsnet.co.uk

Grange-over-Sands	Main Street	(015395) 34026	grangetic@southlakeland.gov.uk
Kendal	Highgate	(01539) 725758	kendaltic@southlakeland.gov.uk
Keswick	Market Square	(017687) 72645	keswicktic@lake-district.gov.uk
Kirkby Lonsdale	24 Main Street	(015242) 71437	kltic@southlakeland.gov.uk
Kirkby Stephen	Market Street	(017683) 71199	ks.tic@eden.gov.uk
Maryport	Senhouse Street	(01900) 812101	maryporttic@allerdale.gov.uk
Millom*	Station Road	(01229) 774819	millomtic@copelandbc.gov.uk
Penrith	Middlegate	(01768) 867466	pen.tic@eden.gov.uk
Rheged		(01768) 860034	tic@rheged.com
Sedbergh	72 Main Street	(015396) 20125	tic@sedbergh.org.uk
Silloth-on-Solway	Liddell Street	(016973) 31944	sillothtic@allerdale.gov.uk
Southwaite	M6 Service Area	(016974) 73445	southwaitetic@visitscotland.com
Ullswater	Glenridding	(017684) 82414	ullswatertic@lake-district.gov.uk
Ulverston	County Square	(01229) 587120	ulverstontic@southlakeland.gov.uk
Whitehaven	Market Place	(01946) 852939	tic@copelandbc.gov.uk
Windermere	Victoria Street	(015394) 46499	windermeretic@southlakeland.gov.uk
Workington	21 Finkle Street	(01900) 606699	workingtontic@allerdale.gov.uk

Greater Manchester

Bolton	Le Mans Crescent	(01204) 334321	tourist.info@bolton.gov.uk
Bury	Market Street	(0161) 253 5111	touristinformation@bury.gov.uk
Manchester Visitor Information Centre	Lloyd Street	0871 222 8223	touristinformation@ marketing-manchester.co.uk
Oldham	12 Albion Street	(0161) 627 1024	ecs.tourist@oldham.gov.uk
Saddleworth	High Street, Uppermill	(01457) 870336	ecs.saddleworthtic@oldham.gov.uk
Salford	Salford Quays	(0161) 848 8601	tic@salford.gov.uk
Stockport	30 Market Place	(0161) 474 4444	tourist.information@stockport.gov.uk
Wigan	62 Wallgate	(01942) 825677	tic@wlct.org

Lancashire

Accrington	Blackburn Road	(01254) 872595	leisure@hyndburnbc.gov.uk
Ashton-under-Lyne	Wellington Road	(0161) 343 4343	tourist.information@mail.tameside.gov.uk
Barnoldswick	Fernlea Avenue	(01282) 666704	tourist.info@pendle.gov.uk
Blackburn	50-54 Church Street	(01254) 53277	visit@blackburn.gov.uk
Blackpool	1 Clifton Street	(01253) 478222	tourism@blackpool.gov.uk
Blackpool*	Central Promenade	(01253) 478222	tourism@blackpool.gov.uk
Burnley	Croft Street	(01282) 664421	tic@burnley.gov.uk
Cleveleys	Victoria Square	(01253) 853378	cleveleystic@wyrebc.gov.uk
Clitheroe	12-14 Market Place	(01200) 425566	tourism@ribblevalley.gov.uk
Fleetwood	The Esplanade	(01253) 773953	fleetwoodtic@wyrebc.gov.uk
Garstang	High Street	(01995) 602125	garstangtic@wyrebc.gov.uk
Lancaster	29 Castle Hill	(01524) 32878	lancastertic@lancaster.gov.uk
Lytham St Annes	67 St Annes Road West	(01253) 725610	touristinformation@fylde.gov.uk

Morecambe	Marine Road Central	(01524) 582808	morecambetic@lancaster.gov.uk
Pendle Heritage Centre	Park Hill	(01282) 661701	heritage.centre@pendle.gov.uk
Preston	Lancaster Road	(01772) 253731	tourism@preston.gov.uk
Rochdale	The Esplanade	(01706) 864928	tic@rochdale.gov.uk

Merseyside

Birkenhead	Woodside Ferry Terminal, Wirral	(0151) 647 6780	touristinfo@wirral.gov.uk
Liverpool	John Lennon Airport	(0151) 907 1057	info@visitliverpool.com
Liverpool 08 Place	Whitechapel	(0151) 233 2008	08place@liverpool.gov.uk
St Helens	Chalon Way East	(01744) 755150	info@sthelenstic.com
Southport	112 Lord Street	(01704) 533333	info@visitsouthport.com

Northumberland

Adderstone	Adderstone Garage	(01668) 213678	adderstone@hotmail.com
Alnwick	2 The Shambles	(01665) 510665	alnwicktic@alnwick.gov.uk
Amble*	Queen Street Car Park	(01665) 712313	ambletic@alnwick.gov.uk
Bellingham	Main Street	(01434) 220616	bellinghamtic@btconnect.com
Berwick-upon-Tweed	106 Marygate	(01289) 330733	tourism@berwick-upon-tweed.gov.uk
Corbridge*	Hill Street	(01434) 632815	corbridgetic@btconnect.com
Craster*	Craster Car Park	(01665) 576007	crastertic@alnwick.gov.uk
Haltwhistle	Station Road	(01434) 322002	haltwhistletic@btconnect.com
Hexham	Wentworth Car Park	(01434) 652220	hexham.tic@tynedale.gov.uk
Morpeth	Bridge Street	(01670) 500700	tourism@castlemorpeth.gov.uk
Once Brewed*	Military Road	(01434) 344396	tic.oncebrewed@nnpa.org.uk
Otterburn	Otterburn Mill	(01830) 520093	tic@otterburnmill.co.uk
Rothbury*	Church Street	(01669) 620887	tic.rothbury@nnpa.org.uk
Seahouses*	Seafield car park	(01665) 720884	seahousestic@berwick-upon-tweed.gov.uk
Wooler*	12 Padgepool Place	(01668) 282123	woolertic@berwick-upon-tweed.gov.uk

Tees Valley

Darlington	13 Horsemarket	(01325) 388666	tic@darlington.gov.uk
Guisborough	Church Street	(01287) 633801	guisborough_tic@redcar-cleveland.gov.uk
Hartlepool	Church Square	(01429) 869706	hpooltic@hartlepool.gov.uk
Middlesbrough	99-101 Albert Road	(01642) 729700	middlesbrough_tic@middlesbrough.gov.uk
Redcar	West Terrace	(01642) 471921	redcar_tic@redcar-cleveland.gov.uk
Saltburn-by-the-Sea	Station Square	(01287) 622422	saltburn_tic@redcar-cleveland.gov.uk
Stockton-on-Tees	Church Road	(01642) 528130	touristinformation@stockton.gov.uk

Tyne and Wear

| Gateshead (Central Library) | Prince Consort Road | (0191) 433 8400 | tic@gateshead.gov.uk |
| Gateshead (Visitor Centre, Quayside) | St Mary's Church | (0191) 478 4222 | tourism@gateshead.gov.uk |

Newcastle International Airport		(0191) 214 4422	niatic@hotmail.com
Newcastle upon Tyne (Grainger St)	8-9 Central Arcade	(0191) 277 8000	tourist.info@newcastle.gov.uk
Newcastle upon Tyne (Guildhall)	Quayside	(0191) 277 8000	tourist.info@newcastle.gov.uk
North Shields	Royal Quays Outlet Shopping	(0191) 200 5895	ticns@northtyneside.gov.uk
South Shields	Ocean Road	(0191) 454 6612	museum.tic@southtyneside.gov.uk
South Shields (Amphitheatre)*	Sea Road	(0191) 455 7411	foreshore.tic@southtyneside.gov.uk
Sunderland	50 Fawcett Street	(0191) 553 2000	tourist.info@sunderland.gov.uk
Whitley Bay	Park Road	(0191) 200 8535	ticwb@northtyneside.gov.uk

Yorkshire

Aysgarth Falls	Aysgarth Falls National Park Centre	(01969) 662910	aysgarth@ytbtic.co.uk
Barnsley	Central Library	(01226) 206757	barnsley@ytbtic.co.uk
Batley	Bradford Road	(01924) 426670	batley@ytbtic.co.uk
Beverley	34 Butcher Row	(01482) 867430	beverley.tic@eastriding.gov.uk
Bradford	City Hall	(01274) 739067	tourist.information@bradford.gov.uk
Bridlington	25 Prince Street	(01262) 673474	bridlington.tic@eastriding.gov.uk
Brigg	Market Place	(01652) 657053	brigg.tic@northlincs.gov.uk
Cleethorpes	42-43 Alexandra Road	(01472) 323111	cleethorpes@ytbtic04.freeserve.co.uk
Danby*	Lodge Lane	(01439) 772737	moorscentre@northyorkmoors-npa.gov.uk
Doncaster	38-40 High Street	(01302) 734309	tourist.information@doncaster.gov.uk
Filey*	John Street	(01723) 383637	fileytic@scarborough.gov.uk
Grassington	Hebden Road	(01756) 752774	grassington@ytbtic.co.uk
Guisborough	Church Street	(01287) 633801	guisborough_tic@redcar-cleveland.gov.uk
Halifax	Piece Hall	(01422) 368725	halifax@ytbtic.co.uk
Harrogate	Crescent Road	(01423) 537300	tic@harrogate.gov.uk
Hawes	Station Yard	(01969) 666210	hawes@ytbtic.co.uk
Haworth	2/4 West Lane	(01535) 642329	haworth@ytbtic.co.uk
Hebden Bridge	New Road	(01422) 843831	hebdenbridge@ytbtic.co.uk
Helmsley	Castlegate	(01439) 770173	helmsley@ytbtic.co.uk
Holmfirth	49-51 Huddersfield Road	(01484) 222444	holmfirth.tic@kirklees.gov.uk
Hornsea*	120 Newbegin	(01964) 536404	hornsea.tic@eastriding.gov.uk
Horton in Ribblesdale	Pen-y-ghent Cafe	(01729) 860333	horton@ytbtic.co.uk
Huddersfield	3 Albion Street	(01484) 223200	huddersfield.tic@kirklees.gov.uk
Hull	1 Paragon Street	(01482) 223559	tourist.information@hullcc.gov.uk
Humber Bridge	Ferriby Road	(01482) 640852	humberbridge.tic@eastriding.gov.uk
Ilkley	Station Road	(01943) 602319	ilkley@ytbtic.co.uk
Ingleton*	The Community Centre Car Park	(015242) 41049	ingleton@ytbtic.co.uk

Knaresborough	9 Castle Courtyard	08453 890177	kntic@harrogate.gov.uk
Leeds	The Arcade, City Station	(0113) 242 5242	tourinfo@leeds.gov.uk
Leeming Bar	The Great North Road	(01677) 424262	leeming@ytbtic.co.uk
Leyburn	4 Central Chambers	(01969) 623069	leyburn@ytbtic.co.uk
Malham	National Park Centre	(01969) 652380	malham@ytbtic.co.uk
Malton	58 Market Place	(01653) 600048	maltontic@btconnect.com
Otley	Nelson Street	(01943) 462485	otleytic@leedslearning.net
Pateley Bridge*	18 High Street	08453 890179	pbtic@harrogate.gov.uk
Pickering	The Ropery	(01751) 473791	pickering@ytbtic.co.uk
Redcar	West Terrace	(01642) 471921	redcar_tic@redcar-cleveland.gov.uk
Reeth	The Green	(01748) 884059	reeth@ytbtic.co.uk
Richmond	Friary Gardens	(01748) 850252	richmond@ytbtic.co.uk
Ripon*	Minster Road	08453 890178	ripontic@harrogate.gov.uk
Rotherham Visitor Centre	40 Bridgegate	(01709) 835904	tic@rotherham.gov.uk
Scarborough	Brunswick Centre	(01723) 383636	tourismbureau@scarborough.gov.uk
Scarborough (Harbourside)	Sandside	(01723) 383636	harboursidetic@scarborough.gov.uk
Scunthorpe	Carlton Street	(01724) 297354	brigg.tic@northlincs.gov.uk
Selby	52 Micklegate	(01757) 212181	selby@ytbtic.co.uk
Settle	Cheapside	(01729) 825192	settle@ytbtic.co.uk
Sheffield	Winter Garden	(0114) 221 1900	visitor@sheffield.gov.uk
Skipton	35 Coach Street	(01756) 792809	skipton@ytbtic.co.uk
Sutton Bank	Sutton Bank	(01845) 597426	suttonbank@ytbtic.co.uk
Thirsk	49 Market Place	(01845) 522755	thirsktic@hambleton.gov.uk
Todmorden	15 Burnley Road	(01706) 818181	todmorden@ytbtic.co.uk
Wakefield	9 The Bull Ring	0845 601 8353	tic@wakefield.gov.uk
Wetherby	17 Westgate	(01937) 582151	wetherbytic@leedslearning.net
Whitby	Langborne Road	(01723) 383637	whitbytic@scarborough.gov.uk
Withernsea*	131 Queen Street	(01964) 615683	withernsea.tic@eastriding.gov.uk
York (De Grey Rooms)	Exhibition Square	(01904) 550099	info@visityork.org
York (Railway Station)	Station Road	(01904) 550099	info@visityork.org

* seasonal opening

Alternatively, you can text **TIC LOCATE** to **64118** to find your nearest Tourist Information Centre

Places to visit in
Northern England

On the following pages you'll find an extensive selection of indoor and outdoor attractions in Northern England. Get to grips with nature, stroll around a museum, have an action-packed day with the kids and a whole lot more...

Attractions are ordered by county, and if you're looking for a specific kind of experience each county is divided into the following sections.

 Family fun

 Nature and wildlife

 Historic England

Outdoor activities

Entertainment and culture

Food and drink

Relaxing and pampering

Look out, too, for the Quality Assured Visitor Attraction sign. This indicates that the attraction is assessed annually and meets the standards required to receive the quality marque. So rest assured, you'll have a great time.

Turn to the maps at the front of the guide to find the location of those attractions displaying a map reference.

The index on page 459 will help you to locate specific attractions with ease. For more great ideas for places to visit contact a local Tourist Information Centre or log on to **enjoyengland.com**.

Please note, as changes often occur after press date, it is advisable to confirm opening times and admission prices before travelling.

KEY TO ATTRACTIONS

Cafe/restaurant	☕
Picnic area	⩌
No dogs except service dogs	✗
Partial disabled access	♿
Full disabled access	♿

Where prices aren't specified, use the following guide for an adult admission:

£	up to £5
££	between £5 and £10
£££	between £10 and £15
££££	more than £15

Fascinating facts and inventions at the Discovery Museum, Newcastle upon Tyne

Cheshire

Enjoy the fun of a special event or visit one of the attractions listed for a great day out. For more inspiring ideas go to **enjoyengland.com**.

26–27 May
Arley Horse Trials & Country Fair
Arley Hall & Gardens, Northwich
(01565) 777353
arleyhallandgardens.com

19–20 Jun
Cheshire County Show
Tabley, Knutsford
(01565) 722050
cheshirecountyshow.org.uk

18–22 Jul
RHS Flower Show at Tatton Park
Tatton Park, Knutsford
(020) 7649 1885
rhs.org.uk

28–30 Sep
Nantwich Food & Drink Festival
Mill Island, Nantwich
(01270) 610983
nantwichfoodfestival.co.uk

May 08
May Festival
Chester Racecourse
(01244) 304600
chester-races.co.uk

FAMILY FUN

Apple Jacks Farm

Stretton Road, Appleton Thorn
t (01925) 268495
w applejacksfarm.co.uk
open 14 Jul-9 Sep, 13-31 Oct, 2-3 and 10 Nov.
admission Adult: From £6.95

Get lost and get scared. Apple Jacks Farm in Cheshire hosts the Amazing Maize Maze Festival in the summer and Spooky World at Halloween. Both events have lots of attractions for all the family that last all day. There are actors, wacky races, animals, adventure and Halloween fun. Includes Jacks Grill, shop and much more.

Map ref 4A2

v *voucher offer – see back section*

Narrow boats on Cheshire Canal

Admission is based on an adult price. Please check opening times and admission before travelling.

Blaze Farm

Wildboarclough,
nr Macclesfield SK11 0BL
t (01260) 227229 **w** blazefarm.com
admission Free

Award-winning farm selling home-made ice
cream using milk from our dairy herd. Enjoy
freshly made cakes and snacks in our tea
rooms. Stroll around the nature trail. See small
animals. Watch lambing in spring. School
parties and coaches by appointment.

                                Map ref 4B2

Cheshire Ice Cream Farm and Tea Rooms
Drumlan Hall, Newton Lane, Tattenhall CH3 9NE
t (01829) 770446 **w** cheshirefarmicecream.co.uk
open Apr-Oct, daily 1000-1730. Nov-Mar, daily
1030-1700.
admission Free
*Over 30 award-winning flavours of ice cream, a
picturesque location, country tearoom, rare breeds,
under 6's play barn and much more.*

Gulliver's World

Warrington WA5 9YZ
t (01925) 230088
w gulliversfun.co.uk
open Apr-Sep, Oct half-term, Bonfire Night,
phone for details. Opening times vary during
the Christmas period.
admission Adult: £9.99

A magical world for families with children aged
two to 13 years of age. With 30 rides and
attractions it will entertain your child all day.
Visit one of our many shows or relax in one of
our many restaurants.

                Map ref 4A2

Jodrell Bank Visitor Centre
Lower Withington SK11 9DL
t (01477) 571339 **w** jb.man.ac.uk/scicen
open Apr-Oct, daily 1030-1730. Nov-Mar, Tue-Fri
1030-1500, Sat-Sun 1100-1600.
admission £
*Home of the Lovell radio telescope. 3D theatre, small
exhibition, observational pathway and 35-acre
arboretum. Shop, picnic areas and space cafe.*

Roman Soldier Patrol
Chester Visitor Centre and Town Hall TIC,
Chester CH1 1QX
t (01244) 351609 **w** romantoursuk.com/
open Jun-Aug, Thu-Sun 1345-1500.
admission £
*Patrol Fortress Deva with Caius Julius Quartus! In full
battle gear, he takes you on patrol and evokes the
exciting adventures of an imperial warrior.*

Tatton Park

Knutsford WA16 6QN
t (01625) 534400
w tattonpark.org.uk
open Parkland: Oct-Mar 1100-1700, last entry
1600. Apr-Sep 1000-1900, last entry 1800.
Attractions: see website.
admission Please see website for full details

Tatton Park is an impressive historic estate with
1,000 acres of stunning deer park to explore.
Visit the neoclassical mansion, 50-acre
gardens, Tudor Old Hall and working historical
farm. Also featuring speciality shops,
restaurant, adventure playground and full
events programme.

                                          Map ref 4A2

View of Cheshire Plains from Mow Cop

NATURE AND WILDLIFE

Arley Hall & Gardens

Northwich CW9 6NA
t (01565) 777353 **w** arleyhallandgardens.com
open 31 Mar-30 Sep 1100-1700. Hall open Tue, Sun and Bank Holidays only.
admission Adult: £5 (gardens only). £7.50 (hall and gardens)

Rich in history and beauty, Arley offers award-winning gardens and a beautiful Victorian/ Jacobean Hall. Marvel at the double herbaceous border, giant Ilex columns and explore the Victorian Rooftree and delightful woodland trails in the Grove. Other attractions: 15thC Cruck barn, working farm, plant nursery, restaurant and gift shop.

Map ref 4A2

Blue Planet Aquarium
Longlooms Road, Cheshire Oaks, Ellesmere Port CH65 9LF
t (0151) 357 8800
w blueplanetaquarium.com
open All year, Mon-Fri 1000-1700, Sat-Sun 1000-1800.
admission £££

The UK's largest aquarium. Experience an exhilarating journey through the waters of the world. Join the moving walkway and observe an underwater carnival.

Chester Zoo
Upton-by-Chester, Chester CH2 1LH
t (01244) 380280 **w** chesterzoo.org.uk
open Daily 1000-1600.
admission £££

One of Europe's leading conservation zoos, with over 7,000 animals in spacious and natural enclosures. Now featuring the 'Tsavo' African Black Rhino Experience.

Cholmondeley Castle Gardens
Cholmondeley Castle, Malpas SY14 8AH
t (01829) 720383
open Apr-Sep, Wed-Thu, Sun 1130-1700.
admission £

Ornamental gardens, lakeside picnic area, a variety of farm animals including llamas. Tearoom and attractive gift shop. Ancient private chapel in the park. Plants for sale.

Cotebrook Shire Horse Centre
Cotebrook, Tarporley CW6 9DS
t (01829) 760506 **w** cotebrookshirehorses.co.uk
open Daily 1000-1700.
admission ££

There are lots of things to see and do at the centre. As well as the magnificent heavy horses, there is also a variety of other animals and birds.

Marbury Country Park
Comberbach CW9 6AT
t (01606) 77741 **w** cheshire.gov.uk/countryside
open Daily.
admission Free

The parkland of Marbury Hall, which was demolished in 1968, with walks, picnicking and a bird hide overlooking the mere.

Ness Botanic Gardens
University of Liverpool, Ness, Neston CH64 4AY
t (0151) 353 0123 **w** nessgardens.org.uk
open Feb-Oct, daily 0930-1700. Nov-Jan, daily 0930-1600.
admission ££

The gardens contain a large collection of trees, shrubs, roses and heathers. Facilities include a visitor centre, tearoom, shop and plant nursery.

HISTORIC ENGLAND

Anderton Boat Lift
Lift Lane, Anderton, Northwich CW9 6FW
t (01606) 780777 **w** andertonboatlift.co.uk
open Apr-Sep, daily 1000-1700. Oct, Wed-Sun 1100-1600. Nov, Mar Thu-Sun 1100-1600.
admission £££

Houses a modern operations centre, interactive exhibition, gift shop, cafe and children's play area. Enjoy a walk in the nearby Anderton Nature Park or along the canal towpath.
map ref 4A2
see ad on p50

Arley Hall & Gardens

Northwich CW9 6NA
t (01565) 777353 **w** arleyhallandgardens.com
open 31 Mar-30 Sep 1100-1700. Hall open
Tue, Sun and Bank Holidays only.
admission Adult: £5 (gardens only). £7.50
(hall and gardens)

Rich in history and beauty, Arley offers award-winning gardens and a beautiful Victorian/
Jacobean Hall. Marvel at the double
herbaceous border, giant Ilex columns and
explore the Victorian Rooftree and delightful
woodland trails in the Grove. Other attractions:
15thC Cruck barn, working farm, plant nursery,
restaurant and gift shop.

 Map ref 4A2

Beeston Castle (English Heritage)
Chapel Lane, Beeston CW6 9TX
t (01829) 260464 **w** english-heritage.org.uk
open See website for details.
admission £
*A ruined 13thC castle situated on top of the
Peckforton Hills, with views of the surrounding
countryside. Exhibitions are also held featuring the
castle's history.*

Capesthorne Hall
Siddington SK11 9JY
t (01625) 861221 **w** capesthorne.com
open Apr-Oct, Wed, Sun, Bank Hols 1330-1600.
admission £
*Sculptures, paintings, furniture and family monuments.
A Georgian chapel, tearooms, gardens, lakes, nature
walks and a touring caravan park.*

Chester Cathedral
St Werburgh Street, Chester CH1 2HU
t (01244) 324756 **w** chestercathedral.com
open All year, Mon-Sat 0900-1700, Sun 1300-1700.
admission £
*A 14thC-15thC cathedral. The 12thC monastic building
has a magnificent refectory, and the church has
spectacular carved choir stalls. Each visitor receives an
audio tour.*

Chester Visitor Centre
Vicars Lane, Chester CH1 1QX
t (01244) 402111 **w** chestertourism.com
open All year, Mon-Fri 1000-1700.
admission Free
*Probably the biggest visitor information centre in Britain,
and the ideal starting point for exploring Chester.
Activities, history displays, gift shop, tourist service and
cafe.*

Dorfold Hall
Nantwich CW5 8LD
t (01270) 625245
open Apr-Oct, Wed, Bank Hols 1400-1700.
admission £
*A Jacobean house built in 1616, with beautifully
plastered ceilings, oak panelling and a woodland
garden.*

Little Moreton Hall (National Trust)
Congleton CW12 4SD
t (01260) 272018 **w** nationaltrust.org.uk
open Mar, Wed-Sun 1130-1600. Apr-Oct, Wed-Sun,
1130-1700. Nov, Sat-Sun 1130-1600.
admission ££
*A perfect example of a half-timbered moated manor
house with Great Hall, Elizabethan long gallery and
chapel. Elizabethan-style knot and herb garden.*

Lyme Park (National Trust)
Disley SK12 2NX
t (01663) 762023 **w** nationaltrust.org.uk
open House: Apr-Oct, Mon-Tue, Fri-Sun 1300-1700.
Park: Apr-Sep, daily 0800-2030. Oct-Feb, daily
0800-1800.
admission ££
*A National Trust country estate set in 1,377 acres of
moorland, woodland and park. The magnificent house
has 17 acres of historic gardens.*

Roman Amphitheatre – Chester
Vicars Lane, Chester CH1 2HS
t (01244) 402260
w chester.gov.uk/amphitheatre/index.html
open Daily.
admission Free
*The largest stone-built amphitheatre in Britain,
discovered in the 1930s. A long-running
archaeological dig has helped to add to knowledge of
Roman history.*

Stretton Watermill

Mill Lane, Stretton SY14 7HS
t (01606) 41331 **w** strettonwatermill.org.uk
open Apr, Sat-Sun 1300-1700. May-Aug, daily
1300-1700. Sep, Sat-Sun 1300-1700.
admission £

*A restored watermill with two wheels and two sets of
machinery in working order. A separate stable block has
displays of the mill and the miller's upstairs rooms.*

Tabley House Stately Home

Tabley House, Tabley Lane, Knutsford WA16 0HB
t (01565) 750151 **w** tableyhouse.co.uk
open Apr-Oct, Thu-Sun, Bank Hols 1400-1700.
admission £

*A fine Palladian house designed by John Carr in 1761,
containing a collection of English paintings, period
furniture and Leicester family memorabilia.*

Tatton Park

Knutsford WA16 6QN
t (01625) 534400
w tattonpark.org.uk
open Parkland: Oct-Mar 1100-1700, last entry
1600. Apr-Sep 1000-1900, last entry 1800.
Attractions: see website.
admission Please see website for full details

Tatton Park is an impressive historic estate with
1,000 acres of stunning deer park to explore.
Visit the neoclassical mansion, 50-acre
gardens, Tudor Old Hall and working historical
farm. Also featuring speciality shops,
restaurant, adventure playground and full
events programme.

 Map ref 4A2

Chester

Anderton Boat Lift

Take a ride on the world's first Boat Lift
An exciting experience for all ages

- Lift trips available
- Option to combine the lift
  trip with a river trip
- Interactive exhibition
- Café and shop
- Access for all

- Open from February to November
- Lift trips and river trips operating
  April to October
- Group rates available for groups of
  12 or more (Pre booking essential)
  (Charges and terms & conditions apply)

an uplifting experience

For bookings and information call
01606 786777
www.andertonboatlift.co.uk

ANDERTON BOAT LIFT

For key to symbols see inside back cover.

OUTDOOR ACTIVITIES

Apple Jacks Farm

Stretton Road, Appleton Thorn
t (01925) 268495
w applejacksfarm.co.uk
open 14 Jul-9 Sep, 13-31 Oct, 2-3 and 10 Nov.
admission Adult: From £6.95

Get lost and get scared. Apple Jacks Farm in Cheshire hosts the Amazing Maize Maze Festival in the summer and Spooky World at Halloween. Both events have lots of attractions for all the family that last all day. There are actors, wacky races, animals, adventure and Halloween fun. Includes Jacks Grill, shop and much more.

                    Map ref 4A2

V voucher offer – see back section

Walk the hills at Tegg's Nose

Gulliver's World

Warrington WA5 9YZ
t (01925) 230088
w gulliversfun.co.uk
open Apr-Sep, Oct half-term, Bonfire Night, phone for details. Opening times vary during the Christmas period.
admission Adult: £9.99

A magical world for families with children aged two to 13 years of age. With 30 rides and attractions it will entertain your child all day. Visit one of our many shows or relax in one of our many restaurants.

   Map ref 4A2

ENTERTAINMENT AND CULTURE

Boat Museum

South Pier Road, Ellesmere Port CH65 4FW
t (0151) 355 5017
w boatmuseum.org.uk
open Apr-Oct, daily 1000-1700. Nov-Mar, daily 1000-1600.
admission ££
Home to the UK's largest collection of inland waterway craft. Working forge, Power Hall, Pump House, seven exhibitions of industrial heritage and waterways objects. Gift shop and cafeteria.

CATALYST: Science Discovery Centre

Gossage Building, Mersey Road, Widnes WA8 0DF
t (0151) 420 1121
w catalyst.org.uk
open All year, Tue-Fri 1000-1700, Sat-Sun 1100-1700.
admission £
A unique, award-winning formula of interactive exhibits and historical displays. Hands-on exploration will allow you to discover the world of chemistry, its heritage and its effect on our lives.

Cheshire Military Museum

The Castle, Chester CH1 2DN
t (01244) 327617
w chester.ac.uk/militarymuseum
open All year, daily 1000-1600.
admission £
A registered museum with stunning displays and collections telling the story of Cheshire's military history through the use of tableaux and hands-on exhibits.

The Cycle Museum
Old Coach House,
Walton Hall Gardens, Walton Lea Road,
Walton WA4 6SN
t (01928) 711395
open Weekdays: by appointment.
Sat-Sun 1000-1630.
admission Free
The museum is housed in the magnificent park and includes cycles from Holland, Germany, Sweden, China, America and France. Many machines are complemented with anecdotes of social history.

Grosvenor Museum
27 Grosvenor Street, Chester CH1 2DD
t (01244) 402008
w grosvenormuseum.co.uk
open All year, Mon-Sat 1030-1700,
Sun 1300-1600.
admission Free
See Chester come to life, from Roman soldiers to a historic house through time. Exciting special exhibitions, events and activities throughout the year.

Hack Green Secret Nuclear Bunker

PO Box 127,
Nantwich CW5 8AQ
t (01270) 629219
w hackgreen.co.uk
open Apr-Oct, daily 1030-1730. Nov, Jan-Mar,
Sat-Sun 1100-1630.
admission ££
Semi-submerged nuclear bunker containing a decontamination dormitory, sick bay, early-warning systems, communications centre, radio room and BBC studio.

Macclesfield Silk Museum

The Heritage Centre, Roe Street,
Macclesfield SK11 6UT
t (01625) 613210
w silk-macclesfield.org
open All year, Mon-Fri 1100-1600, Sat 1100-1700, Sun 1200-1600.
admission £
The museum is situated in a Grade II Listed former Sunday school and presents the story of silk in Macclesfield, told through an award-winning audiovisual programme.

Radio satellite, Jodrell Bank

Admission is based on an adult price. Please check opening times and admission before travelling.

Oulton Park Race Circuit

Little Budworth CW6 9BW
t (01829) 760301 **w** brandshatchcircuits.co.uk
open All year, daily 0900-1730.
admission Free

Car and bike racing March to October. Spectacular racing rally and Early Drive Experiences. Corporate event days, conference and exhibition facilities and hospitality.

Quarry Bank Mill (National Trust)

Styal SK9 4LA
t (01625) 527468 **w** quarrybankmill.org.uk
open Apr-Sep, daily 1100-1700. Oct-Feb, Wed-Sun 1100-1600.
admission ££

A Georgian water-powered cotton-spinning mill, with five floors of displays and demonstrations and 300 acres of parkland surroundings.

Salt Museum

162 London Road, Northwich CW9 8AB
t (01606) 41331 **w** saltmuseum.org.uk
open Apr-Jul, Tue-Fri 1000-1700, Sat-Sun 1400-1700.
Aug, Mon, Bank Hols 1400-1700, Tue-Fri 1000-1700,
Sat-Sun 1400-1700. Sep-Mar, Tue-Fri 1000-1700,
Sat-Sun 1400-1700.
admission £

The museum deals with the history and development of salt making in Cheshire from early times to the present day.

Warrington Museum and Art Gallery

Museum Street, Warrington WA1 1JB
t (01925) 442733 **w** warrington.gov.uk/museum
open All year, Mon-Fri 0900-1700, Sat 0900-1600.
admission Free

A museum combining diverse collections, photographic archive, mainly 19thC British fine art, and one of the best temporary exhibition spaces in the North West.

West Park Museum and Art Gallery

Prestbury Road, Macclesfield SK10 3BJ
t (01625) 613210 **w** silk-macclesfield.org
open Apr-Oct, Tue-Sun 1330-1630. Nov-Mar, Tue-Sun 1300-1600.
admission Free

A collection of paintings by C F Tunnicliffe and other artists. Displays include Egyptian antiquities and items of local historical interest.

FOOD AND DRINK

Blaze Farm

Wildboarclough,
nr Macclesfield SK11 0BL
t (01260) 227229 **w** blazefarm.com
admission Free

Award-winning farm selling home-made ice cream using milk from our dairy herd. Enjoy freshly made cakes and snacks in our tea rooms. Stroll around the nature trail. See small animals. Watch lambing in spring. School parties and coaches by appointment.

Map ref 4B2

RELAXING AND PAMPERING

McArthur Glen Designer Outlet Cheshire Oaks

Kinsey Road,
Ellesmere Port CH65 9JJ
t (0151) 348 5600
w mcarthurglen.com/cheshireoaks
open All year, Mon-Fri 1000-2000,
Sat 1000-1900, Sun 1000-1700,
Bank Hols 1000-1800.
admission Free

The UK's largest designer outlet with over 140 stores offering discounts of up to 50% – all day, every day.

Mow Cop Castle, near Kidsgrove

County Durham

Enjoy the fun of a special event or visit one of the attractions listed for a great day out. For more inspiring ideas go to **enjoyengland.com**.

9–10 Jun
Durham Regatta
Durham
durham-regatta.org

7–8 Jul
City of Durham Summer Festival
Various venues, Durham
(0191) 301 8819
durhamtourism.co.uk

4 Aug
Georgian Fair
Beamish, The North of England Open Air Museum
(0191) 370 4000
beamish.org.uk

8–9 Sep
Stanhope Agricultural Show
Unthank Park, Stanhope, Bishop Auckland
(01388) 529118
stanhopeshow.com

1–2 Dec (provisional date)
City of Durham Christmas Festival
Various venues, Durham
(0191) 301 8819
durhamtourism.co.uk

FAMILY FUN

Bowlees Picnic Area
Newbiggin, Barnard Castle DL12 0XF
t (01913) 833594
w durham.gov.uk
open Daily.
admission Free
The picnic area is in a sheltered side valley of Teesdale. There are four waterfalls within the site and more falls alongside a footpath to Gibsons Cave.

Causey Arch and Picnic Area
The Derwent Centre, Stanley DH8 5SD
t (01913) 833594
w durham.gov.uk
open Daily.
admission Free
The world's oldest-surviving railway bridge, built between 1725 and 1726, stands over a rocky gorge. Woodland walks and access to Tanfield Railway.

Diggerland
Riverside Industrial Estate, Langley Park,
Durham DH7 9TT
t 0870 034 4437
w diggerland.com
open Apr-Nov, Sat-Sun 1000-1700. School Holidays, daily 1000-1700.
admission £££
An adventure park based on JCB diggers and dumpers. Huge variety of equipment. Rides available for children of all ages, and drives from five years and upwards.

Hall Hill Farm
Lanchester DH7 0TA
t (01388) 731333
w hallhillfarm.co.uk
open Apr-Sep, daily 1030-1700. Oct, Sat-Sun 1030-1700. Dec, Sat-Sun 1030-1600.
admission £
Family fun set in attractive countryside with an opportunity to see and touch the animals at close quarters. Farm trailer ride, gift shop, tearoom, picnic and play area.

Splash
Church Road, Stockton-on-Tees TS18 3AZ
t (01642) 527272
w teesactive.co.uk
open All Year, Mon-Fri 0730-2115, Sat 1045-1630, Sun 0900-1630.
admission £
This exciting leisure complex provides fun for all the family, with two flume slides, a spa pool, a learner pool and a cafeteria on site. One visit is never enough!

For key to symbols see inside back cover.

Weardale Railway

Stanhope Station, Station Road,
Bishop Auckland DL13 2YS
t 0845 600 1348
w weardale-railway.org.uk
open Please phone for details.
admission ££

A steam (subject to availability) railway running for eight miles between Wolsingham and Stanhope in beautiful Weardale within the North Pennines Area of Outstanding Natural Beauty.

NATURE AND WILDLIFE

Billingham Beck Valley Country Park

Visitor Centre, Ecology Park, Billingham TS23 1RA
t (01642) 360376
w stockton.gov.uk
open Park: Daily. Visitor Centre: All year, Sun 1000-1600.
admission Free

Country park with wetlands, wildflower meadows, picnic site and a 10-acre ecology park with visitor centre. Also shop, car park, various events and guided walks.

Butterfly World

Preston Park, Yarm Road, Stockton-on-Tees TS18 3RH
t (01642) 791414
open Mar-Oct, daily 1000-1630.
admission £

An indoor tropical garden populated by exotic free-flying butterflies and complemented by a display of fascinating insects.

Castle Eden Dene National Nature Reserve

Oakside Dene Lodge, Stanhope Chase,
Peterlee SR8 1NJ
t (01915) 860004
w naturalengland.org.uk
open Daily, 0830-dusk.
admission Free

Picturesque wooded valley. National Nature Reserve with 550 acres of natural woodland and 12 miles of footpaths. Wild flowers, woodland birds and red squirrels can be seen.

Crook Hall and Gardens

Sidegate, Durham DH1 5SZ
t (01913) 848028
w crookhallgardens.co.uk
open See website for details.
admission £

Medieval hall with Jacobean drawing room, turret and gallery, set in four acres of gardens. Two walled gardens, maze, silver and white garden and Shakespeare garden.

Eggleston Hall Gardens

Garden Cottage, Eggleston DL12 0AG
t (01833) 650115 **w** egglestonhallgardens.co.uk
open All year, Mon-Sun, Bank Hols 1000-1700.
admission £

Old established gardens growing many species of plants. Vegetable garden with organically grown vegetables for sale in season. Also trees, shrubs, hardy perennials and herbs.

Hardwick Country Park

Sedgefield TS21 2EH
t (01913) 833594 **w** durham.gov.uk
open All year, dawn-dusk.
admission Free

A former landscaped garden designed by James Paine in the 18th century. Contains the remains of several follies and the serpentine lake.

High Force Waterfall

Forest-in-Teesdale, Middleton-in-Teesdale,
Barnard Castle DL12 0QG
t (01833) 640209 **w** rabycastle.com/high_force.htm
open Apr-Oct, Mon-Sun 1000-1630. Nov-Mar,
Tue,Thu,Sat,Sun 1000-1500.
admission £

Take a woodland walk to see England's largest waterfall, and the most majestic on the River Tees. Gift shop, picnic area and parking.

Low Barns Nature Reserve and Visitor Centre

Durham Wildlife Trust, Witton-le-Wear DL14 0AG
t (01388) 488728 **w** durhamwildlifetrust.org.uk
open Daily 1000-1600.
admission Free

Forty-hectare nature reserve with nature trail, bird hides, bird-feeding station, observatory, woodland, ponds, meadow, butterfly garden, lake, river, visitor centre and coffee shop.

Pow Hill Country Park

East Cote House Farm, Edmundbyers,
Consett DH8 9ND
t (01913) 833594 **w** durham.gov.uk
open Daily.
admission Free

The country park is a mixed woodland and moorland site on the banks of the Derwent Reservoir, offering panoramic views towards Castleside and the Hownsgill Viaduct.

Teesside White Water Course

Tees Barrage Way, Stockton-on-Tees TS18 2QW
t (01642) 678000 **w** 4seasons.co.uk
open Apr-Oct, daily 0800-2000. Nov-Mar, please phone for details.
admission ££

Britain's finest purpose-built course is a world-class facility, fully adjustable for absolute beginners to world champions. Cafe and shop. Canoeing, kayaking and rafting.

University of Durham Botanic Garden
Hollingside Lane, Durham DH1 3TN
t (01913) 345521
w dur.ac.uk/botanic.garden/
open Apr-Oct, daily 1000-1700. Nov-Feb, daily 1100-1600.
admission £
A botanic garden set in countryside and mature woodland. There are plants from North America, Himalayas and China as well as rainforest and desert plants. Also a Mediterranean conservatory.

Whitworth Hall Country Park
Whitworth, Spennymoor DL16 7QX
t (01388) 811772
w whitworthhall.co.uk
open Daily.
admission Free
Historic parkland with resident deer, ornamental lake, Victorian walled garden, Britain's most northerly vineyard, children's playground and Grade II Listed building.

HISTORIC ENGLAND

Auckland Castle
Bishop Auckland DL14 7NR
t (01388) 601627
w auckland-castle.co.uk
open Apr-Jun, Mon, Sun 1400-1700. Jul-Aug, Mon, Wed 1100-1700, Sun 1400-1700. Sept, Mon, Sun 1400-1700.
admission £
Principal country residence of the Prince Bishops since 1190, the castle is now home to the Bishop of Durham. Visit St Peter's Chapel, state rooms and deer park.

Barnard Castle
Barnard Castle DL12 8PR
t (01833) 638212
w english-heritage.org.uk
open Apr-Sep, daily 1000-1800. Oct, daily 1000-1600. Nov-Mar, Mon, Thu-Sun 1000-1600.
admission £
A ruined castle overlooking the River Tees. Remains include the 14thC great hall, the three-storey keep and the circular round tower which inspired Sir Walter Scott (Rokeby).

Bowes Castle
Bowes, Barnard Castle DL12 9HP
t (01833) 638212
w english-heritage.org.uk
open Daily.
admission Free
Three-storey-high stone keep, dating from 1170 and set within the earthworks of a Roman fort, guarding the strategic Stainmore pass over the Pennines.

Croxdale Hall
Durham DH6 5JP
t (01913) 780911
open Please phone for details.
admission Free
Croxdale, home to the Salvin family since 1402, stands boldly over the River Wear. Mid-Georgian rooms with fine rococo ceilings, chapel, walled gardens and orangery.

Durham Castle
Palace Green, Durham DH1 3RW
t (01913) 344106 **w** durhamcastle.com
open Apr-Sep, daily 1000-1200, 1400-1630. Oct-Mar, Mon, Wed, Sat-Sun 1400-1600.
admission £
Castle founded in 1072. Norman chapel dating from 1080. Kitchens and great hall dating from 1499 and 1284 respectively. A fine example of a motte-and-bailey castle.

Durham Cathedral
The College, Durham DH1 3EH
t (01913) 864266 **w** durhamcathedral.co.uk
open Apr-Jul, Mon-Sat 0930-1800, Sun 0930-1730. Aug, daily 0930-2000. Sep-Mar, Mon-Sat 0930-1800, Sun 0930-1730.
admission Free
Durham Cathedral is thought by many to be the finest example of Norman church architecture in England. The cathedral contains the tombs of St Cuthbert and The Venerable Bede.

Durham Heritage Centre and Museum
St Mary-le-Bow, North Bailey, Durham DH1 3ET
t (01913) 845589
open Apr-May, Sat-Sun, Bank Hols 1400-1630. June, daily 1400-1630. Jul-Sep, daily 1100-1630. Oct, Sat-Sun, Bank Hols 1400-1630.
admission £
Museum of local history which tells the story of Durham from the 10th century to the present day using displays, models and artefacts. Brass rubbing and shop.

Hartlepool Historic Quay
Part of Hartlepool's Maritime Experience, Jackson's Dock, Hartlepool TS24 0XZ
t (01429) 860077
w hartlepoolsmaritimeexperience.com
open Daily 1000-1700.
admission ££
An authentic reconstruction of an 18thC seaport. Step back in time to a remarkable period in British history. A superb day out for all ages.

HM Bark Endeavour
Castlegate Quay, Riverside, Stockton-on-Tees TS18 1BZ
t (01642) 608038 **w** hmbarkendeavour.co.uk
open Pre-bookings only. Please phone for details.
admission Free
Heritage visitor attraction. Full-size replica of Captain James Cook's ship HM Bark Endeavour. Situated on the river with shop, picnic area and children's games area.

HMS Trincomalee
Part of Hartlepool's Maritime Experience, Jackson's Dock, Hartlepool TS24 0XZ
t (01429) 223193
w hms-trincomalee.co.uk
open Apr-Oct, daily 1000-1700. Nov-Mar, daily 1030-1600.
admission ££

HMS Trincomalee, built in 1817, is the oldest ship afloat in the UK. Come aboard for a unique experience of Navy life two centuries ago.

Raby Castle
Staindrop, Darlington DL2 3AH
t (01833) 660202
w rabycastle.com
open Castle: May-Jun, Sep, Wed, Sun 1300-1700. Jul-Aug, Mon-Fri, Sun 1300-1700. Bank Hols including Sat 1300-1700. Park & Gardens: May-Jun, Sept, Wed, Sun 1100-1730. Jul-Aug, Mon-Fri, Sun 1100-1730. Bank Hols including Sat 1100-1730.
admission ££

The medieval castle, home of Lord Barnard's family since 1626, includes a 200-acre deer park, walled gardens, carriage collection, adventure playground, shop and tearoom.

Rokeby Park
Rokeby, Barnard Castle DL12 9RZ
t (01833) 690100
w rokebypark.com
open May-Sep, Mon-Tue 1400-1700.
admission £

A beautiful Palladian-style country house which was the setting for Sir Walter Scott's ballad 'Rokeby', containing a unique collection of 18thC needlework and period furniture.

Summerhill Visitor Centre
Summerhill Lane, Hartlepool TS25 4LL
t (01429) 284584
w sunnysummerhill.com
open All year, Mon-Sun, Bank Hols 0900-1700.
admission Free

A 100-acre country park on the western edge of Hartlepool which has been transformed for conservation and outdoor sports.

OUTDOOR ACTIVITIES

Prince Bishop River Cruiser
Browns Boathouse Ltd, Elvet Bridge, Durham DH1 3AF
t (01913) 869525
w princebishoprc.co.uk
open Apr-Oct, daily, please phone for details.
admission £

Luxury cruiser (seats 150) which sails in all weather, all year round. Observation deck, lower deck saloon, bar, cafe and commentary. Also rowing boats for hire.

ENTERTAINMENT AND CULTURE

Beamish, The North of England Open Air Museum
Beamish DH9 0RG
t (01913) 704000 **w** beamish.org.uk
open Apr-Oct, daily 1000-1700, Nov-Mar, Tue-Thu, Sat-Sun 1000-1600.
admission ££

Visit the town, colliery village, working farm, Pockerley Manor and 1825 railway, recreating life in the North East in the early 1800s and 1900s.

The Bowes Museum
Barnard Castle DL12 8NP
t (01833) 690606 **w** thebowesmuseum.org.uk
open Daily 1100-1700.
admission ££

This fascinating museum houses a collection of outstanding European fine and decorative art and offers an exhibition programme alongside special events and children's activities.

Durham Light Infantry Museum and Durham Art Gallery
Aykley Heads, Durham DH1 5TU
t (01913) 842214 **w** durham.gov.uk/dli
open Apr-Oct, daily 1000-1700. Nov-Mar, daily 1000-1600.
admission £

The museum tells the 200-year-old story of Durham's famous regiment. The art gallery presents an exciting programme of exhibitions and events, including concerts, talks and workshops.

Killhope, The North of England Lead Mining Museum
Weardale, Cowshill DL13 1AR
t (01388) 537505 **w** durham.gov.uk/killhope
open Apr-Oct, daily 1030-1700, Bank Hols 1030-1730.
admission £

National-award-winning Quality Assured Visitor Attraction. The most complete lead mining site in Britain. See the North of England's largest working water wheel and dress up in Victorian-style clothes. Shops and cafe.

Follow the Country Code!

- Be safe – plan ahead and follow any signs
- Leave gates and property as you find them
- Protect plants and animals, and take your litter home
- Keep dogs under close control
- Consider other people

Locomotion: The National Railway Museum at Shildon

Shildon DL4 1PQ
t (01388) 777999 **w** locomotion.uk.com
open Apr-Sep, daily 1000-1700. Sep-Dec, Wed-Sun 1000-1600.
admission Free

The museum incorporates historic monuments and buildings with interactive displays. View approximately 60 vehicles. Play area, picnic area, modern-art monument, gift shop, cafe.

Museum of Hartlepool

Part of Hartlepool's Maritime Experience, Jackson's Dock, Hartlepool TS24 0XZ
t (01429) 860077
w hartlepoolsmaritimeexperience.com
open Daily 1000-1700.
admission Free

Hartlepool Museum, situated beside Hartlepool Historic Quay, includes local historical exhibits, PSS Wingfield Castle, exhibitions and the original lighthouse light.

Preston Hall Museum

Preston Park, Yarm Road,
Stockton-on-Tees TS18 3RH
t (01642) 527375 **w** stockton.gov.uk/museums
open Apr-Sep, daily 1000-1645. Oct-Mar, Mon-Sat 10-1630, Sun 1400-1630.
admission £

A Georgian country house set in over 100 acres of parkland overlooking the River Tees. There is a museum of social history, picnic areas, tropical-bird aviary and children's play area.

Top Gear Indoor Karting

13 Rennys Lane, Durham DH1 2RS
t (01913) 860999 **w** durhamkarting.co.uk
open All year, Mon-Fri 1300-2100, Sat 0900-1900, Sun 1000-1800.
admission ££££

Indoor karting for anyone over eight years old. Fast, safe and exciting fun for all the family. Minimum height 1.4m/4ft 7in.

RELAXING AND PAMPERING

Dalton Park

Murton SR7 9HU
t (01915) 266500 **w** dalton-park.co.uk
open All year, Mon-Wed, Fri 1000-1800, Thu 1000-2000, Sat 0900-1800, Sun 1030-1700, Bank Hols 1000-1700.
admission Free

Retail outlet centre with up to 50% off the best brands. Cafes, creche and children's play area, all within 55 acres of parkland.

Cumbria

Enjoy the fun of a special event or visit one of the attractions listed for a great day out. For more inspiring ideas go to **enjoyengland.com**.

22 Jul
Coniston Country Fair
Coniston Hall
conistoncountryfair.com

3–19 Aug
Lake District Summer Music Festival
Various venues
0845 644 2144
ldsm.org.uk

3–5 Aug
Lowther Horse Driving Trials
Penrith
(01931) 712577
lowther.co.uk

13 Sep
Westmorland County Show
Kendal
(015395) 67804
westmorland-county-show.co.uk

Oct
Kendal Mountain Film Festival
Kendal
mountainfilm.co.uk

FAMILY FUN

Aquarium of the Lakes
Lakeside, Newby Bridge LA12 8AS
t (015395) 30153 **w** aquariumofthelakes.co.uk
open Apr-Oct. daily 0900-1700. Nov-Mar, daily
0900-1700.
admission ££
The UK's largest collection of freshwater fish in naturally themed habitats. Discover an underwater tunnel featuring giant carp and diving ducks. Spot British sharks, otters, harvest mice and voles.

Greystoke Gill Pottery
Greystoke Gill, Penrith CA11 0UQ
t (01768) 483123 **w** greystokegillpottery.co.uk
open Apr-Oct, daily 1000-1700. Nov-Mar, Wed-Sun
1000-1700.
admission Free
Small studio pottery where visitors can see work in progress, and on certain days make their own pot. Handmade individual and domestic pottery and wood-fired stoneware, glazed with rich, multiple colours.

Lake District Coast Aquarium Maryport
South Quay, Maryport CA15 8AB
t (01900) 817760 **w** lakedistrict-coastaquarium.co.uk
open All year, daily 1000-1700.
admission £
An all-year, all-weather attraction. Gift shop, mini-golf, remote-control boats. Cafe with harbour view. Regular fish feeding and talks.

Lakeland Heavy Horse Centre
Craika Farm, Dearham, Maryport CA15 7EH
t (01900) 818023 **w** lakesheavyhorses.co.uk
open Apr-Sep, daily 1000-1600. Oct, Tue-Sun
1000-1600.
admission ££
Heavy-horse demonstrations, pets' corner, cafe and various visitor attractions on a working farm. The centre was only opened to the public in July 2006.

Lakeland Miniature Village
The Coach House, Winder Lane,
Grange-over-Sands LA11 7LE
t (015395) 58500 **w** lakelandminiaturevillage.com
open All year, daily 1030-dusk.
admission £
A fascinating insight into the buildings of Lakeland's yesteryear. Over 120 buildings made from Coniston slate. Houses, farms, barns etc, all hand made.

Lakeside & Haverthwaite Railway
Haverthwaite Station, Ulverston LA12 8AL
t (015395) 31594 **w** lakesiderailway.co.uk
open See website for details.
admission £
Steam trains running a seasonal daily service from Haverthwaite to Lakeside via the Leven valley. Licensed restaurant, engine sheds, shop, picnic area.

The Laurel and Hardy Museum

4c Upper Brook Street, Ulverston LA12 7BH
t (01229) 582292
w laurel-and-hardy-museum.co.uk
open Feb-Dec 1000-1630. Times vary during Christmas period.
admission Adult: £2.50

The world-famous museum devoted to Laurel and Hardy in the town of Stan's birth. Everything you want to know about them is here, including photographs, letters, personal items and furniture. A large extension gives ample room to browse and a small cinema shows films and documentaries all day.

Map ref 5A3

 voucher offer – see back section

View of the Cumbrian mountains, Ullswater

Muncaster

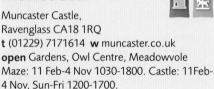

Muncaster Castle,
Ravenglass CA18 1RQ
t (01229) 7171614 **w** muncaster.co.uk
open Gardens, Owl Centre, Meadowvole
Maze: 11 Feb-4 Nov 1030-1800. Castle: 11Feb-
4 Nov, Sun-Fri 1200-1700.
admission Adult: £9.50

Historic haunted castle, home to the
Pennington family for over 800 years. Extensive
gardens with glorious views. Headquarters of
the World Owl Trust with daily bird show and
Heron Happy Hour. Interactive Meadowvole
Maze. Gift shops, cafe, plant centre and
computer suite. B&B accommodation, magical
winter evenings with darkest Muncaster!

                      Map ref 5A3

 voucher offer – see back section

Pots of Fun
Clifton Dykes, Penrith CA10 2DH
t (01768) 892733
open Apr-Oct, daily 1030-1730. Nov-Mar, daily
1000-1630.
admission Free
*Throw your own pot, or paint a pot, figurine, mask, glass
or vase. Make a mosaic and much more. Suitable for all
ages and levels of expertise.*

South Tynedale Railway
The Railway Station, Alston CA9 3JB
t (01434) 381696 **w** strps.org.uk
open See website for details.
admission £
*Travel behind preserved steam and diesel engines, from
Britain and abroad, through this Area of Outstanding
Natural Beauty.*

NATURE AND WILDLIFE

Acorn Bank Garden & Watermill
Temple Sowerby, Penrith CA10 1SP
t (01768) 361893 **w** nationaltrust.org.uk
open Mar-Oct, Wed-Sun 1000-1700.
admission £
*Delightful sheltered garden, with a backdrop of a red
sandstone 17thC house, renowned for its herbs and
orchards growing old English fruit varieties. Over 200
culinary and medicinal herbs.*

Eden Ostrich World
Langwathby Hall Farm, Langwathby, Penrith CA10 1LW
t (01768) 881771 **w** ostrich-world.com
open Mar-Oct, daily 1000-1700. Nov-Feb, daily
1000-1700.
admission £
*Meet African black ostrich and other animals. Tearoom,
Hayloft gallery selling arts and crafts, play areas,
riverside walk, sheep-milking parlour, soft play area.*

Fell Foot Country Park
Newby Bridge, Ulverston LA12 8NN
t (015395) 31273 **w** nationaltrust.org.uk
open All year, daily 0900-1700.
admission Free
*Discover this lakeshore Victorian park – just the place for
families to enjoy access to Windermere with picnic
areas, boat hire and tearoom.*

Graythwaite Hall Gardens
Graythwaite, Ulverston LA12 8BA
t (015395) 31333 **w** graythwaitehall.co.uk
open Apr-Aug, daily 1000-1800.
admission £
*A fine example of Thomas Mawson's architecture
comprising Dutch garden, rose garden, spring-flowering
shrubs and rhododendrons.*

Lakeland Sheep and Wool Centre
Egremont Road, Cockermouth CA13 0QX
t (01900) 822673 **w** sheep-woolcentre.co.uk
open All year, daily 0900-1730.
admission Free
*Live farm show including cows, sheep, dogs and geese,
all displaying their working qualities. Gift shop and
licensed cafe/restaurant. An all-weather attraction.*

Lakeland Wildlife Oasis
Hale, Milnthorpe LA7 7BW
t (015395) 63027 **w** wildlifeoasis.co.uk
open Apr-Jun, daily 1000-1600. Jul-Aug, daily
1000-1700. Sep-Mar, daily 1000-1600.
admission ££
*Wildlife centre with a unique mix of exotic animals and
educational interactive exhibitions. Includes tropical hall
and butterfly house. Free parking.*

Muncaster World Owl Centre
Ravenglass CA18 1RQ
t (01229) 717614 **w** muncaster.co.uk
open Mar-Nov, daily 1030-1800.
admission ££

The centre cares for one of the finest and largest owl collections in the world with over 50 species, from the tiny Pygmy owl to the huge European Eagle owl.

South Lakes Wild Animal Park
Broughton Road, Dalton-in-Furness LA15 8JR
t (01229) 466086 **w** wildanimalpark.co.uk
open All year, daily 1000-1645.
admission £££

A unique concept in zoos, built to put animals first, and probably Britain's finest conservation park. Safari on foot amongst many animals wandering free.

Stagshaw Gardens
Stagshaw Lane, Ambleside LA22 0HE
t (015394) 46027 **w** nationaltrust.org.uk
open Apr-Jun, daily 1000-1830.
admission £

A woodland garden on a slope overlooking Lake Windermere. A superb collection of rhododendrons and azaleas blend perfectly under the hillside oaks.

Trotters World of Animals
Coalbeck Farm, Bassenthwaite CA12 4RD
t (01768) 776239 **w** trottersworld.com
open All year, daily 1000-1730.
admission ££

Wildlife park with collection of rare and interesting animals including primates, antelope, zebra and buffalo. Reptile house and bird of prey centre.

HISTORIC ENGLAND

Birdoswald Roman Fort
Gilsland, Brampton CA8 7DD
t (01697) 747602 **w** english-heritage.org.uk
open See website for details.
admission £

A Roman fort, turret and milecastle on an excellent stretch of Hadrian's Wall. Displaying the best-preserved defences of any wall fort, it was a base for some 1,000 Roman soldiers.

Blackwell, The Arts & Craft House
Bowness-on-Windermere, Windermere LA23 3JT
t (015394) 46139 **w** blackwell.org.uk
open Apr-Oct, daily 1030-1700. Nov-Dec, daily 1030-1600.
admission ££

Elegant arts and crafts house and gardens with spectacular views across Windermere. The restored interiors include many original features. Changing exhibitions of craft in upper galleries.

Carlisle Cathedral
The Abbey, Carlisle CA3 8TZ
t (01228) 548151 **w** carlislecathedral.org.uk
open All year, Mon-Sat 0730-1815, Sun 0730-1700.
admission Free

The cathedral dates from 1122 and has fine medieval stained glass, carved wood and stonework. Gift shop, restaurant, Treasury museum.

Conishead Priory House & Temple Tours
A5087 Coast Road, Ulverston LA12 9QQ
t (01229) 584029 **w** conisheadpriory.org
open Jun-Oct, Sat-Sun, Bank Hols 1400-1700. Nov-Mar, Sat-Sun 1400-1600.
admission £

A fascinating one-hour tour giving the history of the priory since 1160, together with an insight into the Buddhist way of life.

Dalemain Historic House & Gardens
Dalemain, Penrith CA11 0HB
t (01768) 486450 **w** dalemain.com
open Gardens: Apr-Oct, Mon-Thu, Sun 1030-1700. Nov-Mar, Mon-Thu, Sun 1100-1600. House: Apr-Oct, Mon-Thu, Sun 1115-1600.
admission ££

A medieval, Tudor and early-Georgian house. Guided tours available. Wonderful five-acre plantsman garden set against the splendour of the Lakeland Fells.

Dove Cottage and The Wordsworth Museum
Dove Cottage, Grasmere LA22 9SH
t (01539) 435544 **w** wordsworth.org.uk
open All year, daily 0930-1730.
admission ££

Wordsworth's home during his most creative period. Guided cottage tours, award-winning museum displaying manuscripts, portraits, paintings and memorabilia.

Furness Abbey
Abbey Approach, Barrow-in-Furness LA13 0PJ
t (01912) 691200 **w** english-heritage.org.uk
open See website for details.
admission £

A dramatic red sandstone abbey dating from 1123, so beloved by William Wordsworth. The exhibition explains the history of a powerful religious community.

Grizedale Forest Park and Visitor Centre
Grizedale, Hawkshead LA22 0QJ
t (01229) 860010 **w** forestry.gov.uk/northwestengland
open Summer, daily 1000-1700. Winter, daily 1000-1600.
admission Free

The park comprises 2,500 hectacres of Lakeland forest with walking and cycling trails. Sculptures in the forest, Go Ape, bike hire, visitor centre and cafe.

Hill Top
Nr Sawrey,
Ambleside LA22 0LF
t (015394) 36269
w nationaltrust.org.uk
open Apr-May, Mon-Wed, Sat-Sun 1030-1630.
Jun-Aug, Mon-Thu, Sat-Sun 1030-1630. Sep-Oct,
Mon-Wed, Sat-Sun 1030-1630.
admission ££
*Delightful, small 17thC house where Beatrix
Potter wrote many of her famous children's
stories. View her personal treasures.*

Holker Hall and Gardens
Cark-in-Cartmel,
Grange-over-Sands LA11 7PL
t (015395) 58328
w holker-hall.co.uk
open Gardens: Apr-Oct, Mon-Fri, Sun 1030-1730. Hall:
Apr-Oct, Mon-Fri, Sun 1200-1600.
admission ££
*Magnificent hall, award-winning gardens and
museum – three attractions in one setting. There
is also the Courtyard cafe, food hall and free
parking.*

Honister Slate Mine
Honister Pass, Borrowdale,
Keswick CA12 5XN
t (01768) 777230
w honister.com
open All year, daily 1030-1530.
admission ££
*The last working slate mine in England. Fully
guided mine tours. Browse the visitor centre.
Enjoy home-cooked fayre in the Yew Tree pub/
restaurant.*

Lanercost Priory
Lanercost,
Brampton CA8 2HQ
t (01697) 73030
w english-heritage.org.uk
open See website for details.
admission £
*Step back 800 years and explore this wonderful
12thC Augustinian priory which is situated near
Hadrian's Wall.*

Levens Hall & Gardens
Levens,
Kendal LA8 0PD
t (015395) 60321
w levenshall.co.uk
open Gardens: Apr-Sep, Mon-Thu, Sun 1000-1700.
House: Apr-Sep, Mon-Thu, Sun 1200-1600.
admission ££
*Elizabethan mansion and world-famous topiary
gardens designed by M Beaumont in 1694.
Fountain garden and nuttery, licensed restaurant
and gift shop.*

Muscaster
Muncaster Castle,
Ravenglass CA18 1RQ
t (01229) 7171614 **w** muncaster.co.uk
open Gardens, Owl Centre, Meadowvole
Maze: 11 Feb-4 Nov 1030-1800. Castle: 11Feb-
4 Nov, Sun-Fri 1200-1700.
admission Adult: £9.50

Historic haunted castle, home to the
Pennington family for over 800 years. Extensive
gardens with glorious views. Headquarters of
the World Owl Trust with daily bird show and
Heron Happy Hour. Interactive Meadowvole
Maze. Gift shops, cafe, plant centre and
computer suite. B&B accommodation, magical
winter evenings with darkest Muncaster!

Map ref 5A3

V *voucher offer – see back section*

Nenthead Mines Heritage Centre
Nenthead, Alston CA9 3PD
t (01434) 382726 **w** npht.com
open Apr-Oct, Wed-Sun 1030-1700. Apr-Oct, School
Hols daily 1030-1700.
admission Free
*Fantastic underground tour and interactive exhibits
including working water wheels. Centuries of history
interpreted in a unique environment.*

Rydal Mount and Gardens
Rydal, Ambleside LA22 9LU
t (015394) 33002 **w** rydalmount.co.uk
open Apr-Oct, daily 0930-1700. Nov-Dec, Mon,
Wed-Sun 0930-1700.
admission £
*Wordsworth's best-loved home for 37 years. It was here
that he wrote many of his poems. He became Poet
Laureate to Queen Victoria at the age of 74.*

For key to symbols see inside back cover.

St Mary & St Michael's Church
Church Road, Great Urswick, Ulverston LA12 0TA
t (01229) 582053
open Apr-Oct, daily 1000-1600. Nov-Mar, daily
1000-1500.
admission Free

*A 10thC church, the oldest in Furness. Pre-Viking cross
and Georgian gallery. Fine carvings by Alec Miller.
Possible Celtic Roman connections.*

Sizergh Castle and Garden
Sizergh, Kendal LA8 8AE
t (015395) 60951 **w** nationaltrust.org.uk
open Castle: Apr-Oct, Mon-Thu, Sun 1300-1700.
Garden: Apr-Oct, Mon-Thu, Sun 1100-1700.
admission ££

*Occupied by the Strickland family for over 760 years.
View some of the finest Elizabethan carved overmantels,
English and French furniture and Jacobite relics.*

Stott Park Bobbin Mill
Low Stott Park, Ulverston LA12 8AX
t (015395) 31273 **w** english-heritage.org.uk
open See website for details.
admission £

*See the industrial revolution come to life at this Victorian
bobbin mill in an idyllic woodland setting at the south
end of Lake Windermere.*

Wordsworth House
Main Street, Cockermouth CA13 9RX
t (01900) 824805 **w** nationaltrust.org.uk
open Apr-Oct, Mon-Sat 1100-1630.
admission £

*Meet the Wordsworth household. Explore the garden.
Enjoy the sights, sounds and smells of a working 18thC
kitchen. Hands-on activities.*

OUTDOOR ACTIVITIES

Coniston Launch
Coniston Boatlandings, Coniston LA21 8AJ
t (01539) 436216 **w** conistonlaunch.co.uk
open See website for details.
admission £

*Cruise and ferry service calling at seven jetties including
Brantwood. Special-interest cruises, eg Swallows &
Amazons, Campbells on Coniston.*

Steam Yacht Gondola
Pier Cottage, Coniston LA21 8AJ
t (015394) 41288 **w** nationaltrust.org.uk
open All year, daily 1100-1600. Weather permitting.
admission ££

*The unrivalled cruising experience of the Lakes. View
Coniston's spectacular scenery from a unique, rebuilt
steam yacht sailing from Coniston pier.*

Ullswater Steamers – Pooley Bridge
The Pier House, Glenridding, Ullswater CA11 0US
t (017684) 82229
w ullswater-steamers.co.uk
open See website for details.
admission £

*Superb pier house offering tea and coffee overlooking
the lake. Ticket sales and visitor information available.*

Windermere Lake Cruises Bowness
Winander House, Glebe Road,
Bowness-on-Windermere, Windermere LA23 3HE
t (015394) 43360
w windermere-lakecruises.co.uk
open All year, please phone for details.
admission ££

*Steamers and launches sail daily between Ambleside,
Bowness and Lakeside. The steamers have saloons,
promenade decks, teashops and licensed bars.
Additional summer routes. Timetabled services.*

ENTERTAINMENT AND CULTURE

Abbot Hall Art Gallery
Abbot Hall, Kendal LA9 5AL
t (01539) 722464
w abbothall.org.uk
open Mar-Nov, Mon-Sat 1030-1600. Dec-Feb, Mon-Sat
1030-1700.
admission £

*The gallery's fine collection of 18thC, 19thC and 20thC
art is set within an elegant Georgian villa. The
permanent collection is complemented by a programme
of critically acclaimed changing exhibitions.*

Beatrix Potter Gallery
Main Street, Hawkshead LA22 0NS
t (015394) 36355
w nationaltrust.org.uk
open Apr-May, Mon-Wed, Sat-Sun 1030-1630.
Jun-Aug, Mon-Thu, Sat-Sun 1030-1630. Sep-Oct,
Mon-Wed, Sat-Sun 1030-1630.
admission £

*Gallery showing original book illustrations by Beatrix
Potter, once the office of her husband, William Heelis.
An exhibition of sketches and watercolours painted for
her children's stories changes annually.*

Cars of the Stars Motor Museum
Standish Street, Keswick CA12 5LS
t (01768) 773757
w carsofthestars.com
open Apr-Nov, daily 1000-1700. Dec, Sat-Sun
1000-1700.
admission £

*This motor museum features vehicles from TV and film:
Chitty, Batmobiles, James Bond, Fab 1, the A Team van
and many more.*

Cumberland Pencil Museum
Southey Works, Keswick CA12 5NG
t (01768) 773626 **w** pencils.co.uk
open All year, daily 0930-1600.
admission £

Fascinating exhibits and film reveal 170 years of pencil heritage and how pencils are made today. Learn artists' techniques, and browse world-famous products in the gift shop.

The Dock Museum
North Road, Barrow-in-Furness LA14 2PW
t (01229) 876400 **w** dockmuseum.org.uk
open Apr-Oct, Tue-Fri 1000-1700, Sat-Sun 1100-1700.
Nov-Mar, Wed-Fri 1030-1600, Sat-Sun 1100-1630.
admission Free

The museum explores the fascinating history of Barrow-in-Furness and how it grew from a tiny 19thC hamlet to a major shipbuilding force in just 40 years.

Gossipgate Gallery
The Butts, Alston CA9 3JU
t (01434) 381806 **w** gossipgate-gallery.co.uk
open Apr-Aug, Wed-Sat 1000-1700, Sun 1100-1700.
Sep-Oct, Wed-Fri, Sun 1100-1630, Sat 1000-1700.
admission Free

The gallery has a reputation for quality art and craftwork from the north of England, with a continuous programme of exhibitions. Small coffee shop, tea terrace and wildflower garden.

Haig Colliery Mining Museum
Solway Road, Kells, Whitehaven CA28 9BG
t (01946) 599949 **w** haigpit.com
open All year, daily 0930-1630.
admission Free

The museum is situated on the former site of Haig Pit. Suitable for educational, group and corporate visits. Outreach talks, oral history and guided walks all available by booking.

Lake District Visitor Centre at Brockhole
Windermere LA23 1LJ
t (015394) 46601 **w** lake-district.gov.uk
open Gardens: Daily 1000-1700. House: Apr-Oct, daily 1000-1700.
admission Free

Visitor centre with interactive exhibitions, thirty acres of Mawson gardens and grounds, adventure playground, shop and information centre. Lakeshore access for all.

Lakeland Motor Museum
Holker Hall and Gardens, Cark in Cartmel,
Grange-over-Sands LA11 7PL
t (015395) 58328 **w** lakelandmotormuseum.co.uk
open Apr-Oct, daily 1030-1600.
admission ££

An award-winning visitor experience and a great educational resource. Over 30,000 motor-related exhibits including a 1930s garage recreation.

The Laurel and Hardy Museum
4c Upper Brook Street, Ulverston LA12 7BH
t (01229) 582292
w laurel-and-hardy-museum.co.uk
open Feb-Dec 1000-1630. Times vary during Christmas period.
admission Adult: £2.50

The world-famous museum devoted to Laurel and Hardy in the town of Stan's birth. Everything you want to know about them is here, including photographs, letters, personal items and furniture. A large extension gives ample room to browse and a small cinema shows films and documentaries all day.

Map ref 5A3

V *voucher offer – see back section*

Lowes Court Gallery & Egremont TIC
12 Main Street, Egremont CA22 2DW
t (01946) 820693 **w** lowescourtgallery.co.uk
open Mar-Dec, Mon-Tue, Thu-Sat, 1000-1700, Wed 1000-1300.
admission Free

The gallery is housed in an 18thC listed building and is home to Egremont TIC and gift shop with 'Made in Cumbria' goods. The upper gallery has changing exhibitions.

Museum of Lakeland Life
Abbot Hall, Kendal LA9 5AL
t (01539) 722464 **w** lakelandmuseum.org.uk
open Apr-Oct, Mon-Sat 1030-1700. Nov, Feb-Mar, Mon-Sat 1030-1600.
admission £

The award-winning museum, housed in the stable block of the Georgian Abbot Hall Art Gallery, goes back in time to tell the story of the Lake District.

Admission is based on an adult price. Please check opening times and admission before travelling.

Ravenglass Railway Museum

Ravenglass CA18 1SW
t (01229) 717171 **w** ravenglass-railway.co.uk
open Apr-Oct, daily 0900-1700.
admission Free

The history of the Ravenglass and Eskdale railway told with relics, models, photographs and a 20-minute video.

The Rheged Centre

Redhills, Penrith CA11 0DQ
t (01768) 868000 **w** rheged.com
open Daily 1000-1730.
admission ££

International-award-winning centre, and Europe's largest grass-covered building, home to a giant cinema screen showing epic movies daily. Regular events.

The Rum Story

27 Lowther Street, Whitehaven CA28 7DN
t (01946) 592933
w rumstory.co.uk
open All year, daily 1000-1630.
admission ££

The world's first exhibition depicting the story of the UK rum trade, including slavery, the effects of liquor on society, and the shipping and transport of rum.

Threlkeld Quarry & Mining Museum

Threlkeld Quarry, Threlkeld,
Keswick CA12 4TT
t (01768) 779747
w threlkeldminingmuseum.co.uk
open Apr-Oct, daily 1000-1700.
admission £

Museum of mining, quarrying, geology and minerals. A large collection of excavators from the 20th century. Underground guided tours. Narrow-gauge railway.

Tullie House Museum & Art Gallery Museum

Castle Street,
Carlisle CA3 8TP
t (01228) 534781
w tulliehouse.co.uk
open Apr-Jun, Mon-Sat 1000-1700, Sun 1200-1700. Jul-Aug, Mon-Sat 1000-1700, Sun 1100-1700. Sep-Oct, Mon-Sat 1000-1700, Sun 1200-1700. Nov-Mar, Mon-Sat 1000-1600, Sun 1200-1600.
admission ££

Travel through time at Tullie House and discover thousands of years of Carlisle and Border history, from prehistoric to recent times.

View across Ullswater, near Martindale

Greater Manchester

Enjoy the fun of a special event or visit one of the attractions listed for a great day out. For more inspiring ideas go to **enjoyengland.com**.

May
Comfest
Various venues, Manchester
(0161) 200 1500
commonwealthfilm.com

28 Jun–15 Jul
Manchester International Festival
Various venues, Manchester
(0161) 238 7300
manchesterinternationalfestival.com

17–27 Aug
Manchester Pride
The Gay Village, Manchester
(0161) 238 4548
manchesterpride.com

6 Oct–27 Jan 08
Art Treasures
Manchester Art Gallery
(0161) 235 8888
manchestergalleries.org

Mar 08
Manchester Irish Festival
Various venues, Manchester
(0161) 205 4007
irishfestival.co.uk

 FAMILY FUN

East Lancashire Railway
Bolton Street Station,
Bolton Street,
Bury BL9 0EY
t (0161) 764 7790
w east-lancs-rly.co.uk
open All Year, 1000-1600.
admission £££

Beautifully restored, award-winning steam heritage railway. Passenger services run from Bury to Ramsbottom, Rawtenstall and Heywood as well as the villages of Summerseat and Irwell Vale.

Hat Works Museum

Wellington Mill, Wellington Road South, Stockport SK3 0EU
t 0845 833 0975 **w** hatworks.org.uk
open Mon-Fri 1000-1700, Sat-Sun 1300-1700 (excl Christmas period, phone for details). Open Bank Holidays.
admission Free

Hat Works is the UK's only museum dedicated to the hatting industry, hats and headwear. This award-winning heritage attractions offers two floors of interactive exhibits taking you on a journey through the history of Stockport's once-thriving hatting industry. Relax in the cafe or take home a souvenir from our shop.

Map ref 4B2

For key to symbols see inside back cover.

Imperial War Museum North

The Quays, Trafford Wharf Road,
Trafford Park M17 1TZ
t (0161) 836 4000 **w** iwm.org.uk
open Mar-Oct 1000-1800. Nov-Feb 1000-1700
(excl 24-26 Dec).
admission Free

The award-winning Imperial War Museum
North is located at the Quays, a waterfront
destination two miles from Manchester city
centre, and uses dynamic displays to reflect on
how people's lives are shaped by war. Cafe,
shop and viewing platform offering fantastic
views over the area.

                          Map ref 4B1

Staircase House

30-31 Market Place, Stockport SK1 1ES
t (0161) 480 1460 **w** staircasehouse.org.uk
open Mon-Fri 1200-1700, Sat-Sun 1000-1700
(excl 25-26 Dec, 1 Jan). Open Bank Holidays.
admission Adult: £3.50

Time travel through the history of Staircase
House from 1460 to WWII. With the help of a
state-of-the-art audio guide, the fascinating
history of this 18-room town house will unfold
on a fun, accessible and informative journey.
You are invited to smell, touch and listen as the
entire house is fully interactive.

                          Map ref 4B2

Manchester City Experience (Museum and Tour)

Manchester City Football Club, Sportcity,
Manchester M11 3FF
t 0870 062 1894 **w** mcfc.co.uk
open Museum: All year, Mon-Sat 0930-1630, Sun
1100-1500. Tour: Please phone for details.
admission ££

*Tour Britain's stunning new stadium and experience the
atmosphere of one of the country's most passionate
clubs, Manchester City.*

Quality counts

Look out for the Quality Assured
Visitor Attraction sign. These
attractions are assessed annually
and meet the standards required
to receive the quality marque.

Saddleworth Moor

Stockport Story Museum

Market Place, Stockport SK1 1ES
t (0161) 480 1460
w stockportstory.org.uk
open Mon-Sun 1000-1700 (excl 25-26 Dec, 1 Jan). Open Bank Holidays.
admission Free

Stockport Story Museum follows the evolution of Stockport on a time line through the ages from Palaeolithic to the present day. Find out how the hunters and gatherers of Stockport lived, what a thriving market town Stockport became and what a rich social history the town has. Family-friendly with interactives.

Map ref 4B2

NATURE AND WILDLIFE

Etherow Country Park and Local Nature Reserve
George Street,
Compstall SK6 5JD
t (0161) 427 6937
w marple-uk.com/community/etherow2.htm
open Daily, 1000-1600.
admission Free

The park covers approximately 92 hectares on the site of an old cotton mill and offers a variety of leisure pursuits with events and educational services.

Haigh Hall and Country Park
Haigh, Wigan WN2 1PE
t (01942) 832895 **w** haighhall.net
open Daily.
admission Free

Set in 350 acres of wood and parkland. Facilities include a model village, bouncy castle, play area, miniature railway, ladybird ride, mini-golf, craft gallery, information centre, gift shop and cafeteria.

Reddish Vale Country Park
Mill Lane, Reddish, Stockport SK5 7HE
t (0161) 477 5637 **w** stockport.gov.uk
open Daily.
admission Free

Nature reserve offering a wide variety of pursuits. Trails, bridleways and cycle routes link the Thame Valley to the Etherow/Goyt Valley and surrounding area. Butterfly park.

HISTORIC ENGLAND

Bramall Hall
Bramall Park, Bramhall SK7 3NX
t (0161) 485 3708
w stockport.gov.uk/heritageattractions
open Apr-Sep, Mon-Thu, Sun 1300-1700, Fri-Sat 1300-1600. Oct-Dec, Tue-Sun 1300-1600. Jan-Mar, Sat-Sun 1300-1600. Bank Hols 1100-1700.
admission £

A Tudor manor house with 60 acres of landscaped grounds with lakes, woods and gardens. The house contains 16thC wall paintings. Tearoom and gift shop.

Dunham Massey Hall Park and Garden (National Trust)
Altrincham WA14 4SJ
t (0161) 941 1025 **w** thenationaltrust.org.uk
open House: Apr-Oct, Mon-Wed, Sat-Sun 1200-1700. Park: Apr-Oct, Daily 0900-1930. Nov-Feb, Daily 0900-1700.
admission ££

An 18thC mansion in a 250-acre wooded deer park with furniture, paintings and silver. Also, a 25-acre informal garden with mature trees and waterside plantings.

Hall i'th Wood Museum
off Green Way, Crompton Way, Bolton BL1 8UA
t (01204) 332370 **w** boltonmuseums.org.uk
open Apr-Oct, Wed-Sun 1200-1700. Nov-Mar, Sat-Sun 1200-1700.
admission £

A 15thC furnished house with personal items belonging to Samuel Crompton, inventor of the Spinning Mule.

Manchester Cathedral
Cathedral Yard, Manchester M3 1SX
t (0161) 833 2220
open All year, Mon-Fri 0900-1730, Sat 0900-1530, Sun 0900-1830, Bank Hols 0900-1630.
admission Free

Dedicated to St Mary, St Denys and St George, this 15thC perpendicular church became a collegiate church in 1421 and was raised to cathedral status in 1847.

Staircase House

30-31 Market Place, Stockport SK1 1ES
t (0161) 480 1460 **w** staircasehouse.org.uk
open Mon-Fri 1200-1700, Sat-Sun 1000-1700
(excl 25-26 Dec, 1 Jan). Open Bank Holidays.
admission Adult: £3.50

Time travel through the history of Staircase
House from 1460 to WWII. With the help of a
state-of-the-art audio guide, the fascinating
history of this 18-room town house will unfold
on a fun, accessible and informative journey.
You are invited to smell, touch and listen as the
entire house is fully interactive.

Map ref 4B2

Stockport Air Raid Shelters

Chestergate, Stockport SK1 1NE
t (0161) 474 1940
open Mon-Sun 1300-1700 (excl 25-26 Dec,
1 Jan). Open Bank Holidays.
admission Adult: £3.95

Step back in time to 1940s war-torn Britain and
experience the sights and sounds of Britain's
home front. Stockport's unique air raid shelters
have been carved into the natural sandstone
cliffs of Stockport town centre and are the
largest purpose-built WWII civilian
underground air raid shelters in Britain.

Map ref 4B2

'B' of the Bang sculpture

Stockport Story Museum

Market Place, Stockport SK1 1ES
t (0161) 480 1460
w stockportstory.org.uk
open Mon-Sun 1000-1700 (excl 25-26 Dec, 1 Jan). Open Bank Holidays.
admission Free

Stockport Story Museum follows the evolution of Stockport on a time line through the ages from Palaeolithic to the present day. Find out how the hunters and gatherers of Stockport lived, what a thriving market town Stockport became and what a rich social history the town has. Family-friendly with interactives.

Map ref 4B2

Hat Works Museum

Wellington Mill, Wellington Road South, Stockport SK3 0EU
t 0845 833 0975 **w** hatworks.org.uk
open Mon-Fri 1000-1700, Sat-Sun 1300-1700 (excl Christmas period, phone for details). Open Bank Holidays.
admission Free

Hat Works is the UK's only museum dedicated to the hatting industry, hats and headwear. This award-winning heritage attractions offers two floors of interactive exhibits taking you on a journey through the history of Stockport's once-thriving hatting industry. Relax in the cafe or take home a souvenir from our shop.

Map ref 4B2

ENTERTAINMENT AND CULTURE

City of Manchester Stadium
Sport City,
Manchester M11 3FF
t (0161) 224 5000
w mcfc.co.uk
open Please phone for details.
admission ££

Manchester City Football Club moved to City of Manchester Stadium in July 2003. Museum and stadium tour, plus City Social cafe & Reebok City superstore.

Canal boat on Castlefield basin

For key to symbols see inside back cover.

Imperial War Museum North

The Quays, Trafford Wharf Road,
Trafford Park M17 1TZ
t (0161) 836 4000 **w** iwm.org.uk
open Mar-Oct 1000-1800. Nov-Feb 1000-1700
(excl 24-26 Dec).
admission Free

The award-winning Imperial War Museum
North is located at the Quays, a waterfront
destination two miles from Manchester city
centre, and uses dynamic displays to reflect on
how people's lives are shaped by war. Cafe,
shop and viewing platform offering fantastic
views over the area.

                    Map ref 4B1

The Lowry
Pier 8, Salford Quays, Salford M50 3AZ
t (0161) 876 2000 **w** thelowry.com
open All year, Mon-Sat 1000-2000, Sun, Bank Hols
1000-1800.
admission Free
*The Lowry is a spectacular home to the arts and
entertainment with a wealth of activity all under one
roof, including two theatres and an art gallery of
international renown.*

Manchester Art Gallery
Mosley Street, Manchester M2 3JL
t (0161) 235 8888 **w** manchestergalleries.org
open All year, Tue-Sun 1000-1700.
admission Free
*The gallery houses one of the country's finest art
collections in spectacular Victorian and contemporary
surroundings. Exciting exhibitions programme and a
wide range of events.*

Manchester United Museum & Tour
Sir Matt Busby Way, Old Trafford,
Manchester M16 0RA
t 0870 442 1994 **w** manutd.com
open Museum: All year, Mon-Sun 0930-1700.Tours: All
year, Mon-Sun 0940-1630.
admission ££
*The official museum and tour of Old Trafford offers
every football fan a unique insight into Manchester
United Football Club and a fantastic day out.*

The Museum of Science and Industry
Liverpool Road, Castlefield, Manchester M3 4FP
t (0161) 832 2244 **w** msim.org.uk
open All year, Mon-Sun 1000-1700.
admission Free
*The museum is based on the site of the oldest passenger
railway station in the world. Five historic buildings
packed with fascinating exhibitions, hands-on galleries,
historic working machinery and special exhibitions.*

Museum of Transport
Boyle Street, Cheetham, Manchester M8 8UW
t (0161) 205 2122 **w** gmts.co.uk
open Apr-Oct, Wed, Sat-Sun 1000-1700, Nov-Dec
Wed, Sat-Sun 1000-1600.
admission £
*The museum has one of the largest transport collections
in the country, with 90 buses and a small number of
other vehicles.*

Reebok Stadium
Burnden Way, Lostock, Bolton BL6 6JW
t (01204) 673673 **w** bwfc.co.uk
open All year, Mon-Wed, Fri-Sat 0930-1730, Thu
0930-1900, Sun, Bank Hols 1000-1600.
admission £
*Home of Bolton Wanderers Football Club and De Vere
Whites Hotel, with a regional conference and exhibition
centre. Stadium tours, sports hall and a merchandise
store.*

Colourful fun at Manchester Pride Festival

Stockport Air Raid Shelters

Chestergate, Stockport SK1 1NE
t (0161) 474 1940
open Mon-Sun 1300-1700 (excl 25-26 Dec,
1 Jan). Open Bank Holidays.
admission Adult: £3.95

Step back in time to 1940s war-torn Britain and experience the sights and sounds of Britain's home front. Stockport's unique air raid shelters have been carved into the natural sandstone cliffs of Stockport town centre and are the largest purpose-built WWII civilian underground air raid shelters in Britain.

Map ref 4B2

Touchstones Rochdale
Esplanade, Rochdale OL16 1AQ
t (01706) 924492 **w** rochdale.gov.uk/touchstones
open All Year, Mon-Sat 1000-1715, Sun, Bank Hols 1200-1600.
admission Free
The gallery features exhibitions of contemporary art and changing displays from collections of painting and sculpture. Local-history museum and local-studies centre. Cafe, bookshop and tourist information centre.

Urbis
Cathedral Gardens, Manchester M4 3BG
t (0161) 605 8200
w urbis.org.uk
open All year, Mon-Wed, Sun 1000-1800, Thu-Sat 1000-2000.
admission Free
Located at the heart of Manchester, Urbis is an exhibition centre of city life, featuring interactive exhibits and dynamic changing exhibitions.

The Whitworth Art Gallery
The University of Manchester, Oxford Road, Manchester M15 6ER
t (0161) 275 7450
w whitworth.man.ac.uk
open All year, Mon-Sat 1000-1700, Sun 1400-1700.
admission Free
The gallery has a light and spacious modern interior and is home to an internationally famous collection of British watercolours, sculptures, textiles and wallpapers.

Wigan Pier
Trencherfield Mill, Wigan WN3 4EF
t (01942) 323666
w wiganmbc.gov.uk
open All year, Mon-Thu 1000-1700, Sun 1100-1700.
admission ££

The pier combines interaction with displays and reconstructions and performances by the Wigan Pier Theatre Company. Facilities include shops, boats and a cafe.

RELAXING AND PAMPERING

Lowry Outlet Mall
Centre Management Office, The Quays, Salford Quays, Manchester M50 3AH
t (0161) 848 1800
w http://lowryoutletmall.com
open All year, Mon-Fri 1000-0100, Sat 0900-0100, Sun 1000-2330.
admission Free
The new designer outlet for the North West with over 80 shops offering up to 70% discount. Food court, cinema, coffee shops and restaurants.

enjoyEngland.com

A great attraction or activity can often make the perfect holiday. enjoy**England**.com features a comprehensive list of every quality-assured theme park, landmark, museum, national park and activity in England.

Admission is based on an adult price. Please check opening times and admission before travelling.

Lancashire

Enjoy the fun of a special event or visit one of the attractions listed for a great day out. For more inspiring ideas go to **enjoyengland.com**.

20–22 Jul
Royal Lancashire Agricultural Show
Ribchester
(01254) 813769
rlas.co.uk

24–27 Aug
The Great British Rhythm & Blues Festival
Colne
(01282) 661234
bluesfestival.co.uk

31 Aug–3 Sep
Pendle Walking Festival
Pendle
(01282) 661981
pendle.gov.uk

6–9 Sep
The 2nd Pennine Lancashire Festival of Food & Drink
Various venues across the West Pennine Moors
(01254) 683563
visitlancashire.com

31 Oct–4 Nov
Blackpool Illuminations
Blackpool Promenade
(01253) 478222
visitblackpool.com

 FAMILY FUN

Adrenalin Zone
South Pier, Promenade, Blackpool FY4 1BB
t (01253) 298080
w adrenalinezone.co.uk
open Mar-Nov, daily 0900-1700.
admission ££
Thrill to the adrenalin rush of the SkyCoaster, a reverse bungee jump reaching 200kmph in two seconds, the Crazy Mouse Roller Coaster, Sky Screamer or the new Skad Tower.

Blackpool Model Village
East Park Drive, Blackpool FY3 9RB
t (01253) 763827
w blackpoolmodelvillage.com
open Apr-Nov, daily 1000-dusk.
admission £
An enchanting attraction set in 2.5 acres of landscaped gardens. Marvel at the hand-crafted models and figures that depict many scenes of life in miniature.

Blackpool Sandcastle Waterworld
South Promenade, Blackpool FY4 1BB
t (01253) 343602
w sandcastle-waterworld.co.uk
open See website for details.
admission £
A subtropical paradise. Brave the 'Typhoon Lagoon' wave pool; relax in the fun pool with fountains and kiddies' slides; ride the 300ft 'Gentle Giant' waterslide or race down the 'Barracuda'.

Blackpool's Piers
North Pier, The Promenade, Blackpool FY1 1NE
t (01253) 621452
w blackpoollive.com
open Mar-Oct, daily 0900-2300. Nov-Feb, daily 0900-1800.
admission £
On foot or by tram, enjoy the golden sands and the bustle of Blackpool's Golden Mile. From late August until early November the illuminations make it a magical night experience.

Camelot Theme Park
Charnock Richard, Chorley PR7 5LP
t (01257) 452100
w camelotthemepark.co.uk
open May-Jun Sat-Sun 1000-1600. Jul-Aug daily 1000-1630. Sep-Oct, Sat-Sun 1000-1600.
admission ££££
This is a land of great knights and amazing days where you can meet Merlin and King Arthur and his brave Knights of the Round Table.

Lancaster Leisure Park G B Antiques

Wyresdale Road,
Lancaster LA1 3LA
t (01524) 68444
open Daily 1000-1700.
admission £

The leisure park complex includes children's rides set in 42 acres of landscaped parkland. The antique centre is now the second largest in Europe.

Louis Tussaud's Waxworks

97-89 Promenade,
Blackpool FY1 1HW
t (01253) 625953
w louistussaudswaxworks.co.uk
open See website for details.
admission ££

Experience CelebCity. Once you've walked the red carpet, you'll be immersed in a world of celebrity, rubbing shoulders with Hollywood's A List and the tabloid's favourites.

Pleasure Beach, Blackpool

Blackpool FY4 1EZ
t 0870 444 5566
w blackpoolpleasurebeach.com
open Mar-Nov. See website or phone for opening times.
admission Free

Ride fabulous thrill rides, float through river caves and watch spectacular shows, including Hot Ice and Forbidden. Look out for our new white-knuckle ride opening in spring 2007. Rides for all the family, including Beaver Creek for children.

Map ref 4A1

  V *voucher offer – see back section*

NATURE AND WILDLIFE

Beacon Country Park

Beacon Lane, Upholland WN8 7RU
t (01695) 622794
w westlancsdc.gov.uk/tourist_information/
beacon_park.html
open Daily.
admission Free

Three hundred acres of open countryside, staging events and activities throughout the year. Golf course and driving range, visitor centre, cafe and bar, nature trails, orienteering course, heritage trail.

Blackpool Zoo Park

East Park Drive, Blackpool FY3 8PP
t (01253) 830830
w blackpoolzoo.org.uk
open All year, daily 1000-1545.
admission £££

In 32 acres of maturing parkland and lakes, this award-winning zoo is home to over 1,500 beautiful, rare and exotic animals from all around the world. Play areas, crafts, miniature railway, shops and picnic areas.

Bowland Wild Boar Park

Leagram, Chipping PR3 2QS
t (01995) 61554
w wildboarpark.co.uk
open Daily 1100-1600.
admission £

Ideal for young families and grandparents with grandchildren. View wild boar, cattle, llama, wallabies, red squirrels and pet lambs – some of the animals can be fed. Beautiful woodland walks.

Marshside RSPB Nature Reserve

c/o 24 Hoghton Street, Southport PR9 0PA
t (01704) 536378
w rspb.org.uk
open All year, daily 0830-1700.
admission Free

A nature reserve with coastal grasslands, lagoons and hides by the estuary. Thousands of ducks and geese, as well as large flocks of wading birds, gather from autumn to spring.

RSPB Leighton Moss

Myers Farm, Silverdale LA5 0SW
t (01524) 701601
w rspb.org.uk
open All year, daily 0900-dusk.
admission £

An attractive wooded valley below limestone hills, the only place in the North West with breeding bitterns, bearded tits and marsh harriers. Reception centre, RSPB shop and tearoom.

For key to symbols see inside back cover.

Wildfowl & Wetland Trust Martin Mere

Fish Lane, Burscough, Nr Ormskirk L40 0TA
t (01704) 895181 **w** wwt.org.uk
open Apr-Oct, daily 0930-1730. Nov-Mar, daily
0930-1700.
admission ££
The centre is home to over 1,600 ducks, geese and swans.
Special events and exhibitions, visitor centre and gift shop.

Williamson Park

Lancaster LA1 1UX
t (01524) 33318 **w** williamsonpark.com
open All year, daily dawn-dusk.
admission £
Facilities include the Ashton Memorial, viewing and art
gallery, tropical butterfly house, mini-beast cave, free-
flying bird enclosure and small-mammal enclosure.

Witton Country Park

Preston Old Road, Blackburn BB2 2TP
t (01254) 55423 **w** blackburn.gov.uk
open Park: Daily. Visitor Centre: Apr-Sep, Mon-Sat
1300-1630, Sun, Bank Hols 1100-1600. Oct-Mar,
Thu-Sat 1300-1630, Sun 1100-1600.
admission Free
The park covers 480 acres of countryside and is
peppered with pretty picnic spots, walks, nature trails, a
small animal reserve and a visitor centre.

Wyre Estuary Country Park

River Road, Stanah,
Thornton Cleveleys FY5 5LR
t (01253) 857890 **w** wyrebc.gov.uk
open All year, daily.
admission Free

The park and visitor centre offer year-round
activities and events for all the family, including
ranger-led walks, natural-environment activities
and workshops. Visit our gift shop, take
refreshments or walk the network of footpaths
on the river estuary. Tours by arrangement.

Map ref 4A1

HISTORIC ENGLAND

Blackburn Cathedral

Cathedral Offices, Cathedral Close, Blackburn BB1 5AA
t (01254) 51491 **w** blackburn.anglican.org/cathedral
open All year, Mon-Sat 0800-1700.
admission Free
Blackburn Cathedral has a Georgian nave with 20thC
extensions, featuring sculptures by John Hayward and
Josephina De Vasconcellos, and Burne-Jones windows.

Blackpool Tower & Circus

Promenade, Blackpool FY1 4BJ
t (01253) 622242 **w** blackpooltower.co.uk
open See website for details.
admission £££
There's entertainment for all ages, night and day at the
world-famous Blackpool Tower. Don't miss the Tower
Circus, the magnificent Tower Ballroom and Jungle Jim's
Adventure Playground.

Clitheroe Castle Museum

Castle Hill, Castle Gate, Clitheroe BB7 1BA
t (01200) 424635 **w** visitlancashire.com
open Apr-Oct, Mon-Sat, Bank Hols 1115-1630, Sun
1300-1630. Nov, Sat 1115-1630, Sun 1300-1630.
admission £
The museum's displays cover a wide variety of topics
including reconstructions of a Victorian kitchen, a
printer's shop and a clogger's shop, birds of the Ribble
Valley and local geology.

Gawthorpe Hall and Estate Block (National Trust)

Burnley Road, Padiham, Burnley BB12 8UA
t (01282) 771004 **w** lancsmuseums.gov.uk
open Apr-Oct, Tue-Thu, Sat-Sun 1300-1700.
admission £
The house was built in 1600 and restored by Sir Charles
Barry in the 1850s. A loan from the National Portrait
Gallery adds to the notable paintings already displayed.

Hoghton Tower

Hoghton, Preston PR5 0SH
t (01254) 852986 **w** hoghtontower.co.uk
open Jul-Sep, Mon-Thu, Bank Hols 1100-1600, Sun
1300-1700.
admission ££
A historic house with magnificent state apartments,
banqueting hall, ballroom, grounds and dolls' houses on
display. Underground passages and dungeons.

Lancaster Castle

Shire Hall, Castle Parade, Lancaster LA1 1YJ
t (01524) 64998 **w** lancastercastle.com
open All year, daily 1000-1700.
admission £
Shire Hall has a collection of coats of arms, a crown
court, a grand jury room, a 'drop room' and dungeons.
There is also an external tour of the castle.

Lancaster Maritime Museum

Custom House, St George's Quay, Lancaster LA1 1RB
t (01524) 64637 **w** lancsmuseums.gov.uk
open Apr-Oct, daily 1100-1700. Nov-Mar, daily
1230-1800.
admission £
The museum covers the maritime trade of Lancaster, the
history of the port, the Lancaster canal and the fishing
industry of the Lune Estuary and Morecambe Bay.

Leighton Hall

Carnforth LA5 9ST
t (01524) 734474 w leightonhall.co.uk
open May-Jul, Tue-Fri, Bank Hols 1400-1700. Aug, Tue-Fri,
Sun 1230-1700. Sep, Tue-Fri, Bank Hols 1400-1700.
admission ££

*The award-winning hall is the lived-in house of the
famous furniture-making Gillow dynasty. Here, visitors
can unravel the fascinating past of this ancient
Lancashire family.*

Rufford Old Hall

200 Liverpool Road, Rufford, Ormskirk L40 1SG
t (01704) 821254 w nationaltrust.org.uk
open Apr-Oct, Mon-Wed, Sat-Sun 1300-1700.
admission £

*One of the finest 16thC buildings in Lancashire. The
magnificent timber-framed Tudor hall, with impressive
wood carvings, is believed to have hosted the young
William Shakespeare.*

Samlesbury Hall

Preston New Road, Samlesbury,
Preston PR5 0UP
t (01254) 812229 w samlesburyhall.co.uk
open All year, Mon-Fri, Sun 1100-1630.
admission £

*A black and white, oak-timbered medieval manor house
dating from 1325. The hall is home to displays, craft
exhibitions and antique sales.*

Whalley Abbey

Whalley, Clitheroe BB7 9SS
t (01254) 828400 w whalleyabbey.co.uk
open Daily 1000-Dusk.
admission £

*Fourteenth-century Cistercian abbey ruins set in
beautiful countryside beside the River Calder, with mini
woodland trail, riverside path, exhibition centre, gift
shop and coffee shop.*

Forest of Bowland

OUTDOOR ACTIVITIES

Wyre Estuary Country Park

River Road, Stanah,
Thornton Cleveleys FY5 5LR
t (01253) 857890 w wyrebc.gov.uk
open All year, daily.
admission Free

The park and visitor centre offer year-round
activities and events for all the family, including
ranger-led walks, natural-environment activities
and workshops. Visit our gift shop, take
refreshments or walk the network of footpaths
on the river estuary. Tours by arrangement.

   Map ref 4A1

ENTERTAINMENT AND CULTURE

British Commercial Vehicle Museum

King Street, Leyland PR25 2LE
t (01772) 451011 w thevehicleworks.com
open Apr-Sep, Tue-Thu, Sun 1000-1700. Oct, Sun
1000-1700.
admission £

*The museum contains the finest collection of historic
and commercial vehicles in Europe, including the world-
famous Popemobile, horse-drawn and steam vehicles
and fire engines.*

Carnforth Station and Heritage Centre

Warton Road, Carnforth LA5 9TR
t (01524) 735165 w carnforthstation.co.uk
open Apr-Sep, daily 1000-1600. Oct-Mar, Tue-Sun
1000-1600.
admission Free

*Made famous as the setting for David Lean's Brief
Encounter, this once-significant railway station has been
restored and conserved as a 1940s working railway
station, heritage centre and conference venue.*

Doctor Who Museum

Central Promenade, Blackpool FY1 5AA
t (01253) 299982 w doctorwhoexhibitions.co.uk
open Apr-Oct, daily 1030-1730.
admission ££

*The museum boasts the most extensive collection of
Doctor Who exhibits ever, charting four decades of the
memorable BBC science-fiction series.*

The National Football Museum
Sir Tom Finney Way, Deepdale, Preston PR1 6RU
t (01772) 908442
w nationalfootballmuseum.com
open All year, Tue-Sat 1000-1700, Sat 1000-1500, Sun 1100-1700.
admission Free

The museum offers a unique experience by bringing alive the fascinating story of football through a number of interactive and hands-on elements.

Pleasure Beach, Blackpool

Blackpool FY4 1EZ
t 0870 444 5566
w blackpoolpleasurebeach.com
open Mar-Nov. See website or phone for opening times.
admission Free

Ride fabulous thrill rides, float through river caves and watch spectacular shows, including Hot Ice and Forbidden. Look out for our new white-knuckle ride opening in spring 2007. Rides for all the family, including Beaver Creek for children.

Map ref 4A1

V *voucher offer – see back section*

Ribchester Roman Museum
Riverside, Ribchester, Preston PR3 3XS
t (01254) 878261
w ribchestermuseum.org
open All year, Mon-Fri 1000-1700, Sat-Sun 1200-1700.
admission £

Located on the north bank of the beautiful River Ribble, the museum has recently reopened after major development of its facilities. Roman Ribchester is brought to life by dramatic displays.

Worden Park
Worden Lane, Leyland PR25 3EL
t (01772) 625400 **w** southribble.gov.uk/visitors
open Daily 0800-1730.
admission Free

The park is over 150 acres in size. It includes the formal gardens, overlooked by a magnificent conservatory originally built in 1892. Alongside is the famous maze or puzzle garden.

RELAXING AND PAMPERING

Barden Mill Shop
Barden Lane, Burnley BB12 0DX
t (01282) 420333 **w** bardenmillshop.co.uk
open All year, Mon-Fri 0930-1730, Sat 0930-1800, Sun 1030-1700.
admission Free

Over 50 departments in one mill store – serious bargain hunting in the unique surroundings of a converted weaving mill. Plenty of free parking.

Botany Bay Villages and Puddletown Pirates
Canal Mill, Botany Brow, Chorley PR6 9AF
t (01257) 261220 **w** botanybay.co.uk
open Botany Bay: All year, daily 1030-1730. Puddletown Pirates: All year, daily 1000-1800.
admission £

A shopping, leisure and heritage experience housed within a converted Victorian spinning mill. Includes Puddletown Pirates, the North West's largest indoor adventure play centre.

Freeport Fleetwood Outlet Village
Anchorage Road, Fleetwood FY7 6AE
t (01253) 877377 **w** freeport-fleetwood.com
open All year, Mon-Wed, Fri-Sun 1000-1800, Thur 1000-2000.
admission Free

A shopping and leisure village with over 40 retail outlets, selling at discounts of up to 50%. Children's adventure playground and indoor play area.

Sherry's Lancashire Mill Shop
Stockbridge Mill, Stockbridge Road, Burnley BB12 7HA
t (01282) 778416 **w** sherrytex.co.uk
open All year, Mon-Sat 0930-1730, Sun 1000-1630.
admission Free

Large mill shop attached to an existing traditional Lancashire weaving mill. 6,000 sq ft of bargains and gifts with 30-seater coffee shop serving drinks and snacks.

Winfield's
Hazel Mill, Blackburn Road, Haslingden BB4 5DD
t (01706) 831952 **w** winfieldsoutdoor.co.uk
open All year, Mon-Wed, Fri 1000-1730, Thu 1000-2000, Sat 0900-1730, Sun 1100-1700.
admission Free

Footwear, sports and designer wear, fashion, homeware, luggage. Winfield's has the answer, and all at discount prices you won't believe.

Merseyside

Enjoy the fun of a special event or visit one of the attractions listed for a great day out. For more inspiring ideas go to **enjoyengland.com**.

25 Aug
Creamfields
Daresbury, Halton
(0151) 707 1309
creamfields.com

28 Aug
Liverpool 800 Day
Various venues, Liverpool
liverpool08.com

22–23 Sep
Southport Airshow and Military Display
Southport seafront
(01704) 533333
visitsouthport.com

19 Oct–13 Jan 08
Turner Prize
Tate Liverpool, Albert Dock
(0151) 702 7400
tate.org.uk/Liverpool

Apr 08
John Smith's Grand National
Aintree Racecourse
(0151) 522 2929
aintree.co.uk

FAMILY FUN

The Cavern Quarter
Liverpool L2 6RE
t (0151) 227 1963 **w** beatles64.co.uk
open See website for details.
admission Free
The cultural birthplace of the Beatles is the home of many tourism landmarks, including the Cavern Club.

Liverpool Football Club Museum and Stadium Tour
Anfield Road, Liverpool L4 0TH
t (0151) 260 6677 **w** liverpoolfc.tv
open Daily 1000-1700. Match days, last admission one hour before kick-off.
admission ££
You'll never walk alone on the tour of Liverpool Football Club. The tour includes dressing rooms, players' tunnel, coaches' seating area and grandstand.

Face to face with The Beatles

For key to symbols see inside back cover.

National Wildflower Centre

Court Hey Park, Knowsley L16 3NA
t (0151) 738 1913 **w** nwc.org.uk
open 1 Mar-1 Sep 1000-1700, last entry 1600.
admission Adult: £3

A peaceful haven in an otherwise busy world. Full events programme, including Wildflower Heroes events and workshops – all ages and abilities welcome. Pre-booked groups welcome. Seasonal wildflower displays, children's play area (visitor centre charge applies). Award-winning Cornflower Cafe and gift shop on site (cafe open weekdays in winter).

Map ref 4A2

V *voucher offer – see back section*

Spaceport
Victoria Place, Wallasey CH44 6QY
t (0151) 330 1333 **w** spaceport.org.uk
open All year, Tue-Sun 1030-1730.
admission ££
Blast off on a virtual journey through space, from Earth to the farthest reaches of the known universe. Expand your mind at the amazing new £10 million Spaceport in Merseyside.

The World of Glass
Chalon Way East,
St Helens WA10 1BX
t 0870 011 4466
w worldofglass.com
open All year, Tue-Sun 1000-1700.
admission ££
England's best small visitor attraction features live glass blowing, multi-media shows, exhibitions, cafe, gift shop and tourist information centre. It is also a first-class conference and corporate hospitality venue.
map ref 4A2
see ad below

NATURE AND WILDLIFE

Formby Red Squirrel Reserve (National Trust)
Victoria Road, Freshfield,
Formby L37 1LJ
t (01704) 878591
w nationaltrust.org.uk
open Daily.
admission Free
This National Trust property is the home of red squirrels, which are the main attraction at this superb nature reserve.

Knowsley Safari Park

Prescot L34 4AN
t (0151) 430 9009 **w** knowsley.com
open Mar-Oct, daily 1000-1600. Nov-Feb, daily
1030-1500.
admission £££

*A five-mile safari through 500 acres of rolling
countryside and the world's wildest animals roaming
free – that's the wonderful world of freedom you'll find
at the park.*

National Wildflower Centre

Court Hey Park, Knowsley L16 3NA
t (0151) 738 1913 **w** nwc.org.uk
open 1 Mar-1 Sep 1000-1700, last entry 1600.
admission Adult: £3

A peaceful haven in an otherwise busy world.
Full events programme, including Wildflower
Heroes events and workshops – all ages and
abilities welcome. Pre-booked groups
welcome. Seasonal wildflower displays,
children's play area (visitor centre charge
applies). Award-winning Cornflower Cafe and
gift shop on site (cafe open weekdays in
winter).

 Map ref 4A2

v *voucher offer – see back section*

Quality counts

Look out for the Quality Assured
Visitor Attraction sign. These
attractions are assessed annually
and meet the standards required
to receive the quality marque.

HISTORIC ENGLAND

Albert Dock

The Colonnades, Liverpool L2 7SU
t (0151) 708 8854 **w** albertdock.com
open Please see website for details.
admission Free

*A truly stunning architectural triumph, this award-
winning attraction houses cafe bars, restaurants, shops,
The Beatles Story, Merseyside Maritime Museum,
Museum of Liverpool Life and Tate Liverpool.*

Croxteth Hall and Country Park

Croxteth Hall Lane, Muirhead Avenue,
Liverpool L12 0HB
t (0151) 228 5311 **w** croxteth.co.uk
open See website for details.
admission Free

*An Edwardian stately home set in 500 acres of
countryside (woodlands and pasture), featuring a
Victorian walled garden and animal collection.*

Liverpool Anglican Cathedral

St James Mount, Liverpool L1 7AZ
t (0151) 709 6271 **w** liverpoolcathedral.org.uk
open Daily 0800-1800.
admission Free

*The largest cathedral in Britain. A great neo-Gothic
building, designed by Giles Gilbert Scott, started in 1904
and completed in 1978.*

Metropolitan Cathedral of Christ the King

Mount Pleasant, Liverpool L3 5TQ
t (0151) 709 9222 **w** liverpoolmetrocathedral.org.uk
open Daily 0800-1800.
admission Free

*A 20thC circular cathedral famous for its 290ft lantern
tower, stained glass and modern works of art.
Monumental crypt of an earlier incomplete project by
Edwin Lutyens.*

Port Sunlight Village Trust

95 Greendale Road, Port Sunlight CH62 4XE
t (0151) 644 4803 **w** portsunlightvillage.com
open See website for details.
admission Free

*A picturesque Grade II Listed village built for Lever's
19thC soap works. The heritage centre tells the story of
the village and community.*

Speke Hall, Gardens and Woodland (National Trust)

The Walk, Liverpool L24 1XD
t (0151) 427 7231 **w** nationaltrust.org.uk
open Please see website for details.
admission £££

*A wonderful, rambling Tudor mansion with rich
Victorian interiors, set in a wooded estate on the banks
of the Mersey with views of Wirral and North Wales.*

Admission is based on an adult price. Please check opening times and admission before travelling.

OUTDOOR ACTIVITIES

Mersey Ferries
Victoria Place, Seacombe, Wallasey CH44 6QY
t (0151) 330 1444
w merseyferries.co.uk
open See website for details.
admission £

Cruises offering visitors the opportunity to view the spectacular Liverpool waterfront which is now a UNESCO World Heritage Site.

The Yellow Duckmarine
Britannia Vaults, Albert Dock, Liverpool L3 4AD
t (0151) 708 7799
w theyellowduckmarine.co.uk
open Daily 1100-dusk.
admission ££

A one-hour amphibious sightseeing tour of Liverpool's historic city and award-winning waterfront and docks with live commentary throughout.

ENTERTAINMENT AND CULTURE

The Beatles Story
Britannia Vaults, Albert Dock, Liverpool L3 4AD
t (0151) 709 1963
w beatlesstory.com
open Daily 1000-1800.
admission ££

The multi-award-winning attraction dedicated to Liverpool's most famous sons – John, Paul, George and Ringo. Living-history audio guide. A personal journey through the Fab Four's meteoric rise to fame.

Lady Lever Art Gallery
Port Sunlight Village,
Higher Bebington CH62 5EQ
t (0151) 478 4136
w ladyleverartgallery.org.uk
open Daily 1000-1700.
admission Free

The 1st Lord Leverhulme's magnificent collection of British paintings dated 1750-1900, British furniture, Wedgwood pottery and oriental porcelain.

Liverpool Museum
William Brown Street, Liverpool L3 8EN
t (0151) 478 4393
w liverpoolmuseum.org.uk
open Daily 1000-1700.
admission Free

One of Britain's finest museums with collections from all over the world. Features include the planetarium, the space gallery and the hands-on Natural History Centre.

Mendips & 20 Forthlin Road (National Trust)

Speke Hall, The Walk, Speke Hall Avenue,
Speke L24 1XD
t (0151) 427 7231 **w** nationaltrust.org.uk
open Mar-Oct, Wed-Sun, by tour only.
admission £££

Number 20 Forthlin Road is where the Beatles met, rehearsed and wrote many of their earliest songs. Displays include contemporary photographs by Mike McCartney and early Beatles memorabilia.

Merseyside Maritime Museum
Albert Dock, Liverpool L3 4AQ
t (0151) 478 4499
w merseysidemaritimemuseum.org.uk
open Daily 1000-1700.
admission Free

Liverpool's seafaring heritage brought to life in the historic Albert Dock. Visitors can inspect the mueum's collection and, during the summer, explore the adjacent ships and quaysides.

Tate Liverpool

Albert Dock, Liverpool L3 4BB
t (0151) 702 7400 **w** tate.org.uk/liverpool/
open All year, Tue-Sun 1000-1750.
admission Free

Part of the historic Albert Dock, and home to the National Collection of modern art, Tate Liverpool has four floors of art, free daily talks, shop and cafe.

The Walker
William Brown Street, Liverpool L3 8EL
t (0151) 478 4199 **w** thewalker.org.uk
open Daily 1000-1700.
admission Free

The national gallery of the North, The Walker is one of the finest galleries in Europe, housing outstanding collections of British and European art.

Williamson Art Gallery
Slatey Road, Birkenhead CH43 4UE
t (0151) 652 4177 **w** wirral.gov.uk
open All year, Tue-Sun 1000-1700.
admission Free

The gallery features English watercolours, Liverpool school pictures, important collections of Merseyside pottery and porcelain (Liverpool, Seacombe, Della Robbia) and local-history galleries.

World Museum Liverpool
William Brown Street, Liverpool L3 8EN
t (0151) 478 4393
w worldmuseumliverpool.org.uk
open Daily 1000-1700.
admission Free

One of Britain's finest museums, with extensive collections from the Amazonian rain forest to the mysteries of outer space. Special attractions include the award-winning hands-on Natural History Centre and th Planetarium.

Northumberland

Enjoy the fun of a special event or visit one of the attractions listed for a great day out. For more inspiring ideas go to **enjoyengland.com**.

28 May
The Northumberland County Show
Tynedale Park, Corbridge
(01434) 609533
northcountyshow.co.uk

14–16 Jun
Tynedale Beer Festival
Tynedale Park, Corbridge
(01434) 652220
tynedalebeerfestival.org.uk

27 Jun–1 Jul
Alnwick Fair
Alnwick
(01665) 711397

4–11 Aug
Alnwick International Music and Dance Festival
Alnwick
(01665) 510665
alnwickfestival.com

13–21 Oct
Haltwhistle Walking Festival
Haltwhistle
(01434) 321242
haltwhistle.org

 FAMILY FUN

Alnwick Castle

Alnwick Castle Ventures,
Estates Office, Alnwick NE66 1NQ
t (01665) 510777 **w** alnwickcastle.com
open 2 Apr-28 Oct 1000-1800.
admission Adult: £9

Alnwick is one of Europe's finest medieval castles, featuring glorious state rooms, fine art and architecture, fascinating exhibitions, children's activities, special events and the unique Knights Quest interactive games area. Fine food and drink is served by The Sanctuary at The Castle – Restaurant and Wine Bar, and the Courtyard Cafe. Best Large Attraction 2006 – North East Tourism Awards.

Map ref 5C1

V voucher offer – see back section

Prudhoe Waterworld
Front Street,
Prudhoe NE42 5DQ
t (01661) 833144
w leisuretynedale.co.uk
open All year, Mon-Thu 0715-2100,
Fri 0715-1915, Sat 0800-1630,
Sun 0800-1730.
admission £

Leisure pool incorporating wave machine, 40m aqua slide, spa pool and other water features, fitness gym, fitness studio, soft play area, creche and bowling green.

For key to symbols see inside back cover.

Whitehouse Farm Centre

North White House Farm, Morpeth NE61 6AW
t (01670) 789998
w whitehousefarmcentre.co.uk
open Feb-Oct, Dec, Tue-Sun, Bank Hols 1000-1700.
Nov, Jan, Sat-Sun 1000-1700.
admission ££

An all-weather fun attraction with soft play area, licensed restaurant, craft workshops and outdoor play areas. Tractor and trailer rides and lots of animals.

NATURE AND WILDLIFE

The Alnwick Garden

Denwick Lane, Alnwick NE66 1YU
t (01665) 511350
w alnwickgarden.com
open Apr-May, daily 1000-1800. Jun-Sep,daily, 1000-1900. Oct, daily 1000-1800. Nov-Mar, daily 1000-1600.
admission ££

An exciting, contemporary garden with beautiful and unique gardens, features and structures, brought to life with water. Fantastic eating, drinking and shopping. Events throughout the year.

Carlisle Park and Castle Woods

Castle Square, Morpeth NE61 1YD
t (01670) 500777
w castlemorpeth.gov.uk
open Apr-Oct, daily 0730-dusk. Nov-Mar, daily 0730-1600.
admission Free

Formal park containing historic architectural remains, riverside and woodland walks, aviary, tennis courts, bowling greens, paddling pool, boats and play area.

Chesters Walled Garden

The Chesters, Humshaugh, Hexham NE46 4BQ
t (01434) 681483
w chesterswalledgarden.co.uk
open Apr-Oct, daily 1000-1700.
admission £

Beautiful two-acre walled garden containing a unique extensive herb collection, Roman garden, National Collection of thyme, large herbaceous borders, herbal gift shop and nursery.

Druridge Bay Country Park

Red Row, Druridge Bay NE61 5BX
t (01670) 760968
w northumberland.gov.uk
open Daily, dawn-dusk.
admission Free

Lake with woods and meadows plus three miles of beach and sand dunes. Visitor centre, walks, water sports, picnic areas, natural history and birdwatching. Cafe and gift shop.

Howick Hall Gardens

Estate Office, Howick Hall, Alnwick NE66 3LB
t (01665) 577285 **w** howickhallgardens.org.uk
open Apr-Oct, daily 1200-1800. Nov-Mar, Sat-Sun 1200-1600.
admission £

Lovely flower, shrub and rhododendron gardens. Extensive grounds with a collection of shrubs in woodland garden, formal gardens around the house, a bog garden and new arboretum (2006).

Kielder Water Birds of Prey Centre

Leaplish Waterside Park, Falstone, Hexham NE48 1AX
t (01434) 250400 **w** kielderwaterbirdsofpreycentre.com
open Mar-Sep, daily 1030-1700. Oct-Feb, daily 1030-dusk.
admission £

Visit one of the largest and most fascinating collections of birds of prey in the North of England, located within the magnificent forest lakeside surrounding Kielder Water.

Leaplish Waterside Park

Northumbrian Water Ltd, Hexham NE48 1BT
t 0870 240 3549 **w** nwl.co.uk/kielder
open Daily.
admission Free

Situated in the north Tyne Valley and close to the Scottish Borders, with breathtaking scenery around the 27-mile shoreline. Facilities and activities to suit all ages.

Longframlington Gardens

Swarland Road, Longframlington NE65 8BE
t (01665) 570382 **w** longframlingtongardens.co.uk
open Daily 0830-1700.
admission £

Twelve acres of garden and arboretum walks including a wild-flower meadow, rope art, garden design and nursery and plant centre, all in a peaceful countryside setting with fabulous views.

Queen Elizabeth II Jubilee Country Park, Local Nature Reserve

Woodhorn Road, Ashington NE63 9AS
t (01670) 843444
open Daily.
admission Free

Woodhorn Colliery is a heritage museum. The country park, once the site of a colliery spoil heap, features a wide variety of wildlife in its woodland and a 40-acre lake.

Tyne Green Country Park

Tyne Green, Hexham NE46 3SG
t 07811 129525 **w** tynedale.gov.uk
open Daily.
admission Free

Riverside park in a wooded setting with golf, fishing and canoeing on the river. Waymarked country trail, children's play area and picnic and barbecue area.

HISTORIC ENGLAND

Alnwick Castle

Alnwick Castle Ventures,
Estates Office, Alnwick NE66 1NQ
t (01665) 510777 **w** alnwickcastle.com
open 2 Apr-28 Oct 1000-1800.
admission Adult: £9

Alnwick is one of Europe's finest medieval castles, featuring glorious state rooms, fine art and architecture, fascinating exhibitions, children's activities, special events and the unique Knights Quest interactive games area. Fine food and drink is served by The Sanctuary at The Castle – Restaurant and Wine Bar, and the Courtyard Cafe. Best Large Attraction 2006 – North East Tourism Awards.

     Map ref 5C1

 voucher offer – see back section

Aydon Castle
Corbridge NE45 5PJ
t (01434) 632450 **w** english-heritage.org.uk
open See website for details.
admission £
Fine example of a small castle built as a manor house in the late 13th century and fortified shortly after. It was converted to a farmhouse in the 17th century.

Tourist Information Centres

To find your nearest Tourist Information Centre text TIC LOCATE to 64118.

Bamburgh Castle
Bamburgh NE69 7DF
t (01668) 214515 **w** bamburghcastle.com
open Apr-Oct, daily 1000-1700.
admission ££
Magnificent coastal castle completely restored in 1900 housing collections of china, porcelain, furniture, paintings, arms and armour. The castle is home to the Armstrong family.

Barter Books
Alnwick Station, Alnwick NE66 2NP
t (01665) 604888 **w** barterbooks.co.uk
open Apr-Sep, daily 0900-1900. Oct-Mar, Mon-Wed, Fri-Sun 0900-1700, Thu 0900-1900.
admission Free
The bookshop, selling second-hand books, is one of the largest in Britain. Lots of seating, a children's room, light refreshments, free parking.

Belsay Hall, Castle and Gardens
Belsay NE20 0DX
t (01661) 881636 **w** english-heritage.org.uk
open See website for details.
admission ££
Home of the Middleton family for 600 years. Thirty acres of landscaped gardens and winter garden. Fourteenth-century castle, ruined 17thC manor house and neoclassical hall.

Berwick Castle
The Walls, Berwick-upon-Tweed TD15 1HP
t (01289) 304493 **w** english-heritage.org.uk
open See website for details.
admission £
West wall of 12thC castle with 16thC gun tower which survived as a boundary for the railway yard, and late 13thC curtain wall descending to the river.

Brinkburn Priory
Longframlington NE65 8AR
t (01665) 570628 **w** english-heritage.org.uk
open See website for details.
admission £
Founded in 1135, the priory was restored in the 19th century, and now survives in its entirety as Northumberland's finest example of early Gothic architecture.

Chesters Roman Fort (Cilurnum) Hadrian's Wall
Chollerford, Humshaugh NE46 4EU
t (01434) 681379 **w** english-heritage.org.uk
open Apr-Sep, daily 0930-1800. Oct-Mar, daily 1000-1600.
admission £
The best-preserved example of a Roman cavalry fort in Britain, including remains of the bath house. The Clayton Collection Museum houses a fascinating collection of Roman sculpture and inscriptions.

Chillingham Castle
Chillingham, Alnwick NE66 5NJ
t (01668) 215359 **w** chillingham-castle.com
open Castle: Apr-Sep, Mon-Fri, Sun 1300-1700.
Grounds: Apr-Sep, Mon-Fri, Sun 1200-1700.
admission ££
Medieval fortress with Tudor additions. Torture chamber, shop, dungeon, tearoom, woodland walks, beautifully furnished rooms and Italian topiary garden with spectacular herbaceous borders.

Chipchase Castle
Wark, Chillingham NE48 3NT
t (01434) 230203
open Jun, daily 1400-1700.
admission £
One of the best examples of Jacobean architecture in the Borders. Chapel, 14thC pele tower, walled vegetable garden, wild garden with lake, nursery garden selling plants.

Cragside House, Gardens and Estate
Cragside, Rothbury, Morpeth NE65 7PX
t (01669) 620333 **w** nationaltrust.org.uk
open House: Apr-Sep, Tue-Sun 1300-1730. Oct, Tue-Sun 1300-1630. Gardens: Apr-Oct, Tue-Sun 1030-1730. Nov, Wed-Sun 1100-1600.
admission £££
The creation of Lord Armstrong, Cragside is a garden of breathtaking drama, whatever the season. This magnificent estate provides one of the last shelters for the endangered red squirrel.

Dunstanburgh Castle
Craster NE66 3TT
t (01665) 576231 **w** english-heritage.org.uk
open See website for details.
admission £
Romantic ruins of extensive 14thC castle in dramatic coastal situation on 100ft cliffs. Built by Thomas, Earl of Lancaster. Remains include gatehouse and curtain wall.

Etal Castle
Etal Village, Etal TD12 4TN
t (01890) 820332 **w** english-heritage.org.uk
open Apr-Oct, daily 1100-1600.
admission £
Typical compact 14thC border castle comprising four-storey keep, gatehouse, parts of curtain wall and corner tower. The 19thC chapel displays an award-winning exhibition.

Hexham Abbey
Beaumont Street, Hexham NE46 3NB
t (01434) 602031 **w** hexhamabbey.org.uk
open Daily 0930-1700.
admission £
Saxon crypt, 15thC paintings, misericords and Saxon chalice, 7thC Frith stool and Augustinian night stair. Most of the church is in the Early English style of architecture.

Housesteads Roman Fort (Vercovicium) Hadrian's Wall
Haydon Bridge NE47 6NN
t (01434) 344363
w english-heritage.org.uk
open Apr-Sep, daily 1000-1800. Oct-Mar, daily 1000-1600.
admission £
The best-preserved and most impressive of the Roman forts, Vercovicium was a five-acre fort for an extensive 800-strong civil settlement and contains the only example of a Roman hospital in Britain.

Kielder Castle Forest Park Centre
Kielder Castle, Kielder, Hexham NE48 1ER
t (01434) 250209
w forestry.gov.uk
open Apr-Oct, daily 1000-1700. Nov-Dec, Sat-Sun 1100-1600.
admission Free
Kielder Castle is the visitor centre for Kielder Forest. Features include forest shop, information centre, tearoom and exhibitions about forestry and conservation.

National Park Centre Once Brewed
Military Road, Hadrian's Wall, Hexham NE47 7AN
t (01434) 344396
w northumberland-national-park.org.uk
open Apr-Oct, daily 0930-1700. Dec-Mar, Sat-Sun 1000-1500.
admission Free
National Park visitor centre with exhibitions, shop selling refreshments, maps, books, souvenirs and clothing, picnic area, toilets, car park and easy access onto Hadrian's Wall.

Norham Castle
Norham TD15 1DF
t (01289) 382329
w english-heritage.org.uk
open Apr-Sep, Sun, Bank Hols 1000-1700.
admission Free
One of the strongest of Border castles and one of the finest Norman keeps in England. The most famous siege in Sir Walter Scott's Marmion.

Otterburn Mills
Otterburn NE19 1JT
t (01830) 520225
w otterburnmill.co.uk
open Apr-Oct, Mon-Sat 0900-1700, Sun 1000-1630. Nov-Mar, daily 1000-1630.
admission Free
Retailers of high-quality woollen rugs, knitwear, jackets and outdoor leisurewear gifts. Fully licensed coffee shop and exhibition of textile machines and water turbine.

Preston Tower

Chathill NE67 5DH
t (01665) 589227
open Apr-Sep, daily 1000-dusk. Oct-Mar, daily 1000-1600.
admission £

The tower, built by Sir Robert Harbottle in 1392, is one of the few-surviving pele towers. The tunnel-vaulted rooms remain unaltered, and two are furnished in contemporary style.

Wallington House, Walled Garden and Grounds

Wallington, Cambo, Morpeth NE61 4AR
t (01670) 773600
w nationaltrust.org.uk
open House: Apr-Aug, Mon, Wed-Sun 1300-1730.
Sep-Oct, Mon, Wed-Sun 1300-1630. Walled Garden:
Apr-Sep, daily 1000-1900. Oct, daily 1000-1800.
Nov-Feb, daily 1000-1600. Grounds: Daily, dawn-dusk.
admission ££

The country home of the Trevelyan family sits in 100 acres of lawns, lakes and woodland. Visit the beautiful walled garden or enjoy a woodland or riverside walk.

Warkworth Castle

Warkworth NE65 0UJ
t (01665) 711423
w english-heritage.org.uk
open See website for details.
admission £

Dramatic ruins dating from the 12thC-14thC, owned by the Percy family for 600 years. Remains include the 15thC keep, chapel, great hall and lion tower with carved lion.

Warkworth Hermitage

Warkworth NE65 0UJ
t (01665) 711423
w english-heritage.org.uk
open See website for details.
admission £

The hermitage is cut into the rock of the river cliff, hidden away underneath the wooded bank, a short walk upstream from the castle.

OUTDOOR ACTIVITIES

Billy Shiel's Farne Island Boat Trips

Seahouses NE68 7YT
t (01665) 720308
w farne-islands.com
open Daily 1000-1600, weather permitting.
admission £££

Boat trips to the Farne Islands from Seahouses. Visit the grey-seal colonies whilst listening to the commentary. All-day birdwatching trips during the breeding season.

Kielder Water Cruises

Northumbrian Water Ltd, Hexham NE48 1AX
t 0870 240 3549
w nwl.co.uk/leisure
open Apr-Oct, daily 1015-1615, weather permitting.
admission ££

Cruise around Kielder Water in an 80-passenger cruiser with heated lounge, light refreshments, toilets and on-board commentary. Full safety equipment.

Puffin Cruises Dave Gray Boat Trips

21 Broomhill Street, Amble NE65 0AN
t (01665) 711975
open Please phone for details.
admission ££

Take a boat trip around Coquet Island to see the puffins, terns, ducks and seals. A lighthouse, built by monks, and ruins of a monastery window are visible.

ENTERTAINMENT AND CULTURE

Berwick-upon-Tweed Museum and Art Gallery

Ravensdowne Barracks,
Berwick-upon-Tweed TD15 1DG
t (01289) 301869
w english-heritage.org.uk
open Apr-Oct, daily 1000-1700.
admission £

The museum is housed in the historic Berwick Barracks and contains collections of fine and decorative art and local history displayed in innovative ways.

Hadrian's Wall, near Haltwhistle

Cherryburn: Thomas Bewick Birthplace Museum

Cherryburn, Station Bank, Mickley,
Stocksfield NE43 7DD
t (01661) 843276 **w** nationaltrust.org.uk
open Apr-Oct, Mon-Tue, Thu-Sun 1100-1700.
admission £

The birthplace of Thomas Bewick. The 19thC farmhouse houses a small exhibition on his life and work. Farmyard animals including donkeys and lambs, garden with picnic lawn. Demonstrations most days.

Hexham Old Gaol

Hallgate, Hexham NE46 3NH
t (01434) 652349 **w** tynedaleheritage.org
open Mar-Oct, daily 1000-1630. Nov-Feb, Mon-Tue, Sat 1000-1630.
admission £

Tour the Old Gaol (1330AD) which has a glass lift down to the dungeon. Meet the gaoler, see a Reiver raid and try on costumes.

Lady Waterford Hall

Ford Village, Berwick-upon-Tweed TD15 2QA
t (01890) 820503 **w** ford-and-etal.co.uk
open Apr-Oct, daily 1030-1730.
admission £

A beautiful 19thC hall with watercolour paintings by Louisa Anne, Marchioness of Waterford, together with famous and unique 19thC murals and scenes from the Bible.

Vindolanda (Chesterholm) Hadrian's Wall

Chesterholm Museum, Bardon Mill NE47 7JN
t (01434) 344277 **w** vindolanda.com
open Apr-Sep, daily 1000-1800. Oct-Nov, daily 1000-1700.
admission £

Visitors may inspect the remains of the Roman fort and settlement and see its extraordinary finds in the superb museum. Full-scale replicas of Roman buildings.

Woodhorn

QEII Country Park, Ashington NE63 9YF
t (01670) 528080 **w** experiencewoodhorn.com
open Apr-Oct, Wed-Sun 1000-1700. Nov-Mar, Wed-Sun 1000-1600.
admission Free

A fascinating visitor attraction celebrating Northumberland. A stunning new building, inspired by monster coal-cutting machines that once worked underground, houses an emotive display about life in the local mining community.

Wylam Railway Museum

Falcon Centre, Falcon Terrace, Wylam NE41 8EE
t (01661) 852174
open Apr-Mar, Tue, Thu 1400-1930, Sat 0900-1200.
admission Free

This small museum shows the importance of Wylam in the history of railway development and the work of famous local railway pioneers George Stephenson, Timothy Hackworth and William Hedley.

Lion Bridge, Alnwick Castle

Tees Valley

Enjoy the fun of a special event or visit one of the attractions listed for a great day out. For more inspiring ideas go to **enjoyengland.com**.

17 Jun
Middlesbrough Music Live
Middlesbrough town centre
(0114) 247755
middlesbroughmusiclive.co.uk

15 Jul
Middlesbrough Mela
Albert Park, Middlesbrough
boromela.co.uk

28 Jul–4 Aug
Billingham International Folklore Festival
Billingham town centre and Forum Theatre
(01642) 553220
billinghamfestival.co.uk

28 Jul
Cleveland Show
Stewart Park, Middlesbrough
(01642) 312231
middlesbrough.gov.uk

1–5 Aug
Stockton International Riverside Festival
Stockton
(01642) 528130
sirf.co.uk

FAMILY FUN

Darlington Railway Centre and Museum

North Road Station, Darlington DL3 6ST
t (01325) 460532 **w** drcm.org.uk
open Daily 1000-1700 (excl 25 Dec, 1-2 Jan).
admission Adult: £2.50

Step back in time in one of the world's oldest railway stations – see, touch, feel and smell living railway heritage. More than just a museum, enjoy family-friendly events, too. There's always something to see and do, whatever the weather. Fun for everyone, from Grandma to the tiniest tot!

 Map ref 5C3

 V *voucher offer – see back section*

Nature's World
Ladgate Lane, Acklam,
Middlesbrough TS5 7YN
t (01642) 594895
w naturesworld.org.uk
open Apr-Sep, daily 1000-1700. Oct-Mar, daily 1030-1530.
admission £

Demonstration gardens, wildlife pond, white garden, shop, tearoom and unique River Tees model. Futuristic Hydroponicum and Eco Centre now open, powered by renewable energy. Family trails and play areas.

Newham Grange Leisure Farm
Wykeham Way, Coulby Newham,
Middlesbrough TS8 0TG
t (01642) 300202
w middlesbrough.gov.uk
open Apr-Sep, daily 0930-1730. Oct-Mar,
Sat-Sun 1000-1600.
admission £

*A working farm that is recognised as a Rare
Breeds Survival Trust Approved
Conservation Centre with many breeds to
see. A great day out, allowing visitors to
interact with animals.*

Saltburn Miniature Railway
Valley Gardens,
Saltburn-by-the-Sea
t (01642) 502863
w saltburn-miniature-railway.org.uk
open Apr-Sep, Sat-Sun, Bank Hols 1300-1700.
admission £

*A 15''-gauge miniature railway running from the
seafront to the Valley Gardens and Woodland
Centre. First established in 1947 and operated
solely by volunteers.*

NATURE AND WILDLIFE

Flatts Lane Woodland Country Park
Woodland Country Park,
Visitor Centre, Flatts Lane,
Middlesbrough TS6 0NN
t (01642) 459629
w redcar-cleveland.gov.uk/countryside
open All year, Mon-Fri 0830-1630,
Sun 1000-1600.
admission Free

*Country park comprising 100 acres of woodland
and scrub. Visitor centre with exhibition showing
the past, present and future landscape. Shop,
picnic site and play area.*

Guisborough Forest and Walkway Visitor Centre
Pinchinthorpe, Guisborough TS14 8HD
t (01287) 631132 **w** redcar-cleveland.gov.uk
open Summer: Mon-Fri, 0900-1630, Sat-Sun 1000-1700.
Winter: Mon-Fri 0900-1600, Sat-Sun 1000-1630.
admission Free

*Countryside visitor centre with self-guided trails,
orienteering, walks and mountain biking. Situated on the
edge of Guisborough Forest. Picnic areas with fantastic
views of the Tees Valley.*

Kirkleatham Owl Centre
Kirkleatham, Redcar TS10 5NW
t (01642) 480512 **w** jillsowls.co.uk
open See website for details.
admission £

*Bird of prey centre with one of the most significant
collections of owls in the British Isles. Falcons, buzzards
vultures, kites, caracaras, baby owls and flying displays.*

HISTORIC ENGLAND

Guisborough Priory
Church Street, Guisborough TS14 6HG
t (01287) 633801
open All year, Wed-Sun 0900-1700.
admission £

*An Augustinian priory founded by Robert the Bruce in
1119, the remains of which include the gatehouse and
the east end of a 14thC church.*

Ormesby Hall
Church Lane, Ormesby,
Middlesbrough TS7 9AS
t (01642) 324188
w nationaltrust.org.uk
open Apr-Nov, Sat-Sun 1330-1700.
admission £

*Beautiful 18thC mansion with park, gardens, tearoom,
impressive contemporary plasterwork, magnificent
stable block attributed to Carr of York and model railway
exhibition and layout.*

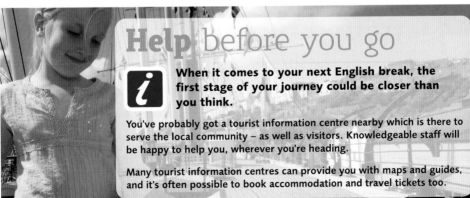

Help before you go

i When it comes to your next English break, the first stage of your journey could be closer than you think.

You've probably got a tourist information centre nearby which is there to
serve the local community – as well as visitors. Knowledgeable staff will
be happy to help you, wherever you're heading.

Many tourist information centres can provide you with maps and guides,
and it's often possible to book accommodation and travel tickets too.

Saltburn's Inclined Tramway

Marine Parade, Saltburn-by-the-Sea TS12 1DP

t (01287) 622528

open Apr-May, daily 1000-1700. Jun-mid Sep, daily 1000-1900. Mid Sep-Oct, daily 1000-1700. Oct, Sat-Sun 1000-1700.

admission £

The oldest remaining water-balanced cliff lift in Britain, recently refurbished, with stained glass windows. It links Saltburn's pier, one of the few left in the country, with the town.

Sir William Turner Alms Houses

1 Sir William Turner's Court, Kirkleatham TS10 4QT

t (01642) 482828

w communigate.co.uk/ne/swthospital

open Group bookings only, please phone for details.

admission £

Founded in 1676 as Almshouses for the poor. They have been lived in continuously to this day. Fine Georgian chapel containing various historical items.

Tocketts Water Mill

Skelton Road, Guisborough TS14 6TC

t (01287) 634437

open Jul-Sep, Sun 1400-1600.

admission £

Fully restored water-driven corn mill and Grade II* Listed building. Flour-grinding and -grading machinery dating from the 18thC and 19thC. Wholemeal flour, stone-ground on some Sundays.

Transporter Bridge and Visitor Centre

Ferry Road, Middlesbrough TS2 1PL

t (01642) 728162 **w** middlesbrough.gov.uk

open Bridge: All Year, Mon-Sat 0500-2300, Sun 1400-2300. Visitor Centre: All Year, Mon-Sat 0900-1700, Sun 1400-1700.

admission Free

A unique structure which can carry nine cars or 200 people on each crossing. Gantry system. Visitor information centre and shop.

ENTERTAINMENT AND CULTURE

Captain Cook Birthplace Museum

Stewart Park, Marton, Middlesbrough TS7 8AT

t (01642) 311211 **w** captcook-ne.co.uk

open Mar-Oct, Tue-Sun 1000-1730. Nov-Feb, Tue-Sun 0900-1600.

admission Free

Discover why Captain Cook is the world's most famous navigator and explorer. Find out about life below decks in the 18th century. Temporary exhibitions and permanent displays.

Cleveland Ironstone Mining Museum

Deepdale, Skinningrove, Saltburn-by-the-Sea TS13 4AP

t (01287) 642877 **w** ironstonemuseum.co.uk

open Apr-Oct, daily 1300-1700.

admission £

Discover the special skills and customs of the miners that helped make Cleveland the most important ironstone-mining district in Victorian and Edwardian England.

Darlington Railway Centre and Museum

North Road Station, Darlington DL3 6ST

t (01325) 460532 **w** drcm.org.uk

open Daily 1000-1700 (excl 25 Dec, 1-2 Jan).

admission Adult: £2.50

Step back in time in one of the world's oldest railway stations – see, touch, feel and smell living railway heritage. More than just a museum, enjoy family-friendly events, too. There's always something to see and do, whatever the weather. Fun for everyone, from Grandma to the tiniest tot!

Map ref 5C3

ⓥ *voucher offer – see back section*

MIMA, Middlesbrough Institute of Modern Art

Middlesbrough Central Square, Middlesbrough TS1 2BG

t (01642) 803434 **w** mima.uk.com

open Apr-Mar, Mon-Sat 1000-1700, Sun 1200-1600, Bank Hols 1000-1700.

admission Free

MIMA is a new gallery of modern and contemporary art in central Middlesbrough. Admission is free. Exhibitions of fine art and craft change every three months.

For key to symbols see inside back cover.

Tyne and Wear

FAMILY FUN

Enjoy the fun of a special event or visit one of the attractions listed for a great day out. For more inspiring ideas go to **enjoyengland.com**.

30 Jun–1 Jul
Sunderland International Kite Festival
Washington
(0191) 553 2000
sunderland-kites.co.uk

13–15 Jul
Whitley Bay International Jazz Festival
Menzies Silverlink Hotel, Wallsend
(0191) 252 3505
whitleybayjazzfest.org

28–29 Jul
Sunderland International Airshow
Seaburn seafront, Sunderland
(0191) 553 2000
sunderland-airshow.com

1–31 Dec
Winter Festival
Various venues, NewcastleGateshead
(0191) 243 8804
newcastlegateshead.com

May 08
Northumbrian Water University Boat Race
River Tyne, Quayside, Newcastle upon Tyne
(0191) 433 6900
gateshead.gov.uk

New Metroland
39 Garden Walk, MetroCentre, Gateshead NE11 9XY
t (01914) 932048 **w** metroland.uk.com
open School Hols: Mon-Sat 1000-2000, Sun 1100-1800. Term Time: Mon-Fri, 1200-2000, Sat 1000-2000, Sun 1100-1800.
admission £££
Europe's largest indoor funfair with twelve major attractions including the New Rollercoaster, Disco Dodgems, Whirling Waltzer and Children's Adventure Play Area.

Ocean Beach Pleasure Park
Sea Road, South Shields NE33 2ld
t (01914) 561617 **w** oceanbeach.co.uk
open Apr-Nov, daily. Please phone for times.
admission Free
This is the only funfair on the north east coast. Guaranteed new attractions every season. A great day out for all the family. See website for details.

Pier Amusements Centre
South Shields NE33 2JS
t (01914) 553885
open Daily 1000-2000.
admission £
The centre has all the latest in amusement equipment including Quasar, a futuristic game where each player is armed with a laser gun and shoots the opposition to win points.

Wet 'N Wild
Rotary Way, Royal Quays, North Shields NE29 6DA
t (01912) 961333 **w** wetnwild.co.uk
open Apr-Jun, Wed-Thu 1200-1930, Fri 1200-2000, Sat 1000-2000, Sun 1000-1900. July-Sep, Bank Hols, Mon-Sat 1000-2000, Sun 1000-1900. Oct-Mar, Wed-Thu 1200-1930, Fri 1200-2000, Sat 1000-2000, Sun 1000-1900.
admission ££
Tropical indoor water park. A fun water playground providing the wildest and wettest indoor rapid experience. Whirlpools, slides and meandering lazy river.

Whickham Thorns Outdoor Activity Centre
Market Lane, Dunston NE11 9NX
t (01914) 335767 **w** gateshead.gov.uk
open Apr-Oct, Mon-Fri 0900-2000, Sat 1100-1830, Sun 1200-1500. Nov-Mar, Mon-Fri 1100-1000, Sat 1100-1830, Sun, 1200-1500.
admission Free
Multi-activity outdoor centre featuring skiing, snowboarding, indoor climbing, archery, assault course, orienteering, mountain biking and team challenges

NATURE AND WILDLIFE

HISTORIC ENGLAND

Blue Reef Aquarium
Grand Parade, Tynemouth NE30 4JF
t (01912) 581031
w bluereefaquarium.co.uk
open Apr-Oct, Mon-Sat 1000-1730, Sun 1200-1730.
Nov-Mar, Mon-Sat 1000-1630, Sun 1200-1630.
admission ££
More than 30 living displays exploring the drama of the
North Sea and the dazzling beauty of a spectacular coral
reef with its own underwater tunnel.

Derwent Walk Country Park
Rowlands Gill NE39 1AU
t (01207) 545212
w gateshead.gov.uk
open All Year, Mon-Fri 1200-1400, Sat-Sun, Bank Hols
1200-1700.
admission Free
Woodlands, riverside meadows and the Derwent Walk
(a disused railway line). Served by Thornley Woodlands
Visitor Centre and Swalwell Visitor Centre.

Gateshead Angel of the North
Durham Road, Low Eighton,
Gateshead NE9 6AA
t (01914) 784222
w gateshead.gov.uk
open Daily.
admission Free
Britain's largest sculpture designed by Antony Gormley,
standing 20m high with a wing span of 54m. The steel
structure can withstand winds of more than 100 miles
per hour.

Saltwell Park
Saltwell Road, Gateshead NE8 4SF
t (01914) 335900
w gateshead.gov.uk
open Daily, dawn-dusk.
admission Free
One of Britain's finest examples of a Victorian Park
offering bedding displays, rose garden, play areas,
shrubbery, a lake with boating and bowls.

WWT Washington Wetland Centre
Pattinson, Washington NE38 8LE
t (01914) 165454
w wwt.org.uk
open Apr-Oct, daily 0930-1700. Nov-Mar, daily
0930-1600.
admission ££
Conservation site with 100 acres of wetland and
woodland. Home to wildfowl, insects and flora. Lakeside
hides, wild bird feeding, station, waterside cafe, picnic
areas and playground.

Gateshead Millennium Bridge
South Shore Road, Gateshead NE8 3AE
t (01914) 784222 **w** gateshead.gov.uk/bridge
open Daily.
admission Free
A stunning pedestrian and cycle bridge which operates
like the giant lid of an eye slowly opening, forming an
arch to allow the passage of river traffic.

Gibside
Burnopfield NE16 6BG
t (01207) 541820 **w** nationaltrust.org.uk
open Grounds: Apr-Oct, daily 1000-1800. Nov-Feb,
daily 1000-1600. Chapel: Apr-Oct, daily 1100-1630.
Stables: Apr-Oct, daily 1100-1630. Nov-Feb, daily
1100-1530.
admission ££
Sixteen miles of riverside and woodland walks beside
the River Derwent. Also there is a beautiful 18thC
Palladian chapel, Georgian stables and greenhouse to
view.

National Glass Centre
Liberty Way, Sunderland SR6 0GL
t (01915) 155555 **w** nationalglasscentre.com
open Daily, 1000-1700.
admission Free
An inspirational visitor experience. Enjoy an ever-
changing programme of exhibitons in glass, live glass
blowing and a stunning restaurant overlooking the River
Wear.

Segedunum (Wallsend) Roman Fort, Baths and Museum
Buddle Street, Wallsend NE28 6HR
t (01912) 369347 **w** twmuseums.org.uk/segedunum
open Apr-Oct, daily 1000-1700. Nov-Mar, daily
1000-1500.
admission £
Discover life on Hadrian's Wall 1,800 years ago. Explore
buildings and excavated ruins, and see original remains
of the wall, fascinating displays and exciting computer
interactives.

Seven Stories, The Centre for Children's Books
30 Lime Street, Ouseburn Valley,
Newcastle upon Tyne NE1 2PQ
t 0845 271 0777 **w** sevenstories.org.uk
open All year, Mon-Sat 1000-1700, Sun 1100-1700.
admission £
Britain's first centre dedicated to children's literature,
bringing together original manuscripts and artwork from
some of the best-loved children's books. There is a
changing programme of exhibitions.

Admission is based on an adult price. Please check opening times and admission before travelling.

Souter Lighthouse and The Leas
Coast Road, Whitburn, Sunderland SR6 7NH
t (01915) 293161
w nationaltrust.org.uk
open Apr-Oct, Mon-Thu, Sat-Sun 1100-1700.
admission £
A magnificent lighthouse located on a beautiful stretch
of coastline. Explore the engine room, and climb the
winding staircase to the top of the tower.

Washington Old Hall
The Avenue, Washington Village, Washington NE38 7LE
t (01914) 166879
w nationaltrust.org.uk
open House: Apr-Oct, Mon-Wed, Sun 1100-1700.
Gardens: Apr-Oct, Mon-Wed, Sun 1000-1700.
admission £
A delightful stone-built manor house on the site of the
home of the ancestors of George Washington. Displays,
gardens and 17thC room recreations. A gem of a
property!

ENTERTAINMENT AND CULTURE

BALTIC Centre for Contemporary Art
Gateshead Quays, South Shore Road,
Gateshead NE8 3BA
t (01914) 781810
w balticmill.com
open Daily 1000-1800.
admission Free
Housed in a landmark industrial building on the River
Tyne is the biggest gallery of its kind in the world
presenting a dynamic, diverse and international
programme of contemporary visual art.

Bede's World
Church Bank, Jarrow NE32 3DY
t (01914) 892106
w bedesworld.co.uk
open Apr-Oct, Mon-Sat 1000-1730, Sun 1200-1730.
Nov-Mar, Mon-Sat 1000-1630, Sun 1200-1630.
admission £
Discover the exciting world of the Venerable Bede, early
medieval Europe's greatest scholar. Church, monastic
site, museum with exhibitions and recreated Anglo-
Saxon farm.

Biscuit Factory
16 Stoddart Street, Newcastle upon Tyne NE2 1AN
t (01912) 611103
w thebiscuitfactory.com
open All year, Mon 1100-1700, Tues-Sat 1000-2000,
Sun 1100-1700.
admission Free
A large commercial art space providing a vibrant, relaxed
environment of the highest quality for a wide range of
art and artists and for the public.

Childhood Memories Toy Museum
Palace Building, Grand Parade,
Tynemouth NE30 4JH
t (01912) 591776
w tynemouthtoymuseum.co.uk
open Apr-May, Sat-Sun 1030-1700. Jun-Sep, Tue-Sun
1030-1700. Oct-Nov, Sat-Sun 1030-1700.
admission £
The museum has over 7,000 toys on display dating from
1890-1970. Childhood memorabilia, dolls, games, pedal
cars, prams, cars, puzzles, clockwork and mechanical
toys.

Discovery Museum

Blandford House, Blandford Square,
Newcastle upon Tyne NE1 4JA
t (01912) 326789
w twmuseums.org.uk/discovery
open All year, Mon-Sat 1000-1700, Sun 1400-1700.
admission Free
The museum offers a wide variety of experiences
for all the family to enjoy. Explore Newcastle
Story, Live Wires, Science Maze and Fashion
Works.

Karting North East
Warden Law Motorsport Centre,
Sunderland SR3 2PR
t (01915) 214050
w kartingnortheast.com
open Daily, 0900-2000.
admission ££££
A 1,250m outdoor karting and off-road centre offering
high standards of safety and professionalism.
Clubhouse with showers, changing facilities and
meeting room.

Laing Art Gallery

New Bridge Street,
Newcastle upon Tyne NE1 8AJ
t (01912) 327734
w twmuseums.org.uk
open All Year, Mon-Sat 1000-1700, Sun 1400-1700.
admission Free
The gallery is home to an important collection of 18thC
and 19thC paintings, which are shown alongside
temporary exhibitions of historic and contemporary
art.

Monkwearmouth Station Museum
North Bridge Street,
Sunderland SR5 1AP
t (01915) 677075
w twmuseums.org.uk/monkwearmouth
open All year, Mon-Sat 1000-1700, Sun 1400-1700.
admission Free
Take a look inside a real Victorian railway station
and visit the fascinating ticket office. Watch trains
pass by and 'drive' a full-size bus cab. Re-opening
in 2007, visitors will be able to enjoy a range of
exciting new displays.

North East Aircraft Museum
Old Washington Road, Sunderland SR5 3HZ
t (01915) 190662
open Daily 1000-1700.
admission £
A collection of aircraft and aero engines. Museum buildings with World War II exhibits. Vulcan bomber and over 30 aircraft under cover.

The Sage Gateshead
St Mary's Square, Gatshead Quays, Gateshead NE8 2JR
t (01914) 434666
w thesagegateshead.org
open Daily, 0900-1100.
admission Free
The pioneering centre for music and musical discovery on the south bank of the River Tyne, presenting leading British and international artists in all kinds of music.

Shipley Art Gallery
Prince Consort Road, Gateshead NE8 4JB
t (01914) 771495
w twmuseums.org.uk/shipley
open All year, Mon-Sat 1000-1700, Sun, 1400-1700.
admission Free
The gallery is home to one of the largest collections of contemporary craft in northern England. Exhibits include jewellery, textiles, ceramics, furniture and glass.

Stephenson Railway Museum
Middle Engine Lane, North Shields NE29 8DX
t (01912) 007146
w twmuseums.org.uk/stephenson
open Apr-Oct, Sat-Sun 1100-1600.
admission Free
Museum covering steam, diesel and electric trains. Use interactive exhibits to discover how trains work, and enjoy our new multi-sensory display.

Sunderland Museum and Winter Gardens
Burdon Road, Sunderland SR1 1PP
t (01915) 532323
w twmuseums.org.uk/sunderland
open All year, Mon-Sat 1000-1700, Sun 1400-1700.
admission Free
Stunning winter gardens, with 1,500 of the world's most exotic flowers, plants and trees. Dramatic 'Museum Street', 11 galleries, tree-top walkway, shop, brasserie and lifts.

Sunderland Wall
Doxford Works, Pallion Quay, Sunderland SR4 6TQ
t (01915) 144234
w sunderlandwall.co.uk
open All year, Mon-Fri 1000-2200, Sat-Sun 1000-2000.
admission ££
The highest and largest indoor climbing centre in Europe, offering a bouldering wall as well as larger, top-roped and lead walls.

Yorkshire

Enjoy the fun of a special event or visit one of the attractions listed for a great day out. For more inspiring ideas go to **enjoyengland.com**.

15–17 Jun
Beverley Folk Festival
Various venues, Beverley
(01377) 217569
beverleyfestival.com

10–12 Jul
The Great Yorkshire Show
Harrogate
(01423) 541000
greatyorkshireshow.com

24–26 Aug
Carling Weekend Leeds Festival
Bramham Park, Leeds
0870 060 3775
carling.com/music/festival

1–2 Sep
Art in the Gardens
Botanical Gardens, Sheffield
sheffield.gov.uk

Feb 08
Jorvik Viking Festival
Jorvik Viking Centre, York
(01904) 543400
jorvik-viking-centre.co.uk

FAMILY FUN

Aerial Extreme
Camp Hill, Kirklington DL8 2LS
t (01845) 567100 **w** aerialextreme.co.uk
open Feb-Nov, Sat-Sun 0900-1700.
admission ££££
Get high above the forest floor travelling from tree to tree encountering rope bridges, log walks, tightropes, scramble nets and zip slides.

Barnsley Metrodome Leisure Complex
Queens Ground, Queens Road, Barnsley S71 1AN
t (01226) 730060 **w** themetrodome.co.uk
open All year, see website for details.
admission £
The Space Adventure is Britain's most exciting and imaginative indoor water attraction featuring the Space Bullet, possibly the fastest water slide in the universe!

Bridlington Leisure World
The Promenade, Bridlington YO15 2QQ
t (01262) 606715 **w** bridlington.net/leisureworld
open Please phone for details.
admission £
One of the East Riding's premier leisure attractions boasts three pools, including a fun pool with waves, slides, rainstorm effect and water features, a 25m training pool and a learner pool.

Brockholes Farm Visitor Centre
Warnington Lane, Branton DN3 3NH
t (01302) 535450 **w** brockholesfarm.co.uk
open All year, daily 1030-1730.
admission ££
Visitor centre housing a selection of farm animals including a pedigree herd of Limousin cattle. Also small animals including rabbits, guinea pigs, hamsters etc. Woodland walk and exotic birds.

Cannon Hall Farm
Bark House Lane, Cawthorne, Barnsley S75 4AT
t (01226) 790427 **w** cannonhallfarm.co.uk
open Apr-Sep, daily 1030-1630. Oct-Mar, daily 1030-1600.
admission £
A multiple-award-winning farm open to visitors all year round. A large variety of animals including donkeys, cows, rabbits, guinea pigs, wallabies and pygmy goats.

Cruckley Animal Farm
Foston-on-the-Wolds YO25 8BS
t (01262) 488337 **w** cruckley.co.uk
open Apr-Sep, daily 1000-1730.
admission £
A working family farm with many kinds of modern and rare breeds of cows, sheep and pigs. See the hatchery, children's paddock, waterfowl lake and daily milking demonstrations.

The Dome Leisure Centre
Doncaster Leisure Park, Bawtry Road, Doncaster DN4 7PD
t (01302) 370777 **w** the-dome.co.uk
open See website for details.
admission Free
The largest leisure facility in the UK with all the facilities under one roof. Activities include bowling, swimming, skating, gym, aerobic studio, saunas, badminton and basketball.

Embsay & Bolton Abbey Steam Railway
Bolton Abbey Station, Bolton Abbey BD23 6AF
t (01756) 710614 **w** embsayboltonabbeyrailway.org.uk
open See website for details.
admission ££
The railway runs between Embsay Station, built in 1888, and the new, award-winning Bolton Abbey Station. The five-mile journey through the Yorkshire Dales passes Holywell Halt.

Flamingo Land Theme Park and Zoo
Kirby Misperton YO17 6UX
t (01653) 668287 **w** flamingoland.co.uk
open Apr-Oct, Mon-Fri 1000-1700. Sat-Sun 1000-1800.
admission ££££
One price family adventure park with over 100 rides and attractions including the UK's only motorbike launch rollercoaster, the free-falling cliff hanger and Kamali, the suspended looping rollercoaster.

The Foundry Climbing Centre
45 Mowbray Street, Sheffield S3 8EN
t (0114) 279 6331 **w** foundryclimbing.com
open Summer, Mon-Fri 1000-2200, Sat-Sun 1000-1800.
Winter, Mon-Fri 1000-2200, Sat-Sun 1000-2000.
admission ££
A dedicated indoor climbing centre offering walls up to 13m high and lead/top rope climbs with 150 routes and bouldering. On-site cafe and climbing shop.

Freeport Hornsea Outlet Village
Rolston Road, Hornsea HU18 1UT
t (01964) 534211 **w** freeporthornsea.info
open All year, daily 0930-1800.
admission Free
Set in 25 acres of landscaped gardens with over 40 quality high street names, all selling stock with discounts of up to 50%. Licensed restaurant. Leisure attractions.

Hazel Brow Visitor Centre
Low Row DL11 6NE
t (01748) 886224 **w** hazelbrow.co.uk
open Apr-Sep, Tue-Thu, Sat-Sun 1030-1630.
admission £
Award-winning 200-acre organic livestock farm in the heart of Swaledale. Crafts and skills demonstrations including spinning and quilting, stick and rug making, butter making and sheepdog training.

Herringthorpe Leisure Complex

Middle Lane South,
Rotherham S65 2HR
t (01709) 388500
open All year, Mon-Fri 0900-2200, Sat 0900-1900, Sun 0900-2000.
admission £

The complex comprises a leisure pool with wave machine and aqua slide, multi-sports facilities including four squash courts and ten badminton courts, fitness suite and five-a-side football pitches.

Keighley and Worth Valley Railway

Haworth Station,
Keighley BD22 8NJ
t (01535) 645214
w kwvr.co.uk
open See website for details.
admission ££

Fully operational, preserved railway branch line, five miles long (Keighley to Oxenhope). Six award-winning stations including Oakworth, 'The Railway Children' station. The location for many film and television productions.

Kirklees Light Railway

Park Mill Way,
Clayton West HD8 9XJ
t (01484) 865727
w kirkleeslightrailway.com
open See website for details.
admission ££

Steam along on Hawk, Owl, Badger or Fox, our four handbuilt steam engines. An enchanting 50-minute return trip on narrow gauge rail takes you through superb scenery.

Knaresborough Castle & Courthouse Museum

Castle Yard, Knaresborough HG5 8AS
t (01423) 556188
w harrogate.gov.uk/museums
open Good Friday-30 Sep 1030-1700.
admission Adult: £2.50

Explore the keep, mysterious underground sallyport and dungeon of this medieval castle. Visit the rare Tudor courthouse and museum to discover Knaresborough's intriguing history. Enjoy the hands-on 'Life in a Castle' gallery - try on clothes and play games.

Map ref 4B1

Laser Quest

29 St Johns Road, Huddersfield HD1 5DX
t (01484) 307040 **w** darkfuture.co.uk
open All year, Mon-Fri 1200-2300, Sat-Sun 1000-2300.
admission £

Laser Quest combines the classic games of tag and hide-and-seek with a high-tech twist. Donning the most sophisticated laser tag equipment available, the game is played in a large, multi-level arena.

Lightwater Valley Theme Park

North Stainley HG4 3HT
t 0870 458 0040 **w** lightwatervalley.net
open See website for details.
admission ££££

Visit Lightwater Valley for the ultimate day out. Experience the fun and thrills of this family-sized theme park. Pay once and enjoy the fun all day long.

Magna Science Adventure Centre

Sheffield Road, Templeborough,
Rotherham S60 1DX
t (01709) 723123 **w** magnatrust.org.uk
open Mar-Nov, daily 1000-1700. Dec-Feb, Tue-Sun 1000-1700.
admission ££

Magna is the UK's first science adventure centre, set in the vast Templeborough steelworks in Rotherham. Within this cavernous space are four pavilions, giving you the ultimate interactive experience.

National Railway Museum

Leeman Road, York YO26 4XJ
t 0870 421 4001 **w** nrm.org.uk
open All year, daily 1000-1800.
admission Free

Explore the three giant halls at the world's largest railway museum with true railway legends such as the Flying Scotsman and Mallard. An unforgettable experience for all the family.

North Yorkshire Moors Railway

Pickering Station, Park Street,
Pickering YO18 7AJ
t (01751) 473799 **w** northyorkshiremoorsrailway.com
open See website for details.
admission £££

The country's most popular heritage railway with an 18-mile line running through the beautiful North York Moors National Park, between the market town of Pickering and the village of Grosmont.

The Norwich Union Yorkshire Wheel

Leeman Road, York YO26 4XJ
t (01904) 621261 **w** nrm.org.uk
open All year, daily 1000-1800.
admission ££

York's new gigantic observation wheel offers unforgettable views of the beautiful city of York and the surrounding countryside as you have never seen it before.

Admission is based on an adult price. Please check opening times and admission before travelling.

Settle-Carlisle Railway
Town Hall, Market Place, Settle BD24 9EJ
t 0800 980 0766 **w** settle-carlisle.co.uk
open See website for details.
admission £

The 72-mile spectacular railway journey takes you through the breathtaking Yorkshire Dales, into the Eden Valley and Appleby, and on to Cumbria's vibrant capital city – Carlisle.

Skipton Castle
Skipton BD23 1AW
t (01756) 792442
w skiptoncastle.co.uk
open Mar-Sep, Mon-Sat 1000-1800,
Sun 1200-1800. Oct-Feb, Mon-Sat 1000-1600,
Sun 1200-1600 (excl 25 Dec).
admission Adult: £5.60

Come and explore one of the most complete medieval castles in England with over 900 years of turbulent history. Picnic areas, licensed tea rooms, shop with a notable book section, plant sales. At the head of the High Street. A great day out in any season. Open every day.

                        Map ref 4B1

(V) *voucher offer – see back section*

---

enjoy**England**.com

A great attraction or activity can often make the perfect holiday. enjoy**England**.com
features a comprehensive
list of every quality-assured
theme park, landmark,
museum, national park
and activity in England.

Thackray Museum
Nr St James's Hospital, Beckett Street,
Leeds LS9 7LN
t (0113) 244 4343 **w** thackraymuseum.org
open Daily 1000-1700 (excl 24-26, 31 Dec,
1 Jan), last entry 1500.
admission Adult: £5.50

The award-winning Thackray Museum has something for everyone. Experience life as a character in the Victorian slums of 1840, where you will be flabbergasted at the incredible lotions and potions once offered as cures, and have fun exploring the human body in the new interactive Life Zone!

                                          Map ref 4B1

(V) *voucher offer – see back section*

Waterworld
Leisure Park, Monks Cross, Huntington YO32 9XX
t (01904) 642111
w courtneys.co.uk
open All year, Mon-Thu 0630-2200, Fri 0630-2100,
Sat-Sun 0800-1700.
admission £

A fun pool where you can surf the waves, ride the slides and float on the 'Lazy River'. Also fitness pool, health suite, sauna, steam room and sunbeds.

Xscape Castleford
Colorado Way, Glasshoughton WF10 4TA
t 0871 200 3221
w xscape.co.uk
open All year, daily 0600-2300.
admission Free

The UK's ultimate family entertainment destination housing the largest indoor real-snow slope, 14-screen cinema complex, 20-lane bowling alley, urban-lifestyle shops, bars, restaurants and more.

York Dungeon
12 Clifford Street, York YO1 9RD
t (01904) 632599
w thedungeons.com
open Apr-Sep, daily 1030-1700. Oct, daily 1030-1630.
Nov-Jan, daily 1100-1600. Feb-Mar, daily 1030-1630.
admission £££
Catch the plague at York Dungeon, take a spine-tingling tour round the plague-ravaged streets of 14thC York. The Black Death wiped out a third of the population in Europe.

York Maze
Grimston Bar Park & Ride Site, Hull Road,
York YO19 5LA
t (01904) 415364
w yorkmaze.co.uk
open Jul-Sep, daily 1000-1800.
admission ££
One of Yorkshire's most popular summer attractions, the maze is carved out of an amazing 1.5 million growing maize plants! Activities include talking sculptures, farm animals and monster tractor rides.

NATURE AND WILDLIFE

Anglers Country Park
Haw Park Lane, Wintersett WF4 2EB
t (01924) 303982
w wakefield.gov.uk
open Apr-Oct, Tue-Sun 1100-1600. Nov-Mar, Tue-Sun 1030-1530.
admission Free
Country park near Wakefield with visitor centre, nature reserve, picnic area and excellent winter wildfowl site. Booster scooters available for loan from discovery centre.

Bolton Abbey Estate
Estate Office, Bolton Abbey BD23 6EX
t (01756) 718009
w boltonabbey.com
open Apr, daily 0900-1900. May-Aug, daily 0900-2100. Sep-Oct, daily 0900-1900. Nov-Mar, daily 0900-1800.
admission ££
Ruins of 12thC priory in a park setting by the River Wharfe. Tearooms, catering, nature trails, fishing, walking and picturesque countryside.

Brimham Rocks (National Trust)
Summer Bridge HG3 4DW
t (01423) 780688
w nationaltrust.org.uk
open All year, daily 0800-dusk.
admission Free
At nearly 300m high, Brimham Rocks enjoys spectacular views. Set within the Nidderdale Area of Outstanding Natural Beauty, this fascinating moorland is filled with strange and fantastic rock formations.

BTCV Wildlife Garden
Hollybush Conservation Centre, Broad Lane,
Kirkstall LS5 3BP
t (0113) 274 2335 **w** btcv.org.uk
open All year, Mon-Fri 1300-1600.
admission Free
The Hollybush Nature Garden has been created on a formerly derelict site and consists of many varied habitats, creating a haven for wildlife and an inspiration to visitors.

Burnby Hall Gardens and Museum Trust
The Balk, Pocklington YO42 2QE
t (01377) 288359 **w** burnbyhallgardens.co.uk
open Apr-Sep, daily 1000-1800.
admission £
Yorkshire in Bloom winner. The gardens are a glorious haven of beauty and tranquillity and include the two lakes that house the National Collection of hardy water lilies.

Chevin Forest Park
White House, Johnny Lane, off Birdcage Walk,
Otley LS21 3JL
t (01943) 465023
open Daily.
admission Free
Chevin Forest Park is a wooded escarpment overlooking Otley, with fabulous views over the Wharfe valley. This local nature reserve comprises 700 acres of woodland and crags.

Constable Burton Hall Gardens
Constable Burton DL8 5LJ
t (01677) 450428 **w** constableburtongardens.co.uk
open Apr-Oct, daily 0900-1800.
admission £
A terraced woodland garden attached to a beautiful Palladian house (not open) designed by John Carr. Near the main entrance drive is a stream, bog garden and rockery.

Dales Countryside Museum
Station Yard, Hawes DL8 3NT
t (01756) 752748
open All year, daily 1000-1700.
admission £
The perfect place to start your visit to the Yorkshire Dales. Unique exhibits from the Stone Age to Victorian times, demonstration of traditional crafts and free exhibitions.

The Forbidden Corner
Tupgill Park Estate, Coverham, Middleham DL8 4TJ
t (01969) 640638
w yorkshirenet.co.uk/theforbiddencorner
open Apr-Oct, Mon-Sat 1200-1800, Sun, Bank Hols 1000-1800.
admission ££
A unique labyrinth of tunnels, chambers, follies and surprises created in a four-acre garden in the heart of the Yorkshire Dales to challenge and delight children of all ages.

For key to symbols see inside back cover.

Hartshill Hayes Country Park
Oldbury Road, Hartshill CV10 0TE
t (024) 7639 5141
w warwickshire.gov.uk
open Apr, daily 0900-1900.
May, daily 0900-2000. Jun-Jul, daily 0900-2100.
Aug, daily 0900-2000. Sep, daily 0900-1900.
Oct, daily 0900-1800. Nov-Dec,
daily 0900-1600.
admission Free
*One hundred and thirty-six acres of woodland
and open hillside, reported site of Queen
Boudicca's defeat by the Romans. Three
waymarked walks and adventure playground for
children.*

Hollies Botanical Garden
off Weetwood Lane, Leeds LS16 5NZ
t (0113) 232 3069
open All year, dawn-dusk.
admission Free
*Twenty-two hectares of land comprising
flowering rhododendrons and azaleas from early
spring to summer, herbaceous borders, mature
plants and large woodland walks on three
different levels.*

Ingleborough Show Cave
Clapham LA2 8EE
t (01524) 251242
w ingleboroughcave.co.uk
open Mar-Sep, daily 1000-1700. Oct-Nov, daily
1000-1600.
admission ££
*The cave is 1.2 miles from Clapham village at the
end of the nature trail through Ingleborough
estate grounds (for which there is a separate
small charge).*

Malham Tarn
Settle BD24 9PT
t (01729) 830416
w nationaltrust.org.uk
open Daily.
admission Free
*The estate extends to over 7,200 acres of moor
and farmland. Malham Tarn and the adjacent
areas of raised bog, fen and woodland are
protected as a National Nature Reserve.*

Newmillerdam Country Park
Barnsley Road, Newmillerdam WF2 6QF
t (01924) 303982
w wakefield.gov.uk
open Daily.
admission Free
*Ninety-five hectares of woodland and water. The
country park was once part of the medieval
'Chevet' estate. Attractions include woodland
walks, easy walks around the lake and
permanent orienteering course.*

Ogden Water Country Park
Ogden Lane, Keighley Road, Ogden HX2 8YA
t (01422) 249136
w ogdenwater.org.uk
open Apr, daily 0800-2000. May, daily 0800-2100.
Jun-Jul, daily 0800-2200. Aug, daily 0800-2100. Sep,
daily 0800-2000. Oct, daily 0800-1900. Nov, daily
0800-1700. Dec, daily 0800-1700.
admission Free
*A Calderdale 'Countryside Gateway' site with 174 acres
of mixed woodland affording excellent views over
Halifax and Calderdale. Reservoir and woodland walks.
Information centre with guide books, leaflets, hot drinks.*

Old Moor Wetland Centre
Old Moor Lane, Off Manvers Way, Broomhill,
Wombwell S73 0YF
t (01226) 751593
w rspb.org.uk
open Feb-Oct, daily 0930-1700. Nov-Jan, daily
0930-1600.
admission £
*An RSPB nature reserve set in 250 acres, including a
visitor centre in converted farm buildings with hands-on,
interactive displays and a film show.*

Paddock Farm Water Gardens
West Lane, Dalton-on-Tees DL2 2PT
t (01325) 378286
w paddock-farm.co.uk
open Apr-Oct, Mon-Sat 1000-1800, Sun 1100-1700.
Mov-Mar, Tue-Sat 1000-1800, Sun 1100-1700.
admission Free
*Nine unique, individually designed gardens, taking
inspiration from the Mediterranean to the Orient.
Bridge, waterfall, pond and pagoda. Garden centre with
experienced, friendly staff. Tearoom overlooking the
gardens.*

Pugneys Country Park
Asdale Road, off Denby Dale Road, Wakefield WF2 7EQ
t (01924) 302360
w wakefield.gov.uk
open All year, daily 0900-dusk.
admission Free
*A 250-acre site with two lakes, the smaller of which is a
nature reserve, and the larger a watersports lake for
canoeing, sailing and windsurfing.*

RHS Garden Harlow Carr
Crag Lane, (off B6162 Otley Road),
Harrogate HG3 1QB
t (01423) 565418
w rhs.org.uk
open Mar-Oct, daily 0930-1800. Nov-Feb, daily
0930-1600.
admission ££
*Spectacular 58 acres offering interest for all seasons –
from vegetables to wildflowers and alpines to woodland.
Bettys Cafe tea rooms and shop offering delicious food
and drinks.*

Rievaulx Terrace & Temples (National Trust)

The National Trust, Rievaulx YO62 5LJ
t (01439) 798340 **w** nationaltrust.org.uk
open Apr-Sep, daily 1100-1800. Oct, daily 1100-1700.
admission £ &

An 18thC grass-covered terrace, landscaped from wooded hillside with views of Rievaulx Abbey. Two classical temples, one furnished and decorated as a dining room. National Trust shop.

Rother Valley Country Park

Mansfield Road, Wales Bar, Rotherham S26 5PQ
t (01709) 856353 **w** rothervalleycountrypark.co.uk
open All year, daily 0830-dusk.
admission Free &

This 750-acre country park offers woods and parkland, a visitor centre, craft centre, cafe and shop. Watersports activities include public hire of sailing dinghies, sailboards, canoes and family rowing boats.

Roundhay Park

Leeds LS8 1ER
t (0113) 266 1850 **w** leeds.gov.uk
open Daily.
admission Free &

One of Europe's largest municipal parks, comprising over 700 acres of rolling parkland with lakes, woodland, the gorge and ravine and specialist gardens. It is also home to Tropical World.

RSPB Blacktoft Sands Nature Reserve

Hillcrest, High Street, Whitgift DN14 8HL
t (01405) 704665 **w** rspb.org.uk
open All year, daily 0900-dusk.
admission £ &

One of North East England's best nature reserves. Nestled between the Yorkshire and Lincolnshire Wolds, the reserve is set on the banks of the Humber Estuary.

Sea Life and Marine Sanctuary

Scalby Mills, Scarborough YO12 6RP
t (01723) 376125 **w** sealife.co.uk
open All year, daily 1000-1600.
admission £££ &

Here, you will meet creatures that live in the oceans of the British Isles, ranging from starfish and crabs to rays and seals. Marine sanctuary and seal-rescue hospital.

Sheffield Botanical Gardens

Clarkehouse Road, Sheffield S10 2LN
t (0114) 267 6496 **w** sbg.org.uk
open Winter: Mon-Fri 0800-1600, Sat-Sun, Bank Hols 1000-1600. Summer: Mon-Fri 0800-dusk, Sat-Sun, Bank Hols 1000-dusk.
admission Free &

Extensive gardens with over 5,500 species of plants. The gardens, which are Grade II Listed by English Heritage, were landscaped by Robert Marnock, a famous 19thC landscape designer.

Sheffield Winter Gardens

Surrey Street, Sheffield S1 2HH
t (0114) 273 6681 **w** sheffield.gov.uk
open Daily 0800-1800.
admission Free &

One of the largest temperate glasshouses to be recently built in the UK, the award-winning Winter Gardens offer a stunning green world in the heart of the city.

Spurn Point

East Riding, Spurn Head YO24 1GN
t (01964) 650533
open Daily, weather permitting.
admission Free &

A unique natural landscape: a narrow headland stretching into the Humber estuary spanning only 50m wide in some places and three and a half miles long.

Sutton Bank Visitor Centre North York Moors

Sutton Bank YO7 2EH
t (01439) 770657 **w** visitthemoors.co.uk
open Apr-Oct, daily 1000-1700. Nov-Feb, Sat-Sun 1100-1600. Mar, daily 1100-1600.
admission Free &

A modern visitor centre set above Whitestone Cliffe with stunning views across the Vale of York. Exhibitions, tearoom, shop, local walks, guide books, tourist information, crafts and souvenirs for sale.

Thorp Perrow Arboretum & Falconry Centre

Thorp Perrow DL8 2PR
t (01677) 425323 **w** thorpperrow.com
open Daily, dawn-dusk.
admission ££ &

One of the largest collections of trees and shrubs in the North of England, set in 85 acres of woodland. Four national collections: ash, lime, walnut and laburnum.

Tropical Butterfly House, Wildlife and Farm

Hungerhill Farm, Woodsetts Road,
North Anston S25 4EQ
t (01909) 569416 **w** butterflyhouse.co.uk
open Apr-Sep, Mon-Fri 1000-1630, Sat-Sun 1000-1730. Nov-Mar, Mon-Fri 1100-1630, Sat-Sun 1000-1700.
admission ££ &

Exotic butterflies, plants and animals in a natural jungle environment. Falconry Centre, farm animals and pets, Unique Native Fauna and Flora Nature Trail, picnic area, formal gardens, gift shop and cafe.

Tropical World

Canal Gardens, Roundhay Park, Leeds LS8 1ER
t (0113) 266 1850 **w** leeds.gov.uk
open Summer: daily 1000-1800. Winter: daily 1000-1600.
admission £ &

An unforgettable, fun adventure on a tropical island. Land on the sandy white beach before forging inland to the rainforest where you will find waterfalls tumbling into jungle pools.

The Walled Garden at Scampston
Scampston Hall, Malton YO17 8NG
t (01944) 758224 **w** scampston.co.uk
open Apr-Oct, daily 1000-1700.
admission £

An inspired contemporary garden designed by the internationally acclaimed Piet Oudolf, winner of Gold and Best in Show at Chelsea in 2000. Rare plants for sale, restaurant.

Wentworth Castle Gardens
Lowe Lane, Stainborough S75 3ET
t (01226) 776040 **w** wentworthcastle.org
open Apr-Sep, daily 1000-1700. Oct-Mar, daily 1000-1600.
admission £

Wentworth Castle Gardens provide a wonderful day out for all the family. A secret Yorkshire treasure awaits you, hidden away in green rolling hills near Barnsley.

White Scar Cave
Ingleton LA6 3AW
t (01524) 241244 **w** whitescarcave.co.uk
open All year, daily 1000-1700, weather permitting.
admission ££

The longest show cave in Britain. A spectacular natural cave in the Yorkshire Dales National Park. See underground streams and waterfalls, thousands of stalactites, and the massive 200,000-year-old Battlefield Cavern.

Wolds Way Lavender
Deer Park Farm, Sandy Lane, Wintringham YO17 8HW
t (01944) 758641 **w** deerparkfarm.com
open Apr-May, daily 1000-1600. Jun-Aug, daily 1000-1700. Sep-Oct, daily 1000-1600.
admission Free

Surrounded by mature woodland, on the edge of the picturesque Yorkshire Wolds, the newly created lavender and herb farm is a wonderful and relaxing place to visit.

Yorkshire Dales Falconry Centre
Crows Nest, Giggleswick LA2 8AS
t (01729) 822832 **w** falconryandwildlife.com
open Daily 1000-dusk.
admission ££

Falconry centre with many species of birds of prey from around the world including vultures, eagles, hawks, falcons and owls. Flying displays, lecture room and aviaries.

Yorkshire Lavender
Terrington YO60 6PB
t (01653) 648008 **w** lavenderland.co.uk
open Apr-Oct, daily 1000-1700.
admission Free

The North of England's premier lavender attraction/herb nursery is set in a hillside farm of 60 acres within the Howardian Hills, an Area of Outstanding Natural Beauty.

Yorkshire Sculpture Park
West Bretton WF4 4LG
t (01924) 832515 **w** ysp.co.uk
open Apr-Oct, daily 1000-1800. Nov-Mar, daily 1000-1700.
admission Free

Set in the beautiful grounds of a 500-acre, 18thC country estate, the park is one of the world's leading open-air galleries and presents a changing programme of international sculpture exhibitions.

Beningbrough Hall & Gardens (National Trust)
Beningbrough, York YO30 1DD
t (01904) 470666 **w** nationaltrust.org.uk
open House: Jun, Mon-Wed, Sat-Sun 1200-1700. Jul-Aug, Mon-Wed, Fri-Sun 1200-1700. Sep-Oct, Mon-Wed, Sat-Sun 1200-1700. Grounds: Mar-June, Sep-Oct, Mon-Wed, Sat-Sun 1100-1730. Jul-Aug, Mon-Wed, Fri-Sun 1100-1730. Nov, Jan-Feb Sat-Sun 1100-1530.
admission ££

Handsome Baroque house, built in 1716, housing 100 portraits from the National Portrait Gallery. The attraction also includes a Victorian laundry, potting shed and restored walled garden.

Beverley Minster
38 Highgate, Beverley HU17 0DN
t (01482) 868540
open Apr-Jul, Mon-Sat 0900-1700, Sun 1200-1630. Aug, Mon-Sat 0900-1730, Sun 1200-1630. Sep-Oct, Mon-Sat 0900-1700, Sun 1200-1630. Nov-Mar, Mon-Sat, 0900-1600, Sun 1200-1630.
admission Free

A splendid example of medieval Gothic architecture, built 1220-1400. Well known for the Percy tomb, burial place of St John of Beverley, Saxon sanctuary chair and large collection of misericords.

Bolling Hall
Bowling Hall Road, Bradford BD4 7LP
t (01274) 723057 **w** bradford.gov.uk
open All year, Wed-Fri, Bank Hols 1100-1600, Sat 1000-1500, Sun 1200-1500.
admission Free

Period house, medieval tower to 18thC wing. Period furnishings and splendid oak furniture, central hall with early stained-glass windows.

Bolton Castle
Leyburn DL8 4ET
t (01969) 623981 **w** boltoncastle.co.uk
open Apr-Sep, daily 1000-1700. Oct-Mar, daily 1000-1600.
admission £

Fortress with nine-foot-thick walls which has dominated Wensleydale since 1379. Mary Queen of Scots was imprisoned here during 1568 and 1569 and the Royalists were besieged here during the Civil War.

Brodsworth Hall and Gardens

Brodsworth Hall, Brodsworth DN5 7XJ
t (01904) 601974
w english-heritage.org.uk
open See website for details.
admission ££

One of the most complete surviving examples of an English Victorian country house set in 15 acres of formal and informal gardens and woodland.

Byland Abbey (English Heritage)

Coxwold YO61 4BD
t (01904) 601974
w english-heritage.org.uk
open See website for details.
admission £

Once one of the great northern monasteries, Byland Abbey's design influenced many other religious buildings throughout Europe. The abbey contains a splendid collection of medieval floor tiles.

Cannon Hall Country Park

Cawthorne S75 4AT
t (01226) 790270
open Daily.
admission Free

An 18thC landscaped parkland and formal gardens with lakes. Educational visits, fishing, important collections in the walled garden including extensive and rare pear trees.

Castle Howard

York YO60 7DA
t (01653) 648444
w castlehoward.co.uk
open Grounds: daily 1000-dusk. House: Mar-Oct, daily 1100-1600.
admission ££

Home to the Howard family since 1699. Extensive collections, breathtaking parkland, outdoor tours, historical-character guides, archaeological dig, exhibition wing and events programme. Cafe, gift shop.

Clifford's Tower

Tower Street, York YO1 9SA
t (01904) 601974
w english-heritage.org.uk/yorkshire
open See website for details.
admission £

Once the central stronghold of York Castle, the tower was at the heart of William the Conqueror's fearsome Harrying of the North campaign after his 1066 invasion.

Duncombe Park

Helmsley YO62 5EB
t (01439) 770213
w duncombepark.com
open Gardens: May-Oct, Mon-Thu, Sun 1100-1730. House: May-Oct, Mon-Thu, Sun 1230-1530.
admission £

A magnificent family home, owned and restored by Lord and Lady Feversham. The original 18thC house was remodelled after a serious fire in the late 19th century.

DIG – An Archaeological Adventure

St Saviour's Church, St Saviourgate, York YO1 8NN
t (01904) 543403 **w** digyork.co.uk
open Daily 1000-1600 (excl 24-26 Dec).
admission Adult: £5.50

JORVIK Viking Centre's sister attraction, DIG – An Archaeological Adventure, is NOW open. Ever fancied getting your hands dirty and learning about York's rich past? DIG offers visitors the opportunity to take part in an excavation, discover genuine artefacts from ancient civilisations and also understand how archaeologists recreate the past.

Map ref 4C1

V *voucher offer – see back section*

East Riddlesden Hall (National Trust)

Bradford Road, Keighley BD20 5EL
t (01535) 607075 **w** nationaltrust.org.uk
open Apr-Jun, Tue-Wed, Sat-Sun 1200-1700. Jul-Aug, Mon-Wed, Sat-Sun 1200-1700. Sep-Oct, Tue-Wed, Sat-Sun 1200-1700.
admission £

A homely 17thC merchant's house with fine plaster ceilings and mullioned windows. The house contains beautiful embroideries, textiles and Yorkshire oak furniture. Delightful garden, shop and tearoom.

Quality counts

Look out for the Quality Assured Visitor Attraction sign. These attractions are assessed annually and meet the standards required to receive the quality marque.

For key to symbols see inside back cover.

Fountains Abbey and Studley Royal Water Garden

Ripon HG4 3DY
t (01765) 608888 **w** fountainsabbey.org.uk
open Mar-Oct, daily 1000-1700. Nov-Feb, daily 1000-1600.
admission ££
The largest monastic ruin in Britain, founded by Cistercian monks in 1132. Landscaped garden laid 1720-1740 with lake, formal water garden, temples and deer park.

Harewood House

Harewood LS17 9LG
t (0113) 218 1010 **w** harewood.org
open Mar-Oct, daily 1000-1600. Winter, please phone for details.
admission £££
The home of the Earl of Harewood is renowned for its stunning architecture and exquisite Adam interiors, and contains a rich collection of Chippendale furniture, fine porcelain and art collections.

Helmsley Castle

Helmsley YO62 5AB
t (01904) 601974 **w** english-heritage.org.uk/yorkshire
open See website for details.
admission £
Helmsley Castle has been in existence for over 900 years. Originally a medieval castle, a Tudor mansion was added in the 1600s before Cromwell's men blew up the great keep.

Jervaulx Abbey

Park House, Jervaulx, Ripon HG4 4PH
t (01677) 460226 **w** jervaulxabbey.com
open All year, dawn-dusk.
admission £
A ruined Cistercian abbey, set in 110 acres of parkland noted for its lovely wallflowers and shrubs. The informal grounds give a true feeling of tranquillity and serenity.

JORVIK Viking Centre

Coppergate, York YO1 9WT
t (01904) 543402 **w** jorvik-viking-centre.co.uk
open Apr-Oct 1000-1700. Nov-Mar 1000-1600 (excl 24-26 Dec).
admission Adult: £7.75

Get face to face with the vikings of JORVIK. Explore York's viking history on the very site where archaeologists uncovered the remains of the viking-age city of 'Jorvik'. Journey through a reconstruction of the actual streets, which stood here 1,000 years ago, complete with sound and smells. See over 800 of the items discovered on site. Learn what life was really like in our Special Exhibitions.

Map ref 4C1

V *voucher offer – see back section*

Sun set at Higger Tor, Peak District

King's Manor
Exhibition Square, York YO1 7EP
t (01904) 433995 w york.ac.uk
open All year, Mon-Sat 0900-dusk.
admission Free

One of historic York's most attractive and unusual sites, enjoying a renaissance which is both physical and intellectual. Home to University of York staff and students.

Kirkstall Abbey
Abbey Road, Kirkstall LS5 3EH
t (0113) 247 8391 w leeds.gov.uk
open All year, daily dawn-dusk.
admission Free

One of the best-preserved medieval Cistercian monasteries in the country. Constructed between 1152 and 1182, many of its buildings still survive virtually intact up to eaves level.

Knaresborough Castle & Courthouse Museum

Castle Yard, Knaresborough HG5 8AS
t (01423) 556188
w harrogate.gov.uk/museums
open Good Friday-30 Sep 1030-1700.
admission Adult: £2.50

Explore the keep, mysterious underground sallyport and dungeon of this medieval castle. Visit the rare Tudor courthouse and museum to discover Knaresborough's intriguing history. Enjoy the hands-on 'Life in a Castle' gallery - try on clothes and play games.

Map ref 4B1

Merchant Adventurers' Hall
Fossgate, York YO1 9XD
t (01904) 654818 w theyorkcompany.co.uk
open Apr-Sep, Mon-Thu 0900-1700, Fri-Sat 0900-1730, Sun 1200-1600. Oct-Mar, Mon-Sat 0900-1530.
admission £

The finest medieval guildhall in Britain, built 1357-1361 and basically unaltered, operates today as a museum. Merchants conducted business and feasted in the superb timbered Great Hall.

Merchant Taylors Hall
Aldwark, York YO1 7BX
t (01904) 624889
open All year, Tue1000-1600.
admission Free

A 14thC craft guildhall maintained in its original condition. To book the venue please contact Taylor Woodcock Conference & Banqueting on (01904) 624889.

Middleham Castle (English Heritage)
Middleham DL8 4QR
t (01904) 601974 w english-heritage.org.uk
open See website for details.
admission £

The castle was the childhood and favourite home of Richard III. The massive keep, one of the largest in England, served as a defensive building and self-contained residence.

Mother Shipton's Cave and Petrifying Well
Prophecy Lodge, High Bridge,
Knaresborough HG5 8DD
t (01423) 864600 w mothershipton.co.uk
open Apr-Oct, daily 1000-1730. Feb-Mar, Sat-Sun 1000-1730.
admission ££

Mother Shipton is England's most famous prophetess. She lived some 500 years ago in the reign of Henry VIII and Queen Elizabeth I and was born in a legendary cave.

Newburgh Priory
Coxwold YO61 4AS
t (01347) 868372 w newburghpriory.co.uk
open Apr-June, Wed, Sun 1430-1645.
admission £

Founded in 1145, and standing on the site of an Augustinian priory, this fine stately home occupies a superb setting with breathtaking views to the Kilburn White Horse.

Newby Hall & Gardens
Ripon HG4 5AE
t 0845 450 4068 w newbyhall.com
open House; Apr-Jun, Tue-Sun1200-1700. Jul-Aug, daily 1200-1700. Sep, Tue-Sun 1200-1700. Gardens; Apr-Jun, Tue-Sun 1100-1730. Jul-Aug, daily 1100-1730. Sep, Tue-Sun 1100-1730.
admission ££

One of England's renowned Adam houses, an exceptional example of 18thC interior decoration. Contents include unique Gobelins tapestry room, classical statuary and fine Chippendale furniture.

Oakwell Hall & Country Park
Nutter Lane, Birstall WF17 9LG
t (01924) 326245 w oakwellhallcountrypark.co.uk
open All year, Mon-Fri 1100-1700, Sat-Sun 1200-1700.
admission £

This Elizabethan manor house has delighted visitors for centuries. Charlotte Brontë was a regular visitor, and Oakwell Hall featured as Fieldhead, the home of the heroine in Charlotte's novel, Shirley.

Pickering Castle (English Heritage)
Pickering YO18 7AX
t (01904) 601974 w english-heritage.org.uk
open See website for details.
admission £

Originally built by William the Conqueror to suppress the rebellious northerners, this castle was used by a succession of medieval Kings as a hunting lodge, holiday home and stud farm.

Admission is based on an adult price. Please check opening times and admission before travelling.

Piece Hall
Halifax HX1 1RE
t (01422) 358087 **w** calderdale.gov.uk
open All year, Mon-Wed 0800-1800, Thu 0700-1800,
Fri 0800-1800, Sat 0700-1800, Sun 0800-1800.
admission Free
*Built in 1779 and restored in 1976, this Grade I Listed
building forms a unique and striking monument to the
wealth and importance of the wool trade before the
industrial revolution.*

Richmond Castle
Richmond DL10 4QW
t (01904) 601974 **w** english-heritage.org.uk
open See website for details.
admission £
*Built shortly after the Battle of Hastings, this is the best-
preserved castle of such scale and age in the country
and alleged to be where the legendary King Arthur lies
sleeping.*

Rievaulx Abbey (English Heritage)
Rievaulx YO62 5LB
t (01904) 601974 **w** english-heritage.org.uk
open See website for details.
admission £
*Experience the beauty of this impressive monastic site. It
was the first Cistercian abbey to be founded in the
North, and one of the most powerful abbeys in Europe.*

Ripley Castle
Ripley HG3 3AY
t (01423) 770152 **w** ripleycastle.co.uk
open Castle: Apr-Oct, daily 1100-1500. Nov, Tue, Thu,
Sat-Sun 1100-1500. Dec-Feb, Sat-Sun 1100-1500. Mar,
Tue-Thu, Sat-Sun 1100-1500.
Gardens: Apr-Oct, daily 0900-1700. Nov-Feb
0900-1630.
admission ££
*Ripley Castle, home to the Ingilby family for over 26
generations, is set in the heart of a delightful estate with
Victorian walled gardens, deer park and pleasure
grounds.*

Scarborough Castle (English Heritage)
Castle Road, Scarborough YO11 1HY
t (01904) 601974 **w** english-heritage.org.uk
open See website for details.
admission £
*This 12thC castle is set high on the cliff tops and
conceals over 2,500 years of turbulent history. It played
a key role in national events up to the 20th century.*

Selby Abbey
The Crescent, Selby YO8 4PU
t (01757) 703123 **w** selbyabbey.org.uk
open All year, daily 1000-1600.
admission Free
*The abbey's foundations date back to 1069. It is
probably the most outstanding example of a monastic
abbey in the North of England. Architectural features
include Norman arches.*

Sewerby Hall and Gardens
Church Lane, Sewerby YO15 1EA
t (01262) 673769 **w** bridlington.net/sewerby
open Hall: Apr-Oct, daily 1000-1700. Gardens: Daily,
dawn-dusk.
admission £
*Situated in a dramatic cliff-top position, forming the
gateway to the Flamborough Heritage Coast, Sewerby
Hall and Gardens, set in 50 acres of early 19thC
parkland, enjoys spectacular views over Bridlington.*

Sheffield Cathedral
Church Street, Sheffield S1 1HA
t (0114) 275 3434 **w** sheffield-cathedral.org.uk
open Mon-Fri 0845-1830, Sat 1000-1500, Sun
0800-1930. School Hols, Mon-Fri 0845-1700, Sat
1000-1500, Sun 0800-1930.
admission Free
*There has been a church on this site since Saxon times.
Rebuilt and modified over the centuries, history is
written into its stones. Guided tours available.*

Skipton Castle

Skipton BD23 1AW
t (01756) 792442
w skiptoncastle.co.uk
open Mar-Sep, Mon-Sat 1000-1800,
Sun 1200-1800. Oct-Feb, Mon-Sat 1000-1600,
Sun 1200-1600 (excl 25 Dec).
admission Adult: £5.60

Come and explore one of the most complete
medieval castles in England with over 900 years
of turbulent history. Picnic areas, licensed tea
rooms, shop with a notable book section, plant
sales. At the head of the High Street. A great
day out in any season. Open every day.

Map ref 4B1

 voucher offer – see back section

Shibden Hall
Lister's Road, Halifax HX3 6XG
t (01422) 352246
w calderdale.gov.uk
open Mar-Nov. Mon-Sat 1000-1700, Sun 1200-1700.
Dec-Feb, Mon-Sat 1000-1600, Sun 1200-1600.
admission £

Dating from c1420, the hall is a distinctive half-timbered building furnished in the styles of the17thC, 18thC and 19thC. An important 17thC aisled barn houses a collection of horse-drawn vehicles.

Sledmere House
Sledmere YO25 3XG
t (01377) 236637
open May, Tue-Thu, Sun 1100-1700. Jun-Aug, Tue-Fri, Sun, Bank Hols 1100-1700. Sep, Tue-Thu, Sun 1100-1700.
admission ££

Georgian house containing Chippendale, Sheraton and French furnishing and many fine pictures. Magnificent plasterwork by Joseph Rose (Adam style). Capability Brown parkland, woodland walks, rose and knot gardens, chapel.

Standedge Visitor Centre
Tunnel End, Marsden HD7 6NQ
t (01484) 844298
w standedge.co.uk
open Apr-Oct, daily 1000-1700.
admission £

The longest, deepest and highest canal tunnel in the country, Standedge – on the Huddersfield Narrow Canal – is nearly three and a half miles long.

Sutton Park
Sutton-on-the-Forest YO61 1DP
t (01347) 810249
w statelyhome.co.uk
open Apr-Sep, daily 1100-1700.
admission £

Georgian stately home with fine furniture, magnificent plasterwork by Cortese and paintings from Buckingham House, now Buckingham Palace. Important collection of porcelain. Wonderful award-winning gardens.

Temple Newsam House and Farm
Temple Newsam, Leeds LS15 0AD
t (0113) 264 5535
w leeds.gov.uk/templenewsam
open Farm: Winter, Tue-Sun 1000-1600. Summer, Tue-Sun 1000-1700. House: Winter, Tue-Sun 1030-1600, Summer, Tue-Sun 1030-1700.
admission ££

The farm has over 400 head of stock including cattle, pigs, sheep, goats and poultry. Piglets, hens and cats run free around the farmyard.

Treasurer's House (National Trust)
Minster Yard, York YO1 7JL
t (01904) 624247 **w** nationaltrust.org.uk
open Apr-Oct, Mon-Thu, Sat-Sun 1100-1630. Nov, Mon-Thu, Sat-Sun 1100-1500.
admission £

Nestled behind the minster, this elegant house was carefully restored by wealthy local Victorian industrialist Frank Green, and contains 16thC-20thC decoration, furniture, china and glass.

Underground RAF Bunker Tours
RAF Holmpton, Rysome Lane, Withernsea HU19 2QR
t (01964) 630208 **w** rafholmpton.co.uk
open See website for details.
admission £

The massive Command Bunker at Royal Air Force Holmpton (built in 1952 and rebuilt in 1985) extends almost 100ft below ground and covers nearly 30,000sq ft.

Wassand Hall, Gardens & Grounds
Seaton HU11 5RJ
t (01964) 534488 **w** wassand.co.uk
open See website for details.
admission £

A fine Regency house in beautiful tranquil surroundings, containing 18thC and 19thC paintings and a collection of English and European silver, furniture and porcelain from the same period.

Whitby Abbey
Whitby YO22 4JT
t (01904) 601974
w english-heritage.org.uk/yorkshire
open See website for details.
admission £

The moody and magnificent Whitby Abbey has drawn successive generations to this site of settlement, and has been responsible for religious devotion and even literary inspiration.

Wilberforce House
25 High Street, Hull HU1 1NQ
t (01482) 613902 **w** hullcc.gov.uk/museums
open All year, Mon-Sat 1000-1700, Sun 1330-1630.
admission Free

The birthplace of William Wilberforce, Hull MP and slavery abolitionist whose campaign made the establishment of Freetown (Sierra Leone) possible. Slavery exhibits, period rooms and furniture.

York Minster
Deangate, York YO1 7HH
t (01904) 557216 **w** yorkminster.org
open All year, Mon-Sat 0900-1700, Sun 1200-1545.
admission £

The largest medieval Gothic cathedral in northern Europe, and a treasure house of 800 years of stained glass. Experience York's finest viewpoint from the top of the central tower's 275 steps.

For key to symbols see inside back cover.

OUTDOOR ACTIVITIES

Fosse Hill Jet Ski Centre
Catwick Lane, Brandesburton YO25 8SB
t (01964) 542608 **w** fossehill.co.uk
open Daily 1000-dusk.
admission Free
Jet-skiing lake on site. Lakeside walk, bar, fast food, ice cream, adventure playground. Seventy-two seasonal pitches for touring caravans.

M/V Yorkshire Belle
28 Roundhay Road, Bridlington YO15 3JY
t (01262) 673582 **w** yorkshire-belle.co.uk
open Apr-Oct, phone for details.
admission £
One-hour, non-landing coastal cruises from Bridlington harbour to Flamborough Head, and longer (at least two hours), non-landing cruises to the Bempton Cliffs RSPB Reserve. Vessel also available for private charter.

YorkBoat Guided River Trips

The Boatyard, Lendal Bridge, York YO1 7DP
t (01904) 628324
w yorkboat.co.uk/buytickets-online.html
open Feb-Dec, daily 1030-1510.
admission ££
Sit back and relax as the sights of York city and country sail by. Trips include floodlit evening cruises, ghost cruises, lunch cruises and the Summer Nights Afloat cruises.

ENTERTAINMENT AND CULTURE

1853 Gallery
Salts Mill, Victoria Road, Saltaire BD18 3LA
t (01274) 531185 **w** saltsmill.org.uk
open All year, Mon-Fri, Bank Hols 1000-1730, Sat-Sun 1000-1800.
admission Free
Four comprehensive art galleries featuring over 400 works by David Hockney. Grade II Listed historic mill building set in a picturesque village which was built for the mill workers in 1853. Salts Mill and Saltaire include various retail outlets.

Abbey House Museum
Kirkstall Road, Leeds LS5 3EH
t (0113) 247 8391 **w** leeds.gov.uk/abbeyhouse
open All year, Tue-Fri, Sun, Bank Hols 1000-1700, Sat 1200-1700.
admission £
Travel through time at Abbey House by walking through three Victorian streets of shops and homes. Visit the Sunday School or dress up in the haberdasher's. Explore nursery rhymes in the Childhood Gallery and visit the new Smelly History Exhibition.

Aeroventure South Yorks Aircraft Museum
Dakota way, Airbourne Road, Doncaster DN4 7PD
t (01302) 761616 **w** aeroventure.org.uk
open Apr-Oct, Wed-Sun 1000-1700. School Hols, Tue-Sun 1000-1700. Nov-Mar, Wed-Sun 1000-1600.
admission £
Housed at former RAF Doncaster, this museum has an interesting collection of 15 British jets and helicopters on display in the historic aircraft hangar built in 1940.

Ashley Jackson Galleries
13-15 Huddersfield Road, Holmfirth HD9 2JR
t (01484) 686460 **w** ashley-jackson.co.uk
open All year, Mon-Sat, Bank Hols 0930-1700.
admission Free
See the work of one of the country's leading and most successful landscape water colourists, Ashley Jackson.

Beverley Art Gallery
Champney Road, Beverley HU17 9HE
t (01482) 392772
open All year, Mon, Wed, Fri 0930-1700, Tue, Thu 0930-2000, Sat 0900-1600.
admission Free
The gallery holds the largest public collection of paintings by Beverley-born artist Fred Elwell. An exciting programme of changing exhibitions.

Bradford Industrial Museum & Horses at Work

Moorside Mills, Moorside Road, Bradford BD2 3HP
t (01274) 435900 **w** bradford.gov.uk
open All year, Tue-Sat, Bank Hols 1000-1700, Sun 1200-1700.
admission Free
An original spinning mill is alive with magnificent machinery which once converted wool into the world's worsted cloth. The shire horses give rides and pull a horse tram.

Bridlington Harbour Heritage Museum
Harbour Road, Bridlington YO15 2NR
t (01262) 608346 **w** bscps.com
open Apr-Oct, daily 1000-1600.
admission £
Located on Bridlington's historic harbourside and operated by the Bridlington Sailing Coble Preservation Society (BSCPS).

Captain Cook Memorial Museum, Whitby

Grape Lane, Whitby YO22 4BA
t (01947) 601900 **w** cookmuseumwhitby.co.uk
open March, daily 1100-1500. Apr-Oct, daily 0945-1700.
admission £
This handsome 17thC harbourside house is where James Cook, the great explorer, served his apprenticeship in 1746. It belonged to Cook's master, the Quaker ship owner, Captain John Walker.

Cusworth Hall
Cusworth Lane, Doncaster DN5 7TU
t (01302) 782342 **w** doncaster.gov.uk
open Apr-Dec, Mon-Sat 1000-1700, Sun 1300-1700.
admission Free
Built in the 1740s, Cusworth Hall is set in 50 acres of parkland and contains displays illustrating everyday life in South Yorkshire over the last 200 years.

Dales Countryside Museum
Station Yard, Hawes DL8 3NT
t (01756) 752748
open All year, daily 1000-1700.
admission £
The perfect place to start your visit to the Yorkshire Dales. Unique exhibits from the Stone Age to Victorian times, demonstration of traditional crafts and free exhibitions.

DIG –
An Archaeological
Adventure
St Saviour's Church, St Saviourgate,
York YO1 8NN
t (01904) 543403 **w** digyork.co.uk
open Daily 1000-1600 (excl 24-26 Dec).
admission Adult: £5.50

JORVIK Viking Centre's sister attraction, DIG – An Archaeological Adventure, is NOW open. Ever fancied getting your hands dirty and learning about York's rich past? DIG offers visitors the opportunity to take part in an excavation, discover genuine artefacts from ancient civilisations and also understand how archaeologists recreate the past.

Map ref 4C1

 voucher offer – see back section

Dewsbury Museum
Crow Nest Park, Heckmondwike Road,
Dewsbury WF13 2SG
t (01924) 325100 **w** dewsburymuseum.co.uk
open All year, Mon-Fri 1100-1700, Sat-Sun 1200-1700.
admission Free
With a busy programme of temporary exhibitions and events and the new 'Toys will be Toys' gallery, Dewsbury Museum is for anyone who's ever been a child.

Dinostar
28-29 Humber Street, Hull HU1 1TH
t (01482) 320424 **w** dinostar.co.uk
open All year, Wed-Sun 1100-1700.
admission £
Dinosaurs have long held a fascination for kids of all ages. At Dinostar, Hull's newest visitor attraction, you can learn about these fascinating creatures close up.

Doncaster Museum & Art Gallery
Chequer Road, Doncaster DN1 2AE
t (01302) 734293 **w** doncaster.gov.uk/museums
open All year, Mon-Sat 1000-1700, Sun 1400-1700.
admission Free
Regional collections of human and natural history, art, glass and ceramics. King's Own Yorkshire Light Infantry Regimental Gallery. New 'By River and Road' gallery telling the history of Doncaster.

Eden Camp Modern History Theme Museum
Malton YO17 6RT
t (01653) 697777 **w** edencamp.co.uk
open All year, daily 1000-1700.
admission £
A look at wartime Britain, depicted through a series of expertly recreated scenes, constructed in the huts of a genuine prisoner of war camp.

Eureka! The Museum for Children
Discovery Road, Halifax HX1 2NE
t (01422) 330069 **w** eureka.org.uk
open Daily 1000-1700.
admission ££
Britain's leading interactive museum for children, opening up a fascinating world of hands-on exploration. Over 400 exhibits invite children to unleash their imaginations and learn about the world around them.

Fast Track Karting
Poorhouse Lane, Preston Road, Hull HU9 5DF
t (01482) 308740 **w** ukfasttrack.com/
open All year, Mon-Fri 1000-2100, Sat-Sun 1000-1600.
admission ££
A purpose-built circuit designed by professional racing drivers. Experience fast straights, chicanes and hairpin bends. Race commentary is provided throughout the day to give that extra special Grand Prix atmosphere.

Admission is based on an adult price. Please check opening times and admission before travelling.

Graves Art Gallery

Surrey Street, Sheffield S1 1XZ
t (0114) 278 2612 **w** sheffieldgalleries.org.uk
open All year, Mon-Sat 1000-1700.
admission Free

The gallery houses an outstanding collection of British and European modern art, including works by Matisse, Picasso and Cézanne, together with a range of first-class touring exhibitions.

The Henry Moore Institute

74 The Headrow, Leeds LS1 3AH
t (0113) 246 7467 **w** henry-moore-fdn.co.uk
open All year, Mon-Tue, Thu-Sun 1000-1730, Wed 1000-2100.
admission Free

The Henry Moore Institute, formerly a neglected group of early Victorian merchants' offices, has been transformed into a unique building devoted to the exhibition, study and promotion of sculpture.

Hornsea Museum

11 Newbegin, Hornsea HU18 1AB
t (01964) 533443 **w** hornseamuseum.com
open Apr-Sep, Tue-Sat, Bank Hols 1100-1700, Sun 1400-1700.
admission £

Folk museum (village life), housed in 18thC farmhouse and associated buildings. Period rooms of the 1880s, village crafts, local history, the farming year, all attractively presented. Occasional craft demonstrations.

Huddersfield Art Gallery

Princess Alexandra Walk, Huddersfield HD1 2SU
t (01484) 221962 **w** kirklees.gov.uk
open All year, Mon-Fri 1000-1700, Sat 1000-1600.
admission Free

The gallery has a changing permanent collection of British paintings, drawings, sculpture and graphics from the mid-19th century to date, as well as exhibitions featuring contemporary art and craft work.

JORVIK
Viking Centre

Coppergate, York YO1 9WT
t (01904) 543402 **w** jorvik-viking-centre.co.uk
open Apr-Oct 1000-1700. Nov-Mar 1000-1600 (excl 24-26 Dec).
admission Adult: £7.75

Get face to face with the vikings of JORVIK. Explore York's viking history on the very site where archaeologists uncovered the remains of the viking-age city of 'Jorvik'. Journey through a reconstruction of the actual streets, which stood here 1,000 years ago, complete with sound and smells. See over 800 of the items discovered on site. Learn what life was really like in our Special Exhibitions.

Map ref 4C1

V voucher offer – see back section

Shopping in the Shambles, York

Last of the Summer Wine Exhibition
30 Huddersfield Road,
Holmfirth HD9 2JS
t (01484) 681408
open Apr-Sep, daily 1100-1600. Oct-Mar, Sat-Sun
1100-1500.
admission £

*A collection of photographs and memorabilia connected
with the television series 'Last of the Summer Wine'.
The exhibition is inside Compo's house next door to
Nora Batty's.*

Leeds City Art Gallery
The Headrow, Leeds LS1 3AA
t (0113) 247 8391
w leeds.gov.uk
open All year, Mon-Tue, Thur-Sat 1000-1700, Wed
1000-2000, Sun 1300-1700.
admission Free

*Since opening in 1888, Leeds City Art Gallery has
acquired a remarkable collection of British 20thC art,
voted by The Times as 'probably the best outside
London'.*

Leeds Industrial Museum at Armley Mills
Canal Road, Leeds LS12 2QF
t (0113) 263 7861
w leeds.gov.uk
open All year, Tue-Sat, Bank Hols 1000-1700, Sun
1300-1700.
admission £

*Formerly the largest woollen mill in the world, the
building now houses Leeds Industrial Museum. Located
beside the River Aire, the museum explores the city's
rich industrial past.*

Maritime Museum Hull
Queen Victoria Square,
Hull HU1 3DX
t (01482) 613902
w hullcc.gov.uk/museums
open All year, Mon-Sat 1000-1700, Sun 1330-1630.
admission Free

*Formerly the Town Docks offices, the impressive
building of the Hull Maritime Museum now
houses a fine collection of paintings, artefacts
and models. Whaling, fishing and trawling
exhibits.*

Millennium Galleries
Arundel Gate, Sheffield S1 2PP
t (0114) 278 2612
w sheffieldgalleries.org.uk
open All year, Mon-Sat 0800-1700, Sun 1100-1700,
Bank Hols 1000-1700.
admission Free

*With four different galleries, there is something
for everyone. Enjoy new blockbuster exhibitions
drawn from the collections of Britain's national
galleries and museums, including the Victoria
and Albert Museum.*

National Coal Mining Museum for England

Caphouse Colliery, New Road,
Overton WF4 4RH
t (01924) 848806 **w** ncm.org.uk
open All year, daily 1000-1700.
admission Free

*Exciting, award-winning museum of the English
coalfields with a unique collection of buildings, displays
and activities revealing the hidden world of mining
through the centuries.*

National Museum of Photography, Film and Television

Bradford BD1 1NQ
t 0870 701 0200 **w** nmpft.org.uk
open All year, Tue-Sun 1000-1800.
admission Free

*The museum includes ten free interactive galleries
where you can ride on a virtual magic carpet, read the
news or look back at your TV favourites from yesteryear.*

Old Penny Memories
2 Marlborough Terrace, Bridlington YO15 2PA
t (01262) 603341 **w** oldpennymemories.co.uk
open Apr-Oct, Sat-Sun, Bank Hols 1000-1600.
admission Free

*One of the largest collections of antique slot machines in
England. Visitors to the museum can actually play the
slot machines, exchanging their money for old pennies.*

Richard III Museum
Monk Bar, York YO1 7LQ
t (01904) 634191 **w** richardiiimuseum.co.uk
open Mar-Oct, daily 0900-1700. Nov-Feb, daily
0930-1600.
admission £

*The museum reconstructs a modern-day trial, presenting
the case for and against England's most notorious king,
Richard III. Afterwards, the visitor is invited to pass
sentence in the comments book.*

Royal Armouries Museum
Armouries Drive, Leeds LS10 1LT
t (0113) 220 1916 **w** armouries.org.uk
open All year, daily 1000-1700.
admission Free

*Spectacular displays, live interpretations, unique
handling collections, jousting tournaments and
thousands of breathtaking exhibitions from one of the
world's most famous collections of arms and armour.*

Scarborough Art Gallery
The Crescent, Scarborough YO11 2PW
t (01723) 367326
open All year, Tue-Sun 1000-1700.
admission £

*This Italianate villa was built in the 1840s as part of The
Crescent. It houses Scarborough's fine-art collection
which features seascapes and views of Scarborough,
including works by Grimshaw.*

For key to symbols see inside back cover.

Sheffield City Museum
Weston Park, Sheffield S10 2TP
t (0114) 278 2612
w sheffieldgalleries.org.uk
open All year, Mon-Sat 1000-1700, Sun 1100-1700.
admission Free

See Sheffield's vast natural and social history,
archaeology and decorative arts collections, together
with a programme of fascinating temporary exhibitions.

Site Gallery (Media, Art, Photography)
1 Brown Street, Sheffield S1 2BS
t (0114) 281 2077
w sitegallery.org
open All year, Wed-Sat 1100-1730.
admission Free

An international centre for contemporary art, offering a
changing exhibitions programme, backed up with
regular publications and a comprehensive calendar of
conferences, artists' talks and events.

Spurn Lightship
River Hull, Museum Quarter, Hull HU1 1PS
t (01482) 613902
w hullcc.gov.uk/museums
open Apr-Oct, Mon-Sat 1000-1700, Sun 1330-1630.
admission Free

Built in 1927, the Spurn served for almost 50 years as a
navigational aid in the treacherous River Humber. See
how the crew lived and worked.

'Streetlife' – Hull Museum of Transport
High Street, Hull HU1 1PS
t (01482) 613902
w hullcc.gov.uk/museums
open All year, Mon-Sat 1000-1700, Sun 1330-1630.
admission Free

Streetlife has some of the finest period displays on
railways, horse-drawn carriages, cycles, cars and trams.
Animated horses, a simulated carriage ride and
costumed figures add to the visual display.

Thackray Museum

Nr St James's Hospital, Beckett Street,
Leeds LS9 7LN

t (0113) 244 4343 **w** thackraymuseum.org
open Daily 1000-1700 (excl 24-26, 31 Dec,
1 Jan), last entry 1500.
admission Adult: £5.50

The award-winning Thackray Museum has
something for everyone. Experience life as a
character in the Victorian slums of 1840, where
you will be flabbergasted at the incredible
lotions and potions once offered as cures, and
have fun exploring the human body in the new
interactive Life Zone!

Map ref 4B1

 voucher offer – see back section

Stunning views over Staithes harbour

University of Hull Art Collection
University of Hull, Cottingham Road, Hull HU6 7RX
t (01482) 465035 **w** hull.ac.uk/artcoll
open All year, Mon-Fri 1000-1600.
admission Free
The collection features British art, paintings, drawings and sculpture from 1890-1940, including works by Sickert, Steer, Lucien Pissarro, Augustus John, Stanley Spencer, Epstein and Moore.

Vintage Carriages Trust – Museum of Rail
Ingrow Railway Station, Ingrow, Keighley BD21 5AX
t (01535) 680425 **w** vintagecarriagestrust.org
open All year, daily 1100-1630.
admission £
The museum houses a collection of beautifully restored railway carriages which evoke memories of rail travel in the past, brought to life by the use of sound presentations called 'Travellers' Tales'.

Wakefield Art Gallery
Wentworth Terrace, Wakefield WF1 3QW
t (01924) 305900 **w** wakefield.gov.uk
open All year, Tue-Sat 1030-1630, Sun 1400-1630.
admission Free
The gallery is housed in an attractive late-Victorian townhouse near the city centre and contains a large collection of sculptures, drawings and paintings by Henry Moore and Barbara Hepworth.

Wakefield Museum
Wood Street, Wakefield WF1 2EW
t (01924) 305356 **w** wakefield.gov.uk
open All year, Mon-Sat 1030-1630, Sun 1400-1630.
admission Free
Explorer and early conservationist Charles Waterton collected rare species from South America. Follow his journey, and also discover how he founded the world's first nature reserve.

Whitby Lifeboat Museum (RNLI)
Pier Road, Whitby YO21 3PU
t (01947) 602001 **w** rnli.org.uk
open Apr-Oct, daily 1000-1700. Nov-Mar 1000-1600, weather permitting.
admission Free
The museum has as its main exhibit the last pulling lifeboat to be in service with the Royal National Lifeboat Institution (RNLI), plus models of lifeboats and other types of vessel.

The World of James Herriot
23 Kirkgate, Thirsk YO7 1PL
t (01845) 524234 **w** worldofjamesherriot.org
open Apr-Oct, daily 1000-1700. Nov-Mar, daily 1100-1600.
admission £
1940s nostalgia, veterinary equipment, TV studios and interactive children's gallery combine to make a fun, interesting and memorable visit to the home and surgery of James Herriot.

York & Lancaster Regimental Museum
Arts Centre, Walker Place, Rotherham S65 1JH
t (01709) 823635 **w** rotherham.gov.uk
open All year, Mon-Sat 0930-1700.
admission Free
At the museum, the York and Lancaster Regiment's history is shown in chronological order through displays of uniforms, campaign relics and over 1,000 medals.

York Castle Museum
The Eye of York, York YO1 9RY
t (01904) 650321 **w** yorkcastlemuseum.org.uk
open Daily, 0930-1700.
admission ££
England's most popular museum of everyday life including reconstructed streets and period rooms, costume and jewellery, arms and armour and craft workshops. Special exhibition 'From Cradle to Grave'.

York City Art Gallery
Exhibition Square, York YO1 7EW
t (01904) 650321 **w** yorkmuseumstrust.org.uk
open Daily 1000-1700.
admission Free
The gallery shows 600 years of painting, from gold-ground panels of 14thC Italy to the art of the 20th century. The collection includes pictures by Parmigianino, Bellotto, Lely and Reynolds.

York Cold War Bunker
Acomb Road, Holgate, York YO24 4HT
t 0870 333 1181 **w** english-heritage.org.uk
open See website for details.
admission £
Royal Observer Corps 20 Group Headquarters is the formal description of the semi-submerged nuclear bunker which is now owned by English Heritage.

Yorkshire Air Museum
Halifax Way, Elvington YO41 4AU
t (01904) 608595 **w** yorkshireairmuseum.co.uk
open Mar-Oct, daily 1000-1700. Nov-Feb, daily 1000-1530.
admission £
The award-winning museum is based on the largest authentic former WWII Bomber Command Station. Experience the tremendous atmosphere as you admire fascinating displays and the extensive collection of 43 historic aircraft.

Yorkshire Motor Museum
Alexandra Mills, Alexandra Road, Batley WF17 6JA
t (01924) 444423
open All year, Mon-Sat 1000-1700, Sun 1100-1630.
admission Free
A magnificent and diverse collection of over 60 types of cars from 1885-1985, including the only surviving Bramham. Live restorations seen in progress.

Yorkshire Museum
Museum Gardens, York YO1 7FR
t (01904) 650321
w yorkmuseumtrust.org.uk
open Daily 1000-1700.
admission £

The award-winning museum is set in ten acres of botanical gardens and displays some of the finest Roman, Anglo-Saxon, Viking and medieval treasures ever discovered in Britain.

RELAXING AND PAMPERING

Bramley Baths
Broad Lane, Bramley LS13 3DF
t (0113) 214 6000
w leeds.gov.uk
open See website for details.
admission £

Built in 1904, historic Bramley Baths has undergone a major refurbishment to restore this beautiful building to its former Edwardian splendour. Russian steam baths.

Lakeside Village
White Rose Way, Doncaster DN4 5JH
t (01302) 366444
w lakeside-village.co.uk
open All year, Mon-Wed, Fri 1000-1800, Thur 1000-2000, Sat 0930-1800, Sun 1030-1700.
admission Free

Lakeside Village, previously The Yorkshire Outlet, has recently undergone a radical and impressive makeover, greatly improving the landscape, centre facilities and range of outlet shops.

McArthurGlen Designer Outlet
St Nicholas Avenue, Fulford YO19 4TA
t (01904) 682705 **w** mcarthurglen.com/york
open All year, Mon-Wed, Fri-Sat 1000-1800, Thu 1000-2000, Sun 1000-1700.
admission Free

This is the designer destination of the north, with over 115 designer and high street stores with discounts of up to 50% off recommended retail prices.

The Mill Batley, Factory Outlet Shopping
Bradford Road, Batley WF17 5LZ
t (01924) 423172 **w** yorkshiremillvillage.com
open All year, Mon-Sat 0930-1730, Sun 1100-1700.
admission Free

The Mill covers four massive floors and offers unbelievable savings on famous high street brands including Puma, Wedgwood, FCUK, Elle, Liz Claiborne and Yorkshire's favourite discount store, Readmans.

Titanic Spa
Low Westwood Lane, Linthwaite HD7 5UN
t (01484) 843544 **w** titanicspa.com
open All year, daily 0900-2100.
admission ££££

Set in a beautifully restored 1900s textile mill, the spa blends organically inspired design features and cutting-edge botanical therapies to provide a stylish sense of escapism.

Turkish Baths & Health Spa
Parliament Street, Harrogate HG1 2WH
t (01423) 556746 **w** harrogate.gov.uk/turkishbaths
open Health Spa: Mon-Fri, Sun 0930-2030, Sat 0930-1630. Turkish Baths: Please phone for details.
admission £££

Unique, traditional Turkish baths built in 1897, plus steam rooms and various beauty treatments and types of massage. Also available: facial, manicure, pedicure, eyelash/eyebrow tint, leg waxing and reflexology.

North York Moors

Beaches in
Northern England

Beaches with have been awarded the prestigious Blue Flag award. For more information, visit **blueflag.org.uk**

A resort beach actively encourages visitors and is normally near a town with recreational facilities.

A rural beach has limited facilities, is generally more remote than a resort beach and will not be actively managed.

Bamburgh Beach

Humber Bridge

County Durham

Seaton Carew Foreshore
t (01429) 266522
Access The nearest town is Hartlepool. The nearest station is Seaton Carew. By bus – Stagecoach 1/1A,12,15. Accessible via the A178, A689 and A179. Designated cycle routes. Disabled facilities via Dial-a-Ride.

Cumbria

Allonby South Saltpans
t (01900) 326333
Access Access is available to the shore along much of this coast adjacent to B5300.

Allonby West Winds
t (01900) 326333
Access Access is available to the shore along much of this coast adjacent to B5300.

Haverigg Beach
t (01946) 852916
Access The nearest town is Millom and is approx one mile south of Haverigg. The beach is accessible off the main A595 through the village. A large car park is located within walking distance of the beach.

Seascale Beach
t (01946) 852916
Access Egremont is the nearest town and is approx ten miles north of Seascale. The beach is accessible off the A595, taking you through the village, where a railway overlooks the beach and is within walking distance. There is also a limited bus service to the village.

Silecroft Beach
t (01946) 852916
Access The nearest town is Millom and is approx three miles south of Silecroft. The beach is accessible from the A595 through the village, where the railway station is within walking distance of the beach.

Silloth West Beach
t (01900) 326333
Access Silloth is within walking distance of the beach car park.

St Bees Beach
t (01946) 852916
Access The beach lies to the west of the village, signposted from the A595, approx three miles from Whitehaven and Egremont. Rail links within easy walking distance.

Lancashire

Boulevard Beach
t (01253) 478222
Access Travelling from north or south on the M6, turn onto the M55 (signs indicate junction for Blackpool). Travel along the M55 and for central beaches follow Yeadon Way onto Seasiders Way.

St Bees Beach

Central Beach
t (0121) 5547 8222
Access Travelling from north or south on the M6, turn onto the M55 (signs indicate junction for Blackpool) travel along the M55 to the end of the motorway and for central beaches follow Yeadon Way onto Seasiders Way. Leave Seasiders Way just before the central car park.

St Annes Pier
t (01253) 725610
Access The nearest town is St Annes on Sea. Buses run from Preston and Blackpool. Accessible via the M55/B5261 – follow tourism signs to St Anne's Pier.

Merseyside

Ainsdale Beach
t (0151) 934 2967
Access A bus runs from Southport to Ainsdale Beach. By road Ainsdale can be accessed from the A565.

Formby Beach
t (0151) 934 2967
Access Formby is seven miles south of Southport and is accessed by car from the A565. Ample car parking is available at Lifeboat Road, off St Luke's Church Road. Formby Station is one mile from the beach. Public transport details are available.

Southport Beach
t (0151) 934 2967
Access Southport is well signposted from the motorway network. A park and ride operates to the south of the beach, adjacent to Southport Ecocentre. Southport railway station is one mile from the beach.

Wallasey Beach
t (0151) 678 5488
Access Accessible via the A554 from junction 1 on the M53 motorway. Grove Road railway station in Wallasey is a 12-minute walk away.

Northumberland

Amble Links
t (01900) 326333
Access Amble Links beach is located on the south side of the town. Bus links to Warkworth, Alnwick and Newcastle. Fifteen minutes' walk from town centre.

Bamburgh Beach
t (01665) 720884
Access Bamburgh Beach is accessible via a number of routes across sand dunes from Bamburgh village.

Beadnell Bay
t (01289) 330733
Access The nearest village is Beadnell with various pathways leading from the town onto the beach.

Low Newton Beach
t (01665) 510665
Access The nearest town is Alnwick, five miles south-west of Low Newton. Low Newton is a small coastal village situated on the Northumberland Heritage Coast and ANOB.

St Aidans Beach
t (01665) 720884
Access Seahouses is the nearest town. The main bus service to and from Newcastle which runs via the A1, detours to pass through.

Warkworth Beach
t (01665) 712313
Access Fifteen minutes' walk from Warkworth village – also good bus links. Access to beach clearly signposted.

Tyne and Wear

Cullercoats Bay Beach
t (01912) 192477
Access Cullercoats Bay is sandwiched between North Tyneside's resorts of Whitley Bay and Tynemouth. It is easily accessible by car from the A19 or by alighting at Cullercoats Metro station.

Roker Beach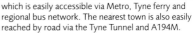
t (01915) 532000
Access The nearest city is Sunderland. Access to the beach is via Roker.

Sandhaven Beach
t (01914) 247989
Access Sandhaven beach is located in South Shields which is easily accessible via Metro, Tyne ferry and regional bus network. The nearest town is also easily reached by road via the Tyne Tunnel and A194M.

Seaburn Beach
t (01915) 532000
Access The nearest city is Sunderland. Access to the beach is via Seaburn.

Tynemouth King Edwards Bay
t (01912) 192477
Access Located to the north of the River Tyne's mouth and neighbouring resort town of Whitley Bay. Accessible by Tyneside's Rapid Transport System (The Metro) by alighting at Tynemouth station.

Southport Beach

Tynemouth Longsands South
t (01912) 192477
Access Located on the north of the River Tyne and neighbouring town resort of Whitley Bay. Accessible from A19 by car or by Metro, alighting at Tynemouth station.

Whitley Bay South
t (01912) 192477
Access Easily accessible from Whitley Bay Metro station or via the A19.

Yorkshire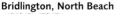

Barmston Beach
t (01262) 673474
Access The nearest town is Bridlington. Access from the south via the A164, A163 and A166 through the Wolds to Bridlington. From the north take the A1, A19 A166 coastal route.

Bridlington, North Beach
t (01262) 673474
Access The nearest town is Bridlington. Access from the south via the A164, A163 and A166 through the Wolds to Bridlington. From the north take the A1, A19 A166 coastal route.

Cayton Bay Beach
t (01723) 383636
Access Scarborough town centre is located three miles to the north. Bus service every 30 minutes in the summer season.

Danes Dyke
t (01262) 678255
Access From Bridlington take the B1255 to Flamborough. A local bus service is also available.

Filey Beach
t (01484) 717200
Access The beach is 200 yards from the town centre.

Hornsea Beach
t (01964) 536404
Access The nearest town is Hornsea. To visit from the west, take the M62, B1230, A1035 and B1244. To visit from York, A1079, A1035, B1244. To visit from Bridlington, A165, B1242. There is a local bus service available.

North Bay Beach
t (01723) 383636
Access One mile from Scarborough town centre. Regular bus service available every 15 minutes.

Redcar Lifeboat Beach
t (01642) 471921
Access Accessible via the A1085 from Middlesbrough. The railway station is approx 0.5 miles from the beach.

Robin Hood's Bay Beach
t (01947) 602674
Access Whitby is located three miles to the north and there is a regular bus service.

Runswick Bay
t (01947) 602674
Access Whitby is located eight miles to the south and there is a regular bus service.

Saltburn Beach
t (01287) 622422
Access From the A19, take the A174 signposted to Saltburn. Railway station is approx 0.5 miles from the beach.

Whitley Bay

Sandsend Beach
t (01947) 602674
Access Whitby is two miles south on the A174. Public transport is available every 30 minutes in the summer season.

Skipsea Beach
t (01262) 678255
Access To get to Skipsea take the B1249 off the A165. Access to the beach can be gained via Ulrome Beach (north) or Hornsea Beach (south). There is no public right of way through Skipsea Caravan Park onto the beach.

South Bay
t (01723) 383636
Access Five minutes' walk from Scarborough town centre with bus and lift services available.

South Beach
t (01262) 673474
Access From the south, take the A164, A163 and A166 through the Wolds. From the north, take the A1, A19, A166 coastal route to Bridlington. From the west, take the A514, A166. To get to Bridlington by rail take the East Coast Line.

South Landing Beach
t (01262) 678255
Access From Bridlington take the B1255 to Flamborough. A local bus service is available from Bridlington to Flamborough.

Tunstall Beach
t (01262) 678255
Access The nearest town is Withernsea to the south of Tunstall. Access to the beach can be gained via the A1033 from Hull or the B1242 from Hornsea.

Whitby West Cliff
t (01947) 602674
Access Whitby town centre is within walking distance of the beach.

Wilsthorpe Beach
t (01262) 678255
Access The beach lies south of Bridlington.

Withernsea Beach
t (01964) 615683
Access Accessible from the west via the M62 or from the north via the A165 then the B1242. There is also a local bus service available.

Yorkshire and The Humber Beach
t (01262) 678255
Access From Bridlington take the B1255 to Flamborough. A local bus service is also available.

enjoyEngland ™

official tourist board publications

OFFICIAL TOURIST BOARD PUBLICATION
Hotels
Guide to quality-assessed accommodation in England
2007

Hotels, including
country house and
town house hotels,
metro and budget
hotels in England 2007

£10.99

OFFICIAL TOURIST BOARD PUBLICATION
Bed & Breakfast
Guide to quality-assessed accommodation in England
2007

Guest accommodation,
B&Bs, guest houses,
farmhouses, inns,
restaurants with rooms,
campus and hostel
accommodation in
England 2007

£11.99

OFFICIAL TOURIST BOARD PUBLICATION
Self Catering
Guide to quality-assessed holiday homes in England
2007

Self-catering holiday
homes, including
serviced apartments and
approved caravan
holiday homes, boat
accommodation and
holiday cottage agencies
in England 2007

£11.99

OFFICIAL TOURIST BOARD PUBLICATION
Britain's Camping & Caravan Parks
Guide to quality-assessed sites
2007

Touring parks, camping
parks and holiday
parks and villages in
Britain 2007

£8.99

informative, easy to use and great value for money

OFFICIAL TOURIST BOARD PUBLICATION
Pets Come Too!
Guide to quality-assessed pet-friendly hotels, B&Bs and self-catering accommodation in England
2007

Pet-friendly hotels,
B&Bs and self-catering
accommodation in
England 2007

£9.99

OFFICIAL TOURIST BOARD PUBLICATION
Days Out For All

Great ideas for places
to visit and stay
in England

£10.99

OFFICIAL TOURIST BOARD GUIDE
Places to Stay and Visit
South West England

Places to stay and visit
in South West England

£9.99

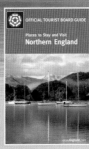

OFFICIAL TOURIST BOARD GUIDE
Places to Stay and Visit
Northern England

Places to stay and visit
in Northern England

£9.99

Britain's
accessible
places to stay
2006

Accessible places
to stay in Britain

£9.99

From good bookshops, online at
enjoyEnglanddirect.com
or by mail order from:

t **0870 606 7204**   e **fulfilment@visitbritain.org**

Places to stay in
Northern England

Accommodation in this section is listed alphabetically by place name (shown in the blue bands), establishment category and establishment name.

All the place names can be found on the maps at the front of this guide – use the map references to locate them.

Accommodation symbols

Symbols give useful information about services and facilities. A key to these symbols can be found on the inside back-cover flap. Keep it open for easy reference.

BAMBURGH, Northumberland Map ref 5C1 | **SELF CATERING**

★★★★–★★★★★★
SELF CATERING

Units **3**
Sleeps **2–28**
Low season per wk
£221.00–£1,666.00
High season per wk
£394.00–£2,362.00

Waren Lea Hall, Bamburgh

contact Carolynn and David Croisdale-Appleby, Abbotsholme, Hervines Road, Amersham HP6 5HS
t (01494) 725194 **f** (01494) 725474 **e** croisdaleappleby@aol.com **w** selfcateringluxury.co.uk

open All year
payment Cash/cheques

Imposing, spacious country house on shore of Budle Bay at Waren Mill near Bamburgh in two acres of waters-edge parkland. Breathtaking, panoramic views of Lindisfarne and the Cheviots. The holiday homes can be booked individually or together. Waren Lea Hall enjoys an unrivalled location with easy access for walking, golf, fishing etc.

⊕ From A1, 15 miles north of Alnwick, turn towards Belford Station on B1342. On reaching Waren Mill turn towards Bamburgh. Cross bridge over river. Property is 100yds on left.

♥ Short breaks available from Nov-Mar. Weekend breaks, 3 nights, Fri-Mon. Mid-week breaks, 4 nights, Mon-Fri.

Children 🐥 🎠 ♨ 🗐 ⚠   Unit ▦ 📺 📼 ☑ 🖥 ▣ 🖬 🗐 🍴 🗓 🖳 🗐 ✿
General **P** 🅂   Leisure U ✈ ► 🚴   Shop 1.5 miles   Pub 1.5 miles

---

BAMBURGH, Northumberland Map ref 5C1 | **CAMPING & CARAVANNING**

★★
HOLIDAY, TOURING
& CAMPING PARK

🚐 (80) £12.00–£15.00
🚏 (80) £12.00–£15.00
🅰 (80) £12.00–£15.00
80 touring pitches

Bradford Kaims Caravan Park

Bradford House, Bamburgh NE70 7JT **t** (01668) 213432 **f** (01668) 213891 **e** lwrob@tiscali.co.uk
w bradford-leisure.co.uk

Beautiful walking country. Close to Bamburgh, Seahouses, Wooler and Cheviot Hills. Pre-booking advised during school holidays. Open March to November. Bradford Kaims Caravan Park is signposted from the B1341.

payment Credit/debit cards, cash/cheques

General 🔌 🚾 🍴 🈁 ☉ 📵 🗑 🐾 🌲 ☼   Leisure ♣ ⚠

Key to symbols

Open the back flap for a key to symbols.

BARMBY MOOR, East Riding of Yorkshire Map ref 4C1 | **SELF CATERING**

★★★★
SELF CATERING

Units **1**
Sleeps **1–6**
Low season per wk
£375.00–£400.00
High season per wk
£440.00–£600.00

Northwood Coach House, York

contact Ann Gregory, Northwood Coach House, St Helens Square, Barmby Moor YO42 4HF
t (01759) 302305 **e** annjgregory@hotmail.com **w** northwoodcoachhouse.co.uk

open All year
payment Cash/cheques, euros

This pretty, three-bedroomed, converted Victorian coach house overlooks open countryside. Warm and cosy in winter, it is ideally situated in a picturesque village on the edge of the Wolds, only 12 miles from York and convenient for the coast and moors. Pubs, shops and restaurants nearby.

⊕ At main crossroads in village take road between the pub and general store. House is up a long drive after sharp bend before school field.

♥ Short breaks (3 days), bookable 28 days in advance, 60% normal weekly rate.

Children ➰ ▥ ♟ ✆ 🐾 ⚠ Unit ▥ TV 🕹 ▦ 🍽 🏠 ⚡ 🔥 🍴 🛋 ❄
General P ⓘ S 🐕 Leisure ∪ ⚓ ► 🚴 Shop < 0.5 miles Pub < 0.5 miles

---

BLACKPOOL, Lancashire Map ref 4A1 | **GUEST ACCOMMODATION**

★★★
GUEST ACCOMMODATION

B&B per room per night
s £20.00–£30.00
d £40.00–£60.00
Evening meal per person
£5.50–£9.00

Sandalwood

3 Gynn Avenue, Blackpool FY1 2LD **t** (01253) 351795 **f** (01253) 351795
e peter.gerald@btconnect.com **w** sandalwoodhotel.co.uk

Small family-run guest accommodation in quiet part of Blackpool, close to seafront, offering a friendly service and good home-cooked meals. Tower, shows and attractions 20 minutes' walk away.

open All year except Christmas
bedrooms 5 double, 2 twin, 2 family
bathrooms 7 en suite
payment Cash/cheques

Children ➰ ▥ ♟ 🛷 ♨ ✎ CM 🗗 Room TV ♨ General 🍴 ⍾ ✗ ▥ ♪ ❄

BRIDLINGTON, East Riding of Yorkshire Map ref 5D3 | **CAMPING & CARAVANNING**

★★★★
HOLIDAY, TOURING
& CAMPING PARK

🚐 £16.00–£19.00
🚎 £16.00–£19.00
⛺ (20) £16.00–£19.00
🏠 (10) £184.00–£440.00
175 touring pitches

South Cliff Caravan Park

Wilsthorpe, Bridlington YO15 3QN **t** (01262) 671051 **f** (01262) 605639
e southcliff@eastriding.gov.uk **w** southcliff.co.uk

Situated 300yds from clean, safe, sandy beaches, one mile south of Bridlington. Bus service to Bridlington, also a shop, takeaway and leisure complex including bars, children's lounge and restaurant. Open March to November.

payment Credit/debit cards, cash/cheques

General P 🚐 🖰 🏕 📶 ☉ ▥ 🗗 🛒 ✗ ☼ Leisure TV ▮ ♪ ⚡ ⚙ ∪ ⚓ ►

Log on to **enjoyengland.com** to find a break that matches your mood. experience scenes that inspire and traditions that baffle. discover the world's most inventive cultural entertainment and most stimulating attractions. explore vibrant cities and rugged peaks. relax in a country pub or on a sandy beach.

enjoyEngland.com

CHESTER, Cheshire Map ref 4A2 — HOTEL

★★
HOTEL

B&B per room per night
s £65.00–£85.00
d £90.00–£120.00
HB per person per night
£60.00–£75.00

Curzon Hotel

52-54 Hough Green, Chester CH4 8JQ t (01244) 678581 f (01244) 680866
e curzon.chester@virgin.net w curzonhotel.co.uk

open All year except Christmas and New Year
bedrooms 8 double, 3 twin, 1 single, 2 family, 2 suites
bathrooms All en suite
payment Credit/debit cards, cash/cheques

The Curzon is a family-run, Victorian townhouse hotel. Unwind in the lounge bar and sample our excellent cuisine in the splendid restaurant. Sleep peacefully in one of the individually designed guest rooms. There is ample private parking, and we are within easy reach of the city centre.

⊕ Junction of A55/A483 follow sign for Chester. At 3rd roundabout take 2nd exit A5104 signposted Saltney. Curzon Hotel 500yds on right-hand side.

♥ Deva Break: any 2 nights' DB&B £60pppn. Winter Warmers (from Nov): third night's DB&B half price. Special breaks our speciality.

Children 🏕 🎠 🎣 🐾 ✏ 🖼 Room 🛏 🔌 📺 🛎 ⛳ General P ♟ 🎱 🎯 ✲ Leisure ➤ 🏊

CRAMLINGTON, Northumberland Map ref 5C2 — SELF CATERING

★★★★
SELF CATERING

Units   9
Sleeps 2–36

Low season per wk
£270.00–£520.00
High season per wk
£430.00–£840.00

Burradon Farm Houses & Cottages, Cramlington

contact Mrs Judith Younger, Burradon Farm Houses & Cottages, Burradon Farm, Cramlington NE23 7ND
t (0191) 268 3203 e judy@burradonfarm.co.uk w burradonfarm.co.uk

open All year
payment Credit/debit cards, cash/cheques

Burradon Farm is located only a few miles from the spectacular Northumbrian coastline and within easy reach of the cultural heritage and dynamic centre which is Newcastle-upon-Tyne. The new barn conversions have become characterful, high-quality houses and cottages boasting every amenity and facility to ensure an enjoyable visit. Dishwasher in houses.

⊕ B1505 to Burradon. Travel 0.3 miles up hill and take 1st left onto Burradon Farm Road. Farmhouse is on right-hand side.

♥ 3-4-night stays welcomed, all year round.

Children 🏕 🎠 🎣 📷 🎮 ⛰ Unit 🎚 📺 🎛 📀 🖨 💻 📠 🍳 🔥 🍽 💡 ✲
General P 🅿 Ⓢ 🔫 Leisure ⤢ ➤ Shop 0.5 miles Pub 0.5 miles

GRASMERE, Cumbria Map ref 5A3 — **SELF CATERING**

★★★★
SELF CATERING

Units **3**
Sleeps **2–5**
Low season per wk
£265.00–£300.00
High season per wk
£435.00–£600.00

Broadrayne Farm Cottages, Grasmere

contact Mr Bev Dennison & Mrs Jo Dennison Drake, Broadrayne Farm, Grasmere, Ambleside LA22 9RU
t (015394) 35055 **f** (015394) 35733 **e** bev@grasmerehostel.co.uk **w** grasmere-accommodation.co.uk

open All year
payment Cash/cheques

With dramatic mountains, rolling fells, glorious lakes and peaceful valleys, Broadrayne Farm is at the heart of the Lake District, superbly located for wonderful views. The traditional farm properties have been lovingly renovated with today's creature comforts, including open coal fires, central heating and off-street parking. Pets welcome by arrangement.

⊕ *Our driveway is directly off the A591, we are 1.25 miles north of the village of Grasmere, 400m after the Travellers Rest Pub.*

❤ *A week booked in the year allows 10% off a second week booked in Mar (excl Easter holidays).*

Children Unit
General P Leisure Shop 1.3 miles Pub 1.25 miles

GREAT ASBY, Cumbria Map ref 5B3 — **SELF CATERING**

★★★★
SELF CATERING

Units **3**
Sleeps **2–5**
Low season per wk
£240.00–£305.00
High season per wk
£336.00–£460.00

Scalebeck Holiday Cottages, Great Asby, Appleby-in-Westmorland

contact Mr K J Budding, Scalebeck Holiday Cottages, Scalebeck, Appleby-in-Westmorland CA16 6TF
t (01768) 351006 **f** (01768) 353532 **e** mail@scalebeckholidaycottages.com
w scalebeckholidaycottages.co.uk

Self-catering cottages in barn conversion. Secluded valley, abundant wildlife. Non-smokers, pets welcome, games room, open all year.

open All year
payment Credit/debit cards, cash/cheques

Children Unit
General P Leisure Shop 5 miles Pub 1 mile

HARROGATE, North Yorkshire Map ref 4B1 — **CAMPING & CARAVANNING**

★★★★★
HOLIDAY &
TOURING PARK

(200) £13.00–£15.00
(57) £13.00–£15.00
200 touring pitches

High Moor Farm Park

Skipton Road, Felliscliffe, Harrogate HG3 2LT **t** (01423) 563637 **f** (01423) 529449
e highmoorfarmpark@btconnect.com

Secluded site surrounded by trees on the edge of the Yorkshire Dales. Open April to October.

payment Credit/debit cards, cash/cheques

General P Leisure

KESWICK, Cumbria Map ref 5A3

★★
HOTEL

B&B per room per night
s £37.50–£42.00
d £75.00–£95.00
HB per person per night
£55.00–£65.00

Crow Park Hotel

The Heads, Keswick CA12 5ER **t** (01768) 772208 **f** (01768) 774776 **e** enquiries@crowpark.co.uk
w crowpark.co.uk

open All year except Christmas
bedrooms 17 double, 7 twin, 4 single
bathrooms 26 en suite, 2 private
payment Credit/debit cards, cash/cheques

Centrally located, but quiet hotel overlooking Crow Park, Derwent Water and Catbells. Hope Park, with its golf course, is 30m away and the Theatre on the Lake 500m. Private parking for 23 cars. The hotel has some of the best views in Keswick.

⊕ *M6 jct 40, A66 to Keswick. Follow signs for the lake and theatre, turning onto The Heads just before the roundabout.*

♥ *3 or 5 nights' DB&B breaks available all year.*

Children 🐄 🛏 🌡 ✐   Room 🛋 📺 🕯 ☎   General 🅿 ✂ 🍷 🍴 🎱 🔥 🐾   Leisure ∪ 🎣 🏌 ⚙

KIRKBY STEPHEN, Cumbria Map ref 5B3

★★★★★
GUEST ACCOMMODATION
SILVER AWARD

B&B per room per night
s £100.00–£140.00
d £120.00–£140.00
Evening meal per person
£35.00–£40.00

Augill Castle

Kirkby Stephen CA17 4DE **t** (017683) 41937

open All year except Christmas
bedrooms 6 double, 4 twin
bathrooms All en suite
payment Credit/debit cards, cash/cheques, euros

A neo-Gothic Victorian fantasy. Romantic, quirky, laid back and utterly beguiling. Anything goes except hushed tones or a false formality. The ultimate escape or the ultimate house party. A real family home where children aren't just tolerated, but welcomed. Be part of the family or keep yourself to yourself.

⊕ *From M6 take jct 38 onto A685 to Brough. Turn right 0.5 miles before village. Exit A66 at Brough then left 0.5 miles outside village.*

Children 🐄 🛏 🌡 🐴 🎲 🎡 ✐ 🖥 🎥   Room 🛋 📺 🕯 ☎   General 🅿 ✂ 🍷 ✗ 🍴 🎱 ▣ 🔥
Leisure ♠ ↻ ∪ 🎣 🏌 ⚙ 🏠

LIVERPOOL, Merseyside Map ref 4A2

★★★
GUEST ACCOMMODATION

B&B per room per night
s £35.00–£45.00
d £54.00–£65.00

Aachen Hotel

89-91 Mount Pleasant, Liverpool L3 5TB **t** (0151) 709 3477 **f** (0151) 709 1126
e enquiries@aachenhotel.co.uk **w** aachenhotel.co.uk

open All year except Christmas
bedrooms 5 double, 5 twin, 2 single, 4 family
bathrooms 9 en suite
payment Credit/debit cards, cash/cheques

Award-winning hotel situated in the heart of the city convenient for all road, rail and air links. Within walking distance of all attractions, and famous for the 'Eat as much as you like' breakfast. Late bar.

⊕ *Follow City Centre signs towards Catholic cathedral. The Aachen is situated 100yds on the left of the main entrance.*

Children 🛏 🌡 ✐ 🖥 🎥   Room 🛋 ☎ 📺 🕯 ☎   General 🍷 ✗ 🍴 🎱 ▣ 🐾 🔥   Leisure 🏠

Rest assured

All accommodation in this guide has been rated, or is awaiting assessment, by a professional assessor.

MALTON, North Yorkshire Map ref 5D3　　　　　　　　　　　　　　　**SELF CATERING**

★★★★
SELF CATERING

Units **1**
Sleeps **1–4**

Low season per wk
£202.00–£246.00
High season per wk
£280.00–£440.00

Walnut Garth, Nr Malton

t (01751) 434261　**f** (01653) 691293　**e** cas@radfords.org　**w** radfords.org

open All year
payment Cash/cheques

Tastefully decorated, two-bedroom cottage furnished to a high standard with all modern conveniences. Walnut Garth is set in the grounds of owner's property at edge of village, yet only two miles from market town of Malton and excellent selection of local amenities and attractions. Easy access to York and coast.

⊕ *From A64, take Malton turn-off, turn onto B1257 toward Hovingham. Travel for 2 miles. Last house on left in Swinton village.*

♥ *10% discount for stays of 2 weeks or longer.*

Children 🧒🛏🏕🖊🗔　Unit 🏚 📺 ▨ ▣ 🗔 ▣ 🗔▣🗔 🗔 🗔 🗔 🗔 🌢　General **P** ⅍ ⊙ 🐴　Leisure 🌢 🗔　Shop < 0.5 miles　Pub < 0.5 miles

MASHAM, North Yorkshire Map ref 5C3　　　　　　　　　　　　　　　　　　**HOTEL**

★★★★
HOTEL
GOLD AWARD

B&B per room per night
s £150.00–£350.00
d £150.00–£350.00
HB per person per night
£120.00–£218.00

Swinton Park

Ripon HG4 4JH　**t** (01765) 680944　**f** (01765) 680901　**e** felicity@swintonpark.com
w swintonpark.com

A family home since the late 1800s, Swinton Park has played host to country-house parties of legendary style and grandeur. Mark and Felicity Cunliffe-Lister are proud to welcome you to join them to continue this tradition.

open All year
bedrooms 26 double, 4 suites
bathrooms All en suite
payment Credit/debit cards, cash/cheques, euros

Children 🧒🛏🏕🔔🗔🐾🖊　🗔🗔　Room 🗔 📺 🗔 🗔 🗔　General **P ♟** 🗔🗔 🌢 🐴
Leisure 🌢 ∪ 🗔 🗔 🗔 🗔

MORPETH, Northumberland Map ref 5C2　　　　　　　　　　　　　　　　　　**HOTEL**

★★★
HOTEL

B&B per room per night
s £45.00–£85.00
d £50.00–£108.00

Longhirst Hall

Longhirst, Morpeth NE61 3LL　**t** (01670) 791348　**f** (01670) 791385　**e** enquiries@longhirst.co.uk
w longhirst.co.uk

open All year
bedrooms 54 double, 19 twin, 4 single
bathrooms All en suite
payment Credit/debit cards, cash/cheques

Nestled in rural Northumberland, Longhirst Hall is an early-19thC, John Dobson-designed building set in 75 acres of woodland and landscaped gardens. All en suite bedrooms in the hall, and 34 dormy houses, each able to accommodate up to eight guests. The perfect blend of business, adventure and tranquillity.

⊕ *Located just off the A1. Take turning marked Hebron, follow road, turn left at T-junction. Longhirst 1 mile along the B1337.*

♥ *Exclusive Alnwick Garden breaks, including tickets and brochure, £118 (£59pp).*

Children 🧒🛏🏕🖊🗔🖊　Room 🗔 🗔 📺 🗔 🗔 🗔　General **P** ⅍ **♟** 🗔🗔 🌢 🐴　Leisure 🗔 ∪ 🗔 🗔 🗔 🗔

It's all quality-assessed accommodation

Our commitment to quality involves wide-ranging accommodation assessment. Ratings and awards were correct at the time of going to press but may change following a new assessment. Please check at the time of booking.

MUNGRISDALE, Cumbria Map ref 5A2 — GUEST ACCOMMODATION

★★★★
GUEST ACCOMMODATION

B&B per room per night
s £30.00–£40.00
d £50.00–£70.00

Near Howe Hotel and Cottages

Mungrisdale, Troutbeck, Penrith CA11 0SH **t** (017687) 79678 **f** (017687) 79678
e enquiries@nearhowe.co.uk **w** nearhowe.co.uk

open All year
bedrooms 2 double, 1 twin, 2 family
bathrooms 3 en suite, 2 private
payment Cash/cheques, euros

The ideal answer for a stress-free, away-from-it-all holiday. Set amidst 350 acres of open moorland. All bedrooms have spectacular views over the Cumbrian fells. The comfortable residents' lounge and bar both have real coal/log fires. Easily accessible, yet isolated enough to ensure peace and tranquillity.

From M6 jct 40 travel west towards Keswick (A66). After 9 miles pass Troutbeck. After 1 mile turn right to Mungrisdale/Caldbeck. Drive is 1 mile on right.

Children Room General P Leisure

MUNGRISDALE, Cumbria Map ref 5A2 — SELF CATERING

★★★★
SELF CATERING

Units **5**
Sleeps **2–7**
Low season per wk
£250.00–£375.00
High season per wk
£350.00–£575.00

Near Howe Cottages, Penrith

contact Steve & Jill Woolley, Near Howe Hotel and Cottages, Near Howe, Mungrisdale, Penrith CA11 0SH
t (01768) 779678 **f** (01768) 779462 **e** wswoolley@tiscali.co.uk **w** nearhowe.co.uk

open All year
payment Cash/cheques, euros

The ideal answer for a stress-free, away-from-it-all holiday, set amidst 350 acres of open moorland. All cottages have spectacular views over the Cumbrian Fells. Comfortable bar with real fire. Large garden with relaxation areas. Easily accessible, yet isolated enough to ensure peace and tranquillity.

From M6 jct 40, travel west towards Keswick (A66). Pass Troutbeck after 9 miles. After 1 mile, turn right to Mungrisdale/Caldbeck. Near Howe is 1 mile on the right.

Children Unit
General P Leisure Shop 5 miles Pub 2 miles

PICKERING, North Yorkshire Map ref 5D3 — SELF CATERING

★★★★
SELF CATERING

Units **9**
Sleeps **2–8**
Low season per wk
£189.00–£380.00
High season per wk
£424.00–£1,050.00

Keld Head Farm Cottages, Pickering

contact Julian & Penny Fearn, Keld Head Farm Cottages, Keld Head, Pickering YO18 8LL
t (01751) 473974 **e** julian@keldheadcottages.com **w** keldheadcottages.com

open All year
payment Cash/cheques, euros

On the edge of Pickering, in open countryside overlooking fields where sheep and cows graze. Beautiful, spacious, character stone cottages with pantile roofs, traditional stone fireplaces and beamed ceilings, tastefully furnished with the emphasis on comfort and relaxation. Some rooms with four-poster beds. Award-winning gardens with garden house. York, moors and coast easily accessible.

Cottages are on western periphery of Pickering, at corner of A170 and road signposted Marton. Turn into this road and the entrance is on the left.

Senior citizen and 2-person discounts. Short breaks.

Children Unit
General P Leisure Shop < 0.5 miles Pub 0.5 miles

ROTHBURY, Northumberland Map ref 5B1   GUEST ACCOMMODATION

★★★★
GUEST ACCOMMODATION

B&B per room per night
s £35.00–£50.00
d £50.00–£56.00
Evening meal per person
£12.50–£22.00

Burnfoot Guest House

Netherton, Rothbury, Morpeth NE65 7EY   t (01669) 631061   f (01207) 900 2173
e burnfootbb@aol.com   w burnfoothouse.co.uk

open All year
bedrooms 2 double, 1 twin, 1 family
bathrooms All en suite
payment Credit/debit cards, cash/cheques, euros

A warm, friendly welcome awaits guests. Enjoy a relaxing and informal visit in our 250-year-old house. Set in the scenic valley of Netherton, just north of Rothbury. The location is ideal for touring the heart of Northumberland. We welcome families and pets.

⊕ *A1 to A697. Proceed to B6344 to Rothbury, continue to Thropton, turning right at Cross Keys pub. Proceed to next T-Junction; turn left.*

♥ *Winter Special Oct-Mar: £40 per room. Christmas/New Year breaks: from £65pp.*

Children 🖼🍴🏃⚠ ✏ 📺📷   Room 📺♿🍵   General P✕🍴🅿☀️🐾   Leisure ∪♪▶🚴🏊

ROTHBURY, Northumberland Map ref 5B1   SELF CATERING

★★★–★★★★★
SELF CATERING

Units   **4**
Sleeps   **4–21**
Low season per wk
£200.00–£300.00
High season per wk
£320.00–£495.00

Low Alwinton Cottages, Nr Rothbury

contact Mr & Mrs Eamonn and Susan Gribben, 12 Parkshiel, South Shields NE34 8BU
t (0191) 420 4919   f (0191) 420 4919   e eamonngribben@blueyonder.co.uk   w lowalwinton.co.uk

open All year
payment Credit/debit cards, cash/cheques, euros

Luxury cottages nestling in a spectacular wooded valley, amidst the glorious National Park. Located beside the River Coquet and ten minutes from Caistron trout fishery. Stunning panoramic views. Otters, birds, squirrel and deer are just some of the wildlife found here. Ideal for nature lovers, walkers, fishermen, cyclists and families.

♥ *If 4 people or less in Byre Cottage (sleeps 8), £50 off.*

Children 🖼🍴🏃📷⚠   Unit 🔥📺📀📷🖥 ▦📶📻   General P🅾🆂🐾   Leisure ♪🚴🏊   Shop 1.5 miles   Pub 1 mile

SALTBURN-BY-THE-SEA, Tees Valley Map ref 5C3   GUEST ACCOMMODATION

★★★★
GUEST HOUSE

B&B per room per night
s £35.00–£40.00
d £60.00–£80.00

The Arches

Low Farm, Ings Lane, Brotton, Saltburn-by-the-Sea TS12 2QX   t (01287) 677512   f (01287) 677150
e hotel@gorallyschool.co.uk   w gorallyschool.co.uk

open All year
bedrooms 4 double, 3 twin, 4 family
bathrooms All en suite
payment Credit/debit cards, cash/cheques, euros

The Arches offers a relaxing environment and overlooks spectacular views of cliffs and golf course. All the rooms are individually furnished with en suite bathrooms.

Children 🖼🍴🏃✏📷   Room ♿📺♿🍵   General P🔑🍴✕🍴🅿☀️🐾   Leisure ∪♪▶🏊

Check it out

Please check prices, quality ratings and other details when you book.

SCARBOROUGH, North Yorkshire Map ref 5D3 — GUEST ACCOMMODATION

◆◆◆◆
GUEST ACCOMMODATION

B&B per room per night
s £22.00–£25.00
d £50.00–£59.00

Howdale

121 Queen's Parade, Scarborough YO12 7HU t (01723) 372696 f (01723) 372696
e mail@howdalehotel.co.uk w howdalehotel.co.uk

open All year except Christmas and New Year
bedrooms 10 double, 2 twin, 1 single, 2 family
bathrooms 13 en suite
payment Credit/debit cards, cash/cheques

Beautifully situated overlooking North Bay and
Scarborough Castle, yet close to town. We are
renowned for cleanliness and the friendly, efficient
service provided in a comfortable atmosphere. Our
substantial breakfasts are deservedly famous.
Thirteen of our excellent bedrooms are en suite,
many have sea views. All have TV, tea/coffee
facilities, hairdryer etc.

⊕ At traffic lights opposite railway station turn left. Next traffic
lights turn right. At 1st roundabout turn left. Property is
0.5 miles on the right.

♥ Mini-breaks (3 nights min) Mar-early Jul, Sep and Oct, from
£23pppn.

Children 🛉🏊🎀✏ Room 📺👤🍵 General P✂🍽♟❀🐕

SCARBOROUGH, North Yorkshire Map ref 5D3 — SELF CATERING

★★★★
SELF CATERING

Units   1
Sleeps   1–4

Low season per wk
Min £250.00
High season per wk
Max £450.00

Lendal House, Scarborough

contact Petra Scott, Lendal House, 34 Trafalgar Square, Scarborough YO12 7PY
t (01723) 372178 e info@lendalhouse.co.uk w lendalhouse.co.uk

Luxury, self-contained ground-floor flat with four-
poster bed. Near cricket ground; five minutes'
walk to North Bay Beach and town centre. Also
great for walks on the North York Moors.

open All year
payment Cash/cheques

Children 🛉🏊🎀📷 Unit 🏠📺📱🍴💻💿📼🔌🔥🧺🔥❀
General ✂ Ⓢ

SCARBOROUGH, North Yorkshire Map ref 5D3 — CAMPING & CARAVANNING

★★★★★
**HOLIDAY, TOURING
& CAMPING PARK**
ROSE AWARD

🚐(220) £13.50–£18.50
🚙(30)   £13.50–£18.50
🛖(50)   £11.00–£18.50
🏠(20) £190.00–£450.00
300 touring pitches

Flower of May Holiday Parks Ltd

Lebberston, Scarborough YO11 3NU t (01723) 584311 f (01723) 581361 e info@flowerofmay.com
w flowerofmay.com

payment Credit/debit cards, cash/cheques

Excellent facilities on family-run park. Luxury indoor
pool, adventure playground, golf course. Ideal for
coast and country. Prices based per pitch, per night
for four people with car. Open April to October.

⊕ From A64 take the A165 Scarborough/Filey coast road.
Well signposted at Lebberston.

♥ Early-booking discount: £25 off full week's hire. 10%
discount off full week's pitch fees, booked by post in
advance.

General P🔌♿♨🐕🛖💿🛒☀ Leisure 🎣📺🍽🎵🎯🎱⛱🏊⚓

enjoyEngland.com

Big city buzz or peaceful panoramas? Take a fresh look at England and you may
be surprised at what's right on your doorstep. Explore the diversity online at
enjoyengland.com.

SEAHOUSES, Northumberland Map ref 5C1   **CAMPING & CARAVANNING**

★★★★★
HOLIDAY &
TOURING PARK
ROSE AWARD

🚐 (18)   £18.00–£35.00
🚚 (18)   £18.00–£35.00
🏕 (37) £295.00–£620.00
18 touring pitches

Seafield Caravan Park

Seafield Road, Seahouses NE68 7SP **t** (01665) 720628 **f** (01665) 720088 **e** info@seafieldpark.co.uk
w seafieldpark.co.uk

payment Credit/debit cards, cash/cheques

Luxurious holiday homes for hire on
Northumberland's premier park. Fully appointed
caravans. Superior, fully serviced touring pitches.
Prices include full use of Ocean Club facilities
(www.ocean-club.co.uk).

⊕ Take the B1340 from Alnwick for 14 miles. East to coast.

♥ Seasonal discounts available on 3-, 4- and 7-day breaks.

General 🗺 P 🔌 🗋 📶 🈂 ⊙ 🗆 ✗ 🐾 🚿 ☼ Leisure ⌇ ⚒ U ♪ ►

SOUTHPORT, Merseyside Map ref 4A1   **SELF CATERING**

★★★★
SELF CATERING

Units   **2**
Sleeps   **1–6**

Low season per wk
£285.00–£350.00
High season per wk
£325.00–£410.00

Martin Lane Farmhouse Holiday Cottages, Burscough

contact Mrs Stubbs, Martin Lane Farmhouse Holiday Cottages, Ormskirk L40 8JH
t (01704) 893527 **f** (01704) 893527 **e** mlfhc@btinternet.com
w martinlanefarmhouse.btinternet.co.uk

open All year
payment Cash/cheques, euros

Beautiful, award-winning country cottages, nestling
in the rich arable farmland of West Lancashire and
just four miles from Southport and the seaside. Our
cottages have a friendly, relaxed, family atmosphere.
The ideal base for visiting all the North West's major
attractions.

⊕ From A59 take B5242. After 2 miles turn right
(Drummersdale Lane). 1st right (Merscar Lane). Right onto
Martin Lane, over canal, 200yds.

♥ 10% discount on 2-week bookings.

Children 🛏 🏛 🎣 🗄 ⚒ Unit 🏭 📺 📼 🗄 🍴 🗇 🖳 ✿
General P 🅂 Leisure U ♪ ►

WHITBY, North Yorkshire Map ref 5D3   **GUEST ACCOMMODATION**

★★★★
GUEST ACCOMMODATION

B&B per room per night
s £45.00–£87.90
d £59.00–£87.90
Evening meal per person
£15.00–£35.00

Seacliffe Hotel

12 North Promenade, Whitby YO21 3JX **t** (01947) 603139 **f** (01947) 600829
e stay@seacliffehotel.co.uk **w** seacliffehotel.co.uk

open All year except Christmas
bedrooms 10 double, 2 twin, 1 single, 2 family
bathrooms All en suite
payment Credit/debit cards, cash/cheques, euros

A very friendly and relaxing seafront hotel with
magnificent sea views. En suite rooms with digital
TV/DVD/CD, Internet, hairdryer, tea/coffee
facilities. Delicious 'Heartbeat'-Country cooking.
Traditional Aidensfield Arms licensed bar, with patio
garden, serving meals and snacks. James Cook
candlelit restaurant for superb wines and fine dining
(booking advised). Golf course nearby.

⊕ From A171 follow signs for West Cliff and West Cliff car
park. The establishment is on the seafront.

♥ Captain Cook country break: 2 nights' DB&B £124pp.
'Heartbeat'-Country break: 3 nights' B&B for the price of 2
– autumn, winter and spring.

Children 🛏 🏛 🎣 ✏ 🖾 🗄 Room 📞 📺 ♨ 🍵 General P ⚟ ✗ 🍴 🛗 ✿ 🐾 Leisure ● U ♪ ► 🚴 🚣

GUEST ACCOMMODATION

★★★★
GUEST HOUSE

B&B per room per night
s £29.00–£37.00
d £58.00–£94.00
Evening meal per person
£20.50

Fairfield Garden Guesthouse

Brantfell Road, Bowness Bay LA23 3AE **t** (015394) 46565 **f** (015394) 46564
e relax@the-fairfield.co.uk **w** the-fairfield.co.uk

open All year except Christmas
bedrooms 5 double, 2 twin, 1 single, 1 family, 2 suites
bathrooms 10 en suite, 1 private
payment Credit/debit cards, cash/cheques, euros

Secluded Georgian house set in own grounds with beautiful garden and private car park. Informally run B&B with exceptional breakfasts. King-size four-poster bedrooms available. All rooms en suite, some with state-of-the-art, deluxe bathrooms. Guest lounge with Internet access. Located central Bowness – close to Lake Windermere, restaurants, shops and pubs.

⊕ *M6 jct 36. Follow signs Kendal, Windermere. Through Windermere town to Bowness. 1st left after roundabout and left in front of Spinnery restaurant.*

♥ *Reduced prices for 3 nights during weekdays, or extended weekends in low season. DB&B available Nov-Mar.*

Children ♿5   Room 🛏 📺 ♨ 🍷   General ⚡ ♥ ✕ 🏠 ♨ ✿ 🐾   Leisure ∪ ♪ ► 🚲

HOTEL

★★★
HOTEL

B&B per room per night
s £85.00–£120.00
d £115.00–£205.00
HB per person per night
£95.00–£123.00

Dean Court Hotel

Duncombe Place, York YO1 7EF **t** (01904) 625082 **f** (01904) 620305 **e** info@deancourt-york.co.uk
w deancourt-york.co.uk

open All year
bedrooms 24 double, 5 twin, 3 single, 4 family, 1 suite
bathrooms All en suite
payment Credit/debit cards, cash/cheques

Superbly appointed hotel opposite York Minster. All the historic attractions of York are within easy walking distance. All public areas have been tastefully refurbished (February 2004) along with the rosette-awarded restaurant, re-launched as DCH. The new decor is contemporary with magnificent design features. The Court Café-Bistro opened April 2006.

⊕ *A1 to A64 York, then city centre signs A19/A1237 Clifton direction to Bootham Bar, through archway, up one-way street or continue to lights and turn left. Hotel at end.*

♥ *2-night, mid-week literary breaks with top authors. 2-night, mid-week wine and food breaks with top wine producers.*

Children ♿ 🏠 🎿 🎠 🍼 ✎ CM 📷   Room 🔌 📺 ♨ 🍷 ⟲   General P ♥ 🏠 🗊   Leisure ∪ ► 🚲 🏊

GUEST ACCOMMODATION

★★★
GUEST ACCOMMODATION

B&B per room per night
s £40.00–£70.00
d £40.00–£105.00

Blossoms York

28 Clifton, York YO30 6AE **t** (01904) 652391 **f** (01904) 652392 **e** ernie@blossomsyork.co.uk
w blossomsyork.co.uk

Set in a Georgian townhouse on a tree-lined avenue, yet only eight minutes' walk from the Minster, with shops, restaurants and bars nearby. Free parking; large family rooms; friendly welcome.

open All year
bedrooms 6 double, 2 twin, 8 family
bathrooms All en suite
payment Credit/debit cards, cash/cheques

Children ♿ 🏠 🎿 🎠 🍼 ✎ CM 📷   Room 🛏 🔌 📺 ♨ 🍷   General P ♥ 🏠 🗊 ✿ 🐾   Leisure 🚲 🏊

YORK, North Yorkshire Map ref 4C1   GUEST ACCOMMODATION

★★★★
GUEST ACCOMMODATION

B&B per room per night
s £35.00–£80.00
d £65.00–£90.00
Evening meal per person
£14.95–£20.00

Warrens

30-32 Scarcroft Road, York YO23 1NF **t** (01904) 643139 **f** (01904) 658297
e info@warrenshotel.co.uk **w** warrenshotel.co.uk

open All year except Christmas
bedrooms 8 double/twin, 1 twin, 3 family
bathrooms All en suite
payment Credit/debit cards, cash/cheques

Excellent location in conservation area, 350m from city walls. Park your car in our private car park and walk into the city. All rooms are en suite and include hospitality tray, trouser-press, hairdryer, colour TV. Four-poster and king-size beds. Enjoy breakfast in our conservatory; vegetarian options available. WI-FI Internet and email access available.

⊕ *Please visit our website for travel directions.*

♥ *Reductions for 3 or more days Sun-Thu inclusive (excl Bank Holidays and race days). Enhance your stay with a champagne and chocolate package.*

Children 🛏🎮♨🐾 ✐ Room 🛁 📺 ☕ 🍴 General P ✂ ♟ ✕ 🍽 🎭 ✿ Leisure 🏠

Country ways

The Countryside Rights of Way Act gives people new rights to walk on areas of open countryside and registered common land.

To find out where you can go and what you can do, as well as information about taking your dog to the countryside, go online at countrysideaccess.gov.uk.

And when you're out and about...

Always follow the Country Code

● **Be safe – plan ahead and follow any signs**
● **Leave gates and property as you find them**
● **Protect plants and animals, and take your litter home**
● **Keep dogs under close control**
● **Consider other people**

Central England

Having a blast at Alton Towers

BERRY JUICER

Bedfordshire, Cambridgeshire, Derbyshire, Essex, Herefordshire, Hertfordshire, Leicestershire, Lincolnshire, Norfolk, Northamptonshire, Nottinghamshire, Rutland, Shropshire, Staffordshire, Suffolk, Warwickshire, West Midlands, Worcestershire

Soak up the drama of
Shakespeare Country

Central **attraction**

**Active pursuits, lazy days and family
fun –** it's all on a plate in Central
England. Put on your walking boots
ready to challenge the Pennines, drift
along one of the many canals that
criss-cross the region or follow the trail
to the Major Oak in Sherwood Forest.

Nose to nose with a lemur at Woburn Safari Park

Keeping up with the kids

You'll have to be game for anything with such a wide choice of fun family days out. Pick up a Thrill Hopper ticket that gives you great value access to four top theme park attractions: Drayton Manor Theme Park, Alton Towers, SnowDome (ski, snowboard, snowblade or toboggan on real snow) and Waterworld (hold your breath as you plummet down Nucleus, the UK's first indoor water rollercoaster). Still standing? Then head off for the National Space Centre, Leicester, where you can test your ability to survive a little more with a voyage on the interactive Human Spaceflight. Hit the assault course at Conkers, Swadlincote, in the heart of the National Forest, dodge the lions at Woburn Safari Park, and hunt for the Lost World Tribe in the Lost World Maze at the Dinosaur Adventure Park near Norwich. Time for a rest? Take a factory tour at Wedgwood Visitor Centre, Stoke-on-Trent, and then browse the shops while your offspring try throwing a pot or two under expert supervision.

> White-knuckle rides, forest trails on a bike or the battle-worn decks of HMS *Victory*. Where to start?

Sporting challenges

Want to push the boundaries? Choose from walking, cycling, climbing and potholing for starters. Cross in and out of Wales on Offa's Dyke Path or tackle part of the Heart of England Way. There's 270 miles of the Pennine Way, stretching from the Peak District all the way to the Scottish Borders, to dip into or explore the long-distance paths that reach East Anglia's numerous sandy beaches. In the west of the region, admire the vistas that stretch to the Malverns. Two wheels more your thing? You're in luck – the East of England is flat, ideal cycling terrain whatever your age. Traffic-free circular rides in Bacton Woods, Norfolk, are excellent for mountain biking and will suit keen youngsters. Follow part of The Fens Cycle Way or, alternatively, zoom through the stunning Derwent Valley, a World Heritage Site, or spin into seven medieval plague villages on the Black Death Challenge. Action and adventure are bywords for the Peak District and Derbyshire. Limestone and gritstone crags offer great choice for climbers of all abilities, while potholers will relish some of most challenging caves in Britain. More of a spectator? Thrill to the sight of high-octane drag racing at Santa Pod or book early for the British Grand Prix at Silverstone. Hold on to your horse and back a winner at Newmarket, the historical home of British horseracing.

Cantering across Holkham Beach

Time and tides

Buckets, spades and binoculars at the ready for mile upon mile of sandy and shingle beaches running from Essex to Lincolnshire. Undeniably beautiful is the National Nature Reserve at Holkham, Norfolk, where creeks, sand dunes, pinewoods, pastures and marshes have merged. Down along the coast at RSPB Minsmere, Suffolk, hush the children and peer from a hide to see just a few of the wading birds and waterfowl. For bustling seaside resorts, try Felixstowe, Southend-on-Sea and Great Yarmouth. For something a bit quieter, seek out the havens of Frinton-on-Sea, Covehithe and Anderby Creek and the coast's numerous quaint fishing villages. Try out a hammock, avoid the rats and beware of the cannon fire in Below Decks, an interactive recreation of HMS *Victory*, at the Norfolk Nelson Museum in Great Yarmouth.

Main The stunning sculpture at Aldeburgh **Left** Shopaholics head for the Bullring, Birmingham; on target at Sherwood Forest Country Park; celebrate Diwali in style in Leicester; cool off in the stunning gardens at Chatsworth House

Moving inland, explore the rivers and dykes in the Fens – spread over Cambridgeshire, Lincolnshire, Norfolk and Rutland. At Fenscape, the interactive Fens discovery centre in Spalding, learn about the unique past of the inhospitable marshland. For lazy days spent with friends and family, what could be more calming than the reed-fringed waterways of the Norfolk Broads? Sailing is child's play off the blustery Lincolnshire coast. Artificial, but no less exhilarating, there's whitewater rafting at Nene Whitewater Centre in Northampton, kayaking at the National Water Sports Centre at Holme Pierrepont, and bell boating at Carsington Water.

UNESCO Ironbridge Gorge World Heritage Site

Artistic roots

With such a rich mix of industry, history, culture and raw natural beauty it's not surprising Central England inspired so much creative energy. Spot a solitary cottage near Flatford Mill in the Stour Valley, the location of *The Hay Wain*, a masterpiece by local boy John Constable. On the streets of Stratford-upon-Avon, you just can't avoid references to the town's greatest son, William Shakespeare. Book a seat at the Swan Theatre – home of the Royal Shakespeare Company. Find out what shaped DH Lawrence's early life at his birthplace in Eastwood, near Nottingham. See at first hand the decadence of Lord Byron in gothic Newstead Abbey and, on a musical note, Benjamin Britten's Aldeburgh Festival at Snape Maltings, Suffolk, is the place for classical concerts in a rural setting. On Aldeburgh's beach, you can't miss a huge sculpture, *The Scallop*, dedicated to the composer.

> Artist, architect, scientist, historian or aviator – whatever your aspirations, there's an attraction to suit

Spotlight on the past

Spend time in the historic cities of Shrewsbury and Worcester – noted for uneven Tudor half-timbered architecture. Reach for your camera as you pass through Much Wenlock, one of the beautiful black and white villages of Shropshire. Castles and grand homes dot the landscape – Kenilworth Castle and Warwick Castle are favourites. For Elizabethan architecture at its most impressive, Hardwick Hall and Chatsworth

are hard to beat. Step back into the area's proud industrial past at the Ironbridge Gorge Museums – at Enginuity let the kids switch on their imaginations in the interactive design and technology centre. Have a chat with the working craftsmen at The Black Country Living Museum. Trace the history of fighter planes at the Imperial War Museum Duxford in Cambridgeshire, Europe's premier aviation museum, or visit the new National Cold War Exhibition at RAF Museum Cosford.

Indulge yourself

There's a great range of hearty foods to try out – succulent Melton Mowbray pork pies, Red Leicester and Stilton, Lincolnshire plumbread and Bakewell pudding – often imitated, never matched. Head for Britain's food capital, pretty Ludlow on the Welsh borders, to discover what lures so many top chefs to the Ludlow Marches Food and Drink Festival. And then there's retail therapy at its best. Remember the Bullring in Birmingham? A space the size of more than 26 football pitches – all dedicated to shopping and entertainment. The upmarket Mailbox is yet another magnet for shoppers. Soak up the colourful atmosphere of multi-cultural Leicester and try on a sari or two.

Further **information**

East Midlands Tourism
w enjoyeastmidlands.com

East of England Tourist Board
t (01284) 727470
w visiteastofengland.com

Heart of England Tourism
t (01905) 761100
w visitheartofengland.com

Tourist Information Centres

When you arrive at your destination, visit a tourist information centre for help with accommodation and information about local attractions and events, or email your request before you go.

Bedfordshire

Bedford	St Pauls Square	(01234) 215226	TouristInfo@bedford.gov.uk
Luton	St George's Square	(01582) 401579	tourist.information@luton.gov.uk

Cambridgeshire

Cambridge	Wheeler Street	0871 226 8006	tourism@cambridge.gov.uk
Ely	29 St Mary's Street	(01353) 662062	tic@eastcambs.gov.uk
Huntingdon		(01480) 388588	hunts.tic@huntsdc.gov.uk
Peterborough	3-5 Minster Precincts	(01733) 452336	tic@peterborough.gov.uk
St Neots	8 New Street	(01480) 388788	stneots.tic@huntsdc.gov.uk
Wisbech	2-3 Bridge Street	(01945) 583263	tourism@fenland.gov.uk

Derbyshire

Ashbourne	13 Market Place	(01335) 343666	ashbourneinfo@derbyshiredales.gov.uk
Bakewell	Bridge Street	(01629) 816558	bakewell@peakdistrict.gov.uk
Buxton	The Crescent	(01298) 25106	tourism@highpeak.gov.uk
Chesterfield	Rykneld Square	(01246) 345777	tourism@chesterfield.gov.uk
Derby City	Market Place	(01332) 255802	tourism@derby.gov.uk
Glossop	Henry Street	(01457) 855920	info@glossoptouristcentre.co.uk
Matlock	Crown Square	(01629) 583388	matlockinfo@derbyshiredales.gov.uk
Matlock Bath*	The Pavillion	(01629) 55082	matlockbathinfo@derbyshiredales.gov.uk
Ripley	Market Place	(01773) 841488	touristinformation@ambervalley.gov.uk

Essex

Braintree	Market Place	(01376) 550066	tic@braintree.gov.uk
Brentwood	44 High Street	(01277) 200300	michelle.constable@brentwood.gov.uk
Clacton-on-Sea	Station Road	(01255) 423400	emorgan@tendringdc.gov.uk
Colchester	1 Queen Street	(01206) 282920	vic@colchester.gov.uk
Harwich Connexions	Iconfield Park	(01255) 506139	harwichtic@btconnect.com
Maldon	Coach Lane	(01621) 856503	tic@maldon.gov.uk
Saffron Walden	1 Market Place	(01799) 510444	tourism@uttlesford.gov.uk
Sandy	5 Shannon Court	(01767) 682728	tourism@sandytowncouncil.gov.uk
Southend-on-Sea	Western Esplanade	(01702) 215620	vic@southend.gov.uk
Waltham Abbey	2-4 Highbridge Street	(01992) 652295	tic@walthamabbey.org.uk

Herefordshire

Bromyard	Cruxwell Street	(01432) 260280	tic-bromyard@herefordshire.gov.uk
Hereford	1 King Street	(01432) 268430	tic-hereford@herefordshire.gov.uk
Ledbury	3 The Homend	(01531) 636147	tic-ledbury@herefordshire.gov.uk
Leominster	1 Corn Square	(01568) 616460	tic-leominster@herefordshire.gov.uk

| Queenswood* | Dinmore Hill | (01568) 797842 | queenswoodtic@herefordshire.gov.uk |
| Ross-on-Wye | Edde Cross Street | (01989) 562768 | tic-ross@herefordshire.gov.uk |

Hertfordshire

Birchanger Green	Welcome Break Service Area	(01279) 508656	
Bishop's Stortford	Windhill	(01279) 655831	tic@bishopsstortford.org
Hemel Hempstead	Marlowes	(01442) 234222	stephanie.canadas@dacorum.gov.uk
Hertford	10 Market Place	(01992) 584322	tic@hertford.gov.uk
Letchworth Garden City	33-35 Station Road	(01462) 487868	tic@letchworth.com
St Albans	Market Place	(01727) 864511	tic@stalbans.gov.uk

Leicestershire

Ashby-de-la-Zouch	North Street	(01530) 411767	ashby@goleicestershire.com
Hinckley	Lancaster Road	(01455) 635106	hinckleytic@goleicestershire.com
Leicester City	7/9 Every Street	0906 294 1113**	info@goleicestershire.com
Loughborough	Market Place	(01509) 218113	loughborough@goleicestershire.com
Market Harborough	Adam & Eve Street	(01858) 821270	harborough@goleicestershire.com
Melton Mowbray	7 King Street	(01664) 480992	melton@goleicestershire.com

Lincolnshire

Boston	Market Place	(01205) 356656	ticboston@boston.gov.uk
Grantham	St Peter's Hill	(01476) 406166	granthamtic@southkesteven.gov.uk
Horncastle	14 Bull Ring	(01507) 526636	horncastleinfo@e-lindsey.gov.uk
Lincoln Castle Hill	9 Castle Hill	(01522) 873213	tourism@lincoln.gov.uk
Lincoln Corn Hill	21 Cornhill	(01522) 873256	tourism@lincoln.gov.uk
Louth	The Market Hall	(01507) 609289	louthinfo@e-lindsey.gov.uk
Mablethorpe	High Street	(01507) 474939	mablethorpeinfo@e-lindsey.gov.uk
Skegness	Grand Parade	(01754) 899887	skegnessinfo@e-lindsey.gov.uk
Sleaford	Carre Street	(01529) 414294	tic@n-kesteven.gov.uk
Spalding	Market Place	(01775) 725468	tic@sholland.gov.uk
Stamford	27 St Mary's Street	(01780) 755611	stamfordtic@southkesteven.gov.uk
Woodhall Spa*	Iddesleigh Road	(01526) 353775	woodhallspainfo@e-lindsey.gov.uk

Norfolk

Aylsham	Norwich Road	(01263) 733903	aylsham.tic@broadland.gov.uk
Burnham Deepdale	Deepdale Farm	(01485) 210256	info@deepdalefarm.co.uk
Cromer	Prince of Wales Road	0871 200 3071	cromertic@north-norfolk.gov.uk
Diss	Mere Street	(01379) 650523	dtic@s-norfolk.gov.uk
Downham Market	78 Priory Road	(01366) 383287	downham-market.tic@west-norfolk.gov.uk
Great Yarmouth	25 Marine Parade	(01493) 846345	tourism@great-yarmouth.gov.uk
Holt*	3 Pound House	0871 200 3071	holttic@north-norfolk.gov.uk
Hoveton*	Station Road	(01603) 782281	hovetoninfo@broads-authority.gov.uk
Hunstanton	The Green	(01485) 532610	hunstanton.tic@west-norfolk.gov.uk
King's Lynn	Purfleet Quay	(01553) 763044	kings-lynn.tic@west-norfolk.gov.uk
Norwich	Millennium Plain	(01603) 727927	tourism@norwich.gov.uk
Sheringham*	Station Approach	0871 200 3071	sheringhamtic@north-norfolk.gov.uk
Swaffham*	Market Place	(01760) 722255	swaffham@eetb.info

Thetford	4 White Hart Street	(01842) 820689	info@thetfordtourism.co.uk
Wells-next-the-Sea*	Staithe Street	0871 200 3071	wellstic@north-norfolk.gov.uk
Wymondham	Market Place	(01953) 604721	wymondhamtic@btconnect.com

Northamptonshire

Brackley	2 Bridge Street	(01280) 700111	tic@southnorthants.gov.uk
Corby	George Street	(01536) 407507	tic@corby.gov.uk
Kettering	Sheep Street	(01536) 410266	tic@kettering.gov.uk
Northampton	St Giles Square	(01604) 838800	tic@northampton.gov.uk
Oundle	14 West Street	(01832) 274333	oundle@east-northamptonshire.gov.uk

Nottinghamshire

Newark	Castlegate	(01636) 655765	gilstrap@nsdc.info
Nottingham	1-4 Smithy Row	0844 477 5678	tourist.information@nottinghamcity.gov.uk
Ollerton	Sherwood Heath	(01623) 824545	sherwoodheath@nsdc.info
Retford	40 Grove Street	(01777) 860780	retford.tourist@bassetlaw.gov.uk
Worksop	Memorial Avenue	(01909) 501148	worksop.tourist@bassetlaw.gov.uk

Rutland

| Oakham | Catmose Street | (01572) 758441 | museum@rutland.gov.uk |
| Rutland Water* | Sykes Lane | (01572) 653026 | tic@anglianwater.co.uk |

Shropshire

Bridgnorth	Listley Street	(01746) 763257	bridgnorth.tourism@shropshire-cc.gov.uk
Church Stretton	Church Street	(01694) 723133	churchstretton.tourism@shropshire-cc.gov.uk
Ellesmere, Shropshire*	Mereside	(01691) 622981	ellesmere.tourism@shropshire-cc.gov.uk
Ironbridge	Ironbridge Gorge Museum Trust	(01952) 884391	tic@ironbridge.org.uk
Ludlow	Castle Street	(01584) 875053	ludlow.tourism@shropshire-cc.gov.uk
Market Drayton	49 Cheshire Street	(01630) 653114	marketdrayton.scf@shropshire-cc.gov.uk
Much Wenlock*	High Street	(01952) 727679	muchwenlock.tourism@shropshire-cc.gov.uk
Oswestry (Mile End)	Mile End	(01691) 662488	tic@oswestry-bc.gov.uk
Oswestry Town (Heritage Centre)	2 Church Terrace	(01691) 662753	ot@oswestry-welshborders.org.uk
Shrewsbury	The Square	(01743) 281200	tic@shrewsburytourism.co.uk
Telford	The Telford Centre	(01952) 238008	tourist-info@telfordshopping.co.uk
Whitchurch	12 St Mary's Street	(01948) 664577	whitchurch.heritage@ukonline.co.uk

Staffordshire

Burton upon Trent	Horninglow Street	(01283) 508111	tic@eaststaffsbc.gov.uk
Leek	Stockwell Street	(01538) 483741	tourism.services@staffsmoorlands.gov.uk
Lichfield	Castle Dyke	(01543) 412112	info@visitlichfield.com
Newcastle-under-Lyme	Ironmarket	(01782) 297313	tic.newcastle@staffordshire.gov.uk
Stafford	Market Street	(01785) 619619	tic@staffordbc.gov.uk
Stoke-on-Trent	Bagnall Street	(01782) 236000	stoke.tic@stoke.gov.uk
Tamworth	29 Market Street	(01827) 709581	tic@tamworth.gov.uk

Suffolk

Aldeburgh	152 High Street	(01728) 453637	atic@suffolkcoastal.gov.uk
Beccles*	Fen Lane	(01502) 713196	becclesinfo@broads-authority.gov.uk
Bury St Edmunds	6 Angel Hill	(01284) 764667	tic@stedsbc.gov.uk
Felixstowe	91 Undercliff Road West	(01394) 276770	ftic@suffolkcoastal.gov.uk
Flatford	Flatford Lane	(01206) 299460	flatfordvic@babergh.gov.uk
Ipswich	St Stephens Lane	(01473) 258070	tourist@ipswich.gov.uk
Lavenham*	Lady Street	(01787) 248207	lavenhamtic@babergh.gov.uk
Lowestoft	Royal Plain	(01502) 533600	touristinfo@waveney.gov.uk
Newmarket	Palace Street	(01638) 667200	tic.newmarket@forest-heath.gov.uk
Southwold	69 High Street	(01502) 724729	southwold.tic@waveney.gov.uk
Stowmarket	Museum of East Anglian Life	(01449) 676800	tic@midsuffolk.gov.uk
Sudbury	Market Hill	(01787) 881320	sudburytic@babergh.gov.uk
Woodbridge	Station Buildings	(01394) 382240	wtic@suffolkcoastal.gov.uk

Warwickshire

Kenilworth	11 Smalley Place	(01926) 748900	kenilworthlibrary@warwickshire.gov.uk
Leamington Spa	The Parade	(01926) 742762	leamington@shakespeare-country.co.uk
Nuneaton	Church Street	(024) 7634 7006	nuneatonlibrary@warwickshire.gov.uk
Rugby	Little Elborow Street	(01788) 534970	visitor.centre@rugby.gov.uk
Stratford-upon-Avon	Bridgefoot	0870 160 7930	stratfordtic@shakespeare-country.co.uk
Warwick	Jury Street	(01926) 492212	touristinfo@warwick-uk.co.uk

West Midlands

Birmingham Rotunda	150 New Street	0870 225 0127	ticketshop@marketingbirmingham.com
Coventry	4 Priory Row	(024) 7622 7264	tic@cvone.co.uk
Dudley	259 Castle Street	(01384) 812345	dudleycouncilplus@dudley.gov.uk
Merry Hill	Merry Hill	(01384) 487900	
Solihull	Homer Road	(0121) 704 6130	ckelly@solihull.gov.uk
Walsall	Lichfield Street	(01922) 653110	reference@walsall.go.uk
Wolverhampton	18 Queen Square	(01902) 556110	wolverhampton.tic@dial.pipex.com

Worcestershire

Bewdley	Load Street	(01299) 404740	bewdleytic@btconnect.com
Bromsgrove	26 Birmingham Road	(01527) 831809	tic@bromsgrove.gov.uk
Droitwich Spa	Victoria Square	(01905) 774312	heritage@droitwichspa.gov.uk
Evesham	Abbey Gate	(01386) 446944	tic@almonry.ndo.co.uk
Malvern	21 Church Street	(01684) 892289	malvern.tic@malvernhills.gov.uk
Redditch	Alcester Street	(01527) 60806	info.centre@redditchbc.gov.uk
Upton-upon-Severn	4 High Street	(01684) 594200	upton.tic@malvernhills.gov.uk
Worcester	High Street	(01905) 726311	touristinfo@cityofworcester.gov.uk

*seasonal opening ** calls to this number are charged at a premium rate*

Alternatively, you can text **TIC LOCATE** to **64118** to find your nearest tourist information centre

What makes the
perfect break?

**Big city buzz or peaceful country panoramas?
Take a fresh look at England and you may be
surprised at what's on your own doorstep.**

experience... paddling on sandy beaches, playing
Poohsticks in the forest, picnics at open-air concerts, tearooms
offering home-made cakes... **discover...** make your own
journey of discovery through England's cultural delights:
surprising contrasts between old and new, traditional and
trendsetting, time-honoured and contemporary...
explore... drink in lungfuls of fresh air on a hillside with
heart-stopping views, wander through the maze in the garden
of a stately home or tug on the sails of a boat skimming across
a lake... **relax...** no rush to do anything or be anywhere,
take time to immerse yourself in your favourite book by a
roaring log fire or glide from a soothing massage to a
refreshing facial, ease away the tension...

**To help you make up
your mind go online at**

enjoyEngland.com

On the following pages you'll find an extensive selection of indoor and outdoor attractions in Central England. Get to grips with nature, stroll around a museum, have an action-packed day with the kids and a whole lot more...

Attractions are ordered by county, and if you're looking for a specific kind of experience each county is divided into the following sections.

 Family fun

 Nature and wildlife

Historic England

Outdoor activities

 Entertainment and culture

 Food and drink

Relaxing and pampering

Look out, too, for the Quality Assured Visitor Attraction sign. This indicates that the attraction is assessed annually and meets the standards required to receive the quality marque. So rest assured, you'll have a great time.

Turn to the maps at the front of the guide to find the location of those attractions displaying a map reference.

The index on page 459 will help you to locate specific attractions with ease. For more great ideas for places to visit contact a local Tourist Information Centre or log on to **enjoyengland.com**.

Please note, as changes often occur after press date, it is advisable to confirm opening times and admission prices before travelling.

KEY TO ATTRACTIONS

Cafe/restaurant	☕
Picnic area	⌒
No dogs except service dogs	🐕
Partial disabled access	♿
Full disabled access	♿

Where prices aren't specified, use the following guide for an adult admission:

£	up to £5
££	between £5 and £10
£££	between £10 and £15
££££	more than £15

Admire the spectacular interior of Lincoln Cathedral

Bedfordshire

 **FAMILY FUN**

Enjoy the fun of a special event or visit one of the attractions listed for a great day out. For more inspiring ideas go to **enjoyengland.com**.

7–8 July
Bedfordshire Country Show
Old Warden Park, Nr Biggleswade
(01767) 627527
shuttleworth.org.uk

17–19 Aug
de Havilland Club Aircraft Rally
Woburn Abbey, Woburn
(01442) 862077
dhmothclub.co.uk

25–27 Aug
Twinwood Festival, incorporating The Glen Miller Festival of Swing
Twinwood Arena & Airfield, Clapham
(01234) 350413
twinwoodevents.com

Apr 08
Easter Thunderball
Santa Pod Raceway, Podington, Nr Bedford
(01234) 782828
santapod.co.uk

Apr 08
St George's Day Festival
Wrest Park Gardens, Silsoe
0870 333 1183
english-heritage.org.uk

Bedford Butterfly Park

Renhold Road, Wilden, Bedford MK44 2PX
t (01234) 772770
w bedford-butterflies.co.uk
open Feb-Oct 1000-1700. Nov-Jan, Thurs-Sun 1000-1600 (excl 18 Dec-3 Jan).
admission Adult: £4.75

Whatever the weather, come and visit us at Bedford Butterfly Park. We have wildflower meadows outside and tropical butterflies in our hot house. There are farm animals, a playground, tea room and gift shop. Follow the nature trail. Children's arts and crafts every weekend and school holiday.

                              Map ref 2D1

 voucher offer – see back section

Mead Open Farm and Rare Breeds

Stanbridge Road,
Billington,
Leighton Buzzard LU7 9HL
t (01525) 852954
w meadopenfarm.co.uk
open Daily 1000-1830.
admission ££
A working farm with a wide range of traditional farm animals and rare breeds, pets' corner, undercover children's play area and a tearoom.

Woodside Farm and Wildfowl Park
Woodside Road,
Slip End LU1 4DG
t (01582) 841044
w woodsidefarm.co.uk
open Apr-Oct, Mon-Sat 0900-1800,
Sun 1000-1800. Nov-Mar, Mon-Sat 0900-dusk,
Sun 1000-dusk.
admission ££

A seven-acre park with farm shop, rare breeds, wildlife, farm animals, adventure play area and coffee shop. Indoor hands-on sessions. Eighteen-hole crazy golf.

NATURE AND WILDLIFE

Bedford Butterfly Park

Renhold Road, Wilden, Bedford MK44 2PX
t (01234) 772770
w bedford-butterflies.co.uk
open Feb-Oct 1000-1700. Nov-Jan, Thurs-Sun 1000-1600 (excl 18 Dec-3 Jan).
admission Adult: £4.75

Whatever the weather, come and visit us at Bedford Butterfly Park. We have wildflower meadows outside and tropical butterflies in our hot house. There are farm animals, a playground, tea room and gift shop. Follow the nature trail. Children's arts and crafts every weekend and school holiday.

Map ref 2D1

 voucher offer – see back section

Dunstable Downs
Whipsnade Road, Dunstable LU6 2TA
t (01582) 608489
w nationaltrust.org.uk
open Daily.
admission Free

Scenic views over the vale of Aylesbury. Countryside centre where kites, souvenirs and publications can be purchased. Site of Special Scientific Interest.

The English School of Falconry Bird of Prey & Conservation Centre
Old Warden Park, Biggleswade SG18 9EA
t (01767) 627527
w birdsofpreycentre.co.uk
open Feb-Oct, daily 1000-1700.
admission ££

One of the country's largest collections of birds of prey (over 300), including rare species. Walk-through barn owl aviary and daily displays featuring different birds of prey.

The Marston Vale Millennium Country Park
The Forest Centre, Station Road, Marston Moretaine,
Bedford MK43 0PR
t (01234) 767037
w marstonvale.org
open Daily.
admission Free

For a naturally great day out – whatever the weather. Cycle, walk, ride, visit the shop, or relax in Lakeside Cafe. Adventure playground. Exciting calendar of events.

Priory Country Park
Barkers Lane, Bedford MK41 9SH
t (01234) 211182
open Daily.
admission Free

Over 300 acres of open space with two lakes and riverside. Fishing facilities, water sports, bird-watching hides, guided walks and talks.

The Swiss Garden
Old Warden Park, Old Warden SG18 9ER
t (01767) 627666
w shuttleworth.org
open Apr-Oct, daily 1000-1700. Nov-Mar, daily 1000-1600.
admission ££

A nine-acre romantic and picturesque garden.

Whipsnade Wild Animal Park
Dunstable LU6 2LF
t (01582) 872171
w zsl.org
open Daily 1000-1600.
admission £££

Whipsnade Wild Animal Park has over 2,500 animals set in 600 acres of beautiful parkland. Fun-filled and informative daily events run throughout the day.

Woburn Safari Park

Woburn MK17 9QN
t (01525) 290407
w discoverwoburn.co.uk
open Apr-Oct, daily 1000-1700. Nov-Mar, Sat-Sun 1100-1500.
admission ££££

Drive through the safari park with 30 species of animals in natural groups just a windscreen's width away, plus the action-packed Wild World Leisure Area.

Wrest Park Gardens

Silsoe MK45 4HS
t (01525) 860152
w english-heritage.org.uk
open Apr-Jun, Sat-Sun, Bank Hols 1000-1800. Jul-Aug, Mon, Thu-Sun 1000-1800. Sep, Sat-Sun 1000-1800. Oct, Sat-Sun 1000-1700.
admission £

One hundred and fifty years of English gardens laid out in the early 18thC including painted pavilion, Chinese bridge, lakes, classical temple, orangery and bath house.

HISTORIC ENGLAND

Bedford Museum

Castle Lane, Bedford MK40 3XD
t (01234) 353323
open Tue-Sat 1100-1700. Sun, Bank Holiday Mon 1400-1700. (Excl 6 Apr, 24-26 Dec, 1 Jan.)
admission Free

Embark on a fascinating journey through the human and natural history of north Bedfordshire, pausing briefly to glimpse at wonders from more distant lands. Go back in time to visit the delightful rural room sets and the Old School Museum.

Map ref 2D1

Elstow Moot Hall

Elstow Green, Church End, Elstow MK42 9XT
t (01234) 266889
open Apr-Sep, Tue-Thu, Sun, Bank Hols 1300-1600.
admission £

A medieval market hall containing exhibits of 17thC life including beautiful period furniture. Publications and antique maps for sale.

Moggerhanger Park

Park Road, Moggerhanger MK44 3RW
t (01767) 641007
w moggerhangerpark.com
open Tea rooms/restaurant: all year 1100-1600. House tours: 16 Jun-9 Sep 1200 & 1430.
admission Adult: From £7.50

Recently restored Grade I Georgian house, as designed by Sir John Soane. Guided tours daily throughout the summer; free access to woodlands and exhibition all year round; conference facilities available. Tea rooms open every day from 1100 to 1600 - do visit the first restaurant to be awarded a Bedfordshire 'Food Mark'!

Map ref 2D1

V *voucher offer – see back section*

Woburn Abbey

Woburn MK17 9WA
t (01525) 290666 **w** discoverwoburn.co.uk
open Apr-Sep, daily 1100-1600.
admission £££

An 18thC Palladian mansion, altered by Henry Holland, the Prince Regent's architect, containing a collection of English silver, French and English furniture and art.

ENTERTAINMENT AND CULTURE

Bedford Museum

Castle Lane, Bedford MK40 3XD
t (01234) 353323
open Tue-Sat 1100-1700. Sun, Bank Holiday
Mon 1400-1700. (Excl 6 Apr, 24-26 Dec, 1 Jan.)
admission Free

Embark on a fascinating journey through the
human and natural history of north
Bedfordshire, pausing briefly to glimpse at
wonders from more distant lands. Go back in
time to visit the delightful rural room sets and
the Old School Museum.

 Map ref 2D1

The Mossman Collection
Stockwood Park Museum, Farley Hill, Luton LU1 4BH
t (01582) 738714 **w** luton.gov.uk
open Apr-Sep, Tue-Sun 1000-1630. Oct-Mar, Sat-Sun
1000-1530.
admission Free
*The Mossman Collection is Britain's largest collection of
horse-drawn carriages illustrating the history of road
transport from Roman times to the 1930s.*

Stockwood Park Museum
Stockwood Park, Farley Hill, Luton LU1 4BH
t (01582) 738714 **w** luton.gov.uk
open Apr-Oct, Tue-Sun 1000-1700. Nov-Mar, Sat-Sun
1000-1700.
admission Free
*The craft museum illustrates the crafts and trades of pre-
industrial Bedfordshire; period gardens; the Mossman
Collection of carriages, sculpture gardens, tea room.*

The magnificent White Lion of Dunstable Downs

Stondon Museum
Station Road,
Lower Stondon,
Henlow Camp SG16 6JN
t (01462) 850339
open Daily 1000-1700.
admission ££
*A museum with transport exhibits from the early
1900s to the 1980s. The largest private collection
in England of bygone vehicles from the
beginning of the century.*

FOOD AND DRINK

Moggerhanger Park

Park Road, Moggerhanger MK44 3RW
t (01767) 641007
w moggerhangerpark.com
open Tea rooms/restaurant: all year 1100-
1600. House tours: 16 Jun-9 Sep 1200 & 1430.
admission Adult: From £7.50

Recently restored Grade I Georgian house, as
designed by Sir John Soane. Guided tours daily
throughout the summer; free access to
woodlands and exhibition all year round;
conference facilities available. Tea rooms open
every day from 1100 to 1600 - do visit the first
restaurant to be awarded a Bedfordshire 'Food
Mark'!

Map ref 2D1

ⓥ *voucher offer – see back section*

Cambridgeshire

Enjoy the fun of a special event or visit one of the attractions listed for a great day out. For more inspiring ideas go to **enjoyengland.com**.

15–17 Jun
East of England Country Show
Peterborough
(01733) 234451
eastofengland.org.uk

7– 8 Jul
Flying Legends Airshow
Imperial War Museum, Duxford
(01223) 835000
iwm.org.uk/duxford

26–29 Jul
Cambridge Folk Festival
Cherry Hinton Hall, Cambridge
(01223) 357851
cambridgefolkfestival.co.uk

8 Oct
East of England Agricultural Society Autumn Show
Peterborough
(01733) 234451
eastofengland.org.uk

5 May 08
Stilton Cheese Rolling Contest
Stilton
(01733) 241206
stilton.org

 FAMILY FUN

The Milton Maize Maze
Rectory Farm Shop, A10 Milton bypass,
Milton CB4 6DA
t (01223) 860374
w themiltonmaizemaze.co.uk
open Jul-Aug, daily 1000-1700.
admission ££
The Milton Maize Maze. A walk-through puzzle to challenge any age! A field full of family fun. Find us on the A10 Milton bypass.

Nene Valley Railway

Wansford Station, Stibbington,
Peterborough PE8 6LR
t (01780) 784444
w nvr.org.uk
open Wansford site: All year (excl 25 Dec). Nov-Easter, Sun. Easter to mid-May, Sat-Sun. Mid-May to Oct, Wed, Sat-Sun. Other mid-week services operate in summer.
admission Adult: £10.50

The golden age of steam comes alive at the Nene Valley Railway, travelling between Yarwell, Wansford and Peterborough. The 7.5 mile track also passes through the heart of the 500-acre Ferry Meadows Country Park. Home of 'Thomas', children's favourite engine. Shop, cafe, bookshop and museum. Special events all year. Disabled visitors welcome

Map ref 3A1

  voucher offer – see back section

For key to symbols see inside back cover.

Sacrewell Farm & Country Centre

Thornhaugh, Peterborough PE8 6HJ
t (01780) 782254 **w** sacrewell.org.uk
open Mar-Sep 0930-1700. Oct-Feb 1000-1600 (excl 24 Dec-2 Jan).
admission Adult: £5.50

Hidden deep in the heart of the countryside nestles a farm and 18thC watermill. Friendly farm animals, shire horses, children's indoor and outdoor play areas, tractor rides, range of listed buildings, working watermill, gardens, farm bygones and farm trails. Excellent Miller's Country Cafe and shop. Dogs allowed.

                        Map ref 3A1

V voucher offer – *see back section*

 NATURE AND WILDLIFE

Cambridge University Botanic Garden

Cory Lodge,
Bateman Street,
Cambridge CB2 1JF
t (01223) 336265
open Daily 1000-1600.
admission £

Forty-acre oasis of beautiful gardens and glasshouses, with some 80,000 plant species. Rock, winter and dry gardens, tropical glasshouse and lake. Unique systematic beds.

Crossing House

78 Meldreth Road, Shepreth SG8 6PS
t (01763) 261071
open Daily, dawn-dusk.
admission Free

The crossing-keeper's cottage and a small plantsman's garden with a very wide variety of plants.

Docwra's Manor Garden

2 Meldreth Road, Shepreth SG8 6PS
t (01763) 261473
w docwrasmanorgarden.co.uk
open All year, Wed-Fri 1000-1600.
admission £

Walled gardens round an 18thC redbrick house approached by 18thC wrought-iron gates. There are barns, a 20thC folly and unusual plants.

Grafham Water

Visitor Centre, Marlow Park, Grafham PE28 0BH
t (01480) 812154
open Apr-Oct, Mon-Fri 1100-1600, Sat-Sun 1100-1700. Nov-Mar, Mon-Fri 1100-1500, Sat-Sun 1100-1600.
admission Free

Water park with extensive views, sailing, trout fishing, nature reserve, trails and walks, picnic areas, play areas, refreshments and gift shop.

Hamerton Zoo Park

Sawtry PE28 5RE
t (01832) 293362
w hamertonzoopark.com
open Apr-Oct, daily 1030-1800. Nov-Mar, daily 1030-1600.
admission ££

A wildlife park with tigers, lemurs, marmosets, meerkats, wallabies and a unique bird collection with rare and exotic species from around the world.

Linton Zoo

Hadstock Road, Linton CB21 4NT
t (01223) 891308
w lintonzoo.com
open Apr-May, daily 1000-1700. Jun-Aug, daily 1000-1800. Sep-Oct, daily 1000-1700. Nov-Apr, daily 1030-1600.
admission ££

The zoo has big cats, tigers, wallabies, lemurs, toucans, parrots and reptiles, a wonderful combination of beautiful gardens and wildlife.

Milton Country Park

Cambridge Road, Milton, Cambridge CB4 6AZ
t (01223) 420060
w scambs.gov.uk
open Apr-Jun, daily 0800-1730. Jul-Sep, daily 0800-1900. Oct-Mar, daily 0800-1630.
admission Free

A haven of peace and quiet with a network of paths over two miles, suitable for bicycles and wheelchairs. Picnic areas, play equipment for children, fishing.

National Stud

Newmarket CB8 0XE
t (01638) 663464
w nationalstud.co.uk
open Mar-Sep, daily 1115-1545.
admission ££

A conducted tour which includes top thoroughbred stallions, mares and foals, and gives an insight into the day-to-day running of a modern stud farm.

The Raptor Foundation

The Heath, St Ives Road, Woodhurst PE28 3BT
t (01487) 741140
w raptorfoundation.org.uk
open Daily 1000-1700 (excl 25-26 Dec, 1 Jan).
admission Adult: £4

Get close to nature's most endearing and stunning creatures: owls, hawks, falcons and eagles. Stroll in gardens with the gentle sound of running water and feed the kio in the pond. Watch one of the three flying displays, with audience participation. Relax in Silent Wings tea room over tea and cake.

Map ref 3A2

 voucher offer – see back section

Shepreth Wildlife Park Willersmill

Station Road, Shepreth SG8 6PZ
t (01763) 262226
w sheprethwildlifepark.co.uk
open Apr-Oct, daily 1000-1800. Nov-Mar, daily 1000-1700.
admission ££

A great day out for the whole family. See tigers, monkeys, wolves, otter, birds, reptiles and much more. Also children's play areas.

Wandlebury Country Park

Wandlebury Ring, Gog Magog Hills, Babraham CB2 4AE
t (01223) 243830
w cpswandlebury.org
open Daily, dawn-dusk.
admission Free

An Iron Age ring ditch, woodlands, footpaths, walks, wildlife and public footpaths to a Roman road and picnic areas.

Wicken Fen National Nature Reserve

The National Trust, Lode Lane, Wicken CB7 5XP
t (01353) 720274
w nationaltrust.org.uk
open Daily, dawn-dusk.
admission £

The last remaining undrained portion of the great Fen levels of East Anglia, rich in plant and invertebrate life and good for birds. Also a working windpump and restored Fen cottage.

Wood Green Animal Shelters

King's Bush Farm, London Road, Godmanchester PE29 2NH
t 0870 190 4090
w woodgreen.org.uk
open Daily 1000-1600.
admission Free

One of Europe's busiest animal rescue and re-homing sites with lots to see, including farm animals, cats, dogs and small animals. Permanent residents; others awaiting new homes.

HISTORIC ENGLAND

Anglesey Abbey, Gardens and Lode Mill

Quy Road, Lode CB5 9EJ
t (01223) 810080
w nationaltrust.org.uk
open Abbey: Apr-Oct, Wed-Sun 1300-1700. Gardens: Apr-Oct, Wed-Sun 1030-1730. Lode Mill: Apr-Oct, Wed-Sun 1300-1700.
admission ££

A 13thC abbey with a later Jacobean style house and the famous Fairhaven collection of paintings and furniture. There is also an outstanding 100-acre garden and arboretum.

Cambridge All Saints

Jesus Lane, Cambridge CB5 8BS
t (020) 7213 0660
w visitchurches.org.uk
open Please phone for details.
admission Free

This spire of this fine Victorian church is a prominent local landmark. The interior is a milestone of the Gothic revival, with richly painted stencil wall decoration and stained glass by William Morris and other Pre-Raphaelites.

Elton Hall
Elton PE8 6SH
t (01832) 280468 **w** eltonhall.com
open Jun, Wed, 1400-1700. Jul-Aug, Wed, Thu, Sun 1400-1700.
admission ££
A historic house and gardens open to the public with a fine collection of paintings, furniture, books and Henry VIII's prayer book. There is also a restored rose garden.

Ely Cathedral
Chapter House, The College, Ely CB7 4DL
t (01353) 667735 **w** cathedral.ely.anglican.org
open Apr-Oct, daily 0700-1900. Nov-Mar, Mon-Sat 0730-1800, Sun 0730-1700.
admission ££
One of England's finest cathedrals with guided tours and tours of the Octagon and West Tower and monastic precincts. Also a brass-rubbing centre and The Stained Glass Museum.

Flag Fen Bronze Age Centre
The Droveway, Northey Road,
Peterborough PE6 7QJ
t (01733) 313414 **w** flagfen.com
open Apr-Oct, Mar, Tue-Sun, Bank Hols 1000-1600.
admission £
Visitor centre with landscaped park, summer archaeological excavations, rare breed animals, roundhouses and museum of the Bronze Age.

Houghton Mill
Houghton PE28 2AZ
t (01480) 301494 **w** nationaltrust.org.uk
open Apr, Sat 1100-1700, Sun 1300-1700. May-Sep, Mon-Wed, 1300-1700, Sat 1100-1700, Sun 1300-1700. Oct, Sat 1100-1700, Sun 1300-1700.
admission £
A large timber-built watermill on an island in the River Ouse with much of the 19thC mill machinery intact and some restored to working order.

Kings College Chapel
Kings College, Cambridge CB2 1ST
t (01223) 331212 **w** kings.cam.ac.uk
open Term Time: Mon-Fri 0930-1530, Sat 0930-1515, Sun 1315-1415. School Hols: Mon-Sat 0930-1630, Sun 1000-1700.
admission £
The chapel, founded by Henry VI, includes the breathtaking fan-vault ceiling, stained-glass windows, a carved-oak screen and Ruben's masterpiece The Adoration of the Magi.

The Manor
Hemingford Grey PE28 9BN
t (01480) 463134
open House: By appointment. Gardens: Apr-Sep, daily 1000-1700. Oct-Mar, daily 1000-dusk.
admission £
The 'Green Knowe' children's books were based on this ancient house. Also see the Lucy Boston patchworks. There is a 4.5-acre garden with topiary.

Nene Valley Railway
Wansford Station, Stibbington,
Peterborough PE8 6LR
t (01780) 784444
w nvr.org.uk
open Wansford site: All year (excl 25 Dec). Nov-Easter, Sun. Easter to mid-May, Sat-Sun. Mid-May to Oct, Wed, Sat-Sun. Other mid-week services operate in summer.
admission Adult: £10.50

The golden age of steam comes alive at the Nene Valley Railway, travelling between Yarwell, Wansford and Peterborough. The 7.5 mile track also passes through the heart of the 500-acre Ferry Meadows Country Park. Home of 'Thomas', children's favourite engine. Shop, cafe, bookshop and museum. Special events all year. Disabled visitors welcome

Map ref 3A1

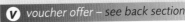
voucher offer – see back section

Ely Cathedral

Oliver Cromwell's House

29 St Mary's Street, Ely CB7 4HF
t (01353) 662062 **w** eastcambs.gov.uk
open Daily (excl 25-26 Dec, 1 Jan).
admission Adult: £4.10

Visit the former Lord Protector's family home and experience an exhibition on 17thC life, the Civil War and Cromwell's connection with Fen life. There are eight period rooms, exhibitions and videos to enjoy. Try dressing up and venture into the Haunted Bedroom if you dare! Also gift shop and Tourist Information Centre.

Map ref 3A2

 voucher offer – see back section

Peckover House and Gardens
North Brink, Wisbech PE13 1JR
t (01945) 583463
w nationaltrust.org.uk
open House: Apr-Oct, Mon-Wed, Sat-Sun
1300-1630. Garden: Apr-Oct, Mon-Wed, Sat-Sun
1200-1700.
admission £

A merchant's house on the north brink of the River Nene, built in 1722 with a plaster and wood rococo interior and a notable and rare Victorian garden with unusual trees.

Peterborough Cathedral
12a Minster Precincts, Peterborough PE1 1XS
t (01733) 343342
w peterborough-cathedral.org.uk
open All year, Mon-Fri 0900-1830, Sat 0900-1700, Sun 0730-1700.
admission £

A Norman cathedral with an early-English west front, a 13thC painted nave ceiling and the tomb of Catherine of Aragon. It was also the former burial place of Mary Queen of Scots.

Sacrewell Farm & Country Centre

Thornhaugh, Peterborough PE8 6HJ
t (01780) 782254 **w** sacrewell.org.uk
open Mar-Sep 0930-1700. Oct-Feb 1000-1600
(excl 24 Dec-2 Jan).
admission Adult: £5.50

Hidden deep in the heart of the countryside nestles a farm and 18thC watermill. Friendly farm animals, shire horses, children's indoor and outdoor play areas, tractor rides, range of listed buildings, working watermill, gardens, farm bygones and farm trails. Excellent Miller's Country Cafe and shop. Dogs allowed.

Map ref 3A1

 voucher offer – see back section

Friendly help and advice

Tourist Information Centres offer suggestions of places to visit and things to do as well as friendly help with accommodation and holiday ideas. To find the one nearest to you text TIC LOCATE to 64118.

For key to symbols see inside back cover.

Wimpole Hall and Home Farm: The National Trust

Arrington SG8 0BW
t (01223) 206000
w nationaltrust.org.uk
open Apr-Jul, Mon-Wed, Sat-Sun 1030-1700.
Aug, Mon-Thu, Sat-Sun 1030-1700. Sep-Oct,
Mon-Wed, Sat-Sun 1030-1700. Nov-Feb, Sat-Sun
1100-1600.
admission ££

An 18thC house in a landscaped park with a folly, Chinese bridge, plunge bath and yellow drawing room in the house, the work of John Soane. Home Farm is a rare breeds centre.

OUTDOOR ACTIVITIES

The Raptor Foundation

The Heath, St Ives Road, Woodhurst PE28 3BT
t (01487) 741140
w raptorfoundation.org.uk
open Daily 1000-1700 (excl 25-26 Dec, 1 Jan).
admission Adult: £4

Get close to nature's most endearing and stunning creatures: owls, hawks, falcons and eagles. Stroll in gardens with the gentle sound of running water and feed the kio in the pond. Watch one of the three flying displays, with audience participation. Relax in Silent Wings tea room over tea and cake.

Map ref 3A2

v *voucher offer – see back section*

ENTERTAINMENT AND CULTURE

Blacked-Out Britain War Museum

1 St Marys Street, Huntingdon PE18 3PE
t (01480) 450998
open All year, Mon-Sat 0930-1730, Sun 1000-1400.
admission Free

The museum has everyday items of life from 1939-1945, from evacuation to rationing, bus tickets to bombs. Capture the feel of what life was like.

Burwell Museum of Fen Edge Village Life

Mill Close, Burwell CB5 0HL
t (01638) 605544 **w** burwellmuseum.org.uk
open Apr-Oct, Thu, Sun, Bank Hols 1400-1700.
admission £

Burwell Museum houses a comprehensive collection which portrays Fen Edge life from the prehistoric through Bronze Age, Iron Age, Roman period and Anglo-Saxon to World War II.

Cambridge and County Folk Museum

2-3 Castle Street, Cambridge CB3 0AQ
t (01223) 355159 **w** folkmuseum.org.uk
open Apr-Sep, Mon-Sat 1030-1700, Sun 1400-1700.
Oct-Mar, Tue-Sat 1030-1700, Sun 1400-1700.
admission £

A part timber-framed 17thC inn, retaining many original fittings. Established as a museum of Cambridgeshire life in 1936. Strong collections.

Cromwell Museum

Grammar School Walk, Huntingdon PE29 3LF
t (01480) 375830
open Nov-Mar, Tue-Fri 1300-1600, Sat 1100-1300,
1400-1600, Sun 1400-1600. Apr-Oct, Tue-Sun
1030-1230, 1330-1600.
admission Free

A museum with portraits, signed documents and other articles belonging to Cromwell and his family.

Ely Museum

The Old Gaol, Market Street, Ely CB7 4LS
t (01353) 666655 **w** elymuseum.org.uk
open Mar-Oct, Mon-Sat 1030-1700, Sun 1300-1700.
Nov-Feb, Mon, Wed-Sat 1030-1600, Sun 1300-1600.
admission £

A chronological account of the history of Ely and the isle from prehistory to the present day. The collections consist of archaeology, social and military history.

The Farmland Museum and Denny Abbey

Ely Road, Waterbeach CB5 9PQ
t (01223) 860988
open Apr-Oct, daily 1200-1700.
admission £

An agricultural estate since medieval times with an abbey and an interactive museum. Remains of a 12thC Benedictine Abbey and a 14thC refectory.

Fitzwilliam Museum
Trumpington Street, Cambridge CB2 1RB
t (01223) 332900 **w** fitzmuseum.cam.ac.uk
open All year, Tue-Sat 1000-1700, Sun 1200-1700.
admission Free
A large, internationally renowned collection of antiques, applied art and paintings. The original buildings are mid-19thC with later additions, including the courtyard development.

Imperial War Museum Duxford

Duxford CB2 4QR
t (01223) 835000 **w** duxford.iwm.org.uk
open Apr-Sep, daily 1000-1800. Oct-Feb, daily 1000-1600.
admission £££
With its air shows, unique history and atmosphere, nowhere else combines the sights, sounds and power of aircraft quite like Duxford.

Kettle's Yard
Castle Street, Cambridge CB3 0AQ
t (01223) 352124 **w** kettlesyard.co.uk
open Apr-Sep, Tue-Sun, Bank Hols 1330-1630.
Oct-Mar, Tue-Sun, Bank Hols 1400-1600.
admission Free
A major collection of 20thC paintings and sculpture exhibited in a house of unique character. Also changing contemporary and modern art exhibitions in the gallery.

Octavia Hill's Birthplace Museum
1 South Brink Place, Wisbech PE13 1JE
t (01945) 476358
open Apr-Oct, Wed, Sat-Sun, Bank Hols 1300-1630.
admission £
Grade II* Listed Georgian house in which Octavia Hill, social reformer and co-founder of the National Trust, was born. The museum commemorates her life, work and legacy.

Oliver Cromwell's House

29 St Mary's Street, Ely CB7 4HF
t (01353) 662062 **w** eastcambs.gov.uk
open Daily (excl 25-26 Dec, 1 Jan).
admission Adult: £4.10

Visit the former Lord Protector's family home and experience an exhibition on 17thC life, the Civil War and Cromwell's connection with Fen life. There are eight period rooms, exhibitions and videos to enjoy. Try dressing up and venture into the Haunted Bedroom if you dare! Also gift shop and Tourist Information Centre.

Map ref 3A2

 voucher offer – see back section

Newmarket races

The Sedgwick Museum of Earth Sciences
University of Cambridge, Downing Street,
Cambridge CB2 3EQ
t (01223) 333456
w sedgwickmuseum.org
open All year, Mon-Fri 1000-1300, 1400-1700, Sat
1000-1600.
admission Free

*Displays include the world's largest spider,
minerals and gemstones, rocks collected by
Charles Darwin, dinosaurs, Jurassic marine reptiles
and local fossils.*

Stained Glass Museum
The South Triforium, Ely Cathedral, Ely CB7 4DL
t (01353) 6603 47247
w stainedglassmuseum.com
open Apr-Oct, Mon-Fri 1030-1700, Sat 1030-1730, Sun
1200-1800. Nov-Mar, Mon-Fri 1030-1700, Sat
1030-1700, Sun 1200-1630.
admission £

*A museum housing examples of stained glass
from the 13thC to the present day in specially lit
display boxes with models of a modern
workshop.*

Taggart Tile Museum
Robin Hood Cottage,
Great Staughton, St Neots PE19 5BB
t (01480) 860314
w taggartgallery.co.uk
open All year, Wed-Sat 0930-1700.
admission Free

*The Taggart Tile Museum is located at Robin Hood, a
15thC cottage next to St Andrews church. The museum
houses an extensive permanent exhibition of tiles from
1650-2000.*

University Museum of Archaeology and Anthropology
Downing Street, Cambridge CB2 3DZ
t (01223) 333516 **w** museum.archanth.cam.ac.uk
open All year, Tue-Sat 1400-1630.
admission Free

*The archaeology gallery surveys world prehistory from
the origins of mankind to the rise of literate civilisation.
The anthropology gallery surveys culture and art from all
continents.*

University Museum of Zoology
Downing Street, Cambridge CB2 3EJ
t (01223) 336650 **w** zoo.cam.ac.uk
open All year, Mon-Fri 1000-1645.
admission Free

*Spectacular displays of internationally important
specimens, including fossils, mammal skeletons, birds,
dinosaurs, shells. Exhibitions throughout the year.*

Whipple Museum of the History of Science
Free School Lane, Cambridge CB2 3RH
t (01223) 330906 **w** hps.cam.ac.uk
open All year, Mon-Fri 1230-1630.
admission Free

*The Whipple Museum houses a designated collection of
scientific instruments and models, dating from the
Middle Ages to the present.*

Wisbech and Fenland Museum
Museum Square, Wisbech PE13 1ES
t (01945) 583817 **w** wisbechmuseum.org.uk
open All year, Tue-Sat 1000-1600.
admission Free

*One of the oldest purpose-built museums in the country,
situated next to Wisbech's fine Georgian crescent.
Displays on Fen landscape, local history, geology and
archaeology.*

Relaxing on the River Cam, Cambridge

Derbyshire

Enjoy the fun of a special event or visit one of the attractions listed for a great day out. For more inspiring ideas go to **enjoyengland.com**.

26–27 May
Chesterfield Walking Festival
Chesterfield
(01246) 345777
visitderbyshire.co.uk

6–22 Jul
Buxton Festival
Various venues, Buxton
(01298) 70395
buxtonfestival.co.uk

31 Aug–2 Sep
Chatsworth Country Fair
Chatsworth House, Nr Bakewell
(01328) 701133
countryfairoffice.co.uk

7–23 Sep
Wirksworth Festival
Various venues, Wirksworth
(01629) 824003
wirksworthfestival.co.uk

22 Dec (provisional date)
Carols by Candlelight
Treak Cliff Cavern, Castleton
(01433) 620571
bluejohnstone.com

 FAMILY FUN

Denby Pottery Visitor Centre
Derby Road, Denby DE5 8NX
t (01773) 740799
w denbypottery.co.uk
open All year, Mon-Sat 0930-1700,
Sun 1000-1700.
admission Free
Factory tours daily, museum, Denby factory shop, Dartington Crystal factory shop, garden centre, gift shop, Cookery Emporium and the Courtyard Restaurant.

Gulliver's Kingdom

Temple Walk,
Matlock Bath DE4 3PG
t (01629) 580540 **w** gulliversfun.co.uk
open Apr-Sep, phone for details. Opening times vary during the Christmas period.
admission Adult: £8.99

A magical kingdom for families with children aged two to 13 years of age. With 30 rides and attractions it will entertain your child all day. Visit one of our many shows or relax in one of our many restaurants.

Map ref 4B2

Middleton Top Cycle Hire

Middleton Top Visitor Centre, Rise End,
Middleton, Matlock DE4 4LS
t (01629) 823204
w derbyshire.gov.uk/countryside
open Easter-Oct, Sat-Sun, school holidays 0930-1700. Jun-Aug 0930-1700.
admission Please phone for pricing details

Cycle hire centre on the High Peak Trail. Miles of traffic-free cycling and longer on-road routes for the more adventurous. Adult and child bikes available as well as trailers for children. Free helmet hire with every bike.

Map ref 4B2

Matlock Farm Park
Jaggers Lane, Nr Two Dales,
Matlock DE4 5LH
t (01246) 590200
w matlockfarmpark.co.uk
open Apr-Nov, daily 1000-1630. Dec, Sat-Sun
1000-1600.
admission £
*Matlock Farm Park is a great day out for all the family.
There are many different animals for you to see and
plenty to do for the kids.*

The Midland Railway, Butterley
Butterley Station, Butterley DE5 3QZ
t (01773) 747674
w midlandrailwaycentre.co.uk
open See website for details.
admission ££
*Over 50 locomotives and over 100 items of historic
rolling stock of Midland and LMS origin with a steam-
hauled passenger service, a museum site, country and
farm park.*

Royal Crown Derby Visitor Centre
194 Osmaston Road,
Derby DE23 8JZ
t (01332) 712800
w royal-crown-derby.co.uk
open All year, Mon-Fri 0930-1600.
admission £
*Guided tours of the working factory and demonstrations
of key skills. Museum, demonstrations and factory shop
open daily.*

NATURE AND WILDLIFE

Belper River Gardens
Matlock Road, Belper
t (01773) 841482
w visitambervalley.com
open Daily.
admission Free
*Beautiful gardens situated by the River Derwent – 'The
National Heritage Corridor' – which flows through the
county of Derbyshire.*

Blue John Cavern and Blue John Mine
Castleton S33 8WP
t (01433) 620638
w bluejohn-cavern.co.uk
open Apr-Oct, daily 0930-1700. Nov-Mar, daily
0930-dusk.
admission ££
*The source of the rare Blue John stone . A fine
range of natural water-worn caverns with
stalactites and stalagmites, set in the spectacular
Peak District.*

BlueBell Arboretum
Annwell Lane, Smisby LE65 2TA
t (01530) 413700 **w** bluebellnursery.com
open Mar-Oct, Mon-Sat 0900-1700, Sun 1030-1630.
Nov-Feb, Mon-Sat 0900-1600.
admission £
*Thriving young arboretum and woodland garden
established in 1992, containing a large selection of
beautiful rare trees, with many species planted for their
autumn colour.*

Foremark Reservoir
Milton DE65 6EG
t 0870 062 7777 **w** stwater.co.uk
open Daily, dawn-dusk.
admission £
*Reservoir with nature reserve, woodland walks and
bridleway. Day-ticket sailing available at weekends.
Game fishing during season. Children's play area.*

Grassmoor Country Park and the Five Pits Trail
Birkin Lane, Grassmoor
t (01246) 345777
open Daily.
admission Free
*A country park on the former site of Grassmoor colliery
with angling ponds, cycleways and woodland
plantations. Also features the Five Pits trail and other
walks and cycle trails.*

The Heights of Abraham Cable Cars, Caverns and Hilltop Park
Matlock Bath DE4 3PD
t (01629) 582365 **w** heights-of-abraham.co.uk
open Apr-Oct, daily 1000-1700.
admission ££
*A spectacular cable car ride takes you to the summit
where, within the grounds, there are a wide variety of
attractions for young and old alike. Gift shop and coffee
shop.*

The Herb Garden
Chesterfield Road, Hardstoft, Pilsley S45 8AH
t (01246) 854268
open Mar-Sep, Wed-Sun, Bank Hols 1000-1700.
admission £
*A herb garden with containerised herb plants of 200
varieties on sale; selling pot pourri, herbal oils scented
gifts and a small selection of locally produced crafts.*

Lea Gardens
Lea DE4 5GH
t (01629) 534380
open Apr-Jun, daily 1000-1730.
admission £
*A 3.5-acre garden of species and hybrid
rhododendrons, azaleas and kalmias in woodland
settings with picturesque walks, extensive rock gardens
and plant sales.*

Linacre Reservoirs
Cutthorpe S42 7JW
t (01246) 567049
open Daily.
admission Free   🔵
Three small reservoirs in an attractive wooded valley. Lakeside walks and a nature trail. Game fishing in season.

Matlock Bath Aquarium and Hologram Gallery
110-114 North Parade, Matlock Bath DE4 3NS
t (01629) 583624
open Apr-Jun, daily 1000-1800, Jul-Aug, daily 1000-2200, Sep-Oct, daily 1000-1800. Nov-Mar, Sat-Sun 1000-1800.
admission £   🔵
An aquarium housed in the original spa bathing pool and outbuildings with a large thermal pool fed by a spring with koi, mirror and common carp, tropical fish and holograms.

Peak Cavern
Peak Cavern Road, Castleton S33 8WS
t (01433) 620285 w cavern.co.uk/
open Apr-Oct, daily 1000-1700. Nov-Mar, Sat-Sun 1000-1700.
admission ££   ⚒
The largest natural cavern in the district with the largest cavern entrance in Europe. Remains of a 400-year-old village and rope walks.

Poole's Cavern and Buxton Country Park
Green Lane, Buxton SK17 9DH
t (01298) 26978 w poolescavern.co.uk
open All year, daily 0930-1730.
admission ££   ☕⚒🔵
One of the finest natural limestone caves, described as the 'first wonder of the Peak' with stalactites, stalagmites, an exhibition area, video show, visitor centre and country park.

Renishaw Hall: Gardens, Arts Centre and Museum
Renishaw Park, Renishaw S21 3WB
t (01246) 432310 w sitwell.co.uk
open Apr-Sep, Thu-Sun, Bank Hols 1030-1630.
admission £   ☕🎬⚒🔵
Italianate gardens with terraces, statues, yew hedges and pyramids. The garden, park and lake were the creation of Sir George Sitwell. Arts centre and museum in Georgian stables.

Shipley Country Park
Slack Lane, Heanor DE75 7GX
t (01773) 719961
open Daily.
admission Free   ☕🎬🔵
A country park with walks, woodland areas, lakes, a visitor centre, coffee shop and gardens on Shipley Hill.

Speedwell Cavern
Winnats Pass, Castleton S33 8WA
t (01433) 620512
w speedwellcavern.co.uk
open All year, daily 1000-1700.
admission ££   ⚒
An 18thC lead mine and natural cavern which is visited by boat.

Treak Cliff Cavern
Castleton S33 8WP
t (01433) 620571
w bluejohnstone.com
open Apr-Sep, daily 1000-1700. Oct-Mar, daily 1000-1600.
admission ££   🎬
An underground show cavern, open to visitors, which is mostly natural but part mine with examples of stalactites and stalagmites, rock and cave formations and Blue John veins.

Upper Derwent Reservoirs
Fairholmes Visitor Centre,
Bamford S33 0AX
t (01433) 650953
w peakdistrict.org.uk
open All year, Sat-Sun 0930-1630.
admission Free   ☕🎬🔵
Ladybower, Derwent and Howden reservoirs with woodland and lakeside walks. Views of the surrounding High Peak moorland. Cycle hire, picnic areas, info centre and game fishing.

HISTORIC ENGLAND

Arkwright's Cromford Mill
Mill Lane, Cromford DE4 3RQ
t (01629) 824297
w cromfordmill.co.uk
open Daily 0900-1700.
admission Free   ☕🎬🔵
Progressive restoration of the world's first successful water-powered cotton spinning mill, built by Richard Arkwright in 1771. Guided tours available. A World Heritage site.

Bolsover Castle
Castle Street, Bolsover S44 6PR
t (01246) 822844
w english-heritage.org.uk
open Apr, Mon, Thu-Fri 1000-1700, Sat 1000-1600. May-Sep, Mon-Fri, Sun 1000-1800, Sat 1000-1600. Oct, Mon, Thu-Fri, Sun 1000-1700, Sat 1000-1600. Nov-Mar, Mon, Thu-Sun 1000-1600.
admission ££   ☕🎬⚒🔵
A 17thC house built on the site of a Norman fortress – enchanting, romantic and magical.

Calke Abbey, Park and Gardens
Ticknall DE73 1LE
t (01332) 863822
w nationaltrust.org.uk
open House: Mar-Oct, Mon-Wed, Sat-Sun 1230-1700.
Garden: Apr-Oct, Mon-Wed, Sat-Sun 1100-1700.
Jul-Aug, daily 1100-1700.
admission ££
*Built 1701-1703, and largely unchanged in 100 years.
Natural-history collections, 750 acres of park, ponds,
trees, woodlands, walled gardens and pleasure gardens.*

Carsington Water
Visitor Centre, Ashbourne DE6 1ST
t (01629) 540696
w stwater.co.uk
open Apr-Oct, daily 1000-1800. Nov-Dec, daily
1000-1700. Jan, daily 1000-1600. Feb-Mar, daily
1000-1700.
admission Free
*A visitor centre with an exhibition on the story of
Carsington. Restaurant, shops, walks and trails,
watersports, cycle hire and brown-trout fishery.*

Chatsworth House, Garden, Farmyard & Adventure Playground
Chatsworth, Bakewell DE45 1PP
t (01246) 582204
w chatsworth.org
open House: Mar-Dec, daily 1100-1730. Garden:
Mar-Dec, daily 1100-1800. Farmyard: Mar-Dec, daily
1030-1730.
admission £££
*Visitors to Chatsworth see more than 30 richly
decorated rooms, the garden with fountains, a cascade
and maze and the farmyard and adventure playground.*

Creswell Crags Museum and Education Centre, Picnic Site, Caves & Gorge
Crags Road, Welbeck S80 3LH
t (01909) 720378
w creswell-crags.org.uk
open Feb-Oct, daily 1030-1630. Nov-Jan, Sun
1030-1630.
admission Free
*A limestone gorge with caves, lake, a museum with
interactive displays and audiovisuals. The world-famous
caves were the most northerly home of Ice Age
hunters.*

Derby Cathedral & Derby Cathedral Centre
18/19 Iron Gate, Derby DE1 3GP
t (01332) 341201
w derbycathedral.org
open Cathedral: Daily 0830-1800. Centre: Daily
0900-1700.
admission Free
*With its splendid medieval tower, historical
monuments and thriving contemporary life, Derby
Cathedral is at once a place of prayer and a unique
visitor experience.*

Derwent Valley Visitor Centre
Belper North Mill, Bridgefoot, Belper DE56 1YD
t (01773) 880474 **w** belpernorthmill.org.uk
open Mar-Oct, Wed-Sun, Bank Hols 1300-1700.
Nov-Feb, Sat-Sun 1300-1700.
admission £
*Strutts North Mill is one of the world's most important
industrial monuments and a central feature of the
Derwent Valley Mills World Heritage Site.*

Haddon Hall
Haddon Estate Office, Bakewell DE45 1LA
t (01629) 812855 **w** haddonhall.co.uk
open Apr, Mon, Sat-Sun 1200-1700. May-Sep, daily
1200-1700. Oct, Mon, Sat-Sun 1200-1700.
admission ££
*Magnificent medieval and Tudor manor house, virtually
untouched since the reign of Henry VIII. Outstanding
terraced gardens. Popular film and television location.*

Hardwick Hall
Doe Lea S44 5QJ
t (01246) 850430 **w** nationaltrust.org.uk
open Apr-Oct, Wed-Thu, Sat-Sun 1200-1630.
admission ££
*Elizabethan country house, gardens and parkland, with
outstanding collections of furniture, tapestry and
needlework.*

Hardwick Old Hall
Doe Lea S44 5QJ
t (01246) 850431 **w** english-heritage.org.uk
open See website for details.
admission £
*Bess of Hardwick's first great house at Hardwick,
finished in 1591, a few years before the 'New Hall'
which displays Bess of Hardwick's innovative planning.*

High Peak Junction Workshop
High Peak Junction, Cromford DE4 5HN
t (01629) 822831
open Apr-Oct, daily 1000-1630.
admission £
*The original workshop of the Cromford and High Peak
railway, now restored to about 1900 with displays on the
railway, a video, model, information centre and canalside picnic area.*

Kedleston Hall
Kedleston DE22 5JH
t (01332) 842191 **w** nationaltrust.org.uk
open Hall: Apr-Oct, Mon-Wed, Sat-Sun 1200-1630.
Park: Apr-Oct, daily 1000-1800. Nov-Feb, daily
1000-1600.
admission ££
*An outstanding Robert Adam house, 1759-1765, with a
unique marble hall, saloon, state rooms, Old Masters,
furniture, Lord Curzon's Indian museum, a 12thC church
and a park.*

Melbourne Hall: Gardens and Visitor Centre
Melbourne DE73 1EN
t (01332) 862502
w melbournehall.com
open Hall: Aug, daily 1400-1630. Gardens: Apr-Sep,
Wed, Sat-Sun, Bank Hols 1330-1730.
admission £

*Queen Victoria's Prime Minister, Lord Melbourne, lived
here as did Byron's friend Lady Caroline Lamb. There
are famous formal gardens and a visitor centre.*

National Stone Centre
Porter Lane, Wirksworth DE4 4LS
t (01629) 824833
w nationalstonecentre.org.uk
open Apr-Oct, daily 1000-1700. Nov-Mar, daily
1000-1600.
admission Free

*The story of stone from prehistoric stone axes to hi-tech
processing, from sculpture to 300 million tonnes of stone
sold annually for construction. Site trail and activities.*

Peveril Castle
Market Place, Castleton S33 8WQ
t (01433) 620613
w english-heritage.org.uk
open Apr, daily 1000-1700. May-Aug, daily 1000-1800.
Sep-Oct, daily 1000-1700. Nov-Mar, Mon, Thu-Sun
1000-1600.
admission £

*A ruined Norman castle on the hill high above Castleton,
built in the 11thC. The curtain wall is almost complete
with a small imposing keep.*

Rosliston Forestry Centre
Burton Road, Rosliston, Swadlincote DE12 8JX
t (01283) 563483
w south-derbys.gov.uk
open All year, dawn-dusk.
admission Free

*National Forest visitor and education facility. The centre
comprises 153 acres of newly planted woodland, plus
play area, hide, picnic area, restaurant and craft units.*

Sharpe's Pottery Visitor Centre
West Street, Swadlincote DE11 9DG
t (01283) 222600
w sharpes.org.uk
open All year, Mon-Sat 1000-1630.
admission Free

*Sharpe's Pottery Visitor Centre is housed in a newly
restored 19thC pottery works in the heart of
Swadlincote and is a registered museum.*

Sudbury Hall (National Trust)
Sudbury DE6 5HT
t (01283) 585305
w nationaltrust.org.uk
open Apr-Oct, Wed-Sun 1300-1700.
admission ££

*A grand 17thC house with plasterwork ceilings, ceiling
paintings, a carved staircase and overmantel. The
Museum of Childhood is in the old servants' wing.*

Wingfield Manor
Garner Lane,
South Wingfield DE5 7NH
t (01773) 832060
w english-heritage.org.uk
open See website for details.
admission £

*A superb vaulted undercroft, medieval barn and high
tower with stunning views.*

OUTDOOR ACTIVITIES

Gulliver's Kingdom

Temple Walk,
Matlock Bath DE4 3PG
t (01629) 580540 **w** gulliversfun.co.uk
open Apr-Sep, phone for details. Opening
times vary during the Christmas period.
admission Adult: £8.99

A magical kingdom for families with children
aged two to 13 years of age. With 30 rides and
attractions it will entertain your child all day.
Visit one of our many shows or relax in one of
our many restaurants.

Map ref 4B2

Middleton Top Cycle Hire

Middleton Top Visitor Centre, Rise End,
Middleton, Matlock DE4 4LS
t (01629) 823204
w derbyshire.gov.uk/countryside
open Easter-Oct, Sat-Sun, school holidays
0930-1700. Jun-Aug 0930-1700.
admission Please phone for pricing details

Cycle hire centre on the High Peak Trail. Miles
of traffic-free cycling and longer on-road routes
for the more adventurous. Adult and child
bikes available as well as trailers for children.
Free helmet hire with every bike.

Map ref 4B2

For key to symbols see inside back cover.

ENTERTAINMENT AND CULTURE

Bakewell Old House Museum
Cunningham Place, Bakewell DE45 1DD
t (01629) 813642
w oldhousemuseum.org.uk
open Apr-Oct, daily 1100-1600.
admission £
An early-16thC house with many original features.
Museum with 19thC costumes displayed on models,
Victorian kitchen, tools, farm implements, toys, lace
work and local items.

Buxton Museum and Art Gallery
Terrace Road, Buxton SK17 6DA
t (01298) 24658
w derbyshire.gov.uk/libraries&heritage
open All year, Tue-Fri 0930-1730, Sat 0930-1700, Sun,
Bank Hols 1030-1700.
admission Free
A ground-floor temporary exhibition space and
reproduction late-Victorian study with an art gallery
that hosts temporary exhibitions by local and national
artists.

Buxton Opera House
Water Street, Buxton SK17 6XN
t 0845 127 2190
w buxton-opera.co.uk
open All year, see website for details.
admission £££
A beautifully restored Frank Matcham-designed theatre
providing comedy, drama, music, opera, ballet,
Christmas pantomime and summer festivals.

Chesterfield Museum and Art Gallery
St Mary's Gate, Chesterfield S41 7TY
t (01246) 345727
w visitchesterfield.info
open All year, Mon-Tue, Thu-Sat 1000-1600.
admission Free
A museum, with a small art gallery, depicting the story
of Chesterfield from Roman times until the present
day.

Crich Tramway Village
Crich DE4 5DP
t (01773) 854321
w tramway.co.uk
open Apr-Oct, daily 1000-1730. Nov, Sat-Sun
1030-1600.
admission ££
A collection of over 70 trams from Britain and overseas
from 1873-1969 with tram rides on a 1-mile route, a
period street scene, depots, a power station, workshops
and exhibitions.

Derby City Museum and Art Gallery
The Strand, Derby DE1 1BS
t (01332) 716659
w derby.gov.uk/museums
open All year, Mon 1100-1700, Tue-Sat 1000-1700,
Sun, Bank Hols 1300-1600.
admission Free
An art gallery with Joseph Wright paintings. The
museum houses Derby porcelain, antiquities, natural
history displays, archaeology and militaria.

Peak District Mining Museum
The Pavilion, Matlock Bath DE4 3NR
t (01629) 583834
w peakmines.co.uk
open Summer: daily 1000-1700. Winter: daily
1100-1600.
admission £
A large exhibition on 3,500 years of lead mining with
displays on geology, mines and miners, tools and
engines. The climbing shafts make it suitable for children
as well.

Pickford's House Museum
41 Friar Gate, Derby DE1 1DA
t (01332) 255363
w derby.gov.uk/museums
open All year, Mon 1100-1700, Tue-Sat 1000-1700, Sun
1230-1600.
admission Free
Built in 1770 by the architect Joseph Pickford with
period room displays. The museum also has a lively
temporary exhibitions programme including costume
and textiles.

Red House Stables and Carriage Museum
Old Road, Darley Dale DE4 2ER
t (01629) 733583
open Mar-Oct, daily 1000-1700. Nov-Feb, daily
1000-1500.
admission £
Collection of harnesses, collars, liveries, horse-drawn
vehicles and equipment. Horse-drawn carriages by
arrangement. Blacksmith at work.

Whinstone Lee Tor, Peak District

The Silk Mill – Derby's Museum of Industry and History

Essex

Silk Mill Lane, off Full Street,
Derby DE1 3AF
t (01332) 255308
w derby.gov.uk/museums
open All year, Mon, 1100-1700, Tue-Sat 1000-1700, Sun 1300-1600.
admission Free 　　　　　　　　　　 ⊞ ✗ ♿
Displays on the Derbyshire industries, Rolls Royce aero engines, power sources, railway engineering and research. On the site of a former silk mill, Britain's first factory.

Sir Richard Arkwright's Masson Mills Working Textile Museum

Derby Road, Matlock Bath DE4 3PY
t (01629) 581001　**w** massonmills.co.uk
open All year, Mon-Fri 1000-1600, Sat 1000-1700, Sun 1100-1600.
admission £ 　　　　　　　　　　 💻 ✗ ♿
Sir Richard Arkwright's 1783 showpiece, Masson Mills – the finest surviving Arkwright Mill. Museum and shopping village. Gateway to the Derwent Valley Mills World Heritage Site.

RELAXING AND PAMPERING

Derwent Crystal

Shaw Croft Car Park, Ashbourne DE6 1GH
t (01335) 345219　**w** derwentcrystal.co.uk
open Factory: Daily 0900-1330. Shops: All year, Mon-Sat 0900-1700.
admission Free 　　　　　　　 💻 ⊞ ✗ ♿
Showing the manufacture, blowing and decorating of full lead English crystal glassware.

Markeaton Park Craft Village

Markeaton Park, Ashbourne Road, Derby DE22 3BG
t (01332) 716272
open All year, Sat-Sun 1000-1600. School Hols, daily 1000-1600.
admission Free 　　　　　　　　　 ⊞ ✗ ♿
A craft village in the old stables set amidst Markeaton Park, Derby's largest park, with formal gardens, a riverside walk and a children's play area.

McArthurGlen Designer Outlet Mansfield

Mansfield Road, South Normanton DE55 2ER
t (01773) 545000　**w** mcarthurglen.com
open All year, Mon-Wed 1000-1800, Thu 1000-2000, Fri 1000-1800, Sat 0900-1800, Sun 1000-1700.
admission Free 　　　　　　　 💻 ⊞ ✗ ♿
Love a bargain? You'll love McArthurGlen Mansfield. With discounts of up to 50% off designer and high street brands in 65 stores, there's something for everyone.

Enjoy the fun of a special event or visit one of the attractions listed for a great day out. For more inspiring ideas go to **enjoyengland.com**.

27–28 May
Southend Air Show
Southend-on-Sea
(01702) 390333
southendairshow.com

23–24 Jun
Wings and Wheels
North Weald Airfield, Nr Epping
(01480) 462265
wingsnwheelsspectacular.com

23–24 Aug
Clacton Airshow
Clacton-on-Sea
(01255) 686633
essex-sunshine-coast.org.uk

1–2 Sep
English Wine Festival
New Hall Vineyard, Purleigh, Maldon
(01621) 828343
newhallwines.co.uk

1 Sep
Oyster Festival
The Waterfront, Maldon
(01621) 856503
hidden-treasures.co.uk

FAMILY FUN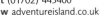

Adventure Island Southend
Western Esplanade, Southend-on-Sea SS1 1EE
t (01702) 443400
w adventureisland.co.uk
open Please phone for details.
admission Free
One of the best-value theme parks in the South East, with over 40 great rides and attractions, for all ages. No admission charge – you only 'pay if you play'!

Audley End Miniature Railway
Audley End CB11 4JB
t (01799) 541354
w audley-end-railway.co.uk
open Apr-Oct, Sat-Sun 1400-1700, Bank Hols 1100-1700.
admission £
Steam and diesel locomotives in 10.25 gauge, running through attractive woodland for 1.5 miles. The railway crosses the River Cam twice.

Barleylands Craft Village and Farm Centre
Barleylands Road, Billericay CM11 2UD
t (01268) 290229
w barleylands.co.uk
open Mar-Oct, daily 1000-1700. Nov-Feb, daily 1000-1600.
admission £
Stroll around over 20 impressive individual specialist working craft villages, including blacksmiths and glass-blowing. Cuddle a rabbit and feed the animals.

Colne Valley Railway
Yeldham Road, Castle Hedingham CO9 3DZ
t (01787) 461174
w colnevalleyrailway.co.uk
open All year, see website for details.
admission ££
An award-winning station. Ride in the most pleasant part of the Colne Valley. A large, interesting collection of operational heritage rolling stock.

East Anglian Railway Museum
Chappel Station, Colchester CO6 2DS
t (01206) 242524
w earm.co.uk
open Apr-Oct, daily 1000-1630. Nov-Mar, daily 1000-1600.
admission ££
A large and varied collection of working and static railway exhibits from the age of steam, set in original surroundings of a once important Victorian country junction station.

Eastbury Manor House
Eastbury Square, Barking IG11 9SN
t (020) 8724 1002
w barking-dagenham.gov.uk
open Mon-Tue weekly, 1st & 2nd Sat of every month 1000-1600.
admission Adult: £2.50

Eastbury Manor House, a Grade II Listed manor in Barking, is a truly magnificent venue for fairs and family days, evening events, medieval weekends and much more. With a gift shop, tea room and beautiful grounds, Eastbury is a hidden gem. Public events organised throughout the year.

 Map ref 2D2

 voucher offer – see back section

Go Bananas
9-10 Mason Road,
Cowdray Centre, Cowdray Avenue,
Colchester CO1 1BX
t (01206) 761762
w go-bananas.co.uk
open Daily 0930-1830.
admission £
Children's indoor adventure playground with a three-storey adventure frame for 5-12 year-olds, an under 5's play village, climbing wall, spaceball ride and cafeteria.

The Original Great Maze
Blake House Craft Centre, Braintree CM77 6RA
t (01376) 553146
w greatmaze.info
open Jul-Sep, daily 1000-1630.
admission £
This challenging maize maze is known as one of the biggest mind benders in the world. Now set in over 10 acres of the idyllic northern Essex countryside.

Southend Planetarium
Southend Central Museum, Victoria Avenue,
Southend-on-Sea SS2 6EW
t (01702) 434449
w southendmuseum.co.uk
open All year, Wed-Sat 1100-1600.
admission £
A projector provides a clear illusion of the night sky with stars and the Milky Way which lasts 40 minutes. No children under five admitted.

Southend-on-Sea Pier
Western Esplanade, Southend-on-Sea SS1 1EE
t (01702) 215620
w southend.gov.uk
open Apr-Sep, Mon-Fri 0930-1700, Sat-Sun 0930-1900. Oct-Mar, Mon-Fri 0930-1500, Sat-Sun 0930-1700.
admission £
The world's longest pleasure pier. Train along the pier. Museum at North Station, amusements, novelty shop, restaurant and licensed public house. Guided tours.

NATURE AND WILDLIFE

BBC Essex Garden
Ongar Road, Abridge RM4 1AA
t (01708) 688479
open Apr-Oct, daily 0900-1730. Nov-Mar, daily 0930-1700.
admission Free
Garden with lawn, borders, small vegetable area, linked to Ken Crowther's BBC programme 'Down to Earth'. Also farmyard pets, tea shop, superb plants and clematis on sale.

The Beth Chatto Gardens
Elmstead Market CO7 7DB
t (01206) 822007
w bethchatto.co.uk
open Apr-Oct, Mon-Sat 0900-1700. Nov-Mar, Mon-Fri 0900-1600.
admission £
Drought-tolerant plants furnish the gravel garden throughout the year, the dappled wood garden is filled with shade lovers, while the water garden fills the spring-fed hollow.

Colchester Zoo
Maldon Road, Stanway CO3 0SL
t (01206) 331292
w colchester-zoo.com
open Apr-Sep, daily 0930-1800. Oct-Mar, daily 0930-dusk.
admission £££
Colchester Zoo has over 250 species and some of the best cat and primate collections in the UK, 60 acres of gardens and lakes, award-winning enclosures and picnic areas.

Cudmore Grove Country Park
Bromans Lane, East Mersea CO5 8UE
t (01206) 383868
w essexcc.gov.uk
open Daily 0800-dusk.
admission Free
Situated next to the entrance of the Colne estuary, the park consists of grassland and a sandy beach, ideally suited to walking, picnics, informal games and wildlife watching.

Feeringbury Manor
Feering CO5 9RB
t (01376) 561946
w ngs.org.uk
open Apr-Jul, Sep, Thu-Fri 0800-1600.
admission £
A well designed 10 acre garden, intensively planted with many rare and interesting plants for both dry and damp areas.

Fingringhoe Wick Nature Reserve
South Green Road, Fingringhoe CO5 7DN
t (01206) 729678
w essexwt.org.uk
open All year, Tue-Sun, Bank Hols 0900-1700.
admission £
One hundred and twenty five acres of woodland, lakes and saltmarsh on the Colne estuary, with nature trails and eight hides. Observation room, tower and gift shop.

The Gardens of Easton Lodge
Warwick House, Easton Lodge,
Great Dunmow CM6 2BB
t (01371) 876979
w eastonlodge.co.uk
open Apr-Oct, Fri-Sun, Bank Hols 1200-dusk.
admission £
Twenty-three acres of beautiful historic gardens famous for their peaceful atmosphere. Featuring the splendid formal gardens created by leading Edwardian designer Harold Peto.

The Gibberd Garden
Marsh Lane, Gilden Way, Harlow CM17 0NA
t (01279) 442112
w thegibberdgarden.co.uk
open Apr-Sep, Wed, Sat-Sun, Bank Hols 1400-1600.
admission £
Important 20thC garden designed by Sir Frederick Gibberd, master planner for Harlow New Town. With some 50 sculptures.

Green Island Garden
Green Island, Park Road, Ardleigh CO7 7SP
t (01206) 230455
w greenislandgardens.co.uk
open Apr-Oct, Wed-Thu, Sun, Bank Hols 1000-1700.
admission £
Beautiful gardens situated in 19 acres of woodland with a huge variety of unusual plants and lots of interest all year.

For key to symbols see inside back cover.

Hadleigh Castle Country Park

Chapel Lane Car Park, Chapel Lane, Hadleigh SS7 2PP
t (01702) 551072 **w** essexcc.gov.uk
open Daily 0800-dusk.
admission Free

Fields and woodland overlooking the Thames estuary. Remains of castle close by, accessible by footpath. Waymarked trails with superb views, horse rides and bird hides.

Hatfield Forest

The National Trust, Hatfield Forest Estate Office, Takeley CM22 6NE
t (01279) 870678 **w** nationaltrust.org.uk
open Apr-Oct, daily 1000-1700. Nov-Mar, Sun 1000-1700.
admission £

Hatfield Forest comprises over 400 hectares of ancient coppice woodland, grassland, magnificent pollarded trees, along with two ornamental lakes, 18thC Shell House and stream.

High Woods Country Park

Visitors Centre, Turner Road, Colchester CO4 5JR
t (01206) 853588 **w** visitcolchester.com
open Park: Daily. Visitor centre: Apr-Sep, daily 1000-1730. Oct-Mar, Sat-Sun 1000-1600.
admission Free

A 330-acre country park situated to the north of central Colchester with a variety of landscape and wildlife, visitor centre, toilets, bookshop and small shop.

Langdon Visitor Centre and Nature Reserve

Third Avenue, Lower Dunton Road, Basildon SS16 6EB
t (01268) 419103
open Nature Reserve: Daily. Visitor Centre: All year, Tue-Sun, Bank Hols 0900-1700.
admission Free

460 acres of meadow, woodland and plotland gardens. Eighteen miles of footpaths and bridleways. A former plotland home, The Haven has been restored to 1930s style.

Little Easton Manor and Barn Theatre

Park Road, Little Easton CM6 2JN
t (01371) 872857
open Please phone for details.
admission ££

Little Easton Manor has gardens, lakes and fountains. The Barn Theatre, angling, a caravan and rally site and refreshments.

Marks Hall Garden and Arboretum

The Thomas Phillips Price Trust, Estate Office, Marks Hall, Coggeshall CO6 1TG
t (01376) 563796 **w** markshall.org.uk
open Apr-Oct, Tue-Sun 1030-1700. Nov-Mar, Fri-Sun 1030-dusk.
admission £

Garden and arboretum for every season of the year. Visitor centre with tea shop, information and gift shop. Admission £4.00 per car.

Marsh Farm Country Park

Marsh Farm Road, South Woodham Ferrers CM3 5WP
t (01245) 321552 **w** marshfarmcountrypark.co.uk
open Apr-Oct, Mon-Fri 1000-1600, Sat-Sun, Bank Hols 1000-1700. Nov-Dec, Sat-Sun 1000-1700.
admission £

A farm with sheep, a pig unit, free-range chickens, milking demonstrations, indoor and outdoor adventure play areas, nature reserve, walks, picnic area and pets' corner.

Mistley Place Park, Animal Rescue Centre

New Road, Mistley CO11 1ER
t (01206) 396483 **w** mistley.org.uk
open All year, Tue-Sun 1000-1730.
admission £

Twenty-five acres of woodlands and lakeside walks with goats, horses, sheep, rabbits, ducks, hens, a tearoom, gift shop and a nature trail.

Mole Hall Wildlife Park

Widdington CB11 3SS
t (01799) 540400 **w** molehall.co.uk
open Daily 1030-1700.
admission ££

Park with otters, chimps, guanaco, lemurs, wallabies, deer, a tropical butterfly pavilion, attractive gardens, picnic and play areas and pets' corner.

Old MacDonalds Educational Farm Park

Weald Road, South Weald CM14 5AY
t (01277) 375177 **w** oldmacdonaldsfarm.org.uk
open Apr, daily 1000-dusk. Jul-Aug, daily 1000-1800. Sep-Mar, daily 1000-dusk.
admission ££

We tell the whole story of British livestock farming, keeping rare breed cattle, pigs, sheep, shire horses and poultry. Red squirrels, owls, otters and lots more.

Red House Visitor Centre

School Road, Messing CO5 9TH
t (01621) 815219
open All year, Mon-Fri 0930-1600.
admission Free

Sensory and artists' gardens, pond, children's play area and junior farm. Coffee shop, plant and craft sales, picnic area and conference venue.

RHS Garden Hyde Hall

Buckhatch Lane, Rettendon, Chelmsford CM3 8ET
t (01245) 400256 **w** rhs.org.uk
open Apr-Sep, daily 1000-1800. Oct-Mar, daily 1000-dusk.
admission £

A 28-acre garden with all-year-round interest including a dry garden, roses, flowering shrubs, ponds, perennial borders and alpines.

Roundwood Garden & Visitor Centre
Bocking Church Street, Bocking CM7 5LJ
t (01376) 551728
open All year, Mon-Fri 0930-1630.
admission Free
Set in seven acres, delightful area for afternoon tea in the tearooms. Unusual plants and crafts for sale all year round. A visitors centre with conservation as its theme.

Southend Sea Life Adventure
Eastern Esplanade, Southend-on-Sea SS1 2ER
t (01702) 442200 **w** sealifeadventure.co.uk
open Daily 1000-1700.
admission ££
The very latest in marine technology brings the secrets of the mysterious underwater world closer than ever before. An amazing underwater tunnel allows an all-round view.

Tropical Wings Butterfly and Bird Gardens
Wickford Road, South Woodham Ferrers CM3 5QZ
t (01245) 425394 **w** tropicalwings.co.uk
open Apr-Oct, daily 0930-1730. Nov-Mar, daily 1030-1630.
admission ££
Butterflies, birds and so much more! Delightful gardens, wallaby paddock, pets' corner, flying displays, tropical house, play area, gift shop, tearoom and farm shop.

Weald Country Park
Weald Road, South Weald CM14 5QS
t (01277) 216343 **w** essexcc.gov.uk
open Daily 0800-dusk.
admission Free
Visitor centre, gift shop, light refreshments, deer paddock, country walks, lakes, horse riding and cycling. Large-group camping available.

HISTORIC ENGLAND

Audley End House and Gardens
Audley End CB11 4JF
t (01799) 522842 **w** english-heritage.org.uk
open Gardens: Apr-Sep, Wed-Sun 1000-1800. Oct, Sat-Sun 1000-1700. Feb-Mar, Sat-Sun 1000-1500. House: Apr-Sep, Wed-Fri 1100-1600, Sat 1200-1400, Sun 1100-1600. Oct, Mar, Sat-Sun 1000-1500.
admission ££
Visit a former wonder of the nation and experience the sumptuous splendour enjoyed by royalty and the aristocracy in one of England's grandest stately homes.

Chelmsford Cathedral
Cathedral Office, 53 New Street, Chelmsford CM1 1TY
t (01245) 294480 **w** chelmsfordcathedral.org.uk
open Daily 0800-1800.
admission Free
A late-medieval church, reordered in 1983 and blending old with new. It became a cathedral in 1914 when the Diocese of Chelmsford was created. Modern sculpture and tapestry.

Coggeshall Grange Barn
The National Trust, Grange Hill, Coggeshall CO6 1RE
t (01376) 562226 **w** nationaltrust.org.uk
open Apr-Oct, Tue,Thu,Sun 1400-1700.
admission £
One of the oldest surviving timber framed barns in Europe, dating from around 1240, and originally part of a Cistercian Abbey. Restored in the 1980s.

Audley End, Essex

Admission is based on an adult price. Please check opening times and admission before travelling.

The Dutch Cottage
Crown Hill,
Rayleigh SS6 7HQ
t (01702) 318150
open All year, Wed 1345-1600.
admission Free

An eight-sided cottage based on the design of 17thC Dutch settlers.

Eastbury Manor House

Eastbury Square, Barking IG11 9SN
t (020) 8724 1002
w barking-dagenham.gov.uk
open Mon-Tue weekly, 1st & 2nd Sat of every month 1000-1600.
admission Adult: £2.50

Eastbury Manor House, a Grade II Listed manor in Barking, is a truly magnificent venue for fairs and family days, evening events, medieval weekends and much more. With a gift shop, tea room and beautiful grounds, Eastbury is a hidden gem. Public events organised throughout the year.

Map ref 2D2

ⓥ voucher offer – see back section

Hadleigh Castle
Hadleigh SS7 2PP
t (01223) 582700
w english-heritage.org.uk
open Daily.
admission Free

Familiar from Constable's painting, the castle stands on a bluff overlooking the Leigh Marshes with a single, large 50ft tower and 13thC and 14thC remains.

Hedingham Castle
Bayley Street, Castle Hedingham CO9 3DJ
t (01787) 460261 **w** hedinghamcastle.co.uk
open Apr-Oct, Mon-Thu, Sun 1000-1700.
admission £

The finest Norman keep in England, built in 1140 by the de Veres, Earls of Oxford. Visited by Kings Henry VII and VIII and Queen Elizabeth I and besieged by King John.

Hylands House
Hylands Park, London Road, Chelmsford CM2 8WQ
t (01245) 605500 **w** chelmsford.gov.uk/hylands
open Apr, Mon 1100-1600, Sun 1100-1800. May-Oct, Mon, Sun 1100-1800. Nov-Mar, Mon 1100-1600, Sun 1100-1800.
admission £

Hylands House is a beautiful Grade II* Listed building, set in 574 acres of parkland.

Ingatestone Hall
Hall Lane, Ingatestone CM4 9NR
t (01277) 353010
open Apr-Jul, Sat-Sun, Bank Hols 1300-1800. Aug, Wed-Sun 1300-1800. Sep, Sat-Sun, Bank Hols 1300-1800.
admission £

Tudor house and gardens, the home of the Petre family since 1540, with a family portrait collection, furniture and other heirlooms on display.

Layer Marney Tower
Layer Marney CO5 9US
t (01206) 330784 **w** layermarneytower.co.uk
open Apr-Sep, Mon-Thu, Sun 1200-1700.
admission £

A 1520 Tudor-brick gatehouse, eight storeys high with Italianate terracotta cresting and windows. Gardens, park and rare breed farm animals and also the nearby church.

Mountfitchet Castle
Stansted Mountfitchet CM24 8SP
t (01279) 813237 **w** mountfitchetcastle.com
open Mar-Nov, daily 1000-1700.
admission ££

A reconstructed Norman motte-and-bailey castle and village of the Domesday period with a Grand Hall, church, prison, siege tower and weapons. Domestic animals roam the site.

The Old House
Rochford District Council, South Street,
Rochford SS4 1BW
t (01702) 318144 **w** rochford.gov.uk
open Please phone for details.
admission Free

History is revealed in the rooms of this elegant house, originally built in 1270, lovingly restored and now housing the District Council offices.

Paycockes
West Street, Coggeshall CO6 1NS
t (01376) 561305
w aboutbritain.com
open Apr-Oct, Tue, Thu, Sun, Bank Hols 1400-1700.
admission £

A half-timbered merchant's house, built in the 16thC with a richly carved interior and a small display of Coggeshall lace. Very attractive garden.

Saint Botolphs Priory
Colchester
t (01206) 282931
open Daily.
admission Free

The remains of a 12thC priory near the town centre with a nave which has an impressive arcaded west end. One of the first Augustinian priories in England.

Tilbury Fort
No 2 Office Block, The Fort, Tilbury RM18 7NR
t (01375) 858489
w english-heritage.org.uk
open Apr-Oct, daily 1000-1700. Nov-Mar, Wed-Sun 1000-1600.
admission £

One of Henry VIII's coastal forts, re-modelled and extended in the 17thC in continental style.

Paper Mill Lock
North Hill, Little Baddow CM3 4BS
t (01245) 225520
w papermilllock.co.uk
open Apr, daily 1000-1500. May-Sep, daily 1000-1700. Oct-Mar, daily 1000-1500.
admission Free

Historic canal with 14 miles of towpath – excellent for walkers, boaters and anglers. Canal centre at Paper Mill Lock offers a teashop, boat hire and river trips.

Central Museum and Planetarium
Victoria Avenue, Southend-on-Sea SS2 6EW
t (01702) 434449
w southendmuseum.co.uk
open Museum: All year, Tue-Sat 1000-1700. Planetarium: All year, Wed-Sat 1000-1700.
admission £

An Edwardian building housing displays of archaeology, natural history, social and local history. Hands-on discovery centre. Planetarium.

Colchester Castle
Castle Park, Colchester CO1 1TJ
t (01206) 282939
w colchestermuseum.org.uk
open All year, Mon-Sat 1000-1700, Sun 1100-1700.
admission £

A Norman keep on the foundations of a Roman temple. The archaeological material includes much on Roman Colchester (Camulodunum). Exciting hands-on displays.

Combined Military Services Museum
Station Road, Maldon CM9 4LQ
t (01621) 841826 **w** cmsm.co.uk
open All year, Wed-Sun, Bank Hols 1030-1700.
admission £

The museum has collections of British military artefacts, and a number of items on display are of national importance, for example: the only surviving MK2 'Cockle' canoe.

Dedham Art and Craft Centre
High Street, Dedham CO7 6AD
t (01206) 322666
w dedhamartandcraftcentre.co.uk
open Daily 1000-1700.
admission Free

Beautiful converted church in the heart of Constable Country featuring three floors of arts and crafts, showrooms and vegetarian/wholefood restaurant and tearooms.

East Essex Aviation Society and Museum
Martello Tower, Point Clear, St Osyth
t (01255) 423400
open All year, Mon 1900-2130. Apr-Oct, Sun 1000-1400. Jun-Sep, Wed 1000-1400.
admission Free

An exhibition of aircraft parts from local recoveries. There are also displays from World War I up to the late 1940s housed in a 19thC Martello tower.

firstsite
@ the minories art gallery, 74 High Street, Colchester CO1 1UE
t (01206) 577067 **w** firstsite.uk.net
open All year, Mon-Sat 1000-1700.
admission Free

Firstsite presents a diverse programme of innovative contemporary art exhibitions and events at the Minories Art Gallery, across the region and on tour.

Fry Public Art Gallery
Bridge End Gardens, Castle Street, Saffron Walden CB10 1BD
t (01799) 513779
open Apr-Oct, Tue, Fri, Sat-Sun, Bank Hols 1400-1700.
admission Free

Permanent exhibition of 20thC British artists who have lived and worked in north west Essex. In addition, two or three changing exhibitions are on show in parallel.

  For key to symbols see inside back cover.

Hollytrees Museum

High Street, Colchester CO1 1UG
t (01206) 282940 **w** colchestermuseums.org.uk
open All year, Mon-Sat 1000-1700, Sun 1100-1700.
admission Free

A collection of toys, costume and decorative arts from the 18th-20thC, displayed in an elegant Georgian townhouse, built in 1718.

House on the Hill Toy Museums Adventure

Stansted Mountfitchet CM24 8SP
t (01279) 813237 **w** mountfitchetcastle.com
open Apr-Nov, daily 1000-1700.
admission ££

An exciting, animated toy museum covering 7,000sq ft and featuring a huge collection of toys from Victorian times to the 1970s. Offers a nostalgic trip back to childhood.

Kelvedon Hatch Nuclear Bunker

Kelvedon Hall Lane, Kelvedon Hatch,
Brentwood CM14 5TL
t (01277) 364883 **w** secretnuclearbunker.co.uk
open Apr-Oct, Mon-Fri 1000-1600, Sat-Sun 1000-1700.
Nov-Mar, Thu-Sun 1000-1600.
admission ££

A large, three-storey, ex-government regional headquarters buried some 100ft below ground, complete with canteen, BBC studio, dormitories, plant room and plotting floor.

Mangapps Railway Museum

Southminster Road, Burnham-on-Crouch CM0 8QQ
t (01621) 784898 **w** mangapps.co.uk
open Apr-Jul, Sat-Sun 1130-1630. Aug, daily
1130-1630. Sep-Oct, Sat-Sun 1130-1630. Dec, Sat-Sun
1130-1630. Feb-Mar, Sat-Sun 1130-1630.
admission £

A large collection of railway relics, two restored stations, locomotives, coaches and wagons with a working railway line.

Mersea Island Museum

High Street, West Mersea CO5 8QD
t (01206) 385191 **w** merseamuseum.org.uk
open May-Sep, Wed-Sun, Bank Hols 1400-1700.
admission £

Museum of local, social and natural history with displays of methods and equipment used in fishing and wildfowling. Fossils and a mineral display. Also special exhibitions.

Royal Gunpowder Mills

Beaulieu Drive, Waltham Abbey EN9 1JY
t (01992) 707370 **w** royalgunpowdermills.com
open Apr-Oct, Sat-Sun, Bank Hols 1100-1700. School
Summer Hols, Sat-Sun, Wed 1100-1700.
admission ££

Combining fascinating history, exciting science and 175 acres of natural parkland, the Royal Gunpowder Mills offers a truly unique day out for the family.

Saffron Walden Museum

Museum Street, Saffron Walden CB10 1JL
t (01799) 510333 **w** uttlesford.gov.uk
open Apr-Oct, Mon-Sat 1000-1700, Sun, Bank Hols
1400-1700. Nov-Feb, Mon-Sat 1000-1630, Sun, Bank Hols
1400-1630. Mar, Mon-Sat 1000-1700, Sun 1400-1700.
admission £

Award-winning 'family friendly' museum. From moccasins and mummy cases to woolly mammoths and Wallace the lion, there is something for all tastes and ages.

The Sir Alfred Munnings Art Museum

Castle House, Castle Hill, Dedham CO7 6AZ
t (01206) 322127 **w** siralfredmunnings.co.uk
open Apr-Jul, Wed, Sun, Bank Hols 1400-1700. Aug,
Wed-Thu, Sat-Sun, Bank Hols 1400-1700. Sep-Oct,
Wed, Sun, Bank Hols 1400-1700.
admission £

The house, studio and grounds where Sir Alfred Munnings, KCVO, lived and painted for 40 years. The collection also includes pictures on loan from private collections.

Thurrock Museum

Thameside Complex, Orsett Road, Grays RM17 5DX
t (01375) 413965 **w** thurrock.gov.uk/museum.
open All year, Mon-Sat 0900-1700.
admission Free

Over 1,500 artefacts interpreting 250,000 years of Thurrock's heritage from prehistory through to our recent industrial developments.

Tiptree Tearoom, Museum and Shop

Tiptree CO5 0RF
t (01621) 814524 **w** tiptree.com
open Apr-Dec, Mon-Sat 1000-1700, Sun 1100-1700.
Jan-Feb, Mon-Sat 1000-1600. Mar, Mon-Sat 1000-1700,
Sun 1100-1700.
admission Free

Tearoom and shop with a museum displaying how life was and how the art of jam-making has advanced over the years at Tiptree.

Tymperleys Clock Museum

Trinity Street, Colchester CO1 1JN
t (01206) 282931 **w** colchestermuseums.org.uk
open Apr-Oct, Tue-Sat 1000-1300, 1400-1700.
admission Free

A fine collection of Colchester-made clocks from the Mason collection, displayed in a 15thC timber-framed house which Bernard Mason restored and presented to the town.

Carter's Vineyards

Green Lane, Boxted CO4 5TS
t (01206) 271136 **w** cartersvineyards.co.uk
open Apr-Oct, daily 1100-1700.
admission £

Vineyards and a winery with an alternative energy project and a conservation area. Fishing facilities (day licence) are available.

Herefordshire

Enjoy the fun of a special event or visit one of the attractions listed for a great day out. For more inspiring ideas go to **enjoyengland.com**.

26 May–4 Jun
Hay on Wye International Book Festival
Hay on Wye
0870 990 1299
hayfestival.com

22–24 Jun
Dore Abbey Music Festival
Abbey Dore
doreabbey.co.uk

2–5 Aug
The Big Chill Festival
Eastnor Castle, Ledbury
(020) 7684 2020
bigchill.net

6–8 Sep
Festival of Flowers
Hereford Cathedral
herefordcathedral.org

May 08
International Cider & Perry Competition
Hereford Cider Museum, Hereford
(01432) 354207
cidermuseum.co.uk

FAMILY FUN

Amazing Hedge Puzzle
The Jubilee Park, Symonds Yat West HR9 6DA
t (01600) 890360
w mazes.co.uk
open Apr-Oct, daily 1000-1700. Nov-Mar, daily 1000-1600.
admission £
A traditional hedge maze with carved stone temple centre piece, created to celebrate Queen Elizabeth's Jubilee in 1977. World's only 'hands-on interactive' Museum of Mazes.

The Hop Pocket Craft Centre
New House Farm, Bishops Frome WR6 5BT
t (01531) 640323
w thehoppocket.com
open Mar-Oct, Tue-Sat 1000-1730, Sun 1200-1700, Bank Hols 1000-1730. Nov-Dec, Mon-Sat 1000-1730, Sun 1200-1700. Jan-Feb, Wed-Sat 1000-1730, Sun 1200-1700.
admission Free
Magnificent large display of crafts and gifts situated in the picturesque Frome Valley. Visit the new shopping village, craft units, plant centre and all day restaurant.

Shortwood Family Farm
Shortwood, Pencombe HR7 4RP
t (01885) 400205
w shortwoodfarm.co.uk
open Apr-Aug, daily from 1000. Sep, Sat-Sun from 1000.
admission ££
A modern dairy farm with trail and pets' corner. Guided tour between 1400 and 1600 every afternoon. Visitors can collect eggs, feed the animals and milk a cow.

The Small Breeds Farm Park and Owl Centre
Kingswood, Kington HR5 3HF
t (01544) 231109
w owlcentre.com
open Daily 1030-1730.
admission ££
A collection of miniature and rare animals including poultry, water fowl, pheasants and owls, many of which are friendly and can be fed and stroked.

Symonds Yat West Leisure Park
Ross-on-Wye HR9 6BY
t (01600) 890770
w symondsyatleisure.co.uk
open Apr-Oct, Mon-Fri 1000-1800, Sat-Sun 1000-2000.
admission ££
An amusement park incorporating fun for all the family in a popular beauty spot. Fun fair, adventure playground, river cruises, restaurant and gift shop.

NATURE AND WILDLIFE

Abbey Dore Court Garden
Abbey Dore HR2 0AD
t (01981) 240419 w abbeydorecourt.co.uk
open All year, Tue, Thu, Sat-Sun, BankHols 1100-1730.
admission Free
Six-acre plant lovers' garden full of interesting trees, shrubs and herbaceous perennials.

Arrow Cottage Garden
Ledgemoor, Weobley HR4 8RN
t (01344) 622181 w arrowcottagegarden.co.uk
open May-Aug, Fri-Sun 1100-1600.
admission £
Set amidst an idyllic landscape in rural Herefordshire, this romantic two-acre garden combines formal design, follies and topiary with exuberant and imaginative planting.

Bryan's Ground Garden
Bryan's Ground, Letchmoor Lane, Stapleton LD8 2LP
t (01544) 260001 w bryansground.co.uk
open May-Jun, Mon, Sun 1400-1700.
admission £
A formal Edwardian garden, restored and extensively developed since 1993, of nearly eight acres with a newly created five-acre arboretum.

The Garden at the Bannut
Bringsty, Bromyard WR6 5TA
t (01885) 482206 w bannut.co.uk
open Apr-Sep, Wed, Sat-Sun, Bank Hols 1230-1700.
admission £
Two and a half acres of gardens with many fascinating features including colour theme gardens, lawns, mixed borders, knot garden, heather gardens, refreshments and 'secret' garden.

Hampton Court Gardens
Hope-under-Dinmore HR6 0PN
t (01568) 797777 w hamptoncourt.org.uk
open Apr-Oct, Tue-Thu, Sat-Sun 1100-1700.
admission £
Stunning organic gardens. Their design blends harmonious planting with innovative water features. Ornamental kitchen garden, flower gardens, waterfalls, follies and a maze.

Hergest Croft Gardens
Kington HR5 3EG
t (01544) 230160 w hergest.co.uk
open Apr-Oct, daily 1200-1730.
admission ££
Spring bulbs in March and April, rhododendrons and azaleas in May and June, roses and herbaceous borders in high summer and spectacular autumn colour.

How Caple Court Gardens
How Caple HR1 4SX
t (01989) 740626
open Apr-Sep, Mar, daily 1000-1700.
admission £
Eleven-acre Edwardian gardens overlooking river Wye. Formal terrace gardens and sunken Florentine water garden.

Ivy Croft Garden
Ivy Croft, Ivington Green, Leominster HR6 0JN
t (01568) 720344
w ivycroft.freeserve.co.uk
open See website for details.
admission £
Beautiful garden in peaceful country setting, full of interesting plants, some of which are available in our small nursery.

Queenswood Arboretum and Country Park
Dinmore Hill, Leominster HR6 0PY
t (01568) 797052
w herefordshire.gov.uk
open Daily, dawn-dusk.
admission Free
A 170-acre woodland including the arboretum with many rare and exotic trees. A look out on the highest point with main features on a toposcope.

Shipley Gardens
Shipley, Holme Lacy HR2 6LS
t (01432) 870356
w shipleygardens.plus.com
open Apr-Oct, daily 1000-1800.
admission £
The gardens, created during the last 40 years, are set within 30 acres of mixed environmental habitats and are managed as a home for birds, insects, butterflies and small mammals.

Stockton Bury Gardens
Stockton Bury, Kimbolton, Leominster HR6 0HB
t (01568) 613432
open Apr-Oct, Wed-Sun, Bank Hols 1200-1700.
admission £
Gardens laid out in ancient setting in unspoiled countryside with fine views. Pigeon house, tithe barn, hop kilns, unusual plants for sale.

Wye Valley Butterfly Zoo
The Jubilee Park, Symonds Yat West HR9 6DA
t (01600) 890360
w butterflyzoo.co.uk
open Apr-Oct, daily 1000-1700. Nov-Mar, daily 1000-1600.
admission £
Experience the delight of nature's most beautiful wildlife, and find out how you can attract butterflies to your own garden.

HISTORIC ENGLAND

Berrington Hall (National Trust)
Leominster HR6 0DW
t (01568) 615721
w nationaltrust.org.uk
open Apr-Nov, Mon-Wed, Sat-Sun 1300-1700.
admission ££

Built in the late 18th century, designed by Henry Holland. Beautifully decorated ceilings and naval battle paintings. Grounds by Capability Brown. Views of Welsh Hills.

Brockhampton Estate National Trust
Brockhampton Estate, Lower Brockhampton,
Bringsty WR6 5TB
t (01885) 482077
w nationaltrust.org.uk
open Apr-Sep, Wed-Sun 1200-1700. Oct, Wed-Sun 1200-1600.
admission £

Late 14thC moated manor house and detached half-timbered 15thC gatehouse; a rare example of this structure.

Croft Castle (National Trust)
Leominster HR6 9PW
t (01586) 780246
w nationaltrust.org.uk
open Apr-Sep, Wed-Sun 1300-1700. Oct, Wed-Sun 1300-1600.
admission ££

Property of the Croft family since Domesday, with a break of 170 years from 1750. Original walls and corner towers of 14th, 15th and 18thC Georgian Gothic staircase and ceiling.

Eastnor Castle
Eastnor HR8 1RL
t (01531) 633160
w eastnorcastle.com
open Apr-Jul, Sun, Bank Hols 1100-1630. Aug, Mon-Fri, Sun 1100-1630. Sep, Sun, Bank Hols 1100-1630.
admission ££

Fairytale Georgian castle, standing at the end of the Malvern Hills. A fine collection of armour, pictures, tapestries and Italian furniture.

Goodrich Castle (English Heritage)
Goodrich HR9 6HY
t (01600) 890538
w english-heritage.org.uk
open Mar-May, daily 1000-1700. Jun-Aug, daily 1000-1600. Sep-Oct, daily 1000-1700. Nov-Feb, Wed-Sun 1000-1600.
admission £

Remarkably complete, magnificent red sandstone castle with 12thC keep and extensive remains from the 13th and 14thC. Stunning views across the Wye Valley.

Hereford Cathedral
Cathedral Office, The Cloisters, Cathedral Close, Hereford HR1 2NG
t (01432) 374202
w herefordcathedral.org
open Daily 0730-1730.
admission Free

Built on a 7thC church site. Mixture of styles from Norman to early English, decorated to Perpendicular.

Kinnersley Castle
Kinnersley HR3 6QF
t (01544) 327407
w kinnersleycastle.co.uk
open See website for details.
admission £

Welsh border castle modernised around 1580 featuring leaded glass and stone-tiled roof, fine plasterwork and panelling. Walled gardens and fine trees.

Mappa Mundi & Chained Library Exhibition
Hereford Cathedral, 5 The Cloisters, Hereford HR1 2NG
t (01432) 374202
w herefordcathedral.co.uk
open Apr-Sep, Mon-Sat 1000-1630, Sun 1100-1530. Oct-Mar, Mon-Sat 1000-1630.
admission £

The new library of Hereford Cathedral is home to the unique Mappa Mundi, the largest and most complete map in the world, drawn in 1289.

The Old House
High Town, Hereford HR1 2AA
t (01432) 260694
w herefordshire.gov.uk/leisure
open Apr-Sep, Tue-Sat 1000-1700, Sun 1000-1600. Oct-Mar, Tue-Sat 1000-1700.
admission Free

Built in 1621, with Jacobean domestic architecture, furnished in the 17thC style, on three floors. The house includes kitchen and bedrooms originally part of Butchers Row.

OUTDOOR ACTIVITIES

Kingfisher Cruises
c/o Wye Rapids Cottage, Symonds Yat West HR9 6BL
t (01600) 891063
open Mar-Oct, daily 1100-1700.
admission ££

Kingfisher Cruises is a family business with two all-weather water buses that take you on a river trip through the valley and village of Symonds Yat.

ENTERTAINMENT AND CULTURE

FOOD AND DRINK

Cider Museum and King Offa Distillery
21 Ryelands Street, Hereford HR4 0LW
t (01432) 354207 **w** cidermuseum.co.uk
open Apr-Oct, Tue-Sat 1000-1700. Nov-Mar, Tue-Sat 1100-1500.
admission £
Explore the history of cider-making and view the working King Offa distillery. Programme of temporary exhibitions and events. Free tasting of distillery products.

Hereford Museum and Art Gallery
Broad Street, Hereford HR4 9AU
t (01432) 260692 **w** herefordshire.gov.uk/leisure
open Apr-Sep, Tue-Sat 1000-1700, Sun, Bank Hols 1000-1600. Nov-Mar, Tue-Sat 1000-1700.
admission Free
Herefordshire history and life, programme of events and activities.

Teddy Bears of Bromyard
The Old Bakery, 12 The Square, Bromyard HR7 4BP
t (01885) 488329 **w** bromyard57.freeserve.co.uk
open Please phone for details.
admission Free
Museum of antique teddy bears, dolls, Disney and old toys together with a museum shop. There is a Thunderbirds puppets exhibition, Captain Scarlet and a talking Dalek from Dr Who.

Coddington Vineyard and Gardens
Coddington Vineyard,
Coddington HR8 1JJ
t (01531) 640668
open Mar-Dec, Thu-Sun 1400-1700.
admission Free
A 17thC farm with threshing barn and cider mill. The gardens include woodland, pool and stream. Two-acre vineyard and winery. Free wine tasting and sales available.

Dunkertons Cider Company
Luntley,
Pembridge HR6 9ED
t (01544) 388653
open All year, Mon-Sat 1000-1700.
admission Free
Ciders and perry on sale, made on the premises from local and home-grown organic cider apples and perry pears. Tastings from the barrel. Also cider bar and restaurant.

Malvern Hills

Hertfordshire

Enjoy the fun of a special event or visit one of the attractions listed for a great day out. For more inspiring ideas go to **enjoyengland.com**.

26–27 May
Hertfordshire County Show
Herts County Showground, Redbourn
(01582) 792676
hertsshow.com

27–28 May
Tring Canal Festival
Tring
(01442) 827702
tringcanalfestival.org.uk

14–15 Jul
Rhythms of the World
Hitchin
(01462) 453335
htci.org.uk

17–19 Aug
Hatfield House County Show
Hatfield
(01707) 287010
hatfield-house.co.uk

2 Sep
Medieval Jousting
Knebworth House, Nr Stevenage
(01438) 812661
knebworthhouse.com

FAMILY FUN

Willows Farm Village
Coursers Road, London Colney AL2 1BB
t (01727) 822444 w willowsfarmvillage.co.uk
open Apr-Oct, daily 1000-1730.
admission ££
At the unique Willows Farm Village, families discover their true animal instincts, roaming free in the countryside and running wild with the adventure activities.

NATURE AND WILDLIFE

Aldenham Country Park
Park Office, Dagger Lane, Elstree WD6 3AT
t (020) 8953 9602 w hertsdirect.org
open Mar-Apr, daily 0900-1700. May-Sep, daily 0900-1800. Oct, daily 0900-1700. Nov-Feb, daily 0900-1600.
admission Free
Meadow and woodland consisting of 175 acres with rare breeds farm, playgrounds, angling, nature trail and toilets. Re-creation of the features in Winnie the Pooh.

Ashridge Estate
Moneybury Hill, Ringshall, Berkhamsted HP4 1LX
t (01442) 851227
open Estate: Daily. Visitor Centre: Apr-Oct, daily 1200-1700. Nov-Dec, daily 1200-dusk. Bridgewater Monument: Mar-Oct, Sat-Sun, Bank Hols 1200-1630.
admission Free
Six square miles of woodlands, commons, chalk downland and farmland with the focal point of the Bridgewater monument, visitor centre and tea shop.

Benington Lordship Gardens
Benington SG2 7BS
t (01438) 869228 w beningtonlordship.co.uk
open See website for details.
admission £
Edwardian garden on historic site. Ornamental, vegetable and rose/water garden. Herbaceous borders, lakes and contemporary sculptures.

Fairlands Valley Park
Six Hills Way, Stevenage SG2 0BL
t (01438) 353241 w stevenage-lesiure.co.uk
open Park: Daily. Sailing Centre: All year, daily 0800-1600.
admission Free
There are 120 acres of parkland including watersports, dinghy, windsurfing and powerboat courses. Private tuition and angling. Play area, cafe and disabled toilets on site.

Admission is based on an adult price. Please check opening times and admission before travelling.

Paradise Wildlife Park
White Stubbs Lane, Broxbourne EN10 7QA
t (01992) 470490 **w** pwpark.com
open Apr-Oct, daily 0930-1800. Nov-Mar, daily 1000-1700.
admission £££
A marvellous day out for all the family with many daily activities, children's rides, catering outlets, picnic areas, paddling pool and an excellent range of animals.

Stanborough Park
Stanborough Road, Welwyn Garden City AL8 6DQ
t (01707) 327655
open Daily.
admission Free
Stanborough Park is a high quality public open space providing a focus of activity for many varied user groups. Watersports centre, nature trail, picnic areas and fishing.

Wilstone Reservoir Nature Reserve
Lower Icknield Way, Tring HP23 4LN
t (01727) 858901 **w** tringreservoirs.com
open Daily.
admission Free
A well-known birdwatching spot. One of the four 'Tring Reservoirs' an important refuge for ducks and gulls, plus large heronry.

HISTORIC ENGLAND

Berkhamsted Castle
Berkhamsted
t (01536) 402840 **w** english-heritage.org.uk
open Apr-Oct, daily 1000-1800. Nov-Mar, daily 1000-1600.
admission Free
The extensive remains of an 11thC motte-and-bailey castle which was the work of Robert of Mortain, half brother of William of Normandy, who learnt he was king here.

British Schools Museum
41 Queen Street, Hitchin SG4 9TS
t (01462) 420144 (01462) 452697
w hitchinbritishschools.org.uk
open Feb-Mar, Nov, Tue 1000-1600. Apr-Oct, Tue 1000-1600, Sat 1000-1300, Sun 1400-1700.
admission Adult: £4

Discover 200 years of elementary education by guided tour or family trail. Explore historic classrooms, trying inkwells, slates and sandtrays. Find out why the Lancasterian Schoolroom is very special. Tea room.

Map ref 2D1

Cathedral and Abbey Church of St Alban
The Chapter House, St Albans AL1 1BY
t (01727) 860780
w stalbanscathedral.org.uk
open Daily 0800-1745.
admission Free
A Norman abbey church on the site of the martyrdom of St Alban, Britain's first Christian martyr. The 13thC shrine has been restored and is a centre of ecumenical worship.

Gorhambury
Gorhambury AL3 6AH
t (01727) 855000
open May-Sep, Thu 1400-1700.
admission ££
A classical-style mansion built 1777-1784 by Sir Robert Taylor with 16thC enamelled glass, 17thC carpet, and historic portraits of the Bacon and Grimston families.

Hatfield House
Hatfield AL9 5NQ
t (01707) 287010 **w** hatfield-house.co.uk
open Apr-Sep, Wed-Sun, Bank Hols 1200-1700.
admission ££
Magnificent Jacobean house, home of the Marquess of Salisbury. Exquisite gardens, model soldiers and park trails. Childhood home of Queen Elizabeth I.

Knebworth House, Gardens and Park
The Estate Office, Knebworth House, Knebworth SG3 6PY
t (01438) 812661 **w** knebworthhouse.com
open See website for details.
admission ££
Tudor manor house, re-fashioned in the 19thC, housing a collection of manuscripts, portraits, and Jacobean banquet hall. Formal gardens, parkland and adventure playground.

Roman Theatre of Verulamium
Gorhambury AL3 6AH
t (01727) 835035 **w** romantheatre.co.uk
open Mar-Oct, daily 1000-1700. Nov-Feb, daily 1000-1600.
admission £
The only completely excavated exposed Roman theatre in Britain with the remains of a townhouse and underground shrine.

Scott's Grotto
Scotts Road, Ware SG12 9JQ
t (01920) 464131 **w** scotts-grotto.org
open Apr-Sep, Sat 1400-1630.
admission Free
Grotto extending 67ft into the hillside, including passages and six chambers decorated with fossils, shells, pebbles and flints. Unlit, so torches are necessary.

Shaw's Corner

Ayot St Lawrence AL6 9BX
t (01438) 820307
w nationaltrust.org.uk
open House: Apr-Oct, Wed-Sun 1300-1700. Garden: Apr-Oct, Wed-Sun 1200-1730.
admission £

The home of George Bernard Shaw from 1906 until his death in 1950, with literary and personal effects on display and a 3.5-acre garden.

ENTERTAINMENT AND CULTURE

British Schools Museum

41 Queen Street, Hitchin SG4 9TS
t (01462) 420144 (01462) 452697
w hitchinbritishschools.org.uk
open Feb-Mar, Nov, Tue 1000-1600.
Apr-Oct, Tue 1000-1600, Sat 1000-1300, Sun 1400-1700.
admission Adult: £4

Discover 200 years of elementary education by guided tour or family trail. Explore historic classrooms, trying inkwells, slates and sandtrays. Find out why the Lancasterian Schoolroom is very special. Tea room.

Map ref 2D1

Bushey Museum and Art Gallery

Rudolph Road, Bushey WD23 3HW
t (02089) 503233
open All year, Thu-Sun 1100-1600.
admission Free

Community museum telling the story of Bushey. Archaeology, social history, local trades and industries. Art galleries show changing exhibitions.

De Havilland Aircraft Heritage Centre

PO Box 107, Salisbury Hall, London Colney AL2 1EX
t (01727) 822051
w dehavillandmuseum.co.uk
open Mar-Oct, Tue, Thu, Sat 1400-1730, Sun, Bank Hols 1030-1730.
admission £

Museum showing the restoration and preservation of a range of de Havilland aircraft; the prototype Mosquito. Also engines, propellers, missiles, memorabilia and storyboard.

Hertford Museum

18 Bull Plain, Hertford SG14 1DT
t (01992) 582686
w hertfordmuseum.org
open All year, Tue-Sat 1000-1700.
admission Free

A 17thC building with main exhibits on the archaeology, natural and local history of Hertfordshire with a collection of Hertfordshire Regiment regalia and changing exhibitions.

Museum of St Albans

Hatfield Road, St Albans AL1 3RR
t (01727) 819340
w stalbansmuseums.org.uk
open All year, Mon-Sat 1000-1700, Sun, Bank Hols 1400-1700.
admission Free

Purpose-built as a museum in 1898, displays include craft tools and local and natural history telling the St Albans story from Roman times to the present day. Wildlife garden.

Saint Albans Organ Theatre

320 Camp Road, St Albans AL1 5PE
t (01727) 873896
w stalbansorganmuseum.org.uk
open All year, Sun 1400-1630.
admission £

A collection of organs by Mortier, DeCap, Bursens; Weber and Steinway duo-art reproducing pianos, Mills violano-virtuoso music boxes, and Wurlitzer and Rutt theatre pipe organs.

Stevenage Museum

St George's Way, Stevenage SG1 1XX
t (01438) 218881
w stevenage.gov.uk
open All year, Mon-Sat 1000-1700, Sun 1300-1600.
admission Free

A lively award-winning museum which tells the story of Stevenage from the Stone Age to the present. Displays include a 1950s living room and a programme of exhibitions.

Verulamium Museum

St Michaels Street, St Albans AL3 4SW
t (01727) 751810
w stalbansmuseums.org.uk
open All year, Mon-Sat 1000-1730, Sun 1400-1730.
admission £

The museum of everyday life in Roman Britain. Award-winning displays of re-created Roman rooms, hands-on areas and video of Roman Verulamium.

The Walter Rothschild Zoological Museum

Akeman Street, Tring HP23 6AP
t (02079) 426171
w nhm.ac.uk/tring
open All year, Mon-Sat 1000-1700, Sun 1400-1700.
admission Free

Once the private collection of Lionel Walter, 2nd Baron Rothschild, now part of The Natural History Museum. More than 4,000 mounted specimens of animals.

For key to symbols see inside back cover.

Leicestershire & Rutland

Enjoy the fun of a special event or visit one of the attractions listed for a great day out. For more inspiring ideas go to **enjoyengland.com.**

4 Jun–25 Aug
Stamford Shakespeare Festival
Rutland Open Air Theatre, Tolethorpe Hall, Little Casterton
(01780) 756133
stamfordshakespeare.co.uk

16 Jun–30 Sep
Picasso Exhibition – Ceramics
New Walk Museum & Art Gallery, Leicester
(0116) 225 4900
leicestermuseums.ac.uk

Oct–Nov
Diwali
Various venues, Leicester
(0116) 266 8266
goleicestershire.com

6–7 Oct
East Midlands Food and Drink Festival
Various venues across Leicestershire
(01664) 562971
eastmidlandsfoodfestival.co.uk

Feb 08
Comedy Festival
Various venues around Leceister
comedy-festival.co.uk

FAMILY FUN

Great Central Railway
Great Central Station,
Great Central Road,
Loughborough LE11 1RW
t (01509) 230726
w greatcentralrailway.com
open Daily 0900-1700.
admission £££
Britain's only double track, main line heritage railway, running through 8 miles of scenic Leicestershire countryside.

Twinlakes Park
Melton Spinney Road,
Melton Mowbray LE14 4SB
t (01664) 567777
w twinlakespark.com
open Daily 1000-1700.
admission ££
A new destination for family fun with a huge variety of activities and multiple play zones for all ages indoors and outdoors. All-weather family fun guaranteed.

NATURE AND WILDLIFE

Barnsdale Gardens
The Avenue, Exton LE15 8AH
t (01572) 813200
w barnsdalegardens.co.uk
open Apr-May, daily 0900-1700. Jun-Aug, daily 0900-1900. Sep-Oct, daily 0900-1700. Nov-Feb, daily 1000-1600.
admission ££
Geoff Hamilton's Barnsdale TV Garden, familiar to BBC2 'Gardeners' World' viewers, consists of 37 individual gardens and features, all blending into an eight-acre garden. Small, specialist nursery, licensed coffee shop.

Bradgate Country Park
Estate Office, Deer Barn Buildings, Bradgate Park, Newtown Linford LE6 0HE
t (0116) 236 2713
open Daily, dawn-dusk.
admission Free
The birthplace and early home of Lady Jane Grey. Natural parkland, river, hills, rock outcrops, woods, heath, bracken, herds of deer, visitor centre, shops, refreshments and information.

Brocks Hill Country Park and Visitor Centre
Washbrook Lane, Oadby LE2 5JJ
t (0116) 271 4514 w oadby-wigston.gov.uk
open Country park: Daily. Visitor centre: All year,
Mon-Fri 1000-1700, Sat-Sun, Bank Hols 1000-1600.
admission Free
Environmentally friendly building promoting energy efficiency and sustainability, set in 67 acres of country park. Play area, cafe and human sun dial.

Broombriggs Farm Trail
Beacon Road, Woodhouse Eaves LE12 8SR
t (01509) 890048 w leics.gov.uk
open Daily.
admission Free
A farm trail set around a 130-acre typical Charnwood forest farm. Windmill Hill is an adjoining wooded area with the remains of a windmill.

Burrough Hill Country Park
Burrough on the Hill
t (0116) 267 1944 w leics.gov.uk
open Daily, dawn-dusk.
admission Free
The 86-acre site of a former Iron Age hill fort with fine views over East Leicestershire, woodland walks and walks through the open countryside.

Foxton Locks Country Park
Gumley Road, Foxton
t (0116) 265 6918 w leics.gov.uk
open Daily, dawn-dusk.
admission Free
Landscaped car park and picnic site with a woodland footpath leading to the Grand Union Canal towpath, a long flight of locks and the remains of barge lifts on a plane.

Jubilee Wood
Woodhouse Lane (off B5350), Nanpantan
t (01509) 890048 w leicester.gov.uk
open Daily.
admission Free
A mixed woodland with rocky outcrops.

Market Bosworth Country Park
The Park, Market Bosworth CV13 0LP
t (01455) 290429 w leics.gov.uk
open All year, 0800-dusk.
admission Free
Eighty-seven acres of rural park including an 11-acre arboretum, a children's adventure playground and a lake. Day fishing tickets available from the warden (Jun-Mar).

Melton Country Park and Visitor Centre
Wymondham Way, Melton Mowbray LE13 1LB
t (01664) 480992
open Daily, dawn-dusk.
admission Free
Waterfowl areas, nature reserves and facilities for football and children's play areas, a visitor centre and the Jubilee way path.

Mill on the Soar Fishing Lake
Coventry Road, Sutton in the Elms LE9 6QD
t (01455) 285924
open Daily, dawn-dusk.
admission ££
Fishing lake with a large variety of species and a good number of specimens. Fishing tackle and bait is available for purchase on site.

Rutland Falconry and Owl Centre
Burley Bushes, Exton Lane, Exton LE15 7TA
t 07778 152814
w rutland-falconry.com
open Apr-Oct, daily, 1000-1730. Nov-Mar, daily 1000-1530.
admission £
Falconry displays throughout the day and evening with static birds and aviaries.

Rutland Water
Tourist Information Centre, Sykes Lane,
Empingham LE15 8PX
t (01572) 653026
w anglianwaterleisure.co.uk
open Daily.
admission Free
An information centre with water- and land-based recreational facilities, a pleasure cruiser, church museum, butterfly and aquatic centre and nature reserve.

Rutland Water Nature Reserve
Anglian Water Bird Watching Centre, Egleton LE15 8BT
t (01572) 770651
w anglianwaterleisure.co.uk
open Apr-Oct, daily 0900-1700. Nov-Mar, daily 0900-1600.
admission £
Important wildfowl sanctuary, SSSI, SPA, Ramsar site, nine miles of reservoir edge, three lagoons and 20 hides.

Twycross Zoo
Atherstone, Twycross CV9 3PX
t (01827) 880250
w twycrosszoo.com
open Apr-Oct, daily 1000-1730. Nov-Mar, daily 1000-1600.
admission ££
A zoo with gorillas, orang-utans, chimpanzees, a modern gibbon complex, elephants, lions, giraffes, a reptile house, pets' corner and rides.

University of Leicester: Botanic Gardens
The Knoll, Glebe Road, Leicester LE2 2LD
t (0116) 271 7725
w le.au.lk/botanicgarden/
open Apr-Nov, daily 1000-1600. Dec-Mar, Mon-Fri 1000-1600.
admission Free
Sixteen acres of rock, herb, water and formal gardens with glasshouses organised for teaching and research.

Admission is based on an adult price. Please check opening times and admission before travelling.

Watermead Country Park
Off Wanlip Road, Syston LE7 8PF
t (0116) 267 1944 **w** leics.gov.uk
open Apr, Sep, daily 0700-1900. May-Aug, daily
0700-2000. Oct, Mar, daily 0700-1800. Nov-Jan, daily
0700-1600. Feb, daily 0700-1700.
admission Free
Two hundred and thirty acres of country park with lakes,
a nature reserve, woodland, walks, footpaths, cycleways
and access to the River Soar and the canal.

Ashby-de-la-Zouch Castle
South Street, Ashby-de-la-Zouch LE65 1BR
t (01530) 413343 **w** english-heritage.org.uk
open Apr-Jun, Mon, Thu-Sun 1000-1700. Jul-Aug, daily
1000-1800. Sep-Oct, Mon, Thu-Sun 1000-1700.
Nov-Mar, Mon, Thu-Sun 1000-1600.
admission £
The remains of a Norman manor house which Lord
Hastings turned into a castle in the 15th century.
Remains of a tower, parts of walls, great hall, private
chambers, kitchen and chapel.

Belvoir Castle
Estate Office, Belvoir NG32 1PE
t (01476) 871000 **w** belvoircastle.com
open Apr, Sat-Sun 1100-1700. May-Jun, Tue-Thu,
Sat-Sun 1100-1700. Jul-Aug, Mon-Thu, Sat-Sun
1100-1700. Sep, Sat-Sun 1100-1700.
admission £££
The fourth castle to have stood on the site since Norman
times, completed in the early 19th century. Sloping
lawns lead to the gardens which are elegantly laid out
around a central fountain.

Bosworth Battlefield Visitor Centre and Country Park
Sutton Cheney CV13 0AD
t (01455) 290429 **w** leics.gov.uk
open Battlefild visitor centre: Apr-Oct 1100-1700.
Country park: Apr, daily 0700-1900. May-Aug, daily
0700-2000. Sep, daily 0700-1900. Oct, daily 0700-1800.
Nov-Dec, daily 0700-dusk.
admission Free
The site of the Battle of Bosworth Field (1485). There is
a battlefield visitor centre with models, exhibitions, flags,
armour, a film theatre and trails to King Richard's well.

Burbage Common and Woods
Burbage Common Road, Hinckley LE10 3DD
t (01455) 633712
open All year, Sat 1400-1600, Sun 1100-1600.
admission Free
A log cabin visitor centre with an exhibition on local
wildlife, history, recreation and conservation, set in
204 acres of wildflower meadows and ancient
woodland.

Conkers: at the Heart of the National Forest
Millennium Avenue, Rawdon Road, Moira,
Swadlincote DE12 6GA
t (01283) 216633 **w** visitconkers.com
open Apr-Oct, daily 1000-1800. Nov-Mar, daily
1000-1600.
admission ££
Innovative interactive exhibits complemented by
woodland trails, lakes, assault course, train, restaurants,
shops, indoor play area and events. All-year activities.

Framework Knitters Museum
42-44 Bushloe End, Wigston LE18 2BA
t (0116) 288 3396
open All year, Sun 1400-1700.
admission £
A mainly 18th and 19thC master hosiers house in the
course of restoration with a 19thC framework knitters
workshop with frames in situ; a unique Leicestershire
survival.

Leicester Cathedral
21 St Martin's, Leicester LE1 5DE
t (0116) 262 5294 **w** cathedral.leicester.anglican.org
open All year, Mon-Sat 0800-1800, Sun 0700-1700.
admission Free
The guild Church of St Martin became Leicester's
cathedral in 1927; a medieval church which was rebuilt
externally in the late 19thC; Herrick monuments and
Richard III memorial.

Lyddington Bede House
Blue Coat Lane, Uppingham LE15 9LZ
t (01572) 822438 **w** english-heritage.org.uk
open Apr-Oct, Mon, Thu-Sun 1000-1700.
admission £
The only surviving part of a medieval palace belonging
to the Bishops of Lincoln, converted to almshouses in
1600 with an elaborate 16thC timber ceiling cornice on
the first floor.

The Manor House
Manor Road, Donington le Heath, Coalville LE67 2FW
t (01530) 831259 **w** leics.gov.uk/museums
open Apr-Dec, daily 1100-1600.
admission Free
A medieval manor house of the early 14thC with 16th-
17thC alterations, oak furniture of the 16th-17thC, a
herb garden and restaurant.

National Space Centre, Leicester
Exploration Drive, Leicester LE4 5NS
t 0870 607 7223 **w** spacecentre.co.uk
open Apr-Jul, Tue-Sun 1000-1700. Aug, daily
1000-1700. Sep-Mar, Tue-Sun 1000-1700.
admission £££
'The universe as you've never seen it before.' The
National Space Centre is the UK's largest attraction
dedicated to space.

Stamford Shakespeare Company
Rutland Open-Air Theatre, Tolethorpe Hall,
Little Casterton PE9 4BH
t (01780) 754381 **w** stamfordshakespeare.co.uk
open Jun-Aug, Mon-Sat 2000-2300.
admission £££
*An annual summer season of Shakespeare plays during
June, July and August in Rutland Open Air Theatre with
a covered auditorium in the grounds of Elizabethan
Tolethorpe Hall.*

Stanford Hall
Stranford-upon-Avon, Lutterworth LE17 6DH
t (01788) 860250 **w** stanfordhall.co.uk
open House: Apr-Sep, Sun, Bank Hols 1330-1730.
Grounds: Apr-Sep, Sun, Bank Hols 1200-1730.
admission ££
*A William and Mary house on the River Avon with family
costumes, furniture, pictures, a replica 1898 flying
machine, rose garden and nature trail.*

OUTDOOR ACTIVITIES

Foxton Boat Services Limited
Bottom Lock, Foxton LE16 7RA
t (0116) 279 2285 **w** foxtonboats.co.uk
open Daily.
admission Free
*Providing boat trips and boat hire. There is a canal
museum and boats using the flight of 10 locks. There is
also a wildlife trail.*

Rutland Water Cruises
Whitwell Park, North Shore, Rutland Water,
Whitwell LE15 8BL
t (01572) 787630 **w** rutlandwatercruises.com
open Apr, Sat-Sun 1300-1500. Sun, Bank Hols
1200-1500. May-Jun, Sep, Mon-Sat 1300-1500, Sun,
Bank Hols 1200-1600. Jul-Aug, Mon-Sat 1300-1600,
Sun, Bank Hols 1200-1700. Easter, Oct School Hols,
daily 1300-1500.
admission ££
*Cruises on the Rutland Belle to enjoy the sights of
Rutland Water with a commentary highlighting points of
interest. Morning, afternoon and private evening cruises
available, also Osprey and Wildlife trips.*

ENTERTAINMENT AND CULTURE

Abbey Pumping Station
Corporation Road, Abbey Lane, Leicester LE4 5PX
t (0116) 299 5111 **w** leicestermuseums.ac.uk
open Apr-Nov, Mon-Wed, Sat 1100-1630, Sun
1300-1630. Feb-Mar, Mon-Wed, Sat 1100-1630, Sun
1100-1630.
admission Free
*The pumping station is Leicester's Museum of Science
and Technology, displaying the city's technological and
scientific heritage. It is also home to fully working
Victorian beam engines.*

Charnwood Museum
Queen's Hall, Granby Street,
Loughborough LE11 3DU
t (01509) 233784 **w** leics.gov.uk
open All year, Mon-Sat, Bank Hols 1000-1630, Sun
1400-1600.
admission Free
*Explore Charnwood's rich and exciting heritage, from
the discovery of some of the world's oldest fossils to the
lives of present-day Charnwood people.*

The City Gallery
90 Granby Street, Leicester LE1 1DJ
t (0116) 223 2060 **w** leicester.gov.uk/citygallery
open All year, Tue-Fri 1100-1800, Sat 1000-1700.
admission Free
*Art gallery showcasing the best in contemporary art and
craft, including pieces for sale. There is a dynamic
education and events programme and a touring
exhibitions scheme.*

Donington Grand Prix Collection
Donington Park, Castle Donington DE74 2RP
t (01332) 811027 **w** doningtoncollection.com
open Daily 1000-1700.
admission ££
*The world's largest collection of single seater racing cars
on display to the public, adjoining Donington Park racing
circuit with a full programme of events.*

Discover Britain's heritage

Discover the history and beauty of over 250 of
Britain's best-known historic houses, castles, gardens
and manor-houses. You can purchase *Britain's Historic
Houses and Gardens – Guide and Map* from good
bookshops and online at enjoy**England**direct.com.

Foxton Canal Museum
Middle Lock, Gumley Road,
Foxton LE16 7RA
t (0116) 279 2657
w fipt.org.uk
open Apr-Sep, daily 1000-1700. Oct-Mar, Mon-Wed,
Sat-Sun 1100-1600.
admission £

A flight of 10 locks, a canal museum and education workshop; the site of a unique inclined plane boat lift. Also on the site is a pub, shop and boat trips.

The Harborough Museum
Council Offices (Fox Yard Entrance),
Adam and Eve Street,
Market Harborough LE16 7AG
t (01858) 821085
w leicester.gov.uk/museums
open All year, Mon-Sat 1000-1630,
Sun 1400-1600.
admission Free

Local history museum for the Harborough area, illustrating the town's role as a market and social focus. Includes items from the Symington Collection of Corsetry.

Leicester Royal Infirmary: History Museum
Knighton Street, Leicester LE1 5WW
t (0116) 254 1414
w uhl-tr.nhs.uk
open All year, Wed 1200-1400.
admission Free

The history of the Royal Infirmary (opened in 1771) with an exhibition of medical and surgical instruments.

Moira Furnace
Furnace Lane, Moira,
Swadlincote DE12 6AT
t (01283) 224667
w nwleicestershire.gov.uk
open Apr-Aug, Tue-Sun, Bank Hols 1000-1700.
Sep-Mar, Wed-Sun, Bank Hols 1130-1600.
admission £

An early 19thC blast furnace with interactive displays and a two-mile industrial heritage trail adjacent to Ashby Canal. Boat trips available all year.

New Walk Museum and Art Gallery
New Walk, Leicester LE1 7EA
t (0116) 225 4900
w leicestermuseums.ac.uk
open All year, Mon-Sat 1000-1700, Sun 1100-1700.
admission Free

A major regional venue featuring various galleries and displays including Ancient Egypt, decorative arts, geology, paintings, the animal world, dinosaurs, children's gallery.

Queen's Royal Lancers Museum
Belvoir Castle, Belvoir NG32 1PD
t (0115) 957 3295
w qrl.uk.com
open Apr, Sat-Sun 1100-1600. May-Jun, Tue-Thu,
1100-1700, Sat-Sun, Bank Hols 1100-1600. Jul-Aug,
Mon-Thu 1100-1700, Sat-Sun 1100-1600. Sep, Sat-Sun
1100-1600.
admission £££

The museum is situated within Belvoir Castle. Weapons, uniforms, paintings, silver, medals and personal artefacts form part of this fine collection.

Rutland County Museum
Catmose Street, Oakham LE15 6HW
t (01572) 758440
w rutnet.co.uk/rcc/rutlandmuseums
open All year, Mon-Sat 1030-1700, Sun 1400-1600.
admission Free

Museum of Rutland life, with farm equipment, rural tradesmen's tools, domestic collections and local archaeology. Late 18thC riding school.

Snibston Discovery Park
Ashby Road, Coalville LE67 3LN
t (01530) 278444
w snibston.com
open Apr-Nov, daily 1000-1700. Dec-Mar, Mon-Fri
1000-1500, Sat-Sun, Bank Hols 1000-1700.
admission ££

An award-winning all-weather science and technology heritage museum, where visitors can get their 'hands-on' the many inter-activities.

RELAXING AND PAMPERING

Ferrers Centre for Arts and Crafts
Staunton Harold, Ashby-de-la-Zouch LE65 1RU
t (01332) 695049
w ferrerscentre.co.uk
open All year, Tue-Sun 1100-1700.
admission Free

An idyllic English setting, splendid buildings, woods, gardens, lakes and parkland. Contemporary design-led arts and crafts centre.

Ye Olde Pork Pie Shoppe and the Sausage Shop
Dickinson & Morris, 10 Nottingham Street,
Melton Mowbray LE13 1NW
t (01664) 562341
w porkpie.co.uk
open All year, Mon-Sat 0800-1600.
admission Free

The oldest and only remaining bakery producing truly authentic Melton Pork Pies. Discover how Melton Mowbray became the original home of the pork pie industry.

Lincolnshire

Enjoy the fun of a special event or visit one of the attractions listed for a great day out. For more inspiring ideas go to **enjoyengland.com.**

19 May–3 Jun
Lincolnshire Wolds Walking Festival
Various venues across Lincolnshire
(01507) 609289
lincswolds.org.uk

12 Aug
Wonders of the Wash
Gilbraltar Point National Nature Reserve, Skegness
lincstrust.org.uk

30 Aug–2 Sep
Burghley Horse Trials
Burghley House, Stamford
(01780) 752131
burghley-horse.co.uk

6–9 Dec
Lincoln Christmas Market
Lincoln Market
(01522) 873213
lincoln.gov.uk

3 May 08
Spalding Flower Parade
Spalding
(01775) 724843
flowerparade.org

FAMILY FUN

Butlins
Roman Bank, Skegness PE25 1NJ
t (01754) 762311
w butlinsonline.co.uk
open See website for details.
admission ££
Butlins has a Skyline Pavilion, Toyland, Sub Tropical Waterworld, tenpin bowling and entertainment centre with live shows.

Cleethorpes Central Beach
Cleethorpes Central DN35 8SE
t (01472) 323356
open Daily.
admission Free
Cleethorpes beaches are unspoilt, gently sloping and sandy. The central beach is flanked by a traditional promenade which runs parallel to Victorian gardens with flowerbeds and a waterfall.

Cleethorpes Coast Light Railway
Lakeside Station, Kings Road, Cleethorpes DN35 0AG
t (01472) 604657
w cleethorpescoastlightrailway.co.uk
open Mar-Sep, daily 1100-1700, Oct-Feb, Sat-Sun 1100-1700.
admission £
A delightful scenic railway journey from Kingsway Station through the country atmosphere of the lakeside, with panoramic views of the Humber Estuary. One of Britain's premier minimum-gauge steam railways.

Fantasy Island
Sea Lane, Ingoldmells PE25 1RH
t (01754) 874668
w fantasyisland.co.uk
open All year, please phone for details.
admission Free
Multi award winning family visitor attraction with amazing array of theme park thrills and experiences in a setting the weather cannot spoil. Free admission for day visitors. Pay-as-you-go ride tokens.

Fun Farm – Grantham
Dysart Road, Grantham NG31 7LE
t (01406) 373444
w funfarm.co.uk
open Daily 1000-1800.
admission Free
Fun Farm has so many attractions, whatever the weather. Children can have hours of fun in this safe, friendly environment whilst adults can relax in the Fun Farm Restaurant and Gift Shop.

Fun Farm – Spalding

High Road, Weston PE12 6JD
t (01406) 373444
w funfarm.co.uk
open Daily 1000-1800.
admission Free

Fun Farm is a large adventure play facility providing a safe, secure play environment. Featuring ball pools, slides, ramps and lots of other soft-play possibilities in an eight metre high play structure.

Hall Farm Park

Thornton Road, South Kelsey LN7 6PS
t (01652) 678698
w hallfarmpark.co.uk
open See website for details.
admission £

Hall Farm Park is set on a working farm but the Farm Park site has been purposely developed to cater for visitors of all ages.

Hardys Animal Farm

Anchor Lane, Ingoldmells PE25 1LZ
t (01754) 872267
w hardysanimalfarm.co.uk
open Apr-Oct, daily 1000-1700.
admission £

An enjoyable way to learn about the countryside and how a farm works. There are animals for the children to enjoy and an opportunity to learn about the traditions of the countryside.

Lakeside Leisure

Trench Lane, Chapel St Leonards PE24 5TU
t (01754) 872631
w ukattractions.com
open Mar-Nov, daily. Please phone for details.
admission Free

Family lakeside fun park next to the beach with fishing, boating, quad biking and crazy golf.

Lindholme Leisure Lakes

Don Farm House, West Carr, Epworth DN9 1LF
t (01427) 872905
w lindhulmelakes.com
open Daily, dawn-dusk.
admission Free

Trout fishing, 4 acres in Epworth near Doncaster, fly only and coarse fishing, 1.5-acre carp fishery, 3-acre silver fish and 12-acre coarse fishing (mixed). Caravan park (touring), tents.

Pleasure Island Family Theme Park

Kings Road, Cleethorpes DN35 0PL
t (01472) 211511
w pleasure-island.co.uk
open Apr-Jun, daily 1030-1600. Jul-Aug, daily 1030-1800. Sep-Oct, daily 1030-1700.
admission £££

Pleasure Island is still the best value day out on the east coast with its fantastic package of over 50 rides and attractions. Adrenaline-draining rides like the Pendulus, Condor and the Alakazam!

Rand Farm Park

Rand, Lincoln LN8 5ND
t (01673) 858904   **w** randfarmpark.com
open Mar-Oct, daily 1000-1800. Nov-Feb, daily 1000-1600.
admission ££

Rand Farm Park is a genuine working farm providing a high quality hands-on learning and fun experience for visitors of all ages. Large variety of animals to hold, feed, touch and cuddle.

Saltburn Smugglers Heritage Centre

Saltburn Smugglers Heritate Centre, Old Saltburn, Saltburn-by-the-Sea TS12 1HF
t (01642) 496418   **w** redcar-cleveland.gov.uk/leisure
open Apr-Sep, daily 1000-1800.
admission £

The award-winning Saltburn Smugglers is set in ancient fishermen's cottages and skillfully blends costumed characters with authentic sounds and smells. Follow the story of John Andrew, 'King of the Smugglers'.

Scalextric Racing

Electric Tracks Ltd,
Angies Plant Centre, Weston Hills Road,
Spalding PE12 6NE
t (01775) 725415   **w** scalextric-racing.co.uk
open Term Time, Tue-Sun 1100-1800. School Hols, daily 1100-1800.
admission ££

Come and race Scalextric cars on five large circuits, Silverstone, Brands Hatch, Catalunya, Edinburgh and Donnington Park. Each circuit has four lanes.

Skegness Pier

Grand Parade, Skegness PE25 2UE
t (01754) 767376
open All year, Mon-Fri 1200-1800, Sat-Sun 1000-2000.
admission Free

Family entertainment centre. Bowling centre with licensed bar. Children and toddlers' indoor adventure playground. Dino's Burger Bar, cash bingo.

Stickney Farm Park

West View Farm, West Fen Lane,
Stickney PE22 8BD
t (01205) 481001   **w** stickneyfarmpark.co.uk
open Mar-Oct, Tue-Sun 1000-1700. Nov-Feb, Tue-Sun 1000-1600.
admission £

A working farm comprising a variety of farm animals and pets, waterfowl pond, lake, picnic areas, play area for ages two to five and playground for ages five to 16. Souvenir shop, tea-room.

The Wragby Maze

Amazing Lodge, Goltho Lane, Wragby LN8 5JS
t (01673) 857372
open Apr-Oct, daily 1000-1700.
admission £

Hedge maze, garden games, picnic area and gardens for all ages to enjoy. Light refreshments are available.

NATURE AND WILDLIFE

Baytree Garden Centre (Owl Centre)
Baytree Nursery, High Road,
Weston PE12 6JU
t (01406) 372840
w baytree-gardencentre.com
open Garden Centre: All year, Mon-Sat 0900-1730, Sun 1100-1700. Owl Centre: Daily 1000-1600.
admission £
A landscaped area with owls from around the world. Daily flying displays will take place in the new indoor arena from March to October (please phone for details).

Butterfly and Wildlife Park
Long Sutton PE12 9LE
t (01406) 363833
w butterflyandwildlifepark.co.uk
open Apr-Oct, daily 1000-1700.
admission ££
One of Britain's largest walk-through butterfly houses with exotic butterflies, reptile land, gift shop, gardens, adventure playground, pets' corner and picnic areas.

Candlesby Herbs
Cross Keys Cottage, Candlesby PE23 5SF
t (01754) 890211
w candlesbyherbs.co.uk
open All year, Tue-Sun, Bank Hols 1000-1700.
admission Free
Specialists in the growing and usage of herbs with plants for sale and display, talks, lectures and demonstrations by arrangement, both on and off site.

Elsham Hall Gardens and Country Park
Elsham Hall, Elsham DN20 0QZ
t (01652) 688698
w elshamhall.co.uk
open Apr-Sep, Wed-Sun 1100-1700.
admission £
Elsham Hall Gardens and Country Park Arboretum. Animal farm, adventure playground, carp and trout lakes with carp feeding jetty and a wild butterfly garden and walkway.

The Garden House
Cliff Road, Saxby, Market Rasen LN8 2DQ
t (01673) 878820
w thegardenhousesaxby.com
open May-Sep, Fri-Sat 1000-1700.
admission £
A large garden with long terrace, Mediterranean, Dutch, damp and dry gardens with woodland, wildflower meadow, ponds, spring bulbs.

Gibraltar Point National Nature Reserve and Visitor Centre
Gibraltar Point Wash Study Centre, Gibraltar Road, Skegness PE24 4SU
t (01754) 762677 **w** lincstrust.org.uk
open Nature reserve: Daily. Visitor Centre: Apr-Oct, daily 1000-1700. Nov-Mar, daily 1000-1600.
admission Free
Nature reserve with 1,500 acres of habitat including sand dunes, salt marsh, sandy shores and freshwater marsh. There is also a visitor and residential centre.

Hartsholme Country Park
Skellingthorpe Road, Lincoln LN6 0EY
t (01522) 873577
open Daily.
admission Free
A 40-hectare country park comprising woodland, lakes and open grassland with a visitor centre and ranger service.

Normanby Hall Country Park
Normanby, Scunthorpe DN15 9HU
t (01724) 720588 **w** northlincs.gov.uk/normanby
open Park: All year 0900-dusk. Hall: Apr-Sep, daily 1300-1700.
admission £
Winners of Yorkshire in Bloom 2001, 2003 & 2004. Whether you love gardens, wildlife or history, or just want a great day out with the family, Normanby is the place to be.

Rose Cottage Water Garden Centre Joinery, Spar and Bird Centre
Glenside North, Pinchbeck PE11 3SD
t (01775) 710882 **w** rosecottagewgc.co.uk
open Apr-Oct, Mon-Fri 0830-1700, Sat 0900-1700, Sun 1000-1600. Nov-Mar, Mon-Fri 0830-1700, Sat 1000-1600, Sun 1100-1500.
admission Free
The UK's largest undercover display of spas and spa buildings. Spa, hot tub and joinery centre. Ponds, pumps, filters, and other aquatic products. Water garden.

RSPB Freiston Shore Nature Reserve
Freiston Shore, Freiston PE22 0LY
t (01205) 724678 **w** rspb.org.uk
open Daily.
admission Free
Freiston Shore is a developing nature reserve with an expanding range of wetland habitats. Situated on the Wash – the most important site in the UK for wintering birds.

Rushmoor Country Park
Louth Road, North Cockerington LN11 7DY
t (01507) 327184 **w** rushmoorpark.co.uk
open Apr-Oct, daily 1000-1700.
admission £
Animal gardens; rare breed poultry with over 40 different breeds. Tearoom and play area for children.

For key to symbols see inside back cover.

Skegness Natureland Seal Sanctuary

North Parade, Skegness PE25 1DB
t (01754) 764345
w skegnessnatureland.co.uk
open Apr-Oct, daily 1000-1700. Nov-Mar, daily 1000-1600.
admission ££

Natureland's work with abandoned seals has become known worldwide. A mix of entertainment and education with feeding time for seals and penguins. A favourite venue for organised party visits.

Skegness Water Leisure Park

Walls Lane, Ingoldmells PE25 1JF
t (01754) 769019
open Mar-Oct, please phone for details.
admission Free

Water leisure park with cable-tow water-skiing and coarse fishing, narrow-gauge railway, touring caravans, tent park and a children's playground.

Tallington Lakes

Barholm Road, Tallington PE9 4RJ
t (01778) 347000
w tallington.com
open See website for details.
admission £

Lakes with windsurfing, water-skiing, adventure playground, beach, picnic area, jet-skiing, a dry ski slope, fishing, canoeing and sailing; also a bar, restaurant and snack bar.

HISTORIC ENGLAND

Belton House, Park and Gardens

Belton NG32 2LS
t (01476) 566116
w nationaltrust.org.uk
open House: Apr-Oct, Wed-Sun 1230-1700. Park: Apr-Jul, Wed-Sun 1100-170.
Aug, daily 1030-1730. Sep-Oct, Wed-Sun 1100-1730.
Garden: Apr-Jul, Wed-Sun 1100-1730. Aug, daily 1030-1730. Sep-Oct, Wed-Sun 1100-1730. Nov, Fri-Sun 1200-1600. Feb, Sat-Sun 1200-1600.
admission ££

The crowning achievement of restoration country house architecture, built 1685-1688 for Sir John Brownlow, with alterations by James Wyatt in 1777. Formal gardens, orangery and landscaped park.

Bolingbroke Castle

Old Bolingbroke PE23 4HJ
t (01529) 461499
w lincsheritage.org
open All year, dawn-dusk.
admission Free

A prime example of 13thC castle design complete with large gatehouse, round towers and moat. Only the ground floors of the towers and the lower parts of the walls remain.

Burghley House

Stamford PE9 3JY
t (01780) 752451
w burghley.co.uk
open Apr-Oct, Mon-Thu, Sat-Sun 1100-1700.
admission ££

The largest and grandest house of the first Elizabethan age. Built between 1555 and 1587, it features fine paintings, tapestries, ceramics and works of art.

Doddington Hall

Doddington, Lincoln LN6 4RU
t (01522) 694308
w doddingtonhall.com
open Hall: May-Sep, Wed, Sun, Bank Hols 1300-1700.
Gardens: May-Sep, Wed, Sun, Bank Hols 1200-1700.
admission ££

Superb Elizabethan mansion by the renowned architect Robert Smythson, standing today as it was completed in 1600 with walled courtyards, turrets, gatehouse. 6 acres of romantic garden.

Ellis Windmill

Burton Road, Lincoln LN1 3LY
t (01522) 528448
w lincolnshire.gov.uk/museumoflincolnshirelife
open Apr-Sep, Sat-Sun 1300-1700. Oct-Mar, Sun 1300-dusk.
admission £

A glorious 18th century working mill next door to the Museum of Lincolnshire Life, run by a dedicated band of volunteer millers who produce and sell flour. Special tours and openings by arrangement.

Epworth Old Rectory

1 Rectory Street,
Epworth DN9 1HX
t (01427) 872268
w epworthrectory.freeserve.co.uk
open Mar-Apr, Oct, Mon-Sat 1000-1230, 1400-1630, Sun 1200-1630. Jun-Aug, Mon-Sat 1000-1630, Sun 1200-1630.
admission £

Epworth Old Rectory, a Queen Anne period house, was the boyhood home of John Wesley founder of World Methodism and his brother Charles who wrote over 700 hymns.

Fenscape

Springfields, Camelgate,
Spalding PE12 6EU
t (01775) 764800
w visitthefens.com
open All year, Mon-Sat 1000-1700, Sun 1030-1600.
admission Free

Discover the fens through interactive and audio visual displays, interpretive sculptures, theatrical sets, graphic panels and more.

Gainsborough Old Hall
Parnell Street,
Gainsborough DN21 2NB
t (01427) 612669
w lincolnshire.gov.uk
open Apr-Oct, Mon-Sat 1000-1700, Sun 1300-1630.
Nov-Mar, Mon-Sat 1000-1700.
admission £

Magnificent medieval manor house in the centre of Gainsborough with original kitchens, great hall and tower. Connections with Richard III, Henry VIII, The Mayflower Pilgrims and John Wesley. Regular exhibitions and events.

Grimsthorpe Castle, Park and Gardens
Estate Office,
Grimsthorpe PE10 0LY
t (01778) 591205
w grimsthorpe.co.uk
open Castle: Apr-Jul, Sep, Thu, Sun, Bank Hols 1300-1700. Aug, Mon-Thu, Sat-Sun 1300-1700. Park: Apr-May, Thu, Sun, Bank Hols 1100-1800. Jun-Sep, Mon-Thu, Sat-Sun 1100-1800.
admission ££

The castle covers four periods of architecture with a collection of portraits and furniture which are mainly 18thC.

Humber Bridge
Ferriby Road,
Hessle HU13 0JG
t (01482) 647161
w humberbridge.co.uk
open Daily.
admission Free

The Humber Bridge is a true masterpiece of civil engineering and the longest single-span suspension bridge in the world.

Julian's Bower
Back Street, Alkborough DN15 9JN
t (01724) 720484
open Daily.
admission Free

Turf-cut maze with explanatory plaque. Panoramic views from the site over the confluence of the rivers Ouse and Trent. Information plaque on places visible from the viewpoint.

Lincoln Castle
Castle Hill, Lincoln LN1 3AA
t (01522) 511068
w lincolnshire.gov.uk/lincolncastle
open Apr-Oct, Mon-Sat 0930-1730, Sun 1100-1730.
Nov-Mar, Mon-Sat 0930-1600, Sun 1100-1600.
admission £

Lincoln Castle is located in the heart of the historic City of Lincoln and is one of the county's leading tourist attractions.

Lincoln Cathedral
Minster Yard, Lincoln LN2 1PX
t (01522) 561600
w lincolncathedral.com
open Apr-Oct, Mon-Fri 0715-2000, Sat-Sun 0715-1800.
Nov-Mar, Mon-Sat 0715-1800, Sun 0715-1700.
admission £

One of the finest medieval buildings in Europe. High on its hill overlooking the ancient city and dominating the skyline for many miles, it has a visual impact nothing less than startling.

Lincoln Medieval Bishops' Palace
Minster Yard, Lincoln LN2 1PU
t (01522) 527468
w english-heritage.org.uk
open See website for details.
admission £

Begun in the 12thC, the Palace reflects the power and wealth of the bishops. Visited by Henry VIII and James I, sacked by Royalists during the Civil War. Medieval vaulting; working vineyard.

Mount Pleasant Windmill
North Cliff Road, Kirton in Lindsey DN21 4NH
t (01652) 640177
w mountpleasantwindmill.co.uk
open All year, Tue-Sun, Bank Hols 1000-1700.
admission £

A traditional four-sailed, brick-tower windmill. Built in 1875 on the Lincoln Cliff overlooking Kirton in Lindsey with extensive views over the Trent Valley and the Yorkshire Wolds. Restored in 1990.

Mrs Smith's Cottage
Craven Cottage, 3 East Road, Navenby LN5 0EP
t (01529) 414294
open See website for details.
admission £

Built in the early 19thC , a remarkable house surviving from a bygone age. The cottage was lived in by Mrs Smith until she was 102 years old.

The Old Smithy and Heritage Centre
High Street, Owston Ferry DN9 1RL
t (01427) 728361
open May-Sep, Sat-Sun 1400-1700.
admission £

The old village blacksmith's shop complete with working forge and old craftsmen's tools and a museum depicting the life of the village.

St Andrews Parish Church
Church Walk, Epworth DN9 1GA
t (01427) 872080
open Daily 0900-1600.
admission Free

Grade I Listed building, 12thC church famous as the church at which Samuel Wesley, father of John and Charles Wesley, was once rector. Many interesting features of church architecture.

Stonebow & Guildhall

Saltergate, Lincoln LN2 1DH
t (01522) 541727 (01522) 873507
w lincoln.gov.uk
open Guided tours: Fri-Sat at 1030 and 1330.
Other times by appointment.
admission Free

The historic Guildhall is the Mayor's official home situated above the Stonebow, once the southern gateway to Roman Lincoln. Tours include the Council Chamber, the City's fine collection of Civic Insignia, the City Charters and much more.

Map ref 4C2

Tattershall Castle

Tattershall LN4 4LR
t (01526) 342543 **w** nationaltrust.org.uk
open Apr-Sep, Mon-Wed, Sun 1100-1730, Sat 1300-1730. Oct, Mon-Wed, Sun 1100-1600, Sat 1300-1600. Nov, Sat, 1300-1600, Sun 1200-1600.
admission £

Tattershall Castle was built in the 15th century, to impress and dominate, by Ralph Cromwell, one of the most powerful men in England.

Waltham Windmill

Brigsley Road, Waltham DN37 0JZ
t (01472) 822236 **w** walthamwindmill.co.uk
open Apr-Jun, Sat-Sun, Bank Hols 1000-1600. Jul-Aug, Tue-Sun 1000-1600. Sep, Sat-Sun, Bank Hols 1000-1600.
admission £

The present six-storey tower windmill was built in 1878-80 by John Saunderson of Louth using light coloured bricks and tarring. Restored in recent years to working order.

Wrawby Windmill

Mill Lane, Wrawby DN20 8RA
t (01652) 653699
open All year, Bank Hols 1400-1700.
admission £

The last working post mill in the North of England. Small museum of old milling tools with postcards and pictures for sale.

OUTDOOR ACTIVITIES

Ancholme Valley Clay Target Club

Kirton in Lindsey Airfield, Kirton in Lindsey DN21 4HZ
t (01777) 818362 **w** ancholme-valley-ctc.org.uk
open All year, Wed 1200-1500, Sat 1200-1500, Sun 1030-1500.
admission £

The club provides clay-pigeon shooting facilities. Disciplines include English skeet, down the line, automatic ball trap and English sporting. Tuition, by appointment, for beginners, individuals or groups.

Cathedral City Cruises

PO Box 832, Lincoln LN1 1WT
t (01522) 546853 **w** lincoln-cruises.co.uk
open All year, Mon-Sun 1100-1600, weather permitting.
admission £

Captain Ian Smith and his crew are pleased to welcome you aboard. Enjoy a relaxing cruise and see Lincoln and its surrounding area from the comfort of the MV 'City of Lincoln'.

ENTERTAINMENT AND CULTURE

20-21 Visual Arts Centre

St John's Church, Church Square, Scunthorpe DN15 6TB
t (01724) 297070 **w** northlincs.gov.uk/20-21
open All year, Tue-Sat 1000-1700.
admission Free

Following four years of research and development and 15 months of construction work, the church, a Grade II* Listed building, has been converted into a visual arts centre, offering exhibitions, activities and events.

Ayscoughfee Hall Museum and Gardens

Churchgate, Spalding PE11 2RA
t (01775) 764555 **w** ayscoughfee.org
open Apr-Sep, Tue, Wed, Fri 1030-1700, Thu 1200-1700, Sat-Sun 1030-1600. Oct-Mar, Tue-Fri 1200-1700, Sat-Sun 0930-1600.
admission Free

A beautiful, late-medieval wool merchant's house on the banks of the River Welland. There have been Regency and Victorian alterations to the original 1420s design.

Battle of Britain Memorial Flight Centre

RAF Coningsby, Coningsby LN4 4SY
t (01526) 344041 **w** lincolnshire.gov.uk/bbmf
open All year, Mon-Fri 1000-1700.
admission £

The flight centre operates a Lancaster, five Spitfires, two Hurricanes, two Chipmunks and a Dakota. Guided tours, permanent gallery, temporary exhibitions, shop.

Baysgarth House Museum

Baysgarth Leisure Park, Caistor Road,
Barton-upon-Humber DN18 6AH
t (01652) 637568
open All year, Fri-Sun 1200-1600.
admission Free

An 18thC townhouse set in over 30 acres of park, containing a fine collection of 18thC and 19thC English and Oriental porcelain and pottery. Changing temporary exhibitions.

Collectors World

Springfields, Camelgate, Spalding PE12 6UE
t (01775) 761161 **w** collectors-world.org
open Daily 1100-1700.
admission ££

Possibly Norfolk's greatest eccentric and prolific collector, the original Mr 'Norfolk Punch' himself, Eric St John-Foti has displayed his extraordinary lifetime collections, which are open to the public all year round.

Gordon Boswell Romany Museum

Clay Lake, Spalding PE12 6BL
t (01775) 710599 **w** boswell-romany-museum.com
open Apr-Oct, Fri-Sun 1030-1700.
admission £

The Gordon Boswell Museum is a unique experience for all the family, containing one of the country's finest collections of Romany vardos (gypsy caravans) carts and harnesses.

Grantham Museum

St. Peters Hill, Grantham NG31 6PY
t (01476) 568783
w lincolnshire.gov.uk/granthammuseum
open All year, Mon-Sat, Bank Hols 1000-1700.
admission Free

'This is a neat, pleasant, well-built and populous town' – Daniel Defoe 1720s. The museum interprets the archaeology and history of this market town and includes Sir Isaac Newton, the Dambusters and Margaret Thatcher.

Immingham Museum

Margaret Street, Immingham DN40 1LE
t (01469) 575777 **w** nelincs.gov.uk
open All year, Mon-Fri 1300-1600.
admission Free

The Great Central Railway and the creation of a port. The impact of GCR on town and area. GCR artefacts, archive material and photographs. Also LNER and later local history; archaeology gallery.

Lincolnshire Road Transport Museum

Whisby Road, North Hykeham LN6 3QT
t (01522) 689497 **w** lvvs.org.uk
open May-Oct, Mon-Fri 1200-1600, Sun 1000-1600.
Nov-Apr, Sun 1300-1600.
admission £

Historic road transport vehicles from the 1920s to the 1980s. Most vehicles have a strong association with Lincolnshire and are in restored condition. Includes cars, lorries, buses and fire engines.

Museum Of Lincolnshire Life

Burton Road, Lincoln LN1 3LY
t (01522) 528448
w lincolnshire.gov.uk/museumoflincolnshirelife
open Apr-Sep, daily 1000-1700. Oct-Mar, Mon-Sat 1000-1700.
admission £

The museum is situated in an old barracks originally built for the Loyal North Lincoln Militia in 1857. The museum contains large and significant collections covering all aspects of social history.

National Bubble & Microcar Museum

The Beeches, Byards Leap, Cranwell NG34 8EY
t (01400) 262637 **w** bubblecarmuseum.co.uk
open See website for details.
admission £

A museum dedicated to bubble and microcars from the 50s, 60s and 70s with over 70 exhibits. Archives and memorabilia. Camping and rally fields.

Gibraltar Point National Nature Reserve

For key to symbols see inside back cover.

National Fishing Heritage Centre

Alexandra Dock, Grimsby DN31 1UZ
t (01472) 323345
open Apr-Oct, Mon-Fri 1000-1700, Sat-Sun 1030-1730.
Nov-Mar, Mon-Fri 1000-1600, Sat-Sun 1100-1500.
admission ££
Prepare to be blasted by freezing winds and lashing rain, feel the trawler decks heave and moan beneath your feet.

North Lincolnshire Museum

Oswald Road, Scunthorpe DN15 7BD
t (01724) 843533
w northlincs.gov.uk
open All year, Tue-Sat, Bank Hols 1000-1600, Sun 1300-1600.
admission Free
Regional museum for North Lincolnshire. Archaeology, local history, plus geology and countryside gallery. Exhibition galleries featuring a constantly-changing programme of temporary exhibitions. Courtyard garden.

Ropewalk Contemporary Art and Craft

Maltkiln Road, Barton upon Humber DN18 5JT
t (01652) 660380
w the-ropewalk.com
open All year, Tue-Sat 1000-1700, Sun, Bank Hols 1000-1600.
admission Free
Opened as an arts centre and heritage display in April 2000. Formerly Hall's rope-making factory, the building sits on the southern bank of the Humber, east of the bridge.

Spalding Flower Bulb Museum

Surfleet Road, Pinchbeck PE11 3XY
t (01775) 680490 **w** birchgrovegc.co.uk
open Apr-Oct, Mon-Sat 0930-1630, Sun 1030-1530.
admission Free
The museum shows how horticulture and agriculture shaped the lives of local people in and around Spalding over the last 120 years, including the famous tulip-growing industry.

Ye Olde Curiosity Museum

61a Victoria Road, Mablethorpe LN12 2AF
t (01507) 472406
open Apr-Oct, daily 1000-1700. Nov-Mar, daily 1000-1600.
admission Free
Old glass lampshades, memorabilia and bygones during the last 100 years such as a Morris Minor estate, irons, kettles, bed warmers, dollypegs, Christmas decorations and lights.

RELAXING AND PAMPERING

Kirton Pottery

36 High Street, Kirton in Lindsey DN21 4LX
t (01652) 648867
open All year, Thu-Sat 1000-1700.
admission Free
The pottery produces colourful earthenware, painted with birds, animals and flowers, and stoneware pottery using the rich effects produced in a reducing gas-fired kiln.

Lincoln Cathedral viewed from the Observatory Tower at Lincoln Castle

Norfolk

Enjoy the fun of a special event or visit one of the attractions listed for a great day out. For more inspiring ideas go to **enjoyengland.com.**

18–24 Jun
George Vancouver 250th Festival
King's Lynn
(01553) 779095
west-norfolk.co.uk

27–28 Jun
Royal Norfolk Show
Norfolk Showground, New Costessey, Norwich
(01603) 748931
royalnorfolkshow.co.uk

11–15 Jul
Lord Mayor's Celebration
Norwich
(01603) 212136
norwich.gov.uk

18 Jul–9 Sep
Hippodrome Summer Spectacular
& Watershow
Great Yarmouth
(01493) 780223
hippodromecircus.co.uk

21 Jul
World Snail Racing Championships
Congham, nr King's Lynn
(01485) 600650
scase.co.uk/snailracing

FAMILY FUN

Bressingham Steam Experience and Gardens
Bressingham IP22 2AB
t (01379) 686900 **w** bressingham.co.uk
open Apr, Sep, Oct, daily 1030-1700. May-Aug, daily 1030-1730.
admission ££
For a fun-packed family day out, you have to go a long way to beat Bressingham Steam Museum and Bressingham Gardens.

Britannia Pier
Marine Parade, Great Yarmouth NR30 2EH
t (01493) 842914 **w** britannia-pier.co.uk
open Apr-Oct, daily 0800-0400.
admission Free
Arcades, children's rides, restaurants and fun fair. Two bars with family rooms and theatre.

Caithness Crystal Visitor Centre
Paxman Road, Hardwick Industrial Estate, King's Lynn PE30 4NE
t (01553) 765111 **w** caithness-crystal.co.uk
open All year, Mon-Sat 0900-1700, Sun 1000-1600.
admission Free
See glass-making at close quarters, watching the skill of our glass makers as they shape and blow the glass in the manner used for centuries. The factory shop sells giftware.

The Dinosaur Adventure Park
Weston Park, Lenwade NR9 5JW
t (01603) 876310 **w** dinosaurpark.co.uk
open Mar-Jun, daily 1000-1700. Jul-Aug, daily 1000-1730. Sep-Oct, daily 1000-1700. Nov-Mar, 1000-1600.
admission ££
A unique family day out. Attractions include the dinosaur trail, woodland maze, secret animal garden, Climb-a-Saurus, adventure play areas and education centre.

Thurne Dyke Wind Pump, Norfolk Broads

Admission is based on an adult price. Please check opening times and admission before travelling.

Ecotech Centre

Turbine Way, Swaffham PE37 7HT
t (01760) 726100 **w** ecotech.org.uk
open Mon-Fri 1000-1600 (excl Bank Holidays).
May-Sep, open on last Sunday in the month.
admission Free

Environmental visitor attraction, with an organic
garden/heritage seed orchard, cafe and shop.
We have an Ecotricity E66 climbable wind
turbine situated in our grounds (subject to
health and safety rules, charges apply and
booking is recommended, please phone
01760 726100).

          Map ref 3B1

Joyland – Coles Amusement Enterprises Ltd

Marine Parade, Great Yarmouth NR30 2EH
t (01493) 844094 **w** joyland.org.uk
open Apr-Oct, see website for details.
admission Free

Joyland is a delightful family fun park for young children, with the world famous snails and tub twist.

Langham Glass

The Long Barn, North Street,
Langham NR25 7DG
t (01328) 830511 **w** langhamglass.co.uk
open Apr-Oct, daily 1000-1700. Nov-Mar, Mon-Fri
1000-1700.
admission £

Glassmakers can be seen working with molten glass from the furnace using blowing irons. Situated in a lovely flint-faced Norfolk barn complex. Seven acre maize maze.

Merrivale Model Village

Marine Parade, Great Yarmouth NR30 3JG
t (01493) 842097
w greatyarmouthmodelvillage.co.uk
open Apr-Oct, daily 1000, please phone for details.
admission £

Step into our miniature world of town and countryside that sits in an acre of landscaped gardens with lake, streams & new garden railway. Not forgetting the Old Penny Museum.

Mid-Norfolk Railway

County School Station, Holt Road,
North Elmham NR20 5LE
t (01362) 668181 **w** mnr.org.uk
open See website for details.
admission ££

Station built in 1884 is northern outpost of Mid-Norfolk Railway. Situated in the heart of the unspoilt Wensum Valley. Tearoom, small exhibition and walks.

North Norfolk Railway Sheringham Station

The Station, Sheringham NR26 8RA
t (01263) 820800
w nnrailway.co.uk
open See website for details.
admission ££

A five-mile long heritage railway with stations at Sheringham, Weybourne and Holt. Steam trains daily through the summer.

The Playbarn

West Green Farm, Shotesham Road,
Poringland NR14 7LP
t (01508) 495526
w theplaybarn.co.uk
open All year, Mon-Fri 0930-1530, Sun 1000-1700.
admission £

Children's indoor and outdoor play centre. Designed for 7s and under. Large barn and courtyards, beach barn, children's farm, riding school and after-school club.

Pleasure Beach

South Beach Parade, Great Yarmouth NR30 3EH
t (01493) 844585
w pleasure-beach.co.uk
open Please phone for details.
admission Free

Rollercoaster, log flume, twister, monorail, galloping horses, caterpillar, ghost train and fun house. Height restrictions are in force on some rides.

Snettisham Park

Snettisham PE31 7NQ
t (01485) 542425
w snettishampark.co.uk
open Feb-Oct, daily 1000-1700.
admission ££

Providing unique safari tours, a visitor centre, crafts centre, art gallery, tearoom and souvenir shop. Indoor and outdoor activities include farm animals and pets.

South Creake Maize Maze

Compton Hall, South Creake NR21 9JD
t (01328) 823224
w amazingmaizemaze.co.uk
open Jul-Sep, daily 1000-1800.
admission £

The amazing South Creake maize maze. Acres of maze and miles of pathways. Come and discover the history of one of our greatest admirals. Ship, cannons and muskets.

Wells Walsingham Railway

Stiffkey Road, Wells-next-the-Sea NR23 1QB
t (01328) 710631
w wellswalsinghamrailway.co.uk
open Apr-Oct, see website for details.
admission ££

Four miles of railway. The longest 10.25-inch railway in the world with a new steam locomotive, Norfolk Hero, now in service, the largest of its kind ever built.

NATURE AND WILDLIFE

Amazonia – World of Reptiles
Central Seafront, Marine Parade,
Great Yarmouth NR30 3AH
t (01493) 842202
w amazonia-worldofreptiles.net
open Apr-Oct, daily 1000-1900. Nov-Mar, daily 1000-1700.
admission £

Amazonia – World of Reptiles has one of the largest collections of reptiles in the country, set in a beautiful tropical garden for the ultimate jungle experience.

Banham Zoo
The Grove, Banham NR16 2HE
t (01953) 887771
w banhamzoo.co.uk
open Apr-Jun, daily 1000-1700. Jul-Aug, daily 1000-1730. Sep-Oct, daily 1000-1700. Nov-Mar, daily 1000-1600.
admission ££

Wildlife spectacular which will take you on a journey to experience tigers, leopards and zebra plus some of the world's most exotic, rare and endangered animals.

Congham Hall Herb Garden
Lynn Road, Grimston PE32 1AH
t (01485) 600250
open Apr-Oct, daily 1400-1600.
admission Free

Garden with over 650 varieties of herbs in formal beds with wild flowers and a potager garden. Over 250 varieties of herbs for sale in pots.

East Ruston Old Vicarage Garden
East Ruston Old Vicarage, East Ruston NR12 9HN
t (01692) 650432
w e-ruston-oldvicaragegardens.co.uk
open Apr-Oct, Wed, Fri, Sat-Sun, Bank Hols 1400-1730.
admission £

A 20-acre exotic garden separated into sections including the Tropical Borders, Mediterranean Garden, Sunken Garden, Autumn Borders, Kitchen Garden and Wildflower Meadows.

Eau Brink Cacti
Eau Brink Road, Tilney All Saints PE34 4SQ
t (01553) 617635
open Mar-Oct, Mon-Thu, Sun 1000-1700. Nov-Feb, please phone for details.
admission Free

Half an acre of greenhouses housing owner's collection of approximately 1000 mature cacti and succulents grown by the owner from seed over the last 40 years.

Fairhaven Woodland and Water Garden
School Road, South Walsham NR13 6DZ
t (01603) 270449 **w** fairhavengarden.co.uk
open May-Aug, daily 1000-1700. Sep-Apr, daily 1000-1600.
admission £

Delightful natural woodland and water garden with private broad and a 950-year-old oak tree. Spring flowers, candelabra primulas, azaleas and rhododendrons.

Fritton Lake Country World
Church Lane, Fritton NR31 9HA
t (01493) 488288
open Apr-Sep, daily 1000-1730.
admission ££

A 250-acre centre with a children's assault course, putting, an adventure playground, golf, fishing, boating, wildfowl, heavy horses, cart rides, falconry and flying displays.

Gooderstone Water Gardens
The Street, Gooderstone PE33 9BP
t (01603) 712913 **w** gooderstonewatergardens.co.uk
open Daily 1000-1800.
admission £

Water gardens covering 6.5 acres, with trout stream, four ponds, waterways, mature trees, colourful plants, nature trails, 13 bridges. Tearoom with home-made cakes & disabled toilets.

Great Yarmouth Sealife
Marine Parade, Great Yarmouth NR30 3AH
t (01493) 330631
open Apr-Sep, daily 1000-1730. Nov-Mar, please phone for details.
admission ££

Great Yarmouth Sealife Centre takes visitors on a fascinating seabed stroll from local waters through to tropical depths.

Hillside Animal Sanctuary
Hill Top Farm, Hall Lane, Frettenham NR12 7LT
t (01603) 736200 **w** hillside.org.uk
open Apr-May, Sun, Bank Hols 1300-1700. Jun-Aug, Mon, Sun, Bank Hols 1300-1700. Sep-Oct, Sun, Bank Hols 1300-1700.
admission £

Visit our rescued farm animals. Information centre and gift shop. Two self-catering holiday cottages onsite for rent.

Hoveton Hall Gardens
Hoveton Hall, Wroxham NR12 8RJ
t (01603) 782798 **w** hovetonhallgardens.co.uk
open Apr, Sun, Bank Hols 1030-1700. May-Aug, Wed-Fri, Sun, Bank Hols 1030-1700. Aug, Sun, Bank Hols 1030-1700.
admission £

Approximately 15 acres of gardens in a woodland setting with a large walled herbaceous garden and a Victorian kitchen garden. There are also woodland and lakeside walks.

 For key to symbols see inside back cover.

Hunstanton Sea Life Sanctuary
Southern Promenade, Hunstanton PE36 5BH
t (01485) 533576 w sealsanctuary.co.uk
open Apr-Sep, daily 1000-1700. Oct-Mar, daily
1000-1500.
admission ££
*Ocean tunnel. See a world which experienced divers
see. See and touch rock pool creatures. Also a
rehabilitation centre for unwell or abandoned seals,
otters and penguin sanctuary.*

Mannington Gardens and Countryside
Mannington Hall, Norwich NR11 7BB
t (01263) 584175 w manningtongardens.co.uk
open Gardens: May, Sep, Sun 1200-1700. Jun-Aug,
Wed-Fri 1100-1700. Countryside: Daily.
admission £
*Gardens with a lake, moat, woodland and an
outstanding rose collection. There is also a Saxon church
with Victorian follies, countryside walks and trails with
guide booklets.*

Norfolk Lavender Limited
Caley Mill, Heacham PE31 7JE
t (01485) 570384 w norfolk-lavender.co.uk
open Apr-Oct, daily 0900-1700. Nov-Mar, daily
0900-1600.
admission Free
*Lavender is distilled from the flowers and the oil made
into a wide range of gifts. There is a slide show when the
distillery is not working.*

Pensthorpe Nature Reserve and Gardens
Pensthorpe NR21 0LN
t (01328) 851465 w pensthorpe.com
open Apr-Dec, daily 1000-1700. Jan-Mar, daily
1000-1600.
admission ££
*Waterfowl and wildfowl collections with information
centre, conservation shop, adventure play area, walks,
nature trails and a licensed restaurant and Wensum
discovery tour.*

Peter Beales Roses
London Road, Attleborough NR17 1AY
t (01953) 454707
open All year, Mon-Sat 0900-1700, Sun, Bank Hols
1000-1600.
admission Free
*Two and a half acres of display rose garden set in rural
surroundings.*

The Plantation Garden
4 Earlham Road, Norwich NR2 3DB
t (01603) 624256 w plantationgarden.co.uk
open Daily 0900-1800.
admission £
*A rare surviving example of a private Victorian town
garden, created between 1856-1897 in a former
medieval chalk quarry and undergoing restoration by
volunteers.*

Raveningham Gardens
The Stables, Raveningham NR14 6NS
t (01508) 548152
w raveningham.com
open Apr-Aug, Mon-Fri 1100-1600, Bank Hols
1400-1700.
admission £
*Extensive gardens surrounding an elegant Georgian
house provide the setting for many rare, variegated and
unusual plants and shrubs, with sculptures, parkland and
a church.*

Redwings Horse Sanctuary

Hapton, Norwich NR15 1SP
t 0870 040 0033 w redwings.co.uk
open Caldecott (Norfolk), Stonham (Suffolk):
1 Apr-28 Oct 1000-1700. Ada Cole (Essex): all
year 1000-1700.
admission Free

Redwings was established in 1984 and has
grown to become the largest horse charity in
the UK. Visit rescued horses, ponies, donkeys
and mules in beautiful surroundings at one of
the charity's three East of England visitor
centres. Free admission.

                          Map ref 3B1

 voucher offer – see back section

RSPB Titchwell Marsh Nature Reserve
Main Road, Titchwell PE31 8BB
t (01485) 210779
w rspb.org.uk
open Daily.
admission Free
*Nature reserve with three bird-watching hides and two
trails. Visitor centre with large shop, food servery, large
car park and toilets.*

Sheringham Park

Upper Sheringham NR28 8TB
t (01263) 821429 **w** nationaltrust.org.uk
open Daily, dawn-dusk.
admission Free

Park with rhododendrons, woodland and spectacular views of the park and coastline. There is a car parking charge.

Thrigby Hall Wildlife Gardens

Thrigby Hall, Filby NR29 3DR
t (01493) 369477
open Apr-Oct, daily 1000-1700. Nov-Mar, daily 1000-1600.
admission ££

A wide selection of Asian mammals, birds, reptiles, tigers, crocodiles and storks. A 250-year-old landscaped garden with play area and willow pattern gardens.

Walpole Water Gardens

Chalk Road, Walpole St Peter PE14 7PH
t 07718 745935 **w** walpolewatergardens.co.uk
open Apr-Oct, daily 1000-1900. Nov-Mar, daily 1000-2100.
admission Free

Dominated by water and rocks, with sub-tropical atmosphere, 0.75 acres. Eucalyptus, rockeries and palms. Koi carp, black swans, ducks and peacocks.

West Acre Gardens

King's Lynn, West Acre PE32 1UJ
t (01760) 755562 **w** west-norfolk.gov.uk
open Feb-Nov, daily 1000-1700.
admission Free

D-shaped walled garden with extensive display beds with year-round interest and beauty.

Wildfowl and Wetlands Trust

Hundred Foot Bank, Welney PE14 9TN
t (01353) 860711 **w** wwt.org.uk
open Mar-Oct, daily 0930-1700. Nov-Feb, Mon-Tue 1000-1700, Wed-Sun 1000-2000.
admission £

A wetland nature reserve of 1,000 acres attracting large numbers of ducks and swans in winter and waders in spring and summer, plus a range of wild plants and butterflies.

Bircham Windmill

Great Bircham PE31 6SJ
t (01485) 578393
open Apr-Sep, daily 1000-1700.
admission £

A Norfolk windmill with working machinery and a small working bakery. There are also tearooms, ponies and cycle hire.

Blakeney Guildhall

Blakeney
t (01223) 582766
w english-heritage.org.uk
open See website for details.
admission Free

The remains of the 14thC basement to a merchant's house, which was most likely used for storage.

Blickling Hall

Blickling NR11 6NF
t (01263) 738030
w nationaltrust.org.uk
open Apr-Jun, Wed-Sun 1300-1700. Jul-Aug, Mon, Wed-Sun 1300-1700. Sep-Oct, Wed-Sun 1300-1700.
admission ££

A Jacobean redbrick mansion with garden, orangery, parkland and lake. Spectacular long gallery, plasterwork ceilings and fine collections of furniture, pictures, books & walks.

Castle Acre Castle

Castle Acre PE32 2AF
t (01760) 755394
w english-heritage.org.uk
open Daily, 0900-dusk.
admission Free

The remains of a Norman manor house which became a castle with earthworks, set by the side of a village.

Castle Rising Castle

Castle Rising PE31 6AH
t (01553) 631330
w english-heritage.org.uk
open Apr-Sep, daily 1000-1800. Nov-Mar, Wed-Sun 1000-1600.
admission £

Castle Rising Castle is a fine example of a Norman castle. The rectangular keep, one of the largest, was built around 1140 by William D'Albini.

Dragon Hall

115-123 King Street, Norwich NR1 1QE
t (01603) 663922
w dragonhall.org
open Mar-Dec, Mon-Fri 1000-1700, Sun 1100-1600.
admission £

Medieval merchant's hall with outstanding timber-framed structure. The 15thC Great Hall has a crown-post roof with an intricately carved and painted dragon.

Felbrigg Hall

Felbrigg NR11 8PR
t (01263) 837444
w nationaltrust.org.uk
open Apr-Oct, Mon-Wed, Sat-Sun 1300-1700.
admission ££

A 17thC country house with original 18thC furniture and pictures. There is also a walled garden, orangery, park and woodland with waymarked walks, shops and catering.

Grimes Graves

The Exhibition Building, Lynford IP26 5DE
t (01842) 810656 **w** english-heritage.org.uk
open See website for details.
admission £

Neolithic flint mines. Five thousand years old and first excavated in the 1870s with over 300 pits and shafts, one open to the public.

Hales Hall Barn and Gardens

Hales Hall, Loddon NR14 6QW
t (01508) 548507 **w** haleshall.com
open Apr-Oct, Wed-Sun 1100-1600. Nov-Mar, Wed-Sat 1100-1600.
admission £

Fortified manor with fabulous 180ft brick barn, built by Henry VII's attorney general, Sir James Hobart. Gardens with topiary, fruit, pottager, greenhouses & exotic plants.

Holkham Hall

Wells-next-the-Sea NR23 1AB
t (01328) 710227
open Jun-Sep, Mon-Thu, Sun 1200-1700.
admission ££

A classic 18thC Palladian-style mansion. Part of a great agricultural estate and a living treasure house of artistic and architectural history along with a bygones collection.

Houghton Hall

Houghton PE31 6UE
t (01485) 528569 **w** houghtonhall.com
open Apr-Sep, Wed-Thu, Sun, Bank Hols 1330-1700.
admission ££

Built in the 18thC with superb staterooms. Five-acre walled garden provides colour all summer. Unique collection of 20,000 model soldiers. Restaurant, shop and picnic area.

Norwich Cathedral

62 The Close, Norwich NR1 4EH
t (01603) 218321 **w** cathedral.org.uk
open May-Sep, daily 0700-1800. Oct-Apr, daily 0730-1800.
admission £

A Norman cathedral from 1096 with 14thC roof bosses depicting bible scenes from Adam and Eve to the Day of Judgement, cloisters, cathedral close, shop and restaurant.

Oxburgh Hall

Oxborough PE33 9PS
t (01366) 328258 **w** nationaltrust.org.uk
open Apr-Jul, Mon-Wed, Sat-Sun 1300-1700. Aug, daily 1300-1700. Sep, Mon-Wed, Sat-Sun 1300-1700. Oct, Mon-Wed, Sat-Sun 1300-1600.
admission ££

A 15thC moated redbrick fortified manor house with an 80ft gatehouse, Mary Queen of Scot's needlework, a Catholic priest's hole, garden, woodland walks and a Catholic chapel.

Roman Catholic Cathedral of St John The Baptist

Unthank Road, Norwich NR2 2PA
t (01603) 624615
w stjohncathedral.co.uk
open Daily 0700-2000.
admission Free

A particularly fine example of 19thC gothic revival by George Gilbert Scott Junior, with fine stained glass, exquisite stonewalk and Frosterley marble.

Sandringham

Sandringham PE35 6EN
t (01553) 612908
w sandringhamestate.co.uk
open House: Apr-Oct, daily 1100-1645. Museum: daily 1100-1700. Gardens: daily 1030-1700.
admission ££

The country retreat of HM The Queen. A delightful house set in 60 acres of gardens and lakes. There is also a museum of royal vehicles and royal memorabilia.

Shrine of our Lady of Walsingham

Holt Road, Walsingham NR22 6BW
t (01328) 820239
open Daily, dawn-dusk.
admission Free

A pilgrimage church containing the Holy House, standing in extensive grounds.

Wymondham Abbey

Vicar Street, Wymondham NR18 0PL
t (01953) 602269
w wymondhamabbey.nildram.co.uk
open Apr, Mon-Sat 1000-1600. May-Oct, Mon-Sat 1000-1700. Nov, Mon-Sat 1000-1600. Dec-Mar, Mon-Sat 1000-1500.
admission Free

Magnificent Norman church, built 1107, with ruins of former Benedictine abbey. Splendid interior with angel roofs, two 18thC organs and gold-faced reredos. Shop on site.

OUTDOOR ACTIVITIES

Broads Tours

The Bridge, Wroxham NR12 8RX
t (01603) 782207
open Apr-May, daily 1130-1400. Jun, Mon-Thu 1030-1500, Fri 1130-1600, Sat 1130-1400, Sun 1130-1400. Jul-Aug, Mon-Thu 1030-1600, Fri-Sat 1130-1600, Sun 1130-1500. Sep, Mon-Thu 1130-1500, Fri-Sun 1130-1400. Oct, daily 1130-1400.
admission ££

Leading passenger-boat company on the Norfolk Broads with a choice of boats including luxury double-deckers with bar facilities and traditional river bus.

Ecotech Centre

Turbine Way, Swaffham PE37 7HT
t (01760) 726100 **w** ecotech.org.uk
open Mon-Fri 1000-1600 (excl Bank Holidays).
May-Sep, open on last Sunday in the month.
admission Free

Environmental visitor attraction, with an organic
garden/heritage seed orchard, cafe and shop.
We have an Ecotricity E66 climbable wind
turbine situated in our grounds (subject to
health and safety rules, charges apply and
booking is recommended, please phone
01760 726100).

                Map ref 3B1

Redwings Horse Sanctuary

Hapton, Norwich NR15 1SP
t 0870 040 0033 **w** redwings.co.uk
open Caldecott (Norfolk), Stonham (Suffolk):
1 Apr-28 Oct 1000-1700. Ada Cole (Essex): all
year 1000-1700.
admission Free

Redwings was established in 1984 and has
grown to become the largest horse charity in
the UK. Visit rescued horses, ponies, donkeys
and mules in beautiful surroundings at one of
the charity's three East of England visitor
centres. Free admission.

                Map ref 3B1

 voucher offer – see back section

Temple Seal Trips
The Anchor, The Street, Morston NR25 7AA
t (01263) 740791 **w** sealtrips.co.uk
open Please phone for details.
admission ££

*Daily boat trips to see common and grey seals basking
on Blakeney Point. Boats leave from Morston Quay
according to tides.*

ENTERTAINMENT AND CULTURE

Bridewell Museum
Bridewell Alley, Norwich NR2 1AQ
t (01603) 629127 **w** museums.norfolk.gov.uk
open Apr-Oct, Tue-Fri 1000-1630, Sat 1000-1700.
admission £

*A museum with displays illustrating local industry during
the past 200 years with a recreated 1920s pharmacy and
a 1930s pawnbroker's shop. There are also temporary
exhibits.*

Charles Burrell Museum
Minstergate, Thetford IP24 1BN
t (01842) 751166
open Please phone for details.
admission Free

*The Charles Burrell Steam Museum draws together an
impressive collection of exhibits to tell the story of
Charles Burrell and Son (1770-1932).*

Cromer Museum
East Cottages, Tucker Street, Cromer NR27 9HB
t (01263) 513543
open Apr-Oct, Mon-Sat 1000-1700, Sun 1400-1700.
Nov-Mar, Mon-Sat 1000-1600.
admission £

*A late-Victorian fisherman's cottage with displays of local
history (fishing, bathing resort), geology, natural history
and archaeology.*

Fenland and West Norfolk Aviation Museum: Bambers Garden Centre
Old Lynn Road, West Walton PE14 7DA
t (01945) 463996
open Mar-Oct, Sat-Sun 0930-1630.
admission £

*Vampire T11 and Lightning aircraft. Uniforms, aero
engines, aircraft components, artefacts, memorabilia,
radio equipment, souvenirs, models and jumbo jet
cockpit.*

Great Yarmouth Row Houses

South Quay, Great Yarmouth NR30 2RQ
t (01493) 857900 **w** english-heritage.org.uk
open See website for details.
admission £

*Typical 17thC townhouses, one with splendid plaster
ceilings containing local original architectural and
domestic fittings salvaged from other row houses.*

For key to symbols see inside back cover.

Iceni Village and Museums
Cockley Cley, Swaffham PE37 8AG
t (01760) 724588
open Apr-Jun, daily 1130-1730. Jul-Aug, daily
1030-1730. Sep-Oct, daily 1130-1730.
admission £
Iceni tribal village reconstruction, believed to be on the original site. Medieval cottage and forge with museum, Saxon church 630AD, carriage, vintage engine and farm museum.

Inspire Discovery Centre
St Michael's Church, Coslany Street, Norwich NR3 3DT
t (01603) 612612 **w** inspirediscoverycentre.com
open All year, Mon-Fri 1000-1700, Sat-Sun 1100-1700.
admission £
Inspire is a hands-on science centre housed in a medieval church. Suitable for all ages, it allows everyone to explore and discover the wonders of science for themselves.

Muckleburgh Collection
Weybourne Old Military Camp,
Weybourne NR25 7EG
t (01263) 588210 **w** muckleburgh.co.uk
open Apr-Oct, daily 1000-1700.
admission ££
Collection of over 130 military vehicles and heavy equipment used by the allied armies during and since World War II, including fighting tanks, armoured cars and artillery.

Mundesley Maritime Museum
Beach Road, Mundesley NR11 8BG
t (01263) 720879
open May-Sep, daily 1100-1300, 1400-1600.
admission £
The former coastguard lookout point contains photographs, prints and artefacts illustrating Mundesley's maritime and village history. The first floor has been reinstated as a lookout.

The Museum of the Broads
Stalham Staithe, Stalham NR12 9BZ
t (01692) 581681
w northnorfolk.org/museumofthebroads/
open Apr-Oct, daily 1030-1700.
admission £
Displays of tools from the traditional Broads industries and many Broads boats.

The Mustard Shop
15 The Royal Arcade, Norwich NR2 1AQ
t (01603) 627889 **w** colmansmustardshop.com
open All year, Mon-Sat 0930-1700, Bank Hols 1100-1600.
admission Free
Nineteenth-century-style shop housing a museum with displays tracing the history of Colman's mustard. Situated in a Victorian arcade decorated in art noveau style.

Norfolk Motor Cycle Museum
Railway Yard, North Walsham NR28 0DS
t (01692) 406266
open Apr-Oct, daily 1000-1630. Nov-Mar, Mon-Sat 1000-1630.
admission £
A museum displaying a wide collection of motorcycles dating from 1920-1960. Also old bicycles and die cast toys.

Norfolk Nelson Museum
21 South Quay, Great Yarmouth NR30 2RG
t (01493) 850698 **w** nelson-museum.co.uk
open Apr-Oct, Mon-Fri 1000-1700, Sat-Sun 1300-1600.
admission £
Visit the Norfolk Nelson Museum to find out about Admiral Lord Horatio Nelson and his life and times, career and life on board ship.

Norwich Castle
Shirehall, Market Avenue, Norwich NR1 3JQ
t (01603) 493625 **w** museums.norfolk.gov.uk
open Term Time: Mon-Fri 1000-1630, Sat 1000-1700, Sun 1300-1700. School Hols: Mon-Sat 1000-1730, Sun 1300-1700.
admission £
The ancient Norman keep of Norwich Castle dominates the city and is one of the most important buildings of its kind in Europe.

Origins Visitor Attraction
The Forum, Millenium Plain, Norwich NR2 1TF
t (01603) 727922 **w** originsnorwich.co.uk
open All year, Mon-Sat 1000-1715, Sun 1100-1645.
admission ££
Origins is Norfolk's most original and interactive experience, equally popular with visitors and local people. It has three floors of imaginative and interactive exhibits.

Roots of Norfolk at Gressenhall
Norfolk Rural Life Museum,
Gressenhall NR20 4DR
t (01362) 860563 **w** museums.norwich.gov.uk
open Apr-Oct, daily 1000-1700. Nov-Mar, please phone for details.
admission ££
Discover 200 years of Norfolk life. Stunning displays housed in magnificent workhouse. Fifty beautiful acres, 1920s farm and animals. Events, activities, cafe and shop.

The Royal Air Force Air Defence Radar Museum
RAF Neatishead, Norwich NR12 8YB
t (01692) 631485 **w** radarmuseum.co.uk
open Apr-Oct, Tue, Thu, Bank Hols 1000-1700.
admission £
History of the development and use of radar in the UK and overseas from 1935 to date. Winner of the Regional Visitor Attraction (under 100,000 visitors), National Silver Award.

Royal Norfolk Regimental Museum
Shirehall, Market Avenue, Norwich NR1 3JQ
t (01603) 493625
w museums.norfolk.gov.uk
open Term Time: Tue-Fri 1000-1630, Sat 1000-1700.
School Hols: Mon-Sat 1000-1700.
admission £
A modern museum with displays about the county regiment from 1685, includes a reconstructed World War I communication trench.

Sainsbury Centre for Visual Arts
University of East Anglia, Norwich NR4 7TJ
t (01603) 593199 **w** scva.org.uk
open All year, Tue, Thu-Sun 1000-1700, Wed 1000-2000.
admission Free
Housing the Sainsbury Collection of works by artists such as Picasso, Bacon and Henry Moore alongside many objects of ceramics and art from across cultures and time.

Shirehall Museum and Abbey Gardens
Common Place, Little Walsingham NR22 6BP
t (01328) 820510
open Apr-Nov, Feb-Mar, daily 1000-1630. Dec, Sat-Sun 1000-1630.
admission £
A Georgian country courthouse, local museum and Tourist Information Centre. Ruins of the Augustinian abbey, peaceful gardens and woodland walks, set in approximately 20 acres.

Strangers' Hall Museum
Charing Cross, Norwich NR2 4AL
t (01603) 667229
open All year, Wed, Sat 1030-1630.
admission £
Medieval townhouse with period rooms. Displays from Tudor to Victorian times. Toy collection on display.

The Straw Museum
Conifer Cottage, Buck Bridge, Colby NR11 7HH
t (01263) 761615
open Apr-Oct, Wed, Sat 1100-1600.
admission Free
Fascinating items from all around the world. Corn dollies, plain and dyed marquetry, Swiss straw lace, plaits, embroidery, jewellery and quilling. Courses are available.

Strumpshaw Old Hall Steam Museum and Farm Machinery Collection
Low Road, Strumpshaw NR13 4HR
t (01603) 714535 **w** strumpshawsteammuseum.co.uk
open Apr-May, Wed, Sun 1100-1600. Jun-Oct, daily 1100-1600.
admission £
Many steam engines, beam engines, mechanical organs, narrow-gauge railway and a working toy train for children. There is also a cafe, gift shop, picnic area and free parking.

Tales of the Old Gaolhouse
Saturday Market Place, King's Lynn PE30 5DQ
t (01553) 774297 **w** west-norfolk.gov.uk
open Apr-Oct, Mon-Sat 1000-1700. Nov-Mar, Tue-Sat 1000-1600.
admission £
A personal stereo tour of the Old Gaol House tells the true stories of Lynn's infamous murderers, highwaymen and even witches.

Thursford Collection
Thursford Green, Thursford NR21 0AS
t (01328) 878477 **w** thursford.com
open Apr-Sep, Mon-Fri, Sun 1200-1700.
admission ££
A live musical show with nine mechanical organs and a Wurlitzer show starring Robert Wolfe.

Time and Tide – Museum of Great Yarmouth Life
Blackfriars Road, Great Yarmouth NR29 3BX
t (01493) 743930 **w** museums.norfolk.gov.uk
open All year, Mon-Fri 1000-1600, Sat-Sun 1200-1600.
admission ££
Set in one of the UK's best preserved Victorian herring curing works, 'Time and Tide' tells the story of Great Yarmouth from its ice age origins to the present day.

RELAXING AND PAMPERING

Wroxham Barns
Tunstead Road, Hoveton NR12 8QU
t (01603) 783762 **w** wroxham-barns.co.uk
open Daily 1000-1700.
admission Free
Rural craft centre with 12 resident craftsmen, tearooms, gift and clothes shop, food and fudge shops. Junior farm and children's funfair.

Friendly help and advice

Tourist Information Centres offer suggestions of places to visit and things to do as well as friendly help with accommodation and holiday ideas. To find the one nearest to you text TIC LOCATE to 64118.

Admission is based on an adult price. Please check opening times and admission before travelling.

Northamptonshire

Enjoy the fun of a special event or visit one of the attractions listed for a great day out. For more inspiring ideas go to **enjoyengland.com**.

16–17 Jun
Althorp Literary Festival
Althorp, Northampton
(01604) 770107
althorp.com

6–8 Jul
Formula One British Grand Prix
Silverstone
0870 458 8300
silverstone.co.uk

17–19 Aug
Northampton Balloon Festival
Racecourse Park, Northampton
(01604) 838222
northamptonballoonfestival.com

14 Oct
World Conker Championships
Ashton
(01293) 889889
worldconkerchampionships.com

May 08
Call to Arms History Fair
Rockingham Castle, nr Corby
0870 789 8778
historyfair.co.uk

FAMILY FUN

Burnums Farmyard Friends

Watling Street, Watford NN6 7UH
t (01788) 822227 **w** burnumsfarm.co.uk
open Apr-31 Aug, Thu-Sun 1000-1700.
Mar, Sep-Oct, Sat-Sun 1000-1700.
admission Adult: £3.50

Hand-feed the farm animals. Hold a baby chick or rabbit. Bottle-feed the lambs from March to the end of August, at 1100 and 1500 daily. Play/picnic area, gift shop, tea room. Groups and birthdays catered for.

Map ref 4C3

West Lodge Rural Centre

Pipewell Road, Desborough NN14 2SH
t (01536) 760552 **w** westlodgeruralcentre.co.uk
open Feb-Dec, daily 1000-1700. Jan, Sat-Sun 1000-1700.
admission £

An open farm and garden centre based around a working family farm which can be seen at work throughout the seasons. Cows, sheep, goats, pigs, poultry and horses.

Wicksteed Park

Barton Road, Kettering NN15 6NJ
t (01536) 512475 **w** wicksteedpark.co.uk
open Daily 0900-1700.
admission £££

The earliest intended leisure park in the UK, first opened in 1921. Set in extensive parkland with a wide range of amusements, recreational and educational opportunities.

NATURE AND WILDLIFE

Barnwell Country Park

Barnwell, Peterborough PE8 5PB
t (01832) 273435 **w** northamptonshire.gov.uk
open Daily.
admission Free

Barnwell Country Park is on the southern boundary of Oundle, nestled in the Nene Valley water meadows.

Brampton Valley Way Linear Park
c/o Brixworth Country Park, Northampton Road,
Brixworth NN6 9DG
t (01604) 883920 **w** northamptonshire.gov.uk
open Daily.
admission Free
*A 14-mile linear park from Northampton to Market
Harborough providing cycling, walking and riding
routes.*

Brixworth Country Park
Northampton Road, Brixworth NN6 9DG
t (01604) 883920 **w** northamptonshire.gov.uk
open Park: Daily. Cafe: Daily 1000-1600.
admission Free
*Visitor centre, toilets, picnic meadows, accessible paths,
cafe, cycle hire, 7.5-mile cycle track, sensory garden and
boules court. Children's play area.*

Burnums Farmyard Friends

Watling Street, Watford NN6 7UH
t (01788) 822227 **w** burnumsfarm.co.uk
open Apr-31 Aug, Thu-Sun 1000-1700.
Mar, Sep-Oct, Sat-Sun 1000-1700.
admission Adult: £3.50

Hand-feed the farm animals. Hold a baby chick
or rabbit. Bottle-feed the lambs from March to
the end of August, at 1100 and 1500 daily.
Play/picnic area, gift shop, tea room. Groups
and birthdays catered for.

 Map ref 4C3

Castle Ashby Gardens
Castle Ashby House, Castle Ashby NN7 1LQ
t (01604) 696187 **w** castleashby.co.uk
open Apr-Sep, daily 1000-1800. Oct-Mar, daily
1000-1630.
admission £
*An Elizabethan mansion with Capability Brown gardens
and an arboretum containing some superb mature trees.
The gardens are renowned for their native wild flowers
and a wide range of flowering bulbs.*

Catanger Llamas
18 High Street, Weston NN12 8PU
t (01295) 768676 **w** llamatrekking.co.uk
open Daily. Please phone for details.
admission ££££
*All-year-round trekking with personal guide, and
everyone getting their very own llama for the entire trek.
Maximum of six llamas.*

Coton Lodge
West Haddon Road, Guilsborough,
Northampton NN6 8QE
t (01604) 740215
w cotonlodge.co.uk
open May-Sep, Thu-Fri, Sun 1200-1700.
admission £
*Mature two-acre garden with panoramic views over
beautiful, unspoilt countryside. Intimate enclosed areas
are complemented by an informal woodland stream and
pond, giving interest throughout the seasons.*

Daventry Country Park
Welton Road, Daventry NN11 2JB
t (01327) 877193
w northamptonshire.gov.uk
open Daily.
admission Free
*The country park is an ideal place to come and enjoy the
countryside with beautiful lakeside scenery, flowery
grassland and shady woodland.*

East Carlton Countryside Park
East Carlton LE16 8YF
t (01536) 770977
w northamptonshire.gov.uk
open Apr-Oct, daily 1000-2000. Nov-Mar, daily
1000-1600.
admission Free
*A countryside park with 100 acres of exceptional
hardwoods, a nature trail, craft workshops and a forge.*

Fermyn Woods Country Park
Lyveden Road, Brigstock NN14 3HS
t (01536) 373186
w northamptonshire.gov.uk
open Daily.
admission Free
*A country park with picnic meadows, forest walks and
wildlife observation. There is a visitor and information
centre and ranger service, a children's play area and
toilets.*

Haddonstone Show Gardens
The Forge House, Church Lane, East Haddon NN6 8DB
t (01604) 770711
w haddonstone.com
open All year, Mon-Fri 0900-1700.
admission Free
*See Haddonstone's classic garden ornaments in the
beautiful setting of the walled manor gardens – planters,
statuary, fountains and even follies.*

Hazelborough Wood
Silverstone NN12 8UZ
t (01780) 444394
w forestry.gov.uk
open Daily.
admission Free
*An ancient woodland site with both majestic oak and
younger conifer plantations. Many species of wildlife
Including roe and fallow deer, badgers, owls,
woodpeckers, and a wide range of butterflies.*

Irchester Country Park
Gipsy Lane, Little Irchester NN29 7DL
t (01933) 276866 **w** northamptonshire.gov.uk
open Daily.
admission Free

In the heart of the Nene Valley, award-winning Irchester Country Park offers something for everyone. Whether it's wandering under towering trees, participating in one of the many exciting events or enjoying a picnic.

Salcey Forest
Hartwell MK16 8LR
t (01780) 444394 **w** forestry.gov.uk
open All year, 0830-dusk.
admission Free

The Royal Forest of Salcey offers excellent walking and opportunities to view an amazing range of wildlife.

Wakerley Great Wood
Wakerley
t (01780) 444394 **w** forestry.gov.uk
open Daily, dawn-dusk.
admission Free

Wakerley Great Wood is an historic ancient woodland. A permanent orienteering course, all-ability woodland path and waymarked trail all leave from the car park.

HISTORIC ENGLAND

78 Derngate
82 Derngate, Northampton NN1 1UH
t (01604) 603408 **w** 78derngate.org.uk
open Apr-Oct, Wed-Sun, Bank Hols. Please phone for details.
admission ££

Charles Rennie Mackintosh transformed a typical terraced house into a startlingly modern house with a striking interior. The adjoining property houses an exhibition about the original design.

Althorp
The Stables, Althorp NN7 4HQ
t (01604) 770107 **w** althorp.com
open Jul-Aug, daily 1100-1700.
admission £££

Built by Sir John Spencer in 1508 and altered by Henry Holland in 1790, with fine pictures, porcelain and furniture. The home of Earl Spencer and his family.

Boughton House
Kettering NN14 1BJ
t (01536) 515731 **w** boughtonhouse.org.uk
open May-Jul, Mon-Fri, Sun 1300-1700. Aug, Mon-Fri, Sun 1400-1700.
admission ££

Northamptonshire home of The Duke of Buccleuch and his Montagu ancestors since 1528. A 500-year-old Tudor monastic building, gradually enlarged until the French-style addition of 1695.

Canons Ashby House
Canons Ashby NN11 3SD
t (01327) 861901
w nationaltrust.org.uk
open House: Apr-Sep, Mon-Wed, Sat-Sun 1300-1730. Oct-Nov, Mon-Wed, Sat-Sun 1300-1630. Dec, Sat-Sun 1200-1600. Church and Park: Apr-Sep, Mon-Wed, Sat-Sun 1100-1730. Oct-Nov, Mon-Wed, Sat-Sun 1100-1630. Dec, Sat-Sun 1100-1600. Gardens: Apr-Sep, Mon-Wed, Sat-Sun 1100-1730. Oct-Nov, Mon-Wed, Sat-Sun 1100-1630. Nov-Dec, Sat-Sun 1100-1600.
admission ££

The home of the Dryden family since its construction, this Elizabethan manor house has remained largely unaltered since 1710. Gardens, parkland, church, tearoom and shop.

Coton Manor Gardens
Nr Guilsborough, Northampton NN6 8RQ
t (01604) 740219
w cotonmanor.co.uk
open Apr-Sep, Tue-Sat , Bank Hols 1200-1730. Apr-May, Sun 1200-1730.
admission £

A ten-acre garden lying in the peaceful Northamptonshire countryside. Originally laid out in the 1920s by the grandparents of the current owner, it comprises a number of smaller gardens.

Cottesbrooke Hall and Gardens
Cottesbrooke NN6 8PF
t (01604) 505808
w cottesbrookehall.co.uk
open May-Jun, Wed-Thu 1400-1730. Jul-Sep, Thu, Bank Hols 1400-1730.
admission ££

A magnificent Queen Anne house dating from 1702, set in delightful rural Northamptonshire. It is reputed to be the pattern for Jane Austen's Mansfield Park.

Deene Park
Deene NN17 3EW
t (01780) 450223
w deenepark.com
open Apr-May, Bank Hols 1100-1600. Jun-Aug, Sun 1400-1700.
admission ££

Acquired by the Brudenell family in 1514 and lived in by their descendants including the 7th Earl of Cardigan (Charge of the Light Brigade). Gardens, teas and gift shop.

Holdenby House Gardens & Falconry Centre
Holdenby House, Holdenby NN6 8DJ
t (01604) 770074
w holdenby.com
open Gardens and Falconry: Apr, Sun 1300-1700. May-Aug, Sun, Bank Hols 1300-1700. Sep, Sun 1300-1700.
admission £

Holdenby's royal connections go back over 400 years. Built by Sir Christopher Hatton to entertain Elizabeth I, later the Palace of James I and the prison of his son, Charles I.

Kelmarsh Hall and Gardens
Estate Office, Kelmarsh Hall,
Kelmarsh NN6 9LY
t (01604) 686543
w kelmarsh.com
open House: Apr-Sep, Thu, Bank Hols 1400-1700.
Gardens: Apr-Sep, Tue-Thu, Sun, Bank Hols
1400-1700.
admission £

*Built 1732 to a James Gibbs design, Kelmarsh
Hall is surrounded by its working estate,
grazed parkland and beautiful gardens.
Successive owners and influences have left
their imprint on the Palladian house and
gardens.*

Kirby Hall
Deene NN17 1AA
t (01536) 203230
w english-heritage.org.uk
open Apr-Jun, Mon, Thu-Sun 1000-1700.
Jul-Aug, daily 1000-1800. Sep-Oct, Mon,
Thu-Sun 1000-1700. Nov-Mar, Mon, Thu-Sun
1000-1600.
admission £

*Kirby Hall is one of the great Elizabethan
houses, built in the hope of receiving the
Queen on her annual 'progresses' round the
country.*

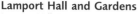

Lamport Hall and Gardens
Lamport Hall, Lamport NN6 9HD
t (01604) 686272
w lamporthall.co.uk
open Apr-Oct, Sun. Aug, Mon-Fri, Sun. Please call for
details.
admission ££

*Home of the Isham family for over four centuries.
During the Commonwealth, the Hall was
developed from a Tudor mansion. Now best
known for its classical frontage, started in 1655
by John Webb.*

Northampton Museum and Art Gallery

Guildhall Road, Northampton NN1 1DP
t (01604) 838111
w northamptonmuseums.com
open Mon-Sat 1000-1700. Sun 1400-1700.
admission Free

Showcasing one of the world's largest
collections of footwear, discover shoe fashions
and the history of shoe making. Other displays:
a fine collection of Italian and British paintings;
British and Oriental ceramics and glass; the
history of Northampton. A dynamic programme
of exhibitions/events promises something for
everyone.

Map ref 2C1

Fotheringhay Church

Admission is based on an adult price. Please check opening times and admission before travelling.

Rockingham Castle

Rockingham LE16 8TH
t (01536) 770240 **w** rockinghamcastle.com
open Apr-May, Sun, Bank Hols 1200-1700. Jun-Sep,
Tue, Sun, Bank Hols 1200-1700.
admission ££

*An Elizabethan house within the walls of a Norman
castle, with fine pictures, extensive views and gardens
with roses and an ancient yew hedge.*

Rushton Triangular Lodge

Rushton NN14 1RP
t (01536) 710761 **w** english-heritage.org.uk
open Apr-Oct, Mon, Thu-Sun 1000-1700.
admission £

*Completed by Sir Thomas Tresham in 1597 to symbolise
the Trinity, with three sides, three floors and trefoil
windows, and reputed meeting place of the Gunpowder
Plot conspirators.*

Southwick Hall

Oundle PE8 5BL
t (01832) 274064 **w** southwickhall.co.uk
open All year, Bank Hols 1400-1700.
admission £

*A manor house dating from the 14th century with
Elizabethan and Georgian additions and an exhibition of
Victorian and Edwardian costumes and country
bygones.*

Stoke Park Pavilions

Stoke Bruerne NN12 7RZ
t (01604) 862329
open Aug, daily 1300-1800.
admission £

*Two 17thC pavilions and a colonnade attributed to Inigo
Jones and restored in 1954. Extensive gardens.*

Sulgrave Manor

Manor Road, Sulgrave OX17 2SD
t (01295) 760205 **w** sulgravemanor.org.uk
open Apr, Sat-Sun 1200-1600. May-Oct, Tue-Thu
1400-1600, Sat-Sun 1200-1600.
admission ££

*An early English home of the ancestors of George
Washington, with Washington souvenirs. A good
example of a small manor house of Shakespeare's time
with furniture of the period and kitchen.*

OUTDOOR ACTIVITIES

Stoke Bruerne Boat Company

29 Main Road,
Shutlanger NN12 7RU
t (01604) 862107
w stokebruerneboats.co.uk
open Please phone for details.
admission £

*Boat trips from the canal museum situated in the famous
canal village of Stoke Bruerne.*

ENTERTAINMENT AND CULTURE

The Canal Museum

Stoke Bruerne,
Towcester NN12 7SE
t (01604) 862229
w thewaterwaystrust.org.uk
open Apr-Oct, daily 1000-1700. Nov-Mar, daily
1030-1530.
admission £

*Housed in a restored cornmill, the museum tells a vivid
story of the inland waterways and the people who
worked on them.*

Harrington Aviation Museum

Sunnyvale Farm & Nursery, off Lamport Road,
Harrington NN6 9PF
t (01604) 686608
w harringtonmuseum.org.uk
open Apr-Oct, Sat-Sun, Bank Hols 1000-1700.
admission £

*Museum set up in administration buildings of a
wartime airfield, used by 8th American Air Force
for secret operations during World War II.
Extensive records of hitherto secret missions
available on site.*

Rockingham Castle

Silverstone Circuit

Silverstone NN12 8TN
t 0870 458 8260
w silverstone-circuits.co.uk
open All year. Please phone for details.
admission ££££

As the home of the Formula 1(TM) Foster's British Grand Prix, Silverstone is recognised as the home of British motor racing.

RELAXING AND PAMPERING

Northampton Museum and Art Gallery

Guildhall Road, Northampton NN1 1DP
t (01604) 838111
w northamptonmuseums.com
open Mon-Sat 1000-1700. Sun 1400-1700.
admission Free

Showcasing one of the world's largest collections of footwear, discover shoe fashions and the history of shoe making. Other displays: a fine collection of Italian and British paintings; British and Oriental ceramics and glass; the history of Northampton. A dynamic programme of exhibitions/events promises something for everyone.

Map ref 2C1

The Old Dairy Farm Country Shopping

Old Dairy Farm,
Upper Stowe NN7 4SH
t (01327) 340525
w old-dairy-farm-centre.co.uk
open Daily 1000-1730.
admission Free

A relaxed shopping experience in a beautiful rural setting. Browse the unique selection of shops and galleries including women's classic clothing and quality lingerie, arts and crafts, traditional sweets and gifts.

The Royal Forest of Salcey

For key to symbols see inside back cover.

Nottinghamshire

Enjoy the fun of a special event or visit one of the attractions listed for a great day out. For more inspiring ideas go to **enjoyengland.com**.

19 May–1 Jul
Exposed! Climate Change in Britain's Backyard – Photography by the National Trust and Magnum Photos
Nottingham Castle
(0115) 915 3700
nottinghamcity.gov.uk/museums

26 Jun–8 Jul
International Byron Festival
Various venues, Hucknall
(01159) 664367
internationalbyronsociety.org

30 Jul–5 Aug
Robin Hood Festival
Sherwood Forest Visitor Centre, Edwinstowe
(01623) 823202
robinhood.co.uk

3–7 Oct
Goose Fair
Forest Recreation Ground, Nottingham
nottinghamgoosefair.co.uk

11–12 Oct
Newark International Antiques Fair
Newark
(01636) 702326
dmgantiquefairs.com

FAMILY FUN

City of Caves
1st Floor, Broad Marsh Shopping Centre, Nottingham NG1 7LS
t (0115) 988 1955 **w** cityofcaves.com
open All year, Mon-Fri 1130-1630, Sat-Sun 1030-1630.
admission £
Enter and explore a whole new world in the caves underneath Nottingham city. Descend into the dark depths of the original Anglo-Saxon tunnels, meeting real cave dwellers from its dramatic past.

The Cornerhouse
Burton Street, Nottingham NG1 4DB
t (0115) 950 5168 **w** cornerhouse.tv
open See website for details.
admission Free
Located in the heart of the city and attracting over 4.5 million visitors every year, an extensive leisure complex combining multiscreen cinema, nightclubs, music venues, restaurants, cafés, bars and health club.

Ghost Tours of Nottingham
Ye Olde Saluation, Maid Marion Way, Nottingham NG1 6AD
t 07850 145642 **w** ghost-walks.co.uk
open All year, Sat 1900-2030.
admission £
The 'Original Nottingham Ghost Walk' was set up in 1993. The walk takes in the older parts of the city near the castle, where the street plan is almost 1,000 years old.

Go Ape High Wire Forest Adventure
Sherwood Forest Pines Visitor Centre, Sherwood Pines Forest Park, Edwinstowe, Mansfield NG21 9JL
t (01284) 850858 **w** goape.co.uk
open Apr-Oct, daily 0900-dusk. Nov, Sat-Sun 0900-dusk.
admission ££££
Go Ape! is a high ropes adventure course of rope bridges, Tarzan swings and zip slides up to almost 40 feet off the forest floor. Ideal for friends, families and corporate groups.

Jumicar
Mansfield Road, White Post Island, Farnborough NG22 8HX
t (0115) 966 9000 **w** ukjumicar.co.uk
open See website for details.
admission ££
Teaches road awareness in a fun and unique way. Children aged 6+ learn to drive junior-sized cars (with younger children as passengers) around a circuit with traffic lights, road signs, zebra crossings.

Making It! Discovery Centre

Littleworth, Mansfield NG18 1AH
t (01623) 473297 **w** makingit.org.uk
open 1000-1700 during Nottinghamshire
school holidays.
admission Adult: £6.95

Fully interactive exhibits where everyone gets
to be busy pushing, bashing, drawing,
designing and testing. Make a working model
to take home - rocket, motorised buggy, ball
launcher, live wire challenge and many more -
the choice is yours - lots of fun and excitement.
Family-friendly cafe, patio and gift shop.

  Map ref 4C2

V voucher offer – see back section

Sherwood Forest Farm Park

Lamb Pens Farm, Edwinstowe, Mansfield,
Mansfield NG21 9HL
t (01623) 823558 **w** sherwoodforestfarmpark.co.uk/
open Apr-Sep, daily 1030-1715.
admission ££

Located within 27 acres of rural Nottinghamshire, home
to more than 30 different rare breeds of farm animals
and several other more unusual species including water
buffalo, Kune Kune pigs and even wallabies.

Sherwood Forest Fun Park

Sherwood Forest Country Park, Edwinstowe NG21 9QA
w experiencenottinghamshire.com
open Mar-Oct, daily 1000-dusk, weather permitting.
admission Free

Fun-packed amusement park catering for families and
children of all ages. Ghost Train, Jumping Jack,
Caterpillar Coaster, Circus Train, Pony Express and
much more.

Sundown Adventure Park

Treswell Road, Rampton, Retford DN22 0HX
t (01777) 248274 **w** sundownadventureland.co.uk
open See website for details.
admission ££

Sundown Adventure Land is a theme park uniquely
designed for under 10s.

The Tales of Robin Hood

30-38 Maid Marian Way, Nottingham NG1 6GF
t (0115) 948 3284 **w** robinhood.uk.com
open Mar-Oct, daily 1000-1630. Nov-Feb, daily
1000-1600.
admission ££

Join the world's greatest medieval adventure. Ride
through the magical green wood and play the Silver
Arrow game, in the search for Robin Hood.

The White Post Farm Centre

White Post Farm, Farnsfield, Newark NG22 8HL
t (01623) 882977 **w** whitepostfarm.co.uk
open Daily 1000-1700.
admission ££

Have a unique day out with lots of opportunities to get
up close to the animals at the East Midlands Visitor
Attraction of the Year 2005.

Wonderland Pleasure Park

White Post Island, Farnsfield,
Mansfield NG22 8HX
t (01623) 882773 **w** wonderlandpleasurepark.com
open All year, Mon-Fri 1000-1630, Sat-Sun 1000-1700.
admission ££

Set in 30 acres of parkland in the heart of
Nottinghamshire, Wonderland Pleasure Park makes the
perfect day out for all the family.

A gentle stroll through a Nottingham park

NATURE AND WILDLIFE

Attenborough Nature Centre

Barton Lane, Chilwell, Nottingham NG9 6DY
t (0115) 972 1777
w attenboroughnaturecentre.co.uk
open Daily (excl 25 Dec). Seasonal hours apply.
admission Free

The reserve features many carefully restored habitats which have become havens for wildlife. Visitors can enjoy the excellent paths, learning about conservation and the flora and fauna. The nature centre offers an education centre, nature shop and an organic/Fair Trade cafe.

                Map ref 4C2

Bestwood Country Park

Alexandra Lodge,
Northern Drive,
Park Road,
Bestwood Village NG6 8UW
t (0115) 927 3674
open Daily.
admission Free   　
A 450-acre park on Nottingham's urban fringe, made up of pleasant grassland and secluded woodlands with adjacent mill lakes, and containing a remarkable range of wildlife habitats.

Brierley Forest Park, Treversal Trails, Portland Park and Kings Mill Reservoir

Ashfield District Council, Urban Road, Kirkby-in-Ashfield NG17 8AD
t (01623) 450000 **w** ashfield-dc.gov.uk
open See the website or phone Ashfield District Council for opening hours.
admission Free

Brierley Forest Park, Treversal Trails, Portland Park and Kings Mill visitor centres are located in beautiful country parks, offering car parking, refreshments and displays. An ideal starting point for short strolls or longer walks, including the Three Centres Trail and the Hidden Valley Circular Walk through Byron and Lawrence countryside.

Map ref 4C2

Sherwood Pines Forest Park, Mansfield

Burntstump Country Park
Mansfield Road, Arnold
t (0115) 901 3603
open Daily.
admission Free   📖♿

A country park with 22 acres of woodlands and park with hard-surface footpaths, space for informal games and picnicking, a cricket pitch and a pond.

Colwick Country Park
off Mile End Road, Colwick, Nottingham NG4 2DW
t (0115) 987 0785
open Apr-Sep, daily 0700-2030. Oct-Mar, daily 0830-1630.
admission £   ⊓♿

A haven for wildlife, formed from former gravel workings with grassland and water course which offer fishing, water sports and many other leisure activities.

Felley Priory Garden
Underwood NG16 5FL
t (01773) 810230
open All year, Tue, Wed, Fri 0900-1300.
admission £   📖✕♿

A plantman's garden full of unusual and old-fashioned perennials, shrubs and trees.

Meditation Centre and Japanese Garden
Pureland, North Clifton NG23 7AT
t (01777) 228567
open Meditation centre: All year, Tue-Fri 1030-1730, Sat-Sun 1000-1730. Japanese Garden: Mar-Jul, Oct, Tue-Fri 1030-1730, Sat-Sun 1000-1730. Aug-Sep, Tue-Fri 1030-1730, Sat-Sun 1000-1730, 1900-2200.
admission £   📖✕♿

A traditional Japanese garden open to the public.

National Water Sports Centre and Country Park
Adbolton Lane, Holme Pierrepont,
Nottingham NG12 2LU
t (0115) 982 1212
w nationalsportscentres.co.uk
open Apr-Oct, daily 0800-2100. Nov-Mar, daily 0800-1630.
admission Free   📖⊓♿

An Olympic-standard water sports course of 2000m with rowing, canoeing, artificial canoe slalom course, water-ski lagoon and a country park for picnics and walks.

Naturescape Wildflower Farm
Coach Gap Lane, Off Harby Road,
Langar NG13 9HP
t (01949) 860592
w naturescape.co.uk
open Apr-Sep, daily 1130-1700.
admission Free   📖♿

Range of wild flowers in bloom over 30 acres of fields which attract associated butterflies, birds and mammals, and a wildlife garden featuring many habitats.

Rufford Country Park and Craft Centre
Ollerton NG22 9DF
t (01623) 822944
w ruffordcraftcentre.org.uk
open Mar-Dec, daily 1030-1700. Jan-Feb, daily 1030-1600.
admission Free   ⊓✕♿

Rufford includes a country park with the picturesque remains of 12thC Rufford Abbey. Craft centre with gallery. Lakeside garden shop. Outdoor Living centre.

Rushcliffe Country Park
Mere Way, Ruddington
t (0115) 921 5865
w rushcliffe.gov.uk
open Daily.
admission Free   ⊓♿

Park with 210 acres of grassland, conservation areas, lake and amenity areas with over 150,000 trees. Information point and refreshments available at the heritage centre.

Sherwood Forest Country Park
Edwinstowe, Mansfield NG21 9HN
t (01623) 821327
w sherwood-forest.org.uk
open Daily.
admission Free   📖⊓♿

Once part of a royal hunting forest, Sherwood Forest Country Park covers 450 acres and incorporates some truly ancient areas of native woodland where slender birches grow alongside over one thousand veteran oaks.

Discover Britain's heritage

Discover the history and beauty of over 250 of Britain's best-known historic houses, castles, gardens and manor-houses. You can purchase *Britain's Historic Houses and Gardens – Guide and Map* from good bookshops and online at enjoy**England**direct.com.

       For key to symbols see inside back cover.

Sywell Country Park

Washbrook Lane, Ecton NN6 0QX
t (01604) 810970
w northamptonshire.gov.uk/leisure.countryside
open Daily.
admission Free

A welcome refuge for wildlife and visitors with picturesque waterside walks, arboretum, butterfly garden, play area and visitor centre.

Teversal Manor Gardens

Buttery Lane, Teversal Old Village,
Teversal NG17 3JN
t (01623) 554569
open Apr-Dec, Thu-Sat 1000-1730, Sun, Bank Hols 1100-1700.
admission £

A handsome 18th century manor house set in the small unspoilt village of Old Teversal.

Wetlands Animal Park

Off Loundlow Road, Sutton-cum-Lound,
Retford DN22 8SB
t (01777) 818099
w wetlandswildlife.co.uk
open All year, 1030-1630.
admission £

A unique experience featuring many exotic animals. Touch, hear, see and smell the residents at Wetlands. Set in 32 acres of lakes and woodland.

HISTORIC ENGLAND

D H Lawrence Durban House Heritage

Mansfield Road, Eastwood NG16 3DZ
t (01773) 717353 **w** broxtowe.gov.uk
open Apr-Oct, daily 1000-1600. Nov-Mar, daily 1000-1700.
admission £

Come and visit the renovated offices of the local coal owners, Barber, Walker and Co, where as a boy D. H. Lawrence would pick up his father's wages. Now a Heritage Centre.

Newstead Abbey

Newstead Abbey Park, Ravenshead NG15 8NA
t (01623) 455900
open Park: All year, daily 0900-dusk. Abbey: Apr-Sep, daily 1200-1700.
admission £

The 800-year-old remains of a priory church, converted into a country house in the 16thC; the home of Lord Byron with possessions, manuscripts, parkland, a lake and gardens.

Nottingham City Council

w nottinghamcity.gov.uk/enjoy
map ref 4C2
see ad below

Southwell Minster

The Minster Office,
The Minster Centre,
Church Street,
Southwell NG25 0HD
t (01636) 817282
w southwellminster.org.uk
open Mar-Oct, daily 0800-1900. Nov-Feb, daily 0800-dusk.
admission £

Southwell Minster is a superb cathedral and minster church with a Norman nave which is one of the finest in Europe.

OUTDOOR ACTIVITIES

Attenborough Nature Centre

Barton Lane, Chilwell, Nottingham NG9 6DY
t (0115) 972 1777
w attenboroughnaturecentre.co.uk
open Daily (excl 25 Dec). Seasonal hours apply.
admission Free

The reserve features many carefully restored habitats which have become havens for wildlife. Visitors can enjoy the excellent paths, learning about conservation and the flora and fauna. The nature centre offers an education centre, nature shop and an organic/Fair Trade cafe.

  Map ref 4C2

Brierley Forest Park, Treversal Trails, Portland Park and Kings Mill Reservoir

Ashfield District Council, Urban Road, Kirkby-in-Ashfield NG17 8AD
t (01623) 450000 **w** ashfield-dc.gov.uk
open See the website or phone Ashfield District Council for opening hours.
admission Free

Brierley Forest Park, Treversal Trails, Portland Park and Kings Mill visitor centres are located in beautiful country parks, offering car parking, refreshments and displays. An ideal starting point for short strolls or longer walks, including the Three Centres Trail and the Hidden Valley Circular Walk through Byron and Lawrence countryside.

  Map ref 4C2

Dragon Boat Festival, River Trent, Newark-on-Trent

Admission is based on an adult price. Please check opening times and admission before travelling.

Sherwood Pines Forest Park

Forest Enterprise, Sherwood and Lincs Forest District, Edwinstowe, Mansfield NG21 9JL
t (01623) 822447
w forestry.gov.uk/england
open Summer 0800-2000. Winter 0800-1800.
admission Free

A centre for activities and outdoor play, including cycling on waymarked trails, mountain biking through the forest, walking on our all-ability waymarked woodland trails, or just a bite to eat at our visitor centre cafe.

                                    Map ref 4C2

ENTERTAINMENT AND CULTURE

Angel Row Gallery
Central Library Building, 3 Angel Row, Nottingham NG1 6HP
t (0115) 915 2869
w angelrowgallery.com
open All year, Mon-Tue, Thu-Fri 1000-1700, Wed 1000-1900, Sat 1000-1700.
admission Free
One of the region's leading galleries of contemporary art, showing a changing programme of temporary exhibitions which reflect the diversity of trends within contemporary visual arts practice.

Bassetlaw Museum
Amcott House, 40, Grove Street, Retford DN22 6LD
t (01777) 713749
w bassetlawmuseum.org.uk
open All year, Mon-Sat 1000-1700.
admission Free
The museum's collections include local history, archaeology, decorative and fine art, agriculture, costume and textiles. It is situated in an 18thC town house which retains many of its original features.

Brewhouse Yard Museum
Castle Boulevard, Nottingham NG7 1FB
t (0115) 915 3600
w nottinghamcity.gov.uk/museums
open All year, daily 1000-1630.
admission £
In these picturesque 17thC cottages and grounds, you can experience a Victorian home, peer into the 1920s shop windows and relive World War II in the cave air-raid shelter.

D H Lawrence Birthplace Museum
8a Victoria Street, Eastwood NG16 3AW
t (01773) 717353 **w** broxtowe.gov.uk
open Apr-Oct, daily 1000-1600. Nov-Mar, daily 1000-1700.
admission £
Step back in time and soak up the atmosphere of the author's early home as a Victorian time capsule unfolds before your eyes.

Galleries of Justice
Shire Hall, High Pavement, Nottingham NG1 1HN
t (0115) 952 0555 **w** galleriesofjustice.org.uk
open All year, Tue-Fri 1000-1600, Sat-Sun 1100-1700.
admission ££
The HM Prison Service Collection. This important national collection is now on permanent display in the 1833 wing.

The Harley Gallery
Welbeck, Worksop S80 3LW
t (01909) 501700 **w** harleygallery.co.uk
open All year, Tue-Sun, Bank Hols 1000-1700.
admission Free
Leading UK gallery showing work by internationally renowned artists and designers. Custom-built vault showing historical objects from the Portland Collection of fine and decorative arts. Award-winning gallery shop.

The Lace Centre
Severn's Building, Castle Road, Nottingham NG1 6AA
t (0115) 941 3539
open Apr-Oct, Mon-Sat 1000-1700, Sun 1100-1600. Nov-Mar, Mon-Sat 1000-1600, Sun 1100-1600.
admission Free
A lace exhibition and retail of locally made laces, housed in a medieval building dating from about 1450.

Mansfield Museum and Art Gallery
Leeming Street, Mansfield NG18 1NG
t (01623) 463088 **w** mansfield-dc.gov.uk
open All year, Mon-Sat 1000-1700.
admission Free
Permanent displays use unique objects and photographs to illustrate the local, natural and social history of Mansfield. Temporary exhibitions and events for everyone.

Robin Hood Festival, Sherwood Forest

Making It! Discovery Centre

Littleworth, Mansfield NG18 1AH
t (01623) 473297 **w** makingit.org.uk
open 1000-1700 during Nottinghamshire
school holidays.
admission Adult: £6.95

Fully interactive exhibits where everyone gets
to be busy pushing, bashing, drawing,
designing and testing. Make a working model
to take home - rocket, motorised buggy, ball
launcher, live wire challenge and many more -
the choice is yours - lots of fun and excitement.
Family-friendly cafe, patio and gift shop.

                Map ref 4C2

 voucher offer – see back section

Newark Air Museum

The Airfield, Winthorpe, Newark, Newark NG24 2NY
t (01636) 707170
w newarkairmuseum.co.uk
open Mar-Oct, daily 1000-1700. Nov-Feb, daily
1000-1600.
admission ££

*An extensive collection of aircraft and cockpit sections
from across the history of aviation, featuring transport,
training and reconnaissance aircraft, jet fighters,
bombers and helicopters. Many exhibits displayed
under cover.*

Newark Millgate Museum

48 Millgate, Newark NG24 4TS
t (01636) 655730
w newark-sherwooddc.gov.uk
open All year, Tue-Sun 1030-1630.
admission Free

*Collections of archaeology, the local history of the area,
some natural history, militaria and exhibits which reflect
the Newark district.*

Nottingham City Council

w nottinghamcity.gov.uk/enjoy
map ref 4C2
see ad on p207

Papplewick Pumping Station

Off Longdale Lane, Ravenshead NG15 9AJ
t (0115) 963 2938
w papplewickpumpingstation.org.uk
open Apr-Oct, Sun 1200-dusk.
admission £

*Britain's finest working Victorian water pumping station
with range of buildings, ornate engine house and
landscaped grounds. Steam days every Bank Holiday
weekend.*

View across the city from Nottingham Castle

For key to symbols see inside back cover.

Sherwood Forest Art and Craft Centre
Forest Corner, Mansfield NG21 9RN
t (01636) 950 1185 **w** newark-sherwoodc.gov.uk
open Daily.
admission Free

Adjacent to Sherwood Forest Youth Hostel, this superb centre was created in a Victorian coach house and stables. An all-weather attraction with glazed atrium.

Thoresby Gallery (Pierrepont Gallery)
Thoresby Park, Ollerton, Newark NG22 9EF
t (01623) 822009 **w** thoresby.com/gallery
open Daily 1030-1700.
admission Free

Inspiring arts and crafts. Working craftspeople side by side with elegant retail outlets.

Vina Cooke Museum: Dolls & Bygone Child
The Old Rectory, Cromwell, Newark NG23 6JE
t (01636) 821364
open Please phone for details.
admission £

Large collection of dolls, prams and costumes. Handmade dolls by Vina Cooke depicting royalty, stars of stage and screen and historical personalities. Rooms full of nostalgia, thousands of childhood memories on display.

Wollaton Hall, Natural History Museum & The Industrial Museum
Wollaton Park, Nottingham NG8 2AE
t (0115) 915 3900
w nottinghamcity.gov.uk/museums
open Apr-Sep, daily 1100-1700. Nov-Mar, daily 1100-1600.
admission Free

An Elizabethan house built by Sir Francis Willoughby and now housing the Natural History Museum and the Industrial Museum, set in grounds and gardens, a deer park and lake.

Nottingham

The Workhouse
Upton Road,
Southwell NG25 0PT
t (01636) 817250
w nationaltrust.org.uk/places/theworkhouse/
open Apr, Mon, Wed-Sun 1200-1700.
Jun-Jul, Thu-Sun 1200-1700. Aug, Mon, Wed-Sun 1200-1700. Sep, Thu-Sun 1200-1700. Oct, Sat-Sun 1200-1700.
admission ££

Follow the path trodden by hundreds of 19th-century paupers at The Workhouse. Explore the segregated work yards, dayrooms, dormitories, masters quarters and cellars using the audio guide, based on archive records.

FOOD AND DRINK

Sherwood Pines Forest Park

Forest Enterprise, Sherwood and Lincs Forest District, Edwinstowe, Mansfield NG21 9JL
t (01623) 822447
w forestry.gov.uk/england
open Summer 0800-2000. Winter 0800-1800.
admission Free

A centre for activities and outdoor play, including cycling on waymarked trails, mountain biking through the forest, walking on our all-ability waymarked woodland trails, or just a bite to eat at our visitor centre cafe.

Map ref 4C2

RELAXING AND PAMPERING

Longdale Craft Centre
Longdale Lane, Ravenshead NG15 9AH
t (01623) 794858
w longdale.co.uk
open Daily 0900-1800.
admission Free

The award-winning craft centre is located in the heart of Sherwood Forest and was established in 1972 by Gordon Brown – royal sculptor and Fellow of the Royal Society of Arts.

Shropshire

Enjoy the fun of a special event or visit one of the attractions listed for a great day out. For more inspiring ideas go to **enjoyengland.com**.

10 Jun
The Cosford Air Show
Royal Air Force Museum, Cosford
(01902) 377922
cosfordairshow.co.uk

13–16 Jul
121st Wenlock Olympian Games Weekend
Various venues, Much Wenlock
(01952) 727679
wenlock-olympian-society.org.uk

18–19 Aug
V Festival
Weston Park, Weston-under-Lizard, Shifnal
0871 220 0260
vfestival.com

7–9 Sep
Ludlow Marches Food and Drink Festival
Various venues, Ludlow
(01584) 873957
foodfestival.co.uk

24–25 Nov
Ludlow Medieval Christmas Fayre
Ludlow Castle
(01584) 875053
ludlowcraftevents.co.uk

FAMILY FUN

Acton Scott Historic Working Farm
Wenlock Lodge, Acton Scott, Church Stretton SY6 6QN
t (01694) 781306 **w** shropshire.gov.uk
open Apr-Oct, Tue-Sun, Bank Hols 1000-1700.
admission £
Acton Scott Historic Working Farm near Church Stretton demonstrates life on a Shropshire upland farm at the turn of the last century.

Bridgnorth Cliff Railway
6a Castle Terrace, Bridgnorth WV16 4AH
t (01746) 762124 **w** bridgnorthcliffrailway.co.uk
open All year, Mon-Sat 0800-1830, Sun 1200-1830.
admission £
This remarkable funicular railway is the oldest and steepest inland electric cliff railway in the country.

Enginuity
Coach Road, Coalbrookedale, Telford TF8 7DQ
t (01952) 435900 **w** ironbridge.org.uk
open Daily 1000-1700.
admission ££
At Enginuity you can turn the wheels of your imagination, test your horse power and discover how good ideas are turned into real things.

Hoo Farm Animal Kingdom
Preston-on-the-Weald-Moors, Telford TF6 6DJ
t (01952) 677917 **w** hoofarm.com
open Apr-Sep, Tue-Sun, Bank Hols 1000-1800. Oct-Dec, Tue-Sun 1000-1700.
admission ££
Hoo Farm Animal Kingdom is a real children's paradise where, between March and December, there is always something happening.

Rays Farm Country Matters
Rays Farm, Billingsley WV16 6PF
t (01299) 841255 **w** raysfarm.com
open Apr-Oct, daily 1000-1730. Feb, Sat-Sun 1000-1730.
admission ££
A farm visitor attraction with many unusual farm animals and birds and a Myth and Magic wood-carving trail.

Rednal Paintball Arena
Rednal Airfield, Rednal, West Felton SY11 4HT
t 0845 121 1947 **w** rednalpaintballarena.com
open All year, Wed-Sun 1000-1800.
admission ££
A first-class paintballing venue, utilising an ex-airfield control tower, with 16 rooms and three floors, surrounded by trenches, fortresses, convoys of vehicles and a jungle village.

Admission is based on an adult price. Please check opening times and admission before travelling.

Telford Steam Railway
The Old Loco Shed, Bridge Road, Horsehay,
Telford TF4 2NF
t 07765 858348
w telfordsteamrailway.co.uk
open Apr-Sep, Sat-Sun, Bank Hols 1100-1630.
admission £
*The railway is based at Horsehay and Dawley station
and goods yard in Telford, the birthplace of the
Industrial Revolution. Many enthusiast and family special
events.*

Wonderland
Telford Town Park Wonderland, Telford TF3 4AY
t (01952) 591633
w wonderlandtelford.com
open Apr-Sep, daily 1030-1800. Oct-Mar, Sat-Sun
1030-1600.
admission ££
*Children's tourist attraction based on nursery rhymes
and fairy tales, set in beautiful woodland. Teddy Bear
tearoom, indoor play area, gift shop, children's rides and
more.*

NATURE AND WILDLIFE

Angel Gardens
Springfield, Angel Lane, Ludlow SY8 3HZ
t (01584) 890381
w stmem.com/angelgardens
open Apr-Oct, Mon, 1200-1700, Sat, 1400-1700, Sun,
Bank Hols 1200-1700.
admission £
*Angel Gardens are beautiful ornamental gardens located
in an Area of Outstanding Natural Beauty near Ludlow.*

Burford House Gardens
Burford Garden Company,
Tenbury Wells WR15 8HQ
t (01584) 810777
w burford.co.uk
open Apr-Dec, Mon-Sun 0900-dusk. Jan-Mar, Mon-Sun
0900-dusk.
admission £
*Seven acres of beautiful riverside gardens, containing
the National Clematis Collection. Garden centre bursting
with interesting gifts for home and garden.*

Carding Mill Valley
Church Stretton SY6 6JG
t (01694) 722631
w nationaltrust.org.uk
open Apr-Oct, daily 1100-1630. Nov, Mon-Tue, Sat-Sun
1030-1600. Dec-Feb, Mon-Fri 1030-1600.
admission Free
*The area includes part of the great ridge, the Long
Mynd, with stunning views across the Shropshire and
Cheshire plains and the Black Mountains.*

David Austin Roses
Bowling Green Lane,
Albrighton,
Wolverhampon WV7 3HB
t (01902) 376334
w davidaustinroses.co.uk
open Daily 0900-1700.
admission Free
*World-famous rose garden containing over 700
roses of all types, including the Renaissance
Garden which is devoted entirely to English
roses.*

Goldstone Hall Gardens
Goldstone TF9 2NA
t (01630) 661202
w goldstonehall.com
open Daily.
admission Free
*Walled garden with acacia, an incomparable stand of
hornbeams, natural green beech and views of
Staffordshire.*

Meres Visitor Centre
Mere SY12 0DQ
t (01691) 622981
open Apr-Jun, Sep, daily 1100-1600.
Jul-Aug, daily 1030-1630. Oct-Dec,
Sat-Sun 1100-1600.
admission Free
*A 114-acre mere noted for its wildfowl.
Contrasting gardens, large picnic area, rowing
boats, playground, visitor centre and woodland
walks.*

Park Hall Countryside Experience
Park Hall,
Oswestry SY11 4AS
t (01691) 671123
w parkhallfarm.co.uk
open Apr-Aug, daily 1000-1700. Sep, Sat-Sun
1000-1700. Oct, daily 1000-1600. Nov, Sat-Sun
1000-1600. Dec, daily 1000-1600. Jan-Mar, Sat-Sun
1000-1600.
admission ££
*One of Shropshire's most exciting all-weather visitor
attractions with animals large and small. Animal feeding,
milking, pony grooming and indoor and outdoor play
areas.*

Wollerton Old Hall Garden
Wollerton, Market Drayton TF9 3NA
t (01630) 685760
w wollertonoldhallgarden.com
open Apr-Sep, Fri, Sun, Bank Hols 1200-1700.
admission £
*An example of horticultural excellence, set in the
Shropshire countryside. This formal garden,
created on a centuries-old site, comprises
individual garden rooms, each with its own
dazzling display of perennials.*

HISTORIC ENGLAND

Attingham Park
Atcham, Shrewsbury SY4 4TP
t (01743) 708123
w nationaltrust.org.uk
open House: Apr-Oct, Mon-Tue, Fri-Sat 1300-1730.
Grounds: Apr-Oct, daily 1000-1730. Nov-Feb, daily
0900-1600.
admission ££
For a meagre sum you may have the house and grounds to enjoy for a whole day. You'll see a late 18thC house commanding views over 500 acres of wonderful parkland.

Benthall Hall
Broseley TF12 5RX
t (01952) 882159
w nationaltrust.org.uk
open House: Apr-Jun, Tue-Wed 1400-1730.
Jul-Sep, Tue-Wed, Sun 1400-1730. Grounds: Apr-Jun,
Tue-Wed 1330-1730. Jul-Sep, Tue-Wed, Sun
1330-1730.
admission £
Handsome 16thC house and restored gardens located on a plateau over looking the River Severn.

Darby Houses (Ironbridge)
Darby Rd, Coalbrookdale, Telford TF8 7DQ
t (01952) 435900
w ironbridge.org.uk
open Apr-Oct, daily 1000-1700.
admission £
In the Darby houses, Dale House and Rosehill House, you can delve into the everyday life of Quaker families.

Dudmaston Hall
Quatt, Bridgnorth WV15 6QN
t (01746) 782821
w nationaltrust.org.uk
open House: Apr-Sep, Tue-Wed, Sun 1400-1730.
Grounds: Apr-Sep, Mon-Wed, Sun 1200-1800.
admission ££
Dudmaston is a 17th C mansion with art collection, lakeside garden and estate.

Hawkstone Hall and Gardens
Marchamley SY4 5LG
t (01630) 685242
w hawkstone-hall.com
open Aug, daily 1300-1700.
admission £
Visit this beautiful Georgian mansion, set in Shropshire 's spacious parkland. Ancestral home of the famous Hill family from 1556 until 1906.

Hawkstone Historic Park and Follies
Weston-Under-Redcastle, Shrewsbury SY4 5UY
t (01939) 200611 **w** hawkstone.co.uk
open Apr-May, Sep-Oct, Wed-Sun, Bank Hols
1000-1530. Jun-Aug, daily 1000-1600.
admission ££
Hawkstone Historic Park & Follies is a unique place. Created in the 18th century by the Hill family (Sir Rowland and his son Richard), Hawkstone became one of the greatest historic parklands in Europe.

Ludlow Castle
Castle Square, Ludlow SY8 1AY
t (01584) 873355 **w** ludlowcastle.com
open Apr-Jul, daily 1000-1700. Aug, daily 1000-1900.
Sep, daily 1000-1700. Oct-Dec, daily 1000-1600.
admission £
The construction of Ludlow Castle began in the late 11th century as the border stronghold of one of the Marcher Lords, Roger De Lacy.

Much Wenlock Priory
Much Wenlock TF13 6HS
t (01952) 727466
w english-heritage.org.uk/wenlockpriory
open See wbsite for details.
admission £
The spectacular ruins of the priory, with its stunning clipped topiary, has a pastoral setting on the edge of lovely Much Wenlock.

Shrewsbury Abbey
Abbey Foregate, Shrewsbury SY2 6BS
t (01743) 232723 **w** shrewsburyabbey.com
open Apr-Oct, daily 1000-1600. Nov-Mar, Mon-Sat
1030-1500, Sun 1100-1430.
admission Free
The abbey was founded in 1083 by the Norman Roger de Montgomery. The Chronicles of Brother Cadfael, written by Ellis Peters, are inspired by medieval Shrewsbury.

Stokesay Castle
Stokesay, Craven Arms SY7 9AH
t (01588) 672544
w english-heritage.org.uk/stokesaycastle
open Mar-Apr, Wed-Sun 1000-1700. May-Jun, daily
1000-1700. Jul-Aug, daily 1000-1800. Sep-Oct,
Wed-Sun 1000-1700. Nov-Feb, Thu-Sun 1000-1600.
admission £
The castle is the finest and best-preserved 13thC manor house in England, nestling in peaceful South Shropshire countryside near the Welsh border.

The Tar Tunnel
The Wharfage, Ironbridge, Telford TF8 7DQ
t (01952) 433522 **w** ironbridge.co.uk
open Apr-Oct, daily 1000-1700.
admission £
Enter this narrow, dimly lit tunnel to see a geological curiosity, where bitumen still oozes through the walls.

For key to symbols see inside back cover.

Wroxeter Roman City

Wroxeter, Shrewsbury SY5 6PH
t (01743) 761330
w english-heritage.org.uk/wroxeter
open See website for details.
admission £

Viroconium (Roman name) is thought to have been one of the largest Roman cities in the UK with over 200 acres of land, two miles of walls and a population of approximately 5,000.

ENTERTAINMENT AND CULTURE

Blists Hill Victorian Town

Legges Way, Madeley, Telford TF8 7DQ
t (01952) 884391 **w** ironbridge.org.uk
open Apr-Oct, daily 1000-1700. Nov-Mar, daily 1000-1600.
admission ££

Watch the world go by over 100 years ago.

Bridgnorth Costume & Childhood Museum

Postern Gate, Bridgnorth WV16 4AA
t (01746) 766666
open All year, Tue, Wed, Fri 1030-1630, Sat 0930-1630, Sun 1130-1630.
admission £

Striking Victorian Italianate building housing collection of dolls, toys, costumes, textiles, fashion accessories and much more. Many illuminate the local social history.

Wrekin Reservoir

Broseley Clay Tobacco Pipe Works

Duke Street, Broseley TF8 7DQ
t (01952) 435900 **w** ironbridge.org.uk
open May-Sep, daily 1300-1700.
admission £

This clay pipe factory looks and feels just like it did when the doors closed behind the last pipe maker in 1957.

Coalbrookdale Museum of Iron

Coalbrookdale, Telford TF8 7DQ
t (01952) 884391 **w** ironbridge.org.uk
open Daily 1000-1700.
admission £

Here, iron is the business. Take a look at the pioneering spirit and revolutionary thinking that made the Gorge the 'silicon valley' of its time.

Coalport China Museum

Coalport, Telford TF8 7DQ
t (01952) 435900 **w** ironbridge.org.uk
open Daily 1000-1700.
admission £

At the Coalport China Museum you can see the vibrant National Collections of Coalport and Caughley.

Ironbridge Gorge Museums

Coalbrookdale, Telford TF8 7DQ
t (01952) 435900 **w** ironbridge.org.uk
open Daily 1000-1700.
admission £

Whether you are interested in fine china, fun interactives or a 'Victorian' town, it's all to be found in this World Heritage Site.

Jackfield Tile Museum

Jackfield, Telford TF8 7DQ
t (01952) 435900 **w** ironbridge.org.uk
open Daily 1000-1700.
admission £

At the Jackfield Tile Museum there are tiles everywhere! The Victorians were on a mission to not only make them, but also to use them.

Mythstories Museum

The Morgan Library, Aston Street, Wem SY4 5AU
t (01939) 235500 **w** mythstories.com
open Apr-Aug, Mon-Fri 1430-1830. Sep-Nov, Sat-Sun 1100-1600.
admission Free

The museum is set in the historic Morgan Library in Wem. Here you can discover living legends that have inspired writers throughout the centuries.

Royal Air Force Museum

Cosford, Shifnal, Telford TF11 8UP
t (01902) 376200 **w** rafmuseum.org
open Daily 1000-1600.
admission Free

Transport, research and development, warplanes, missiles and aero-engine collections. Art gallery, temporary-exhibition gallery and interactives in the Fun 'n' Flight area. Gift shop, restaurant and flight simulator.

Secret Hills – Shropshire Hills Discovery Centre
School Road, Craven Arms SY7 9RS
t (01588) 676000
w shropshirehillsdiscoverycentre.co.uk
open Apr-Oct, daily 1000-1730. Nov-Mar, daily 1000-1630.
admission £
Visit Shropshire's only grass-roofed public building and discover how to read the clues to the mysteries of our landscape. Also activities, walks and trails.

Shrewsbury Castle & Shropshire Regimental Museum
Castle Street,
Shrewsbury SY1 2AT
t (01743) 361196
w shrewsburymuseums.com
open Apr-May, Tue-Sat 1000-1600. Jun-Aug, Mon-Sat 1000-1700, Sun 1000-1600. Sep-Dec, Tue-Sat 1000-1600.
admission £
The castle, built by Roger de Montgomery in 1070, houses the Shropshire Regimental Museum including spectacular collections of pictures, weapons, uniforms and other memorabilia from the 1700s to the present.

FOOD AND DRINK

Bird On The Rock Tearoom
Rock Cottage, Clungunford,
Craven Arms SY7 0PX
t (01588) 660631
w birdontherock.com
open All year, Thu-Sun 1000-1700.
admission Free
Bird on the Rock is now considered to be one of the most exclusive and unique tea rooms in the world (Top 50 Tea Rooms Independent newspaper 2001).

RELAXING AND PAMPERING

Wenlock Pottery
Shineton Street,
Much Wenlock TF13 6HT
t (01952) 727600
w wenlockpottery.co.uk
open All year, Mon-Sat 0900-1630, Sun 1000-1600.
admission ££
Visit a working pottery and create a masterpiece in the Ceramic Cafe or browse in beautiful surroundings for that special gift.

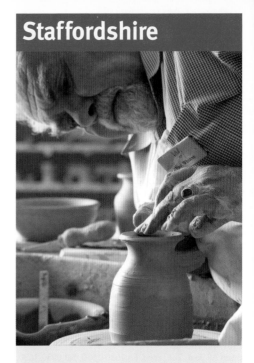

Staffordshire

Enjoy the fun of a special event or visit one of the attractions listed for a great day out. For more inspiring ideas go to **enjoyengland.com**.

28 Jun–14 Jul
Stafford Festival
Stafford Castle
(01785) 619619
staffordbc.gov.uk

5–15 Jul
Lichfield Festival
Lichfield
(01543) 306270
lichfieldfestival.org

1–8 Sep
Longnor Well Dressing
Longnor
(01298) 83495
staffsmoorlands.gov.uk

15 Sep–28 Oct
Walsall Illuminations
Walsall Aboretum
0845 111 2900
walsall-lights.com

5–7 Oct
Stoke-on-Trent Ceramics Festival
Various venues, Stoke-on-Trent
(01782) 236000
visitstoke.co.uk

Admission is based on an adult price. Please check opening times and admission before travelling.

FAMILY FUN

Alton Towers Theme Park
Alton ST10 4DB
t 0870 520 4060
w altontowers.com
open Apr-Oct, daily 0930-dusk.
admission ££££   💻 🎪 🍴 ♿
Britain's number one theme park with rides and attractions such as Air, Oblivion, Nemesis, Congo River Rapids and many children's attractions including Tweenies live show.

Blackbrook Zoological Park
Winkhill ST13 7QR
t (01538) 308293
w blackbrookzoologicalpark.co.uk
open Daily 1030-1730.
admission ££   💻 🎪 ♿
Many unusual species of birds including wildfowl, pheasants, storks and cranes. Also children's farm, pets' area, insect and reptile house, shop and information areas.

Chasewater Railway
Chasewater Country Park, Pool Road,
Nr Brownhills WS8 7NL
t (01543) 452623
w chaserail.com
open See website for details.
admission £   💻 🍴 ♿
The volunteer-run Chasewater Railway operates vintage steam and diesel trains in Chasewater Country Park, just off the A5.

Drayton Manor Theme Park
Tamworth B78 3TW
t 0870 872 5252
w draytonmanor.co.uk
open Daily 1000-1600.
admission ££££   💻 🍴 ♿
Everyone's favourite theme park featuring some of the biggest, wettest and scariest rides around! Don't miss the incredible G-Force, a rollercoaster experience you've never had before!.

Foxfield Steam Railway
Caverswall Road Station, Blythe Bridge ST11 9EA
t (01782) 396210
w foxfieldrailway.co.uk
open Apr-Oct, Sun, Bank Hols 1130-1600. Dec, Sat-Sun 1130-1600.
admission ££   💻 🎪 ♿
Working steam railway, giving a five-mile round trip through Staffordshire countryside. Large collection of locomotives and rolling stock.

Leeds Pottery (Hartley Greens & Co)
Anchor Road, Longton ST3 5ER
t (01782) 599959 **w** hartleygreens.com
open Apr-Oct, Mon-Thu 0900-1630, Fri 0900-1400, Sat 1000-1400. Nov-Mar, Mon-Thu 0900-1630, Fri 0900-1400.
admission Free   ♿
Pottery producing traditional English Creamware, made by hand to original 18thC designs. Factory tours and shop selling own products.

Royal Stafford Factory Shop & Ceramic Cafe

Wedgwood Place, Burslem ST6 4EE
t (01782) 525419 **w** royalstaffordtableware.co.uk
open All year, Mon-Sat 0930-1700.
admission Free   💻 🍴 ♿
The factory shop offers a wide variety of tableware, giftware, glassware and florals. The Ceramic Cafe is where visitors paint items with their own design or message.

Spode Visitor Centre
Spode, Church Street, Stoke-on-Trent ST4 1BX
t (01782) 744011 **w** spode.co.uk
open All year, Mon-Sat 0900-1700, Sun 1000-1600.
admission Free   💻 🍴 ♿
Visitors are shown the various processes in the making of bone china. Fully guided factory tour, magnificent collection in the museum. Italian restaurant, assorted high street concession shops.

Staffordshire Enamels
Weston Coyney Road, Longton ST3 5JT
t (01782) 599948 **w** staffordshire-enamels.com
open All year, Mon-Sat 1000-1600.
admission Free   ♿
The only enamellers whose workshops are open to the public by appointment. Gallery shop, factory tour, shop, seconds and discontinued lines.

Tutbury Crystal Glass
Burton Street, Tutbury DE13 9NG
t (01283) 813281 **w** tutburycrystal.co.uk
open All year, Mon-Fri 0900-1700.
admission Free   💻 ♿
Fully guided factory tours showing the traditional, hand-made crystal glassware manufacturing. The visitors' centre includes information, displays and glass demonstrations.

NATURE AND WILDLIFE

Baggeridge Country Park
Gospel End, Sedgley DY3 4HB
t (01902) 882605 **w** sstaffs.gov.uk
open Apr-Sep, daily 0900-2000. Oct-Mar, daily 0900-1700.
admission Free   💻 🎪 🍴 ♿
Baggeridge Country Park is a haven for wildlife with many trails to explore. The 152-acre site was part of a former coal mine and part of the Earl of Dudley's estate.

Biddulph Grange Garden (National Trust)
Grange Road, Biddulph ST8 7SD
t (01782) 517999 **w** nationaltrust.org.uk
open Apr-Oct, Wed-Sun 1130-1800. Nov, Sat-Sun
1100-1500.
admission ££
An exciting and rare survival of a high Victorian garden, acquired by the Trust in 1988.

Branston Water Park
Burton upon Trent DE14 3HD
t (01283) 508657
open Apr-Sep, daily 0800-2100. Oct-Mar, daily
0800-1700.
admission Free
Forty-acre lake including woodland, wetland and wildflower meadow. The lake is popular with model boating and angling clubs. Walks, birdwatching and picnicking.

British Wildlife Rescue Centre
Amerton Working Farm, Stowe-by-Chartley ST18 0LA
t (01889) 271308 **w** thebwrc.co.uk
open Daily 1000-1700.
admission £
Centre for treatment of sick and injured British wildlife.

Chasewater Country Park
Pool Road, Brownhills WS8 7NL
t (01543) 308859
open Apr-Oct, daily 0800-dusk. Nov-Mar, 0800-1630.
admission Free
Chasewater hosts many leisure opportunities including water-skiing, sailing, angling and a steam railway.

Doxey Marshes Nature Reserve
Doxey Marshes, Stafford
t (01889) 880100 **w** staffs-wildlife.org.uk
open Daily.
admission Free
Wetland habitat for a variety of birds, plants and insects. Bird hides looking over a scrape, area of shallow water and mud flats attracting waders.

Greenway Bank Country Park
Bemmersley Road, Knypersley, Biddulph ST8 7QY
t (01782) 518200
open Daily, dawn-dusk.
admission Free
The park offers a variety of attractive scenery within its 110 acres. Easy access to lawns and shrubberies. Extensive areas of quiet woodland around the Serpentine Pool.

Ilam Park (National Trust)
Ilam DE6 2AZ
t (01335) 350503 **w** nationaltrust.org.uk
open Daily.
admission Free
Park and woodland on both banks of the river Manifold.

National Memorial Arboretum
Croxall Road, Alrewas DE13 7AR
t (01283) 792333
w nationalmemorialarboretum.org.uk
open Daily 0900-dusk.
admission Free
A 150-acre arboretum planted as a tribute to the people of the 20th century. Plots include those planted for the Armed and Merchant Services, the police and fire service.

RSPB Coombes Valley Nature Reserve
Six Oaks Farm, Bradnop ST13 7EU
t (01538) 384017
w rspb.org.uk
open Daily, dawn-dusk.
admission Free
The reserve lies in a wooded valley covering 261 acres. It is a refuge for a large number of woodland birds and a wide variety of other wildlife.

Trentham Leisure
Stone Road, Trentham ST4 8AX
t (01782) 657341
w trenthamleisure.co.uk
open Garden: Apr-Sep, daily 1000-1800. Nov-Mar, daily 1000-1600. Woodlands: Daily, dawn-dusk.
admission ££
Seven-hundred-and-fifty acres of scenic gardens, woodlands and lake, currently undergoing major redevelopment work.

HISTORIC ENGLAND

Arthur's Stone (English Heritage)
Dorstone
t (0121) 625 6820
w english-heritage.org.uk
open Daily, dawn-dusk.
admission Free
An impressive prehistoric burial chamber, formed of large blocks of stone, in the hills above Herefordshire's Golden Valley.

Chillington Hall
Codsall Wood,
Wolverhampton WV8 1RE
t (01902) 850236
w chillingtonhall.co.uk
open Jul, Thu, Sun 1400-1700. Aug, Wed-Fri, Sun 1400-1700.
admission £
Georgian house, part-1724 Francis Smith, part-1785 Sir John Soane, fine saloon, grounds and lake by Capability Brown. Extensive woodland walks, lakeside temples and folly.

The Complete Working Historic Estate of Shugborough (The National Trust)
Shugborough, Milford ST17 0XB
t (01889) 881388
w shugborough.org.uk
open Apr-Oct, daily 1000-1700.
admission ££

Eighteenth-century mansion house with fine collection of furniture. Gardens and park contain beautiful neo-classical monuments.

Ford Green Hall
Ford Green Road, Smallthorne ST6 1NG
t (01782) 233195
w stoke.gov.uk
open All year, Mon-Thu, Sun 1300-1700.
admission £

A 17thC timber-framed farmhouse with 18thC additions. Fully furnished with items from the 17th and 18thC.

Himley Hall & Park
Himley DY3 4DF
t (01384) 817817
w dudley.gov.uk
open Park: Daily, dawn-dusk. Hall: Apr-Aug, Tue-Sun, Bank Hols 1400-1700.
admission Free

Historic house offering an excellent programme of temporary exhibitions during the spring and summer months and outdoor events throughout the year.

Lichfield Cathedral
The Visitors' Centre, The Close,
Lichfield WS13 7LD
t (01543) 306240
w lichfield-cathedral.org
open All year, daily 0815-1815.
admission Free

A medieval cathedral with three spires. See the 8thC Lichfield Gospels manuscript, superb 16thC Flemish glass, sculptures by Chantrey & Epstein and modern silver collection.

Moseley Old Hall (National Trust)
Moseley Old Hall Lane, Fordhouses WV10 7HY
t (01902) 782808
w nationaltrust.org.uk
open Apr-Oct, Wed, Sat-Sun 1200-1700. Nov, Sun 1200-1600.
admission ££

An Elizabethan house where Charles II hid after the Battle of Worcester. A small reconstructed 17thC garden with formal box parterre or knot garden.

The Museum of Cannock Chase
Valley Road, Hednesford WS12 1TD
t (01543) 877666
w museumofcannockchase.co.uk
open Please phone for details.
admission Free

A former mining site housing a local-history museum and temporary exhibitions. Special events are staged throughout the year.

Stafford Castle and Visitor Centre
Castle Bank, Newport Road, Stafford ST16 1DJ
t (01785) 257698
w staffordbc.gov.uk
open Apr-Oct, Tue-Sun 1000-1700. Nov-Mar, Sat-Sun 1000-1600.
admission Free

On the site of one of the earliest castles, a typical example of a Norman fortress. Field work has revealed a deserted village site.

Tamworth Castle
The Holloway, Tamworth B79 7NA
t (01827) 709626   **w** tamworth.gov.uk
open All year, Thu-Sun 1200-1715.
admission £

Enter a world of history, magic and ghosts! Dramatic Norman castle with 15 rooms to explore. Free quizzes and lots of hands-on activities for children.

Tittesworth Visitor Centre
Buxton Road, Leek ST13 8SW
t (01538) 300400   **w** stwater.co.uk
open Apr-Sep, daily 1000-1800. Oct, daily 1000-1700. Nov-Jan, daily 1000-1600. Feb-Mar, daily 1000-1700.
admission Free

Nature trail, bird hide, trout fishing and adventure playground for children. Also visitors centre, restaurant and barbecue. Sensory garden, wheelchair-accessible areas.

Tutbury Castle
Castle Street, Tutbury DE13 9JF
t (01283) 812129   **w** tutburycastle.com
open Apr-Sep, Wed-Sun 1100-1700.
admission £

A ruined castle, mostly 15th century, the first prison of Mary Queen of Scots. The Great Hall is furnished in the Elizabethan style. Tearoom, gift shop and children's play area.

Wall Roman Site (Letocetum)
Watling Street, Lichfield WS14 0AW
t (01543) 480768
w english-heritage.org.uk
open Apr-Oct, daily dawn-dusk.
admission Free

The remains of a staging post, including the foundations of public baths and lodging house. A small museum showing items found on site stands alongside the site.

The Wedgwood Visitor Centre
Barlaston ST12 9ES
t 0870 606 1759
w thewedgwoodvisitorcentre.com
open All year, Mon-Fri 0900-1700, Sat-Sun 1000-1700.
admission ££

With displays, factory tours and sweeping parkland, the Wedgwood Visitor Centre is a living memorial to one of the greatest Englishmen of all time.

 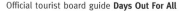

Weston Park

Weston-under-Lizard TF11 8LE
t (01952) 852100 **w** weston-park.com
open See website for details.
admission £

The grounds of Weston Park combine 1,000 acres of natural beauty with three centuries of garden design.

ENTERTAINMENT AND CULTURE

Borough Museum and Art Gallery

The Brampton, Newcastle-under-Lyme ST5 0QP
t (01782) 619705 **w** newcastle-staffs.gov.uk
open All year, Mon-Sat 1000-1730, Sun 1400-1740.
admission Free

Local history, ceramics, militaria, gallery of childhood, clocks, Victorian street scene and an aviary. Frequent art and craft demonstrations and an active temporary-exhibition programme.

Churnet Valley Railway

Cheddleton Station, Station Road,
Cheddleton ST13 7EE
t (01538) 360522 **w** churnetvalleyrailway.co.uk
open See website for details.
admission ££

Station building is a Grade II Listed house, shop and museum, set in Churnet Valley. Steam locomotives, diesel locos, coaches and other rolling stock. Steam days throughout year.

Gladstone Pottery Museum

Uttoxeter Road, Longton ST3 1PQ
t (01782) 237777
w stoke.gov.uk
open Daily 1000-1700.
admission ££

A complete Victorian pottery factory from the days of coal-fired bottle ovens where visitors can get their hands on the history and skills of the Potteries.

The Potteries Museum & Art Gallery

Bethesda Street, Hanley ST1 3DW
t (01782) 232323
w stoke.gov.uk/museums
open Mar-Oct, Mon-Sat 1000-1700, Sun 1400-1700.
Nov-Feb, Mon-Sat 1000-1600, Sun 1300-1600.
admission Free

The finest collection of Staffordshire ceramics in the world. A flagship art gallery within the region. Mark XVI Spitfire and lots of hands-on activities.

Shire Hall Gallery

Market Square, Stafford ST16 2LD
t (01785) 278345
w staffordshire.gov.uk/sams
open All year, Mon 0930-1700, Tue 1000-1700,
Wed-Sat 0930-1700, Sun 1300-1600.
admission Free

Visual arts and crafts venue in fascinating Grade II Listed building. Annual programme of contemporary art, craft and photography exhibitions. Craft shop with work from leading British craftsmen.

Sunnyside Farm, near Cellarhead

The Snowdome Leisure Island

River Drive, Tamworth B79 7ND
t 0870 500 0011 **w** snowdome.co.uk
open Daily 0900-2300.
admission ££

Indoor, real-snow centre. Skiing, snowboarding, tobogganing, snow-tubing and ice-skating available. Tuition and equipment. Warm clothing and gloves essential.

FOOD AND DRINK

Coors Visitor Centre

PO Box 220, Horninglow Street,
Burton upon Trent DE14 1YQ
t 0845 600 0598 **w** coorsvisitorcentre.com
open Daily 1000-1700.
admission ££

Established in 1977, the centre offers a unique blend of living heritage, historic galleries and family entertainment.

Halfpenny Green Vineyards

Tom Lane, Bobbington DY7 5EP
t (01384) 221122 **w** halfpenny-green-vineyards.co.uk
open Daily 1030-1700.
admission Free

Vineyards open to the public. Visitor centre with history of English wine, morning coffees, lunches, off wine sales, afternoon teas, vineyard trail, guided tours and wine bar.

RELAXING AND PAMPERING

Amerton Farm

Stowe-by-Chartley ST18 0LA
t (01889) 270294 **w** amertonfarm.co.uk
open Apr-Dec, daily 0900-1730. Jan-Mar, daily 0900-1700.
admission Free

Irresistible shopping, working crafts and delicious home-made food, all to be enjoyed in beautiful surroundings, set in the lovely Staffordshire countryside.

Heart of the Country Village

Swinfen, Lichfield WS14 9QR
t (01543) 481612 **w** heartofthecountryvillage.co.uk
open All year, Tue-Sun, Bank Hols, Tues-Sun 1000-1700.
admission £

Country shopping village offering the visitor a choice of crafts, food, herbs, country clothing and art gallery. Two restaurants on site.

Slater's Craft Village

Slater's Country Inn, Stone Road,
Baldwins Gate ST5 5ED
t (01782) 680052 **w** slaterscountryinn.co.uk
open Daily 1000-1700.
admission Free

A fully covered Victorian village comprising 15 individual craft units, garden shop and tearoom. Also bars, restaurant and accommodation.

Stunning views across the Roaches

Suffolk

Enjoy the fun of a special event or visit one of the attractions listed for a great day out. For more inspiring ideas go to **enjoyengland.com**.

Jun
Aldeburgh Music Festival
Aldeburgh
(01728) 687110
aldeburgh.co.uk

17 Jun–8 Jul
Great Annual Recreation of Tudor Life
Kentwell Hall, Long Melford
(01787) 310207
kentwell.co.uk

1 Jul
Ipswich Music Day
Ipswich
(01473) 433155
ip-art.com

5 Aug
National Amber Hunt
Southwold
(01502) 723394
ambershop.co.uk

12 Aug
Annual British Open Crabbing Championship
Walberswick
(01502) 722359
walberswick.ws/crabbing

FAMILY FUN

Easton Farm Park

Easton, Woodbridge IP13 0EQ
t (01728) 746475
w eastonfarmpark.co.uk
open 17 Mar-30 Sep 10.30-18.00.
Feb & Oct half-terms, 10.30-16.00.
Weekends in Dec, 11.00-15.00.
admission Adult: £6.25

Easton Farm Park offers an opportunity for the whole family to enjoy life on the farm. Daily activities include pony and train rides, hug-a-bunny, egg collecting and much more. Pedal and electric tractors and diggers; indoor and outdoor playgrounds. Riverside cafe and gift shop. Holiday accommodation. Monthly Farmers' Market (4th Saturday).

 Map ref 3C2

 voucher offer – see back section

Go Ape! High Wire Forest Adventure

High Lodge Forest Centre, Santon Downham, Brandon IP27 0TJ
t 0870 444 5562
w goape.co.uk
open Apr-Oct, Mon-Fri 0900-dusk. Nov, Mon-Sun 0900-dusk.
admission ££££

Go Ape! and tackle a high wire forest adventure course of rope bridges, Tarzan swings and zip slides up to 35 feet above the forest floor.

For key to symbols see inside back cover.

Ipswich Town Football Club Stadium Tour
Portman Road, Ipswich IP1 2DA
t 0870 1110555
w itfc.co.uk
open All year, Mon, 1930-2100.
admission ££

See behind the scenes at a top football club. From the dressing room to the directors' box – the tour gives you unique access 'behind the Blues'.

Manning's Amusement Park
Sea Road, Felixstowe IP11 2DW
t (01394) 282370
open Arcade: Daily 1000-2200. Rides: Apr-Sep, Sat-Sun, School Hols 1100-1800.
admission Free

Crazy Charlie's junior theme park plus a nightclub, sports bar, quasar arena and sun market.

Pleasurewood Hills Leisure Park
Leisure Way, Corton, Lowestoft NR32 5DZ
t (01502) 586000
open Apr-May, Sep, Sat-Sun 1000-1700. Jun, Wed, Sat-Sun 1000-1700.Jul, daily 1000-1700. Aug, daily 1000-1800. School Hols, daily from 1000.
admission £££

Tidal wave watercoaster, log flume, chairlift, two railways, pirate ship, parrot/sealion shows, go-karts and three rollercoasters. Mega-Drop Tower and new circus theatre shows.

Southwold Pier
North Parade, Southwold IP18 6BN
t (01502) 722105
w southwoldpier.co.uk
open Daily from 1000.
admission Free

Pier and amusements. New pier completed 2002 – the first pier to be built in the UK for over 45 years. Exhibition, gift emporium and restaurant.

NATURE AND WILDLIFE

Africa Alive – African Animal Adventure
White's Lane, Kessingland NR33 7TF
t (01502) 740291 **w** africa-alive.co.uk
open Apr-Jun, daily 1000-1700. Jul-Sep, daily 1000-1730. Oct-Mar, daily 1000-1600.
admission £££

Take your family on a walking safari at one of the UK's largest and most exciting wildlife attractions, set in 80 acres of dramatic coastal parkland.

Alton Water
Holbrook Road, Stutton IP9 2RY
t (01473) 589105 **w** altonwater.co.uk
open All year, 0800-dusk.
admission Free

Water park with sailing, rowing, fishing, nature reserves and extensive walks. Visitor centre, cycle hire and catering.

Brandon Country Park
Visitor Centre, Bury Road, Brandon IP27 0SU
t (01842) 810185
open Mar-Oct, Mon-Fri 1000-1700, Sat-Sun 1000-1730. Nov-Feb, daily 1000-1600.
admission Free

Thirty acres of landscaped parkland with tree trail and forest walks. Visitor centre open daily. Play area, walled garden and off-road cycle loops, 20.75km.

Dunwich Heath Coastal Centre and Beach
National Trust, Dunwich Heath, Dunwich IP17 3DJ
t (01728) 648505 **w** nationaltrust.org.uk
open Apr-Jul, Wed-Sun 1000-1600. Aug, daily 1000-1700. Sep-Dec, Wed-Sun 1000-1700. Jan, Sat-Sun 1000-1600. Feb-Mar, Wed-Sun 1000-1600.
admission £

Remnant of the once extensive Sandling Heaths and one of Suffolk's most important nature conservation areas. Many excellent walks and access to beach.

Southwold pier

East Bergholt Place Garden
East Bergholt Place, East Bergholt CO7 6UP
t (01206) 299224
open Apr-Sep, daily 1000-1700.
admission £
The Place Garden was laid out at the turn of the century and covers 15 acres with fine trees, shrubs, rhododendrons, camellias and magnolias.

Easton Farm Park

Easton, Woodbridge IP13 0EQ
t (01728) 746475
w eastonfarmpark.co.uk
open 17 Mar-30 Sep 10.30-18.00.
Feb & Oct half-terms, 10.30-16.00.
Weekends in Dec, 11.00-15.00.
admission Adult: £6.25

Easton Farm Park offers an opportunity for the whole family to enjoy life on the farm. Daily activities include pony and train rides, hug-a-bunny, egg collecting and much more. Pedal and electric tractors and diggers; indoor and outdoor playgrounds. Riverside cafe and gift shop. Holiday accommodation. Monthly Farmers' Market (4th Saturday).

                              Map ref 3C2

(v) *voucher offer – see back section*

Helmingham Hall Gardens
Estate Office, Helmingham IP14 6EF
t (01473) 890799 **w** helmingham.com
open May-Sep, Wed, Sun 1400-1800.
admission £
Moated and walled garden with many rare roses and possibly the best kitchen garden in Britain. With new rose garden and herb and knot garden created in the early 1980s.

High Lodge Forest Centre
Forestry Commission, Santon Downham,
Brandon IP27 0TJ
t (01842) 815434 **w** forestry.gov.uk
open Please phone for details.
admission ££
High Lodge houses a shop and restaurant and the centre offers walking, cycling, high ropes course, adventure playground and much more.

Needham Lake and Nature Reserve
Needham Market
t (01449) 676800
open Daily.
admission Free
A large man-made lake and nature reserve with picnic and educational facilities on the outskirts of Needham Market with a tarmac pathway around the lake.

RSPB Minsmere Nature Reserve
Westleton IP17 3BY
t (01728) 648281 **w** rspb.org.uk
open Daily 0900-dusk.
admission £
RSPB reserve on Suffolk coast with bird-watching hides and trails, year-round events and guided walk and visitor centre with large shop and welcoming tearoom.

The Thornham Walled Garden
Thornham Field Centre Trust, Red House Yard,
Thornham Magna IP23 8HH
t (01379) 788700 **w** thornhamfieldcentre.org
open Apr-Oct, Mar, daily 0900-1700. Nov-Feb, daily 0900-1600.
admission Free
Restored Victorian glasshouses in the idyllic setting of a two-acre walled garden with fruit trees, wide perennial borders, collection of East Anglian geraniums and fern house.

The Walled Garden
Park Road, Benhall IP17 1JB
t (01728) 602510 **w** thewalledgarden.co.uk
open Apr-Nov, Mar,Tue-Sun 0930-1700. Dec-Feb, Tue-Sat 0930-1700.
admission Free
A retail nursery and garden selling almost 1,500 varieties of plants, nestling in the warmth of the high wall of an old kitchen garden.

Woottens Plants

Blackheath, Wenhaston, Halesworth IP19 9HD
t (01502) 478258
w woottensplants.co.uk
open Daily 0930-1700.
admission Free

Plantsman's nursery with huge range of stock. Frequently featured in the press and on television. Unique for the range and quality of its plants.

HISTORIC ENGLAND

Bridge Cottage

Flatford, East Bergholt CO7 6UL
t (01206) 298260
w nationaltrust.org.uk
open Apr-Sep, daily 1030-1730. Oct-Dec, Wed-Sun 1100-1530. Jan-Feb, Sat-Sun 1100-1530. Mar, Wed-Sun 1100-1700.
admission Free

A 16thC thatched cottage , just upstream from Flatford Mill, and housing an exhibition on landscape painter John Constable. Tearoom, shop, information centre & guided walks.

Bungay Castle

Bungay
t (01986) 896156
open Apr, Mon-Sat 1000-1600. May-Nov, daily 1000-1600. Dec-Mar, Mon-Sat 1000-1600.
admission Free

The remains of an original Norman castle with Saxon mounds. Built by the Bigods in 1165. Massive gatehouse towers and curtain walls. Visitor centre with cafe.

Clare Castle Country Park

Malting Lane, Clare CO10 8NW
t (01787) 277491
open Daily.
admission Free

A small country park incorporating the remains of a castle and a Victorian railway station in a 30-acre site fronting onto the River Stour.

The East Point Pavilion Visitor Centre

Royal Plain, Lowestoft NR33 0AP
t (01502) 533600
w visit-sunrisecoast.co.uk
open Apr-Sep, daily 1000-1730. Oct-Mar, daily 1000-1700.
admission £

A glass, all-weather Edwardian-style structure with a large indoor play platform called Mayhem. Small souvenir shop, restaurant and tearooms.

Euston Hall

Euston Estate Office, Thetford IP24 2QP
t (01842) 766366
w eustonhall.co.uk
open Jun-Sep, Thu 1430-1700.
admission ££

Hall housing paintings by Van Dyck, Lely and Stubbs, with pleasure grounds designed by John Evelyn and Capability Brown, and the 17thC Church of St Genevieve.

Eye Castle

Castle Street, Eye
t (01449) 676800
open Apr-Oct, daily 0900-dusk.
admission Free

A Norman motte-and-bailey with medieval walls and a Victorian folly. The castle has always had close associations with royalty since the Norman conquest.

Framlingham Castle

Framlingham IP13 9BP
t (01728) 724189
w english-heritage.org.uk
open See website for details.
admission £

A magnificent castle, the home of Mary Tudor in 1553, with 12thC curtain walls, 13 towers, Tudor brick chimneys and a wall walk.

Guildhall

Market Place, Hadleigh IP7 5DT
t (01473) 823884
open Jul-Sep, Mon-Fri, Sun 1430-1700.
admission Free

A medieval, Grade I Listed timber-framed complex dating from the 15th century. There is a timbered guild room, an old town hall, a Georgian assembly room and a Victorian ballroom.

Haughley Park

Haughley IP14 3JY
t (01359) 240701
w haughleyparkbarn.co.uk
open May-Sep, Tue 1400-1700.
admission £

Grade I Jacobean manor house with gardens and woods set in parkland. House by appointment only. Grade II barn venue for meetings, marriages etc.

Ickworth House, Park and Gardens

The Rotunda, Horringer IP29 5QE
t (01284) 735270
w nationaltrust.org.uk
open House: Apr-Sep, Mon-Tue, Fri-Sun 1300-1700. Oct-Nov, Mon-Tue, Fri-Sun 1300-1630. Gardens: Apr-Sep, Mon-Tue, Fri-Sun 1000-1700. Oct-Feb, Mon-Tue, Fri-Sun 1100-1600. Park: Daily, 0800-2000.
admission ££

An extraordinary oval house with flanking wings, begun in 1795. Fine paintings, a beautiful collection of Georgian silver, an Italian garden and stunning parkland.

The Ipswich Unitarian Meeting House
Friars Street, Ipswich IP1 1TD
t (01473) 218217
open May-Sep, Tue, Thu 1200-1600. Sun 1000-1600.
admission Free
A Grade I Listed building, built 1699, opened in 1700. One of the finest surviving meeting houses and one of the most important historic structures in Ipswich.

Kentwell Hall and Garden
Kentwell Hall, Long Melford CO10 9BA
t (01787) 310207 **w** kentwell.co.uk
open See website for details.
admission ££
Moated Tudor mansion, 'a little great house of magical beauty'. Exterior almost unaltered. The present owners have recovered and extended the once noted gardens.

Lavenham Guildhall of Corpus Christi
Market Place, Lavenham CO10 9QZ
t (01787) 247646 **w** nationaltrust.org.uk
open Apr-Oct, Tue-Sun 1100-1700. Nov-Dec, Sat-Sun 1100-1600.
admission £
An impressive timber-framed building dating from 1530s. Originally the hall of the Guild of Corpus Christi, now a local museum with information on the medieval cloth trade.

Little Hall
Market Place, Lavenham CO10 9QZ
t (01787) 247179
open Apr-Oct, Wed-Thu, Sat-Sun 1400-1730, Bank Hols 1100-1730.
admission £
A 14thC hall house with a crown-post roof which contains the Gayer-Anderson collection of furniture, pictures, sculpture and ceramics. There is also a small walled garden.

Melford Hall
Long Melford CO10 9AA
t (01787) 379228 **w** nationaltrust.org.uk
open Apr, Sat-Sun 1330-1700. May-Sep, Wed-Sun 1330-1700. Oct, Sat-Sun 1330-1700.
admission ££
Turreted brick Tudor mansion with connections to Beatrix Potter. Collection of Chinese porcelain, gardens and a walk in the grounds. Dogs on leads, where permitted.

Orford Castle
Orford IP12 2ND
t (01394) 450472 **w** english-heritage.org.uk
open Apr-Sep, daily 1000-1800. Nov-Mar, Mon, Thu-Sun 1000-1600.
admission £
A 90ft-high polygonal keep with views across the River Alde to Orford Ness, built by Henry II for coastal defence in the 12thC.

Saint Edmundsbury Cathedral
The Cathedral Office, Angel Hill,
Bury St Edmunds IP33 1LS
t (01284) 754933
w stedscathedral.co.uk
open Daily 0800-1800.
admission Free
Come and see the magnificent Millennium Tower which now completes the last unfinished Anglican cathedral in England.

Snape Maltings
Snape IP17 1SR
t (01728) 688303
w snapemaltings.co.uk
open Apr-Oct, Mon-Fri 1000-1730, Sat-Sun 1000-1600. Nov-Mar, Mon-Fri 1000-1700, Sat-Sun 1000-1730.
admission Free
Maltings on the banks of the River Alde with shops, galleries, restaurants, river trips, painting and craft courses in the summer and a world-famous concert hall.

Somerleyton Hall and Gardens
Somerleyton NR32 5QQ
t (01502) 730224
w somerleyton.co.uk
open Hall: Apr-Jun,Thu, Sun, Bank Hols 1200-1600. Jul-Aug, Tue-Thu, Sun 1200-1600. Sep-Oct, Thu, Sun, Bank Hols 1200-1600. Gardens: Apr-Jun,Thu, Sun, Bank Hols 1000-1700. Jul-Aug, Tue-Thu, Sun 1000-1700. Sep-Oct, Thu, Sun, Bank Hols 1000-1700.
admission £
Early Victorian stately mansion in Anglo-Italian style, with lavish features and fine state rooms. Beautiful 12-acre gardens, with historic yew hedge maze, gift shop.

South Elmham Hall
St Cross, South Elmham IP20 0PZ
t (01986) 782526
w batemansbarn.co.uk
open Tours only: May-Sep, Thu 1400, Sun, Bank Hols 1500.
admission ££
A ruined Norman chapel in a fortified enclosure. Wildlife walks around a conservation-award-winning farm. Coffee, lunches and cream teas served in a converted barn.

Sutton Hoo Burial Site
Tranmer House, Sutton Hoo,
Woodbridge IP12 3DJ
t (01394) 389700
w nationaltrust.org.uk
open See website for details.
admission ££
Sutton Hoo, owned by the National Trust, is an Anglo-Saxon royal burial site made up of low, grassy mounds overlooking the River Deben in Suffolk. A new exhibition tells the story.

ENTERTAINMENT AND CULTURE

The Amber Museum
15 Market Place, Southwold IP18 6EA
t (01502) 723394
w ambershop.co.uk
open All year, Mon-Sat 0900-1700, Sun 1100-1600.
admission Free
A purpose-built museum telling the story of amber, the precious gem found on the Suffolk shores. From how it is formed through historical uses to spectacular modern pieces.

Christchurch Mansion
Christchurch Park, Soane Street, Ipswich IP4 2BE
t (01473) 433554
w ipswich.gov.uk
open Apr-Oct, Tue-Sat 1000-1700, Sun 1430-1630.
Nov-Jan, Tue-Sat 1000-1600, Sun 1430-1600. Feb-Mar,
Tue-Sat 1000-1700, Sun 1430-1630.
admission Free
Fine Tudor mansion built between 1548 and 1550. Collection of furniture, panelling, ceramics, clocks and paintings from the 16th-19thC. Art exhibitions in Wolsey Art Gallery.

Clare Ancient House Museum
26 High Street, Clare CO10 8NY
t (01787) 277662
w clare-ancient-house-museum.co.uk
open May-Sep, Thu-Fri, Sun 1400-1700, Sat, Bank Hols
1130-1700.
admission £
Set in a 14thC building, showing the history of Clare with graphic displays, computerised records and census returns.

East Anglia Transport Museum
Chapel Road, Carlton Colville NR33 8BL
t (01502) 518459
w eatm.org.uk
open Apr-Sep, see website for details.
admission ££
A working museum with one of the widest ranges of street transport vehicles on display and in action. Developing street scene and a 2ft-gauge railway.

Gainsborough's House
46 Gainsborough Street, Sudbury CO10 2EU
t (01787) 372958
w gainsborough.org
open All year, Mon-Sat 1000-1700.
admission £
The birthplace of Thomas Gainsborough. An elegant townhouse with paintings by the artist, a garden, print workshop and a programme of temporary exhibitions.

Ipswich Museum
High Street, Ipswich IP1 3QH
t (01473) 433550 **w** ipswich.gov.uk
open All year, Tue-Sat 1000-1700.
admission Free
Displays of Roman Suffolk, Suffolk wildlife, Suffolk and world geology, the Ogilvie bird gallery, 'People of the World' and 'Anglo-Saxons come to Ipswich'.

Ipswich Transport Museum
Old Trolleybus Depot, Cobham Road, Ipswich IP3 9JD
t (01473) 715666 **w** ipswichtransportmuseum.co.uk
open Apr-Nov, Sun, Bank Hols 1100-1600. School Hols,
daily 1300-1600.
admission £
Over 100 historic vehicles housed in a former trolleybus depot. All have been built or used in the area. Also history and products of local engineering companies.

Long Shop Museum
Main Street, Leiston IP16 4ES
t (01728) 832189 **w** longshop.care4free.net
open Apr-Oct, Mon-Sat 1000-1700, Sun 1100-1700.
admission £
Award-winning museum, Grade II* listed Long Shop. Leiston's unique history and home of the Garrett collection. First production line to the first woman doctor.

Lowestoft and East Suffolk Maritime Museum
Sparrows Nest Park, Whapload Road,
Lowestoft NR32 1XG
t (01502) 561963
open Apr-Oct, daily 1000-1700.
admission £
The museum houses models of fishing and commercial ships, shipwrights' tools, fishing gear, a lifeboat display, an art gallery and a drifter's cabin with models of fishermen.

Mechanical Music Museum and Bygones Trust
Blacksmith Road, Cotton IP14 4QN
t (01449) 613876 **w** cottonmusic.co.uk
open Jun-Sep, Sun 1430-1730.
admission £
A selection of fairground organs and pipe organs, street pianos, music boxes, polyphons and many other musical items.

Mid-Suffolk Light Railway Museum
Brockford Station, Wetheringsett IP14 5PW
t (01449) 766899 **w** mslr.org.uk
open Apr-Jul, Sep, Sun, Bank Hols 1100-1700. Aug,
Wed, Sun, Bank Hols 1100-1700.
admission £
A recreated light railway station with exhibits relating to Mid-Suffolk Light Railway and restoration of the station and trackwork on part of the original route.

Moyse's Hall Museum
Cornhill, Bury St Edmunds IP33 1DX
t (01284) 757034 **w** stedmundsbury.gov.uk
open All year, Mon-Fri 1030-1630, Sat-Sun 1100-1600.
admission £

Dating back over 800 years, Moyse's Hall contains local history and archaeology collections, Murder in the Red Barn and highlights from the Suffolk Regiment.

Museum of East Anglian Life
Stowmarket IP14 1DL
t (01449) 612229 **w** eastanglianlife.org.uk
open Apr-Oct, Mon-Sat 1000-1700, Sun 1100-1700.
admission ££

East Anglia's open-air museum, set in 70 acres of Suffolk countryside. Displays and special events to interest visitors of all ages. Historic buildings.

National Horseracing Museum and Tours
99 High Street, Newmarket CB8 8JH
t (01638) 667333 **w** nhrm.co.uk
open Apr-Oct, daily 1100-1630.
admission ££

Award-winning display of the people and horses involved in racing's amazing history. Minibus tours to gallops, stables and equine pool. Hands-on gallery with horse simulator.

Norfolk and Suffolk Aviation Museum – East Anglia's Aviation Heritage Centre
Buckeroo Way, The Street, Flixton NR35 1NZ
t (01986) 896644
open Apr-Oct, Mon-Thu, Sun 1000-1700. Nov, Feb-Mar, Tue-Wed, Sun 1000-1600.
admission Free

A museum with 40 aircraft on display together with a large indoor display of smaller items connected with the history of aviation. Donations are encouraged.

Royal Naval Patrol Service Association Museum
Sparrows Nest, Lowestoft NR32 1XG
t (01502) 586250
open May-Oct, Mon, Wed, Fri 0900-1200.
admission Free

A museum with photographs of models of World War II officers and crews, minesweepers and anti-submarine vessels. Also models of American and British mine sweepers.

Wattisham Airfield Museum
Wattisham IP7 7RA
t (01449) 678189
w wattishamairfieldmuseum.fsnet.co.uk
open Apr-Oct, Sun 1400-1630.
admission Free

The museum houses an extensive photographic record, together with models, artefacts and memorabilia depicting the history and squadrons based at the station.

FOOD AND DRINK

St Peter's Brewery and Visitor Centre
St Peter's Hall, St Peter,
South Elmham NR35 1NQ
t (01986) 782322
open Brewery Talk: Mar-Dec, Sat-Sun 1200-1600. Visitor Centre: All year, Mon-Fri 0900-1700, Sat-Sun 1100-1600.
admission £

A small brewery in the grounds of a 13thC hall, with 19thC farm buildings containing the visitor centre.

Pirate party, Thorpeness

Admission is based on an adult price. Please check opening times and admission before travelling.

Warwickshire

Enjoy the fun of a special event or visit one of the attractions listed for a great day out. For more inspiring ideas go to **enjoyengland.com**.

Daily
Stratford Town Walk
Stratford-upon-Avon
(01789) 292478
stratfordtownwalk.co.uk

26 May–3 Jun
Warwickshire Walking Festival
Various venues throughout Warwickshire
(01926) 413419
warwickshire.gov.uk/walkingfestival

24 Jun
Warwick Racecourse 300th Anniversary Celebration
Warwick
(01926) 491553
warwickracecourse.co.uk

Dec
Skating at the Castle
Warwick Castle
0870 442 2000
warwick-castle.co.uk

Apr 08
Shakespeare Birthday Celebrations
Stratford-upon-Avon
(01789) 204016
shakespeare.org.uk

Ash End House Children's Farm
Ash End House Farm, Middleton Lane,
Middleton B78 2BL
t (0121) 329 3240
w childrensfarm.co.uk
open Apr-Oct, daily 1000-1700. Nov-Dec, Feb-Mar daily 1000-1600.
admission £
Small family-owned farm for children with undercover activities, play areas, picnic barns, gift shop and cafe. Admission includes all activities – no hidden extras!

Broomey Croft Childrens Farm
Broomey Croft Farm, Bodymoor Heath Lane,
Bodymoor Heath B76 0EE
t (01827) 873844
w childrens-farm.com
open All year, Sat-Sun 1000-1600, School Hols, daily 1000-1600.
admission £
A family-run farm with lots of friendly farm animals which can be hand-fed and stroked. Set in 600 acres. Groups and schools welcome.

Dobbies World
Nuneaton Road, Mancetter CV9 1RF
t (01827) 713438
w visitplantasia.co.uk
open Mar-Oct, Mon-Sat 0930-1800, Sun 0930-1700. Nov-Feb, daily 0930-1600.
admission ££
A 30-acre site including Maze World, Plantasia and a deer park with a hide and picnic area. A great day out.

Stratford Town Walk, Stratford Town Ghost Walk
Swan Fountain, Waterside,
Stratford-upon-Avon CV37 6BA
t (01789) 292478
w stratfordtownwalk.co.uk
open Town Walk: Mon-Wed, 1100-1330, Thu-Sun 1400-1530. Ghost Walk: phone for details.
admission £
Daily guided walks. Explore Stratford and its history, including the historic Holy Trinity Church with its cursed tomb.

Umberslade Farm
Butts Lane, Tanworth in Arden B94 5AE
t (01564) 742251
w umbersladefarm.co.uk
open Apr-Sep, daily 1000-1700. Oct-Mar, daily 1000-1600.
admission £
A traditional working farm forming part of an extensive beef, sheep and arable business, situated in beautiful Warwickshire countryside.

Warwick District Parks and Gardens
t (01926) 456214
w warwickdc.gov.uk
map ref 4B3
see ad on p234

NATURE AND WILDLIFE

Burton Dassett Hills Country Park
Burton Dassett CV47 2AB
t (01827) 872660
w warwickshire.gov.uk
open Daily.
admission Free
One hundred acres of open hill top, with magnificent views in all directions.

Coombe Country Park
Brinklow Road, Binley CV3 2AB
t (024) 7645 3720
w coventry.gov.uk
open Daily.
admission Free
Over 400 acres of country park with nature reserve, public bird hide, formal gardens, angling, woodland, lakeside walks. Restaurant and shop.

Draycote Water Country Park
Kites Hardwick, Dunchurch CV23 8AB
t (01788) 811107
w stwater.co.uk
open Daily 0730-2000.
admission Free
Country park covering 21 acres on southern side of Draycote Water reservoir.

Greenway and Milcote Picnic Area
Stratford-upon-Avon CV37 6GR
t (01827) 872660
w warwickshire.gov.uk
open Daily.
admission Free
Five miles of disused railway line converted to cycleway and footpath.

Jephson Gardens
Parade, Leamington Spa CV32 4AB
t (01926) 456211
w warwickdc.gov.uk
open Daily 0800-dusk.
admission Free
World-famous prestigious floral displays. Notable and rare specimen trees and shrubs. Lake and fountain replicas as at Hampton Court. Grade II Listed garden.

Kingsbury Water Park
Bodymoor Heath Lane, Bodymoor Heath,
Sutton Coldfield B76 0DY
t (01827) 872660
w warwickshire.gov.uk/countryside
open Apr, daily 0800-1830. May, daily 0800-1930. Jun, daily 0800-2030. Jul, daily 0530-2030. Aug, daily 0630-1930. Sep, daily 0700-1830. Oct, daily 0800-1730. Nov-Jan, daily 0800-1600. Feb, daily 0800-1700. Mar, daily 0800-1800.
admission Free
Six-hundred acres of countryside, 30 lakes featuring various watersports, fishing, sailing, jet bikes. Waymarked walks, cycle hire and adventure playgrounds. Nature trail.

Redwings Horse Sanctuary

Oxhill Rescue Centre, Oxhill,
nr Stratford-upon-Avon
t 0870 040 0033 w redwings.co.uk
open Daily 1000-1700, last entry 1630.
admission Free

The centre is home to more than 50 rescued horses, ponies and donkeys that visitors can meet and adopt. There is a brand new gift shop and cafe, plus the chance to find out all about the charity's equine welfare work. Free admission.

Map ref 2C1

Stratford-upon-Avon Butterfly Farm
Tramway Walk, Swans Nest Lane,
Stratford-upon-Avon CV37 7LS
t (01789) 299288
w butterflyfarm.co.uk
open Apr-Oct, daily 1000-1800. Nov-Mar, daily 1000-dusk.
admission ££
Hundreds of free-flying exotic butterflies in a jungle setting of tropical plants, cascading waterfalls and fish- filled pools. A strange and fascinating selection of animals can be seen in 'Insect City'.

Ufton Fields Nature Reserve
Ufton CV33 9PU
t (024) 7630 8979
w warwickshire.gov.uk
open Daily.
admission Free
A 77-acre nature reserve with lakes, marshes, grassland and woodland and a wide range of birds, wild flowers and insects. Nature trail with all-weather surface and two bird hides.

For key to symbols see inside back cover.

HISTORIC ENGLAND

Anne Hathaway's Cottage
Cottage Lane, Shottery CV37 9HH
t (01789) 292100 **w** shakepeare.org.uk
open Apr-May, Mon-Sat 0930-1700, Sun 1000-1700.
Jun-Aug, Mon-Sat 0900-1700, Sun 0930-1700. Sep-Oct,
Mon-Sat 0930-1700, Sun 1000-1700. Nov--Mar, daily
1000-1600.
admission ££
This world famous thatched cottage is the childhood
home of Anne Hathaway, Shakespeare's wife, and
remained in the Hathaway family until the 19th century.

Arbury Hall
Nuneaton CV10 7PT
t (024) 7638 2804
open Hall: Easter-Aug Bank Hols, Sun, Mon 1400-1700.
Gardens: Easter-Aug Bank Hols, Sun, Mon, 1330-1800.
admission ££
Elizabethan building gothicised by Sir Roger Newdigate
during the second half of the 18th century. Magnificent
ceilings in Georgian plaster and landscaped gardens.

Baddesley Clinton (National Trust)
Rising Lane, Baddesley Clinton,
Knowle B93 0DQ
t (01564) 783294 **w** nationaltrust.org.uk
open House: Apr, Wed-Sun 1330-1700. May-Sep,
Wed-Sun 1330-1730. Oct, Wed-Sun 1330-1700.
Grounds: Apr, Wed-Sun 1200-1700. May-Sep,
Wed-Sun 1200-1730. Oct, Wed-Sun 1200-1700. Nov,
Wed-Sun 1200-1600.
admission ££
A medieval moated manor house with 120 acres, dating
back to the 14thC. Little changed since 1634. Due to
popularity, visits are timed.

Charlecote Park (National Trust)
Wellesbourne CV35 9ER
t (01789) 470277 **w** nationaltrust.org.uk
open House: Apr-Oct, Mon-Tue, Fri-Sun 1200-1700.
Dec, Sat-Sun 1200-1600. Gardens: Mar-Oct, Mon-Tue,
Fri-Sun 1030-1800. Nov-Dec, Sat-Sun 1100-1600.
admission ££
Home of Lucy family since 1247, present house built
1550. Park landscaped by Capability Brown, supports a
herd of fallow deer. Tudor gatehouse.

Collegiate Church of St Mary
Old Square, Warwick CV34 4RA
t (01926) 400771 **w** stmaryswarwick.org.uk
open Apr-Oct, daily 1000-1800. Nov-Mar, daily
1000-1630.
admission £
Famous for its incomparable 15thC Beauchamp Chapel
with superb glass and medieval/Tudor tombs. Norman
crypt. Fourteenth-century chancel and chapter house.

Hall's Croft
Old Town CV37 6BG
t (01789) 204016
w shakespeare.org.uk
open Apr-May, daily 1100-1700. Jun-Aug, Mon-Sat
0930-1700, Sun 1000-1700. Sep-Oct, daily 1100-1700.
Nov-Mar, daily 1100-1600.
admission £
Tudor house, once home of Shakespeare's elder
daughter and her doctor husband. Contains Elizabethan
and Jacobean furniture, paintings and exhibition of
medicine.

Kenilworth Castle
Castle Green, Kenilworth CV8 1NE
t (01926) 852078
w english-heritage.org.uk
open Apr-May, daily 1000-1700. Jun-Aug, daily
1000-1800. Sep-Oct, daily 1000-1700. Nov-Feb, daily
1000-1600. Mar, daily 1000-1700.
admission ££
Edward II signed his abdication here, John of Gaunt
created the banqueting hall, and Elizabeth I was
entertained by Robert Dudley.

Mary Arden's House and the Shakespeare Countryside Museum
Wilmcote CV37 9UN
t (01789) 293455
w shakespeare.org.uk
open Apr-May, daily 1000-1700. Jun-Aug, daily
0930-1700. Sep-Oct, daily 1000-1700. Nov-Mar, daily
1000-1600.
admission ££
The childhood home of Shakespeare's mother,
and an example of a Tudor farmstead. Also
Palmer's Farm, the countryside museum and
falconry demonstrations.

Nash's House & New Place
Chapel Street, Stratford-upon-Avon CV37 6EP
t (01789) 292325
w shakespeare.org.uk
open Apr-May, daily 1100-1700. Jun-Aug, Mon-Sat
0930-1700, Sun 1000-1700. Sep-Oct, daily 1100-1700.
Nov-Mar, daily 1000-1600.
admission £
The site of Shakespeare's last home, including an
Elizabethan-style knot garden. Nash's House
contains fine period furniture. Also, a museum of
local history.

Packwood House
Packwood Lane, Lapworth B94 6AT
t (01564) 783294
w nationaltrust.org.uk
open Mar-Oct, Wed-Sun 1200-1630.
admission ££
Built in about 1560, a timber-framed house, substantially
renovated in the early 1900s, containing a wealth of
tapestries and furniture.

The Shakespeare Houses

Henley Street, Stratford-upon-Avon
CV37 6QW
t (01789) 204016 **w** shakespeare.org.uk
open Daily (excl 23-26 Dec). See website for
opening times of individual houses.
admission Adult: £7 (£14 to visit all five houses)

The Shakespeare Houses are five beautiful
historic houses in and around Stratford-upon-
Avon, all linked with William Shakespeare and
his family. Experience the Elizabethan way of
life and sights, smells and lost skills of
Shakespeare's time. Shakespeare's Birthplace,
Anne Hathaway's Cottage, Nash's House &
New Place, Hall's Croft and Mary Arden's
House.

See ad on p233

Map ref 2B1

 voucher offer – see back section

Shakespearience

Waterside Theatre, 13 Waterside,
Stratford-upon-Avon CV37 6BA
t (01789) 290111 **w** shakespearience.co.uk
open Daily 1030-1700.
admission ££

*A dynamic new visitor attraction based at Waterside
Theatre, telling the story of William Shakespeare's life
and works in a thrilling two-part show.*

Stratford Brass Rubbing Centre

The Summer House of Royal Shakespeare,
Theatre, Avon Bank Gardens,
Stratford-upon-Avon CV37 6XP
t (01789) 297671
w stratfordbrassrubbing.co.uk
open Apr-Oct, daily 1100-1600. Nov-Mar, daily
1000-1800.
admission Free

*A collection of medieval brasses, facsimiles of the
characters from Shakespeare's time and town. Materials
are supplied to visitors, who are shown how to make
their own pictures.*

Upton House

Banbury OX15 6HT
t (01295) 670266
w nationaltrust.org.uk
open Mar-Oct, Mon-Wed, Sat-Sun 1200-1700. Nov,
Sat-Sun 1200-1600.
admission ££

*A late-17thC house, remodelled from 1927-1929 for the
2nd Viscount Bearsted, containing his internationally
important collection of paintings and porcelain.
Spectacular garden.*

Warwick Castle

Warwick CV34 4QU
t 08704 422000
w warwick-castle.co.uk
open Jan-Mar, daily 1000-1700. Apr-Sep, daily
1000-1800. Oct-Dec, daily 1000-1700.
admission ££££

*Set in 60 acres of grounds with state rooms, armoury,
dungeon, torture chamber, 'A Royal Weekend Party
1898', 'Kingmaker' and the new Mill and Engine House.*

OUTDOOR ACTIVITIES

Avon Boating

Swans Nest Boathouse, Swans Nest Lane,
Stratford-upon-Avon CV37 7LS
t (01789) 267073
w avon-boating.co.uk
open Apr-Oct, daily 0900-dusk.
admission £

*Victorian and Edwardian passenger launches offering
30-minute cruises on River Avon. Rowing boats, punts
and self-drive motor boats for hire.*

Friendly help and advice

Tourist Information Centres offer suggestions of places to visit and
things to do as well as friendly help with accommodation and holiday
ideas. To find the one nearest to you text TIC LOCATE to 64118.

Admission is based on an adult price. Please check opening times and admission before travelling.

Redwings Horse Sanctuary

Oxhill Rescue Centre, Oxhill,
nr Stratford-upon-Avon
t 0870 040 0033 **w** redwings.co.uk
open Daily 1000-1700, last entry 1630.
admission Free

The centre is home to more than 50 rescued horses, ponies and donkeys that visitors can meet and adopt. There is a brand new gift shop and cafe, plus the chance to find out all about the charity's equine welfare work. Free admission.

 Map ref 2C1

Warwick District Parks and Gardens
t (01926) 456214 **w** warwickdc.gov.uk
map ref 4B3
see ad below

ENTERTAINMENT AND CULTURE

Compton Verney House
Compton Verney CV35 9HZ
t (01926) 645500 **w** comptonverney.org.uk
open Apr-Nov, Tue-Sun 1000-1700.
admission ££
Founded by British philanthropist Sir Peter Moores, through the Peter Moores Foundation, as a way of offering visitors informal and enjoyable ways of experiencing art.

Heritage Motor Centre
Banbury Road, Gaydon CV35 0BJ
t (01926) 641188 **w** heritage-motor-centre.co.uk
open All year, daily 1000-1700.
admission ££
The world's largest collection of historic British cars, 4x4 off-road experience, outdoor go-kart track, children's miniature roadway, picnic and play area, cafe and gift shop.

Midland Air Museum

Coventry Airport, Baginton CV8 3AZ
t (024) 7630 1033 **w** midlandairmuseum.co.uk
open Apr-Oct, daily 1000-1700. Nov-Mar, daily
1030-1630.
admission £
*A collection of over 40 historic aeroplanes. The
completed Sir Frank Whittle Jet Heritage Centre
includes early jet aircrafts and aero engines.*

Royal Shakespeare Company

Waterside, Stratford-upon-Avon CV37 6BB
t 0870 609 1110 **w** rsc.org.uk
open See website for details.
admission £££
*Stratford-upon-Avon is the home of the Royal
Shakespeare Company who perform the great works of
Shakespeare and other leading writers throughout the
year.*

The Shakespeare Houses

Henley Street, Stratford-upon-Avon
CV37 6QW
t (01789) 204016 **w** shakespeare.org.uk
open Daily (excl 23-26 Dec). See website for
opening times of individual houses.
admission Adult: £7 (£14 to visit all five houses)

The Shakespeare Houses are five beautiful
historic houses in and around Stratford-upon-
Avon, all linked with William Shakespeare and
his family. Experience the Elizabethan way of
life and sights, smells and lost skills of
Shakespeare's time. Shakespeare's Birthplace,
Anne Hathaway's Cottage, Nash's House &
New Place, Hall's Croft and Mary Arden's
House.

See ad on p233
Map ref 2B1

voucher offer – see back section

Warwickshire Yeomanry Museum

The Court House, Jury Street, Warwick CV34 4EW
t (01926) 492212
open Apr-Oct, Sat-Sun, Bank Hols 1000-1300,
1400-1600.
admission Free
*Uniforms, arms, swords, sabres and selected silver.
Display of photographs from 1794 to the present day.*

RELAXING AND PAMPERING

Hatton Country World

Hatton House, Hatton CV35 7LD
t (01926) 843411 **w** hattonworld.com
open Daily 1000-1700.
admission ££
*Two unique attractions. Hatton Shopping Village with
factory outlet, antique centre and 25 craft and gift
shops. Hatton Farm Village with animals and adventure
playground.*

Hoar Park Craft Village and Antiques Centre

Hoar Park Farm, Ansley, Nuneaton CV10 0QU
t (024) 7639 4433
open Apr-Oct, Tue-Sun 1000-1700. Nov-Mar, Tue-Sun
1000-1630.
admission Free
*Craft and antiques centre, garden centre, children's
farm, licensed restaurant, country walks, fishing pools,
children's play area. Regular craft and antique fairs.*

Warwick Castle

West Midlands

Enjoy the fun of a special event or visit one of the attractions listed for a great day out. For more inspiring ideas go to **enjoyengland.com**.

13–15 Jul
Godiva Festival
Memorial Park, Coventry
(024) 7622 7264
visitcoventry.co.uk/godiva

1–2 Sep
Coventry Festival of Motoring
Coventry
(024) 7623 4270
festival-of-motoring.co.uk

14–16 Sep
Artsfest
Various venues, Birmingham
0870 225 0127
artsfest.org.uk

16 Nov–23 Dec
Frankfurt Christmas Market
Various venues, Birmingham
(0121) 202 5000
beinbirmingham.com

May 08
Coventry Jazz Festival
Various venues, Coventry
(024) 7622 7264
coventryjazzfestival.com

The Birmingham Botanical Gardens & Glasshouses

Westbourne Road, Edgbaston,
Birmingham B15 3TR
t (0121) 454 1860
w birminghambotanicalgardens.org.uk
open Apr-Sep, Mon-Sat 0900-1900,
Sun 1000-1900, last entry 1830.
Oct-Mar, Mon-Sat 0900-1700,
Sun 1000-1700, last entry 1630 (excl 25 Dec).
admission Adult: £6.50

Four glasshouses take visitors from tropical rainforest to arid desert conditions with insectivorous plants, giant cacti, tree ferns and cycads, orchids and citrus fruits. Outside, 15 acres of beautiful, landscaped, historic, themed gardens. Adventure playground, Discovery Garden, walkabout trails, exotic birds, gift shop, plant sales, gallery, art trail, tea room.

Map ref 4B3

 voucher offer – see back section

Quality counts

Look out for the Quality Assured Visitor Attraction sign. These attractions are assessed annually and meet the standards required to receive the quality marque.

Coventry Transport Museum

Millennium Place, Hales Street,
Coventry CV1 1PN
t (024) 7623 4270
w transport-museum.com
open Daily 1000-1700, last entry 1630.
(Excl 24-26 Dec.)
admission Free

Coventry Transport Museum is full of inspiration, thrills and fun, with something to keep everyone in the family happy. With a world-renowned collection and dynamic displays, the museum is one of the major attractions in the region and a must-see for visitors of all ages.

 Map ref 4B3

Earlswood Lakes Craft Centre
Wood Lane, Earlswood B94 5JH
t (01564) 702729 **w** earlswoodlakes.co.uk
open Daily 1000-1600.
admission Free
Working family farm. Adjacent craft workshops all in a compact courtyard setting. There are 25 retail/craft units including Emporium and cafe.

Forge Mill Farm
Forge Lane, West Bromwich B71 3SZ
t (0121) 588 7210
open Apr-Oct, daily 1100-1730. Nov-Mar, daily 1000-1630.
admission Free
Working dairy farm with Jersey cows, farm trail and milking parlour with viewing gallery.

mac

Cannon Hill Park, Edgbaston,
Birmingham B12 9QH
t (0121) 440 3838
w macarts.co.uk
open Daily 0900-2300.
admission Free

As well as theatre, music, comedy, courses, exhibitions, films, children's and literary events, we have a great cafe, free parking and a stunning location in Cannon Hill Park. For more information please phone or visit our website.

Map ref 4B3

Royal Brierley Crystal Experience
Tipton Road, Dudley DY1 4SQ
t (0121) 530 5600
w royalbrierley.com
open All year, Mon-Sat 0900-1700.
admission Free
See crystal being hand made. Museum, large factory shop selling hand-made crystal, other giftware shops selling famous branded tableware and giftware. Coffee shop.

Sandwell Park Farm Visitors Centre
Salters Lane, West Bromwich B71 4BG
t (0121) 553 0220
w sandwellvalley.com
open Daily 1000-1630.
admission £
A restored 19thC working farm with livestock breeds of the period, traditional farming methods, displays and exhibitions. Also tearooms and Victorian kitchen garden.

enjoyEngland.com

A great attraction or activity can often make the perfect holiday. Enjoyengland.com features a comprehensive list of every quality-assured theme park, landmark, museum, national park and activity in England.

NATURE AND WILDLIFE

The Birmingham Botanical Gardens & Glasshouses

Westbourne Road, Edgbaston,
Birmingham B15 3TR
t (0121) 454 1860
w birminghambotanicalgardens.org.uk
open Apr-Sep, Mon-Sat 0900-1900,
Sun 1000-1900, last entry 1830.
Oct-Mar, Mon-Sat 0900-1700,
Sun 1000-1700, last entry 1630 (excl 25 Dec).
admission Adult: £6.50

Four glasshouses take visitors from tropical rainforest to arid desert conditions with insectivorous plants, giant cacti, tree ferns and cycads, orchids and citrus fruits. Outside, 15 acres of beautiful, landscaped, historic, themed gardens. Adventure playground, Discovery Garden, walkabout trails, exotic birds, gift shop, plant sales, gallery, art trail, tea room.

Map ref 4B3

V *voucher offer – see back section*

Quality counts

Look out for the Quality Assured Visitor Attraction sign. These attractions are assessed annually and meet the standards required to receive the quality marque.

Brandon Marsh Nature Centre
Brandon Lane, Coventry CV3 3GW
t (024) 7630 8999
w wildlifetrust.org.uk
open All year, Mon-Fri 0900-1700, Sat-Sun 1000-1600.
admission £

Two-hundred acre nature reserve with lakes, marshes and woodland. Ideal place to see natural wildlife. Nature trail with disabled access. Nature centre with displays and shop.

Dudley Zoological Gardens
2 The Broadway, Dudley DY1 4QB
t (01384) 215313
w dudleyzoo.org.uk
open Apr-Sep, daily 1000-1600. Oct-Mar, daily 1000-1500.
admission ££

From lions and tigers to snakes and spiders, there's something for all ages at Dudley Zoo. Animal feeding, encounters, face painting, land train and fair rides.

Kings Heath Park
Vicarage Road, Kings Heath B14 7TQ
t (0121) 444 2848
w brimingham.gov.uk
open Daily 0730-dusk.
admission Free

Traditional urban park demonstration garden. Also includes the horticultural training school, playground, bowls and tennis areas.

National Sea Life Centre
The Water's Edge, Brindley Place, Birmingham B1 2HL
t (0121) 643 6777
w sealifeeurope.com
open All year, Mon-Fri 1000-1600, Sat-Sun 1000-1700.
admission £££

Marvel at over 3,000 sea creatures displayed in a magical underwater world, complete with the world's first 360-degree transparent, tubular underwater walk-through tunnel. Amazonia exhibition.

Ryton Organic Gardens
Wolston Lane, Ryton-on-Dunsmore, Coventry CV8 3LG
t (024) 7630 3517
w gardenorganic.org.uk
open Daily 0900-1700.
admission £

The UK's national centre for organic gardening with ten acres of glorious gardens and the Vegetable Kingdom, an exciting £2-million interactive visitors' centre.

Sandwell Valley Country Park
Salters Lane, West Bromwich B71 4BG
t (0121) 553 0220
w sandwellvalley.com
open Daily 0730-dusk.
admission Free

Formerly part of the Earl of Dartmouth Estate. Seventeen-hundred acres of farms, woodlands, meadows and lakes for formal and informal recreation.

For key to symbols see inside back cover.

Sutton Park Visitor Centre
Park Road, Towngate, Sutton Park B74 2YT
t (0121) 355 6370
w birmingham.gov.uk
open Apr-Sep, daily 1000-1900. Oct-Mar, daily 1000-1630.
admission Free
A National Nature Reserve comprising 2,400 acres of woodland and lakes with the ancient Roman Ryknild Street running through. Walks, cycling, play areas, angling, golf and picnic area.

Walsall Arboretum
Lichfield Street, Walsall
t (01922) 653148
w walsallarboretum.co.uk
open Summer: Daily 0700-2130. Winter: Daily 0700-1600.
admission Free
A picturesque Victorian park with over 170 acres of gardens, lakes and parkland. Home to the famous Walsall Illuminations each autumn.

Woodgate Valley Country Park
Clapgate Lane, Bartley Green B32 3DS
t (0121) 421 7575
w birmingham.gov.uk/parks
open Apr-Oct, daily 1000-1900. Nov-Mar, daily 1000-1630.
admission Free
A 450-acre country park of meadows, woodland, hedgerows and wetland. Visitor Centre with cafe. Pony-trekking centre and small urban farm.

HISTORIC ENGLAND

Birmingham Cathedral (St Philips)
Colmore Row, Birmingham B3 2QB
t (0121) 262 1840
open Apr-Jul, Mon-Fri 0800-1800, Sat 0930-1600, Sun 0900-1730. Aug, Mon-Sun 0800-1600. Sep-Mar, Mon-Fri 0800-1800, Sat 0930-1600, Sun 0900-1730.
admission Free
A beautiful historic building at the heart of the city, Birmingham Cathedral contains four famous Pre-Raphaelite windows by Burne-Jones, surrounded by a restored churchyard.

Coventry Cathedral
Priory Street, Coventry CV1 5ES
t (024) 7652 1200
w coventrycathedral.org.uk
open Daily 0900-1700.
admission £
Glorious 20thC cathedral rising above the stark ruins of the medieval cathedral destroyed in 1940. The visitor centre includes audio-visual shows.

Galton Valley Canal Heritage Centre
Brasshouse Lane, Smethwick B66 1AP
t (0121) 558 8195
open All year, Mon-Thu, Sun 1000-1500.
admission Free
Thomas Telford's 1820s masterpiece in cast iron, reputed to be the longest single-span canal bridge still in existence. Also canal buildings by Brindley, Smeaton and Telford.

Haden Hill House
Off Barrs Road, via Lee Road, Cradley Heath B64 7JX
t (01384) 569444 **w** lea.sandwell.gov.uk/museums
open Apr-Dec, Feb-Mar, Tue-Fri 1000-1700, Sat-Sun 1400-1700.
admission Free
A restored Grade II Listed Victorian house, built for George Alfred Haden-Best, last of the Haden family connected with the estate and part of a family that is 900 years old.

Red House Glass Cone
High Street, Wordsley DY8 4AZ
t (01384) 812750 **w** redhousecone.co.uk
open Apr-Oct, daily 1000-1700. Nov-Mar, daily 1000-1600.
admission Free
A late-18thC glass cone, one of only four surviving in the UK. Facilities include audio tour around the tunnels and furnace, changing displays and craft studios.

St Chad's Cathedral
Queensway, Birmingham B4 6EU
t (0121) 236 2251 **w** stchadscathedral.org.uk
open All year, Mon-Fri 0800-1700, Sat 0900-1700, Sun, Bank Hols 0900-1300.
admission Free
A Gothic-style cathedral with German or Belgian influences – notably fine twin spires. Fifteenth-century German and Flemish artwork. Excellent John Hardman stained glass.

Sarehole Mill
Cole Bank Road, Hall Green B13 0BD
t (0121) 777 6612 **w** bmag.org.uk
open All year, Tue-Sun, Bank Hols 1130-1600.
admission Free
An 18thC water-powered mill containing displays illustrating milling, blade grinding and agriculture. Tolkein is thought to have used Sarehole as his model for the Mill at Hobbitton in the Hobbit.

Soho House Museum
Soho Avenue, Off Soho Road, Handsworth B18 5LB
t (0121) 554 9122 **w** bmag.org.uk
open Apr-Oct, Tue-Sun, Bank Hols 1130-1600.
admission Free
The former home of industrial pioneer, Matthew Boulton. Displays show the story of the Lunar Society and Boulton's businesses. Community Gallery with changing exhibitions. Period-style garden and tearoom.

Stuart Crystal

Wordsley DY8 4AA
t (01384) 828282
open Shop: All year, Mon-Sat 0900-1700, Sun 1000-1600. Museum: Apr-Oct, Mon-Sat 100-1700, Sun 1000-1600. Nov-Mar, daily 1000-1600.
admission Free

A 19thC glassmaking site with the famous Redhouse Cone kiln, one of only four remaining glass cones in the UK, dominating the local skyline. Museum, factory shop, glass repair service.

Wightwick Manor (National Trust)

Wightwick Bank, Wolverhampton WV6 8EE
t (01902) 761400
w nationaltrust.org.uk
open House: Apr-Dec, Thu-Sat 1230-1700. Gardens: Apr-Dec, Wed-Sat 1100-1800.
admission ££

Begun in 1887, a notable example of William Morris-influenced original wallpapers and fabrics, Kempe glass, de Morgan ware, yew-hedge gardens, pottery studio and William Morris shop.

OUTDOOR ACTIVITIES

Dudley Canal Trust (Trips) Ltd

Blowers Green Pumphouse, Pear Tree Lane, Dudley DY2 0XP
t (01384) 236275
w dudleycanaltrust.org.uk
open Apr-Oct, Mon-Fri 1000-1700. Nov, Wed-Sun 1000-1600. Feb-Mar, Wed-Sun 1000-1600.
admission £

Dudley Canal Tunnel and Singing Cavern experience, a subterranean journey into the past. Travelling by electrically-powered narrow boat into the underground canal.

Second City Canal Cruises Limited

The Canalside Souvenir Shop, Gas Street Basin, Birmingham B1 2JU
t (0121) 236 9811
w secondcityboats.co.uk
open Daily 1000-1800.
admission £

Differing cruises which show off Birmingham's canal ethos. Canal walkabouts and visits to canalside attractions.

ENTERTAINMENT AND CULTURE

Bantock House and Park

Finchfield Road, Wolverhampton WV3 9LQ
t (01902) 552195 **w** wolverhamptonart.org.uk
open Apr-Oct, Tue-Sun 1100-1700. Nov-Mar, Tue-Sun 1200-1600.
admission Free

Restored period house and gardens. Displays include historical and industrial development of Wolverhampton, japanned ware, enamels, steel jewellery, locks and keys.

Barber Institute of Fine Arts

University of Birmingham, Edgbaston B15 2TS
t (0121) 414 7333 **w** barber.org.uk
open All year, Mon-Sat 1000-1700, Sun 1200-1700.
admission Free

British and European paintings, drawings and sculpture from the 13thC to mid-20C.

Birmingham Museum & Art Gallery

Chamberlain Square, Birmingham B3 3DH
t (0121) 303 2834 **w** bmag.org.uk
open All year, Mon-Thu, Sat 1000-1700, Fri 1030-1700, Sun 1230-1700.
admission Free

Fine and applied art, archaeology, local history collections, all displayed in the same building. World-famous collection of work by the pre-Raphaelites.

Birmingham Railway Museum

670 Warwick Road, Tyseley B11 2HL
t (0121) 707 4696 **w** vintagetrains.co.uk
open All year, Sat-Sun 1000-1600.
admission £

A live steam museum featuring a fine collection of locomotives, specialist coaches and goods wagons. Home of the Shakespeare Express.

Black Country Living Museum

Tipton Road, Dudley DY1 4SQ
t (0121) 557 9643 **w** bclm.co.uk
open Apr-Oct, daily 1000-1700. Nov-Feb, Wed-Sun 1000-1600. Mar, daily 1000-1700.
admission £££

A warm welcome awaits you at Britain's friendliest open-air museum. Wander around original shops and houses, ride on fair attractions, take a look down the underground coalmine.

Friendly help and advice

Tourist Information Centres offer suggestions of places to visit and things to do as well as friendly help with accommodation and holiday ideas. To find the one nearest to you text TIC LOCATE to 64118.

Admission is based on an adult price. Please check opening times and admission before travelling.

Broadfield House Glass Museum

Compton Drive, Kingswinford DY6 9NS
t (01384) 812745
w glassmuseum.org.uk
open All year, Tue-Sun, Bank Hols 1200-1600.
admission Free

Internationally famous collection of British glass from 17th century to the present day, focusing on achievements of local Stourbridge glass industry.

Cadbury World

Linden Road, Bournville B30 2LU
t 0845 450 3599
w cadburyworld.co.uk
open See website for details.
admission £££

Story of Cadbury's chocolate includes chocolate-making demonstration and attractions for all ages, with free samples, free parking, shop and restaurant.

Coventry Transport Museum

Millennium Place, Hales Street, Coventry CV1 1PN
t (024) 7623 4270
w transport-museum.com
open Daily 1000-1700, last entry 1630. (Excl 24-26 Dec.)
admission Free

Coventry Transport Museum is full of inspiration, thrills and fun, with something to keep everyone in the family happy. With a world-renowned collection and dynamic displays, the museum is one of the major attractions in the region and a must-see for visitors of all ages.

                           Map ref 4B3

The Coventry Toy Museum

Whitefriars Gate, Much Park Street, Coventry CV1 2LT
t (024) 7622 7560
open Daily 1100-1730.
admission Free

The museum is housed in a building of historic interest, Whitefriars Gate built in 1352. Various toys, dolls, trains and tin plate toys.

Dudley Museum and Art Gallery

St James's Road, Dudley DY1 1HU
t (01384) 815575
w dudley.gov.uk/dudleymuseum
open All year, Mon-Sat 1000-1600.
admission Free

Permanent display in Geological gallery, also changing exhibition programme including items from collection.

Ikon Gallery

1 Oozells Square, Brindleyplace, Birmingham B1 2HS
t (0121) 248 0708
w ikon-gallery.co.uk
open All year, Tue-Sun, Bank Hols 1100-1800.
admission Free

Ikon is one of Europe's premier contemporary art galleries, situated in the heart of canalside Brindleyplace. Ikon houses Birmingham's best tapas restaurant and a bookshop.

mac

Cannon Hill Park, Edgbaston, Birmingham B12 9QH
t (0121) 440 3838
w macarts.co.uk
open Daily 0900-2300.
admission Free

As well as theatre, music, comedy, courses, exhibitions, films, children's and literary events, we have a great cafe, free parking and a stunning location in Cannon Hill Park. For more information please phone or visit our website.

   Map ref 4B3

The Museum of the Jewellery Quarter

75-79 Vyse Street, Hockley B18 6HA
t (0121) 554 3598
w bmag.org.uk
open All year, Tue-Sun, Bank Hols 1130-1600.
admission Free

A 'time capsule' jewellery factory, little changed since 1914 and left undisturbed after closure, is brought back to life. The story of jewellery making in Birmingham.

National Motorcycle Museum
Coventry Road, Bickenhill B92 0EJ
t (01675) 443311 **w** nationalmotorcyclemuseum.co.uk
open Daily 0930-1730.
admission ££
This is recognised as the finest and largest motorcycle museum in the world, with five exhibition halls housing a collection of 650 British machines from 1898-1993.

Royal Birmingham Society of Artists
4 Brook Street, St Paul's Square, Birmingham B3 1SA
t (0121) 236 4353 **w** rbsa.org.uk
open All year, Mon-Fri 1030-1730, Sat 1030-1700.
admission Free
The gallery sells designer-made jewellery, ceramics, glassware, silverware, textiles, original prints and handmade cards. There is an exciting and changing programme of exhibitions.

Thinktank – Birmingham's Museum of Science and Discovery
Millennium Point, Curzon Street,
Birmingham B4 7XG
t (0121) 202 2222 **w** thinktank.ac
open Daily 1000-1700.
admission £££
Birmingham's new £50-million museum where you can investigate everything from locomotives and aircraft to intestines and taste buds!

Walsall Leather Museum
Littleton Street West, Walsall WS2 8EQ
t (01922) 721153
w walsall.gov.uk/leathermuseum
open Apr-Sep, Tue-Sat, Bank Hols 1000-1700, Sun 1200-1700. Oct-Mar, Tue-Sat, Bank Hols 1000-1600, Sun 1200-1600.
admission Free
An award-winning working museum in the saddlery and leather goods 'capital' of Britain. Watch skilled craftsmen and women at work in this restored Victorian leather factory.

Wednesbury Art Gallery and Museum
Holyhead Road, Wednesbury WS10 7DF
t (0121) 556 0683 **w** lea.sandwell.gov.uk/museums
open Apr-Sep, Tue-Fri 1000-1700, Sat 1400-1700. Oct-Mar, Tue-Fri 1000-1700.
admission Free
The gallery and museum houses Edwin Richard's collection of 19thC paintings and the world's largest public collection of Ruskin pottery.

Wolverhampton Art Gallery
Lichfield Street, Wolverhampton WV1 1DU
t (01902) 552055 **w** wolverhamptonart.org.uk
open All year, Mon-Sat 1000-1700.
admission Free
A multi-award-winning gallery with cafe, shop and temporary exhibitions. Explore 300 years of art in this newly refurbished city-centre gallery.

Worcestershire

Enjoy the fun of a special event or visit one of the attractions listed for a great day out. For more inspiring ideas go to **enjoyengland.com**.

15–17 Jun
Three Counties Countryside Show
Three Counties Showground, Malvern
(01684) 584900
threecounties.co.uk

23–24 Jun & 30 Jun–1 Jul
1940s Severn Valley Railway Weekend
Kidderminster
(01299) 403816
svr.co.uk

11–27 Aug
Worcester Festival
Various venues, Worcester
(01905) 611427
worcesterfestival.co.uk

29–30 Sep
Malvern Autumn Show
Three Counties Showground, Malvern
(01684) 584900
threecounties.co.uk

29 Nov–2 Dec
Worcester Christmas Fayre
Various venues, Worcester
(01905) 726311
worcestershire-tourism.org

For key to symbols see inside back cover.

FAMILY FUN

Royal Worcester
Severn Street, Worcester WR1 2NE
t (01905) 74600 **w** royalworcester.com
open Apr-Nov, Mon-Sat 1000-1700, Sun 1100-1700.
Dec-Feb, Mon-Sat 1000-1600, Sun 1100-1700.
admission £
Take a guided tour of the working factory or Museum of Worcester Porcelain. Antler Luggage and Woods of Windsor are new additions to the shopping court.

Severn Valley Railway
The Railway Station, Bewdley DY12 1BG
t (01299) 403816 **w** svr.co.uk
open See website for details.
admission £££
A preserved standard-gauge steam railway running 16 miles between Kidderminster, Bewdley and Bridgnorth. Also a collection of locomotives and passenger coaches.

Wyre Forest Glades Leisure Centre and Glades Arena
Bromsgrove Street, Kidderminster DY10 1PP
t (01562) 515151
open Daily 0715-2230.
admission £
A leisure pool with wave machine and water slides in Mediterranean environment. Also squash and fitness courts, toning suite, sauna, solarium, bar and restaurant.

NATURE AND WILDLIFE

Arley Arboretum
Arley, Bewdley DY12 1SQ
t (01299) 861368 **w** arley-arboretum.org.uk
open Apr-Oct, Wed-Sun, Bank Hols 1100-1700.
admission £
One of the oldest privately owned arboretums in the country with listed walled garden containing Italianate garden, herbaceous borders, picnic area, tea room and plant sales.

Bodenham Arboretum
Wolverley DY11 5SY
t (01562) 852444 **w** bodenham-arboretum.co.uk
open Mar-Sep, Wed-Sun 1100-1700. Oct, daily 1100-1700. Nov-Dec, Wed-Sun 1100-1700. Jan-Feb, Sat-Sun 1100-1700.
admission £
This award winning arboretum, set within a working farm of 156 acres, contains over 2,700 species of trees and shrubs.

Croome Landscape Park
High Green, Severn Stoke WR8 9JS
t (01905) 371006
w nationaltrust.org.uk
open Apr, Wed-Sun 1000-1730. May-Aug, daily 1000-1730. Sep-Oct, Wed-Sun 1000-1730. Nov-Dec, Sat-Sun 1000-1600.
admission £
Landscape park containing water features and park buildings.

Eastgrove Cottage Garden Nursery
Sankyns Green, Nr Shrawley, Little Witley WR6 6LQ
t (01299) 896389
w eastgrove.co.uk
open Apr, Thu-Sat, Bank Hols 1400-1700. May, Mon, Thu-Sun, Bank Hols 1400-1700. Jun, Thu-Sat, Bank Hols. Sep, Thu-Sat 1400-1700.
admission £
Old-world English cottage garden full of scent and colour in country setting. Plants for sale. Owners available for advice. An RHS Partnership garden.

The Falconry Centre
Hurrans Garden Centre, Kidderminster Road South, Hagley DY9 0JB
t (01562) 700014
w thefalconrycentre.co.uk
open All year, Mon-Sat 1000-1700, Sun 1100-1700.
admission £
Owls, hawks, falcons and aviaries. Hawking and falconry courses. Falconry displays at 1300 and 1500, weather permitting.

Hartlebury Common
Hartlebury WR5 1ES
t (01905) 766493
w worcestershire.gov.uk/countryside
open Daily.
admission Free
Hartlebury Common local nature reserve which comprises over 200 acres of sandy lowland heath including Hillditch pool and coppice.

Kingsford Country Park
Blakeshall, Wolverley BH11 5SL
t (01562) 710025
w worcestershire.gov.uk/countryside
open Daily.
admission Free
Two hundred acres of mainly evergreen coniferous woodland and open heath adjacent to Kinver Edge which provides a further 400 acres of heathland access.

Knapp and Papermill Nature Reserve
The Knapp House, Bridges Stone, Alfrick WR6 5HR
t (01886) 832065
w worcswildlifetrust.co.uk
open Daily.
admission Free
Sixty-three acres of woodland, meadow, orchards, marsh and stream. The apple orchard contains old lichen-encrusted trees above a pasture containing many herbs and occasional wild daffodils.

Lickey Hills Visitor Centre and Country Park
Warren Lane, Rednal B45 8ER
t (0121) 447 7106
w birmingham.gov.uk
open Apr-Sep, daily 1000-1900. Oct-Mar, daily 1000-1630.
admission Free
A 524-acre country park of woodland, heathland and shrubs giving views over Birmingham. Green Flag park for 2003 and 2004.

Spetchley Park Gardens

Spetchley Park, Spetchley WR5 1RS
t (01453) 810303
w spetchleygardens.co.uk
admission Adult: £6

The Gardens are amongst the finest in the country. Set in lovely countryside three miles east of Worcester, they extend over 30 acres and include many rare trees, shrubs and plants of interest, both to the professional gardener and to the amateur.

Map ref 2B1

Stone House Cottage Gardens
Stone DY10 4BG
t (01562) 69902
w shcn.co.uk
open Apr-Sep, Wed-Sat 1000-1700.
admission £
A very beautiful old walled garden with rare wall shrubs and climbers, herbaceous plants. In an adjacent nursery, there is a large selection of unusual plants for sale.

Waseley Hills Country Park
Gannow Green Lane, Rubery B45 9AT
t (01562) 710025
w worcestershire.gov.uk/countryside
open Park: Daily. Visitor Centre: Daily, 1000-1700.
admission Free
One-hundred-and-fifty acres of grass-covered hills, spectacular views, small woods and ponds. Visitor Centre, cafe and meeting room available.

Webbs of Wychbold, Garden Centre
Wychbold WR9 0DG
t (01527) 860000
w webbsofwychbold.co.uk
open All year, Mon-Sat 0900-1800, Sun 1030-1630.
admission Free
Fifty acres of gardening, leisure and pleasure. Inspirational riverside gardens, book, card and gift shop, vast range of plants and a relaxing cafe restaurant.

West Midland Safari and Leisure Park
Spring Grove, Bewdley DY12 1LF
t (01299) 402114 **w** wmsp.co.uk
open Feb-Nov, Mon-Fri 1000-1600, Sat, Sun, Banks Hols, School Hols 1000-1700.
admission ££
Two hundred acres incorporating drive-through safari, Discovery Trail, reptile house, sea-lion theatre, hippo lakes, animal and reptile encounters, amusements and shops.

Worcester Woods Country Park
Wildwood Drive, Worcester WR5 2LG
t (01905) 766493 **w** worcestershire.gov.uk/countryside
open Daily.
admission Free
Over 110 acres of ancient woodland and traditional wildflower meadow with self-guided trails, countryside exhibits, shop and cafe.

Wyre Forest Visitor Centre
Callow Hill, Rock DY14 9XQ
t (01299) 266944 **w** wyreforest.net
open All year, Mon-Fri 1000-1530, Sat-Sun 0900-1800.
admission Free
A warm welcome all year round. Guides to the forest, marked trails suitable for wheelchairs and buggies, forest restaurant, tearoom and children's trails.

HISTORIC ENGLAND

Droitwich Spa Heritage Centre
St Richard's House, Victoria Square, Droitwich WR9 8DS
t (01905) 774312
open All year, Mon-Sat 1000-1600.
admission Free
See the fascinating history of Droitwich from salt settlement to luxury spa. Tourist Information Centre and brass rubbing centre.

The Greyfriars (National Trust)
Friar Street, Worcester WR1 2LZ
t (01905) 23571 **w** nationaltrust.org.uk
open Mar-Jun, Wed-Sat 1300-1700. Jul-Aug, Wed-Sun 1300-1700. Aug-Nov, Wed-Sat 1300-1700.
admission £
Mainly late 15th-17thC and late 18thC additions, timber-framed and tiled house of specialist architectural interest. Pretty walled garden.

Hagley Hall
Hagley DY9 9LG
t (01562) 882408 **w** hagleyhall.info
open See website for details.
admission £
The last of the great Palladian houses, completed in 1760. Superb Italian plasterwork. Home of Viscount Cobham.

Hanbury Hall (National Trust)

School Road, Hanbury WR9 7EA
t (01527) 821214 **w** nationaltrust.org.uk
open Mar-Oct, Mon-Wed, Sat-Sun 1300-1700.
Nov-Feb, Sat-Sun 1300-1700.
admission ££

Beautiful English country house with tranquil 18thC gardens and views over 400 acres of parkland. Unusual features include outstanding murals, mushroom house and bowling green.

Harvington Hall

Harvington DY10 4LR
t (01562) 777846 **w** harvingtonhall.com
open Apr-Sep, Wed-Sun 1130-1700. Oct, Mar, Sat-Sun 1130-1700.
admission £

Moated Elizabethan manor house with priests' hiding holes, and rare wall paintings. Georgian Chapel in garden.

Pershore Abbey

Church Street, Pershore WR10 1DT
t (01386) 561520 **w** pershoreabbey.fsnet.co.uk
open Apr-Oct, Mon-Sat 0800-1700. Nov-Mar, Mon-Sat 0800-1600.
admission Free

Ancient abbey church with Norman crossing, 13thC chancel with decorated vault, rare triforium with clerestory and fine lantern tower with unique ringing platform.

Spetchley Park Gardens

Spetchley Park, Spetchley WR5 1RS
t (01453) 810303
w spetchleygardens.co.uk
admission Adult: £6

The Gardens are amongst the finest in the country. Set in lovely countryside three miles east of Worcester, they extend over 30 acres and include many rare trees, shrubs and plants of interest, both to the professional gardener and to the amateur.

Map ref 2B1

The Ark Animal Sanctuary

Evesham Country Park, Evesham WR11 4TP
t (01386) 443348
open Apr-Oct, daily 1030-1730. Nov-Mar, daily 1030-1600.
admission £

Native British wildlife including hedgehogs, foxes, barn owls and red and grey squirrels, together with reptiles and other exotic animals.

Witley Court

Great Witley WR6 6JT
t (01299) 896636 **w** english-heritage.org.uk
open Apr-May, Sep-Oct, Mar, daily 1000-1700. June-Aug, daily 1000-1700. Nov-Feb, Mon, Thu-Sun 1000-1600.
admission ££

Spectacular ruins of one of England's great country houses surrounded by magnificent landscaped gardens designed by Nesfield, and featuring the great Perseus and Andromeda fountain.

Worcester Cathedral

10a College Green, Worcester WR1 2LH
t (01905) 611002 **w** cofe-worcester.org.uk
open All year, Mon-Sat 0730-1800, Sun 0730-1830.
admission £

One of England's loveliest cathedrals with medieval cloisters, an ancient crypt and Chapter House and magnificent Victorian stained glass.

OUTDOOR ACTIVITIES

AZTEC Watersports

The Spring Holiday Park, Salters Lane, Lower Moor WR10 2PD
t (01386) 860013 **w** aztecwatersports.com
open Mar-Oct, daily 1000-1800.
admission ££££

Beautiful countryside setting, ideal learning environment – safe, shallow, clean spring water for windsurfing, sailing, canoeing and lots more.

Croft Farm Leisure and Water Park

Bredon's Hardwick GL20 7EE
t (01684) 772321 **w** croftfarmleisure.co.uk
open Mar-Dec, daily 0900-1700.
admission £

We have sailing, canoeing and windsurfing tuition by qualified instructors on our own lake. We have day tickets for spectators and a picnic area.

ENTERTAINMENT AND CULTURE

Avoncroft Museum of Historic Buildings

Stoke Heath B60 4JR
t (01527) 831363 **w** avoncroft.org.uk
open Mar, Tue-Thu, Sat-Sun 1030-1600. Apr-Jun, Tue-Fri 1030-1630, Sat-Sun 1030-1700. Jul-Aug, daily 1030-1700. Sep-Oct, Tue-Sun 1030-1600.
admission ££

Re-erected historic buildings saved from destruction including a working windmill, furnished houses and the National Telephone Kiosk Collection.

Bewdley Museum
Load Street, Bewdley DY12 2AE
t (01299) 403573
w wyreforestdc.gov.uk
open Apr-Sep, daily 1000-1630. Oct, daily 1100-1600.
admission Free
Local history, craft and trades of the Wyre Forest.

Birmingham & Midland Museum of Transport
Chapel Lane, Wythall B47 6JX
t (01564) 826471
w bammot.org.uk
open Apr-Jun, Aug-Oct, Sat-Sun 1100-1630. Jul, Wed 1300-1630, Sat-Sun 1100-1630.
admission £
The museum houses a broad collection of 100 buses and other vehicles from the Midlands. Classic buses and miniature steam railway provide rides on event days.

The Commandery
Sidbury, Worcester WR1 2HU
t (01905) 721143
w cityofworcester.gov.uk
open Please phone for details.
admission ££
A delightful timber-framed building which offers period rooms depicting Tudor and Stuart life and exciting exhibitions.

The Elgar Birthplace Museum
Crown East Lane, Lower Broadheath WR2 6RH
t (01905) 333224
w elgarmuseum.org
open Daily 1100-1700.
admission £
Country cottage birthplace of Sir Edward Elgar and featuring the new Elgar Centre, giving a fascinating insight into his life, music, family, friends and inspirations.

Farncombe Estate Centre
Broadway WR12 7LJ
t (01386) 854100
w farncombeestate.co.uk
open Sat-Sun (excl Christmas and New Year).
admission Free

This award-winning centre offers a wide range of events and day schools including crafts, art, alternative therapies, walks, history, wine, photography and music. Visitors enjoy stunning views over Broadway and the Cotswolds, good food and wonderful, caring service, all in the tranquillity of a 300-acre private estate.

Map ref 2B1

 voucher offer – see back section

The Four Stones, Clent Hills

For key to symbols see inside back cover.

The Museum of Worcester Porcelain
Severn Street, Worcester WR1 2NE
t (01905) 23221 **w** worcesterporcelainmuseum.org
open All year, Mon-Sat 0900-1730, Sun 1100-1700.
admission £
*The largest and most comprehensive collection of
Worcester porcelain in the world, covering the period
from the start of manufacture in 1751 to the present day.*

Worcester City Art Gallery & Museum
Foregate Street, Worcester WR1 1DT
t (01905) 25371
w worcestercitymuseums.org.uk
open All year, Mon-Fri 0930-1730, Sat 0930-1700.
admission Free
*The museum and art gallery contains temporary
exhibitions and collections of the Worcestershire
Regiment and Yeomanry Cavalry. The art gallery
exhibitions are changed monthly.*

FOOD AND DRINK

Tiltridge Vineyard
Upper Hook Road, Upton-upon-Severn WR8 0SA
t (01684) 592906 **w** elgarwine.com
open Apr-Oct, Mon-Sat 1100-1700, Sun 1200-1700.
Nov-Mar, please phone for details.
admission Free
*A small family vineyard producing award-winning quality
white and rose wines, both still and sparkling. Wine
tasting and shop.*

RELAXING AND PAMPERING

Conderton Pottery
The Old Forge, Conderton GL20 7PP
t (01386) 725387 **w** toffmilway.co.uk
open All year, Mon-Sat 0900-1700.
admission Free
*Handmade salt-glazed stoneware made by the
craftsman on the premises, and displayed in own barn
gallery setting. All parts of workshop open to view.*

Droitwich Spa Brine Baths Complex
St Andrews Road, Droitwich WR9 8DN
t (01905) 793446 **w** brinebath.co.uk
open All year, Mon-Fri 1130-2100, Sat 1000-1700, Sun
1000-1600.
admission ££
*Unique experience of floating weightless in natural
Droitwich brine. Fitness and health facilities such as
rehabilitation, physiotherapy, hydrotherapy & sports
injury.*

Lower Smite Farm
Worcestershire Wildlife Trust, Hindlip WR3 8SZ
t (01905) 754919 **w** worcswildlifetrust.co.uk
open See website for details.
admission Free
*A restored 17thC granary. Interpreted farm trail. Wildlife
information, and information on other trust sites.*

New Road Cricket Ground, Worcester

Beaches in
Central England

Beaches with have been awarded the prestigious Blue Flag award. For more information, visit **blueflag.org.uk**

 A resort beach actively encourages visitors and is normally near a town with recreational facilities.

A rural beach has limited facilities, is generally more remote than a resort beach and will not be actively managed.

Thorpeness Beach

Essex

Albion Beach
t (01255) 686868
Access The nearest train station is Walton-on-the-Naze. By road from the B1034.

Bell Wharf Beach
t (01702) 215620
Access Close to a historical, working fishing village, the beach is ten minutes' walk from Leigh railway station.

Brightlingsea Beach
t (01255) 686868
Access Located along the western promenade at Brightlingsea, adjacent to the town centre. Access by road via the B1027 and B1029.

Chalkwell Beach
t (01702) 215620
Access The nearest railway station is Chalkwell (12 minutes' walk). The beach is situated at Chalkwell Esplanade.

Dovercourt Bay
t (01255) 686868
Access Located adjacent to the town of Dovercourt. Accessible via the A120. Mainline rail from London and Ipswich, Dovercourt or Harwich Station. Bus services from Colchester, Clacton and Ipswich.

East Beach, Shoeburyness
t (01702) 215620
Access Via Southend-on-Sea, Eastern Esplanade and Thorpe Bay. Shoeburyness railway station is five minutes' walk.

Frinton Beach
t (01255) 686868
Access Frinton beach is located adjacent to the town of Frinton-on-Sea on the Essex Sunshine Coast. Access by mainline railway to Frinton-on-Sea. Bus service from Clacton-on-Sea and Walton-on-the-Naze. Albion Beach is located adjacent to Walton-on-the-Naze.

Frinton Beach

Jubilee Beach
t (01702) 215620
Access The nearest railway station is Southend Central (ten minutes' walk). The beach is situated on Marine Parade to the east of the pier.

Martello Bay
t (01255) 686868
Access Located close to Clacton-on-Sea town centre. The town is served by mainline railway connections to London and Ipswich and road connections from the north (Ipswich) and south (London and Colchester) via the A12, A120 and A133.

Shoebury Common Beach
t (01702) 215620
Access Nearest railway station is Southend Central (ten minutes' walk). The beach is on Western Esplanade adjacent to the pier.

Three Shells Beach
t (01702) 215620
Access The nearest railway station is Southend Central (ten minutes' walk). The beach is situated on Western Esplanade adjacent to the pier.

West Beach, Clacton
t (01255) 686868

Access Located adjacent to Clacton-on-Sea, which is served by mainline railway connections to London and Ipswich. Accessible via the A12, A120 and A133 from London and Colchester.

Lincolnshire

Cleethorpes Central Beach
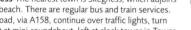
t (01472) 323356
Access Take the A180 motorway link through Grimsby and follow signs for Cleethorpes. A46 from Lincoln, follow signs for Grimsby then signs for Cleethorpes. A16 from Boston, follow signs for Grimsby then signs for Cleethorpes. Main rail services from Doncaster and Manchester.

Mablethorpe Central Beach
t (01507) 474939

Access The nearest town is Mablethorpe, from which there is a regular bus service. By car approach the town via the A1104 which leads to the High Street Directions to the beach are from the eastern end. There is a sand train which takes visitors directly to the beach.

Sutton on Sea Central Beach
t (01507) 474939
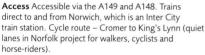
Access East coast location on the A52, approx two miles from Mablethorpe and 15 miles from Skegness. Daily National Express coach service. Access by road via the A16 and A1111.

Tower Esplanade Beach
t (01507) 601111

Access The nearest town is Skegness, which adjoins the beach. There are regular bus and train services. By road, via A158, continue over traffic lights, turn right at mini-roundabout, left at clock tower in Tower Esplanade.

Norfolk

Cromer Beach
t (01263) 51147
Access Accessible via the A149 and A148. Trains direct to and from Norwich, which is an Inter City train station. Cycle route – Cromer to King's Lynn (quiet lanes in Norfolk project for walkers, cyclists and horse-riders).

Gorleston Beach
t (01493) 846345
Access Adjoining the lower promenade/esplanade with adjacent free parking. Clearly signed from the town centre.

Cromer Beach

Hunstanton Beach

Great Yarmouth Central Beach

t (01493) 846345
Access Only a few minutes' walk from the town centre by pedestrianised Regent Road. Central Beach is located between the Britannia and Wellington Piers. There are car parks adjacent to the beach and large overspill car parks only minutes from the beach.

Heacham Beach

t (01485) 535150
Access Nearest town is Hunstanton. There is a bus service to and from Hunstanton and Kings Lynn with a short walk from the village centre (half a mile to the beach).

Hunstanton Beach

t (01485) 535150
Access Bus services to and from Hunstanton to Kings Lynn with a short walk from the resort beach to the nearest town centre of Hunstanton. By car follow the A149 from Kings Lynn.

Mundesley Beach

t (01263) 51147
Access Vehicle access is via the B1159 and B1145 (from Cromer and North Walsham). The nearest train station is North Walsham (Norwich to Cromer line). Local bus service connects with trains. Quiet lanes for cyclists, pedestrians and horse-riders.

Sea Palling Beach

t (01263) 51147
Access Located approx five miles from Stalham – the gateway to the Broads. Good connections to coastal cycle route (Great Yarmouth to Cromer). Local bus to Stalham and main towns Great Yarmouth and North Walsham.

Sheringham Beach
t (01263) 516007
Access Norwich is an Inter City train station.
Sheringham vehicle access is via the A149 and A148.
Cycle route (quiet lanes project) Cromer to King's Lynn.
Coastal bus routes and local bus service inland.

Suffolk

Aldeburgh Beach
t (01394) 444659
Access Aldeburgh can be accessed from the A12,
then by the A1094. The nearest train station is Saxmundham.

Felixstowe South Beach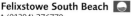
t (01394) 276770
Access Access by rail to Felixstowe. Access by road
via A14 to Felixstowe then follow signs for seafront.
Coach/bus stop at seafront.

Kessingland Beach
t (01502) 533600
Access Kessingland beach is located between
Lowestoft (three miles) and Southwold (eight miles).
Access from the A12 via the B1437. The beach is adjacent
to the village. The local bus service has a bus stop, which
is a short walk from the beach area.

Lowestoft Beach North of Claremont Pier
t (01502) 533600
Access Located centrally in Lowestoft, adjacent to
main A12 trunk road, approx 400 yards from main
train station. Adjacent to coach drop-off point (Royal Plain)
and bus stop.

Lowestoft Beach South of Claremont Pier
t (01502) 533600
Access Located centrally in Lowestoft adjacent to
the A12, approx half a mile from the train station.

Sizewell Beach
t (01394) 444659
Access Take the A12, A1094 and B1122 from the
south. Take the A12 and B1122 from the north via
Yoxford. The V1119 from the north via Saxmundham.
Sizewell is signed from Leiston via High Street/Lovers Lane
(leading to Sizewell Road).

Southwold Denes
t (01502) 724729
Access Located in the town of Southwold, the beach
can be found adjacent to the harbour. Access to
Southwold from the A12 via the A1095 (follow signs to the
harbour through the town). Local bus service available.

Southwold Pier Beach
t (01502) 724729
Access Access to Southwold from the A12 via the
A1095. Local bus service. Beach adjacent to coach
drop-off point and parking.

The Dip (Brackenbury Cliffs)
Access Located on Suffolk Heath's Stour and Orwell
walk. Take the A14 to Felixstowe, the A154 towards
the town centre and High Road East to The Dip on
Cliff Road (signed Old Felixstowe). Bus services are
also available.

Thorpeness Beach
t (01394) 444659
Access The nearest towns are Aldeburgh and Leiston.
Via Aldeburgh (A12, A1094) take coastal Thorpeness
Road North. Via Leiston (A1094/B1122/B1119) take
B1122 to Aldringham, then B1353. A bus service is
also available.

Southwold Pier Beach

Places to stay in
Central England

Accommodation in this section is listed alphabetically by place name (shown in the blue bands), establishment category and establishment name.

All the place names can be found on the maps at the front of this guide – use the map references to locate them.

Accommodation symbols
Symbols give useful information about services and facilities. A key to these symbols can be found on the inside back-cover flap. Keep it open for easy reference.

ASHBOURNE, Derbyshire Map ref 4B2   **HOTEL**

★★
HOTEL

B&B per room per night
s £35.00–£75.00
d £55.00–£105.00
HB per person per night
£52.50–£70.00

The Dog and Partridge Country Inn with Rooms in the Grounds

Ashbourne DE6 2HS **t** (01335) 343183 **f** (01335) 342742 **e** info@dogandpartridge.co.uk **w** dogandpartridge.co.uk

Family-run,17thC inn with purpose-built rooms in the grounds. Log fires, real ales, good food. Pets and children welcome. Ideal Peak District location. Very close to Alton Towers.

open All year
bedrooms 8 double, 4 twin, 2 single, 15 family
bathrooms All en suite
payment Credit/debit cards, cash/cheques

Children 🐧🛏🎣🐾🐕🎿🖉 CM 🎦   Room 🛏📞📺♿🍴   General ♇🍽🎱✿🐾   Leisure ∪♐🏃🚵

ASHBOURNE, Derbyshire Map ref 4B2   **SELF CATERING**

★★★★
SELF CATERING

Units   **5**
Sleeps **2–6**
Low season per wk
£234.00–£430.00
High season per wk
£430.00–£677.00

Paddock House Farm Holiday Cottages, Alstonefield, Ashbourne

contact Mr & Mrs Mark & Melissa Redfern, Paddock House Farm Holiday Cottages, Alstonefield, Ashbourne DE6 2FT
t 0870 027 2500 **f** 0870 027 2400 **e** info@paddockhousefarm.co.uk **w** paddockhousefarm.co.uk

open All year
payment Cash/cheques

Luxury holiday cottages in the heart of the Peak District National Park. Cottages have either three bedrooms, two bedrooms or one bedroom. Wonderful views of the open countryside in a very peaceful location. Excellent attractions, including Alton Towers, Chatsworth and Dovedale.

⊕ From Alstonefield village head for Hulme End, 1.5 miles on the left. At the end of our drive turn left to the main courtyard.

♥ 20% reduction for 2 adults booking a 3-bedroom cottage only using 1 bedroom (off-peak only).

Children 🐧🛏🎣🎦🚲   Unit 🛏📺📻🍴📺📷🧺📞🗄💺✿
General ♇✂🖉Ⓢ🐕   Leisure ♦∪♐🏃🚵🛶   Shop 1.5 miles   Pub 1.5 miles

---

Confirm your booking
It's always advisable to confirm your booking in writing.

ASHBOURNE, Derbyshire Map ref 4B2 — SELF CATERING

★★★★
SELF CATERING

Units	**1**
Sleeps	**1–2**

Low season per wk
£140.00–£200.00
High season per wk
£210.00–£385.00

Turlow Fields Farm, Hognaston, Ashbourne

contact Mandy & Adrian Hunter, Barnclose Cottage, Turlow Fields Farm, Ashbourne DE6 1PW
t (01335) 370834 **e** aahunter@uk2.net

open All year
payment Cash/cheques

Cottage on small organic farm. Double bedroom with bunk bed (can be separated), full underfloor heating, private garden with beautiful views, private picnic areas (picnics prepared by arrangement), farm walks (cattle, sheep, pigs and more to see). Carsington Water is a short, quiet walk away, and Ashbourne and Dovedale a five- to ten-minute drive.

⊕ A517 towards Belper. After 4.5 miles, turn left (signposted Carsington Water and Hognaston). After 1.3 miles, Turlow Fields Farm on right.

Children 🛏 🎠 🖼 Unit 🛏 TV 🖥 💻 🔔 🔌 🎛 ❄
General P ✂ S Leisure 🚣 🚴 ⛰ Shop 1.5 miles Pub 1 mile

BAKEWELL, Derbyshire Map ref 4B2 — SELF CATERING

★★★★
SELF CATERING

Units	**1**
Sleeps	**1–4**

Low season per wk
£220.00–£260.00
High season per wk
£295.00–£420.00

Braemar Cottage, Youlgrave, Nr Bakewell

contact c/o Mrs Irene Shimwell, Braemar Cottage, Crimble House, Main Street, Youlgrave DE45 1UW
t (01629) 636568 & 07929 396525 **e** braemarcottage@fsmail.net **w** braemarcottage.co.uk

Recently restored, luxuriously appointed cottage lying in the heart of the beautiful village of Youlgrave – an ideal base for walking and sightseeing. Pubs and shops close by.

open All year
payment Cash/cheques

Children 🛏 🎠 🚶 🖼 ⛰ Unit 🛏 TV 🖥 💻 🔔 🔌 🎛 ❄
General P ✂ S 🐾 Shop < 0.5 miles Pub < 0.5 miles

BEWDLEY, Worcestershire Map ref 4A3 — SELF CATERING

★★★
SELF CATERING

Units	**1**
Sleeps	**1–4**

Low season per wk
Min £190.00
High season per wk
Max £390.00

Manor Holding, Bewdley

contact Mr & Mrs Nigel & Penny Dobson-Smyth, 32 Church Street, Hagley, Stourbridge DY9 0NA
t 07970 260010 **e** nds@landscapeconsultancy.freeserve.co.uk

Secluded 17thC farmhouse in tranquil, ancient forest (National Nature Reserve) laced with traffic-free foot, cycle and bridle paths. Enchanting, rolling countryside sprinkled with historic market towns. Near Birmingham, Ironbridge and Ludlow.

open All year
payment Cash/cheques, euros

Children 🛏 🎠 ⛰ Unit 🛏 TV 🖥 💻 🔔 🔌 🎛 ❄
General P ✂ S 🐾 Leisure U 🚣 🚴 ⛰ Shop 2 miles Pub 2 miles

BEWDLEY, Worcestershire Map ref 4A3 — SELF CATERING

★★★★
SELF CATERING &
SERVICED APARTMENTS

Units	**1**
Sleeps	**1–5**

Low season per wk
£285.00–£335.00
High season per wk
£345.00–£450.00

Peacock Coach House, Bewdley

contact Mrs Prisca Hall, Peacock House, Lower Park, Bewdley DY12 2DP
t (01299) 400149 **e** priscahall@hotmail.com

Restored, 17thC, oak-beamed coach house, five minutes from Bewdley town centre and River Severn. Private walled garden with patio and barbecue.

open All year
payment Cash/cheques

Children 🛏 🎠 🚶 ⛰ Unit 🛏 TV 🖥 💻 🔌 🎛 ❄
General P S 🐾 Leisure U 🚣 Shop < 0.5 miles Pub < 0.5 miles

♿ **If you have access needs...** 🏷🏷🏷🏷🏷🏷🏷🏷

Look for the National Accessible Scheme symbols if you have special hearing, visual or mobility needs.

CLEOBURY MORTIMER, Shropshire Map ref 4A3 — GUEST ACCOMMODATION

♦♦♦
GUEST ACCOMMODATION

B&B per room per night
s £35.00
d £60.00
Evening meal per person
£10.00–£15.00

Broome Park Farm

Catherton Road, Cleobury Mortimer, Kidderminster DY14 0LB t (01299) 270647
e catherine@broomeparkfarm.co.uk w broomeparkfarm.co.uk

Family-friendly, recently restored farmhouse accommodation. Peaceful location on working farm. Spacious en suite rooms, guest sitting and dining rooms. Evening meals by arrangement. Excellent facilities for families.

open All year
bedrooms 1 double, 1 family
bathrooms All en suite
payment Cash/cheques

Children 🧒 🛏 🎠 🐾 ✏ 🖥 📷   Room 🍴   General P ⚡ ✕ 🍽 🅿 ✿   Leisure ▶ 🚴 ⛵

DISS, Norfolk Map ref 3B2 — GUEST ACCOMMODATION

★★★★★
BED & BREAKFAST
GOLD AWARD

B&B per room per night
s £60.00–£70.00
d £90.00–£100.00
Evening meal per person
£25.00

Old Rectory Hopton

High Street, Hopton, Diss IP22 2QX t (01953) 688135 e llewellyn.hopton@btinternet.com
w theoldrectoryhopton.com

open All year except Christmas and New Year
bedrooms 2 double, 1 twin
bathrooms 2 en suite, 1 private
payment Cash/cheques

The Old Rectory is a listed building, dating from the 16thC, standing in walled grounds. The house is well situated to explore East Anglia, being on the Norfolk/Suffolk border. The house is beautifully furnished, and many period features add to the charm of this lovely home. A non-smoking house.

⊕ *From Bury take the A143. In Stanton take the B1111 signed to Garboldisham. The Old Rectory is immediately after the church in Hopton.*

♥ *10% discount on B&B rate for 3 or more nights 1 Nov to 31 Mar.*

Children 🧒8   Room 🍴 ♨   General P ⚡ 🍷 🍽 🅿 ✿ 🐾   Leisure ▶ ⛵

FLAGG, Derbyshire Map ref 4B2 — SELF CATERING

★★★–★★★★★
SELF CATERING

Units   **3**
Sleeps   **2–12**

Low season per wk
£260.00–£425.00
High season per wk
£400.00–£695.00

Taddington Barns, Buxton

contact Mrs Elizabeth Charboneau, Taddington Barns, Moor Grange Farm, Moor Lane, Flagg SK17 9RA
t (01298) 85020 & 07974 258765 e tony@moorgrangefarm.co.uk w moorgrangefarm.co.uk

open All year
payment Credit/debit cards, cash/cheques

A beautiful rural retreat with stunning views and indoor, 37ft swimming pool. Ideal for family gatherings. Badger's Wood has two en suite bedrooms (one double, one twin), bunk room and bathroom. Robin's Nest has two en suite bedrooms (one double, one twin). Chicken Coop has one bedroom (king-size bed) and bathroom.

⊕ *Five miles equidistant Bakewell and Buxton, off A6. Into Taddington village, onto School Lane, onto Slipperlow Lane. Follow to top, bends to right, 1st farm on right.*

♥ *Short breaks available.*

Children 🧒 🛏 🎠 📷 ⛰   Unit 🍽 📺 🎮 🖥 🧺 🍽 ♨ 🔥 🍴 🧹 ✿
General P ⚡ 🅿 Ⓢ 🐾   Leisure 🎣 🏊 ▶ 🚴 ⛵   Shop 4.5 miles   Pub 1.2 miles

Check the maps

Colour maps at the front pinpoint all the places you will find accommodation entries in the regional sections. Pick your location and then refer to the place index at the back to find the page number.

GREAT YARMOUTH, Norfolk Map ref 3C1 — CAMPING & CARAVANNING

★★★★
HOLIDAY PARK
(72) £159.00–£629.00

Cherry Tree Holiday Park

Burgh Castle, Great Yarmouth NR31 9QR t 0870 420 2997 f (0191) 268 5986
e enquiries@parkdeanholidays.co.uk w parkdeanholidays.co.uk

payment Credit/debit cards, cash/cheques

With the picturesque Norfolk Broads on your doorstep, and popular Great Yarmouth just two miles away, Cherry Tree has the best location for a traditional family holiday! There's lots to do without even leaving the park! Facilities include outdoor and indoor pools, kids' clubs and The Orchard family entertainment venue. Open March to October.

⊕ *A47 to Great Yarmouth. Take 3rd exit at 1st roundabout across bridge. At next roundabout take 3rd exit, 3rd exit again, then turn left at t-junction.*

♥ *Short breaks available.*

General P 🛉 🖰 🖸 👒 ✕ 🐎   Leisure 🎣 🏊 ♨ ♪ ● 🎱 🚶 ⛳

HADLEIGH, Suffolk Map ref 3B2 — SELF CATERING

★★★★
SELF CATERING

Units **3**
Sleeps **1–8**
Low season per wk
£350.00–£470.00
High season per wk
£580.00–£1,000.00

Wattisham Hall Holiday Cottages, Wattisham, Ipswich

contact Mrs Jo Squirrell, Wattisham Hall, Wattisham, Ipswich IP7 7JX
t (01449) 740240 f (01449) 744535 e jhsquirr@farming.co.uk w wattishamhall.co.uk

open All year
payment Cash/cheques

Charming barn conversion within an ancient moat, surrounded by tranquil countryside. The cottages are beautifully furnished, having exposed beams, oak floors, wood-burning stoves and plenty of character. Enclosed patio gardens, shared games room and outdoor play area. Within easy reach of Constable Country and many picturesque villages such as Lavenham.

⊕ *For full travel directions please visit our website or contact us.*

♥ *Short breaks available all year excl May and Oct half-terms, school summer holidays, Christmas and New Year.*

Children 🛝 🎡 🏃 🖰 ⅏   Unit 🛏 📺 🗑 ▯ ● 🗄 🍴 🍳 🌀
General P ✂ 🖸 Ⓢ 🐎   Leisure 🎣   Shop 2 miles   Pub 2 miles

HEMINGFORD ABBOTS, Cambridgeshire Map ref 3A2 — CAMPING & CARAVANNING

★★★★
HOLIDAY, TOURING
& CAMPING PARK
🚐(20) £12.00–£15.00
🚙(20) £12.00–£15.00
⛺(20) £12.00–£15.00
(9) £235.00–£355.00
20 touring pitches

Quiet Waters Caravan Park

Hemingford Abbots, Huntingdon PE28 9AJ t (01480) 463405 f (01480) 463405
e quietwaters.park@btopenworld.com w quietwaterscaravanpark.co.uk

A quiet riverside park situated in centre of picturesque village. Many local walks and cycle routes. Ideal for fishing from own banks. Family run. Open April to October.

payment Credit/debit cards, cash/cheques

General P 🔌 🖱 🛉 🖰 ☺ 🖰 🗑 🐎 ☼   Leisure ∪ 🚣

HICKLING, Norfolk Map ref 3C1 — GUEST ACCOMMODATION

★★★★
FARMHOUSE
SILVER AWARD

The Dairy Barns

Lound Farm, Hickling, Norwich NR12 0BE t (01692) 598243 f (01692) 598243
e enquiries@dairybarns.co.uk w dairybarns.co.uk

B&B per room per night
s £35.00–£40.00
d £56.00–£62.00

The accommodation is in self-contained, converted barns. Breakfast is the best farmhouse cooking using local produce. Spacious en suite rooms. One mile from beaches and Norfolk Broads. Disabled facilities. Children welcome.

open All year
bedrooms 3 double, 3 twin
bathrooms All en suite
payment Cash/cheques

Children 🛝 🎡 🏃 ✐ 🖽 🖰   Room 👒 📺 🛁 🗑   General P ✕ 🏵 ☼   Leisure 🚣 ⛳ ⛵

HUNSTANTON, Norfolk Map ref 3B1 · SELF CATERING

★★★★
SELF CATERING

Units **1**
Sleeps **2–8**

Low season per wk
£295.00–£395.00
High season per wk
£625.00–£825.00

Blue Skies, Hunstanton

contact Ms Debbie Harrington, 45 Burrettgate Road, Walsoken, Wisbech PE14 7BN
t (01945) 588055 **f** (01945) 474397 **e** debs.harrington@btinternet.com
w hunstantonholidaycottages.co.uk

Spacious Victorian house in a peaceful, residential area between town and Old Hunstanton, only a five-minute walk from a beautiful sandy beach. Everything for a family holiday, including Sky TV.

open All year
payment Cash/cheques, euros

Children 🐕 🛏 ⚓ 🗄 Unit ⊞ 📺 🗄 💻 🔋 🎣 🔑 📻 🛎 ✿
General Ⓢ 🐾 Leisure 🌙 🏴 🚲 Shop < 0.5 miles Pub 0.5 miles

ILAM, Staffordshire Map ref 4B2 · SELF CATERING

★★★★
SELF CATERING

Units **3**
Sleeps **6–24**

Low season per wk
£290.00–£450.00
High season per wk
£640.00–£800.00

Lower Damgate Barns, Reuben's Roost, Bremen's Barn, Hope's Hideaway, Ilam, Ashbourne

contact Mrs Carolyn Wilderspin, Lower Damgate Farm, Stanshope, Ashbourne DE6 2AD
t (01335) 310367 & 07779 210791 **e** damgate@hotmail.com **w** damgate.com

open All year
payment Cash/cheques

A 16thC, Grade II Listed rural farm in a stunning setting in the Peak District National Park. The farm is surrounded by National Trust land, and there is excellent walking from the door. The barns retain individuality and have luxury fittings. Games room, patio, barbecue, picnic and playing field. Pet sheep, ducks and chickens.

⊕ Directions provided once booking is confirmed.

Children 🐕 🛏 ⚓ 🗄 🛶 Unit ⊞ 📺 📻 🗄 💻 🔋 🎣 🔑 📻 🛎 ✿
General P 🐾 ⦿ Ⓢ 🐾 Leisure 🔍 ∪ 🌙 🚲 ⛵ Shop 4 miles Pub 1 mile

LEEK, Staffordshire Map ref 4B2 · SELF CATERING

★★★★
SELF CATERING

Units **3**
Sleeps **4–10**

Low season per wk
£233.00–£538.00
High season per wk
£381.00–£939.00

Foxtwood Cottages, Foxt, Froghall

contact Mr & Mrs Clive & Alison Worrall, Foxtwood Cottages, Foxt Road, Foxt, Stoke-on-Trent ST10 2HJ
t (01538) 266160 **e** info@foxtwood.co.uk **w** foxtwood.co.uk

open All year
payment Cash/cheques, euros

Orchids in the flower meadow, a kingfisher flashing by, a fleeting glimpse of a deer in the woods. Relax and watch canal boats chug past, hear the steam trains whistle along the valley. Come and explore this fascinating area. Foxtwood is unique and stunning.

⊕ Between Derby and Stoke-on-Trent on the A52. At Froghall take local road to Foxt for 0.25 miles. We are on the left past the canal.

♥ Special winter breaks for the retired. 4 nights mid-week for less than a 3-night weekend.

Children 🐕 🛏 ⚓ Unit ⊞ 📺 🗄 💻 🔋 🎣 🗄 🛎 ✿
General P 🐾 ⦿ Ⓢ 🐾 Leisure 🌙 🚲 Shop 2 miles Pub < 0.5 miles

Check it out

Information on accommodation listed in this guide has been supplied by proprietors. As changes may occur you should remember to check all relevant details at the time of booking.

LONG MELFORD, Suffolk Map ref 3B2 — GUEST ACCOMMODATION

★★★★
**BED & BREAKFAST
SILVER AWARD**

High Street Farmhouse

High Street, Long Melford, Sudbury CO10 9BD **t** (01787) 375765 **e** mail@gallopingchef.co.uk
w highstreetfarmhouse.co.uk

B&B per room per night
s £35.00–£54.00
d £50.00–£70.00

Charming 16thC farmhouse offers cosy rooms
with pretty gardens. Set on the edge of a
picturesque Tudor village.

open All year
bedrooms 2 double, 1 twin
bathrooms All en suite
payment Cash/cheques

Children ⛺ ▥ ⩕ 🐄 ✿ ⌀ 🖷 ☺ Room ♨ 📺 ✎ ੧ General P ⚡ 🛏 ⚕ ✿ ☏ Leisure ∪ ♪ ⏱ ♿

LOUTH, Lincolnshire Map ref 4D2 — SELF CATERING

★★★
SELF CATERING

Station Masters House, Ludborough, Nr Louth

t (01507) 363470 **f** (01507) 363633 **e** info@raileisure.com **w** raileisure.com

Units **1**
Sleeps **2–8**
Low season per wk
£325.00–£479.00
High season per wk
£479.00–£649.00

open All year
payment Credit/debit cards, cash/cheques

High-quality self-catering accommodation within the
Lincolnshire Wolds. Peace and tranquillity, ideal for
railway, walking and cycling enthusiasts. A most
unique holiday home, ideal for the larger family or
family reunions, within picturesque surroundings.

⊕ *Please see our website for comprehensive travel directions.*
♥ *Off-season short breaks available for a whistle-stop holiday.*

Children ⛺ ▥ ⩕ ☺ Unit ▥ 📺 ⌂ ⊟ ▭ 🗄 🖭 🖳 ✿
General P ⚡ Ⓢ 🛏 Leisure ♪ ♿ 🚲 Shop 2 miles Pub 2 miles

NORFOLK BROADS

See under Great Yarmouth, Hickling, Norwich, Wroxham

NORWICH, Norfolk Map ref 3C1 — SELF CATERING

★★★★
SELF CATERING

The Apartment at City Heights, Norwich

contact Mrs Susan Potter, 6 Stanley Avenue, Norwich NR7 0BE
t (01603) 700438 **e** sueno6p@aol.com **w** number-6.co.uk

Units **1**
Sleeps **1–4**
Low season per wk
£250.00–£300.00
High season per wk
£300.00–£480.00

open All year
payment Cash/cheques

New two-bedroom executive apartment within
walking distance of the city centre, riverside inns and
restaurants. Ultra-modern interior with new facilities.

⊕ *A47, signs for Norwich football ground. Go around Carrow
Road Stadium, take right-hand lane round one-way system
onto Yarmouth Road. City Heights left-hand side.*

Children ⛺ ▥ ⩕ Unit ▥ 📺 ⌂ ▭ 🗄 🖭 ੧ 🖳 ✿
General P ⚡ Ⓢ 🛏 Leisure ∪ ♪ ⏱ 🚲 ♿ Shop 0.5 miles Pub < 0.5 miles

PEAK DISTRICT

See under Ashbourne, Bakewell

Friendly help and advice

Tourist Information Centres offer friendly help with accommodation and holiday
ideas as well as suggestions of places to visit and things to do. You'll find
contact details at the beginning of each regional section.

RIPLEY, Derbyshire Map ref 4B2

★★★
TOURING &
CAMPING PARK

🚐 £15.00–£20.00
🛏 £15.00–£20.00
⛺ £7.50–£10.00
24 touring pitches

Golden Valley Caravan & Camping

The Tanyard, Coach Road, Golden Valley, Ripley DE5 3QU t (01773) 513881 & 07971 283643
e enquiries@goldenvalleycaravanpark.co.uk w goldenvalleycaravanpark.co.uk

payment Cash/cheques

Secluded woodland hideaway. All-weather children's play facilities. Electric hook-ups on individual landscaped sites. Jacuzzi, gymnasium, cafe and takeaway. Fishing on site. Next to Butterley Railway. Function room. Open March to October.

⊕ *A610 to Codnor. Follow signs to Alfreton. Bottom of hill, site on left.*

General 🖭P🚭🛱🍴🚼🏧☉💳 🛁🐕🎠. Leisure ⚑🎵🎯🎢⛵🎣🏊

SEDGEFORD, Norfolk Map ref 3B1

★★★★
SELF CATERING

Units   1
Sleeps   8

Low season per wk
£414.00–£511.00
High season per wk
£556.00–£673.00

Cobble Cottage, Sedgeford

Norfolk Country Cottages, Carlton House, Market Place, Reepham, Norwich NR10 4JJ
t (01603) 871872 f (01603) 870304 e info@norfolkcottages.co.uk
w norfolkcottages.co.uk/properties/841

open All year
payment Credit/debit cards, cash/cheques, euros

Sedgeford is close to both the sandy beaches of the North Norfolk Heritage Coast and the west-facing coastline of the Wash, and the RSPB reserves of Titchwell Marsh and Snettisham. Recently refurbished with two car-parking bays, parts of the cottage are thought to date from the late 1700s.

⊕ *Take A149 from King's Lynn, then B1454 towards Docking. Left onto gravel track 200yds past 30mph sign. Access to cottage at the rear.*

♥ *3- to 6-night stays available Oct-Apr (excl Bank Holidays and school half-terms) and sometimes from Apr-Oct.*

Children 🛏🍴🎠 Unit 🖭 📺💿🗑🍽🖥📼🔲🔲❄
General P✂️🅾️Ⓢ🐕 Leisure ∪♫🎣 Shop 2 miles Pub < 0.5 miles

STOKE-ON-TRENT, Staffordshire Map ref 4B2

★★★★★
HOLIDAY, TOURING
& CAMPING PARK
ROSE AWARD

🚐(60) £12.00–£14.00
🛏(30) £12.00–£14.00
⛺(30) £12.00–£14.00
🚐(9) £280.00–£400.00
120 touring pitches

The Star Caravan and Camping Park

Star Road, Cotton, Stoke-on-Trent ST10 3DW t (01538) 702219 f (01538) 703704
w starcaravanpark.co.uk

payment Cash/cheques

The closest touring park to Alton Towers. Strict 11pm-all-quiet rule on site. No single-sex groups allowed. Families and mixed couples always welcomed. Set in stunning countryside surrounded by mature trees and hedgerows. Ten miles from four market towns, and only four miles from the Peak District National Park. Open March to October.

⊕ *From M6 jct 16 or M1 jct 23a follow signs for Alton Towers. Go past and follow the road (Beelow Lane) for 0.75 miles to crossroad. Turn right up hill. Site on right after 400m.*

♥ *Early-season discounts on caravan holidays homes. Free 2nd-day admission to Alton Towers for 2 persons (ring for information).*

General 🖭P🚭🛱🍴🏧☉💳 🐕🎠.☼ Leisure 🎢∪🎣🚲

SWADLINCOTE, Derbyshire Map ref 4B3

★★★
SELF CATERING

Units **4**
Sleeps **6–10**

Low season per wk
£359.00–£419.00
High season per wk
£419.00–£798.00

Forest Lodges, Rosliston, Swadlincote

contact Mrs Marie Hall, Rosliston Forest Centre, Burton Road, Rosliston, Swadlincote DE12 8JX
t (01283) 519119 **f** (01283) 565494 **e** enquiries@roslistonforestrycentre.co.uk
w roslistonforestrycentre.co.uk

open All year
payment Credit/debit cards, cash/cheques

Luxury, fully equipped lodges nestling in a 154-acre young woodland. Our lodges are fully accessible, with additional features including electric beds, hoist and extra-large shower rooms. Large range of activities available on site from fishing, walking and cycling to archery, falconry and laser combat. Pets welcome by arrangement in one lodge.

⊕ *Nearest train station Burton on Trent. Bus service (Arriva, No. 22) from Burton and Swadlincote.*

Children 🐿 ⛺ ♿ 🅰 Unit 🛏 📺 🖨 💻 🖲 🍴 🎛 ✿
General **P** ⛽ 🅾 🆂 Leisure 🎣 ✈ 🚲 Shop < 0.5 miles Pub < 0.5 miles

TANWORTH-IN-ARDEN, Warwickshire Map ref 4B3

◆◆◆◆
GUEST ACCOMMODATION
SILVER AWARD

B&B per room per night
s £35.00–£45.00
d £70.00–£80.00

Mows Hill Farm

Mows Hill Road, Kemps Green, Tanworth-in-Arden B94 5PP **t** (01564) 784312 **f** (01564) 783378
e mowshill@farmline.com **w** b-and-bmowshill.co.uk

open All year
bedrooms 1 double, 1 family
bathrooms 1 en suite, 1 private
payment Cash/cheques, euros

Ideally situated for visiting Stratford-upon-Avon, Warwick, the Cotswolds, the NEC and NAC. Comfortable family farmhouse with one double and one family room. Peaceful setting with wonderful rural views. Fresh farm produce served for breakfast. Sitting room with books and games and a log fire for colder evenings. New conservatory breakfast room.

⊕ *A3400 towards Stratford/Henley-in-Arden. At Hockley Heath, right onto B4101 (Spring Lane), over bridge, next left (Kemps Green). 2nd right (Mows Hill Road). Farm on right-hand side.*

Children 🐿 ⛺ ♿ 🐾 ✎ 📷 Room 📺 🛁 🍵 General **P** ⛽ 🍴 🅿 ✿ Leisure 🎿 🏇 🚲 🏛

TENBURY WELLS, Worcestershire Map ref 4A3

★★★★
SELF CATERING

Units **2**
Sleeps **3–8**

Low season per wk
Min £180.00
High season per wk
Max £600.00

Rochford Park Cottages, Tenbury Wells

contact Mrs J Robinson, Rochford Park, Tenbury Wells WR15 8SP
t (01584) 781392 **f** (01584) 781392 **e** mrs.j.robinson@fwi.co.uk **w** rochfordpark.co.uk

Former stable and barn, now stylish, comfortable accommodation for an active family in one or a group of friends/family in the other. Bookable together.

open All year
payment Cash/cheques

Children 🐿 ⛺ 📷 🅰 Unit 🛏 📺 📻 💻 🖲 🍴 🎛 🎛 ✿
General **P** ⛽ 🆂 Leisure ♻ 🎿 🏇 🚲 🏛 Shop 3 miles Pub 1.5 miles

Take a break

Look out for special promotions and themed breaks. This could be your chance to indulge an interest, find a new one, or just relax and enjoy exceptional value! Offers are highlighted in colour (and are subject to availability).

WARWICK, Warwickshire Map ref 2B1 GUEST ACCOMMODATION

★★★★
**GUEST ACCOMMODATION
SILVER AWARD**

B&B per room per night
s £40.00–£50.00
d £55.00–£65.00

Shrewley Pools Farm

Haseley, Warwick CV35 7HB **t** (01926) 484315 **w** s-h-systems.co.uk/hotels/shrewley.html

open All year except Christmas
bedrooms 1 twin, 1 family
bathrooms All en suite
payment Cash/cheques

Glorious 17thC traditional family farmhouse with log fires, oak floors, beams etc, set in an acre of outstanding garden featuring herbaceous borders and unusual trees and shrubs. Two spacious en suite bedrooms and own sitting room with books and games. Perfectly situated for numerous attractions. Surrounded by picturesque farmland. Private fishing.

⊕ *A46, take A4177 from Warwick through Hatton, past Falcon Inn. At roundabout take 1st exit. After 0.5 miles we are on left.*

♥ *Four-acre lake stocked with carp and tench: £7 per day.*

Children 🧸 🛏 👶 🐾 ✎ CM 📷 Room TV ♨ ☕ General P ✂ ♨ ❄ Leisure U ♪ ► ⌂

WEST RUNTON, Norfolk Map ref 3B1 HOTEL

★★★
HOTEL

B&B per room per night
s £60.00–£85.00
d £120.00–£180.00
HB per person per night
£80.00–£110.00

The Links Country Park Hotel & Golf Club

Sandy Lane, West Runton NR27 9QH **t** (01263) 838383 **f** (01263) 838264 **e** sales@links-hotel.co.uk
w links-hotel.co.uk

open All year
bedrooms 11 double, 7 twin, 6 single, 15 family, 10 suites
bathrooms All en suite
payment Credit/debit cards, cash/cheques, euros

Norfolk's oldest and longest-established leisure, conference and golfing hotel, The Links combines modern comforts with reassuringly traditional levels of personal service and attention. Situated on the stunningly peaceful North Norfolk coast, but close to the lively towns and cities of Cromer, Sheringham and Norwich, it's the ideal base for all.

⊕ *Midway between Cromer and Sheringham on the A149 – the North Norfolk coastal road.*

♥ *Short getaways, golf breaks and a wide variety of offers and special-interest breaks available all year round – call us!*

Children 🧸 🛏 👶 🐾 ✎ CM Room 🔌 📞 TV ♨ ☕ ⊛ General P ▼ 🍴 ♨ ❄ 🐕 Leisure ⌇ ✺ U ♪ ► 🚲 ⌂

WROXHAM, Norfolk Map ref 3C1 SELF CATERING

★★★★
SELF CATERING

Units **6**
Sleeps **2–6**

Low season per wk
£270.00–£580.00
High season per wk
£670.00–£893.00

Old Farm Cottages, Tunstead, Nr Wroxham

contact Mrs Kay Paterson, Old Farm Cottages, Tunstead, Norwich NR12 8HS
t (01692) 536612 **e** kay@oldfarmcottages.fsnet.co.uk **w** oldfarmcottages.com

payment Cash/cheques

Beautifully furnished cottage barn conversions, providing outstandingly comfortable and well-appointed accommodation. Indoor swimming pool, spa, fitness room, play area and games room. Perfectly situated for coast, countryside, riverside pubs, boat/canoe hire, stately homes and Norwich. Closed 18 November to 22 December, open Christmas and New Year. Closed 6 January to 10 February.

⊕ *A1151 through Wroxham. After 4 miles branch left, signposted Dilham. Left at crossroad and follow this road until you come to Old Farm Cottages.*

♥ *See website.*

Children 🧸 🛏 👶 📷 ⚠ Unit 🛏 TV 📀 📺 📠 💻 🍴 🍳 ♨ 🍽 🔌 ❄ General P 🅿 S 🐕 Leisure ⌇ ✺ ♪ 🚲 ⌂ Shop 1.5 miles Pub 1.5 miles

---

South West England

Waiting for a ride, Polzeath, Cornwall

Bristol, Cornwall, Devon, Dorset, Gloucestershire, Isles of Scilly, Somerset, Wiltshire

Still waters deep underground at
Cheddar Caves & Gorge

Wonders **of the west**

Go rock pooling in hidden bays and sandy
coves. Indulge your love of cream teas and
clotted cream fudge. Tackle part of the
South West Coast Path. Brave the waves
surfing in Newquay. Wonder at the Cerne
Abbas Giant and the stunning landscaped
gardens at Stourhead, Warminster.
**There's so much to experience in South
West England.**

A walk on the wild side

The South West is truly a walker's paradise. Pull on the walking boots and head off for the day along part of the South West Coast Path. It stretches for 630 miles from Minehead to Poole with dramatic views of the coastline along the way (that's if the kids stop for breath for a moment!). For a shorter stroll, wander through shady St Nectan's Glen, near Tintagel, to discover a cascading 60ft waterfall. Arm the children with fossil hammers for an ammonite hunt on the Jurassic Coast, a World Heritage Site, where you'll see 185 million years of earth history along 95 miles of spectacular coastline. Not quite as old is mystical Silbury Hill near Marlborough, Wiltshire, only dating back to 2,780 BC. No one quite knows the reason behind this largest human-built mound in Europe – any ideas?

Down by the sea

How's this for the perfect antidote to modern life? With more Blue Flag beaches than anywhere else in England, the region's sandy bays, sheltered coves and wilder stretches are perfect for buckets and spades, or hitting the waves. The hip centres of Newquay, Bude, Croyde and Woolacombe are great places to learn to surf or even kitesurf. Europe's first artificial surf reef opens at Boscombe seafront in summer 2007, delivering rollers on the calmest of days, while you can try sailing and windsurfing in nearby Poole. Discover Devon's English Riviera – the bustling seaside towns of Torquay, Paignton and Brixham are ideal for families. Get to know some friendly coastal creatures from penguins and puffins to playful fur seals at Living Coasts in Torquay. Away from the beach charming fishing villages, such as Clovelly, Port Isaac and Beer, are a picturesque maze of narrow streets and unbelievably steep roads.

Rock pooling on Woolacombe beach

Spot sleeping giants at the Lost Gardens of Heligan

Secret gardens

The South West boasts three of the most extraordinary gardens in Britain. Its balmy subtropical climate is a perfect for more exotic flora. Start with the remarkable Eden Project, near St Austell, home to thousands of plants. Wander around the enormous glass biomes, where nature and technology meet, or set the children off on one of the fun, interactive trails. Delight in the Lost Gardens of Heligan at Pentewan – an 80-acre garden neglected for more than 70 years until 1991 – or take a helicopter ride to Tresco, one of the Scilly Isles, to see more unexpected exotic plants at the Abbey Garden.

> Spectacular coastlines, perfect beaches, enchanting gardens and tasty treats – indulge your every whim in the South West

Yum yum!

Indulge yourself in the South West's delicious specialities. The Cornish pasty tastes especially good washed down with a pint of sweet cider. Enjoy mouthwatering scones straight from the oven and topped with indulgent clotted cream. Cheese is synonymous with the region. Think Cheddar, Double Gloucester and Somerset Brie, while Cornish Yarg, a unique, nettle-wrapped cheese graces the best cheeseboards. Get the best catch of the day at Rick Stein's Seafood Restaurant and end your culinary quest with Julian Temperley's award-winning Somerset cider brandy. Truly scrumptious!

Main Rooftop indulgence at the Bath Thermae Spa **Left** Uncover the mystery of Stonehenge; follow a timeline on the Jurassic Coast; reflect on the sculptures in the Forest of Dean; make a slithery friend at Longleat Safari Park

Magic and mystery

Quirky customs and mysterious places abound in the South West. Strange rock formations, mystical festivals, outrageous fertility symbols – even cheese rolling! If you look hard enough you may spot Gwyn ap Nudd, King of the Fairies, at Glastonbury Tor or the Witch of Wookey deep in Wookey Hole Caves where pagan and Christian legends intermingle. Ponder the mysteries of the ancient stone circles of Stonehenge and Avebury – just how were such enormous stones transported and arranged?

Chipping Campden in Gloucestershire is the location of the Cotswolds' unique version of the Olimpick Games. A day of rustic activities is topped off with fireworks and a torchlit procession. Gloucestershire is also the home of the annual Cheese Rolling Festival at Cooper's Hill. Competitors from all over the world chase a 7lb Double Gloucester cheese down the hill. What's the reward? You've guessed it – more cheese! Hear the sound of trampling feet at the annual International Worm Charming Festival in Blackawton, Devon. The team that persuades the most worms to rise to the surface, wins!

> Non-stop excitement – animal encounters, llama trekking, worm charming, fairy hunting and witch dodging!

Great days out

If you're looking for even more inspiration on great days out, try these for starters. Uncover the history of the railway at Swindon's interactive attraction Steam – Museum of the Great Western Railway, and find out about the abolition of slavery at the Breaking Chains exhibition at Bristol's British Empire & Commonwealth Museum. See how many animals the kids can spot at Longleat's famous Safari Park and enjoy a close encounter with friendly mute swans and their fluffy cygnets at Abbotsbury Swannery. Relive the seafaring history of the South West at the National Maritime Museum Cornwall in Falmouth, or catch a performance at the stunning cliffside setting of The Minack Theatre at Porthcurno. Hire bikes for all the family and enjoy

a leisurely cycle along part of the Tarka Trail, named after Henry Williamson's Tarka the Otter. Or, if four wheels are more your style, take a driving tour around the honey-coloured limestone villages of the Cotswolds, exploring the beautiful towns of Cheltenham and Cirencester, and the lovely villages of Bourton-on-the-Water and Castle Combe on the way. Saddle up on Exmoor, Dartmoor or Bodmin, soar skywards in a hot-air balloon, and for something completely different, why not try llama-trekking? Phew!

See into the future at At-Bristol

City splendours

The buzzing cities of Bristol and Bath are filled with attractions. Revel in the Georgian beauty of Bath; tour round the best-preserved Roman religious spa from the ancient world, lying under the watchful gaze of Bath Abbey; or sink into the natural thermal waters of the newly opened Thermae Bath Spa. Cappuccino? Sample Bristol's infectious vitality and head for the rejuvenated harbour front to discover vibrant bars and restaurants. Treat the kids to an interactive adventure of a lifetime at magical At-Bristol – a unique destination bringing science, nature and art to life. Check out the feat of engineering that is the Clifton Suspension Bridge, the brainchild of Isambard Kingdom Brunel, and then continue your journey with a trip to some of the West's other great cathedral cities. Discover Exeter, Wells and Gloucester and marvel at Salisbury Cathedral with the tallest spire in Britain.

Further information

South West Tourism
t 0870 442 0880
w visitsouthwest.co.uk

Tourist Information Centres

When you arrive at your destination, visit a Tourist Information Centre for help with accommodation and information about local attractions and events, or email your request before you go.

Bristol & Bath

Bath	Abbey Church Yard	0906 711 2000**	tourism@bathnes.gov.uk
Bristol	Harbourside	0906 711 2191**	ticharbourside@destinationbristol.co.uk

Cornwall & the Isles of Scilly

Bodmin	Mount Folly Square	(01208) 76616	bodmintic@visit.org.uk
Bude	The Crescent	(01288) 354240	budetic@visitbude.info
Camelford*	The Clease	(01840) 212954	manager@camelfordtic.eclipse.co.uk
Falmouth	11 Market Strand	(01326) 312300	info@falmouthtic.co.uk
Fowey	5 South Street	(01726) 833616	info@fowey.co.uk
Isles of Scilly	Hugh Street, Hugh Town	(01720) 422536	tic@scilly.gov.uk
Launceston	Market Street	(01566) 772321	launcestontica@btconnect.com
Looe*	Fore Street	(01503) 262072	looetic@btconnect.com
Newquay	Marcus Hill	(01637) 854020	info@newquay.co.uk
Padstow	North Quay	(01841) 533449	padstowtic@btconnect.com
Penzance	Station Road	(01736) 362207	pztic@penwith.gov.uk
St Austell	Southbourne Road	0845 094 0428	tic@cornish-riviera.co.uk
St Ives	Street-an-Pol	(01736) 796297	ivtic@penwith.gov.uk
Truro	Boscawen Street	(01872) 274555	tic@truro.gov.uk
Wadebridge	Eddystone Road	0870 122 3337	wadebridgetic@btconnect.com

Devon

Axminster*	Church Street	(01297) 34386	axminstertic@btopenworld.com
Barnstaple	The Square	(01271) 375000	info@staynorthdevon.co.uk
Bideford	Victoria Park	(01237) 477676	bidefordtic@torridge.gov.uk
Braunton	Caen Street	(01271) 816400	info@brauntontic.co.uk
Brixham	The Quay	0870 707 0010	brixham.tic@torbay.gov.uk
Budleigh Salterton	Fore Street	(01395) 445275	budleigh.tic@btconnect.com
Combe Martin*	Cross Street	(01271) 883319	mail@visitcombemartin.co.uk
Crediton	High Street	(01363) 772006	info@devonshireheartland.co.uk
Dartmouth	Mayor's Avenue	(01803) 834224	holidays@discoverdartmouth.com
Dawlish	The Lawn	(01626) 215665	dawtic@Teignbridge.gov.uk
Exeter	Dix's Field	(01392) 265700	tic@exeter.gov.uk
Exmouth	Alexandra Terrace	(01395) 222299	info@exmouthtourism.co.uk
Honiton	Lace Walk Car Park	(01404) 43716	honitontic@btconnect.com
Ilfracombe	The Seafront	(01271) 863001	info@ilfracombe-tourism.co.uk
Ivybridge	19 Fore Street	(01752) 897035	bookends.ivybridge@virgin.net
Kingsbridge	The Quay	(01548) 853195	advice@kingsbridgeinfo.co.uk

Lynton and Lynmouth	Lee Road	0845 660 3232	info@lyntourism.co.uk
Modbury*	5 Modbury Court	(01548) 830159	modburytic@lineone.net
Newton Abbot	6 Bridge House	(01626) 215667	natic@Teignbridge.gov.uk
Okehampton	3 West Street	(01837) 53020	okehamptontic@westdevon.gov.uk
Ottery St Mary	10a Broad Street	(01404) 813964	info@otterytourism.org.uk
Paignton	The Esplanade	0870 707 0010	paignton.tic@torbay.gov.uk
Plymouth (Discovery Centre)	Crabtree	(01752) 266030	mtic@plymouth.gov.uk
Plymouth (Plymouth Mayflower)	3-5 The Barbican	(01752) 306330	barbicantic@plymouth.gov.uk
Salcombe	Market Street	(01548) 843927	info@salcombeinformation.co.uk
Seaton	The Underfleet	(01297) 21660	info@seatontic.freeserve.co.uk
Sidmouth	Ham Lane	(01395) 516441	sidmouthtic@eclipse.co.uk
South Molton	1 East Street	(01769) 574122	visitsouthmolton@btconnect.com
Tavistock	Bedford Square	(01822) 612938	tavistocktic@westdevon.gov.uk
Teignmouth	The Den	(01626) 215666	teigntic@teignbridge.gov.uk
Tiverton	Phoenix Lane	(01884) 255827	tivertontic@btconnect.com
Torquay	Vaughan Parade	0870 707 0010	torquay.tic@torbay.gov.uk
Torrington	Castle Hill	(01805) 626140	info@great-torrington.com
Totnes	Coronation Road	(01803) 863168	enquire@totnesinformation.co.uk
Woolacombe	The Esplanade	(01271) 870553	info@woolacombetourism.co.uk

Dorset

Blandford Forum	1 Greyhound Yard	(01258) 454770	blandfordtic@north-dorset.gov.uk
Bournemouth	Westover Road	(01202) 451700	info@bournemouth.gov.uk
Bridport	47 South Street	(01308) 424901	bridport.tic@westdorset-dc.gov.uk
Christchurch	49 High Street	(01202) 471780	enquiries@christchurchtourism.info
Dorchester	11 Antelope Walk	(01305) 267992	dorchester.tic@westdorset-dc.gov.uk
Lyme Regis	Church Street	(01297) 442138	lymeregis.tic@westdorset-dc.gov.uk
Poole	Poole Quay	(01202) 253253	info@poole.gov.uk
Shaftesbury	8 Bell Street	(01747) 853514	shaftesburytic@north-dorset.gov.uk
Sherborne	3 Tilton Court	(01935) 815341	sherborne.tic@westdorset-dc.gov.uk
Swanage	Shore Road	(01929) 422885	mail@swanage.gov.uk
Wareham	South Street	(01929) 552740	tic@purbeck-dc.gov.uk
Weymouth	The Esplanade	(01305) 785747	tic@weymouth.gov.uk
Wimborne Minster	29 High Street	(01202) 886116	wimbornetic@eastdorset.gov.uk

Gloucestershire & the Cotswolds

Bourton-on-the-Water	Victoria Street	(01451) 820211	bourtonvic@cotswold.gov.uk
Cheltenham	77 Promenade	(01242) 522878	tic@cheltenham.gov.uk
Cirencester	Market Place	(01285) 654180	cirencestervic@cotswold.gov.uk
Coleford	High Street	(01594) 812388	tourism@fdean.gov.uk
Gloucester	28 Southgate Street	(01452) 396572	tourism@gloucester.gov.uk
Newent	7 Church Street	(01531) 822468	newent@fdean.gov.uk
Stow-on-the-Wold	The Square	(01451) 831082	stowvic@cotswold.gov.uk
Stroud	George Street	(01453) 760960	tic@stroud.gov.uk

Tetbury	33 Church Street	(01666) 503552	tourism@tetbury.org
Tewkesbury	64 Barton Street	(01684) 295027	tewkesburytic@tewkesburybc.gov.uk
Winchcombe*	High Street	(01242) 602925	winchcombetic@tewkesbury.gov.uk

Somerset

Bridgwater	King Square	(01278) 436438	bridgwater.tic@sedgemoor.gov.uk
Burnham-on-Sea	South Esplanade	(01278) 787852	burnham.tic@sedgemoor.gov.uk
Cartgate	A303/A3088 Cartgate Picnic Site	(01935) 829333	cartgate.tic@southsomerset.gov.uk
Chard	Fore Street	(01460) 65710	chardtic@chard.gov.uk
Cheddar*	The Gorge	(01934) 744071	cheddar.tic@sedgemoor.gov.uk
Frome	Justice Lane	(01373) 467271	frome.tic@ukonline.co.uk
Glastonbury	9 High Street	(01458) 832954	glastonbury.tic@ukonline.co.uk
Minehead	17 Friday Street	(01643) 702624	info@mineheadtic.co.uk
Sedgemoor Services	M5 Southbound	(01934) 750833	somersetvisitorcentre@somserset.gov.uk
Shepton Mallet	48 High Street	(01749) 345258	sheptonmallet.tic@ukonline.co.uk
Street	Farm Road	(01458) 447384	street.tic@ukonline.co.uk
Taunton	Paul Street	(01823) 336344	tauntontic@tauntondeane.gov.uk
Wellington	30 Fore Street	(01823) 663379	wellingtontic@tauntondeane.gov.uk
Wells	Market Place	(01749) 672552	touristinfo@wells.gov.uk
Weston-super-Mare	Beach Lawns	(01934) 888800	westontouristinfo@n-somerset.gov.uk
Yeovil Heritage & Visitor Information Centre	Hendford	(01935) 845946	yeoviltic@southsomerset.gov.uk

Wiltshire – Salisbury & Stonehenge

Amesbury	Smithfield Street	(01980) 622833	amesburytic@salisbury.gov.uk
Avebury	Green Street	(01672) 539425	all.atic@kennet.gov.uk
Bradford-on-Avon	50 St Margaret's Street	(01225) 865797	tic@bradfordonavon.co.uk
Chippenham	Market Place	(01249) 665970	tourism@chippenham.gov.uk
Corsham	31 High Street	(01249) 714660	corshamheritage@northwilts.gov.uk
Devizes	Market Place	(01380) 729408	all.dtic@kennet.gov.uk
Malmesbury	Market Lane	(01666) 823748	malmesburyip@northwilts.gov.uk
Marlborough	High Street	(01672) 513989	all.tic's@kennet.gov.uk
Melksham	Church Street	(01225) 707424	info@visit-melksham.com
Mere	Barton Lane	(01747) 861211	MereTIC@Salisbury.gov.uk
Salisbury	Fish Row	(01722) 334956	visitorinfo@salisbury.gov.uk
Swindon	37 Regent Street	(01793) 530328	infocentre@swindon.gov.uk
Trowbridge	St Stephen's Place	(01225) 710535	tic@trowbridge.gov.uk
Warminster	off Station Rd	(01985) 218548	visitwarminster@westwiltshire.gov.uk

* seasonal opening   ** calls to this number are charged at premium rate

Alternatively, you can text **TIC LOCATE** to **64118** to find your nearest Tourist Information Centre

Places to visit in
South West England

On the following pages you'll find an extensive selection of indoor and outdoor attractions in South West England. Get to grips with nature, stroll around a museum, have an action-packed day with the kids and a whole lot more...

Attractions are ordered by county, and if you're looking for a specific kind of experience each county is divided into the following sections.

 Family fun

 Nature and wildlife

Historic England

Outdoor activities

Entertainment and culture

 Food and drink

Relaxing and pampering

Look out, too, for the Quality Assured Visitor Attraction sign. This indicates that the attraction is assessed annually and meets the standards required to receive the quality marque. So rest assured, you'll have a great time.

Turn to the maps at the front of the guide to find the location of those attractions displaying a map reference.

The index on page 459 will help you to locate specific attractions with ease. For more great ideas for places to visit contact a local Tourist Information Centre or log on to **enjoyengland.com**.

Please note, as changes often occur after press date, it is advisable to confirm opening times and admission prices before travelling.

KEY TO ATTRACTIONS

Cafe/restaurant	☕
Picnic area	⛩
No dogs except service dogs	🐕
Partial disabled access	♿
Full disabled access	♿

Where prices aren't specified, use the following guide for an adult admission:

£	up to £5
££	between £5 and £10
£££	between £10 and £15
££££	more than £15

Blooming marvellous fun, The Eden Project, Cornwall

Bristol & Bath

FAMILY FUN

Enjoy the fun of a special event or visit one of the attractions listed for a great day out. For more inspiring ideas go to **enjoyengland.com**.

25 May–10 Jun
Bath Fringe Festival
Various venues, Bath
(01225) 480079
bathfringe.co.uk

28 Jun–1 Jul
Taste of Bath
Royal Victoria Park
visitbath.co.uk

28–29 Jul
Bristol Harbour Festival
Bristol Harbour
bristol-city.gov.uk28–29 Jul

9–12 Aug
Bristol International Balloon Fiesta
Ashton Court
(0117) 953 5884
bristolfiesta.co.uk

1–2 Sep
Bristol International Festival of Kites and Air Creations
Ashton Court
kite-festival.org

Bristol Blue Glass Ltd
Unit 7, Whitby Road, Brislington BS4 3QF
t (0117) 972 0818 **w** bristol-glass.co.uk
open All year, Mon-Sat 1000-1600.
admission £   ♿
Watch Bristol blue glass being made by a skilled team of glassmakers in the new visitor centre, and purchase direct from the factory shop.

Destination Bristol
t 0906 711 2191 **w** visitbristol.co.uk
map ref 2A2
see ad on p8

Roman Baths

Abbey Churchyard,
Bath BA1 1LZ
t (01225) 477785
w romanbaths.co.uk
open Jan-Feb, Nov-Dec 0930-1630 (excl 25-26 Dec). Mar-Jun, Sep-Oct 0900-1700. Jul-Aug 0900-2000. Exit one hour after these times.
admission Adult: £11.25

The Roman Baths and Temple of Sulis Minerva are among the finest Roman remains in Britain. State-of-the-art computer reconstructions of Roman Britain bring the experience to life. Free personal hand-held audioguides are available in eight languages. Enjoy tea or lunch in the magnificent 18thC Pump Room.

Map ref 2B2

 voucher offer – see back section

Admission is based on an adult price. Please check opening times and admission before travelling.

NATURE AND WILDLIFE

Bristol Zoo Gardens
Clifton BS8 3HA
t (0117) 974 7399 **w** bristolzoo.org.uk
open Apr-Oct, daily 0900-1730. Nov-Mar, daily 0900-1700.
admission £££

Voted Zoo of the Year 2004 by the Good Britain Guide, Bristol Zoo Gardens has something for everyone, from the world's smallest and rarest tortoise to the largest ape.

HorseWorld Visitor Centre
Staunton Manor Farm, Staunton Lane,
Whitchurch BS14 0QJ
t (01275) 540173 **w** horseworld.org.uk
open Apr-Oct, daily 1000-1700. Nov-Mar, Tue-Sun 1000-1600.
admission ££
Meet our friendly horses, ponies and donkeys and enjoy our touch-and-groom areas, pony rides, live shows, adventure playground, slides, nature trail and video theatre.

HISTORIC ENGLAND

Assembly Rooms
Bennett Street, Bath BA1 2QH
t (01225) 477789 **w** museumofcostume.co.uk
open Mar-Oct, daily, Bank Hols 1100-1700.
admission ££
Designed by John Wood the Younger in 1769. One of Bath's finest Georgian buildings. Includes Museum of Costume.

Bath Abbey
Abbey Church Yard, Bath BA1 1LT
t (01225) 422462 **w** bathabbey.org
open Apr-Oct, daily 0900-1800. Nov-Mar, daily 0900-1630.
admission £
Late 15thC abbey built on the site of a Saxon and Norman abbey. Magnificent example of the Perpendicular period of English Gothic architecture. Display in vaults.

Bristol Cathedral
College Green, Bristol BS1 5TJ
t (0117) 926 4879 **w** bristol-cathedral.co.uk
open Daily 0800-1730.
admission Free
Once an Augustinian abbey and splendid 12thC Norman Chapter House. Magnificent 13thC and 14thC architecture.

Bristol St John the Baptist
Broad Street, Bristol BS1 2EZ
t (020) 7213 0660 **w** visitchurches.org.uk
open Daily, please phone for details.
admission Free
The elegant perpendicular spire of St John's rises above the Gothic city gate, and the interior of the church is impressively tall and graceful. A fine collection of monuments testifies to the wealth of Bristol in medieval times and later.

Pump Room
Abbey Church Yard, Bath BA1 1LZ
t (01225) 477785 **w** romanbaths.co.uk
open Mar-Jun, daily 0900-1800. Jul-Aug, daily 0900-2100. Sep-Oct daily 0900-1800. Nov-Feb, daily 0930-1730.
admission £££
With its elegant interior of c1795, the Pump Room is the social heart of Bath. Stop for refreshments or lunch and sample a glass of spa water from the fountain.

Roman Baths

Abbey Churchyard,
Bath BA1 1LZ
t (01225) 477785
w romanbaths.co.uk
open Jan-Feb, Nov-Dec 0930-1630 (excl 25-26 Dec). Mar-Jun, Sep-Oct 0900-1700. Jul-Aug 0900-2000. Exit one hour after these times.
admission Adult: £11.25

The Roman Baths and Temple of Sulis Minerva are among the finest Roman remains in Britain. State-of-the-art computer reconstructions of Roman Britain bring the experience to life. Free personal hand-held audioguides are available in eight languages. Enjoy tea or lunch in the magnificent 18thC Pump Room.

Map ref 2B2

ⓥ *voucher offer – see back section*

ss Great Britain & Maritime Heritage Centre

Great Western Dock, Gas Ferry Road, Bristol BS1 6TY
t (0117) 926 0680 **w** ss-great-britain.com
open Apr-Oct, daily, Bank Hols 1000-1730. Nov-Mar, daily Bank Hols 1000-1630.
admission ££

Designed by Brunel, ss Great Britain was the first of the great steamships when launched in 1843. She is now being restored at the Great Western Dock in which she was built.

OUTDOOR ACTIVITIES

The Bristol Packet Boat Trips

Wapping Wharf, Gas Ferry Road, Bristol BS1 6UN
t (0117) 926 8157 **w** bristolpacket.co.uk
open All year, Sat-Sun 1100-1600. School holidays, daily 1100-1600.
admission £

Trips around the historic harbour and up and down the River Avon. Suitable and available for the general public, for private charter and educational cruises.

ENTERTAINMENT AND CULTURE

Bath Aqua Theatre of Glass

105-107 Walcot Street, Bath BA1 5BW
t (01225) 428146 **w** bathaquaglass.com
open All year, Mon-Sun, Bank Hols 0930-1700.
admission £

Discover the Bath Aqua Theatre of Glass, Bath's newest visitor centre in the heart of the city's artisan quarter.

Bath Postal Museum

27 Northgate Street, Bath BA1 1AJ
t (01225) 460333 **w** bathpostalmuseum.org
open Mar-Nov, Mon-Sat 1100-1700. Dec-Feb, Mon-Sat 1100-1630.
admission £

To discover the truly fascinating story of 4,000 years of written communication, visit the Bath Postal Museum in the very building from which the first stamp in the world, the Penny Black, was posted.

Bristol City Museum & Art Gallery

Queen's Road, Bristol BS8 1RL
t (0117) 922 3571 **w** bristol-city.gov.uk/museums
open Daily 1000-1700.
admission Free

Collection representing applied, oriental and fine art, archaeology, geology, natural history, ethnography and Egyptology.

Bristol Hippodrome

St Augustine's Parade, Bristol BS1 4UZ
t (0117) 302 3333 **w** getlive.co.uk/Bristol
open All year. See website for details.
admission ££££

The West's main theatrical venue for large-scale West End musicals, opera, ballet, comedy, children's shows and much more.

Bristol Old Vic Theatre

Theatre Royal, King Street, Bristol BS1 4ED
t (0117) 987 7877 **w** bristol-old-vic.co.uk
open Jan-Jul, Mon-Sat. Sep-Dec, Mon-Sat. See website for details.
admission ££

Britain's oldest working theatre dates from 1766. Renowned for excellent productions.

British Empire & Commonwealth Museum

Clock Tower Yard, Temple Meads BS1 6QH
t (0117) 925 4980 **w** empiremuseum.co.uk
open Daily 1000-1700.
admission ££

A major new national museum exploring the dramatic history and heritage of the British Empire and its development into the modern Commonwealth.

Brunel's ss Great Britain

Great Western Dockyard, Gas Ferry Road, Bristol BS1 6TY
t (0117) 926 0680 **w** ssgreatbritain.org
open Apr-Oct, daily 0900-1730. Nov-Mar, daily 0900-1630.
admission ££

Brunel's steam ship, the ss Great Britain, is a unique survival from Victorian times and the forerunner of all modern shipping. The world's first iron-hulled, screw propeller-driven, steam-powered passenger liner.

Building of Bath Museum

The Huntingdon Chapel, The Vineyards, Bath BA1 5NA
t (01225) 333895 **w** bath-preservation-trust.org.uk
open All year, Tue-Sun, Bank Hols 1030-1700.
admission £

The Building of Bath Museum tells the story of how Georgian Bath was built. Exhibitions include a huge model of the entire city.

Destination Bristol

t 0906 711 2191 **w** visitbristol.co.uk
map ref 2A2
see ad on p8

Herschel House Museum

19 New King Street, Bath BA1 2BL
t (01225) 446865 **w** bath-preservation-trust.org.uk
open All year, Mon-Tue, Thu-Fri 1300-1700, Sat-Sun, Bank Hols 1100-1700.
admission £

The 18thC house of distinguished astronomer, scientist, musician and composer, William Herschel.

Admission is based on an adult price. Please check opening times and admission before travelling.

Holburne Museum of Art

Great Pulteney Street, Bath BA2 4DB
t (01225) 466669 **w** bath.ac.uk/holburne
open All year, Tue-Sat 1000-1700, Sun 1100-1700, Bank Holidays 1100-1700.
admission ££

Fine collection of sliver, porcelain, miniatures and furniture. Picture gallery contains paintings by Turner, Stubbs and Gainsborough, including The Byam Family.

The Jane Austen Centre

40 Gay Street, Queen Square, Bath BA1 2NT
t (01225) 443000 **w** janeausten.co.uk
open Apr-Sep, daily 1000-1730. Oct-Mar, Mon-Fri, Sun 1000-1630, Sat 1000-1730.
admission ££

Celebrating Bath's most famous resident, the centre offers a snapshot of life during Regency times and explores how living in this magnificent city affected Jane Austen's life and writing.

Museum of Costume

Assembly Rooms, Bennett Street,
Bath BA1 2QH
t (01225) 477785 **w** museumofcostume.co.uk
open Daily 1100-1700.
admission ££

Displays of fashionable dress for men, women and children, from 16thC to present day.

Royal West of England Academy

Queens Road, Clifton, Bristol BS8 1PX
t (0117) 973 5129 **w** rwa.org.uk
open All year, Mon-Sat 1000-1730, Sun 1400-1700.
admission £

Bristol's first art gallery, showing a varied programme of exhibitions all year round.

Victoria Art Gallery

Pulteney Bridge, Bridge Street, Bath BA2 4AT
t (01225) 477233 **w** victoriagal.org.uk
open All year, Tue-Sat 1000-1700, Sun 1330-1700.
admission Free

Permanent collection of British and European fine and decorative art from 15th-21stC. Also major touring exhibitions from national museums and other places.

Watershed Media Centre

1 Canons Road, Harbourside,
Bristol BS1 5TX
t (0117) 927 6444
w watershed.co.uk
open Daily 0900-2300.
admission Free

Watershed offers an electric programme of independent film, digital media and events with a relaxed and welcoming cafe/bar overlooking Bristol's harbourside.

FOOD AND DRINK

Sally Lunn's House

4 North Parade Passage, Bath BA1 1NX
t (01225) 461634
w sallylunns.co.uk
open All year, Mon-Sat, Bank Hols 1000-2200, Sun 1100-2200.
admission Free

The oldest house in Bath. A Tudor-style building on a monastic site with excavations showing early medieval and Roman building. Now a licensed restaurant.

RELAXING AND PAMPERING

Thermae Bath Spa

Hot Bath Street, Avon BA1 1SJ
t (01225) 331234
w thermaebathspa.com
open All year, daily, Bank Hols 0900-2200.
admission ££££

Britain's original and most remarkable spa. The only place in the UK where you can bathe in natural hot waters.

The Clifton Suspension Bridge spanning the River Avon

Cornwall & the Isles of Scilly

Enjoy the fun of a special event or visit one of the attractions listed for a great day out. For more inspiring ideas go to **enjoyengland.com**.

16–24 Jun
Golowan Festival Incorporating Mazey Day
Various venues, Penzance
(01736) 365520
golowan.com

6–12 Aug
Ripcurl Boardmasters
Newquay
(020) 8789 6655
ripcurlboardmasters.com

11–18 Aug
Henri Lloyd Falmouth Week
Falmouth
falmouthweek.co.uk

Mar–Apr 08
Walk Scilly
Throughout the islands
(01720) 422316
walkscilly.co.uk

May 08
Daphne du Maurier Festival
Fowey
dumaurierfestival.co.uk

FAMILY FUN

Bodmin and Wenford Railway
Bodmin General Station, Lostwithiel Road,
Bodmin PL31 1AQ
t (01208) 73666
w bodminandwenfordrailway.co.uk
open See website for details.
admission ££
Cornwall's only preserved standard-gauge steam railway which combines the nostalgia of a branch line in the heyday of steam with the beauty of the Fowey and Camel River valleys.

Cornwall's Crealy Great Adventure Park

Tredinnick PL27 7RA
t (01841) 540276
w crealy.co.uk/cornwall_pages
open Apr-Oct, daily 1000-1800. Nov-Mar, daily 1000-1700.
admission ££
Maximum magical fun and unforgettable adventures. Discover Cornwall's best value all-weather family attraction.

Dairyland Farm World

Tresillian Barton, Summercourt TR8 5AA
t (01872) 510246
w dairylandfarmworld.com
open Apr-Oct, daily 1000-1700.
admission ££
Adventure playground, country life museum, nature trail, farm park, pets and daily events, including 120 cows milked in Clarabelle's space-age orbiter.

Delabole Slate Quarry
Pengelly, Delabole PL33 9AZ
t (01840) 212242
w delaboleslate.co.uk
open May-Aug, Mon-Fri 1400-1600.
admission £
Visit our showroom and viewing platform then see a presentation or take a short guided tour of the quarry's operation.

The Extreme Academy
On the Beach, Watergate Bay, Newquay TR8 4AA
t (01637) 860840
w watergatebay.co.uk
open Apr-Sep, daily, Bank Hols 0830-1830. Oct-Mar, daily, Bank Hols 0930-1630.
admission £££
Cornwall's ski resort on a beach. Take your pick from waveski, kitesurf, mountain board, kite buggy, land board or traction kite lessons, or try them all with an awesome Extreme Day.

For key to symbols see inside back cover.

Flambards Experience
Culdrose Manor, Helston TR13 0QA
t (01326) 573404 **w** flambards.co.uk
open Apr-Oct, daily 1030-1730. Winter: please call for details.
admission £££

Experience a Victorian village, Britain in the blitz and the best thrill rides in Cornwall.

Geevor Tin Mine
Pendeen TR19 7EW
t (01736) 788662 **w** geevor.com
open Apr-Oct, daily 0900-1600. Nov-Mar, Mon-Fri, Sun 0900-1500.
admission ££

Cornish mining museum, tours of surface plant and underground tours of the site. Magnificent mine model.

Goonhilly Satellite Earth Station Experience

The Visitors Centre, Goonhilly Downs TR12 6LQ
t 0800 679 593 **w** goonhilly.bt.com
open Apr-May, daily, Bank Hols 1000-1700. Jun-Sep, daily, Bank Hols 1000-1800. Oct, daily 1000-1700. Nov-Mar, please call for details.
admission ££

The world's largest satellite earth station. Guided bus tour around the complex. Visitor centre with film show, and interactive displays. Children's play area.

Holywell Bay Fun Park
Holywell Bay, Newquay TR8 5PW
t (01637) 830531 **w** holywellbay.co.uk
open Apr-Oct, daily. Please see website for details.
admission Free

Landscaped park with quality rides. Includes go-karts, crazy golf, battle boats, maze. Indoor adventure play area and fun rides, bumper boats, Bugs Buggies, climbing wall, golf.

Isles of Scilly Travel
Quay Street, Penzance TR18 4BZ
t 0845 710 5555
w ios-travel.co.uk
open Office: Mon-Sat. Skybus: All year. Scillonian III: 26 Mar-3 Nov, Mon-Sat. Aug, daily.
admission Please phone for pricing details

Discover the beautiful Isles of Scilly. Fly with Skybus from Southampton, Bristol, Exeter, Newquay or Land's End (shuttle service available) and experience a bird's eye view. Alternatively relax and sail with Scillonian III from Penzance. You'd be scilly to miss it.

Map ref 1A3

The catch of the day, Porthloe

Lappa Valley Steam Railway

St Newlyn East TR8 5HZ
t (01872) 510317 **w** lappavalley.co.uk
open Apr-Sep, School Hols, daily. Oct, Tue-Thu, Sun, daily. Please see website for details.
admission ££

A two-mile steam train journey. Leisure park, paddle boats, canoes, miniature railways, crazy golf, maze. Listed mine building, video of mine disaster.

National Maritime Museum Cornwall

Discovery Quay, Falmouth TR11 3QY
t (01326) 313388 **w** nmmc.co.uk
open Daily 1000-1700 (excl 25-26 Dec).
admission Adult: £7

Located on the edge of Falmouth's stunning harbour, this museum is a hands-on, new generation of visitor attraction that will appeal to landlubbers and sailors alike. More than just a museum about boats, it's all about the sea, boats and Cornwall. Full disability access, waterside cafe and shop.

   Map ref 1B3

 voucher offer – see back section

Newquay Zoo

Trenance Gardens,
Newquay TR7 2LZ
t (01637) 873342 **w** newquayzoo.org.uk
open Oct-Mar 1000-1700 (excl 25 Dec).
Apr-Sep 0930-1800.
admission Adult: £8.95

EXPERIENCE THE WILDLIFE. Discover hundreds of animals from all around the world set amongst lakeside gardens, from the smallest monkey, the Pygmy Marmoset, to African lions. Enjoy talks and feeding times throughout the day. Events are run throughout the year. Phone or see the website for details.

Map ref 1B2

 voucher offer – see back section

Poldark Mine

Wendron TR13 0ER
t (01326) 573173 **w** poldark-mine.co.uk
open Apr, Jul-Aug, daily 1000-1730. May-Jun, Sep-Oct, Mon-Fri, Sun 1000-1730.
admission Free

Genuine 18thC Cornish tin mine featuring guided underground tours. Museum, entertainment, gardens, restaurant, gift shops and craft workshops.

Discover Britain's heritage

Discover the history and beauty of over 250 of Britain's best-known historic houses, castles, gardens and manor-houses. You can purchase *Britain's Historic Houses and Gardens – Guide and Map* from good bookshops and online at enjoy**England**direct.com.

Admission is based on an adult price. Please check opening times and admission before travelling.

Shire Horse Farm and Carriage Museum
Lower Gryllis Farm, Treskillard TR16 6LA
t (01209) 713606
open Apr-Oct, Mon-Fri, Sun 1000-1730.
admission ££
Over 40 commercial and pleasure horse-drawn vehicles. All three breeds of heavy English horses – Shire, Suffolk Punch and Clydesdale.

Spirit of the West American Theme Park
Retallack, Winnards Perch TR9 6DE
t (01637) 881160
w chycor.co.ukspirit-of-the-west
open All year, Mon-Fri, Sun 1030-1700.
admission ££
Wild West theme park, museums of cowboys, Indians and American collections. Live action shows, a complete living history museum of the 1800s set in 100 acres.

Springfields Fun Park and Pony Centre
Ruthvoes TR9 6HU
t (01637) 882132
w springfieldsponycentre.co.uk
open Please see website for details.
admission ££
Lots of indoor and outdoor activities. Springfields is not just a day out, it's what childhood memories are made of.

Trethorne Leisure Farm
Kennards House PL15 8QE
t (01566) 86324
w trethorne.co.uk
open Daily 1000-1800.
admission ££
All-weather attraction for all ages. Large indoor and outdoor play areas plus animal activities. Tenpin bowling, restaurant, bars, gift shop, and games room.

Waterworld
Trenance Leisure Park, Newquay TR7 2LZ
t (01637) 853828
w newquaywaterworld.co.uk
open Daily. Please see website for details.
admission ££
Two swimming pools, 25m fun pool, Wooden Waves ramp park, superb life fitness gym and aerobics classes.

World of Model Railways
Meadow Street, Mevagissey PL26 6UL
t (01726) 842457
w model-railway.co.uk
open Apr-Oct, daily 1000-1700. Nov-Feb, Sat-Sun 1000-1600.
admission £
Extensive layout with detailed scenery. Nearly 50 trains automatically programmed. A world in miniature with over 2,000 models of trains from many countries.

Westward Airways & Land's End Flying School

Land's End Airport, St Just TR19 7RL
t (01736) 788771
w landsendairport.co.uk
open Daily
admission Please phone for pricing details

Experience flying over the Penwith Peninsula for an unforgettable bird's eye view with Westward Airways. Alternatively have a go yourself with a trial flying lesson at Land's End Flying School. Gift vouchers, refreshments, information, toilet facilities and internet access are available, as is, of course, a great view.

Map ref 1A3

NATURE AND WILDLIFE

Blue Reef Aquarium
Towan Promenade,
Newquay TR7 1DU
t (01637) 878134
w bluereefaquarium.co.uk
open Mar-Oct, daily 1000-1700. Nov-Feb, daily 1000-1600.
admission ££
Blue Reef Aquarium brings the magic of the undersea world alive. Enjoy close encounters with tropical sharks, rays and seahorses.

Caerhays Castle Gardens
Caerhays, Gorran PL26 6LY
t (01872) 501310 **w** caehays.co.uk
open Feb-May, daily 1000-1700.
admission ££
A 60-acre woodland garden renowned for its collections of camellias, magnolias, rhododendrons and oaks.

Carnglaze Slate Caverns
Carnglaze, St Neot PL14 6HQ
t (01579) 320251 **w** carnglaze.com
open Apr-Jul, Mon-Sat 1000-1700. Aug, Mon-Sat 1000-2000. Sep-Mar, Mon-Sat 1000-1700.
admission ££
Centuries-old caverns, created by local slate miners. Famous subterranean lake with crystal-clear blue-green water. The Rum Store concert and theatre venue.

Colliford Lake Park
Bolventor, Bodmin Moor, St Neot PL14 6PZ
t (01208) 821469 **w** collifordlakepark.com
open See website for details.
admission ££
An all-weather adventure park with over 30,000 sq ft undercover offering loads of fun and exciting entertainment for all the family. Set in a beautiful country park on Bodmin Moor.

Cornish Birds of Prey Centre
Meadowside Farm, Winnards Perch,
St Columb Major TR9 6DH
t (01637) 880544 **w** cornishbirdsofprey.co.uk
open Daily 1000-1700.
admission ££
Birds of prey centre, animal park and fishing lakes set in a beautiful valley. Flying displays twice daily, over 60 birds to see, plus much more!

Eden Project
Bodelva, St Austell PL24 2SG
t (01726) 811911 **w** edenproject.com
open Apr-Oct, daily 1000-1800. Nov-Mar, daily 1000-1630.
admission £££
An unforgettable experience in a breathtaking epic location. A gateway into the fascinating world of plants and people.

Glendurgan Garden
Mawnan Smith TR11 5JZ
t (01326) 250906 **w** nationaltrust.org.uk
open Mar-Oct, Tue-Sat 1030-1730.
admission £
A valley garden of great beauty, created in the 1820s and running down to the tiny village of Durgan and its beach. There are many fine trees and rare and exotic plants.

Kit Hill Country Park
Kit Hill Office, Clitters, Callington PL17 8HW
t (01579) 370030 **w** cornwall.gov.uk
open Daily.
admission Free
A wild, rugged, granite hilltop, famous for its fine views and fascinating history. Kit Hill Country Park forms a dominating feature, to be seen for miles around.

The Lost Gardens of Heligan
Heligan, Pentewan PL26 6EN
t (01726) 845100 **w** heligan.com
open Mar-Oct, daily 1000-1800. Nov-Feb, daily 1000-1700.
admission ££
The nation's favourite garden offers 200 glorious acres of exploration, which include extensive productive gardens and pleasure grounds, sustainably-managed farmland, wetlands, ancient woodlands and a pioneering wildlife conservation project.

The Monkey Sanctuary Trust
Looe PL13 1NZ
t (01503) 262532 **w** monkeysanctuary.org
open Apr-Sep, Mon-Thu, Sun 1100-1630. Oct, School hols, Mon-Thu, Sun 1100-1630.
admission ££
Protected colony of woolly monkeys. Talks given throughout the day and monkeys can be seen in extensive enclosures and trees.

Newquay Zoo

Trenance Gardens,
Newquay TR7 2LZ
t (01637) 873342 **w** newquayzoo.org.uk
open Oct-Mar 1000-1700 (excl 25 Dec). Apr-Sep 0930-1800.
admission Adult: £8.95

EXPERIENCE THE WILDLIFE. Discover hundreds of animals from all around the world set amongst lakeside gardens, from the smallest monkey, the Pygmy Marmoset, to African lions. Enjoy talks and feeding times throughout the day. Events are run throughout the year. Phone or see the website for details.

 Map ref 1B2

 voucher offer – see back section

For key to symbols see inside back cover.

National Seal Sanctuary
Gweek TR12 6UG
t (01326) 221361
w sealsanctuary.co.uk
open All year. Please phone for details.
admission ££
Britain's leading marine mammal rescue centre, the National Seal Sanctuary, rescues over 30 abandoned and injured seal pups every year.

Paradise Park
Glanmor House, Trelissick Road, Hayle TR27 4HB
t (01736) 751020
w paradisepark.org.uk
open Daily 1000-1800.
admission ££
Award-winning sanctuary specialising in rare birds, otters and red squirrels. Huge aviaries, daily events, cafe and shop. Great for bird, animal and garden lovers.

Pine Lodge Gardens & Nursery
Holmbush, St Austell PL25 3RQ
t (01726) 73500
w pine-lodge.co.uk
open Daily 1000-1800.
admission ££
Thirty acres with over 6,000 plants. Herbaceous and shrub borders, many water features. Lake with waterfowl and black swans. Plant hunting expeditions every year.

Porfell Animal Land
Trecangate, Nr Lanreath, Liskeard PL14 4RE
t (01503) 220211
w PorfellAnimalLand.co.uk
open Apr-Oct, daily, Bank hols 1000-1800.
admission ££
Porfell Animal Land with its gently sloping fields, streams, woodland walks and a variety of exotic wild and domesticated animals allows visitors to enjoy close contact with nature.

Screech Owl Sanctuary
Trewin Farm, Goss Moor, St Columb TR9 6HP
t (01726) 860182
w screechowlsanctuary.co.uk
open Feb-Oct, daily 1000-1800.
admission ££
Owl rescue and rehabilitation centre. Guided tours of sanctuary, approximately 160 owls and an education centre on a conservation theme. Flying displays twice daily.

Tamar Otter Sanctuary
North Petherwin PL15 8LW
t (01566) 785646
open Apr-Oct, daily, Bank Hols 1030-1800.
admission ££
Wooded valley with collection of otters in large, open, natural enclosures. Water-fowl lakes, aviaries, woodland trail with deer, peacocks and pheasants. Breeding owls.

Tamar Valley Donkey Park
St Ann's Chapel, Gunnislake PL18 9HW
t (01822) 834072 **w** donkeypark.com
open Apr-Oct, daily 1000-1730. Nov-Mar, Sat-Sun, School Hols 1030-1630.
admission ££
Donkey rides, feed the animals, rabbit warren, goat mountain, large indoor play barn, two outdoor playgrounds, cafe, shop, picnic garden and adopt a donkey.

Trebah Garden
Trebah, Mawnan Smith TR11 5JZ
t (01326) 250448 **w** trebah-garden.co.uk
open All year. Please see website for details.
admission ££
A 26-acre ravine garden leading to private beach on Helford River. Extensive collection of rare and sub-tropical plants and trees. Water garden with koi carp.

Trelissick Garden
Feock TR3 6QL
t (01872) 862090 **w** nationaltrust.org.uk
open Apr-Oct. Mar, daily 1030-1730. Nov-Feb, daily 1100-1600.
admission ££
Large garden, lovely in all seasons. Superb views of estuary and Falmouth harbour. Woodland walks beside the River Fal.

Trengwainton Garden
Madron TR20 8RZ
t (01736) 363148 **w** nationaltrust.org.uk
open Feb-Oct, Mon-Thu, Sun 1000-1700.
admission £
Garden rich in exotic plants, views to Mount's Bay, stream and walled gardens with many plants which cannot be grown anywhere else on mainland UK.

Trewithen
Grampound Road TR2 4DD
t (01726) 883647 **w** trewithengardens.co.uk
open Feb-May, daily 1000-1630. Jun-Sep, Mon-Sat 1000-1630.
admission £
Gardens renowned for camellias, rhododendrons, magnolias and many rare plants. An 18thC landscaped parkland. House built in 1720. Audiovisual on history of Trewithen.

HISTORIC ENGLAND

The Arthurian Centre
Slaughterbridge, Camelford PL32 9TT
t (01840) 212450 **w** arthur-online.co.uk
open Apr-Oct, daily 1000-1700.
admission £
Site of King Arthur's last battle. Nature and history trail, exhibition room, video loop, brass rubbings, gift shop. A totally unique experience. Beautiful riverside walks.

Charlestown Shipwreck and Heritage Centre
Quay Road, Charlestown PL25 3NJ
t (01726) 69897
w shipwreckcharlestown.com
open Mar-Oct, daily 1000-1700.
admission ££
Visual history of Charlestown including life-size tableaux of old inhabitants, blacksmith and cooper. Outstanding display of shipwreck material. Diving and RNLI exhibitions.

Cornish Mines & Engines
Pool TR15 3NP
t (01209) 315027 w nationaltrust.org.uk
open Apr-Nov, Mon, Wed-Fri, Sun 1100-1700.
admission £
Cornwall's engine houses are dramatic reminders of the time when the county was a powerhouse of tin, copper and china-clay mining.

Cotehele
St Dominick PL12 6TA
t (01579) 351346 w nationaltrust.org.uk
open Mar-Oct, Mon-Thu, Sat-Sun 1100-1630.
admission ££
Medieval house with superb collections of textiles, armour and furniture, set in extensive grounds. Home of the Edgcumbe family for centuries, its granite and slatestone walls contain intimate chambers adorned with tapestries.

The Courtroom Experience
Shire Hall, Mount Folly, Bodmin PL31 2DQ
t (01208) 76616
w bodminmoor.co.uk/bodmintic
open Apr-Oct, Mon-Sat 1100-1600. Nov-Mar, Mon-Fri 1100-1600.
admission £
Guilty or not guilty: you must decide! What will the verdict be in this Victorian murder trial?

King Arthur's Great Halls
Fore Street, Tintagel PL34 0DA
t (01840) 770526 w kingarthursgreathalls.com
open Summer: daily 1000-1700. Winter: daily 1100-1500.
admission £
Dedicated to the Arthurian legend, this is the home of Robert Powell's narrated light show about the deeds of the Knights of the Round Table.

Land's End
Sennen TR19 7AA
t (08704) 580099 w landsend-landmark.co.uk
open Apr-Sep, daily 1000-1700. Oct-Mar, daily 1000-1500.
admission ££
Spectacular cliffs with breathtaking vistas. Superb multi-sensory Last Labyrinth show and other exhibitions.

Lanhydrock
Bodmin PL30 5AD
t (01208) 265950
w nationaltrust.org.uk
open House: Apr-Sep, Tue-Sun 1100-1730. Oct, Tue-Sat 1100-1700. Gardens: Daily 1000-1800.
admission ££
A 17thC house largely rebuilt after a fire in 1881. The 116ft gallery with magnificent plaster ceiling illustrates scenes from the Old Testament. Park, gardens, walks.

Mount Edgcumbe House and Park
Cremyll PL10 1HZ
t (01752) 822236
w mountedgcumbe.gov.uk
open Apr-Sep, Mon-Thu, Sun 1100-1630.
admission £
Restored Tudor mansion, past home of Earl of Mount Edgcumbe. French, Italian and English formal gardens with temples and 800 acres of parkland.

Pencarrow House and Gardens
Washaway PL30 3AG
t (01208) 841369
w pencarrow.co.uk
open Apr-Oct, Mon-Thu, Sun 1100-1700.
admission ££
Historic Georgian house, superb collection of paintings, furniture and china. Extensive grounds, picnic area, craft centre, children's play area and pets' corner, tearooms.

Pendennis Castle
Falmouth TR11 4LP
t (01326) 316594
w english-heritage.org.uk/pendennis
open See website for details.
admission £
Guards the entrance to the Fal estuary, along with its sister castle, St Mawes. Well-preserved coastal fort built by Henry VIII c1540.

Prideaux Place
Padstow PL28 8RP
t (01841) 532411
w prideauxplace.co.uk
open May-Oct, Mon-Thu, Sun 1230-1700.
admission ££
A 16thC Elizabethan mansion with contemporary embossed plaster ceiling in the Great Chamber. Forty acres of grounds including deer park.

Roseland St Anthony's Church
St. Anthony, Roseland, Portscatho TR2 5EY
t (020) 7213 0660
w visitchurches.org.uk
open Daily 1000-1630.
admission Free
Picturesquely situated looking across the creek to St Mawes, the church retains its original medieval plan and appearance. It also features notable Victorian work, and impressive monuments to members of the Spry family.

St Mawes Castle
St Mawes TR2 3AA
t (01326) 270526 **w** english-heritage.org.uk/stmawes
open See website for details.
admission £
On edge of Roseland Peninsula, erected by Henry VIII for coastal defence. Clover-leaf shaped and still intact. Fine example of military architecture. Lovely gardens.

St Michael's Mount
Marazion TR17 0EF
t (01736) 710507 **w** stmichaelsmount.co.uk
open Apr-Nov, Mon-Fri, Sun 1030-1730.
admission ££
Rocky island crowned by medieval church and castle, home to a living community.

Tintagel Castle
Tintagel PL34 0HE
t (01840) 770328 **w** english-heritage.org.uk/tintagel
open See website for details.
admission £
Medieval ruined castle on wild, wind-swept coast. Famous for associations with Arthurian legend. Built largely in 13thC by Richard, Earl of Cornwall.

Truro Cathedral
The Cathedral Office, 14 St Mary's Street,
Truro TR1 2AF
t (01872) 276782 **w** trurocathedral.org.uk
open All year, Mon-Sat 0730-1800, Sun 0900-1900.
admission Free
Outstanding example of the work of Victorian architect, John Pearson, who favoured the Gothic style, with strong influences from French churches.

Fisherman's Bay

OUTDOOR ACTIVITIES

Isles of Scilly Travel

Quay Street, Penzance TR18 4BZ
t 0845 710 5555
w ios-travel.co.uk
open Office: Mon-Sat. Skybus: All year.
Scillonian III: 26 Mar-3 Nov, Mon-Sat.
Aug, daily.
admission Please phone for pricing details

Discover the beautiful Isles of Scilly. Fly with Skybus from Southampton, Bristol, Exeter, Newquay or Land's End (shuttle service available) and experience a bird's eye view. Alternatively relax and sail with Scillonian III from Penzance. You'd be scilly to miss it.

Map ref 1A3

Tamar Cruising
Cremyll Quay,
Cremyll PL10 1HX
t (01752) 822105
w tamarcruising.com
open Daily. Please see website for details.
admission ££
Cruises from the Mayflower Steps, Barbican and Plymouth around the dockyard to see warships. Also along the River Tamar and River Yealm. Ferry lands at Mount Edgcumbe Country Park.

Westward Airways & Land's End Flying School

Land's End Airport, St Just TR19 7RL
t (01736) 788771
w landsendairport.co.uk
open Daily
admission Please phone for pricing details

Experience flying over the Penwith Peninsula for an unforgettable bird's eye view with Westward Airways. Alternatively have a go yourself with a trial flying lesson at Land's End Flying School. Gift vouchers, refreshments, information, toilet facilities and internet access are available, as is, of course, a great view.

Map ref 1A3

ENTERTAINMENT AND CULTURE

Barbara Hepworth Museum and Sculpture Garden
Barnoon Hill, St Ives TR26 1AD
t (01736) 796226
w tate.org.uk/stives
open Apr-Oct, Mon-Sun 1000-1720.
Nov-Feb, Tue-Sun 1000-1620.
Mar, Mon-Sun 1000-1720.
admission £
Home of the late Dame Barbara Hepworth from 1949-75. Sculptures in wood, stone and bronze inside the museum and in the sub-tropical garden. Archive section with photographs.

British Cycling Museum
The Old Station, Camelford PL32 9TZ
t (01840) 212811 **w** chycorco.uk/britishcyclingmuseum
open All year, Sun-Thu 1000-1700.
admission £
A history of cycles and cycling memorabilia from c1818 to modern times. The nation's foremost museum of cycling history.

Falmouth Art Gallery
Municipal Buildings, The Moor, Falmouth TR11 2RT
t (01326) 313863 **w** falmouthartgallery.com
open All year, Mon-Sat 1000-1700.
admission Free
Family-friendly exhibitions, internationally acclaimed artists and one of the best collections in the South West featuring Pre-Raphaelites and British Impressionists.

The Minack Theatre and Visitor Centre
Porthcurno TR19 6JU
t (01736) 810181 **w** minack.com
open Apr-Oct, daily, Bank Hols 0930-1730. Nov-Mar, daily, Bank Hols 1000-1600.
admission £
Open-air cliff-side theatre with breathtaking views, presenting a 17-week season of plays and musicals. Visitor centre telling the theatre's story.

The Museum of Witchcraft
The Harbour, Boscastle PL35 0HD
t (01840) 250111 **w** museumofwitchcraft.com
open Apr-Oct, Mon-Sat 1030-1800, Sun 1130-1800.
admission £
Museum devoted to the study of witchcraft in England during the past and present day. Home to the world's largest collection dedicated to witchcraft.

North Cornwall Museum and Gallery
The Clease, Camelford PL32 9PL
t (01840) 212954
open Apr-Sep, Mon-Sat 1000-1700.
admission £
Reconstruction of the upstairs and downstairs of a Cornish cottage. Farm tools, carpentry, cobbling and quarrying tools. Wagons, domestic bygones and clothes.

Cromwells Castle, Tresco

For key to symbols see inside back cover.

National Maritime Museum Cornwall

Discovery Quay, Falmouth TR11 3QY
t (01326) 313388 **w** nmmc.co.uk
open Daily 1000-1700 (excl 25-26 Dec).
admission Adult: £7

Located on the edge of Falmouth's stunning harbour, this museum is a hands-on, new generation of visitor attraction that will appeal to landlubbers and sailors alike. More than just a museum about boats, it's all about the sea, boats and Cornwall. Full disability access, waterside cafe and shop.

  Map ref 1B3

V *voucher offer – see back section*

Porthcurno Telegraph Museum
Eastern House, Porthcurno TR19 6JX
t (01736) 810966
w porthcurno.org.uk
open Apr-Oct, Mon-Tue, Thu-Sun 1000-1700, Wed 1000-1930.
admission £
Award-winning museum housed in secret underground communications bunker. Superb collection tells the story of Empire communications from 1850 to World War II.

Royal Cornwall Museum
River Street, Truro TR1 2SJ
t (01872) 272205
w royalcornwallmuseum.org.uk
open All year, Mon-Sat 1000-1700 (excl Bank Hols).
admission Free
World-famous mineral collection, Old Master drawings, ceramics, oil paintings by the Newlyn School and others, archaeology, local history, national history, genealogy library.

Tate St Ives
Porthmeor Beach, St Ives TR26 1TG
t (01736) 796226 **w** tate.org.uk/stives
open Apr-Oct, Mon-Sun 1000-1720. Nov-Feb, Tues-Sun 1000-1620. Mar, Mon-Sun 1000-1720.
admission ££
Opened in 1993 and offering a unique introduction to modern art. Changing displays focus on the modern movement St Ives is famous for. Major contemporary exhibitions.

Tunnels Through Time
St Michael's Road, Newquay TR7 1RA
t (01637) 873379 **w** tunnelsthroughtime.co.uk
open Apr-Oct, Mon-Fri, Sun. Please phone for details.
admission £
Exhibition of over 70 full-sized characters portraying Cornish stories and legends.

FOOD AND DRINK

Camel Valley Vineyards
Nanstallon PL30 5LG
t (01208) 77959 **w** camelvalley.com
open Apr-Sep, Mon-Sat 1000-1700. Oct-Mar, Mon-Fri 1000-1700.
admission Free
Cornwall's largest vineyard. New modern winery, tours, tasting. Wine by the glass, bottle or case. International Gold Medal winner.

Cornish Cyder Farm
Penhallow TR4 9LW
t (01872) 573356 **w** thecornishcyderfarm.co.uk
open All year, Mon-Sun. See website for details.
admission Free
Visit a real working cider farm and take a guided tour to learn the art of cider making. Taste the international award-winning cider. Complete your visit with a home-made cream tea.

RELAXING AND PAMPERING

Boscastle Pottery
The Old Bakery, Boscastle PL35 0HE
t (01840) 250291
open All year, Mon-Sun, Bank Hols 0930-1730.
admission Free
The world's only dedicated mocha-ware maker, with an on site showroom. Visitors can watch trees grow on the pots as if by magic.

Cornish Goldsmiths
Tolgus Mill, New Portreath Road, Portreath TR16 4HN
t (01209) 218198 **w** cornishgoldsmiths.com
open All year, Mon-Sat 0930-1730, Sun 1030-1630.
admission Free
Showroom offering the largest collection of gold and silver jewellery in the South West, with many hand finished and carefully crafted pieces.

Devon

Enjoy the fun of a special event or visit one of the attractions listed for a great day out. For more inspiring ideas go to **enjoyengland.com**.

15–17 Jun
Gold Coast Oceanfest
Croyde
goldcoastoceanfest.co.uk

3–10 Aug
Sidmouth Folk Week
Various venues, Sidmouth
(01395) 578627
sidmouthfolkweek.co.uk

30 Aug–1 Sep
Port of Dartmouth Royal Regatta
Various venues, Dartmouth
(01803) 834912
dartmouthregatta.co.uk

10–16 September
Agatha Christie Week
Torquay
englishriviera.co.uk

Mar–Apr 08
Exeter Festival of South West Food & Drink
Exeter
visitsouthwest.co.uk/foodfestival

FAMILY FUN

Babbacombe Model Village
Hampton Avenue, Babbacombe TQ1 3LA
t (01803) 315315 **w** babbacombemodelvillage.co.uk
open See website for details.
admission ££
A unique journey into a miniature world. Picturesque by day, magical at night.

The Big Sheep

Abbotsham, nr Bideford EX39 5AP
t (01237) 472366
w thebigsheep.co.uk
open 1 Apr-31 Oct 1000-1800. 1 Nov-31 Mar, Sat-Sun 1000-1800.
admission Adult: £8.50

A world-famous family attraction for all ages. Hilarious sheepy shows to entertain all, such as the sheep racing, duck trials, shearing demonstrations and sheepdog trials and training. Garden centre for mums, brewery for dads, battlefield shooting for teenagers, and cute cuddly animals for everyone.

Map ref 1C1

 voucher offer – see back section

Quality counts

Look out for the Quality Assured Visitor Attraction sign. These attractions are assessed annually and meet the standards required to receive the quality marque.

Cardew Teapottery
Newton Road, Bovey Tracey TQ13 9DX
t (01626) 832172 w cardewdesign.com
open Daily 1000-1700.
admission Free

Tour of working pottery with painting area, pottery studio, shops, licensed restaurant with sundeck, children's woodland and 10-acre playground with train. Free large car park.

Cascades Tropical Adventure Pool
Ruda Holiday Park, Croyde Bay EX33 1NY
t (01271) 890671 w ruda.co.uk
open Apr-Sep, daily 0900-2000, Oct-Mar, Mon, Tue, Thu, Sat 0900-2000, Sun, Tue, Thu.
admission £

Tropical adventure pool with giant 230ft flume and rapids ride. Safe pools and mini-waterfalls for younger children. Award-winning spectacular sandy beach.

Dartington Crystal Limited
Linden Close, Torrington EX38 7AN
t (01805) 626242 w dartington.co.uk
open Mon-Fri 0900-1700, Sat-Sun 1000-1600.
admission £

Watch skilled craftsmen creating the world-famous crystal. Enjoy the fascinating history of glass in the visitor centre, and browse the dazzling collection in the factory shops.

Devon Railway Centre
The Station, Bickleigh EX16 8RG
t (01884) 855671 w devonrailwaycentre.co.uk
open See website for details.
admission £

Set in the Exe Valley, this railway attraction includes a preserved GWR station, a passenger-carrying 2ft gauge railway, model railways and a museum.

Devon's Crealy Great Adventure Park
Sidmouth Road, Clyst St Mary, Exeter EX5 1DR
t (01395) 233200 w crealy.co.uk
open Apr-Oct, daily 1000-1800. Nov-Mar, Thu-Sun 1000-1700.
admission ££

An unforgettable day with magic, fun and adventure for all the family. Exciting rides, all-weather attractions and the friendliest animals!

Diggerland
Verbeer Manor, Cullompton EX15 2PE
t 0870 034 4437 w diggerland.com
open Feb-Sep, see website for details.
admission £££

An adventure park based on JCBs, where children of all ages can ride and drive diggers and small dumpers. A huge variety of equipment is available for a day of family fun.

Exeter's Underground Passages

Paris Street, Exeter EX4 3PZ
t (01392) 665887 w exeter.gov.uk/visiting
open Please phone for details.
admission Adult: £5

Re-opening in autumn 2007. Tours of medieval vaulted passages, built to bring water into Exeter. A brand new visitor centre will help bring the experience to life.

                         Map ref 1D2

The Gnome Reserve and Wild Flower Garden
West Putford EX22 7XE
t (01409) 241435 w gnomereserve.co.uk
open Mar-Oct, daily 1000-1800.
admission £

Over 1,000 gnomes and pixies in woodland garden with stream. Wild-flower garden with 250 species. Studio making pottery pixies.

Hedgehog Hospital at Prickly Ball Farm
Prickly Ball Farm, Denbury Road, East Ogwell, Newton Abbot TQ12 6BZ
t (01626) 362319 w pricklyballfarm.co.uk
open Apr-Jul, daily 1000-1700, Aug, daily 1000-1730, Sep-Oct, daily 1000-1730.
admission ££

See hedgehogs and other small mammals, meet some patients, stroll in the wildlife garden, cuddle a rabbit, ride a pony or cart.

House of Marbles and Teign Valley Glass
The Old Pottery, Pottery Road, Bovey Tracey TQ13 9DS
t (01626) 835358 w houseofmarbles.com
open All year, Mon-Sat 0930-1700, Sun 1100-1700.
admission Free

Former pottery where visitors may watch glass-blowing and learn of the history of the pottery, glass and the making of glass marbles, in the museums.

The Milky Way Adventure Park
Downland Farm, Clovelly EX39 5RY
t (01237) 431255 w themilkyway.co.uk
open Apr-Oct, daily 1030-1800. Nov-Mar, Sat-Sun, School Hols 1030-1800.
admission ££

All-weather family attraction featuring Clone Zone, Europe's first interactive adventure ride, Time Warp indoor adventure play area, pets' corner, toddlers' area.

Norman Lockyer Observatory and James Lockyer Planetarium
Salcombe Hill Road, Sidmouth EX10 0NY
t (01395) 579941
w ex.ac.uk/nlo
open See website for details.
admission £
An opportunity to observe the planets, moon and sunspots through 10 Victorian telescopes, planetarium and much more. A must for those interested in astronomy, radio and weather.

North Down Farm
Yeoford EX17 5EU
t (01363) 84289
w northdownfarm.com
open Daily.
admission Free
A traditional working farm specialising in rare breeds of British livestock, reflecting bygone rural life from the early 20th century.

Paignton and Dartmouth Steam Railway
Queen's Park Station, Torbay Road, Paignton TQ4 6AF
t (01803) 553760
w paignton-steamrailway.co.uk
open See website for details.
admission ££
Steam train trip from Paignton to Kingswear (for ferry to Dartmouth). Coastal and country scenery. Services combine with trips on the River Dart.

Paignton Pier
Paignton Sands, Paignton TQ4 6BW
t (01803) 522139
w paigntonpier.co.uk
open Daily 1000-1800.
admission Free
Amusements, children's rides and prize bingo.

Pecorama Pleasure Gardens and Exhibition
Underleys, Beer EX12 3NA
t (01297) 21542
w peco-uk.com
open Apr-May, Mon-Sat 1000-1730. May-Sep, daily 1000-1730. Sep-Oct, Mon-Sat 1000-1730.
admission ££
Spectacular Millennium Celebration Gardens, passenger-carrying miniature railway with steam and diesel locomotives, Peco Model Railway exhibition, shop and play areas.

Pennywell – Devon's Farm and Wildlife Centre
Buckfastleigh TQ11 0LT
t (01364) 642023
w pennywellfarm.co.uk
open Feb-Oct, daily 0900-1700.
admission ££
Hands-on activities, shows and displays. The biggest farm activity park in the South West. Fun for all the family!

Quaywest Waterpark
Quaywest, Goodrington Sands, Paignton TQ4 6LN
t (01803) 555550
w quaywest.co.uk
open May-Jun, Mon-Sun, Bank Hols 1100-1700. Jul-Aug, Mon-Sun, Bank Hols 1000-1800. Sep, Mon-Sun, Bank Hols 1100-1700.
admission £
Enjoy the wettest and wildest fun at the English Riviera's outdoor water park. Choose from eight different flumes. Also go-karts, amusement rides, bumper boats and crazy golf.

The Riviera International Centre
Chestnut Avenue, Torquay TQ2 5LZ
t (01803) 299992
w rivieracentre.co.uk
open See website for details.
admission £
Waves leisure pool, flume and wave machine. Children's water spray area, health and fitness suite and restaurant.

Seaton Tramway
Harbour Road, Seaton EX12 2NQ
t (01297) 20375
w tram.co.uk
open See website for details.
admission ££
Journey through East Devon's beautiful Axe valley by open-top or enclosed tramcar. A great way to enjoy panoramic views of the estuary and wildlife.

Sorley Tunnel Adventure Worlds
Loddiswell Road, Kingsbridge TQ7 4BP
t (01548) 854078
w sorleytunnel.co.uk
open Daily 1000-1800.
admission ££
Working organic dairy farm with hands-on experience of farm animals. Picturesque walks, large indoor and outdoor play areas, craft workshops, riding stables and farm shop.

South Devon Railway
The Station, Buckfastleigh TQ11 0DZ
t (01364) 642338
w southdevonrailway.org
open See website for details.
admission ££
A seven-mile Great Western Railway country branch line through the superb scenery of the River Dart. Picnic grounds at Buckfastleigh. Now accessible from Totnes over footbridge.

Tuckers Maltings
Teign Road, Newton Abbot TQ12 4AA
t (01626) 334734
w tuckersmaltings.com
open Apr-Oct, Mon-Sat 1000-1600.
admission ££
A guided tour of England's only working malthouse open to the public. Speciality bottled beer shop. View Teignworthy Brewery and sample 'real' ale.

Watermouth Castle
Berrynarbor EX34 9SL
t (01271) 863879
w watermouthcastle.com
open Apr-Oct, see website for details.
admission ££
Mechanical music demonstrations, model railway, domestic dairy, cider-making exhibits, cycle museum, smugglers' dungeon and gardens. Children's animations and more.

Woodlands Leisure Park
Blackawton TQ9 7DQ
t (01803) 712598
w woodlandspark.com
open Mar-Nov, daily. See website for details.
admission ££
All-weather fun guaranteed. Unique combination of indoor and outdoor attractions, three water coasters, toboggan run, indoor venture centre with rides. Falconry and animals.

NATURE AND WILDLIFE

Becky Falls Woodland Park
Manaton TQ13 9UG
t (01647) 221259
w beckyfalls.com
open Mar-Oct, 1000-1700.
admission ££
Over 60 acres of natural oak woodland with a 70ft waterfall and river walks. Site of Special Scientific Interest. One of Devon's most beautiful places.

Bicton Park Botanical Gardens
East Budleigh, Budleigh Salterton EX9 7BJ
t (01395) 568465
w bictongardens.co.uk
open Apr-Oct, daily 1000-1800. Nov-Mar daily 1000-1700.
admission ££
Grade I Listed historical gardens featuring palm house, Italian and American gardens, indoor and outdoor play areas, shell house, museum, glass houses, garden centre, train ride.

Buckfast Butterfly Farm and Dartmoor Otter Sanctuary
Buckfastleigh Steam and Leisure Park,
Buckfastleigh TQ11 0DZ
t (01364) 642916
w ottersandbutterflies.co.uk
open See website for details.
admission ££
Tropical landscaped garden with waterfalls and large undercover pond where exotic butterflies and moths from all over the world fly free. Also otters, birds, terrapins and fish.

Canonteign Falls
Canonteign, Christow EX6 7NT
t (01647) 252434 **w** canoteignfalls.com
open Mar-Oct, daily 1030-1730. Nov-Dec, Sat-Sun 1030-1600.
admission £
Highest waterfall in England, situated in private parkland and ancient woodland in the Teign Valley. Lakes, grounds, natural gardens and lots of wildlife. Cafe and shop.

Cockington Country Park
Cockington Court, Cockington TQ2 6XA
t (01803) 606035 **w** countryside-trust.org.uk
open Daily, dawn-dusk.
admission Free
A country park of 450 acres with a Craft Centre at its heart, featuring demonstrations of a wide range of craft skills.

Combe Martin Wildlife and Dinosaur Park
Combe Martin EX34 0NG
t (01271) 882486 **w** dinosaur-park.com
open Mar-Oct, Mon-Sun 1000-1500.
admission £££
The land that time forgot. A subtropical paradise with hundreds of birds and animals, and animatronic dinosaurs, so real they're alive!

The Donkey Sanctuary

Slade House Farm, Sidmouth EX10 0NU
t (01395) 578222
w thedonkeysanctuary.org.uk
open Daily 0900 to dusk.
admission Free

The Donkey Sanctuary is open 365 days a year from 0900 until dusk. Admission and parking are free. Visitors return time and again to meander among the donkeys and absorb the serene and relaxed surroundings.

 Map ref 1D2

Escot Fantasy Gardens, Maze and Woodland
Escot Park EX11 1LU
t (01404) 822188 **w** escot-devon.co.uk
open All year, Mon-Sun 1000-1700.
admission ££
Enjoy the natural historical gardens and fantasy woodland which surround the ancestral home of the Kennaway family. Here, in 220 acres of parkland, you'll find an arkful of animals with paths, trails and vistas.

Exmoor Zoological Park

South Stowford, Bratton Fleming EX31 4SG
t (01598) 763352 **w** exmoorzoo.co.uk
open See website for details.
admission ££

Twelve acres of landscaped gardens with tropical and exotic birds, animals, waterfowl and penguins. Tarzan-Land for children.

Grand Western Canal Country Park

The Moorings, Canal Hill, Tiverton EX16 4HX
t (01884) 254072 **w** devon.gov.uk
open See website for details.
admission Free

Opened in 1814, this peaceful, 11 mile canal is great for walking, boating, angling, cycling, picnics and nature walking.

High Moorland Visitor Centre

Tavistock Road, Princetown PL20 6QF
t (01822) 890414 **w** dartmoor-npa.gov.uk
open Daily 1000-1600.
admission Free

Dartmoor's major visitor and interpretation centre in the heart of the moor. Exciting displays for all the family about Dartmoor's natural and cultural heritage.

Ilfracombe Aquarium

The Old Lifeboat House, The Pier,
Ilfracombe EX34 9EQ
t (01271) 864533
open Feb-Mar, daily 1000-1500. Apr-Jun, daily 1000-1630. Jul-Aug, daily, 1000-1730. Sep-Oct, daily 1000-1600.
admission £

Award-winning, all-weather family attraction provides a fascinating journey of discovery into the aquatic life of North Devon.

Jungleland

St John's Garden Centre, St John's Lane,
Barnstaple EX32 9DD
t (01271) 343884 **w** stjohnsgardencentre.co.uk
open All year, Mon-Sat 0900-1800, Sun 1030-1630.
admission Free

Chipmunks, terrapins, birds and fish in an exotic setting of giant cacti, tropical jungle plants and waterfalls. All under cover.

Kents Cavern Prehistoric Caves

Ilsham Road, Wellswood, Torquay TQ1 2JF
t (01803) 215136 **w** kents-cavern.co.uk
open Mar-Jun, daily 1000-1600, Jul-Aug, daily 1000-1630, Sep-Oct daily 1000-1600, Nov-Feb 1000-1530.
admission ££

The most important Stone Age cave in Britain reveals more about Palaeolithic Britain than anywhere else.

Living Coasts

Torquay Harbourside, Beacon Quay,
Torquay TQ1 2BG
t (01803) 202470 **w** livingcoasts.org.uk
open Daily 1000-dusk.
admission ££

Living Coasts features a range of fascinating coastal creatures from loud and loveable penguins to playful fur seals, colourful puffins to waders and sea ducks.
map ref 1D2
see ad on p289

Lydford Gorge

The Stables, Lydford EX20 4BH
t (01822) 820441 **w** nationaltrust.org.uk
open Jan--Mar, Sat-Sun 1030-1500. Apr-Sep, daily 1000-1700. Oct, daily 1000-1600. Nov-Dec, Sat-Sun 1100-1530.
admission £

On the western edge of Dartmoor, a beautiful woodland walk along the top of the gorge leads down to the spectacular 90ft White Lady waterfall.

Marwood Hill Gardens

Marwood Hill, Marwood EX31 4EB
t (01271) 342528 **w** marwoodhillgarden.co.uk
open Daily 0930-1730.
admission £

An 18-acre garden with three small lakes, unusual trees and shrubs, bog garden, national collection of astilbes, iris ensata and tulbaghias.

The Miniature Pony Centre

Wormhill Farm, North Bovey TQ13 8RG
t (01647) 432400 **w** miniatureponycentre.com
open See website for details.
admission ££

Miniature ponies, donkeys and many other animals. Indoor and outdoor play area for the children. A wealth of wildlife in and around the ponds and Willow Garden.

National Marine Aquarium

Rope Walk, Coxside, Plymouth PL4 0LF
t (01752) 600301 **w** national-aquarium.co.uk
open Jan-Mar, daily 1000-1700, Apr-Oct, daily 1000-1800, Nov-Dec, daily 1000-1700.
admission ££

Britain's biggest aquarium has just got even bigger thanks to their brand new three-floor, multi-million-pound interactive centre at the National Marine Aquarium, Plymouth.

Northam Burrows Country Park

Northam EX39 1LY
t (01237) 479708 **w** torridge.gov.uk
open Daily.
admission Free

Coastal country park with visitor centre, beach access and golf course. Walks and activities programme available from ranger staff in the summer.

Admission is based on an adult price. Please check opening times and admission before travelling.

Paignton Zoo Environmental Park

Totnes Road, Paignton TQ4 7EU
t (01803) 697500
w paigntonzoo.org.uk
open Daily 1000-1630.
admission ££

One of England's largest zoos with over 1,200 animals in the beautiful setting of 75 acres of botanical gardens. One of Devon's most popular family days out.

map ref 1D2
see ad below

RHS Garden Rosemoor

Great Torrington EX38 8PH
t (01805) 624067
w rhs.org.uk/rosemoor
open Apr-Sep, daily 1000-1800, Oct-Mar, daily 1000-1700.
admission ££

Rosemoor, an enchanting 65-acre garden, offers year-round interest. Visit us for inspiration, tranquillity or simply a marvellous day out.

River Dart Adventures

Holne Park, Ashburton TQ13 7NP
t (01364) 652511
w riverdart.co.uk
open See website for details.
admission ££

A 90-acre Victorian country estate offering parkland, picnic meadow, nature/tree trails and woodland adventure playgrounds.

Totnes Rare Breeds Farm

Totnes TQ9 6LW
t (01803) 840387 **w** totnesrarebreeds.co.uk
open Mar-Oct, daily 0930-1700.
admission Free

An ideal place for all the family to visit. Good food, beautiful views, lovely animals and spectacular owls.

HISTORIC ENGLAND

Arlington Court

Arlington EX31 4LP
t (01271) 850296 **w** nationaltrust.org.uk
open Mar-Oct, Mon-Fri, Sun 1030-1700.
admission ££

Historic house with interesting collection. Gardens with rhododendrons, azaleas and hydrangeas. Carriage collection and rides. Extensive estate walks.

Berry Pomeroy Castle

Berry Pomeroy TQ9 6NJ
t (01803) 866618
w english-heritage.org.uk/berrypomeroy
open Apr-Jun, Oct, daily 1000-1700. Jul-Aug, daily 1000-1800. Sep, daily 1000-1700.
admission £

A romantic ruined castle set in a picturesque Devon valley. The gatehouse dates from the late 15thC with Elizabethan remains behind. Steeped in folklore.

Buckfast Abbey

Buckfastleigh TQ11 0EE
t (01364) 645500 **w** buckfast.org.uk
open All year, Mon-Thur 0900-1800, Fri 1000-1800, Sun 1200-1800.
admission Free

Large Benedictine monastery rebuilt on medieval foundations. Many art treasures in the Abbey church. Also unusual shops, exhibition and excellent restaurant.

Buckland Abbey

Yelverton PL20 6EY
t (01822) 853607 **w** nationaltrust.org.uk
open See website for details.
admission ££

Originally a Cistercian monastery, then home of Sir Francis Drake. Ancient buildings, exhibitions, herb garden, craft workshops and estate walks. Elizabethan garden.

Cadhay

Ottery St Mary EX11 1QT
t (01404) 812432 **w** cadhay.org.uk
open May-Sep, Fri 1400-1730.
admission £

Historic Elizabethan manorhouse built c1550 around a courtyard. Fine timber roof of Great Hall and Elizabethan Long Gallery. Magnificent gardens.

Castle Drogo

Drewsteignton EX6 6PB
t (01647) 433306 **w** nationaltrust.org.uk
open Mar-Oct, Wed-Sun 1100-1700. Dec, Sat-Sun 1200-1600.
admission ££

Granite castle, built between 1910 and 1930 by Sir Edwin Lutyens, standing at over 900ft overlooking the wooded gorge of the River Teign. Views of Dartmoor.

Crownhill Fort

Crownhill Fort Road, Plymouth PL6 5BX
t (01752) 793754 **w** crownhillfort.co.uk
open See website for details.
admission Free

Tunnels of fun for everyone! Underground tunnels to explore. Step back to 1890 to experience history and adventure. Daily gun firings at 1330.

Dartmouth Castle

Castle Road, Dartmouth TQ6 0JN
t (01803) 833588
w english-heritage.org.uk/dartmouth
open Apr-Jun, Sep, daily 1000-1700, Jul-Aug, daily 1000-1800, Oct-Mar daily 1000-1600.
admission £

This brilliantly positioned defensive castle juts out into the narrow entrance to the Dart Estuary. One of the first castles constructed with artillery in mind.

Exeter Quay House Visitor Centre

46 The Quay, Exeter EX2 4AN
t (01392) 271611 **w** exeter.gov.uk/visiting
open Apr-Oct 1000-1700. Nov-Mar, Sat-Sun 1100-1600.
admission Free

The history and development of Exeter's Quayside is brought to life with lively displays, illustrations and artefacts. Watch 'Exeter – 2,000 years of history', an exciting audio-visual presentation highlighting Exeter's history from Roman times to the present day. Free admission.

Map ref 1D2

Exeter Red Coat Guided Tours

Tourist Information Centre,
Dix's Field, Exeter EX1 1RQ
t (01392) 265203 **w** exeter.gov.uk/visiting
open Daily (excl 25-26 Dec).
admission Free

Free guided walking tours of historic Exeter. Explore a catacomb by torchlight, visit a house that moved and learn why Exeter is reputed to be one of England's most haunted cities! No booking required. Tours last 90 minutes.

Map ref 1D2

Exeter's Underground Passages

Paris Street, Exeter EX4 3PZ
t (01392) 665887 **w** exeter.gov.uk/visiting
open Please phone for details.
admission Adult: £5

Re-opening in autumn 2007. Tours of medieval vaulted passages, built to bring water into Exeter. A brand new visitor centre will help bring the experience to life.

Map ref 1D2

Exeter Cathedral – Church of Saint Peter
The Cloisters, Exeter EX1 1HS
t (01392) 255573
w exeter-cathedral.org.uk
open Daily 0930-1700.
admission £

Medieval cathedral. Fine example of Gothic Decorated style. Longest unbroken stretch of Gothic vaulting in the world.

Hartland Abbey and Gardens
Hartland EX39 6DT
t (01237) 441234
w hartlandabbey.com
open Apr-May, Wed-Thur, Sun and Bank Hols 1230-1700. May-Sep, Mon-Thur, Sun 1230-1700.
admission ££

Family home since the dissolution in 1539. Woodland gardens leading to bog garden and 18th century walled gardens. Beautiful walk to beach.

Hemyock Castle
Hemyock EX15 3RJ
t (01823) 680745
w hemyockcastle.co.uk
open Mar-Sep, Bank Hols 1400-1700.
admission Free

Medieval moated castle and gatehouse remains. Interpretation centre illustrating the history of the site. Life-size historical tableaux including extended Civil War display.

Killerton House and Garden
Broadclyst EX5 3LE
t (01392) 881345
w nationaltrust.org.uk
open See website for details.
admission ££

An 18thC house built for the Acland family. Hillside garden of 18 acres with rare trees and shrubs.

Knightshayes Court
Bolham, Tiverton EX16 7RQ
t (01884) 254665
w nationaltrust.org.uk
open Mar-Nov, Mon-Thu, Sat-Sun 1100-1700.
admission ££

House built c1870 by William Burges. Celebrated garden features a water lily pool, topiary, fine specimen trees, formal terraces, spring bulbs and rare shrubs.

Okehampton Castle
Castle Lodge, Okehampton EX20 1JB
t (01837) 52844
w english-heritage.org.uk/okehampton
open Apr-Jun, daily 1000-1700, Jul-Aug, daily 1000-1800, Sep, daily 1000-1700.
admission £

The ruins of the largest castle in Devon, including the jagged remains of the keep. Picnic area and enchanted woodland walks.

Powderham Castle
Kenton EX6 8JQ
t (01626) 890243
w powderham.co.uk
open Apr-Oct, daily 1000-1730.
admission ££

Built c1390 and restored in the 18thC. Georgian interiors, china, furnishings and paintings. Family home of the Courtenays for over 600 years. Fine views across deer park and River Exe.

St Mary's Church
The College, Ottery St Mary EX11 1DQ
t (01404) 812062
w otterystmary.org.uk
open See website for details.
admission Free

Dating from the 13thC, the church was enlarged and modelled on Exeter Cathedral c1342. Given five star rating in England's Thousand Best Churches.

Saltram
Plympton PL7 1UH
t (01752) 333500
w nationaltrust.org.uk
open See website for details.
admission ££

George II mansion with magnificent interiors designed by Robert Adam. Fine period furniture, china and paintings. Garden with orangery. Art gallery and play area.

Tapeley Park
Instow EX39 4NT
t (01271) 342558
w tapeleypark.com
open Mar-Oct 1000-1700.
admission £

Devon home of the Christie family of Glyndebourne, overlooking the estuary to the sea. Beautiful Italian garden with many rare plants and woodland walk.

Tiverton Castle
Park Hill, Tiverton EX16 6RP
t (01884) 253200
w tivertoncastle.com
open Apr-Oct, Thu, Sun, Bank Hols 1430-1730.
admission £

All ages of architecture from medieval to modern. Important Civil War armoury – try some on. Beautiful gardens with romantic ruins.

Torrington 1646
Castle Hill, South Street, Great Torrington EX38 8AA
t (01805) 626146
w torrington-1646.co.uk
open Mar-Sep, Mon-Sat 1030-1700, Oct-Feb, Mon-Fri 1100-1630.
admission ££

At Torrington 1646 meet colourful 17thC characters and learn what it was like to live, work and play during the Civil War.

Totnes Castle
Castle Street, Totnes TQ9 5NU
t (01803) 864406
w english-heritage.org.uk/totnes
open Apr-Jun, daily 1000-1700. Jul-Aug, daily 1000-1600. Sep, daily 1000-1700. Oct, daily 1000-1600.
admission £
One of the best-preserved Norman shell keeps, this motte and bailey castle offers splendid views over the River Dart.

Ugbrooke House and Park
Chudleigh TQ13 0AD
t (01626) 852179
w ugbrooke.co.uk
open Jul-Sep, Tue, Wed, Thur, Sun, Bank Hols 1300-1730.
admission ££
Robert Adam-designed house and chapel, Capability Brown-designed park and grounds. Fine furniture, paintings, needlework, costume and uniforms.

OUTDOOR ACTIVITIES

Balloons over Britain
Southbrook House, Southbrook, Whimple, Exeter EX5 2PG
t (01404) 822489 **w** balloonsoverbritain.com
open Office: 0900-1730. Main flying season: Mar-Oct.
admission Please phone for full pricing details

Experience the awesome thrill and peaceful serenity of hot air ballooning. Balloons Over Britain offer hot air balloon rides from more than 70 launch sites throughout the UK. Please visit our website.

Map ref 1D2

Dart Pleasure Craft Limited (River Link Operators)
5 Lower Street, Dartmouth TQ6 9AJ
t (01803) 834488
w riverlink.co.uk
open See website for details.
admission ££
Operating between Dartmouth and Totnes, dependent on tide. Circular trips in Dartmouth for one hour. Large boats with covered accommodation and commentary given.

The Grand Western Horseboat Company
The Wharf, Canal Hill, Tiverton EX16 4HX
t (01884) 253345
w horseboat.co.uk
open Apr-Oct, see website for details.
admission ££
Indulge your senses and relax on this rare horse-drawn barge, now one of only five in Britain today. Daytime and evening trips.

Sound Cruising Ltd
Hexton Quay, Hooe, Plymouth PL9 9RE
t (01752) 408590
w soundcruising.com
open Please phone for details.
admission £
Daily cruises around the naval harbour, also regular cruises to Calstock on the River Tamar and sea trips to the River Yealm, east of Plymouth. Ferries from Saltash to Plymouth.

Stuart Line Cruises
Exmouth Marina, Exmouth Docks, Exmouth EX8 1DU
t (01395) 222144
w stuartlinecruises.co.uk
open See website for details.
admission £
Sailing from Exmouth, enjoy relaxing River Exe cruises and trips along the beautiful East Devon coastline. Sailing throughout the year.

ENTERTAINMENT AND CULTURE

Balloons over Britain
Southbrook House, Southbrook, Whimple, Exeter EX5 2PG
t (01404) 822489 **w** balloonsoverbritain.com
open Office: 0900-1730. Main flying season: Mar-Oct.
admission Please phone for full pricing details

Experience the awesome thrill and peaceful serenity of hot air ballooning. Balloons Over Britain offer hot air balloon rides from more than 70 launch sites throughout the UK. Please visit our website.

Map ref 1D2

Admission is based on an adult price. Please check opening times and admission before travelling.

Barometer World

Quicksilver Barn,
Merton EX20 3DS
t (01805) 603443
w barometerworld.co.uk
open Please phone for details.
admission £

New exhibition housing an incredible variety of weather predictors from the normal to the very bizarre.

The Big Sheep

Abbotsham, nr Bideford EX39 5AP
t (01237) 472366
w thebigsheep.co.uk
open 1 Apr-31 Oct 1000-1800. 1 Nov-31 Mar, Sat-Sun 1000-1800.
admission Adult: £8.50

A world-famous family attraction for all ages. Hilarious sheepy shows to entertain all, such as the sheep racing, duck trials, shearing demonstrations and sheepdog trials and training. Garden centre for mums, brewery for dads, battlefield shooting for teenagers, and cute cuddly animals for everyone.

Map ref 1C1

 voucher offer – see back section

Bygones

Fore Street, St Marychurch,
Torquay TQ1 4PR
t (01803) 326108
w bygones.co.uk
open See website for details.
admission ££

Life-size Victorian exhibition street with period rooms. Large Hornby railway layouts, medals and militaria. Illuminated Fantasyland.

City Museum and Art Gallery

Drake Circus, Plymouth PL4 8AJ
t (01752) 304774
w plymouthmuseum.gov.uk
open All year, Tue-Fri 1000-1730, Sat and Bank Hols 1000-1730.
admission Free

Collections of fine and decorative arts, costume, archaeology, coins, local and natural history, and world cultures.

Coldharbour Mill Museum

Coldharbour Mill, Uffculme, Cullompton EX15 3EE
t (01884) 840960
w coldharbourmill.org.uk
open Daily 1100-1600.
admission Free

Museum of the Devon textiles industry in an 18thC woollen mill. Working demonstrations of traditional textile machinery. Waterwheel and steam engines. Riverside walks.

The Devon Guild of Craftsmen

Riverside Mill, Bovey Tracey TQ13 9AF
t (01626) 832223
w crafts.org.uk
open Daily 1000-1730.
admission Free

The largest contemporary craft centre in the South West. A Grade II Listed building with shop, exhibition gallery and cafe.

Dingles Steam Village

Milford, Lifton PL16 0AT
t (01566) 783425
w dinglesteam.co.uk
open Apr-Oct, Mon, Thu-Sun 1030-1700.
admission ££

Indoor live steam and working displays for all the family. The National Fairground Collection. Shop and cafeteria in a rural setting.

Exeter Quay House Visitor Centre

46 The Quay, Exeter EX2 4AN
t (01392) 271611 **w** exeter.gov.uk/visiting
open Apr-Oct 1000-1700. Nov-Mar, Sat-Sun 1100-1600.
admission Free

The history and development of Exeter's Quayside is brought to life with lively displays, illustrations and artefacts. Watch 'Exeter – 2,000 years of history', an exciting audio-visual presentation highlighting Exeter's history from Roman times to the present day. Free admission.

Map ref 1D2

Exeter Red Coat Guided Tours

Tourist Information Centre,
Dix's Field, Exeter EX1 1RQ
t (01392) 265203 **w** exeter.gov.uk/visiting
open Daily (excl 25-26 Dec).
admission Free

Free guided walking tours of historic Exeter. Explore a catacomb by torchlight, visit a house that moved and learn why Exeter is reputed to be one of England's most haunted cities! No booking required. Tours last 90 minutes.

  Map ref 1D2

Marine House at Beer
Fore Street, Beer EX12 3EF
t (01297) 625257
w marinehouse-at-beer.co.uk
open Jan-Jun, Tue-Sun 1000-1730. Jul-Aug, daily 1000-1730. Sep-Dec, Tue-Sun 1000-1730.
admission Free
Two existing galleries in the historic fishing village of Beer. A constantly changing range of paintings, sculpture, ceramics, glassware and jewellery.

Monks Withecombe Gallery
Monks Withecombe, Chagford TQ13 8JY
t (01647) 432854
w strategic-art.com
open All year, Tue-Sun 1100-1800.
admission Free
The Monks Withecombe Gallery exhibits the work of outstanding contemporary artists in the beautiful surroundings of the Dartmoor National Park.

Morwellham Quay The Morwellham & Tamar Valley Trust
Morwellham Quay, Tavistock PL19 8JL
t (01822) 832766
w morwellham-quay.co.uk
open Jan-Mar, daily 1000-1630. Mar-Oct, daily 1000-1730. Nov-Dec, daily 1000-1630.
admission ££
An award-winning, evocative museum and visitor centre based around the historic port and mine workings on the River Tamar.

Museum of Barnstaple and North Devon
The Square, Barnstaple EX32 8LN
t (01271) 346747
w devon.gov.uk
open All year, Tue-Sat 1030-1630.
admission Free
Major regional museum displaying and interpreting the natural and human history of North Devon. Housed in a fine Victorian brick building.

North Devon Maritime Museum
Odun House, Odun Road, Appledore EX39 1PT
t (01237) 422064
w devon.gov.uk
open Apr, daily 1400-1730. May-Sep Mon-Fri 1100-1300, daily 1400-1730. Oct, daily 1400-1730.
admission Free
All aspects of North Devon's maritime history illustrated by models, photographs, paintings and film show. Interpretation centre for the area and museum.

Plymouth Pavilions
Millbay Road, Plymouth PL1 3LF
t (01752) 222200
w plymouthpavilions.com
open See website for details.
admission £
A fun pool and ice rink complement this leading rock, pop and entertainment venue.

Plymouth Ski Centre – John Nike Leisuresport Complex
Alpine Park, Marsh Mills, Plymouth PL6 8LQ
t (01752) 600220
w jnll.co.uk
open See website for details.
admission ££££
Largest ski slope in the South West. Main slope 150m long and 20m wide and two nursery slopes. Largest toboggan run of its type in the South West.

Royal Albert Memorial Museum and Art Gallery

Queen Street, Exeter EX4 3RX
t (01392) 665858
w exeter.gov.uk/museums
open All year, Mon-Sat 1000-1700.
admission Free
Sixteen galleries of displays and a lively activity programme take visitors on a voyage of discovery from pre-history to the present day.

Tiverton Museum of Mid Devon Life
Beck's Square, Tiverton EX16 6PJ
t (01884) 256295
w tivertonmuseum.org.uk
open Feb-Dec, Mon-Fri 1030-1630, Sat 1000-1300, Aug, Sat 1000-1630.
admission £
Comprehensive regional museum. Railway gallery contains a Great Western Railway locomotive. Heathcote lace machine gallery. Collection of agricultural and domestic implements.

Totnes Elizabethan House Museum
70 Fore Street, Totnes TQ9 5RU
t (01803) 863821
w devonmuseums.net/totnes
open Mon-Fri 1030-1700.
admission Free
A 16thC Tudor merchant's house. Period furniture, costumes, dolls' houses, toys and archaeology. Victorian grocer's shop. Charles Babbage (father of the computer) room.

Yelverton Paperweight Centre

Leg O'Mutton, Yelverton PL20 6AD
t (01822) 854250
w paperweightcentre.co.uk
open Apr-Oct, daily 1030-1700. Dec, daily 1030-1700.
admission Free

Exhibition of the Broughton Collection of hundreds of antique and modern glass paperweights.

FOOD AND DRINK

Plymouth Gin Distillery

Black Friars Distillery, 60 Southside Street, Barbican PL1 2LQ
t (01752) 665292
w plymouthgin.com
open Daily 0900-1730.
admission Free

Tour the Black Friars Distillery, England's oldest working gin distillery, where Plymouth Gin has been distilled for over 200 years.

Sharpham Vineyard

Sharpham Estate, Ashprington TQ9 7UT
t (01803) 732203
w sharpham.com
open Mar-Jun, Mon-Sat 1000-1700, Jun-Aug, daily 1000-1700, Sep-Dec, Mon-Sat 1000-1700.
admission £

A beautifully situated working vineyard and winery on the edge of the River Dart, renowned for the quality of its wine. Self-guided vineyard trail.

RELAXING AND PAMPERING

Abbot Pottery

Hopkins Lane, Newton Abbot TQ12 2EL
t (01626) 334933
w abbotpottery.com
open See website for details.
admission Free

A working craft pottery producing traditional Devon slipware by throwing, turning, decorating and glazing.

Atlantic Village

Clovelly Road, Bideford EX39 3QU
t (01237) 473901 **w** atlanticvillage.co.uk
open All year, Mon-Wed, Fri-Sat 1000-1800, Thu 1000-2000, Sun 1030-1630.
admission Free

North Devon's largest discount shopping outlet with themed leisure attractions. A family day out.

Barbican Glassworks

The Old Fish Market, Barbican, Plymouth PL1 2LT
t (01752) 224777 **w** dartington.co.uk
open All year, Mon-Sat 0900-1800, Sun, Bank Hols 1100-1700.
admission Free

Watch glass-blowing at close quarters in the beautifully restored Victorian fishmarket. Large retail shop offering exquisite gifts.

The Famous Lee Mill

Lee Mill, Plymouth Road, Ivybridge PL21 9EE
t (01752) 691100
open All year, Mon-Sat 0930-1700, Sun 1000-1600.
admission Free

Factory outlet offering a wide selection of branded goods at significantly reduced prices including fashion, golf, homeware, gifts and souvenirs.

Otterton Mill

Fore Street, Otterton EX9 7HG
t (01395) 568521 **w** ottertonmill.com
open Daily 1000-1700.
admission Free

Watermill, art gallery, craft centre, restaurant, bakery and four artists' studios.

The Pixie Kiln and Gallery

West Putford EX22 7XE
t (01409) 241435 **w** gnomereserve.co.uk
open Mar-Oct, daily 1000-1800.
admission £

Individually modelled, kiln-fired, hand-painted pottery pixies celebrating all human activities. Gnomes for the garden. Prints of landscape paintings inhabited by gnomes.

Trago Mills

Shopping and Leisure Centre, Stover TQ12 6JD
t (01626) 821111 **w** trago.co.uk
open Mon-Sat 0900-1730, Sun 1000-1600.
admission Free

Large shopping complex with superb leisure attractions, including super karts, trawler boats, steam and model railways plus an interactive animal enclosure.

Friendly help and advice

Tourist Information Centres offer suggestions of places to visit and things to do as well as friendly help with accommodation and holiday ideas. To find the one nearest to you text TIC LOCATE to 64118.

Dorset

Enjoy the fun of a special event or visit one of the attractions listed for a great day out. For more inspiring ideas go to **enjoyengland.com**.

8–10 Jun
Wimborne Folk Festival
Wimborne Minster
(01202) 623740
wimbornefolkfestival.co.uk

27–29 Jul
Weymouth National Beach Volleyball
The Beach, Pavilion End, Weymouth
(01305) 785747
weymouth.gov.uk

10–12 Aug
Weymouth Regatta
Weymouth Bay and Portland Harbour
weymouth-regatta.org

29 Aug–2 Sep
Great Dorset Steam Fair
South Down Farm, Tarrant Hinton
(01258) 860361
gdsf.co.uk

14–16 Sep
Poole Animal Windfest
Sandbanks, Poole
(01202) 708555
poolewindfest.co.uk

FAMILY FUN

Adventure Wonderland
Merritown Lane, Hurn BH23 6BA
t (01202) 483444 **w** adventurewonderland.co.uk
open Apr-Aug, daily 1000-1800. Sep-Oct, Sat-Sun 1000-1800.
admission ££
Exciting Adventure Wonderland with rides and attractions galore including £1-million indoor play centre, scary ghostly galleon plus lots more besides.

The Bournemouth Eye
The Lower Gardens, Bournemouth BH1 2AQ
t (01202) 317697 **w** bournemouthballoon.com
open Apr-Sep, see website for details.
admission ££
Tethered balloon flight to 500ft, giving spectacular views of the coastline, town and countryside for over 20 miles.

Childrens Farm and Smugglers Barn
New Barn Road, Abbotsbury DT3 4JG
t (01305) 871130 **w** abbotsbury-tourism.co.uk
open Apr-Aug, daily 1000-1800. Sep-Oct, see website for full details.
admission ££
Children's farm and soft play with a smuggling theme for children under 11 years. Activities include rabbit and guinea pig handling and pony rides (extra charge).

Corfe Castle Model Village and Gardens
The Square, Corfe Castle BH20 5EZ
t (01929) 481234 **w** corfecastlemodelvillage.co.uk
open Apr-Oct, Mon-Thu, Sat-Sun 1000-1700. Nov-Mar, Sat-Sun 1000-1700. School Hols, daily 1000-1800.
admission £
Detailed scale model of Corfe Castle and village before its destruction by Cromwell. Old English country garden.

Dorset Quadbiking
Manor Farm, East Bloxworth, Wareham BH20 7EB
t (01929) 459083 **w** dorsetquadbiking.co.uk
open All year, phone for details.
admission ££££
Quadbike trekking perfect for all times of the year. With challenging terrain and capable quads, a unique outdoor adventure.

The Dorset Teddy Bear Museum
East Gate, Corner of High East Street/Salisbury Street, Dorchester DT1 1JU
t (01305) 266040 **w** teddybearmuseum.co.uk
open Apr-Oct, daily 1000-1730. Nov-Mar, daily 1000-1630.
admission ££
A museum devoted to the wonderful world of the teddy bear, which contains a wealth of bears for you to delight in.

Farmer Palmer's Farm Park

Organford, Poole BH16 6EU
t (01202) 622022 **w** farmerpalmers.co.uk
open 17 Feb-24 Mar 1000-1600,
25 Mar-27 Oct 1000-1730, 28 Oct-30 Dec,
Fri-Sun 1000-1600.
admission Adult: £5.95

National Farm Attraction of the Year 2006. The attention to detail is obvious. Family-run and designed for children eight years and under. There are hands-on animal events, many play facilities and fresh farmhouse fayre in the large, child-friendly restaurant. Your children will have a fun day whatever the weather!

 Map ref 2B3

Lulworth Castle & Park

East Lulworth, Wareham BH20 5QS
t 0845 450 1054 **w** lulworth.com
open Summer: Sun-Fri 1030-1800. Winter:
Sun-Fri 1030-1600 (excl 24-25 Dec, 7-20 Jan).
admission Adult: £7 (22 Jul-27 Aug £9)

Idyllic castle set in extensive park, 18thC chapel, animal farm, adventure play area, woodland walks, picnic area, stable cafe and courtyard shop. Special events throughout the year, including The Knights of Lulworth (performed by Horses Impossible), with dramatic medieval jousting displays throughout the summer. Fun for all the family.

 Map ref 2B3

V *voucher offer – see back section*

Go Ape!
Moors Valley Country Park, Horton Road,
Ashley Heath BH24 2ET
t 0870 444 5562 **w** goape.co.uk
open Apr-Nov, daily 0800-1730.
admission ££££

Tackle a high-wire forest adventure course of rope bridges, Tarzan swings and zip slides up to 35ft above the forest floor.

The choice is yours

Whether it's indoor or outdoor fun you're after, a relaxing treat or something a little more cultural, this guide will help you find the perfect solution.

Swanage Railway
Station House, Swanage BH19 1HB
t (01929) 425800
w swanagerailway.co.uk
open Apr-Oct, daily 0950-1630. Nov, Sat-Sun
0950-1630. December, Sat-Sun 0950-1630.
admission ££

Enjoy a nostalgic steam-train ride on the Purbeck line.

The Tutankhamun Exhibition
High West Street, Dorchester DT1 1UW
t (01305) 269571
w tutankhamun-exhibition.co.uk
open Apr-Oct, daily 0930-1730. Nov-Mar, Mon-Fri
0930-1700, Sat-Sun 1000-1630.
admission ££

Tutankhamun's tomb and treasures perfectly reconstructed for the first time outside Egypt. Facsimiles of his magnificent treasures including his golden burial mask.

Wimborne Model Town and Gardens
16 King Street, Wimborne Minster BH21 1DY
t (01202) 881924 **w** wimborne-modeltown.com
open Apr-Oct, daily 1000-1700.
admission £

Charming scale recreation of 1950s Wimborne, a delightful historic market town, set in beautiful award-winning gardens. Tearooms and gift shop.

NATURE AND WILDLIFE

Abbotsbury Sub Tropical Gardens
Bullers Way, Abbotsbury DT3 4LA
t (01305) 871387 **w** abbotsbury-tourism.co.uk
open Apr-Aug, daily 1000-1800. Sep-Oct, Feb-Mar, daily 1000-1700. Nov-Jan, daily 1000-1600.
admission ££

Twenty acres of woodland valley. Exotic plants from all over the world, teahouse and gift shop, aviary and children's play area.

Abbotsbury Swannery
New Barn Road, Abbotsbury DT3 4JG
t (01305) 871858 **w** abbotsbury-tourism.co.uk
open Apr-Aug, daily 1000-1800. Sep-Oct, daily 1000-1700.
admission ££

The only place in the world where up to 1,000 swans can be visited during their nesting and hatching time (end May-end June). Audiovisual presentation. Ugly duckling trail.

Bennett's Water Gardens
Putton Lane, Chickerell DT3 4AF
t (01305) 785150 **w** waterlily.co.uk
open Apr-Sep, Tue-Fri, Sun, Bank Hols 1000-1700.
admission ££

Eight acres of gardens. Outstanding displays of water lilies in summer. Monet-style bridge and gazebo. Nursery, gift shop and tearooms.

The Blue Pool
Furzebrook, Wareham BH20 5AR
t (01929) 551408 **w** bluepooluk.com
open Mar-Nov, daily 0930-1700.
admission £

A unique 25 acres of pine trees, gorse and heather. A traditional teahouse, gift shops, museum and plant centre.

Brownsea Island
Poole Harbour, Poole BH13 7EE
t (01202) 707744 **w** nationaltrust.org.uk/brownsea
open Mar-Jul, daily 1000-1700. Aug, daily 1000-1800. Sep, daily 1000-1700. Oct, daily 1000-1600.
admission £

Beautiful island with wonderful views, wildlife and history including rare red squirrels and birds. The birthplace of Scouting and Guiding.

Compton Acres
164 Canford Cliffs Road, Canford Cliffs BH13 7ES
t (01202) 700778 **w** comptonacres.co.uk
open Mar-Oct, daily 0900-1800. Nov-Feb, daily 1000-1600.
admission ££

Eleven distinct gardens of the world. The gardens include Italian, Japanese, water and rock garden and the new amateur-gardening garden.

The Dorset Heavy Horse Centre
Grains Hill, Edmondsham, Verwood BH21 5RJ
t (01202) 824040 **w** dorset-heavy-horse-centre.co.uk
open Apr-Oct, daily 1000-1700.
admission ££

Various breeds of heavy horses plus miniature and Shetland ponies, pets and aviaries. Old farm wagons and implements. Demonstrations of plaiting and harnessing.

Durlston Country Park
Durlston, Lighthouse Road, Swanage BH19 2JL
t (01929) 424443 **w** durlston.co.uk
open Daily.
admission Free

Countryside, cliffs, sea and wildlife. Visitor centre with exhibits, information, live cliff camera and underwater sounds. Theme trails and ranger-guided walks.

Corfe Castle, Isle of Purbeck

For key to symbols see inside back cover.

Farmer Palmer's Farm Park

Organford, Poole BH16 6EU
t (01202) 622022 **w** farmerpalmers.co.uk
open 17 Feb-24 Mar 1000-1600,
25 Mar-27 Oct 1000-1730, 28 Oct-30 Dec,
Fri-Sun 1000-1600.
admission Adult: £5.95

National Farm Attraction of the Year 2006. The attention to detail is obvious. Family-run and designed for children eight years and under. There are hands-on animal events, many play facilities and fresh farmhouse fayre in the large, child-friendly restaurant. Your children will have a fun day whatever the weather!

                    Map ref 2B3

Kingston Maurward Gardens and Animal Park

Kingston Maurward College,
Kingston Maurward DT2 8PY
t (01305) 215003
w kmc.ac.uk
open Jan-Dec, daily 1000-1730.
admission £
Set deep in Hardy's Dorset and listed by English Heritage, these gardens include a croquet lawn, rainbow beds and borders.

Lyme Regis Marine Aquarium and Cobb History

Oakfield, Launchycroft Estate, Lyme Regis DT7 3NF
t (01297) 444230
open Mar-Oct, daily 1000-1700.
admission £
Small marine aquarium with exhibits caught in local waters. History displays of the cobb and ale.

Mapperton

Beaminster DT8 3NR
t (01308) 862645
w mapperton.com
open Gardens: Mar-Oct, Mon-Fri, Sun 1100-1700.
House: May, Bank Hols 1400-1630. July, Mon-Fri 1400-1630. Aug, Bank Hols 1400-1630.
admission £
Valley gardens beside 16th-17thC manor. Pools, orangery, fine views and walks.

Minterne Gardens

Minterne Magna DT2 7AU
t (01300) 341370
w minterne.co.uk
open Mar-Oct, daily 1000-1800.
admission £
Important rhododendron garden with many fine and rare trees, landscaped in the 18th century, with lakes, cascades and streams. The setting of Great Hintock House in Hardy's 'The Woodlanders'.

Moors Valley Country Park

Horton Road, Ashley Heath BH24 2ET
t (01425) 470721
w moors-valley.co.uk
open Daily 0800-dusk.
admission Free
A 1,000-acre country park. Lake and riverside walks, steam railway, golf course, fishing and an adventure play area. Visitor centre housing tearoom and country shop.

Studland Beach and Nature Reserve

Countryside Office, Middle Beach, Studland BH19 3AX
t (01929) 450259
w nationaltrust.org.uk
open Daily.
admission Free
Fine sandy beaches stretch continuously for three miles. The heathland behind the beach is a National Nature Reserve with many rare birds.

Upton Country Park

Upton Road, Upton BH17 7BJ
t (01202) 672625
w boroughofpoole.com
open Daily 0930-dusk.
admission Free
Formal gardens, meadows, woodlands, and marshland. Heritage centre with nature trails. Upton House, historic Grade II Listed building.

Weymouth Sea Life Park and Marine Sanctuary

Lodmoor Country Park, Weymouth DT4 7SX
t (01305) 788255
w sealifeeurope.com
open Daily, 1000-1600.
admission £££
An amazing array of the world's most fascinating marine life, offering a day of fun and amazement whatever the weather.

HISTORIC ENGLAND

Athelhampton House and Gardens
Athelhampton DT2 7LG
t (01305) 848363
w athelhampton.co.uk
open Apr-Oct, Mar, Mon-Thu, Sun 1030-1700.
Nov-Feb, Sun 1030-1700.
admission ££
Legendary site of King Athelstan's palace. One of the finest 15thC manorhouses, surrounded by glorious Grade I Listed garden with fountains, pools and waterfalls.

Brewers Quay and Timewalk Journey
Hope Square, Weymouth DT4 8TR
t (01305) 777622
w brewers-quay.co.uk
open Daily 1000-1730.
admission £
Converted Victorian brewery with indoor speciality shopping village, courtyard restaurant and award-winning Timewalk attraction recreating the sights, sounds and smells of history.

Cerne Abbas Giant
Cerne Abbas
t (01297) 561900
w nationaltrust.org.uk
open Daily.
admission Free
The 180ft-tall club-wielding man has long been regarded as a sign of fertility. He was probably created during the Roman occupation of Britain in the second century AD.

Christchurch Priory Church
Quay Road, Christchurch BH23 1BU
t (01202) 485804
w christchurchpriory.org
open Apr-Oct, daily 0930-1700. Oct-Mar, daily 0930-1600.
admission Free
Longest parish church in England, dating from 1094. The west tower can be climbed. Legendary Miraculous Beam. Memorial to the poet Shelley.

Corfe Castle
The Square, Corfe Castle BH20 5EZ
t (01929) 477063
w nationaltrust.org.uk
open Apr-Sep, daily 1000-1800. Nov-Feb, daily 1000-1600. March, Oct, daily 1000-1700.
admission £
Ruins of former royal castle sieged and slighted in 1646 by parliamentary forces.

Edmondsham House and Garden
Edmondsham House, Edmondsham,
Cranborne BH21 5RE
t (01725) 517207
open House: Apr, Wed 1400-1700. Oct, Wed 1400-1700. Bank Hols, 1400-1700. Gardens: Apr-Oct, Wed, Sun 1400-1700.
admission £
Fine Tudor/Georgian manorhouse, with Victorian stables and dairy. Six-acre garden and one-acre walled garden.

Forde Abbey and Gardens
Chard TA20 4LU
t (01460) 221290 w fordeabbey.co.uk
open Abbey: Apr-Oct, Tue-Fri, Sun 1200-1600. Gardens: daily, 1000-1630.
admission ££
Founded 850 years ago, Forde Abbey was converted into a private house in 1649. Thirty acres of world-famous gardens, interesting plants and stunning vistas.

Highcliffe Castle
Rothesay Drive, off Lymington Road,
Highcliffe BH23 4LE
t (01425) 278807 w highcliffecastle.co.uk
open Feb-Dec, daily 1100-1700.
admission £
Grade I Listed c1830 picturesque and romantic seaside mansion. Now fully repaired to exterior only. Six staterooms open as visitor and exhibition centre.

Kingston Lacy House and Gardens
Wimborne Minster BH21 4EA
t (01202) 883402 w nationaltrust.org.uk
open House: Apr-Oct, Wed-Sun 1100-1600. Gardens: Apr-Oct, daily 1030-1800. Nov-Dec, Fri-Sun 1030-1600. Feb-Mar, Sat-Sun 1030-1600.
admission ££
A 17thC house designed for Sir Ralph Bankes by Sir Roger Pratt, altered by Sir Charles Barry in the 19thC. Collection of paintings, 250-acre wooded park, herd of Devon cattle.

The geological wonder of Durdle Door on the Jurassic coast

Lulworth Castle & Park

East Lulworth, Wareham BH20 5QS
t 0845 450 1054 **w** lulworth.com
open Summer: Sun-Fri 1030-1800. Winter:
Sun-Fri 1030-1600 (excl 24-25 Dec, 7-20 Jan).
admission Adult: £7 (22 Jul-27 Aug £9)

Idyllic castle set in extensive park, 18thC
chapel, animal farm, adventure play area,
woodland walks, picnic area, stable cafe and
courtyard shop. Special events throughout the
year, including The Knights of Lulworth
(performed by Horses Impossible), with
dramatic medieval jousting displays throughout
the summer. Fun for all the family.

                             Map ref 2B3

V *voucher offer – see back section*

Maumbury Rings
Weymouth Avenue, Dorchester
t (01305) 266861
w dorchester-town.co.uk
open Daily.
admission Free   ㅠ
*Originally a sacred circle of the Stone Age, the
Romans later turned the rings into a coliseum
where 13,000 spectators could watch gladiatorial
combats.*

Max Gate
Alington Avenue, Dorchester DT1 2AA
t (01305) 262538
w maxgate.co.uk
open Apr-Sep, Mon, Weds, Sun 1400-1700.
admission £   ఉ
*Victorian house designed by Thomas Hardy, and his
home from 1885 until his death in 1928. Contains
several pieces of Hardy's furniture.*

Nothe Fort
The Nothe, Barrack Road, Weymouth DT4 8UF
t (01305) 766626 **w** fortressweymouth.co.uk
open May-Sep, daily 1030-1730.
admission £   ♿ㅠ♪ఉ
*Mid-Victorian coastal defence fort with ramparts, gun
deck and magazines. Models, displays and exhibitions.
Views over town, harbour and Jurassic Coast.*

Portland Castle
Portland DT5 1AZ
t (01305) 820539
w english-heritage.org.uk/portlandcastle
open Apr-June, daily 1000-1700. Jul-Aug, daily
1000-1800. Sep, daily 1000-1700. Oct, daily 1000-1600.
admission £   ♿♪ఉ
*A well-preserved coastal fort built by Henry VIII to defend
Weymouth Harbour against possible French and Spanish
attack. Exhibition detailing 400 years of the castle's history.*

Sherborne Abbey
The Close, Sherborne DT9 3LQ
t (01935) 812452 **w** sherborneabbey.com
open Apr-Oct, daily 0900-1800. Nov-Mar, daily
0900-1600.
admission Free   ♪ఉ
*Historic abbey church dating from Saxon times. Wealth of
15thC fan vaulting built of hamstone. Fine monuments.*

Sherborne Castle
Sherborne Castle Estates, New Road,
Sherborne DT9 5NR
t (01935) 813182 **w** sherbornecastle.com
open Apr-Oct, Tue-Thur, Sat-Sun, Bank Hols
1100-1630.
admission £   ♿ㅠఉ
*Built by Sir Walter Raleigh in 1594. Home to the Digby
family since 1617. Splendid collections of decorative
arts. Capability Brown lake, gardens and grounds.*

Wimborne Minster
Church House, High Street,
Wimborne Minster BH21 1HT
t (01202) 884753 **w** wimborneminster.org.uk
open Mar-Dec, daily 0930-1730. Jan-Feb, daily
0930-1600.
admission Free   ㅠ♪ఉ
*Medieval church, Ethelred brass, astronomical clock,
quarterjack, chained library and gift shop.*

OUTDOOR ACTIVITIES

The Dorset Belles Ltd
Boat Booking Office, Bournemouth Pier,
Bournemouth BH2 5AA
t (01202) 558550 **w** dorsetcruises.co.uk
open Apr-Oct, daily 0700-2200. Nov-Mar, daily
0800-1700.
admission £   ♿ㅠ♪ఉ
*Glorious coastal and harbour cruises from Bournemouth,
Poole and Swanage. Visit islands or view the Purbeck
heritage coast and Poole Harbour. Dorset's finest scenery.*

ENTERTAINMENT AND CULTURE

Bridport Museum
South Street, Bridport DT6 3NR
t (01308) 422116 **w** bridportmuseum.co.uk
open Apr-Dec, Mon-Sat 1000-1700.
admission £
Learn the unique history of the town, from Romans to rope-making. A gateway to the Jurassic Coast World Heritage Site.

The Dinosaur Museum
Icen Way, Dorchester DT1 1EW
t (01305) 269880 **w** thedinosaurmuseum.com
open Apr-Oct, daily 0930-1730. Nov-Mar, daily 1000-1630.
admission ££
Award-winning museum devoted to dinosaurs. Features fossils, actual-size dinosaur reconstructions, video gallery and audiovisual/hands-on displays.

Dinosaurland
Coombe Street, Lyme Regis DT7 3PY
t (01297) 443541 **w** dinosaurland.co.uk
open All year, Mon-Sun, Bank Hols 1000-1700.
admission £
Jurassic fossil museum. Guided fossil-hunting walks, fossil shop.

Hardy's Cottage
Higher Bockhampton DT2 8QJ
t (01297) 561900 **w** nationaltrust.org.uk
open Apr-Oct, Mon-Thu, Sun 1100-1700.
admission £
Thomas Hardy was born here in 1840. It is where he wrote 'Under the Greenwood Tree' and 'Far from the Madding Crowd'.

The Keep Military Museum
The Keep, Bridport Road, Dorchester DT1 1RN
t (01305) 264066 **w** keepmilitarymuseum.org
open Apr-Sep, Mon-Sat 0930-1700. Oct-Mar, Tue-Sat 0930-1700.
admission £
Touch-screen computers and interactive and creative displays tell the stories of the courage, tradition and sacrifice of those who served in the regiments of Devon and Dorset.

Museum of Electricity
The Old Power Station, Bargates, Christchurch BH23 1QE
t (01202) 480467
w scottish-southern.co.uk//sseinternet/museum/
open Apr-Sep, Mon-Thu 1200-1600.
admission £
One of the most extensive collections of historic electrical equipment in Great Britain, the restored 1903 building houses more than 700 exhibits.

The Priest's House Museum and Garden
23-27 High Street, Wimborne Minster BH21 1HR
t (01202) 882533
open Apr-Oct, Mon-Sat 1000-1630.
admission £
Award-winning museum. Period rooms, Victorian kitchen, walled garden, East Dorset villages gallery, childhood and archaeology galleries and hands-on activities for all ages.

The Red House Museum and Gardens
Quay Road, Christchurch BH23 1BU
t (01202) 482860
w hants.gov.uk/museum/redhouse
open All year, Tue-Sat 1000-1700, Sun 1400-1700.
admission Free
Museum showing the archaeology, social and domestic history of Christchurch. Changing temporary exhibitions, costume gallery, rose and herb gardens.

RNLI Headquarters and Display
West Quay Road,
Poole BH15 1HZ
t (01202) 663000
w rnli.org.uk
open All year, Mon-Fri 0900-1700.
admission Free
History and development of RNLI shown by pictures, models and paintings.

Royal Signals Museum
Blandford Camp, Blandford Forum DT11 8RH
t (01258) 482248
w royalsignalsmuseum.com
open All year, Mon-Fri 1000-1700, Sat-Sun, Bank Hols 1000-1600.
admission ££
History of army communication from Crimean War to Gulf War. Vehicles, uniforms, medals and badges on display.

Russell-Cotes Art Gallery & Museum
East Cliff, Bournemouth BH1 3AA
t (01202) 451800
w russell-cotes.bournemouth.gov.uk
open All year, Tue-Sun 1000-1700.
admission Free
Houses important collections of paintings, sculpture, furniture, ceramics, world-wide collections and contemporary craft commissions.

Shaftesbury Abbey Museum and Garden
Park Walk, Shaftesbury SP7 8JR
t (01747) 852910
w shaftesburyabbey.co.uk
open Apr-Oct, daily 1000-1700.
admission £
Explore one site of Saxon England's foremost Benedictine nunnery, founded by King Alfred.

For key to symbols see inside back cover.

Shaftesbury Town Museum and Garden

Gold Hill, Shaftesbury SP7 8JW
t (01747) 852157
open Apr-Oct, daily 1030-1630.
admission £

Take a step back in time and discover the story of Shaftesbury, the highest market town in Wessex.

The Tank Museum

Bovington,
Wareham BH20 6JG
t (01929) 405096
w tankmuseum.co.uk
open Apr-Oct, daily 1000-1700.
admission ££

The world's finest display of armoured fighting vehicles. Experimental vehicles, interactive displays.

Tolpuddle Martyrs Museum

Tolpuddle DT2 7EH
t (01305) 848237
w tolpuddlemartyrs.org.uk
open Apr-Oct, Tue-Sat 1000-1700, Sun, Bank Hols 1100-1700. Nov-Mar, Thu-Sat 1000-1600, Sun, Bank Hols 1100-1600.
admission Free

Colourful banners and touch-screen computers tell the story of the six Martyrs of Tolpuddle who were transported to Australia in 1834.

RELAXING AND PAMPERING

Poole Pottery Factory Shop Outlet

The Quay, Poole BH15 1RF
t (01202) 668681 **w** poolepottery.co.uk
open All year, Mon-Sat 0930-1630, Sun 1030-1630.
admission Free

Factory shop, teashop and Poole Pottery Experience with design-your-own area.

Stapehill Abbey, Crafts and Gardens

Wimborne Road West, Stapehill,
Wimborne Minster BH21 2EB
t (01202) 861686
open Jan-Mar, daily 1000-1600. Apr-Sep, daily 1000-1700. Oct-Dec 1000-1600.
admission £

Stapehill has magnificent award-winning gardens, 19thC buildings, nuns' chapel, cloister garden, working crafts people and 12,000 sq ft museum depicting life in bygone days.

Walford Mill Craft Centre

Stone Lane, Wimborne BH21 1NL
t (01202) 841400 **w** walfordmillcrafts.co.uk
open Apr-Dec, Mon-Sat 1000-1700, Sun 1100-1600.
admission Free

A converted mill building by the river with a gallery and shop showing the best in contemporary British design. Also has workshops, a craft school and a bistro.

Walk up the ancient cobbled street of Gold Hill, Shaftesbury

Gloucestershire

FAMILY FUN

Enjoy the fun of a special event or visit one of the attractions listed for a great day out. For more inspiring ideas go to **enjoyengland.com**.

14–15 Jul
Royal International Air Tattoo
RAF Fairford
airtattoo.com

21–22 & 28–29 Jul
Joust Festival of Medieval Mayhem
Berkeley Castle
joust.info

5–14 October
Cheltenham Literature Festival
Cheltenham
(01242) 227979
cheltenhamfestivals.co.uk

May 08
Badminton Horse Trials
Badminton
0870 242 3436
badminton-horse.co.uk

May 08
Cheltenham Jazz Festival
Various venues, Cheltenham
(01242) 227979
cheltenhamfestivals.co.uk

Avon Valley Railway
Bitton Station, Bath Road, Bitton BS30 6HD
t (0117) 932 7296 **w** avonvalleyrailway.co.uk
open Apr-Oct, Sun 1100-1600. May, Aug, Oct School Hols, Tue-Thu 1100-1600.
admission ££
A 2.5-mile standard-gauge steam railway offering a journey back in time to the glorious days of steam, and a collection of locomotives and rolling stock.

Butts Farm Rare Farm Animals and Farm Shop
The Butts Farm, Cricklade Road,
Near South Cerney GL7 5QE
t (01285) 869414 **w** buttsfarmshop.com
open See website for details.
admission £
A traditional farm where you can enjoy a unique hands-on experience amongst our friendly farm animals. A must for all animal lovers.

Cotswold Farm Park
Guiting Power GL54 5UG
t (01451) 850307 **w** cotswoldfarmpark.co.uk
open Apr-Aug, daily 1030-1700. Sep-Oct, Sat-Sun 1030-1700.
admission ££
Over 50 flocks and herds of British rare breeds of farm animals, seasonal farming demonstrations, lots of fun children's activities, cafe and gift shop.

Dean Forest Railway
Forest Road GL15 4ET
t (01594) 843423 **w** deanforestrailway.co.uk
open See website for details.
admission ££
Preserved steam railway running between Lydney Junction and Parkend. Besides the regular timetable there are also special events, a luxury dining train, museum, gift shop and cafe.

The Dick Whittington Family Leisure Park
Blakemore Park, Little London GL17 0PH
t (01452) 831137 **w** dickwhittington.info
open All year, Tue-Sun 1000-1700.
admission £
Fun for all the family with an indoor play barn, toy corner, aquarium, outdoor play/adventure zones, giant sandpit, pedal course, farm animals and deer, small pets corner, walks and views.

Forest Model Village and Gardens
Old Park, Lydney Park Estate, Aylburton GL15 6BU
t (01594) 845244 **w** forest-model-village.co.uk
open See website for details.
admission £
Discover a miniature Forest of Dean set within five spectacular landscaped gardens in a shady woodland glade. Come face to face with what makes the Forest of Dean a magical, special place.

Gloucestershire Warwickshire Railway
The Railway Station, Toddington GL54 5DT
t (01452) 539062
w gwsr.com
open See website for details.
admission ££

*Fully operational narrow-gauge railway.
Exhibits from Britain and abroad. Steam rides
available.*

St Augustine's Farm
High Street, Arlingham GL2 7JN
t (01452) 740720
open Mar-Oct, Tue-Sun 1100-1700.
admission £

*Organic dairy farm lying in the middle of a horseshoe
bend in the River Severn. Visitor centre, cafe and
museum.*

Wildfowl &
Wetlands Trust
Slimbridge

WWT Slimbridge Wetland Centre,
Slimbridge GL2 7BT
t (01453) 891900 **w** wwt.org.uk
open Apr-Oct 0930-1700. Nov-Mar 0930-1630
(excl 25 Dec).
admission Please see website

WWT Slimbridge Wetland Centre is a fantastic
day out for everyone. Visit our wonderful
reserve, relax in our restaurant, browse in our
gallery and shop, or enjoy one of our many
events and activities. With plenty to see and do
throughout the year, you'll never be bored!

Map ref 2B1

 voucher offer – see back section

NATURE AND
WILDLIFE

Batsford Arboretum
Batsford Park, Batsford GL56 9QB
t (01386) 701441
w batsarb.co.uk
open Feb-Nov, daily 1000-1600. Dec-Jan, Mon-Tue,
Thu-Sun 1000-1600.
admission £

*Fifty-acre arboretum containing one of the largest
private collections of rare trees in the country, most
spectacular in spring and autumn. Falconry, nursery and
tearooms.*

Birdland Park
Rissington Road, Bourton-on-the-Water GL54 2BN
t (01451) 820480
w birdland.co.uk
open Apr-Oct, daily 1000-1800. Nov-Mar, daily
1000-1600.
admission ££

*A natural setting of woodland, river and gardens,
Birdland is home to over 500 birds of 130 different
species.*

Cotswold Falconry
Batsford Park, Moreton-in-Marsh GL56 9QB
t (01386) 701043
w cotswold-falconry.co.uk
open Mar-Mid Nov, daily 1030-1700.
admission ££

*Collection of over 90 birds of prey. Flying
demonstrations of eagles, owls, hawks and
falcons. Breeding aviaries, owl wood, hawk walk
and gift shop.*

Hidcote Manor Garden (National Trust)
Hidcote Bartrim GL55 6LR
t (01386) 438333
w nationaltrust.org.uk
open Apr-Jun, Mon-Wed, Sat-Sun 1000-1800. Jul-Aug,
Mon-Wed, Fri-Sun 1000-1800. Sep, Mon-Wed, Sat-Sun
1000-1800. Oct, Mon-Wed, Sat-Sun 1000-1700.
admission ££

*One of England's great gardens, famous for its rare trees
and shrubs, outstanding herbaceous borders and
unusual plants from all over the world.*

Keynes Country Park/Cotswold Water Park
Cotswold Water Park, Spratsgate Lane,
Shorncote GL7 6DF
t (01285) 861459
w waterpark.org
open See website for details.
admission £

*Includes nature reserve. Facilities for angling, bathing,
windsurfing and sailing.*

Mill Dene Garden

Mill Dene, School Lane, Blockley GL56 9HU
t (01386) 700457
w milldenegarden.co.uk
open Apr-Oct, Tue-Fri 1000-1730.
admission £

Cotswold garden surrounding a water mill with millpond, stream and grotto. Steep valley hides surprises of colour, views and planting ideas.

Painswick Rococo Garden Trust

Painswick GL6 6TH
t (01452) 813204
w rococogarden.co.uk
open Jan-Dec, daily, Bank Hols 1100-1700.
admission £

Eighteenth-century Rococo garden, set in a hidden combe, with garden buildings, vistas and woodland paths.

Prinknash Bird Park

Prinknash Park, Cranham GL4 8EU
t (01452) 812727
w prinknash-bird-and-deerpark.com
open Apr-Oct, daily 1000-1700. Nov-Mar, daily 1000-1600.
admission £

A deer park with fallow deer, pygmy goats and peacocks, both Indian blue and white and crown cranes. New aviary. Numerous species of waterfowl and exotic pheasants.

Robinswood Hill Country Park

Reservoir Road, Gloucester GL4 6SX
t (01452) 303206
open Daily, Bank Hols 0800-dusk.
admission Free

Open countryside park of 250 acres with viewpoint, pleasant walks, way-marked nature trails and Gloucestershire visitor centre.

Wildfowl & Wetlands Trust Slimbridge

WWT Slimbridge Wetland Centre,
Slimbridge GL2 7BT
t (01453) 891900 **w** wwt.org.uk
open Apr-Oct 0930-1700. Nov-Mar 0930-1630 (excl 25 Dec).
admission Please see website

WWT Slimbridge Wetland Centre is a fantastic day out for everyone. Visit our wonderful reserve, relax in our restaurant, browse in our gallery and shop, or enjoy one of our many events and activities. With plenty to see and do throughout the year, you'll never be bored!

Map ref 2B1

V *voucher offer – see back section*

Broadway Tower, the Cotswolds

For key to symbols see inside back cover.

Westbury Court Garden (National Trust)

Westbury-on-Severn GL14 1PD
t (01452) 760461 w nationaltrust.org.uk
open Mar-Jun, Wed-Sun 1000-1700. Jul-Aug, daily
1000-1700. Sep-Oct, Wed-Sun 1000-1700.
admission £
Formal water garden with canals and yew hedges laid
out between 1696 and 1705.

Westonbirt Arboretum

Forest Enterprise, Westonbirt GL8 8QS
t (01666) 880220 w forestry.gov.uk/westonbirt
open All year, daily 0900-dusk.
admission £
Six-hundred acres with the finest collections of trees,
beautiful spring flowers, stunning autumn colours and a
wide range of events.

Berkeley Castle

Berkeley GL13 9BQ
t (01453) 810332 w berkeley-castle.com
open Apr-Sep, Tue-Sat, Bank Holiday Mon
1100-1600, Sun 1400-1700. Oct, Sun 1400-
1700. Regular special events and concerts.
admission Adult: £7.50

Berkeley Castle is England's oldest inhabited
castle. Over 24 generations the Berkeleys have
transformed a savage Norman fortress into a
stately home full of treasures. Learn about
murder, intrigue and plotting, then enjoy the
grounds, adjacent butterfly farm and church.

                    Map ref 2B2

Clearwell Caves and Ancient Iron Mines

Clearwell, Coleford GL16 8JR
t (01594) 832535 w clearwellcaves.com
open Mar-Oct, daily 1000-1700.
admission £
A natural cave system tunnelled into by miners for over
5,000 years. There are nine large caverns and geological
displays throughout. A great underground experience.

Dyrham Park

Dyrham SN14 8ER
t (0117) 937 2501 w nationaltrust.org.uk
open Park: Daily 1100-1700. House: Mar-Oct, Mon-Tue,
Fri-Sun 1200-1700.
admission ££
Mansion built between 1691 and 1710 for William
Blathwayt. A herd of deer has roamed the 263-acre
parkland since Saxon times.

Gloucester Cathedral

Westgate Street, Gloucester GL1 2LR
t (01452) 528095
w gloucestercathedral.org.uk
open All year, Mon-Fri 0730-1815, Sat 0730-1715, Sun
0730-1600.
admission £
An architectural gem made of honey coloured limestone
with crypt, cloisters and Chapter House set in its
precincts.

Historic Gloucester Docks

1 Albion Cottages, The Docks, Gloucester GL1 2ER
t (01452) 311190
w glosdocks.co.uk
open Daily.
admission Free
Collection of restored Victorian warehouses, with shops,
museums, restaurants and cafe bars. Boat trips and
guided walks in summer months.

Kingswood Abbey Gatehouse

Kingswood
t (01452) 396572
w english-heritage.org.uk
open See website for details.
admission Free
This 16thC gatehouse, with carved mullioned window, is
all that remains of the Cistercian abbey which prospered
in the middle ages due to the wool trade.

Lodge Park & Sherborne Estate

Aldsworth GL54 3PP
t (01451) 844130
w nationaltrust.org.uk
open Daily.
admission £
Lodge Park is part of the Sherborne Estate, an ornate
building dating from 1635, overlooking the deer course
and surrounding countryside.

Odda's Chapel (English Heritage)

Deerhurst
t (01684) 295027
w english-heritage.org.uk
open Apr-Oct, daily 1000-1800. Nov-Mar, daily
1000-1600.
admission Free
Rare Saxon chapel dating back to 1056, attached to a
half-timbered farmhouse. It lay undiscovered for many
years and has been partly rebuilt and restored.

Pittville Pump Room

Pitville Park, Cheltenham GL52 3JE
t (01242) 523852
open All year, Mon, Wed-Sun 1000-1600.
admission Free
Pittville Pump Room is a beautiful, historic Grade I Listed
property set in parkland at Pitville used for cultural,
commercial and community events.

Sezincote House and Garden

Nr Moreton-in-Marsh GL56 9AW
t (01386) 700444 **w** sezincote.co.uk
open Garden: Jan-Nov, Thur-Fri,
Bank Holiday Mon 1400-1800.
House: May-Jul, Sep, Thur-Fri 1430-1730.
admission Adult: £6

Sezincote is a unique Indian house, built in
1805 in the Mogul style of Rajasthan. The
garden, with its Hindu Temple, seven pools and
Persian Paradise Garden, is one of the most
remarkable examples of the Picturesque style in
the UK.

Map ref 2B1

Snowshill Manor (National Trust)
Snowshill WR12 7JU
t (01386) 852410
w nationaltrust.org.uk
open House: Apr-Oct, Wed-Sun 1200-1700. Gardens:
Apr-Oct. Wed-Sun 1100-1730.
admission ££
*Cotswold manorhouse with eclectic collection of
craftsmanship and arts and crafts garden.*

Stanway Water Gardens
Stanway GL54 5PQ
t (01386) 584469
w stanwayfountain.co.uk
open House and Fountain: Jun-Aug, Tue, Thu
1400-1700.
Fountain only: Aug, Sat 1400-1700.
admission ££
*Golden-stoned Jacobean manorhouse with exquisite
gatehouse set amid 20 acres of landscaped grounds.
Important 14thC tythe barn. Tudor great hall with
shuffleboard.*

Sudeley Castle Gardens and Exhibition
Winchcombe GL54 5JD
t (01242) 602308 **w** sudeleycastle.co.uk
open Apr-Oct, daily, Bank hols 1030-1700.
admission ££
*Last home and burial place of Catherine Parr, with royal
connections spanning the centuries. Seasonal
exhibitions and award-winning organic gardens.*

Tewkesbury Abbey
Church Street, Tewkesbury GL20 5RZ
t (01684) 850959 **w** tewkesburyabbey.org.uk
open All Year, daily 0800-1800.
admission Free
*Superb Norman abbey with 14thC vaulting and
windows. Largest surviving Norman tower in the
country. Formerly a Benedictine monastery, it is larger
than many cathedrals.*

Westonbirt School, Gardens & House
Westonbirt School, Westonbirt GL8 8QG
t (01666) 881338 **w** westonbirt.gloucs.sch.uk
open Easter, Summer School Hols, Thu-Sun 1100-1630.
Oct School Hols, Daily 1100-1630.
admission £
*Exquisite gardens surrounding the splendid country seat
of Robert Holford, the great Victorian collector of plants
who founded Westonbirt Arboretum.*

OUTDOOR ACTIVITIES

Telstar Cruises
Riverside Walk, Tewkesbury GL20 5UR
t (01684) 294088
open Apr-Sep, daily 1100-1700.
admission £
*Take a leisurely cruise along the beautiful River Avon in
peace and tranquillity to the village of Twyning. Or enjoy
the river at your own pace and hire a self-drive boat for
half a day, a day, a weekend or longer.*

'The Giant's Throne', Forest of Dean

ENTERTAINMENT AND CULTURE

Berkeley Castle

Berkeley GL13 9BQ
t (01453) 810332 **w** berkeley-castle.com
open Apr-Sep, Tue-Sat, Bank Holiday Mon 1100-1600, Sun 1400-1700. Oct, Sun 1400-1700. Regular special events and concerts.
admission Adult: £7.50

Berkeley Castle is England's oldest inhabited castle. Over 24 generations the Berkeleys have transformed a savage Norman fortress into a stately home full of treasures. Learn about murder, intrigue and plotting, then enjoy the grounds, adjacent butterfly farm and church.

                        Map ref 2B2

Burlington Contemporary Art
The Courtyard,
Montpellier Street,
Cheltenham GL50 1SR
t (01242) 515165
w burlingtoncontemporaryart.com
open All year, Mon-Sat 1000-1730.
admission Free
Gallery selling paintings and original etchings, glass, jewellery, sculpture and ceramics. Crafts Council selected.

Cheltenham Art Gallery and Museum
Clarence Street,
Cheltenham GL50 3JT
t (01242) 237431
w cheltenhammuseum.org.uk
open All year, Mon-Sat 1000-1720.
admission Free
World-renowned arts and crafts collection, inspired by William Morris. Three-hundred years of painting by Dutch and British artists. Special exhibitions throughout the year.

Corinium Museum
Park Street,
Cirencester GL7 2BX
t (01285) 655611
w cotswold.gov.uk
open All year, Mon-Sat 1000-1700, Sun 1400-1700.
admission £
Award-winning museum, featuring one of the finest collections of antiquities from Roman Britain.

Cotswold Motoring Museum & Toy Collection
Bourton-on-the-Water GL54 2BY
t (01451) 821255 **w** cotswold-motor-museum.com
open March-Nov, daily 1000-1800.
admission £
Wonderful cars, motorbikes, toys and pedal cars. A large collection of enamel signs and fascinating motoring memorabilia. Home to Brum, the children's TV character.

Gloucester City Museum and Art Gallery
Brunswick Road, Gloucester GL1 1HP
t (01452) 396131
open All year, Tue-Sat 1000-1700.
admission Free
Housed in a fine Victorian building in the heart of the city, among the spectacular collection are the archaeological finds, fine and decorative arts, and natural history specimens representing Gloucester's rich heritage.

Gloucester Folk Museum
99-103 Westgate Street, Gloucester GL1 2PG
t (01452) 396467 **w** livinggloucester.co.uk
open All year, Tue-Sat 1000-1700.
admission Free
A 15th-17thC timber-framed museum. Pin factory, Victorian agricultural implements and Civil War armour. Also includes wheelwright, carpenter and ironmonger.

Holst Birthplace Museum
4 Clarence Road, Pittville, Cheltenham GL52 2AY
t (01242) 524846 **w** holstmuseum.org.uk
open Apr-Dec, Tue-Sat 1000-1600.
admission £
This Regency terraced house, where the composer of 'The Planets' was born, shows the upstairs/downstairs way of life in Victorian times.

The House of the Tailor of Gloucester
9 College Court, Gloucester GL1 2NJ
t (01452) 422856
open Apr-Dec, daily 0900-1700.
admission Free
House chosen by Beatrix Potter as scene for The Tailor of Gloucester. Also shop featuring Beatrix Potter books and gifts.

Museum in the Park
Stroud District Museum Service,
Stratford Park, Stratford Road, Stroud GL5 4AF
t (01453) 763394 **w** stroud.gov.uk/museum
open Apr-July, Tue-Fri 1000-1700, Sat-Sun, Bank Hols 1100-1700. August, daily 1000-1700. Sep, Tue-Fri 1000-1700, Sat-Sun 1100-1700. Oct-Nov, Tue-Fri 1000-1600, Sat-Sun, Bank Hols 1100-1600. Jan-Mar, Tue-Fri 1000-1600, Sat-Sun, Bank Hols 1100-1600.
admission Free
Family-friendly museum in historic parkland setting. Colourful displays including dinosaur remains, a Roman temple, the world's first lawnmower and much more.

National Waterways Museum
Llanthony Warehouse, Gloucester Docks,
Gloucester GL1 2EH
t (01452) 318200 **w** nwm.org.uk
open Apr-Oct, daily 1000-1700. Nov-Mar, daily
1100-1600.
admission ££
Three floors of a Victorian warehouse with interactive
displays and galleries, charting the story of Britain's
waterways. Historic craft, working forge, cafe and shop.

Nature in Art
Wallsworth Hall, Sandhurst Lane, Sandhurst GL2 9PA
t 0845 450 0233 **w** nature-in-art.org.uk
open All year, Tue-Sun, Bank Hols 1000-1700.
admission £
The world's first museum dedicated exclusively to fine,
decorative and applied art inspired by nature from any
period, any culture and in any media.

Soldiers of Gloucestershire Museum
Custom House, Gloucester Docks, Gloucester GL1 2HE
t (01452) 522682 **w** glosters.org.uk
open Apr-May, Tue-Sun 1000-1700. Jun-Sep, daily,
Bank Hols 1000-1700. Oct-Mar, Tue-Sun 1000-1700.
admission £
Listed Victorian building in historic docks. The story of
Gloucestershire's foot and horse soldiers in the last 300
years.

Winchcombe Folk and Police Museum
Town Hall, High Street, Winchcombe GL54 5LJ
t (01242) 609151 **w** winchcombemuseum.org.uk
open Apr-Oct, Mon-Sat 1000-1630.
admission £
The heritage and history of the ancient town of
Winchcombe and its people with the Police Collection of
British and International Uniforms and Equipment.

Winchcombe Railway Museum and Garden
23 Gloucester Street, Winchcombe GL54 5LX
t (01242) 620641
open Please phone for details.
admission £
A hands-on museum of railway life. Includes working
signals, signal box and booking office. Set in half an acre
of Victorian Cotswold gardens.

FOOD AND DRINK

Three Choirs Vineyards
Baldwins Farm, Newent GL18 1LS
t (01531) 890223 **w** threechoirs.com
open All year, Mon-Fri 0900-1700.
admission £
Home of internationally awarded Three Choirs Wine.
Self-guided tours take visitors around the vineyards and
into the winery for a video, story of winemaking and
viewing gallery.

RELAXING AND PAMPERING

Prinknash Abbey Visitors Centre
Cranham GL4 8EX
t (01452) 812066 **w** prinknashabbey.org.uk
open Apr-Nov, daily, Bank Hols 0900-1730. Dec-Mar,
daily, Bank Hols 0900-1730.
admission Free
Benedictine abbey set in the heart of the Cotswolds. Gift
shop, tearoom, bird and deer park, Roman mosaic
exhibition and children's play area.

Traditional stone cottages in the village of Bibury

For key to symbols see inside back cover.

Somerset

Enjoy the fun of a special event or visit one of the attractions listed for a great day out. For more inspiring ideas go to **enjoyengland.com**.

30 May–2 Jun
Royal Bath & West Show
Bath & West Showground, Shepton Mallet
(01749) 822200
bathandwest.com

21–29 Jul
Westival Arts Festival
Taunton
(01823) 336344
westival.co.uk

3–5 Aug
Glastonbury Abbey Musical Extravaganza
Glastonbury
(01458) 834596
glastonburyfestivals.co.uk

10–13 Aug
Glastonbury Children's Festival
Abbey Park Playground, Fishers Hill,
Glastonbury
(01458) 832925
childrensworldcharity.org

9 Nov
Bridgwater Guy Fawkes Carnival
Various venues, Bridgwater
(01278) 421795
bridgwatercarnival.org.uk

FAMILY FUN

Animal Farm Adventure Park
Red Road, Berrow TA8 2RW
t (01278) 751628
w animal-farm.co.uk
open All year, daily 1000-1730.
admission ££
Set in 25 acres of Somerset countryside with views across to the Mendip Hills. Feed and hold many friendly animals. Indoor play area now open.

Brean Leisure Park
Coast Road, Brean Sands, Burnham-on-Sea TA8 2QY
t (01278) 751595
w brean.com
open See website for details.
admission Free
Fun park with over 30 rides and attractions from roundabouts to rollercoasters. Pool complex with five waterslides, golf course, garden centre, bars and restaurants.

Butlins Minehead
Warren Road, Minehead TA24 5SH
t 0870 145 0045
w butlins.com
open May-Dec, daily 0930-1800.
admission £££
Amusement park, outdoor splash pool and traditional funfair. Skyline pavilion, splash swimming pool, outdoor adventure play area, Hotshots ten-pin bowling alley. Fantastic live entertainment.
map ref 1D1
see ad on inside front cover

The East Somerset Railway
Cranmore Station, Cranmore BA4 4QP
t (01749) 880417
w eastsomersetrailway.com
open Mar-Dec, Tue-Fri 0930-1400, Sat-Sun, Bank Hols 1000-1600.
admission ££
The station complex houses a licensed restaurant, shop and art gallery as well as the museum, goods box and engine sheds.

Exmoor Falconry & Animal Farm
West Lynch Farm, Allerford TA24 8HJ
t (01643) 862816
w exmoorfalconry.co.uk
open Daily, Bank Hols 1000-1700.
admission ££
Falconry centre with owls, hawks, eagles, falcons and other animals set in medieval farmyard.

Fleet Air Arm Museum

RNAS Yeovilton, Ilchester BA22 8HT
t (01935) 840565 **w** fleetairarm.com
open Apr-Oct 1000-1730. Nov-Mar,
Wed-Sun 1000-1630.
admission Adult: £10.50

A must-see attraction when in the South West.
See Europe's largest collection of naval aircraft,
plus Concorde, Harriers, helicopters and the
award-winning Aircraft Carrier Experience.
There's even a nuclear bomb! Adventure
playground, shop, restaurant, excellent parking
and disabled facilities.

                    Map ref 2A3

Grand Pier

Marine Parade,
Weston-super-Mare BS23 1AL
t (01934) 620238
w grandpierwsm.co.uk
open Mar-Dec, daily 1000-1800.
admission Free

*Covered amusement park over the sea.
Deck trains, dodgems, spaceflight
simulator, ghost train, children's adventure
play area, big wheel, slot machines and
videos.*

Noah's Ark Zoo Farm

Moat House Farm,
Failand Road,
Wraxall BS48 1PG
t (01275) 852606
w noahsarkzoofarm.co.uk
open Feb-Oct, Mon-Sat 1030-1700.
admission ££

*The most varied zoo and farm in North
Somerset with hands-on animal experiences for
everyone. Only five miles from Bristol, it's a
beautiful, peaceful and fun place for adults and
children.*

Shakspeare Glass

Foundry Road, Riverside Place,
Taunton TA1 1JJ
t (01823) 333422
w shakspeareglass.co.uk
open All year, Mon, please phone for details, Tue-Sat
0900-1700.
admission Free

*Studio-glass workshop and gallery. One of the
country's leading studio-glass workshops
showing a wide range of Shakspeare's own
work.*

West Somerset Railway

The Railway Station, Minehead TA24 5BG
t (01643) 704996
w west-somerset-railway.co.uk
open Jun-Sep, daily. Mar-May, Oct, Tue-Thu,
Sat-Sun.
admission Adult: £13

The longest Heritage railway in the country, the
West Somerset Railway runs from Bishops
Lydeard, three miles outside Taunton, through
the Quantock Hills before turning along the
Somerset coastline and arriving in Minehead
after a 20-mile journey. A day out for both the
enthusiast and the family.

                    Map ref 1D1

V *voucher offer – see back section*

Weston Miniature Railway

Marine Parade, Weston-super-Mare BS23 1AL
t (01934) 643510
w westonprom.com
open Apr-May, Sat-Sun 1030-1700. June-Sep, daily
1030-1700. Oct, Sat-Sun 1030-1700.
admission £

*Passenger-carrying miniature railway over half a mile on
the seafront. Eighteen-hole putting course.*

Wookey Hole Caves and Papermill

Wookey Hole BA5 1BB
t (01749) 672243
w wookey.co.uk
open Apr-Oct, daily, Bank Hols 1000-1700. Nov-Mar,
daily, Bank Hols 1000-1600.
admission £££

*Spectacular caves and legendary home of the Witch of
Wookey. Working Victorian paper mill including Old
Penny Arcade, Magical Mirror Maze and Cave Diving
Museum.*

NATURE AND WILDLIFE

Ashton Court Estate
Long Ashton BS41 9JN
t (0117) 963 9174
open Apr, daily 0730-2015. May-Aug, daily 0730-2115.
Sep, daily 0730-2015. Oct, daily 0730-1915. Nov-Jan,
daily 0730-1715. Feb, daily 0730-1815.
admission Free
*Woodlands, mansion, stables cafe, garden, pitch and
putt golf courses, nature trail, orienteering course,
miniature railway, deer park, visitor centre, horse-riding
trail.*

Avon Valley Country Park
Pixash Lane, Bath Road, Keynsham BS31 1TS
t (0117) 986 4929
w avonvalleycountrypark.co.uk
open See website for details.
admission ££
*A great day out for all the family. A river-based park with
animals and birds, children's play area and assault
course, boating and fishing. Undercover soft play area
and falconry.*

Barrington Court
Barrington TA19 0NQ
t (01460) 241938
w nationaltrust.org.uk
open Apr-Sep, Mon-Tue, Thu-Sun 1100-1700. Oct,
Mon-Tue, Thu-Sun 1100-1630. Dec, Sat-Sun 1100-1600.
admission ££
*Series of beautiful gardens influenced by Gertrude Jekyll
including a large kitchen garden designed to support the
house.*

Cheddar Caves & Gorge
Cheddar BS27 3QF
t (01934) 742343
w cheddarcaves.co.uk
open Jul-Aug, daily 1000-1700. Sep-Jun, daily
1030-1630.
admission £££
*Nature, culture and adventure. Britain's finest caves and
deepest gorge. Victorian Gothic splendour and how our
Stone Age ancestors survived.*

Chew Valley Lake and Blagdon Lake
Wally Court Road, Chew Stoke BS40 8XN
t (0117) 966 5881
w bristolwater.co.uk
open Daily, dawn-dusk.
admission Free
*Situated on the northern edge of the beautiful Mendip
Hills, the picturesque surroundings make this a popular
destination. Chew Valley Lake is the biggest inland
waterway in South West England.*

East Lambrook Manor Gardens
East Lambrook, South Petherton TA13 5HH
t (01460) 240328 **w** eastlambrook.co.uk
open Daily, Bank Hols 1000-1700.
admission £

*The garden at East Lambrook Manor is recognised
throughout the world as the home of English cottage
gardening, having been created in the 1940s, 50s and
60s by the late gardening icon, Margery Fish.*

Ebbor Gorge National Nature Reserve
Wookey Hole BA5 3AH
t (01749) 679546 **w** english-nature.org.uk
open Daily 0800-dusk.
admission Free
*Woodland walk with excellent spring flowers,
summer butterflies and autumn colour.
Limestone outcrops and towering cliffs surround
the gorge itself with great views across the
Somerset Levels to Glastonbury Tor.*

Ferne Animal Sanctuary
Chard TA20 3DH
t (01460) 65214 **w** ferneanimalsanctuary.org
open Daily 1000-1700.
admission Free
*Fifty-one-acre sanctuary for some 300 animals. Nature
trails, picnic tables and light refreshments. Tearoom and
well-stocked gift shop.*

Hestercombe Gardens
Cheddon Fitzpaine TA2 8LG
t (01823) 413923 **w** hestercombegardens.com
open All year, daily 1000-1800.
admission ££
*A unique combination of Georgian landscape, Victorian
terrace and Edwardian garden. Walks, streams, temples,
vivid colours, formal terraces, woodlands, lakes and
cascades.*

Seaquarium
Marine Parade, Weston-super-Mare BS23 1BE
t (01934) 613361 **w** seaquarium.co.uk
open All year, daily, Bank Hols 1000-1700.
admission ££
*It's a whole new world. See some of the weirdest and
deadliest animals on the planet, from sharks to
seahorses.*

The Wildlife Park at Cricket St Thomas
Cricket St Thomas TA20 4DB
t (01460) 30111 **w** wild.org.uk
open Apr-Sep, daily, Bank Hols 1000-1800. Oct-Mar,
daily, Bank Hols 1000-1600.
admission ££

*Set in a scenic valley, over 600 species of exotic animals
and birds are kept in a natural setting as part of world
conservation programmes.*

Willows & Wetlands Visitor Centre

Meare Green Court, Stoke St Gregory,
Taunton TA3 6HY
t (01823) 490249
w englishwillowbaskets.co.uk
open Mon-Sat 0900-1700.
admission Free

In the heart of the Somerset Levels a warm welcome and the story of the willow industry, past and present, awaits. All our baskets and willow products are handcrafted from home-grown willow by our skilled basketmakers.

                              Map ref 1D1

Wimbleball Lake

Haddon Hill, Dulverton TA22 9AB
t (01398) 371372
w swlakestrust.org.uk/pages/lakes/wimbleball.asp
open Daily.
admission Free

This scenic lake lies within Exmoor National Park and is surrounded by woodland and meadows. It offers a variety of activities including water sports, angling and walking.

Yeovil Country Park

Yeovil
t (01935) 462462 **w** southsomerset.gov.uk
open Daily.
admission Free

Managed by South Somerset District Council, an area of 127 acres of woodland, grassland, lake and river, open to all.

HISTORIC ENGLAND

The Bishop's Palace & Gardens

Wells BA5 2PD
t (01749) 678691 **w** bishopspalacewells.co.uk
open Apr-Oct, Mon-Fri 1030-1800, Sun 1200-1800.
admission £

Medieval palace and gardens surrounded by a moat and fortified walls.

Castle Neroche

Blackdown Hills,
Taunton TA20 3AB
t (01392) 832262
w forestry.gov.uk
open Daily.
admission Free

A visit to the Forest of Neroche will offer you spectacular views over the Vale of Taunton towards the Quantock Hills and Exmoor and a place to enjoy a stroll with the family.

Cleeve Abbey

Washford TA23 0PS
t (01984) 640377
w english-heritage.org.uk/cleeve
open See website for details.
admission £

One of the few 13thC monastic sites left with such a complete set of cloister buildings.

Cothay Manor

Greenham,
Wellington TA21 0JR
t (01823) 672283
w visitourgardens.co.uk/gardens/cothay.htm
open Apr-Sep, Wed-Thu, Sun, Bank Hols 1400-1800.
admission £

Hidden for centuries, and virtually untouched since it was built in 1480. Said to be the finest example of a small classic medieval manorhouse remaining today.

Dunster Castle

Dunster TA24 6SL
t (01643) 821314
w nationaltrust.org.uk
open Apr-Jul, Mon-Wed, Fri-Sun 1100-1600. Aug, Mon-Wed, Fri-Sun 1100-1700. Sep-Oct, Mon-Wed, Fri-Sun 1100-1600.
admission ££

Fortified home of the Luttrells for 600 years, remodelled 100 years ago. Fine 17thC staircase, plaster ceilings and garden of rare shrubs.

Glastonbury Tor

Glastonbury
t (01985) 843600
w nationaltrust.org.uk
open Daily.
admission Free

Remains of 15thC tower. Hill overlooks Glastonbury town and beyond.

Travel update

Get the latest travel information – just dial the RAC on 1740 from your mobile phone.

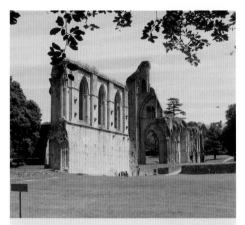

Glastonbury Abbey

Abbey Gatehouse, Magdalen Street,
Glastonbury BA6 9EL
t (01458) 832267 **w** glastonburyabbey.com
open Mar-May, Sep-Nov 0930-1800 (or dusk if
earlier). Jun-Aug 0900-1800. Dec-Feb 1000-
18.00.
admission Adult: £4.50

Magnificent abbey ruins and grounds.
Legendary burial place of King Arthur, it was
here in 1191 that the monks dug to find his
bones; these bones were reburied in the abbey
church in 1278, which was then the largest and
richest abbey in England. Modern museum.
Living history presentations. Outdoor summer
cafe.

                    Map ref 2A2

V *voucher offer – see back section*

Ham Hill Country Park
The Rangers Office, Stoke sub Hamdon TA14 6RW
t (01935) 823617 **w** southsomerset.gov.uk
open All year, Mon-Fri 0730-1630.
admission Free
Open access country park of 400 acres. Superb
countryside walks with Iron Age and Roman earthworks.
Panoramic views of Somerset.

Montacute House
Montacute TA15 6XP
t (01935) 823289 **w** nationaltrust.org.uk
open Apr-Oct, Mon, Wed-Sun 1100-1700.
admission ££
Late 16thC house built of local golden hamstone, by Sir
Edward Phelips. The Long Gallery houses a collection of
Tudor and Jacobean portraits. Formal gardens. Park.

Peat Moors Centre
Shapwick Road, Westhay BA6 9TT
t (01458) 860697
open Apr-Oct, Mon-Tue, Thu-Sun 1000-1630.
admission £
Replica Iron Age settlement and wooden trackways.
Traditional peat-cutting display, archaeology, peat and
wildlife exhibition.

West Somerset Railway

The Railway Station, Minehead TA24 5BG
t (01643) 704996
w west-somerset-railway.co.uk
open Jun-Sep, daily. Mar-May, Oct, Tue-Thu,
Sat-Sun.
admission Adult: £13

The longest Heritage railway in the country, the
West Somerset Railway runs from Bishops
Lydeard, three miles outside Taunton, through
the Quantock Hills before turning along the
Somerset coastline and arriving in Minehead
after a 20-mile journey. A day out for both the
enthusiast and the family.

                    Map ref 1D1

V *voucher offer – see back section*

Wells Cathedral
Chain Gate, Cathedral Green, Wells BA5 2UE
t (01749) 674483
w wellscathedral.org.uk
open Apr-Sep, daily 0700-1900. Oct-Mar, daily
0700-1800.
admission ££
Dating from 12th century and built in the early English
Gothic style. Magnificent West Front with 296
medieval groups of sculpture. Chapter House and
Lady Chapel.

Willows & Wetlands Visitor Centre

Meare Green Court, Stoke St Gregory,
Taunton TA3 6HY
t (01823) 490249
w englishwillowbaskets.co.uk
open Mon-Sat 0900-1700.
admission Free

In the heart of the Somerset Levels a warm welcome and the story of the willow industry, past and present, awaits. All our baskets and willow products are handcrafted from home-grown willow by our skilled basketmakers.

Map ref 1D1

OUTDOOR ACTIVITIES

Middlemoor Waterpark
The Causeway, Woolavington, Bridgwater TA7 8DN
t (01278) 685578 **w** middlemoor.co.uk
open All year, Tue-Sat 1000-1800, Sun 1300-1700.
admission ££££
Middlemoor Waterpark, Somerset's premier venue for jet-skiing, wake-boarding, water-skiing and pro-karting.

Yeovil Alpine Village
Addlewell Lane, Yeovil BA20 1QW
t (01935) 421702 **w** yeovilalpinevillage.co.uk
open Please phone for details.
admission ££
The leading skiing and snowboarding venue in the South West, offering something for everyone whatever their ability. Slopes are set on a natural hillside and have been innovatively designed to create an interesting and exciting facility.

ENTERTAINMENT AND CULTURE

Dunster Dolls Museum
Memorial Hall,
High Street,
Dunster TA24 6SF
t (01643) 821220
open Apr-Sep, Mon-Fri, Bank Hols 1030-1630, Sat-Sun 1400-1700.
admission £
Varied collection of over 900 dolls, period costume, baby gowns and dolls' houses. New themed displays each year.

Fleet Air Arm Museum

RNAS Yeovilton, Ilchester BA22 8HT
t (01935) 840565 **w** fleetairarm.com
open Apr-Oct 1000-1730. Nov-Mar, Wed-Sun 1000-1630.
admission Adult: £10.50

A must-see attraction when in the South West. See Europe's largest collection of naval aircraft, plus Concorde, Harriers, helicopters and the award-winning Aircraft Carrier Experience. There's even a nuclear bomb! Adventure playground, shop, restaurant, excellent parking and disabled facilities.

Map ref 2A3

Porlock Bay, Exmoor National Park

Admission is based on an adult price. Please check opening times and admission before travelling.

Glastonbury Abbey

Abbey Gatehouse, Magdalen Street, Glastonbury BA6 9EL

t (01458) 832267 **w** glastonburyabbey.com

open Mar-May, Sep-Nov 0930-1800 (or dusk if earlier). Jun-Aug 0900-1800. Dec-Feb 1000-18.00.

admission Adult: £4.50

Magnificent abbey ruins and grounds. Legendary burial place of King Arthur, it was here in 1191 that the monks dug to find his bones; these bones were reburied in the abbey church in 1278, which was then the largest and richest abbey in England. Modern museum. Living history presentations. Outdoor summer cafe.

                Map ref 2A2

Haynes International Motor Museum
Sparkford BA22 7LH
t (01963) 440804 **w** haynesmotormuseum.co.uk
open Apr-Oct, daily 0930-1730. Nov-Mar, daily 1000-1630.
admission ££
Awarded Motor Museum of the Year. New exhibition halls now open. Over 300 cars and 100 motorcycles, commercial and military vehicles, play area, cinema and new restaurant.

The Helicopter Museum
The Heliport, Locking Moor Road, Weston-super-Mare BS24 8PP
t (01934) 635227 **w** helicoptermuseum.co.uk
open Apr-Jul, Wed-Sun 1000-1730. Aug, daily 1000-1730. Sep, Wed-Sun 1000-1730. Nov-Mar, Wed-Sun 1000-1630.
admission ££
Unique collection of helicopters and autogyros with background displays on history, developments, how they work and their uses. The only helicopter museum in the UK.

Montacute TV & Radio Memorabilia Museum
1 South Street, Montacute TA15 6XD
t (01935) 823024 **w** montacutemuseum.co.uk
open Apr-Oct, Wed-Sat, Bank Hols 1230-1700, Sun 1400-1700.
admission £
Relive your favourite TV programmes. Probably the largest book, game and toy memorabilia collection in the UK. Also over 500 radios.

Museum of South Somerset
Hendford, Yeovil BA20 1UN
t (01935) 462855 **w** southsomerset.gov.uk
open Apr-Oct, Mon-Sat 0900-1700. Nov-Mar, Mon-Fri 0900-1700.
admission Free
Collections of glassware, costumes, agricultural and domestic bygones, reconstructed period room and temporary exhibitions.

North Somerset Museum
Burlington Street, Weston-super-Mare BS23 1PR
t (01934) 621028 **w** n-somerset.gov.uk/museum
open All year, Mon-Sat, Bank Hols 1000-1630.
admission £
Edwardian gaslight company building with central glazed courtyard. Seaside gallery, costumes, Victorian cottage, doll collection, local archaeology and natural history.

Perry's Cider Farm
Dowlish Wake TA19 0NY
t (01460) 52681 **w** perryscider.co.uk
open All year, Mon-Fri 0900-1730, Sat 0930-1630, Sun 1000-1300, Bank Hols 0930-1630.
admission Free
Working cider farm, with museum of cider presses, wagons, farm tools and photographic displays. Video on cider-making. A 16thC thatched barn.

Tourist Information Centres

To find your nearest Tourist Information Centre text TIC LOCATE to 64118.

Radstock, Midsomer Norton and District Museum
The Market Hall, Waterloo Road, Radstock BA3 3EP
t (01761) 437722
w radstockmuseum.co.uk
open Feb-Nov, Tue-Fri, Bank Hols 1400-1700, Sat 1100-1700.
admission £
Features reconstructed coal face, miner's cottage, Victorian schoolroom, 1930s Co-op, joiner's shop and blacksmith.

Somerset County Museum
Taunton Castle, Castle Green, Taunton TA1 4AA
t (01823) 320201
w somerset.gov.uk
open All year, Tue-Sat, Bank Hols 1000-1700.
admission Free
Housed in Taunton Castle, the displays feature archaeology, ceramics, costume, silver, the Somerset Military Museum and a 16thC almshouse.

Somerset Cricket Museum
7 Priory Avenue, Taunton TA1 1XX
t (01823) 275893
open Please phone for details.
admission £
Display of Somerset County Cricket Club memorabilia housed in a renovated 16thC priory barn.

Somerset Rural Life Museum
Abbey Farm, Chilkwell Street, Glastonbury BA6 8DB
t (01458) 831197
w somerset.gov.uk/museums
open Apr-Oct, Tue-Fri 1000-1700, Sat-Sun 1400-1800. Nov-Feb, Tue-Sat 1000-1700.
admission Free
Magnificent 14thC abbey barn, also Victorian farmhouse and yard. Permanent exhibitions. Events programme throughout the summer.

Wells Museum
8 Cathedral Green, Wells BA5 2UE
t (01749) 673477
w wellsmuseum.org.uk
open Apr-Oct, Mon-Sat, Bank Hols 1000-1730, Sun 1100-1600. Nov-Mar, daily 1100-1600.
admission £
Local archaeology and cave finds. Minerals, fossils, samplers. Display of Wells Cathedral statues.

West Somerset Rural Life Museum
The Old School, Allerford TA24 8HN
t (01643) 862529
w hornermill.co.uk
open May-Oct, Wed-Fri 1030-1600, Sun, Bank Hols 1330-1600.
admission £
Museum housed in the old school building with a large hall, smaller schoolroom, thatched roof and garden by the river. Exhibition of past local rural life. Croquet lawn.

FOOD AND DRINK

Avalon Vineyard
The Little House, East Pennard BA4 6UA
t (01749) 860393
w pennardorganicwines.co.uk
open Daily, please phone for details.
admission Free
Working organic vineyard and fruit farm. Purpose-built winery and underground cellar. Self-guided vineyard walk, free wine and cider tasting.

Sheppy's Cider Farm Centre
Three Bridges, Bradford-on-Tone TA4 1ER
t (01823) 461233 **w** sheppyscider.com
open All year, Mon-Sat 0830-1800.
admission £
Visitors may wander through orchards, visit the press room and farm/cider museum. Children's play area. Licensed tearoom open in season.

The Somerset Distillery
Burrow Hill, Kingsbury, Martock TA12 6BU
t (01460) 240782 **w** ciderbrandy.co.uk
open All year, Mon-Sat, Bank Hols 0900-1730.
admission Free
Barrels of cider and Somerset cider brandy, all pressed and distilled from vintage apples grown in Somerset.

RELAXING AND PAMPERING

Clarks Village
Farm Road, Street BA16 0BB
t (01458) 840064 **w** clarksvillage.co.uk
open Apr-Oct, Mon-Wed, Fri, Sat 0900-1800, Thu 0900-2000. Nov-Mar, Mon-Wed, Fri, Sat 0900-1730, Thu 0900-2000.
admission Free
Factory shopping village including over 80 high street name outlets plus a variety of attractions including a shoe museum, landscaped walkways, children's play area and art studio.

London Cigarette Card Company Showroom and Shop
West Street, Somerton TA11 6NB
t (01458) 273452 **w** londoncigcard.co.uk
open All year, Mon-Tue,Thu-Fri 0930-1300, 1400-1700, Wed, Sat 0930-1300.
admission Free
Over 4,000 different sets of cigarette and trade cards on view, from 1890s to the present day.

For key to symbols see inside back cover.

Wiltshire

Enjoy the fun of a special event or visit one of the attractions listed for a great day out. For more inspiring ideas go to **enjoyengland.com**.

25 May–10 Jun
Salisbury International Arts Festival
Various venues, Salisbury
(01722) 320333
salisburyfestival.co.uk

25–28 May
Chippenham Folk Festival
Various venues, Chippenham
(01249) 657190
chippfolk.co.uk

6–24 Jun
Devizes Festival
Devizes
devizesfestival.co.uk

26–28 Jul
West Wilts Show
Town Park, Trowbridge
westwiltsshow.net

27–29 Jul
Womad
Charlton Park, Malmesbury
0870 720 2128
womad.org

FAMILY FUN

Bush Farm Bison Centre
Bush Farm, West Knoyle BA12 6AE
t (01747) 830263 **w** bisonfarm.co.uk
open Apr-Sep, Wed-Sun 1000-1700.
admission ££
Bison, wapiti and red deer in 100 acres of grass fields and 30 acres of old oak woods. Gallery of North American wildlife and Native American artefacts.

Cholderton Rare Breeds Farm Park
Amesbury Road, Cholderton, Salisbury SP4 0EW
t (01980) 629438 **w** rabbitworld.co.uk
open Apr-Sep, daily 1000-1800. Oct-Mar, daily 1000-1600.
admission ££
Rare farm animals in paddocks, undercover sheep unit, poultry unit and rabbit unit, pets' park, ponds and nature trail, water gardens, adventure playground, cafe and shop.

Farmer Giles Farmstead
Teffont SP3 5QY
t (01722) 716338 **w** farmergiles.co.uk
open Apr-Oct, daily 1000-1800. Nov-Mar, Sat-Sun 1000-dusk.
admission £
Family leisure farm with large selection of animals, set in acres of glorious rolling Wiltshire downland. Working dairy farm. Watch cows being milked or bottle-feed lambs.

River Kennett, Marlborough

Longleat

Estate Office, Longleat,
Warminster BA12 7NW
t (01985) 844400 **w** longleat.co.uk
open 17-25 Feb, 31 Mar-4 Nov, daily. 3 Mar-25
Mar, Sat-Sun. See website or phone for
opening times and further details.
admission Adult: From £10

Set in more than 9,000 acres of beautiful
Wiltshire countryside, Longleat combines the
magic of the old with the marvels of the new.
From safari park to stately home, mazes to
murals and simulator rides to safari boats,
there's always something to discover round
every corner... your day at Longleat will never
be long enough!

                        Map ref 2B2

Salisbury Cathedral

Visitor Services, 33 The Close,
Salisbury SP1 2EJ
t (01722) 555120 **w** salisburycathedral.org.uk
open Daily 0715-1815. 11 Jun-24 Aug,
Mon-Sat, late opening until 1915.
admission Adult: £5

Britain's finest 13thC Gothic cathedral.
Discover nearly 800 years of history, including
Britain's tallest spire, the world's best preserved
Magna Carta (AD1215) and Europe's oldest
working clock (AD1386). Built in just 38 years
(AD1220-1258), the cathedral offers guided
tours and a modern restaurant and shop.
Donation requested.

                        Map ref 2B3

 voucher offer – see back section

Oasis Leisure Centre

North Star Avenue,
Swindon SN2 1EP
t (01793) 445401
w swindon.gov.uk
open Centre: All year, Mon, Fri 0630-2300,
Tue-Thu 0900-2300, Sat 0800-1900,
Sun 0800-2130. Pool: Please phone for
details.
admission £
*Lagoon pool with wave machine, water
cannon, three giant water slides, four
outdoor multiplayer pitches and soft play
area.*

NATURE AND WILDLIFE

The Courts

Holt BA14 6RR
t (01225) 782340
open Apr-Oct, Mon-Tue, Thu-Sun 1100-1730.
admission £
*This delightful and tranquil seven-acre English country
garden is full of charm, variety and colour with herbaceous
borders, water gardens, topiary and arboretum.*

Quality counts

Look out for the Quality Assured Visitor Attraction sign. These attractions are assessed annually
and meet the standards required to receive the quality marque.

Lackham Country Park
Wiltshire College Lackham, Lacock SN15 2NY
t (01249) 466800 **w** lackhamcountrypark.co.uk
open Aug, Mon-Fri, Sun 1000-1700.
admission £

Idyllically situated in the Wiltshire countryside. Discover formal and historic walled gardens, a rural-life museum housed in thatched buildings and woodland walks.

Longleat

Estate Office, Longleat,
Warminster BA12 7NW
t (01985) 844400 **w** longleat.co.uk
open 17-25 Feb, 31 Mar-4 Nov, daily. 3 Mar-25 Mar, Sat-Sun. See website or phone for opening times and further details.
admission Adult: From £10

Set in more than 9,000 acres of beautiful Wiltshire countryside, Longleat combines the magic of the old with the marvels of the new. From safari park to stately home, mazes to murals and simulator rides to safari boats, there's always something to discover round every corner... your day at Longleat will never be long enough!

Map ref 2B2

Stourhead House and Garden
The National trust, The Estate Office,
Stourton BA12 6QD
t (01747) 841152 **w** nationaltrust.org.uk
open Garden: All year, daily 0900-1900. House: Apr-Oct, Mon-Tue, Fri-Sun 1130-1630.
admission £££

Landscaped garden laid out c1741-80, with lakes, temples, rare trees and plants. House, begun c1721 by Colen Campbell, contains fine paintings and Chippendale furniture.

HISTORIC ENGLAND

Avebury Manor and Garden
Avebury SN8 1RF
t (01672) 539250
open House: Apr-Oct, Mon-Tue, Sun 1400-1640.
Garden: Apr-Oct, Mon-Tue, Fri-Sun 1100-1700.
admission £

Manorhouse of monastic origins. Present buildings date from early 16thC with Queen Anne alterations and Edwardian renovations. Gardens.

Avebury Stone Circles
Avebury SN8 1RF
t (01672) 539250 **w** nationaltrust.org.uk
open Daily.
admission Free

Originally from 4,500 years ago, many of the stones were located and re-erected in the 1930s by Alexander Keiller. The circles and henge encircle part of the village.

Bowood House and Gardens
The Estate Office, Bowood, Calne SN11 0LZ
t (01249) 812102 **w** bowood-house.co.uk
open Apr-Oct, daily 1100-1730.
admission ££

An 18th century house by Robert Adam. Collections of paintings, watercolours, Victoriana and porcelain. Landscaped park with lake, terraces, waterfall and grotto.

Lacock Abbey
Lacock SN15 2LG
t (01249) 730227 **w** nationaltrust.org.uk
open Apr-Oct, Mon, Wed-Sun 1300-1730.
admission ££

Founded in the 13thC and dissolved in 1539 since when it has been the home of the Talbot family. Medieval cloisters, 18thC Gothic hall and 16thC stable court.

Malmesbury Abbey
Parish Office, The Old Squash Court,
Malmesbury SN16 0AA
t (01666) 826666 **w** malmesburyabbey.com
open Daily 1000-1600.
admission Free

Norman/Romanesque abbey, now the parish church. Founded by St Aldhelm in Saxon times c676.

Mompesson House
The Cathedral Close, Salisbury SP1 2EL
t (01722) 335659 **w** nationaltrust.org.uk
open Apr-Oct, Mon-Wed, Sat-Sun 1100-1700.
admission £

Built c1701 for Charles Mompesson, the house has a graceful staircase and magnificent plasterwork. Collection of English 18thC drinking glasses. Delightful walled garden.

Old Sarum

Castle Road,
Salisbury SP1 3SD
t (01722) 335398
w english-heritage.org.uk/oldsarum
open Apr-Jun, daily 1000-1700.
Jul-Aug, daily 0900-1800. Sep, daily 1000-1700.
Oct, daily 1000-1600. Nov-Feb, daily 1100-1500.
Mar, daily 1000-1600.
admission £

*Huge ramparts and earthworks covering
56 acres. First an Iron Age hill fort, later
inhabited by Romans, Saxons and
Normans.*

Sheldon Manor Gardens

Sheldon Manor,
Chippenham SN14 0RG
t (01249) 653120
w sheldonmanor.co.uk
open Apr-Oct, Thu, Sun, Bank Hols 1400-1800.
admission £

*Sheldon Manor is Wiltshire's oldest
inhabited manorhouse with a 13thC porch
and a 15thC chapel. Gardens with ancient
yews, a mulberry tree and a profusion of
old-fashioned roses blooming in May and
June.*

Stonehenge

Amesbury SP4 7DE
t (01722) 343834
w english-heritage.org.uk/stonehenge
open See website for details.
admission ££

*World-famous prehistoric monument built as a
ceremonial centre. Started 5,000 years ago and
remodelled several times over the next 1,500
years.*

Salisbury Cathedral

Visitor Services, 33 The Close,
Salisbury SP1 2EJ
t (01722) 555120 **w** salisburycathedral.org.uk
open Daily 0715-1815. 11 Jun-24 Aug,
Mon-Sat, late opening until 1915.
admission Adult: £5

Britain's finest 13thC Gothic cathedral.
Discover nearly 800 years of history, including
Britain's tallest spire, the world's best preserved
Magna Carta (AD1215) and Europe's oldest
working clock (AD1386). Built in just 38 years
(AD1220-1258), the cathedral offers guided
tours and a modern restaurant and shop.
Donation requested.

Map ref 2B3

V *voucher offer – see back section*

River Bybrook, Castle Combe

For key to symbols see inside back cover.

Wilton House

The Estate Office,
Wilton SP2 0BJ
t (01722) 746720
w wiltonhouse.com
open House: Apr-Aug, Mon-Fri, Sun, Bank Hols
1030-1730. Garden: Apr-Sep, daily 1030-1730.
admission £££

Magnificent state rooms, world famous art collection, introductory film, recreated Victorian laundry and Tudor kitchen, landscaped parks, gardens and adventure playground.

OUTDOOR ACTIVITIES

Kennet and Avon Canal Boat Trips

K & A Cottage by Lock, 15 Frome Road,
Bradford-on-Avon BA15 1LE
t (01225) 868683
w katrust.org
open Please phone for details.
admission £

Boat trips along the Kennet and Avon canal. Travel along the scenic Avon Valley and Avoncliff aqueduct.

ENTERTAINMENT AND CULTURE

Alexander Keiller Museum

High Street,
Avebury SN8 1RF
t (01672) 529203
w english-heritage.org.uk/server/show/
conProperty.413
open See website for details.
admission £

One of the most important prehistoric archaeological collections in Britain. Includes the National Trust's Barn Gallery, which uses interactive exhibits to tell the story of the landscape and its people over the past 6,000 years.

Athelstan Museum

Cross Hayes,
Malmesbury SN16 9BZ
t (01666) 829258
w northwilts.gov.uk
open Apr-Oct, daily 1030-1630. Nov-Mar, daily 1130-1530.
admission Free

Exhibits of local history including coins minted in Malmesbury, lace-making displays, early fire engines and tricycles and a drawing of Malmesbury by Thomas Girtin.

Atwell-Wilson Motor Museum Trust

Downside, Stockley Lane, Calne SN11 0NF
t (01249) 813119 **w** atwellwilson.org.uk
open Apr-Oct, Mon-Thu, Sun 1100-1700. Nov-Mar,
Mon-Thu, Sun 1100-1600.
admission £

Motor museum with vintage, post-vintage and classic cars, including American models and classic motorbikes. Water meadow walk. Car clubs welcome for rallies. Play area.

Fox Talbot Museum of Photography

Lacock SN15 2LG
t (01249) 730459 **w** nationaltrust.org.uk/lacock
open Apr-Oct, Mar, daily 1100-1730. Nov-Feb, Sat-Sun
1100-1600.
admission £

Displays of apparatus and photographs related to Fox Talbot. Gallery with changing exhibitions each season.

The Kennet and Avon Canal Museum

The Canal Centre, Couch Lane, Devizes SN10 1EB
t (01380) 721279 **w** katrust.org
open Apr-Sep, daily 1000-1700. Winter: Please phone
for details.
admission £

Exhibition telling of the creation of the waterways link connecting London and Bristol, which emerged as a direct result of the Industrial Revolution.

The Royal Gloucestershire, Berkshire and Wiltshire Regiment (Salisbury) Museum

The Wardrobe, 58 The Close, Salisbury SP1 2EX
t (01722) 414536 **w** thewardrobe.org.uk
open Feb-Mar, Tue-Sun 1000-1700. Apr-Oct, daily,
Bank Hols 1000-1700. Nov, Tue-Sun 1000-1700.
admission £

Collections include Victoria Crosses, uniforms, weapons and militaria. Buildings of historic interest and landscaped garden.

Salisbury and South Wiltshire Museum

The King's House, 65 The Close, Salisbury SP1 2EN
t (01722) 332151 **w** salisburymuseum.org.uk
open Apr-Jun, Mon-Sat 1000-1700. Jul-Aug, Mon-Sat
1000-1700, Sun 1400-1700. Sep-Mar, Mon-Sat
1000-1700.
admission £

Grade I Listed building. Home of the award-winning Stonehenge Gallery. Fascinating displays of history of Salisbury, costume, ceramics, pictures and changing temporary exhibitions. All in the glorious setting of Salisbury Cathedral Close.

STEAM – Museum of the Great Western Railway

Kemble Drive, Swindon SN2 2TA
t (01793) 466646 **w** swindon.gov.uk/steam
open All year, daily 1000-1700.
admission ££

Displays celebrating the Great Western Railway include footplate access on locomotives and detailed reconstructions of life on the railways.

Swindon Museum and Art Gallery
Bath Road,
Swindon SN1 4BA
t (01793) 466556
w swindon.gov.uk
open All year, Mon-Sat 1000-1700.
admission Free

Archaeology, geology and social history of Swindon and North Wiltshire. Also modern 20thC and 21stC British art and ceramic collection, with temporary exhibition programme.

Trowbridge Museum
The Shires, Court Street,
Trowbridge BA14 8AT
t (01225) 751339
w trowbridgemuseum.co.uk
open All year, Tue-Fri 1000-1600,
Sat 1000-1700.
admission Free

The history of Trowbridge and its people. Includes working looms and displays on the West of England woollen industry and local history. Housed in a former woollen mill.

RELAXING AND PAMPERING

McArthurGlen Designer Outlet
Kemble Drive, Swindon SN2 2DY
t (01793) 507622 **w** mcarthurglen.com/swindon
open All year, Mon-Wed, Fri 1000-1800, Thu 1000-2000, Sat 1000-1900, Sun 1000-1700.
admission Free

McArthurGlen Great Western is the largest undercover outlet, offering top brand names at up to 50% off high street prices.

Wilton Shopping Village
Wilton, Salisbury SP2 0RS
t (01722) 741211 **w** wiltonshoppingvillage.co.uk
open All year, Mon-Sat 0930-1730, Sun 1030-1630.
admission Free

The whole family will enjoy a visit to the unique riverside setting of Wilton Shopping Village and its beautifully restored 18thC courtyard. Take a tour of the world-famous Wilton Carpet Factory and Town Museum.

Ancient stone circle, Stonehenge

Admission is based on an adult price. Please check opening times and admission before travelling.

Beaches in
South West England

Beaches with have been awarded the prestigious Blue Flag award. For more information, visit **blueflag.org.uk**

 A resort beach actively encourages visitors and is normally near a town with recreational facilities.

A rural beach has limited facilities, is generally more remote than a resort beach and will not be actively managed.

Polzeath Beach

Constantine Bay

Cornwall

Carbis Bay
t (01736) 796297
Access The beach is reached via the A30 signposted to Carbis Bay. The main road leads along the back of Carbis Bay and the beach is accessed via signposted roads at either end.

Constantine Bay
t (01841) 533449
Access The nearest access point is Wadebridge or St Merryn Village.

Crackington Haven Beach
t (01840) 779084
Access The nearest town is Tintagel.

Crooklets Beach
t (01288) 354240
Access The nearest access point is Bude.

Fistral Beach
t (01637) 850584
Access Within ten minutes' walk of Newquay town centre. Continuous public footpaths to beach. Vehicular access via public roads to car parks. (NB vehicular access can be curtailed at peak periods.) Bus service during season. The Cornwall Coastal Path runs behind the beach.

Fowey Harbour Beach
t (01726) 833616
Access Public transport is available to Fowey.

Godrevy/Gwithian Beach
t (01736) 796297
Access Take the A30 down to the east end of Hayle. Access via coastal road to Portreath via the B3301.

Great Western Beach
t (01637) 879058
Access The beach is on the northern edge of Newquay and is close to the east end of the town. The railway station is very close, as are taxi ranks and bus stops. There is restricted access from the town, down a steep road that ends as a slipway.

Gyllyngvase Beach
t (01326) 312300
Access Coming into Falmouth from the A39, follow the visitors' signs to the beaches. Twenty minutes' walk from town centre and ten minutes' walk from Falmouth Town railway station. Local bus services stop at Gyllyngvase Beach.

Harlyn Bay
t (01841) 533449
Access The nearest access point is Wadebridge or St Merryn village.

Marazion Beach
t (01736) 798090
Access From the A30 to Penzance take the exit marked Marazion at the first roundabout. Follow the road to Marazion where car parks are signposted.

Mawgan Porth Beach
t (01726) 223300
Access Situated between Newquay and Padstow. The nearest town is Newquay (approx five miles away). Public transport is available to the beach entrance.

Par Sands
t (01726) 223300
Access Par Sands adjoins the small town/village of Par which is approx five miles from the town of St Austell. There is ample car parking on site. Public transport exists to main entrance of site, with public footpath/South West Coastal Path access. Par mainline railway station is nearby.

Polzeath Beach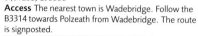
t (01208) 893333
Access The nearest town is Wadebridge. Follow the B3314 towards Polzeath from Wadebridge. The route is signposted.

Porth Beach
t (01726) 223300
Access Located approx 0.75 miles from the town of Newquay, with direct access from classified road. Council car park on the beach. Pedestrian access via South West Coast Path. Some of the beach remains dry even during high water, spring tides.

Porthcothan Bay
t (01841) 533449
Access The nearest town is Padstow.

Porthcurno Beach
t (01736) 362207
Access Take the A30 from Penzance. Follow signs to Lands End. Take B3315 to Porthcurno and follow signs to beach.

Porthleven Beach
t (01326) 573154
Access Porthleven is easily accessed and is situated off the A394 between Helston (two miles) and Penzance (seven miles). It is serviced by a local and national bus service. Penzance is also on the main rail network.

Porthmeor Beach
t (01736) 796297
Access Porthmeor beach is on the west-facing side of the seaside town of St Ives, taking pride of place below the world-famous Tate Gallery. By road, the car park overlooking the beach can be reached by following the A30 to St Erth and then following the signpost.

Porthminster Beach
t (01736) 796297
Access At the entrance to St Ives on B3074, near to railway and bus station.

Porthpean Beach
t (01726) 223300
Access The beach is located approx two miles from St Austell. Public transport is available to within 0.25 miles of the beach. Access is also possible via South West Coast Path. Large privately owned car park 80 yards from beach.

Porthtowan Beach
t (01872) 224723
Access The nearest railway station is Truro. Bus 304 connects Truro to Porthtowan (no service on Sundays). At Chiverton Cross roundabout on the A30 take the exit signposted St Agnes (B3277). Turn left after 400 yards and follow the signs for Porthtowan (approx three miles).

Portreath Beach
t (01209) 614397
Access Portreath is situated between the towns of Redruth and Camborne on the B3300 and is signposted from the main A30 dual carriageway. It is also serviced by bus from both Redruth and Camborne.

Praa Sands
t (01209) 614397
Access Situated between two major towns, Penzance and Helston on the A394. Praa Sands has a bus route to both towns and other surrounding villages. Penzance is also on the major railway network.

Readymoney Beach
t (01726) 223300
Access Located 0.5 miles to the seaward side of Fowey. Large car park approx 300 yards from beach, with pleasant and safe footpath access. There is no parking available at the beach and vehicular access is difficult. Public transport is available to Fowey.

St Michael's Mount, Marazion

Sandymouth Bay
t (01288) 354240
Access If you are travelling from Bude it is advisable to take the A39 heading for Bideford, turn left just before Kilkhampton and it will then be signposted to Sandymouth Bay.

Seaton Beach
t (01579) 341000
Access Seaton is near Looe and Torpoint and is reached using the A387 (Looe - Torpoint Road) and turning off at Hessenford. Regular bus service from Plymouth.

Sennen Cove
t (01736) 362207
Access Take the A30 from Penzance distributor road signposted Lands End. At Sennen turn right to Sennen Cove. Beach is on the right.

Summerleaze Beach
t (01288) 354240
Access The nearest town is Bude.

The Towans
t (01736) 796297
Access Accessible from the town of Hayle – follow signposts to Phillack and Towans.

Towan Beach
t (01637) 878134
Access The beach lies on the northern edge of Newquay and is close to the Rown Centre. There are several car parks within ten minutes' walk of the beach. Pedestrian access to the beach. There is a bus stop and taxi rank nearby and the railway station is 1km away.

Trebarwith Strand
t (01840) 779084
Access The nearest train station is Bodmin, which is 14 miles away. By car, the beach can be accessed from the A39. There are buses from Tintagel, but the service operates on a two-hourly basis.

Trevone Beach
t (01841) 533449
Access The nearest town is Padstow. Take the A389 leading onto the B3276.

Treyarnon Bay
t (01841) 533449
Access The nearest access point is Wadebridge or St Merryn village via the B3276.

Widemouth Sands
t (01288) 354240
Access The nearest access point is Bude.

Babbacombe Beach

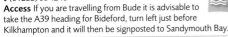

Devon

Anstey's Cove
t (01803) 207975
Access The nearest town is Torquay.

Babbacombe Beach
t (01803) 207975
Access Located next to Oddicombe beach, accessible from the Cliff Railway, and Oddicombe Beach Road.

Bantham Beach
t (01548) 853195
Access Follow the signs for Bantham at the roundabout on the A379 between Churchstow and Aveton Gifford.

Beacon Cove
t (01803) 207975
Access Beacon Cove is a short walking distance from Torquay harbourside, adjacent to Living Coasts. There is a car park situated close by providing convenient access to a gentle slope leading down to the beach.

Bigbury on Sea Beach
t (01548) 830159
Access From the A379 between Modbury and Aveton Gifford turn onto the B3392 to Bigbury. Pass through Bigbury and follow road to Bigbury on Sea. Large car park is on left just past Sedgewell slipway.

Blackpool Sands
t (01803) 770606
Access Signposted from Dartmouth on the A379 between Stoke Fleming and Strete. A side road leads to the car parks. Western National bus 93 to and from Dartmouth and Kingsbridge.

Breakwater Beach
t (01803) 207975
Access Access is from the main road to Berry Head and also by an easy level walk around the harbourside from the town centre. There is a local bus service nearby (17). There are disabled ramps to the promenade.

Broadsands
t (01803) 207975
Access The nearest town is Paignton. Local bus route is on the nearby main road, ten minutes' walk away (14, 118). Very large car parks serve the beach and provide access to the extensive coastal walks in the area.

Challaborough Beach
t (01548) 830159
Access From the A379 between Modbury and Aveton Gifford, turn onto the B3392 towards Bigbury. At St Annes Chapel, turn right – signposted Ringmore and Challaborough.

Combe Martin Beach
t (01271) 883319
Access The nearest town is Ilfracombe. There is a scheduled bus service throughout the day which runs from Barnstaple through Ilfracombe to Combe Martin. Barnstaple is served by both rail and the National Express coach service.

Corbyn Head (Torre Abbey) Beach
t (01803) 207975
Access The nearest town is Torquay. The beach is south of Torre Abbey Sands and is accessible by buses 2, 3, 12, 118 and 122 from Torquay railway station.

Coryton Cove
t (01626) 215601
Access Take the M4/M5 to Exeter, the A303 to Exeter or the A379 from Exeter to Dawlish. Mainline railway station nearby. From the town head directly towards the viaduct, go under the viaduct and follow the signs.

Croyde Bay

Croyde Bay
t (01271) 890671
Access From the A361 take the B231 at Braunton, follow signs for Croyde. Take bus 308 from Barnstaple.

Dawlish Warren Beach
t (01626) 215601
Access From the M5 follow the signs for Dawlish A379, turning left into Cockwood, following the road for approx two miles to Dawlish Warren. From Newton Abbot, Torquay follow the A381 into Teignmouth, follow signs for Dawlish.

Goodrington South Sands
t (01803) 207975
Access Paignton is the nearest town with good main road access. There is ample car parking as well as local rail and bus services (4, 118). Disabled access is easy.

Hele Beach
t (01271) 862728
Access Hele is in North Devon, just over a mile from Illfracombe on the A399 towards Combe Martin (about one hour's drive from the M5). The nearest bus station is in Ilfracombe and the nearest railway station is in Barnstaple.

Hollacombe Beach
t (01803) 207975
Access Hollacombe is on the main coast road and is easily accessible from both Paignton and Torquay. There is some on-street parking close to the beach, but it is in walking distance from nearby Preston. There is a regular local bus service (3,12,118,122).

Hope Cove
t (01548) 853195
Access Hope Cove is signposted off the A381 between Kingsbridge and Salcombe.

Maidencombe Beach
t (01803) 207975
Access The nearest town is Torquay. Maidencombe is on the main bus route to Teignmouth (85). Access is via a footpath and steep steps. There is a small car park at the entrance to the beach and a narrow path and a set of steps lead down to the cafe and beach.

Meadfoot Beach
t (01803) 207975
Access The nearest town is Torquay. There is main road access and a local bus service (x80). Parking is available on street and also in a small car park above the beach.

Ness Cove
t (01626) 215601
Access Take the M4/M5 and then A303 to Exeter. Take the A38, then A380 and head in the direction of Torquay. Take the turn off for Teignmouth and follow signs for Shaldon. Follow the B3220 from Shaldon towards Torquay. Turn left into Ness Drive. Mainline railway station in nearby Teignmouth. Good bus/coach links Torquay and Newton Abbot.

Oddicombe Beach
t (01803) 207975
Access The nearest town is Torquay. There is main road access and local bus services (32, 122). Parking is 0.5 miles from the beach. Access is via a steep footpath or the very popular Babbacombe Cliff Railway.

Paignton Beach
t (01803) 207975
Access The nearest town is Paignton which is an easy level walk of five minutes from the beach. There is main road access and local bus and train stations nearby. There is level access to the promenades and the harbour.

Preston Beach
t (01803) 207975
Access Close to Paignton, clearly signposted. There is easy access via local bus routes (3, 12, 118, 122). Preston can easily be reached on foot from nearby Paignton. The area is quite flat and has excellent access for disabled people.

Putsborough Sands
t (01271) 890230
Access The nearest town is Braunton, which is 4.5 miles away. There is little public transport available.

Salcombe North Sands

Salcombe North Sands
t (01548) 843927
Access Salcombe North Sands may be reached by turning right at the end of the A381.

Salcombe South Sands
t (01548) 843927
Access Salcombe South Sands may be reached by turning right at the end of the A381 and using the coastal road after Salcombe North Sands.

Slapton Sands
t (01548) 853195
Access Torcross is on the A379, Dartmouth to Kingsbridge Road.

St Mary's Bay
t (01803) 207975
Access The nearest town is Brixham. Bus 17 runs from St Mary's Holiday Camp.

Woolacombe Sands

Teignmouth Town Beach

t (01626) 215601
Access Mainline rail services and coach transport links from Exeter. Access via the M4/M5 and A303 to Exeter, A38, A380 and A31 from Exeter to Teignmouth.

Thurlestone Beach
t (01548) 853195
Access On the A381 between West Alvington and Malborough turn where signposted to South Milton. Turn left at the post office. This road leads to the car park.

Tunnels Beaches
t (01271) 879882
Access Tunnels beaches are accessed from the heart of Ilfracombe at Bath Place. From outside the town, follow signs for Ilfracombe. Once within the town follow signs for the seafront and Tunnels Beaches.

Watcombe Beach
t (01803) 207975
Access A small cove, north of Torquay and on the main bus route to Teignmouth.

Westward Ho!
t (01237) 477676
Access From the A39 at Bideford take the A386 to Westward Ho! and then the B3236, also signposted to Westward Ho! Bus service from Barnstaple and Bideford goes to the seafront.

Woolacombe Sands
t (01272) 870234
Access The nearest town is Ilfracombe. Regular bus services connect Ilfracombe, Woolacombe and Barnstaple. Good rail and National Express links to Barnstaple. Access to Barnstaple and Ilfracombe M25 jct 27, then the A361. Leave the A361 and take the A3343 for Wolacombe

Dorset

Alum Chine Beach
t (01202) 451781
Access The nearest major town is Bournemouth. Principle road access routes are the A338 from Ringwood and the A35 from Poole.

Boscombe Pier Beach
t (01201) 451781
Access The nearest major town is Bournemouth. Principal road access routes are the A338 from Ringwood and the A35 from Poole. Railway connections are very good. Once in Bournmouth, the seafront land-train service links all of Bournmouth's beaches.

Bournemouth Pier Beach
t (01202) 451781
Access The nearest major town is Bournemouth. Principal road access routes are the A338 from Ringwood and the A35 from Poole. Railway communications are very good. Once in Bournemouth, the seafront land-train service links all of Bournemouth's beaches.

Branksome Chine
t (01202) 708181
Access Located five miles from the centre of Poole, there is a bus service from Poole and Bournemouth during the summer season and excellent seafront car parking facilities with easy access to the beach.

Canford Cliffs Beach
t (01202) 708181
Access Located approx four miles from the centre of Poole. Accessible by various well-signposted routes from the town centre. A regular bus service runs throughout the year. There is ample car parking within easy reach of the beach.

Bournemouth Pier Beach

Charmouth West Beach
t (01297) 560826

Access Charmouth is signposted from both Lyme Regis and Bridport. Beach access is via Lower Sea Lane. Bus route runs through Charmouth hourly.

Durley Chine Beach
t (01202) 451781

Access The nearest major town is Bournemouth. Principle road access routes are the A338 from Ringwood and the A35 from Poole. Drivers should leave the A35 Wessex Way. Railway connections are good. Durley Chine is located to the west of Bournemouth's Central Beach.

Fisherman's Walk Beach
t (01202) 451781

Access The nearest major town is Bournemouth. Principle road access routes are the A338 from Ringwood and the A35 from Poole.

Hamworthy Park Beach
t (01202) 261303

Access Located approx two miles from the centre of Poole, Dorset. Accessible by various, well-signposted routes (A350 and B3068) from the town centre.

Lake Pier (Ham Common) Beach
t (01202) 253253

Access From the town centre, follow signs to Hamworthy. After crossing lifting bridge stay on the main road and follow signs to Rockley Park. Lake Pier is situated just before entering Rockley Park. There is a local bus service from Poole town centre.

Rockley Sands
t (01202) 680691

Access Rockley Sands is a privately sponsored beach to which the public has access and is located through Rockley Park Holiday Centre. The park is located west of Poole and is clearly signposted from all directions. Bus 152 operates between Sandbanks ferry and Rockley Park via Poole bus station.

Sandbanks Peninsular
t (01202) 708181

Access Located four miles from Poole centre and accessible by various well-signposted routes from the town centre. A regular bus service runs throughout the year and a large car park is available with easy access to this beach. Cycle racks are also available.

Shore Road Beach
t (01202) 708181

Access Located three miles from the centre of Poole, the beach can be reached by various well-signposted routes from the town centre. There is a bus service every 30 minutes during the summer period and good car parking facilities with easy access to the beach.

Southbourne Beach
t (01202) 451781

Access The nearest major town is Bournemouth. Principle road access routes are the A338 from Ringwood and the A35 from Poole. Railway connections are good. From Bournemouth Pier, Alum Chine is located one mile west along a level promenade. A land-train service is provided.

Swanage Central Beach
t (0870) 442 0680

Access Rail links from London Waterloo to Wareham where a connecting bus runs to the beach. Accessible via the M3, then the M27, the A35 and the A351.

Weymouth Central Beach
t (01305) 838511

Access Weymouth is signposted from junction 25 of the M5. Regular national coach service and an hourly train service from London Waterloo. Also good rail links with North West, Bristol and Wales.

Somerset

Berrow Beach
t (01278) 793525

Access The nearest town is Burnham-on-Sea. There is a coast road, and bus and coach services. The railway station is five miles away.

Brean Beach
t (01278) 793525

Access Access is via the Burnham-on-Sea coast road. The railway station is six miles away and there are many buses and coaches.

Brean Cove
t (01278) 793525

Access Access is via the Burnham-on-Sea coast road. The railway station approx six miles away, but there are many buses and coaches running to the area.

Burnham-on-Sea Beach
t (01278) 795083

Access Situated at Burnham-on-Sea, with a coach stop and large car park adjacent. The railway station is 2.5 miles away at Highbridge. Road access is via the A38 from junction 22 of the M5.

Weston-Super-Mare Beach
t (01934) 634994

Access Weston-super-Mare has excellent access via the M5 (jct 21) and the A370.

Weston-Super-Mare Beach

Places to stay in
South West England

Accommodation in this section is listed alphabetically by place name (shown in the blue bands), establishment category and establishment name.

All the place names can be found on the maps at the front of this guide – use the map references to locate them.

Accommodation symbols
Symbols give useful information about services and facilities. A key to these symbols can be found on the inside back-cover flap. Keep it open for easy reference.

ASHWATER, Devon Map ref 1C2 · **SELF CATERING**

★★–★★★
SELF CATERING

Units **6**
Sleeps **2–16**
Low season per wk
£100.00–£400.00
High season per wk
£420.00–£1,350.00

Braddon Cottages and Forest, Ashwater

contact Mr & Mrs George & Anne Ridge, Braddon Cottages, Ashwater, Beaworthy EX21 5EP
t (01409) 211350 **e** holidays@braddoncottages.co.uk **w** braddoncottages.co.uk

For country lovers, cottages in secluded location. Games field, adults' snooker and children's games rooms. Wood fires. New three-mile path suitable for pedestrians and bicycles. Colour brochure, extensive website.

open All year
payment Credit/debit cards, cash/cheques

Children ♥ ⊞ ⚐ Unit ⛭ TV ⚑ ▢ ◻ 🖥 🖨 ♨ 🔲 🗑 🗐 ❄
General P ⚒ ◎ S ♞ Leisure ◕ ⚘ ∪ ♪ ▶ 🚲 🏊 Shop 2 miles Pub 2 miles

---

BAMPTON, Devon Map ref 1D1 · **SELF CATERING**

★★★★
SELF CATERING

Units **5**
Sleeps **2–6**
Low season per wk
£150.00–£285.00
High season per wk
£355.00–£910.00

Three Gates Farm, Tiverton

contact Mrs Alison Spencer, Three Gates Farm, Huntsham, Tiverton EX16 7QH
t (01398) 331280 **e** threegatesfarm@hotmail.com **w** threegatesfarm.co.uk

open All year
payment Cash/cheques

Relax in one of our excellent converted barns, in the beautiful Devonshire countryside. Spend hours in our superb indoor heated pool, sauna or fitness room. Play in the grounds, with play tower and games rooms. The perfect place to unwind and explore the beaches, river valleys and attractions of Devon.

⊕ Jct 27 M5 A362. 1st Tiverton exit. Right Chettiscombe. Over A361 right, 3.5 miles right Huntsham, 1 mile Three Gates on right.

♥ Short breaks available Oct–May (excl school holidays).

Children ♥ ⊞ ⚐ ▢ ⚏ Unit ⛭ TV ⚑ ▢ 🖥 🖨 ♨ 🔲 🗑 🗐 ❄
General P ◎ S ♞ Leisure ⚘ ∪ ♪ 🚲

Look at the maps
Colour maps at the front pinpoint the location of all accommodation found in the regional sections.

BATH, Somerset Map ref 2B2 — SELF CATERING

★★★★
SELF CATERING

Units **7**
Sleeps **2–4**

Low season per wk
£275.00–£645.00

High season per wk
£465.00–£875.00

Church Farm Country Cottages, Bradford-on-Avon

contact Mrs Trish Bowles, Church Farm, Winsley, Bradford-on-Avon BA15 2JH
t (01225) 722246 **f** (01225) 722246 **e** stay@churchfarmcottages.com **w** churchfarmcottages.com

open All year
payment Credit/debit cards, cash/cheques, euros

Well-equipped, single-storey, traditional cow byres. Bath four miles. Working farm with sheep, free-range hens and horses. Swim in our luxurious, heated indoor pool (12m x 5m), whatever the weather! Pub/shop 500m. Kennet & Avon Canal nearby for boating, cycling and walking. Regular buses. Welcome cream tea.

⊕ M4 jct 18, take A46 to Bath, then A363 to Bradford-on-Avon. B3108 to Winsley (2 miles). At roundabout, 2nd exit to Bath/Limpley Stoke. Farm 0.75 miles on right.

♥ 4-night mid-week break (Mon-Thu) available at same price as 3-night weekend break (Fri-Sun), excl school holidays.

Children 🐕 ▥ ♿ 🛏 📺 Unit ▥ 📺 📻 🍴 💺 🖥 ▦ 🎮 🗄 🧺 💧 ❄
General P ✂ ⃝ S 🐾 Leisure ✎ 🔍 ♨ 🚶 🎣 ▶ 🚲 🚣 Shop < 0.5 miles Pub < 0.5 miles

BATHEASTON, Somerset Map ref 2B2 — SELF CATERING

★★★★–★★★★★★
SELF CATERING

Units **2**
Sleeps **1–8**

Low season per wk
£350.00–£580.00

High season per wk
£475.00–£850.00

Avondale Riverside, Bath

contact Mr & Mrs Pecchia, Avondale Riverside, 104 Lower Northend, North End, Batheaston, Bath BA1 7HA
t (01225) 852226 **f** (01225) 852226 **e** sheilapex@questmusic.co.uk **w** riversapart.co.uk

Balconied riverside apartments overlooking nature reserve. Private garden, secure parking, widescreen TV, whirlpool bath, en suite bedrooms, hot tub. Short breaks. Special rates for parties of eight. Ten minutes' drive to city centre.

open All year
payment Cash/cheques

Children 🐕 ▥ ♿ 🛏 /▥ Unit ▥ 📺 📻 🍴 📻 ▦ 🖥 💺 🗄 🧺 🎮 ❄
General P ✂ S 🐾 Leisure ♨ 🎣 🚲 Shop < 0.5 miles Pub < 0.5 miles

BERRYNARBOR, Devon Map ref 1C1 — SELF CATERING

★★★
SELF CATERING

Units **4**
Sleeps **2–8**

Low season per wk
£110.00–£320.00

High season per wk
£550.00–£900.00

Smythen Farm Coastal Holiday Cottages, Ilfracombe

contact Mr & Ms Thompson & Elstone, Smythen Farm Coastal Holiday Cottages, Symthen, Sterridge Valley, Berrynarbor, Ilfracombe EX34 9TB
t (01271) 882875 **f** (01271) 882875 **e** jayne@smythenfarmholidaycottages.co.uk
w smythenfarmholidaycottages.co.uk

open All year except Christmas and New Year
payment Cash/cheques

Near golden sands with sea and coastal views. Heated, covered swimming pool in a suntrap enclosure, gardens and games room with pool table, table tennis, football machine. Tree-house on two levels. Free pony rides, ball pond and bouncy castle, 14-acre recreation field and dog walk. For colour brochure phone Jayne.

⊕ A361 to Barnstaple then A39 for 1 mile towards Lynton. Left onto B3230, through Muddiford and Milltown. Right by garage onto A3123, next left to Sterridge Valley.

Children 🐕 ▥ ♿ 🛏 /▥ Unit ▥ 📺 📻 🍴 💺 🖥 ▦ 🎮 🗄 🧺 ❄
General P ⃝ S 🐾 Leisure ✎ 🔍 ♨ 🚶 🚲 🚣 Shop 1.5 miles Pub 1.5 miles

It's all quality-assessed accommodation

Our commitment to quality involves wide-ranging accommodation assessment. Ratings and awards were correct at the time of going to press but may change following a new assessment. Please check at the time of booking.

BIDEFORD, Devon Map ref 1C1 — SELF CATERING

★★★★
SELF CATERING

Units **6**
Sleeps **4–6**

Low season per wk
£325.00–£450.00
High season per wk
£790.00–£1,060.00

Robin Hill Farm Cottages, Bideford

contact Mr & Mrs Rob & Sue Williams, Robin Hill Farm, Littleham, Bideford EX39 5EG
t (01237) 473605 **e** r.hillcotts@amserve.net **w** robinhillcottages.co.uk

open All year
payment Cash/cheques

Cottages approached by a 0.5-mile leafy lane through 14 acres of woodland and pasture. Set away from the cottages is a leisure complex with an indoor pool and games room. Enjoy the peace and tranquillity, with spectacular views to Exmoor, in rolling countryside close to the coast.

⊕ Full directions will be sent on receipt of final payment for holiday.

♥ Short breaks available all year (excl school holidays).

Children 🚲 🛏 🕯 ⚠ Unit 📺 💻 🗄 🔥 🍳 🧺 ✳
General P 🅿 Ⓢ Leisure 🎣 🔌 U 🎵 🏇 🚴 ⛵ Shop 1.5 miles Pub 1.5 miles

BIGBURY-ON-SEA, Devon Map ref 1C3 — SELF CATERING

★★★★★
SELF CATERING &
SERVICED APARTMENTS

Units **1**
Sleeps **1–4**

Low season per wk
£429.00–£958.00
High season per wk
£1,068.00–£1,497.00

Apartment 5, Burgh Island Causeway, Bigbury-on-Sea

Helpful Holidays, Mill Street, Chagford, Newton Abbot TQ13 8AW
t (01647) 433593 **f** (01647) 433694 **e** help@helpfulholidays.com

open All year
payment Credit/debit cards, cash/cheques

Luxury, modern, ground-floor apartment set into cliff with panoramic southerly views from large patio. Facilities include pool, gym, sauna, cafe/bar, grassy cliff-top grounds and direct access to beautiful large sandy beach and coastal path. Popular for surfing and near golf course and village shop/post office.

⊕ From A38 at Ivybridge, take the 'B' road to Modbury then the A379 towards Kingsbridge. Very soon leave on B3392 for Bigbury-on-Sea.

♥ Bargain weekend and short-stay breaks available in autumn and winter months.

Children 🚲 🛏 🕯 🔔 ⚠ Unit 🧺 📺 🗄 🔥 💻 🍳 Leisure 🎣 🔌 🎵 Shop < 0.5 miles Pub < 0.5 miles
General P Ⓢ 🍴 Leisure 🎣 🔌 🎵 Shop < 0.5 miles Pub < 0.5 miles

BIRDLIP, Gloucestershire Map ref 2B1 — SELF CATERING

★★★★
SELF CATERING

Units **1**
Sleeps **4**

Low season per wk
£250.00–£350.00
High season per wk
£400.00–£475.00

Sidelands Farm, Gloucester

contact Ms Harriet Saunders, Sidelands Farm Holidays, Sidelands Farm, Brimpsfield Road, Gloucester GL4 8LJ
t (01452) 864826 **e** saunders@sidelands.fsnet.co.uk **w** sidelandsfarm.co.uk

Self-catering accommodation providing spacious family cottage in a rural but well-connected location in the heart of the beautiful Cotswolds.

open All year
payment Cash/cheques

Children 🚲 🛏 🕯 🔔 ⚠ Unit 🧺 📺 🗄 🔥 💻 🍳 Leisure U Shop 4 miles Pub 1 mile
General P 🍴 🅿 Ⓢ 🐕 Leisure U Shop 4 miles Pub 1 mile

enjoyEngland.com

Big city buzz or peaceful panoramas? Take a fresh look at England and you may be surprised at what's right on your doorstep. Explore the diversity online at enjoyengland.com.

BOSCASTLE, Cornwall Map ref 1B2 — HOTEL

★★
HOTEL
SILVER AWARD

B&B per room per night
s £40.00–£45.00
d £80.00–£130.00
HB per person per night
£60.00–£85.00

Wellington Hotel

The Harbour, Boscastle PL35 0AQ t (01840) 250202 e info@boscastle-wellington.com
w boscastle-wellington.com

open All year
bedrooms 8 double, 1 twin, 4 single, 2 family
bathrooms All en suite
payment Credit/debit cards, cash/cheques

Listed 16thC coaching inn in the Elizabethan harbour of Boscastle. Fantastic fine-dining restaurant. Traditional pub with Cornish ales, home-cooked food and log fire. Ten acres of private woodland walks and close to coastal path. Ideal location for discovering Cornwall. Recently refurbished after the Boscastle floods.

⊕ *From Exeter, A30 to Launceston. At Kennards House junction, A395 to Camelford. At Davidstowe, B3262 to A39. Turn left, then right onto B3266. Follow signs to Boscastle.*

♥ *Special breaks available throughout the year. 10% discount for 4 or more nights; 15% discount for 7 or more nights.*

Children 🛏🍳🎠🐕🛝✏🖨📷 Room 🛎📺👜🔌🔥 General 🅿🍴🍽🎯🖥♿ Leisure ∪🏊♣🏇🎣🚲

BRADFORD-ON-AVON, Wiltshire Map ref 2B2 — SELF CATERING

★★★★★
SELF CATERING

Units **2**
Sleeps **11**

Low season per wk
£700.00–£925.00
High season per wk
£1,040.00–£1,386.00

Fairfield Barns, Atworth

contact Mr & Mrs Taff & Gilly Thomas, Bradford Road, Atworth, Melksham SN12 8HZ
t (01225) 703585 f 0870 051490 e gilly@fairfieldbarns.com w fairfieldbarns.com

open All year
payment Credit/debit cards, cash/cheques

In a quiet village near Bath, luxurious barn conversions. Panoramic views of the Wiltshire countryside. Superbly equipped, wood-burning stoves, beamed throughout, en suite bedrooms with foreign theme. Indoor swimming pool, gym, tennis court, sauna and children's playhouse and adventure playground. Perfect for touring and sightseeing.

⊕ *A350 to Chippenham, then A4 to Atworth. Right after BP garage (Bradford Road). Pass school on left. Follow road to left. Fairfield Barns is last driveway on left.*

♥ *Short breaks available Sep-Jun.*

Children 🛏🍳🎠📷⛰ Unit 🍳📺🔌🎥📻📺🖥♿🔌🔔💡📠❄
General 🅿✂Ⓢ Leisure 🎣🎾∪🏇🚲 Shop < 0.5 miles Pub 0.5 miles

BREAN, Somerset Map ref 1D1 — CAMPING & CARAVANNING

★★★★
HOLIDAY, TOURING & CAMPING PARK

🚐 £6.00–£13.00
🚋 £6.00–£13.00
⛺ £6.00–£13.00
🏠 (11) £170.00–£440.00
575 touring pitches

Warren Farm Holiday Centre

Warren Road, Brean Sands, Burnham-on-Sea TA8 2RP t (01278) 751227 f (01278) 751033
e enquiries@warren-farm.co.uk w warren-farm.co.uk

payment Credit/debit cards, cash/cheques

Award-winning, family-run holiday centre close to the beach offering a friendly atmosphere, with high standards of cleanliness, modern facilities and excellent value. Spacious, level grass pitches are complemented by indoor and outdoor play facilities, pub, restaurant and nightly entertainment in high season. No pets in caravan holiday homes. Open March to October.

⊕ *M5 south. Jct 22 onto B3140 through Burnham-on-Sea, to Berrow and Brean. 1.5 miles past Brean Leisure Park, on the right.*

General 🖥🅿🚰🚿🚻♨🔌💧🔋🛒✖🔪☀ Leisure 📺🍴🎵♣🎡∪🚣🚲

BRIDGWATER, Somerset Map ref 1D1 | CAMPING & CARAVANNING

★★★
TOURING &
CAMPING PARK

⊡ £9.00–£16.50
⊟ £9.00–£16.50
Å £6.00–£55.00
200 touring pitches

Fairways International Touring Caravan and Camping Park

Bath Road, Bawdrip, Bridgwater TA7 8PP t (01278) 685569 f (01278) 685569
e fairwaysint@btinternet.com w fairwaysint.btinternet.co.uk

payment Credit/debit cards, cash/cheques, euros

International touring park in countryside, two miles off motorway in Glastonbury direction. On-site accessory centre for tents, caravans and motor homes. Storage, store and stay, storage on pitch, seasonals and rallies welcomed. Tents charged on size; caravans and motor homes charged on length. Fishing one mile, seaside six miles. Open 1 March to mid-November.

⊕ From M5 take signs towards Glastonbury/Street. At junction, again head towards Glastonbury/Street. Take left turning to Woolavington, approx 75yds on right. Park is behind garage.

♥ 7 nights for 6. For Senior Citizens only: 7-day booking during Mar, Jun, Sep, Oct 2007/Mar 2008 – £55 per week (with this advert only).

General ▣ P ⊕ ⊙ ☎ 🄍 ☉ ⊞⊟ ≟ ⅙ ☼ Leisure 📺 ⚲ ⚏ ♪

BRIXHAM, Devon Map ref 1D2 | SELF CATERING

★★
SELF CATERING

Units   6
Sleeps   1–5
Low season per wk
£299.00–£300.00
High season per wk
£299.00–£499.00

Devoncourt Holiday Flats, Brixham

contact Mr Robin Hooker, Devoncourt Holiday Flats, Berry Head Road, Brixham TQ5 9AB
t (01803) 853748 e bookings@devoncourt.net w devoncourt.info

open All year
payment Credit/debit cards, cash/cheques, euros

Panoramic sea views from your balcony and lounge over Torbay, Brixham harbour and marina. The beach is opposite, only 50m. Each flat is fully self-contained and carpeted, with colour TV and full cooker. Private gardens. Car park. Children, pets and credit cards welcome. For colour brochure telephone (01803) 853748 or 07050 853748.

⊕ Follow main road from Paignton into Brixham. Follow the Berry Head road, with the sea on your left, until white block of flats on right marked 'Devoncourt'.

♥ 10% discount for Senior Citizens.

Children 🕭 🏛 ⅍ Unit ⊞ 📺 📷 ☎ 🍳 ✿
General P ⊙ ⅙ Leisure ♪ ⚴ Shop 0.5 miles   Pub 0.5 miles

Log on to **enjoyengland.com** to find a break
that matches your mood. experience scenes
that inspire and traditions that baffle.

discover the world's most inventive cultural
entertainment and most stimulating attractions.

explore vibrant cities and rugged peaks.

relax in a country pub or on a sandy beach.

 enjoyEngland.com

BUDE, Cornwall Map ref 1C2 — GUEST ACCOMMODATION

★★★★★
GUEST ACCOMMODATION
SILVER AWARD

Kings Hill Meadow

Bagbury Road, Bude EX23 8SR t (01288) 355004 f (01288) 352494
e kingshillmeadow@btinternet.com w kingshillmeadow.co.uk

B&B per room per night
s £30.00–£50.00
d £50.00–£80.00
Evening meal per person
£9.95–£14.95

open All year
bedrooms 2 double, 3 family
bathrooms All en suite
payment Credit/debit cards, cash/cheques

Luxuriously appointed B&B, set in three acres overlooking Bude nature reserve. All are en suite rooms and equipped to the highest standards. Peaceful location, yet five minutes' walk from Bude town and its beautiful beaches, and ideally located to explore Devon and Cornwall. Ample parking and storage for the sports enthusiast.

⊕ M5, A30, turn for North Cornwall (A395), right B3262, right onto A39 to Bude. Left onto A3073 – 1 mile, left into Bagbury Road, 300m to entrance.

♥ Discounts on stays of 4 or more days (excl Sat). Special price, low-season breaks available – please telephone for details.

Children 🐾 🏛 ♿ ⚑ ⌀ 📷 📱 Room 📺 ♨ 🍷 General P ✄ ✕ 🎱 🎿 🍽 ❄ Leisure ∪ ♪ ♪ 🚴 🚶

CHEDDAR, Somerset Map ref 1D1 — CAMPING & CARAVANNING

★★★★
HOLIDAY, TOURING
& CAMPING PARK
ROSE AWARD

Broadway House Holiday Touring Caravan and Camping Park

Axbridge Road, Cheddar BS27 3DB t (01934) 742610 f (01934) 744950
e info@broadwayhouse.uk.com w broadwayhouse.uk.com

🚐 (100) £13.00–£23.00
🚗 (20)   £10.00–£21.00
▲ (80)   £10.00–£21.00
🏕 (37) £180.00–£600.00
200 touring pitches

payment Credit/debit cards, cash/cheques, euros

Nestling at the foot of the Mendip Hills, this family-run park is only one mile, and the closest of its kind, to England's Grand Canyon: Cheddar Gorge. We have every facility your family could ever want: shop, bar, launderette, swimming pool, BMX track, skateboard park, nature trails, archery, caving and canoeing. Open March to November.

⊕ M5 jct 22. Eight miles. Midway between Cheddar and Axbridge on A371.

General 🖼 P ⟳ 🅱 🍷 🚐 ⟲ ⊙ 📼 🖥 ⚙ ✕ 🗡 🔧 ☼ Leisure ↯ 📺 ♈ ◉ ♬ ∪ ♪ ♪ 🚴

CHELTENHAM, Gloucestershire Map ref 2B1 — GUEST ACCOMMODATION

★★★
INN

Colesbourne Inn

Colesbourne, Cheltenham GL53 9NP t (01242) 870376 e info@thecolesbourneinn.co.uk
w thecolesbourneinn.co.uk

B&B per room per night
s £55.00–£70.00
d £75.00–£90.00
Evening meal per person
£5.00–£25.00

A warm welcome, fabulous food, superb wine (20 by the glass), fine ales, roaring log fires, lovely bedrooms, stunning terrace set in two acres of garden. Midway between Cirencester and Cheltenham … .Heaven!

open All year
bedrooms 6 double, 2 twin, 1 family
bathrooms All en suite
payment Credit/debit cards, cash/cheques, euros

Children 🐾 🏛 ♿ ⚑ ⌀ 📷 Room 🛏 📺 ♨ 🍷 General P ♈ ⚙ ❄ Leisure ♪ ♪ 🚶

COTSWOLDS

See under Birdlip, Cheltenham, Tetbury, Winchcombe

What's in an award

Further information about awards can be found at the front of this guide.

CROYDE BAY, Devon Map ref 1C1   CAMPING & CARAVANNING

★★★★
HOLIDAY, TOURING
& CAMPING PARK
ROSE AWARD

Ruda Holiday Park

Croyde Bay EX33 1NY **t** 0870 420 2997 **f** (0191) 268 5986 **e** enquiries@parkdeanholidays.co.uk
w parkdeanholidays.co.uk

🚐(92)   £13.00–£37.00
🚛(92)   £11.00–£33.00
⛺(220)   £8.00–£29.00
🏠(289)   £179.00–
           £899.00
92 touring pitches

payment Credit/debit cards, cash/cheques

Ruda is a firm favourite with families who return year after year to Croyde Bay's coveted Blue Flag beach, a stunning beach for surfing. You can also enjoy coastal walks with superb views. The excellent facilities include the Cascades Tropical Adventure Pool, mountain boarding and surfing lessons. Open March to November and over Christmas.

⊕ *In the centre of Braunton, turn left after 2nd traffic lights onto B3231. Enter Croyde village and follow signs.*

♥ *Short breaks available.*

General 🔥P🅿️🛗🚻👥📶🖨️🛒✕☼   Leisure 🌳📺🍷🎵🍴🎡🔍🛶🏊‍♂️🚴

DAWLISH, Devon Map ref 1D2   CAMPING & CARAVANNING

Key to symbols

Symbols at the end of each entry help you pick out the services and facilities which are most important for your stay. A key to the symbols can be found inside the back-cover flap. Keep this open for easy reference.

★★★
SMALL HOTEL

B&B per room per night
s £40.00–£65.00
d £60.00–£110.00
HB per person per night
£50.00–£75.00

Yarn Market Hotel (Exmoor)

25 High Street, Dunster, Minehead TA24 6SF   t (01643) 821425   f (01643) 821475
e yarnmarket.hotel@virgin.net   w yarnmarkethotel.co.uk

open All year
bedrooms 10 double, 2 twin, 1 single, 2 family
bathrooms All en suite
payment Credit/debit cards, cash/cheques

Within Exmoor National Park, our hotel is ideal for walking, riding, fishing etc. Family run with a friendly, relaxed atmosphere. All rooms en suite with colour TV etc. Four-poster and Superior rooms available. Totally non-smoking. Home-cooked dishes to cater for all tastes. Group bookings welcomed. Conference facilities. Special Christmas and New Year breaks.

⊕ *From M5 jct 25 follow signs for Exmoor/Minehead A358/A39. Dunster signed approx 0.5 miles from A39 on left. Hotel in centre of village beside Yarn Market.*

♥ *Discounted rates for longer stays and mid-week bookings. Ring for newsletter with information on special events.*

Children 🕭 🎠 ♿ CH 💷   Room ☎ TV 👜 🍵 🔥   General ✂ 🍴 ☕ ♨ ● 🐴   Leisure ∪ ⌨ ► 🚲 🏛

★★★★
SELF CATERING

Units   **12**
Sleeps **2–12**

Low season per wk
£220.00–£1,100.00
High season per wk
£420.00–£2,010.00

Duddings Country Cottages, Minehead

contact Mr Richard Tilke, Duddings Country Holidays, Timberscombe, Minehead TA24 7TB
t (01643) 841123   f (01643) 841165   e richard@duddings.co.uk   w duddings.co.uk

open All year
payment Cash/cheques

Thatched longhouse and eleven cottages, tastefully converted from old stone barns on small country estate in stunning location in Exmoor National Park. Heated indoor pool, tennis court, putting green, pool, table tennis, football net, trampoline, swings and slide. Families and pets welcome. Attentive resident owners.

⊕ *From Dunster, take the A396 (signposted Tiverton). Duddings is on the right just before Timberscombe (approx 2 miles).*

♥ *Short breaks available (excl main school holidays).*

Children 🕭 🎠 ♿ ⚠   Unit 🛏 TV 📼 🍴 ⬛ 📷 🔥 🔌 🍳 ❄
General P S 🐴   Leisure 🎣 🏊 🎾 ∪ ⌨ ► 🚲   Shop 2 miles   Pub 0.5 miles

---

★★★★
SELF CATERING

Units   **1**
Sleeps **6–8**

Low season per wk
£275.00–£495.00
High season per wk
£545.00–£750.00

Brook Cottage, Budleigh Salterton

contact Mrs Jo Simons, Foxcote, Noverton Lane, Prestbury, Cheltenham GL52 5BB
t (01242) 574031   e josimons@tesco.net   w brookcottagebudleigh.co.uk

open All year
payment Cash/cheques

Spacious thatched cottage. Two showers and bathroom. Beaches, walking, golf, karting, bird-watching, riding nearby – but the cottage is so comfortable it's a pleasure to be indoors. Two living rooms with TVs, one for the adults, and a snug, with sofa bed, for the children! Visit our website for more photos.

⊕ *From A376 take B3179 signed for Woodbury and Budleigh Salterton; proceed through Woodbury and Yettington; right after Bicton gates and again on entering East Budleigh.*

♥ *Reduced-rate winter breaks for 3-night stays with or without linen (excl Christmas and New Year).*

Children 🕭 🎠 ♿ ⚠   Unit 🛏 TV 📼 🍴 ⬛ 📷 🔥 🔌 🍳 ❄
General P ✂ S 🐴   Leisure ∪ ⌨ ► 🏛   Shop 1 mile   Pub < 0.5 miles

EAST LOOE, Cornwall Map ref 1C3 — SELF CATERING

★★★–★★★★★
SELF CATERING

Units **11**
Sleeps **2–6**

Low season per wk
£175.00–£330.00
High season per wk
£600.00–£1,470.00

Fox Valley Cottages, Looe

contact Mr & Mrs Andy & Linda Brown, Lanlawren, Trenewan, Looe PL13 2PZ
t (01726) 870115 **e** lanlawren@lycos.com **w** foxvalleycottages.co.uk

open All year
payment Credit/debit cards, cash/cheques

The cottages are set in beautiful countryside – an idyllic location for your holiday in Cornwall. Indoor heated pool, spa, sauna, solarium, games room. Open fires in most of the cottages for those cosy or romantic nights in winter. Dishwashers in large cottages.

⊕ Three miles west of Polperro. Map sent with directions.

♥ Out-of-season short breaks (mid-week or long weekends).

Children 🖙 🏠 🧍🍴🗕 🛝 Unit 🛏 📺 🗄 🖂 🗌 🖲 🗎 🗯 ✿
General P 🖸 S 🐾 Leisure ⚓ 🏊 ♨ ∪ 🎣 Shop 3 miles Pub 3 miles

EXMOOR

See under Dunster

EYPE, Dorset Map ref 1D2 — HOTEL

★★
COUNTRY HOUSE HOTEL

B&B per room per night
s £50.00–£70.00
d £82.00–£100.00
HB per person per night
£55.00–£80.00

Eype's Mouth Country Hotel

Eype, Bridport DT6 6AL **t** (01308) 423300 **f** (01308) 420033 **e** info@eypesmouthhotel.co.uk
w eypesmouthhotel.co.uk

open All year
bedrooms 12 double, 3 twin, 2 single, 1 family
bathrooms All en suite
payment Credit/debit cards, cash/cheques, euros

Set in the picturesque small village of Eype, the hotel nestles amidst the downland and cliff tops that form the Heritage Coastline. Stunning sea views in a peaceful setting are matched by excellent hospitality. Good food and drink, served in the comfortable surroundings of this family-run hotel, make the perfect venue for a relaxing break.

⊕ A35, Bridport bypass, take turning to Eype, also signed to service area, then 3rd right to beach. Hotel 0.5 miles down lane.

♥ Special DB&B 3-night breaks available throughout the year.

Children 🖙 🏠 🧍🐾 ✐ 🖾 Room 📞 📺 🍵 General P 🍷 🍽 🄼 ✿ 🐾 Leisure 🎣 ►

GLASTONBURY, Somerset Map ref 2A2 — SELF CATERING

★★★★
SELF CATERING

Units **8**
Sleeps **2–6**

Low season per wk
£205.00–£300.00
High season per wk
£430.00–£770.00

MapleLeaf Middlewick Holiday Cottages, Glastonbury

Middlewick Holiday Cottages, Wick Lane, Glastonbury BA6 8JW
t (01458) 832351 **f** (01458) 832351 **e** middlewick@btconnect.com
w middlewickholidaycottages.co.uk

open All year
payment Credit/debit cards, cash/cheques

The cottages within this Grade II Listed farmstead have been restored to provide comfortable, well-equipped accommodation. Walk to Glastonbury Tor from the back door, and after a day of exercising, sight-seeing or just communing, relax in the heated indoor swimming pool. WI-FI Internet access.

⊕ Wick Lane runs between A361 and A39. From A39 we are 1 mile on your right. From A361 1.5 miles on your left.

♥ Online booking for last-minute discounts for weekly or short breaks. Optional breakfasts available in the Meadow Barn dining room.

Children 🖙 🏠 🧍🗕 Unit 🛏 📺 🖭 🗌 🖂 🗌 🖳 🗂 🗎 🗯 ✿
General 🖸 S Leisure ⚓ ∪ 🎣 Shop 2 miles Pub 3 miles

HELSTON, Cornwall Map ref 1B3 — SELF CATERING

★★★
SELF CATERING

Units **3**
Sleeps **1–6**

Low season per wk
£150.00–£250.00
High season per wk
£250.00–£425.00

Mudgeon Vean Farm Holiday Cottages, Helston

contact Mr & Mrs Trewhella, Mudgeon Vean Farm Holiday Cottages, St Martin, Helston TR12 6DB
t (01326) 231341 **f** (01326) 231341 **e** mudgeonvean@aol.com
w cornwall-online.co.uk/mudgeon-vean/ctb.htm

open All year
payment Cash/cheques

Cosy cottages on small 18thC farm producing apple juice and cider, near Helford River. Equipped to high standard and personally supervised. Night storage heaters and log fires. National Trust walk to the river, outdoor play area for children, games room. Peaceful location in an Area of Outstanding Natural Beauty.

⊕ A3083 Helston, B3293 Mawgan village. Through Mawgan to St Martins Green. Left at St Martins Green, to next crossroads. Turn left. We are 2nd turning on right down lane.

Children 🐕 🏊 🎠 👶 🅰 Unit 📺 🖥 🍴 💻 🔌 🗄 🔥 🗑 🎮 ✳
General P Ⓢ 🎣 Leisure ♦ U ♪ ⛵ Shop 1 mile Pub 2 miles

HELSTON, Cornwall Map ref 1B3 — SELF CATERING

★★★★
SELF CATERING

Units **1**
Sleeps **9**

Low season per wk
Min £878.00
High season per wk
Max £2,117.00

Tregoose Farmhouse, Helston

contact Mrs Hazel Bergin, Tregoose Farmhouse, The Downes, Foundry Hill, Hayle TR27 4HW
t (01736) 751749 **e** arcj88@dsl.pipex.com **w** tregooselet.co.uk

open All year
payment Cash/cheques

A spacious and luxuriously renovated farmhouse in a peaceful, rural setting. Indoor swimming pool, games room, ground-floor bedroom and wet room, far-reaching views. Conveniently positioned for touring South and West Cornwall's coastline, gardens and attractions.

⊕ From A394 (Helston to Penzance), turn right onto B3302. Take 2nd right signposted Gwavas/Lowertown. Left at crossroad. 30yds turn right. Top of hill on left.

Children 🐕 🏊 🎠 👶 Unit 🏊 📺 🖥 🍴 💻 🔌 🗄 🔥 🗑 🎮 📷 ✳
General P ♿ 🎣 Leisure 🎣 ♦ ♪ ⛵ Shop 1 mile Pub 2 miles

HELSTON, Cornwall Map ref 1B3 — CAMPING & CARAVANNING

★★★★
HOLIDAY PARK
ROSE AWARD

🚐 (132)   £159.00–
          £779.00

Sea Acres Holiday Park

Kennack Sands, Nr Helston TR12 7LT **t** 0870 420 2997 **f** (0191) 268 5986
e enquiries@parkdeanholidays.co.uk **w** parkdeanholidays.co.uk

payment Credit/debit cards, cash/cheques

From the park's cliff-top position you can savour the stunning sea views over Kennack Sands. Explore the dramatic coastline of The Lizard; there's even a PADI diving centre on site! Other facilities include an indoor pool and kids' clubs. Enjoy light evening entertainment in the Family Club House. Open March to October.

⊕ Take the A3083 from Helston, then the B3293 to Coverack, turn right at crossroads signed Kennack Sands, site on right overlooking beach.

♥ Short breaks available.

General P 🛏 🔥 🛒 ✕ 🐕 Leisure 🎣 📺 🍴 🎵 ♦ 🎢 🏇 🚴

To your credit

If you book by credit card it's advisable to check the proprietor's policy in case you have to cancel.

HURN, Dorset Map ref 2B3 | GUEST ACCOMMODATION

★★★★
INN

B&B per room per night
s £50.00–£55.00
d £60.00–£90.00
Evening meal per person
£5.95–£60.00

Avon Causeway Inn

Hurn, Christchurch BH23 6AS **t** (01202) 482714 **f** (01202) 477416
e avoncauseway@wadworth.co.uk **w** avoncauseway.co.uk

The inn has been developed on the site of Hurn train station which was part of the 1870s' Bournemouth to Ringwood railway. Close to Bournemouth Airport.

open All year
bedrooms 10 double, 1 single, 1 family
bathrooms All en suite
payment Credit/debit cards, cash/cheques

Children 🏖 🏨 🔥 🛗 ✐ 🖥 Room 📺 👜 🗜 General P 🍴 🍽 ✕ ✳ Leisure ◢ ►

KINGSBRIDGE, Devon Map ref 1C3 | CAMPING & CARAVANNING

★★★★
HOLIDAY PARK
ROSE AWARD

🏕 (64) £179.00–£779.00

Challaborough Bay Holiday Park

Challaborough Beach, Nr Bigbury-on-Sea TQ7 4HU **t** 0870 420 2997 **f** (0191) 268 5986
e enquiries@parkdeanholidays.co.uk **w** parkdeanholidays.co.uk

payment Credit/debit cards, cash/cheques

An intimate park, nestling in a quiet, sheltered bay on South Devon's Heritage Coast. Located in an Area of Outstanding Natural Beauty, take time to explore the scenery and coastal walks. Excellent leisure facilities, including an indoor pool, gym, sauna and solarium, ensure your stay will be totally relaxing. Open March to October.

General 🔥 P 📷 📺 🐾 ✕ 🐕 Leisure ≋ 🍽 🎵 🍸 ∪ ◢ ►

LAUNCESTON, Cornwall Map ref 1C2 | SELF CATERING

★★★★
SELF CATERING

Units **8**
Sleeps **2–8**
Low season per wk
£210.00–£320.00
High season per wk
£535.00–£1,185.00

Bamham Farm Cottages, Launceston

contact Mrs Jackie Chapman, Bamham Farm Cottages, Higher Bamham Farm, Launceston PL15 9LD
t (01566) 772141 **f** (01566) 775266 **e** jackie@bamhamfarm.co.uk **w** bamhamfarm.co.uk

open All year
payment Credit/debit cards, cash/cheques

Individually designed cottages, ideally situated in beautiful countryside one mile from Launceston, the ancient capital of Cornwall, dominated by its Norman castle. The north and south coasts are easily accessible as are both Dartmoor and Bodmin Moor. Facilities include a heated indoor swimming pool, sauna, solarium, video recorders and trout fishing.

✦ *Leave A30 at Launceston. Farm situated on the Polson Road just 1 mile from the town.*

❤ *For special offers see our website.*

Children 🏖 🏨 🔥 🗝 🔥 Unit 🛏 📺 📻 📺 🍽 🗄 🍽 🖥 ✳
General P ◎ Ⓢ Leisure ≋ 🍸 ∪ ◢ ► Shop 1 mile Pub 1 mile

LOOE, Cornwall Map ref 1C3 | SELF CATERING

★★★★
SELF CATERING

Units **6**
Sleeps **2–5**
Low season per wk
£175.00–£350.00
High season per wk
£350.00–£595.00

Summercourt Coastal Cottages, Looe

contact Mr Hocking, Summercourt Coastal Cottages, Bodigga Cliff, St Martin PL13 1NZ
t (01503) 263149 **e** sccottages@freenet.co.uk **w** holidaycottagescornwall.tv

Stone barns converted to comfortable and well-equipped cottages in a rural Area of Outstanding Natural Beauty. Close to sea and beaches.

open All year
payment Credit/debit cards, cash/cheques

Children 🏖 🏨 🔥 🗝 🔥 Unit 🛏 📺 📺 📻 📺 🍽 🗄 🖥 ✳
General P ◎ Ⓢ 🐕 Leisure ∪ ◢ ► Shop 2 miles Pub 2 miles

LOSTWITHIEL, Cornwall Map ref 1B2 — SELF CATERING

★★★–★★★★★
SELF CATERING

Units **8**
Sleeps **1–6**

Low season per wk
Min £200.00
High season per wk
Max £855.00

Lanwithan Cottages, Lostwithiel

contact Mr V B Edward-Collins, Lanwithan Cottages, Lerryn Road, Lostwithiel PL22 0LA
t (01208) 872444 **f** (01208) 872444 **e** lanwithan@btconnect.com **w** lanwithancottages.co.uk

open All year
payment Cash/cheques, euros

Charming selection of Georgian estate cottages nestling in the Fowey Valley with two delightful waterside properties. Cottages with leaded-light windows, crackling log fires, four-poster bed and glass-topped well. Parkland, river frontage and boat. Woodland and riverside walks from your garden gate. Come and relax and soak up the Cornish atmosphere.

⊕ Liskeard to Lostwithiel on A390, pass National garage on left. 1st left, Great Western units, and 1st left again. Sign after 300yds – follow to house, not farm.

♥ Short breaks out of season. Reduced green fees. Pets accepted in some cottages. Canoe trips available with safety boat.

Children 🛍 🏚 🛖 🖼 ⚠ Unit 🛏 📺 📻 🖥 🍽 ☕ ⛊ 🔌 🔊 🧺 ✿
General **P** ⓟ 🐾 Leisure 🔍 ⚲ U ♂ ▶ 🚲 ⛵ Shop 0.5 miles Pub 0.5 miles

MENHENIOT, Cornwall Map ref 1C2 — SELF CATERING

Units **3**
Sleeps **1–5**

Low season per wk
£150.00–£275.00
High season per wk
£400.00–£600.00

Trewint Farm, Liskeard

contact Mrs Rowe, Trewint Farm, Menheniot, Liskeard PL14 3RE
t (01579) 347155 **f** (01579) 347155 **e** holidays@trewintfarm.co.uk **w** trewintfarm.co.uk

Recently converted cottages with all the extras to make your holiday special. Cornish cream tea on arrival. Children can enjoy the games room, play area and pet corner. Ideal for exploring Looe and Polperro.

open All year
payment Credit/debit cards, cash/cheques

Children 🛍 🏚 🛖 🖼 ⚠ Unit 🛏 📺 📻 🖥 🍽 ☕ ⛊ 🔊 🧺 ✿
General **P** ⓟ Leisure 🔍 U ♂ 🚲 Shop 1 mile Pub 1 mile

MILVERTON, Somerset Map ref 1D1 — SELF CATERING

★★★★★
SELF CATERING

Units **1**
Sleeps **14**

Low season per wk
Min £1,243.00
High season per wk
Max £2,779.00

Wellisford Manor Barn, Wellisford

contact Ms Sarah Campos, Wellisford Manor Barn, Wellington TA21 0SB
t (01823) 672794 **f** (01823) 673229 **e** sjcampos.martyn@btinternet.com **w** wellisfordmanorbarn.com

Luxury, contemporary, converted barn/coach house set around private landscaped garden with hot tub and barbecue. Three bathrooms (two en suite), media room with four-foot plasma screen, kitchen and utility room. All bedrooms have real linen bed linen and plasma TVs.

open All year
payment Cash/cheques, euros

Children 🛍 🏚 🛖 🖼 ⚠ Unit 🛏 📺 📻 🖥 🍽 🎱 ☕ ⛊ 🔊 🧺 🖥 🍴 // ✿
General **P** ✂ ⓟ Ⓢ 🐾 Leisure 🔍 U ♂ ▶ 🚲 ⛵ Shop 6 miles Pub 1 mile

Friendly help and advice

Did you know there are more than 500 tourist information centres throughout England? It adds up to a lot of friendly help and advice. You'll find contact details at the beginning of each regional section.

★★★★
SELF CATERING

Units **4**
Sleeps **2–6**

Low season per wk
£300.00–£495.00
High season per wk
£795.00–£1,185.00

Cornwall Coast Holidays, Newquay

contact Mrs Deborah Spencer-Smith, Cornwall Coast Holidays
t (020) 8440 7518 & 07910 583050 **e** debbie@cornwallcoastholidays.com
w cornwallcoastholidays.com

open All year
payment Cash/cheques

Cornwall Coast Holidays offer apartments and cottages that are in the perfect location for wonderful beach holidays. The cottages are modern, and the apartments have stunning sea views. Both apartments and cottages have one en suite bathroom and are close to the town centre, golf course and other amenities.

Children 🛏 🎋 🛏 🚪   Unit 🛏 📺 🖥 🖥 🗄 🎛 🍴 🔌   General P ⚒

★★★★
HOLIDAY PARK
ROSE AWARD

⛺ (142)   £159.00–
£799.00

Crantock Beach Holiday Park

Crantock, Newquay TR8 5RH **t** 0870 420 2997 **f** (0191) 268 5986
e enquiries@parkdeanholidays.co.uk **w** parkdeanholidays.co.uk

payment Credit/debit cards, cash/cheques

Resting just outside the charming village of Crantock, this tranquil park is the perfect location to get away from it all. The park overlooks secluded Crantock beach, with its rock pools and hidden caves, and is a great base for exploring. Enjoy light evening entertainment in the Wavecrest Pub. Open March to October.

⊕ *A30 to Newquay, then the A392. A3075 to Redruth, then take right turn to Crantock beach.*

♥ *Short breaks available.*

General P 🏠 🗄 🐕   Leisure 📺 🍴 🎵 🔍

★★★★
HOLIDAY PARK
ROSE AWARD

🚐 (244) £10.00–£28.00
🚙 (244) £10.00–£28.00
⛺ (244) £7.00–£25.00
⛺ (162) £149.00–
£689.00

244 touring pitches

Holywell Bay Holiday Park

Holywell Bay, Newquay TR8 5PR **t** 0870 420 2997 **f** (0191) 268 5986
e enquiries@parkdeanholidays.co.uk **w** parkdeanholidays.co.uk

payment Credit/debit cards, cash/cheques

Nestling in the Ellenglaze Valley, this park is small, friendly and simply perfect for beach lovers, being a short stroll from the stunning beach of Holywell Bay. The excellent facilities include heated outdoor pools with waterslide, kids' clubs and evening entertainment. Newquay is just a few miles away. Open March to October.

⊕ *Turn right off the A3075, signposted Holywell Bay, 3 miles west of Newquay.*

♥ *Short breaks available.*

General 🛡 🗄 P 🚐 🚿 👤 🏠 🗄 🗄   Leisure 🎣 📺 🍴 🎵 🔍 ⛰ 🏌

Using map references

Map references refer to the colour maps at the front of this guide.

NEWQUAY, Cornwall Map ref 1B2 — CAMPING & CARAVANNING

★★★★
HOLIDAY PARK
ROSE AWARD

🚐 (60) £12.00–£30.00
🚍 (60) £10.00–£28.00
⛺ (60) £7.00–£25.00
🏕 (104) £159.00–£749.00
60 touring pitches

Newquay Holiday Park

Newquay TR8 4HS t 0870 420 2997 f (0191) 268 5986 e enquiries@parkdeanholidays.co.uk
w parkdeanholidays.co.uk

payment Credit/debit cards, cash/cheques

A spacious park surrounded by luscious rolling countryside, Newquay Holiday Park is ideal for all the family! There's so much to do! Three heated outdoor pools, a giant waterslide, amusements and children's playground keep the kids happy, whilst the bar and entertainment complex are great for some evening family fun. Open March to October.

⊕ Follow A30 Bodmin to Redruth road, after iron bridge turn right signed RAF St Mawgan. 2nd exit off roundabout signposted Newquay A3059. Right at bottom of hill.

♥ Short breaks available.

General P 🔌 🚼 🏨 🛏 📶 📷 🛒 ✕ 🐕   Leisure ⌇ 📺 🍺 🎵 🔍 ⚙ ⚑

PANCRASWEEK, Devon Map ref 1C2 — SELF CATERING

★★★
SELF CATERING

Units **1**
Sleeps **7**
Low season per wk
Min £265.00
High season per wk
Max £560.00

Tamarstone Farm, Holsworthy

contact Mrs Megan Daglish, Tamarstone Farm, Bude Road, Pancrasweek, Holsworthy EX22 7JT
t (01288) 381734 e cottage@tamarstone.co.uk w tamarstone.co.uk

Tastefully extended, centrally heated, three-bedroomed cob cottage. Peacefully situated on the Devon/Cornwall borders, ideal for touring both counties. One double, one twin, one with bunks and a single.

open All year
payment Cash/cheques

Children 🐕 🛏 🎎 🎏   Unit 🔆 📺 📻 🍴 💻 🍽 🛢 🔥 🍳   General P Ⓢ 🐕   Leisure 🎣 🚶 🚲   Shop 1.25 miles Pub 1.25 miles

POLPERRO, Cornwall Map ref 1C3 — GUEST ACCOMMODATION

♦♦♦
GUEST ACCOMMODATION

B&B per room per night
s £40.00–£45.00
d £60.00–£70.00
Evening meal per person
£6.00–£12.00

Crumplehorn Inn and Mill

Crumplehorn, Polperro, Looe PL13 2RJ t (01503) 272348 f (01503) 273148
e host@crumplehorn-inn.co.uk w crumplehorn-inn.co.uk

open All year
bedrooms 6 double, 3 twin, 2 family, 8 suites
bathrooms All en suite
payment Credit/debit cards, cash/cheques

14thC character Cornish inn and mill in quaint, historic fishing village. B&B and self-catering available. En suite, non-smoking rooms with TV, telephone, clock radio and tea and coffee. Local ales and scrumpy. Varied bar menu with daily specials featuring locally caught fish. Pets welcome. Car parking on site.

⊕ Full directions (via car, train and taxi) available on our website.

♥ Winter-break scheme in operation.

Children 🐕 🛏 🎎 ✐ 📺   Room 🛏 ☎ 📺 ♨ 🍵   General P 🍺 🎰 ✿ 🐕   Leisure ∪ 🎣

Check the maps

Colour maps at the front pinpoint all the places you will find accommodation entries in the regional sections. Pick your location and then refer to the place index at the back to find the page number.

POOLE, Dorset Map ref 2B3 — **HOTEL**

★★★★
**HOTEL
SILVER AWARD**

B&B per room per night
s £66.00–£122.00
d £132.00–£244.00
HB per person per night
£75.00–£133.00

The Sandbanks Hotel

Banks Road, Poole BH13 7PS **t** (01202) 707377 **f** (01202) 708885
e reservations@sandbankshotel.co.uk **w** fjbhotels.co.uk

open All year
bedrooms 41 double, 29 twin, 25 single, 14 family
bathrooms All en suite
payment Credit/debit cards, cash/cheques

Set on the Sandbanks peninsula with direct access to the superb Blue Flag beach. Stunning views across Poole Bay and yacht harbour. Most rooms have sea or harbour view and balcony. Extensive range of leisure facilities, children's entertainers and restaurant available in high season and school holidays.

⊕ From the M27 take A31 to Ringwood, at the Ashley Heath roundabout take A338 for 11 miles to Liverpool Victoria roundabout then follow signs for Sandbanks Ferry.

♥ Contact us for details of our current special promotions and offers.

Children 🛝 🎠 🛋 🎁 🐾 🚣 ⚲ ✐ 🖥 🎬   Room 🛏 🌙 📺 👜 ✎   General P 🍽 🏧 🛗 🈂 ⚘   Leisure ⚘ ∪ ▶ 🚲

PORTREATH, Cornwall Map ref 1B3 — **CAMPING & CARAVANNING**

★★★★
**HOLIDAY, TOURING
& CAMPING PARK**

🚐 (18)   £8.00–£12.00
🚍 (3)   £8.00–£12.00
▲ (18)   £8.00–£12.00
🏠 (20) £115.00–£455.00

Tehidy Holiday Park

Harris Mill, Illogan, Redruth TR16 4JQ **t** (01209) 216489 **e** holiday@tehidy.co.uk **w** tehidy.co.uk

payment Credit/debit cards, cash/cheques

Come and visit our beautifully landscaped, family-run park set in a peaceful wooded valley. Ideally situated to explore north and south coastlines. Accommodation includes static caravans and bungalows – two wheelchair friendly. Tents and tourers welcome. Facilities include new ablution block, play area, launderette, games room and licensed shop. Open April to October.

⊕ Off A30 at Redruth, turn right to Porthtowan. After 300 yds turn left onto B3300 (Portreath). Straight over at crossroads. Uphill, past Cornish Arms. Site is 500 yds on left.

General 🔌 P 🔌 🖐 🏠 🍴 ⊙ 🅿 🔳 🛒   Leisure 📺 ❀ /◺

RUAN HIGH LANES, Cornwall Map ref 1B3 — **GUEST ACCOMMODATION**

◆◆◆
GUEST ACCOMMODATION

B&B per room per night
s £26.00–£38.00
d £52.00–£56.00

Trenona Farm Holidays

Ruan High Lanes, Truro TR2 5JS **t** (01872) 501339 **f** (01872) 501253
e info@trenonafarmholidays.co.uk **w** trenonafarmholidays.co.uk

bedrooms 1 double, 3 family
bathrooms 3 en suite, 1 private
payment Credit/debit cards, cash/cheques

Enjoy a warm welcome in our Victorian farmhouse on a working farm on the beautiful Roseland Peninsula. Our guest bedrooms have en suite or private bathrooms, and we welcome children and pets. Public footpaths lead to Veryan and the south coast (three miles). Open between March and November.

⊕ A390 to Truro. At Hewaswater take B3287 to Tregony then A3078 to St Mawes at Tregony Bridge. After 2 miles, pass Esso garage. 2nd farm on left-hand side.

♥ Discounts for stays of 4 or more nights for children and for family rooms.

Children 🛝 🎠 🛋 🎁 ✐   Room 📺 👜 ✎   General P 🍴 🈂 ⚘ 🐾   Leisure ∪

ST AUSTELL, Cornwall Map ref 1B3   **CAMPING & CARAVANNING**

Trewhiddle Village

🚐 (105)   £5.50–£20.00
🚍 (105)   £5.50–£20.00
⛺ (105)   £5.50–£20.00
🚲 (40) £149.00–£600.00
105 touring pitches

Pentewan Road, St Austell PL26 7AD   **t** (01726) 879420   **f** (01726) 879421
e holidays@trewhiddle.co.uk   **w** trewhiddle.co.uk

open All year
payment Credit/debit cards, cash/cheques

Under new management! A great family park superbly situated for beaches, the Eden project, Lost Gardens of Heligan and for touring Cornwall. A fantastic escape for a peaceful and relaxing holiday.

⊕ From the A390 turn south on B3273 to Mevagissey, site 0.75 miles from the roundabout on the right-hand side.

General 🔌🖥️🏕️P🔌🚿♨️🍴🗑️🐾😊🍳🍽️🏪❌🐎♿🔆   Leisure ⚡🍽️🎯⚓🎡⛵🚶🏌️🚴

ST IVES, Cornwall Map ref 1B3   **SELF CATERING**

★★★★
SELF CATERING

Units   **1**
Sleeps   **10**
Low season per wk
£595.00–£895.00
High season per wk
£995.00–£1,995.00

Accommodation Orla-Mo, St Ives

PO Box 6704, Poole BH4 0BW
t 0845 644 2833   **f** 0871 277 2773   **e** info@surfives.co.uk   **w** surfives.co.uk

Stunning, luxuriously refurbished captain's house, centrally located, with breathtaking harbour/bay views. Three king-size beds, two twin beds, three en suites, bathroom, designer kitchen, parking. Spacious and well equipped. WI-FI Internet access (2Mb).

open All year
payment Cash/cheques, euros

Children 👶🖥️🚸🏠🎡   Unit 🏠📺🍳🗑️🧺🖥️🍽️🔌🛁🍳🚰🍴❄️
General P✂️Ⓢ   Leisure ⚓⛵🚶🚴   Shop < 0.5 miles   Pub < 0.5 miles

ST IVES, Cornwall Map ref 1B3   **SELF CATERING**

★★★★
SELF CATERING

Units   **4**
Sleeps   **2–6**
Low season per wk
£195.00–£370.00
High season per wk
£230.00–£600.00

Trevalgan Holiday Farm, St Ives

contact Mrs Melanie Osborne, Trevalgan Holiday Farm, Trevalgan, St Ives TR26 3BJ
t (01736) 796529   **f** (01736) 796529   **e** holidays@trevalgan.co.uk   **w** trevalgan.co.uk

open All year
payment Cash/cheques

Set in an idyllic location, this working farm combines first-class accommodation and breathtaking scenery with a friendly atmosphere. Attention to detail means the cottages are decorated, furnished and equipped to a very high standard. The farm trail joins the South West Coast Path, and the A30 is close, making it easy to explore.

⊕ Leave A30 for St Ives. Follow day visitors' route for B3311. At 2nd T-junction turn left onto B3306 – follow signs for Trevalgan Holiday Farm.

♥ Short breaks available Oct-Apr. Special packages for families with pre-school children.

Children 👶🖥️🚸🏠🎡   Unit 🏠📺🍳🍽️🔌🚰❄️
General P🅿️🐾   Leisure ⚓⚓⛵🚴   Shop 1.5 miles   Pub 1.5 miles

Check it out

Information on accommodation listed in this guide has been supplied by proprietors. As changes may occur you should remember to check all relevant details at the time of booking.

ST MINVER, Cornwall Map ref 1B2 — CAMPING & CARAVANNING

★★★★
HOLIDAY, TOURING
& CAMPING PARK
ROSE AWARD

(87) £159.00–£999.00

St Minver Holiday Park

St Minver, Wadebridge PL27 6RR t 0870 420 2997 f (01208) 268 5986
e enquiries@parkdeanholidays.co.uk w parkdeanholidays.co.uk

payment Credit/debit cards, cash/cheques

A delightful woodland park nestled in the grounds of an old manor-house, St Minver provides a base for exploring the pretty fishing harbours of Padstow and Port Isaac, or the famous beaches of Rock and Polzeath. Facilities include an indoor heated pool, kids' clubs and evening family entertainment. Open March to October.

⊕ Head for Port Isaac on the B3314. After 3.5 miles turn left towards Rock. The park is 250yds along on the right-hand side.

♥ Short breaks available.

General ⛴ P 🗐 🖥 🖳 ✕ 🐕 Leisure 📶 📺 🍷 🎵 🔥 ⚒

SIDMOUTH, Devon Map ref 1D2 — SELF CATERING

★★★★
SELF CATERING

Units   5
Sleeps   2–4
Low season per wk
£174.00–£216.00
High season per wk
£243.00–£544.00

Leigh Farm, Sidmouth

contact Mr & Mrs Geoff & Gill Davis, Leigh Farm, Weston, Sidmouth EX10 0PH
t (01395) 516065 f (01395) 579582 e leigh.farm@virgin.net w streets-ahead.com/leighfarm

open All year except Christmas and New Year
payment Credit/debit cards

We are 150yds from a National Trust valley which leads to the South West Coast Path and Weston beach. Excellent walking and touring area. Our bungalows face south onto a lawn, and each has a patio table and chairs for your use. The perfect location for an interesting and relaxing holiday.

⊕ M5 jct 30, join A3052. At Sidford straight on then right at top of hill, signposted Weston. Follow signs to hamlet, 1st property on right.

Children 👶 🛏 ♿ ⚒ Unit 🖳 📺 🖥 💻 🍵 🖨 🗄❄
General P ✂ 🖨 🐕 Leisure 🔾 ♪ ▶ ♿ Shop 1.5 miles Pub 1.5 miles

SWANAGE, Dorset Map ref 2B3 — CAMPING & CARAVANNING

★★★★
HOLIDAY, TOURING
& CAMPING PARK

🚐   £16.00–£36.00
🏕   £16.00–£36.00
⛺   £16.00–£36.00
🚐 (140)   £330.00–£600.00
77 touring pitches

Ulwell Cottage Caravan Park

Ulwell, Swanage BH19 3DG t (01929) 422823 f (01929) 421500 e enq@ulwellcottagepark.co.uk
w ulwellcottagepark.co.uk

payment Credit/debit cards, cash/cheques

Quiet site in picturesque setting adjoining Purbeck Hills. One and a half miles from Swanage and two miles from Studland, the entrance is on the Swanage to Studland road. Open 1 March – 7 January.

General 🖾 🚐 P 🖭 🛱 🍵 🗐 📞 ⊙ 🗐 🖳 ✕ 🐕 ☼ Leisure 📶 🍷 ⚒ 🔾 ♪ ▶ ♿

What's in a quality rating?

Information about ratings can be found at the back of this guide.

TETBURY, Gloucestershire Map ref 2B2 — HOTEL

★★★★
COUNTRY HOUSE HOTEL
GOLD AWARD

Calcot Manor Hotel & Spa

Calcot, Tetbury GL8 8YJ t (01666) 890391 f (01666) 890394 e reception@calcotmanor.co.uk
w calcotmanor.co.uk

B&B per room per night
s £170.00–£195.00
d £195.00–£370.00
HB per person per night
£120.00–£230.00

A charming English farmhouse, elegantly converted into a stylish hotel. Beautifully furnished bedrooms, a choice of two restaurants and a luxurious spa, including outdoor hot tub and beauty-treatment rooms.

open All year
bedrooms 5 double, 18 twin, 10 family, 1 suite
bathrooms All en suite
payment Credit/debit cards, cash/cheques

Children ⬚⬚⬚⬚⬚⬚⬚ ⬚⬚⬚ Room ⬚⬚⬚⬚⬚⬚ General ⬚⬚⬚⬚
Leisure ⬚⬚⬚⬚⬚⬚⬚

THREE LEGGED CROSS, Dorset Map ref 2B3 — SELF CATERING

★★★★
SELF CATERING

Units 1
Sleeps 4–5
Low season per wk
£280.00–£480.00
High season per wk
£400.00–£690.00

Foresters, Nr Ringwood

contact Mrs Jean Baylis, Cottage Farm, Verwood Road, Three Legged Cross BH21 6RN
t (01202) 820203 e cottagefarm@sagainternet.co.uk

Detached, ground-level cottage on farm. Gas central heating, double/twin bedrooms, both en suite, linen and towels included, washer/dryer, DVD, video, CD, radio, TV. Close to sea and New Forest. Dogs and horses by arrangement.

open All year
payment Cash/cheques, euros

Children ⬚⬚⬚⬚⬚⬚ Unit ⬚⬚⬚⬚⬚⬚⬚⬚⬚⬚⬚
General ⬚⬚⬚⬚ Leisure ⬚⬚⬚⬚⬚ Shop 0.5 miles Pub 0.5 miles

TORQUAY, Devon Map ref 1D2 — CAMPING & CARAVANNING

★★★★
HOLIDAY PARK
⬚ (221)   £169.00–
              £759.00

Torquay Holiday Park

Kingskerswell Road, Torquay TQ2 8JU t 0870 420 2997 f (0191) 268 5986
e enquiries@parkdeanholidays.co.uk w parkdeanholidays.co.uk

payment Credit/debit cards, cash/cheques

A great park which enjoys a countryside hillside setting just minutes from Torquay. As well as being a great base for exploring South Devon and the English Riviera, the park offers fantastic facilities, a range of accommodation, an indoor pool, kids' clubs, family entertainment and much more! Open March to November.

⊕ Take A380 towards Torquay, continue to A3022. Turn left at Currys. At roundabout, turn left onto Barton Road. Continue up hill and turn left.

♥ Short breaks available.

General ⬚⬚⬚⬚⬚ Leisure ⬚⬚⬚⬚⬚⬚

VERYAN, Cornwall Map ref 1B3 | SELF CATERING

★★★★
SELF CATERING

Units **2**
Sleeps **6**

Low season per wk
£240.00–£470.00
High season per wk
£470.00–£760.00

Trenona Farm Holidays, Veryan

contact Mrs Pamela Carbis, Trenona Farm, Ruan High Lanes, Truro TR2 5JS
t (01872) 501339 **f** (01872) 501253 **e** pam@trenonafarmholidays.co.uk
w trenonafarmholidays.co.uk

open All year
payment Credit/debit cards, cash/cheques

The former farmhouse, and old stone workshop, have been tastefully converted to provide quality accommodation with modern furnishings and appliances for relaxing holidays on a mixed working farm on the beautiful Roseland Peninsula. Private gardens and patios. Many public gardens and attractions nearby. Children/pets welcome. Disabled access.

⊕ *A30 past Bodmin, A391 to St Austell, A390 towards Truro. Just beyond Probus take A3078 to St Mawes. After 8 miles pass Esso garage, Trenona Farm 2nd on left.*

♥ *Short breaks available Oct–Mar.*

Children ⏰ 🏊 🎿 📷 Unit 🛏 📺 📱 🍴 📶 🖥 🧺 🍳 🔔 📅 🎮 ❄
General **P** ⚡ 🐕 Leisure ∪ Shop 1 mile Pub 2 miles

WARMWELL, Dorset Map ref 2B3 | CAMPING & CARAVANNING

★★★★
HOLIDAY PARK

🚐 (185)
🏕 (185) **£199.00–**
£1,089.00

Warmwell Holiday Park

Warmwell, Nr Weymouth DT2 8JE **t** 0870 420 2997 **f** (0191) 268 5986
e enquiries@parkdeanholidays.co.uk **w** parkdeanholidays.co.uk

payment Credit/debit cards, cash/cheques

Combine relaxation and fun at Warmwell! With lodges set in peaceful, landscaped woodland and unrivalled leisure facilities, you really can enjoy the best of both worlds. Try skiing and snowboarding on our 110m SnowFlex ski slope. Other facilities include an indoor pool, roller rink, fishing lakes and much more. Open February to December.

General 🔌 **P** 📱 🖥 🛒 ✕ 🐕 Leisure 🎣 📺 🍴 🎵 ♦ ⛰ ♪

WEST BAY, Dorset Map ref 2A3 | CAMPING & CARAVANNING

★★★★
HOLIDAY, TOURING
& CAMPING PARK

🚐 (131) £12.00–£30.00
🚐 (131) £12.00–£30.00
⛺ (131) £9.00–£27.00
🏕 (39) £159.00–£769.00
131 touring pitches

West Bay Holiday Park

West Bay, Bridport DT6 4HB **t** 0870 420 2997 **f** (0191) 268 5986
e enquiries@parkdeanholidays.co.uk **w** parkdeanholidays.co.uk

payment Credit/debit cards, cash/cheques

Set in the heart of a pretty harbour village, just two minutes' walk to the beach at West Bay and the stunning coastline. There's so much to do! Facilities include an indoor pool, crazy golf and the Riverside Entertainment Club, where the whole family can enjoy some evening fun. Open March to November.

⊕ *M5 jct 25, leave main Dorchester road (A35), heading for Bridport. 1st exit at 1st roundabout, 2nd exit at 2nd roundabout into West Bay. Park on right.*

♥ *Short breaks available.*

General 🔌 **P** 📱 🖥 🍴 🏪 🛒 ✕ 🐕 Leisure 🎣 📺 🍴 🎵 ♦ ⛰ ▶

Key to symbols

Open the back flap for a key to symbols.

WESTON-SUPER-MARE, Somerset Map ref 1D1 — HOTEL

Arosfa Hotel

★★
HOTEL

B&B per room per night
s £40.00–£52.50
d Min £69.50
HB per person per night
Min £52.50

Lower Church Road, Weston-super-Mare BS23 2AG t (01934) 419523 f (01934) 636084
e info@arosfahotel.co.uk w arosfahotel.co.uk

A privately owned hotel, close to all amenities. The ideal place for business or pleasure, with traditional hospitality and ambience.

open All year
bedrooms 12 double, 14 twin, 15 single, 5 family
bathrooms All en suite
payment Credit/debit cards, cash/cheques

Children 🐥 🎱 🎿 🍴 Room 📞 📺 ♿ 🍵 General 🍷 🏛 Leisure ▶

WHITE CROSS, Cornwall Map ref 1B2 — CAMPING & CARAVANNING

White Acres Country Park

★★★★★
HOLIDAY, TOURING
& CAMPING PARK
ROSE AWARD

🚐 (40) £15.00–£35.00
🚗 (40) £13.00–£33.00
⛺ (40) £10.00–£29.00
🏠 (254) £189.00–
£849.00
40 touring pitches

White Cross, Newquay TR8 4LW t 0870 420 2997 f (0191) 268 5986
e enquiries@parkdeanholidays.co.uk w parkdeanholidays.co.uk

payment Credit/debit cards, cash/cheques

This park is the perfect place to escape to. Surrounded by tranquil countryside, White Acres is also a premier UK fishing destination. The unrivalled park facilities include indoor heated pool, kids' clubs and family entertainment. The lively resort of Newquay is just a few minutes' drive away. Open March to November and over Christmas.

⊕ Take the Indian Queens exit from A30. Follow A392 towards Newquay. White Acres Holiday Park is approx 1 mile on right-hand side.

♥ Short breaks available.

General 🔌 P 🅿 🚻 📶 ♿ 🔥 ⊙ 🧺 🍽 ✕ 🐾 Leisure 🎣 📺 🍷 🎵 🍺 ⛰ ∪ ⚓ ▶

WINCHCOMBE, Gloucestershire Map ref 2B1 — SELF CATERING

Misty View, Cheltenham

★★★★
SELF CATERING

Units **1**
Sleeps **1–4**

Low season per wk
£225.00–£375.00
High season per wk
£375.00–£575.00

contact Mr Bob Turner, 32 North Street, Winchcombe, Cheltenham GL54 5PS
t (01242) 603583 & 07831 212501 e bobturner@mistyview.wannadoo.co.uk

open All year
payment Cash/cheques, euros

Modern Cotswold-stone cottage, close to heart of the delightful Saxon town of Winchcombe. Farmhouse-style kitchen, stone floors, beamed ceilings. One twin en suite bedroom, one 5ft king-size en suite bedroom. Five minutes' walk to historic pubs, restaurants and beautiful Sudeley Castle, once home of an English queen.

⊕ Railway station: Ashchurch for Tewkesbury, 7 miles. Motorway: M5 jct 9, 7.3 miles. Airport: Birmingham, 35.7 miles.

♥ Short breaks available – email or phone for details and brochure.

Children 🐥 🎱 🎿 📷 ⛰ Unit 🛏 📺 ▣ 🖥 🧺 🔥 🍵 🧊 🍽 ❄
General ✂ Ⓢ Leisure ∪ ⚓ ▶ 🚲 Shop < 0.5 miles Pub < 0.5 miles

Friendly help and advice

Tourist Information Centres offer friendly help with accommodation and holiday ideas as well as suggestions of places to visit and things to do. You'll find contact details at the beginning of each regional section.

WOOLACOMBE, Devon Map ref 1C1 | HOTEL

★★★
HOTEL
SILVER AWARD

Woolacombe Bay Hotel

Woolacombe EX34 7BN t (01271) 870388 f (01271) 870613
e woolacombe.bayhotel@btinternet.com w woolacombe-bay-hotel.co.uk

B&B per room per night
s £65.00–£105.00
d £130.00–£210.00
HB per person per night
£95.00–£125.00

open All year
bedrooms 20 double, 18 twin, 26 family
bathrooms All en suite
payment Credit/debit cards, cash/cheques, euros

Gracious hotel set in six acres of gardens leading to three miles of Blue Flag golden sands. Free use of unrivalled sporting facilities including heated indoor and outdoor pools, squash, tennis, approach golf, short-mat bowls, gym, aerobics, sauna, steam room, creche and children's club. Award-winning cuisine, excellent accommodation, first-class service.

⊕ *Off M5 jct follow Tiverton bypass onto A361. At Barnstaple follow road to Ilfracombe, at roundabout take 1st exit to Woolacombe (B3343), to centre of village, turn left.*

Children ... Room ... General ... Leisure ...

Help before you go

i **When it comes to your next English break, the first stage of your journey could be closer than you think.**

You've probably got a tourist information centre nearby which is there to serve the local community – as well as visitors. Knowledgeable staff will be happy to help you, wherever you're heading.

Many tourist information centres can provide you with maps and guides, and it's often possible to book accommodation and travel tickets too.

Across the country there are more than 500 TICs. You'll find the address of your nearest centre in your local phone book, or look at the beginning of each regional section in this guide.

South East England

I spy at HMS *Gannet*,
Chatham Historic Dockyard, Kent

**Berkshire, Buckinghamshire, East Sussex,
Hampshire, Isle of Wight, Kent, London,
Oxfordshire, Surrey, West Sussex**

XV

XIV

Run for your life at
Dinosaur Isle, Isle of Wight

Southern **delight**

The South East is your quintessential slice of England. And whilst there's plenty for singles and couples to enjoy, this region is bursting with great family days out that the kids will treasure forever. From 400 miles of glorious coastline to the sands of Egypt and Tutankhamun, your feet won't touch the ground!

High spirits

Where to start? London? Capital idea! Did you know that Kylie is the only person, other than the Queen, who has been recreated in wax four times for Madame Tussauds? Swashbuckle with Captain Jack Sparrow and croon with Robbie Williams at this world-famous attraction. Submerge yourself in one of Europe's largest displays of aquatic life at the London Aquarium, then come up for air on the British Airways London Eye for a bird's-eye view of this buzzing city. Surreal! Check out surreal for real at the Dali Universe on the South Bank, where mind-boggling furniture and original sculptures will puzzle and amuse. Watch the kids stare in awe at the Tutankhamun exhibition at The O2 – it's thirty years since this boy-king last left Egypt. On rainy days, cower at the dinosaurs at the Natural History Museum – admission is free.

Kings and queens, castles and palaces, museums and zoos, boats and beaches; the South East has them all.

the captain's bridge to the boiler room. Discover the world-famous HMS *Victory* at Portsmouth Historic Dockyard, where you can also go into battle with the Royal Marines at Action Stations, an interactive showcase of the modern navy.

Delight in seeing some of the country's most familiar landmarks: the gleaming White Cliffs of Dover, magnificent Canterbury cathedral, Big Ben and the spires of Oxford. Oxfordshire celebrates its 1,000th birthday in 2007 so watch out for a stream of exciting events, including the UK's first ever Children's Food Festival.

Brush up on your history at Windsor Castle

Oxford's stunning skyline

Is the Queen at home? Peer into Buckingham Palace's windows at Legoland, Windsor, or prepare for a wet and wild voyage on the Vikings' River Splash ride! Get nose to nose with a multitude of furry and feathered friends at Drusillas Park, Alfriston, where children can learn as they have fun with hands-on activities.

Who killed Harold?

Explore a region that has witnessed some of the most momentous events of British history, from the Battle of Hastings in 1066 to the air raids of the Second World War, the Gunpowder Plot of 1605 and the Great Fire of London in 1666. At Battle Abbey stand on the exact spot where tradition says King Harold fell and take the interactive audio tour of the battlefield. Quake at the knees at the Tower of London where Guy Fawkes was tortured. Put on your sea legs to board HMS *Belfast* – explore all nine decks from

A shore thing

Leave the hurly-burly behind and head to the beaches of the south coast. Eastbourne, Bournemouth, Brighton and Margate were all popular playgrounds for the Victorians – Queen Victoria would frequently stay at her Isle of Wight home, Osborne House. Save your small change for the slot machines on the pier where it's hot doughnuts or fish and chips all round. If you're looking for something a bit more peaceful, there are still many gems on this stretch of coastline. Run in and out of the sand dunes at West Wittering, just down the Sussex coast from Bognor Regis and watch the zigzagging kite-surfers at Pevensey Bay. Too quiet? Liven things up a little at the Calshot Activities Centre where you can try your hand at an unrivalled number of watersports, including sailing on the Solent.

Main Notting Hill Carnival hits town, London **Left** Enjoy glorious countryside, South Downs; how's it done? World Sand Sculpture Festival, Brighton; the friendliest of creatures, Surrey Hills Llamas; present meets past at Winchester Cathedral

Raise the drawbridge

Discover a life of privilege when you explore the South East's many awe-inspiring castles. Hever, Bodiam, Scotney and Arundel, to name but four. Dreamy Leeds Castle in Kent, 'the loveliest castle in the world', was restored by Henry VIII for his first queen, Catherine of Aragon. It might have been the ultimate romantic gesture, but it didn't stop him marrying his second wife, Anne Boleyn, whose childhood home was beautiful Hever Castle. Henry VIII also lived in magnificent Hampton Court Palace. Last one out of the ingenious garden maze buys lunch!

Beware at Bodiam Castle

At one with nature

It's not for nothing that Kent is called the Garden of England. Sample the beauty of country gardens such as Sissinghurst Castle Garden near Cranbrook, the loving creation of Vita Sackville-West. Play hide and seek in and out of the paths and bridleways of the New Forest, now a National Park, and watch out for wild ponies as they gently graze. Follow the ancient tracks of the South Downs Way or the Ridgeway that eventually meets the Thames Path. Spend hours in the Royal Botanic Gardens at Kew, the jewel in the crown of English gardens. Explore the 300 incredible acres or wonder at the exotic plants in the world-famous Palm House. Feeling full of beans? Hop over to the Isle of Wight where you can cycle Round the Island in eight hours.

Never a quiet moment

Catch the buzz of a festival or event, whatever the time of year. From rock 'n' pop to hops, from

> Indulge your love of the open air in glorious countryside or thrill to the sights and sounds of a festival.

rowing to sailing, from Dickens to dancing round a maypole – the rich tapestry of life. In London, there's the Notting Hill Carnival or The Lord Mayor's Show. The Brighton Festival comes to the hip seaside town every May – a true celebration of the arts. If you're looking for the epitome of elegance, dress up for Glyndebourne's season of opera, or see the streets of Broadstairs thronged with Victorian costumes during the Dickens Festival. There's rock, pop and hip hop mixed with a liberal dose of mud at August's Reading Festival. Don't forget the Henley Royal Regatta or Cowes Week – two internationally famous spectacles. Get ready to cheer on your heroes at the London Marathon, Lord's cricket ground and Wimbledon.

Who can resist?

Had your fill of city sightseeing? Shopaholics can head for Oxford Street, Bond Street and Knightsbridge or one of the 83 eclectic markets such as Brick Lane, Camden, Borough and Spitalfields. The Mall antiques arcade in Islington is set in a former tram station and is packed with specialist dealers. The Lanes, Brighton, is also a favourite haunt for antique hunters. Pop into Oxford Castle where boutique stalls, pulsating bars and a feast of visual arts are set against a prison backdrop. You'll need to top up your energy levels, so embark on an epicurean journey through the vineyards, breweries, orchards, oyster houses and fine restaurants of South East England.

Further **information**

Tourism South East
t (023) 8062 5505
w visitsoutheastengland.com

Visit London
t 0870 156 6366
w visitlondon.com

Tourist Information Centres

When you arrive at your destination, visit a tourist information centre for help with accommodation and information about local attractions and events, or email your request before you go.

Berkshire

Bracknell	Nine Mile Ride	(01344) 354409	TheLookOut@bracknell-forest.gov.uk
Maidenhead	St Ives Road	(01628) 796502	maidenhead.tic@rbwm.gov.uk
Newbury	The Wharf	(01635) 30267	tourism@westberks.gov.uk
Reading	Chain Street	(0118) 956 6226	touristinfo@reading.gov.uk
Windsor	24 High Street	(01753) 743900	windsor.tic@rbwm.gov.uk

Buckinghamshire

Aylesbury	Kings Head Passage	(01296) 330559	tic@aylesburyvaledc.gov.uk
Buckingham	Market Hill	(01280) 823020	buckingham.t.i.c@btconnect.com
High Wycombe	Paul's Row	(01494) 421892	tourism_enquiries@wycombe.gov.uk
Marlow	31 High Street	(01628) 483597	tourism_enquiries@wycombe.gov.uk
Wendover	High Street	(01296) 696759	tourism@wendover-pc.gov.uk

East Sussex

Battle	High Street	(01424) 773721	battletic@rother.gov.uk
Brighton	10 Bartholomew Square	0906 711 2255**	brighton-tourism@brighton-hove.gov.uk
Eastbourne	Cornfield Road	0871 663 0031	tic@eastbourne.gov.uk
Hastings (Old Town)*	The Stade	(01424) 781111	hic@hastings.gov.uk
Hastings	Queens Square	(01424) 781111	hic@hastings.gov.uk
Lewes	187 High Street	(01273) 483448	lewes.tic@lewes.gov.uk
Rye	Strand Quay	(01797) 226696	ryetic@rother.gov.uk
Seaford	25 Clinton Place	(01323) 897426	seaford.tic@lewes.gov.uk

Hampshire

Aldershot	39 High Street	(01252) 320968	mail@rushmoorvic.com
Alton	7 Cross and Pillory Lane	(01420) 88448	altoninfo@btconnect.com
Andover	6 Church Close	(01264) 324320	andovertic@testvalley.gov.uk
Basingstoke	Market Place	(01256) 817618	basingstoket.i.c@btconnect.com
Fareham	West Street	(01329) 221342	touristinfo@fareham.gov.uk
Fordingbridge*	Salisbury Street	(01425) 654560	fordingbridgetic@tourismse.com
Gosport	South Street	(023) 9252 2944	tourism@gosport.gov.uk
Havant	1 Park Road South	(023) 9248 0024	tourism@havant.gov.uk
Hayling Island*	Seafront	(023) 9246 7111	tourism@havant.gov.uk
Lymington	New Street	(01590) 689000	information@nfdc.gov.uk
Lyndhurst & New Forest	Main Car Park	(023) 8028 2269	information@nfdc.gov.uk
Petersfield	27 The Square	(01730) 268829	petersfieldinfo@btconnect.com
Portsmouth	Clarence Esplanade	(023) 9282 6722	vis@portsmouthcc.gov.uk
Portsmouth	The Hard	(023) 9282 6722	vis@portsmouthcc.gov.uk
Ringwood	The Furlong	(01425) 470896	information@nfdc.gov.uk

Romsey	13 Church Street	(01794) 512987	romseytic@testvalley.gov.uk
Southampton	9 Civic Centre Road	(023) 8083 3333	tourist.information@southampton.gov.uk
Southsea	Clarence Esplanade	(023) 9282 6722	vis@portsmouthcc.gov.uk
Winchester	High Street	(01962) 840500	tourism@winchester.gov.uk

Isle of Wight

Cowes	9 The Arcade	(01983) 813818	info@islandbreaks.co.uk
Newport	High Street	(01983) 813818	info@islandbreaks.co.uk
Ryde	81-83 Union Street	(01983) 813818	info@islandbreaks.co.uk
Sandown	8 High Street	(01983) 813818	info@islandbreaks.co.uk
Shanklin	67 High Street	(01983) 813818	info@islandbreaks.co.uk
Yarmouth	The Quay	(01983) 813818	info@islandbreaks.co.uk

Kent

Ashford	18 The Churchyard	(01233) 629165	tourism@ashford.gov.uk
Broadstairs	2 Victoria Parade	0870 264 6111	
Canterbury	12/13 Sun Street	(01227) 378100	canterburyinformation@canterbury.gov.uk
Deal	129 High Street	(01304) 369576	info@deal.gov.uk
Dover	Biggin Street	(01304) 205108	tic@doveruk.com
Faversham	13 Preston Street	(01795) 534542	fata@visitfaversham.com
Folkestone	Harbour Street	(01303) 258594	doverfolkestone@btconnect.com
Gravesend	18a St George's Square	(01474) 337600	info@towncentric.co.uk
Herne Bay	Central Parade	(01227) 361911	hernebayinformation@canterbury.gov.uk
Hythe*	Scanlons Bridge Road	(01303) 266421	
Maidstone	High Street	(01622) 602169	tourism@maidstone.gov.uk
Margate	12-13 The Parade	0870 264 6111	margate.tic@visitor-centre.net
New Romney	New Romney Station	(01797) 362353	
Ramsgate	17 Albert Court	0870 264 6111	ramsgate.tic@visitor-centre.net
Rochester	95 High Street	(01634) 843666	visitor.centre@medway.gov.uk
Royal Tunbridge Wells	The Pantiles	(01892) 515675	touristinformationcentre@tunbridgewells.gov.uk
Sandwich*	Cattle Market	(01304) 613565	info@ticsandwich.wanadoo.co.uk
Sevenoaks	Buckhurst Lane	(01732) 450305	tic@sevenoakstown.gov.uk
Tenterden*	High Street	(01580) 763572	tentic@ashford.gov.uk
Tonbridge	Castle Street	(01732) 770929	tonbridge.castle@tmbc.gov.uk
Whitstable	7 Oxford Street	(01227) 275482	whitstableinformation@canterbury.gov.uk

London

Bexley (Hall Place)	Bourne Road	(01322) 558676	hallplaceshoptic@tiscali.co.uk
Britain & London Visitor Centre	1 Regent Street	08701 566 366	blvcenquiry@visitlondon.com
Croydon	Katharine Street	(020) 8253 1009	tic@croydon.gov.uk
Greenwich	2 Cutty Sark Gardens	0870 608 2000	tic@greenwich.gov.uk
Harrow	Station Road	(020) 8424 1102	info@harrow.gov.uk
Hillingdon	14-15 High Street	(01895) 250706	libraryinfoteam@hillingdongrid.org
Hounslow	High Street	0845 456 2929	tic@cip.org.uk
Kingston	Market Place	(020) 8547 5592	tourist.information@rbk.kingston.gov.uk
Lewisham	199-201 Lewisham High Street	(020) 8297 8317	tic@lewisham.gov.uk
Richmond	Whittaker Avenue	(020) 8940 9125	info@visitrichmond.co.uk

Southwark	Bankside	(020) 7401 5266	tourisminfo@southwark.gov.uk
Swanley	London Road	(01322) 614660	touristinfo@swanley.org.uk
Twickenham	44 York Street	(020) 8891 7272	info@visitrichmond.co.uk
Waterloo International	Arrivals Hall	(020) 7620 1550	london.visitorcentre@iceplc.com

Oxfordshire

Banbury	Spiceball Park Road	(01295) 259855	banbury.tic@cherwell-dc.gov.uk
Bicester	Bicester Village	(01869) 369055	bicester.vc@cherwell-dc.gov.uk
Burford	Sheep Street	(01993) 823558	burford.vic@westoxon.gov.uk
Didcot	118 Broadway	(01235) 813243	didcottic@tourismse.com
Faringdon	5 Market Place	(01367) 242191	tourism@faringdontowncouncil.org.uk
Henley-on-Thames	Kings Road	(01491) 578034	henleytic@hotmail.com
Oxford	15/16 Broad Street	(01865) 726871	tic@oxford.gov.uk
Witney	26a Market Square	(01993) 775802	witney.vic@westoxon.gov.uk
Woodstock	Park Street	(01993) 813276	woodstock.vic@westoxon.gov.uk

Surrey

Dorking	Reigate Road	(01306) 879327	visitorinformation@molevalley.gov.uk
Guildford	14 Tunsgate	(01483) 444333	tic@guildford.gov.uk
Haslemere	78 High Street	(01428) 645425	vic@haslemere.com
Woking	Peacocks Centre	(01483) 720103	tourist@woking.gov.uk

West Sussex

Arundel	61 High Street	(01903) 882268	arundel.vic@arun.gov.uk
Bognor Regis	Belmont Street	(01243) 823140	bognorregis.vic@arun.gov.uk
Burgess Hill	96 Church Walk	(01444) 238202	touristinformation@burgesshill.gov.uk
Chichester	29a South Street	(01243) 775888	chitic@chichester.gov.uk
Crawley	County Mall	(01293) 846968	vip@countymall.co.uk
Horsham	9 The Causeway	(01403) 211661	tourist.information@horsham.gov.uk
Littlehampton	63-65 Surrey Street	(01903) 721866	littlehampton.vic@arun.gov.uk
Midhurst	North Street	(01730) 817322	midtic@chichester.gov.uk
Petworth*	The Old Bakery	(01798) 343523	
Worthing	Chapel Road	(01903) 221307	tic@worthing.gov.uk
Worthing*	Marine Parade	(01903) 221307	tic@worthing.gov.uk

* seasonal opening

Alternatively, you can text **TIC LOCATE** to **64118** to find your nearest Tourist Information Centre

Places to visit in
South East England

On the following pages you'll find an extensive selection of indoor and outdoor attractions in South East England. Get to grips with nature, stroll around a museum, have an action-packed day with the kids and a whole lot more...

Attractions are ordered by county, and if you're looking for a specific kind of experience each county is divided into the following sections.

Family fun   **Entertainment and culture**

Nature and wildlife   **Food and drink**

Historic England   **Relaxing and pampering**

Outdoor activities

Look out, too, for the Quality Assured Visitor Attraction sign. This indicates that the attraction is assessed annually and meets the standards required to receive the quality marque. So rest assured, you'll have a great time.

Turn to the maps at the front of the guide to find the location of those attractions displaying a map reference.

The index on page 459 will help you to locate specific attractions with ease. For more great ideas for places to visit contact a local Tourist Information Centre or log on to **enjoyengland.com**.

Please note, as changes often occur after press date, it is advisable to confirm opening times and admission prices before travelling.

KEY TO ATTRACTIONS

Cafe/restaurant	☕
Picnic area	🪑
No dogs except service dogs	✕🐕
Partial disabled access	♿
Full disabled access	♿

Where prices aren't specified, use the following guide for an adult admission:

£	up to £5
££	between £5 and £10
£££	between £10 and £15
££££	more than £15

Become a jousting knight at spectacular Penshurst Place, Kent

Berkshire

Enjoy the fun of a special event or visit one of the attractions listed for a great day out. For more inspiring ideas go to **enjoyengland.com**.

12–26 May
Newbury Spring Festival
Newbury
(01635) 528766
newburyspringfestival.org.uk

19–23 Jun
Royal Ascot
Ascot Racecourse
0870 727 1234
ascot.co.uk

23 Jun
Reading Water Fest
On the Kennet, Reading
(0118) 939 0771
reading.gov.uk/news/whatson

7–14 Jul
Newbury Comedy Festival
Newbury
(01635) 522733
newburycomedyfestival.com

May 08
Royal Windsor Horse Show
Windsor Home Park
(01753) 860633
royal-windsor-horse-show.co.uk

FAMILY FUN

Go Ape! High Ropes Forest Adventure
Look Out Discovery Centre,
Nine Mile Ride, Swinley Forest,
Bracknell RG12 7QW
t 0870 444 5562 **w** goape.co.uk
open Apr-Oct, daily 0900-1700. Nov, Sat-Sun 0900-1700.
admission ££££
Go Ape! and tackle a high-wire forest adventure course of rope bridges, Tarzan swings and zip slides up to 35 feet above the forest floor.

LEGOLAND Windsor
Winkfield Road, Windsor SL4 4AY
t 0870 504 0404 **w** legoland.co.uk
open See website for details.
admission ££££
A family park with hands-on activities, more than 50 interactive rides, themed playscapes and more LEGO bricks than you ever dreamed possible.

The Look Out Discovery Centre
Nine Mile Ride, Bracknell RG12 7QW
t (01344) 354400
w bracknell-forest.gov.uk/lookout
open All year, Mon-Sun, Bank Hols 1000-1700.
admission ££
A hands-on, interactive science exhibition with over 70 exhibits, set in 2,600 acres of Crown woodland. Ideal for school and family visits. Fun and educational!

Monkey-Mates
Old Forest Road, Wokingham RG41 1JA
t (0118) 989 2111 **w** monkeymates.co.uk
open All year, Mon-Sat 0930-1800, Sun 1000-1700.
admission £
Monkey Mates is a children's indoor soft play facility with an outdoor playground. We have an extensive catering facility and seating area.

NATURE AND WILDLIFE

The Living Rainforest
Hampstead Norreys, Thatcham, Newbury RG18 0TN
t (01635) 202444 **w** livingrainforest.org
open Daily 1000-1715.
admission ££
Two tropical rainforests, all under cover, approximately 20,000 sq ft. Collection of rare and exotic tropical plants together with small representation of wildlife.

Admission is based on an adult price. Please check opening times and admission before travelling.

Trilakes Country Park
Yateley Road,
Sandhurst GU47 8JQ
t (01252) 873191
w blackwater-valley.org.uk
open All year, daily 0930-1830.
admission £

Trilakes Country Park incorporates an animal park, nationally renowned fishing lakes, cafe and a new indoor children's adventure playworld.

HISTORIC ENGLAND

Basildon Park
Lower Basildon RG8 9NR
t (0118) 984 3040
w nationaltrust.org.uk
open House: Apr-Oct, Wed-Sun 1200-1700. Grounds: Apr-Oct, Wed-Sun 1100-1700.
admission ££

A classical 18thC house by John Carr of York, with an unusual octagon room, fine plasterwork and the decorative shell room. Situated in 400 acres of parkland and woodland.

Windsor Castle
Windsor SL4 1NJ
t (020) 7766 7304
w royalcollection.org.uk
open Apr-Oct, daily 0945-1715. Nov-Feb, daily 0945-1615.
admission £££

The oldest and largest occupied castle in the world and Official residence of HM The Queen and royal residence for nine centuries. State apartments, Queen Mary's Doll's House.

ENTERTAINMENT AND CULTURE

Ascot Racecourse
High Street, Ascot SL5 7JX
t 0870 727 1234 **w** ascot.co.uk
open See website for details.
admission ££££

Founded in 1711 by Queen Anne, and reopened following an 18-month redevelopment project, Ascot Racecourse stages high quality flat and jump racing throughout the year.

Eton College
Eton SL4 6DW
t (01753) 671177 **w** etoncollege.com
open Apr-Jun, Sep, daily 1400-1630. Jul-Aug, daily 1030-1630.
admission £

The historic buildings are an integral part of the heritage of the British Isles. Visitors are invited to share the unique experience and beauty of Eton College.

Museum of Reading
Blagrave Street, Reading RG1 1QH
t (0118) 939 9800 **w** readingmuseum.org.uk
open All year, Tue-Sat 1000-1600, Sun, Bank Hols 1100-1600.
admission Free

Twelve hands-on galleries including Roman Silchester, changing art gallery, Box Room, Britain's Bayeux Tapestry and the world's only biscuit gallery, Huntley & Palmers.

REME Museum of Technology
Isaac Newton Road (off Biggs Lane), Arborfield, Reading RG2 9NJ
t (0118) 976 3375 **w** rememuseum.org.uk
open All year, Mon-Thu 0900-1630, Fri 0900-1600, Sun 1100-1600.
admission £

The museum shows the developing technology used by the Royal Electrical and Mechanical Engineers in maintaining and repairing the army's equipment since 1942.

Relaxing on the banks of Virginia Water in the Great Park at Windsor

Buckinghamshire

FAMILY FUN

Enjoy the fun of a special event or visit one of the attractions listed for a great day out. For more inspiring ideas go to **enjoyengland.com**.

16 Jun–15 Jul
Bucks Open Studios
Stoke Mandeville
(01296) 614238
bucks-open-studios.org.uk

16–17 Jun
Marlow Town Regatta and Festival
Dorney Lake, Marlow
marlowtownregatta.org.uk

7 Jul
Roald Dahl Festival
Aylesbury
(01296) 585310
aylesburyvaledc.gov.uk

30 Aug
Buckinghamshire County Show
Wingrave
(01296) 680400
buckscountyshow.co.uk

16 Dec
Victorian Christmas
Wycombe Museum, High Wycombe
(01494) 461000
wycombe.gov.uk/museum

Bekonscot Model Village & Railway

Warwick Road, Beaconsfield HP9 2PL
t (01494) 672919 **w** bekonscot.com
open 10 Feb-28 Oct 1000-1700.
admission Adult: £6.50

Be a giant in a miniature wonderland. This unique piece of our heritage depicting rural England in the 1930s is just waiting to be explored by children and adults alike! The ultimate train set runs round the village, and there is a sit-on miniature railway at weekends and holidays. Refreshments, play area, picnic areas.

Map ref 2C2

V *voucher offer – see back section*

Stroll through the poppy fields in Turville

Admission is based on an adult price. Please check opening times and admission before travelling.

Gulliver's Land

Livingstone Drive,
Newlands,
Milton Keynes MK15 0DT
t (01908) 609001 **w** gulliversfun.co.uk
open Apr-Sep, phone for details. Opening
times vary during the Christmas period.
admission Adult: £10.99

A magical land for families with children aged
two to 13 years of age. With 30 rides and
attractions it will entertain your child all day.
Visit one of our many shows or relax in one of
our many restaurants.

                                    Map ref 2C1

Hell-Fire Caves

West Wycombe, High Wycombe
HP14 3AH
t (01494) 533739 **w** hellfirecaves.co.uk
open Apr-Oct daily 1100-1730. Nov-Mar,
Sat-Sun 1100-1730.
admission Adult: £5

The Caves, excavated in the 1750s, extend half
a mile underground along passages leading
down through the Banqueting Hall, and finally
reaching the Inner Temple by the River Styx.
Visit our tea room and gift shop with award-
winning murals.

                                    Map ref 2C2

Willen Lake and Park

Willen Lake, Brickhill Street, Milton Keynes MK15 0DS
t (01908) 691620 **w** whitecap.co.uk
open Daily 0900-1730.
admission Free
*Beautiful lakeside park, offering all types of watersports
including water-skiing, cycle hire, fishing, miniature
railway, children's play area and seasonal attractions.*

NATURE AND WILDLIFE

Boarstall Duck Decoy and Nature Reserve

Boarstall HP18 9UX
t (01844) 237488
w nationaltrust.org.uk
open Apr-Aug, Wed 1530-1830, Sat-Sun, Bank Hols
1000-1600.
admission £

*A 17thC duck decoy in working order in 13 acres of
natural woodland, with nature trail and information
centre.*

Stowe Landscape Gardens

The National Trust, Stowe Landscape
Gardens, Stowe MK18 5EH
t (01280) 822850 (01280) 818825
w nationaltrust.org.uk/stowegardens
open 1 Mar-4 Nov, Wed-Sun 1030-1730. 10
Nov-24 Feb 08, Sat-Sun 1030-1600. Gardens
closed 26 May.
admission Adult: £6

Discover Stowe, a garden full of mystery and
hidden meanings - one of Europe's most
beautiful and influential landscape gardens.
Perfect for a family picnic or for those seeking
peace and tranquillity, with walks and trails for
all to enjoy. Visit our website for news of events
throughout the year.

                                    Map ref 2C1

HISTORIC ENGLAND

Bekonscot Model Village & Railway

Warwick Road, Beaconsfield HP9 2PL
t (01494) 672919 **w** bekonscot.com
open 10 Feb-28 Oct 1000-1700.
admission Adult: £6.50

Be a giant in a miniature wonderland. This unique piece of our heritage depicting rural England in the 1930s is just waiting to be explored by children and adults alike! The ultimate train set runs round the village, and there is a sit-on miniature railway at weekends and holidays. Refreshments, play area, picnic areas.

 Map ref 2C2

 voucher offer – see back section

Claydon House

Middle Claydon MK18 2EY
t (01296) 730349
w nationaltrust.org.uk
open Apr-Oct, Mon-Wed,
Sat-Sun 1300-1700.
admission ££

An 18thC house containing a series of magnificent and unique rococo staterooms with important carvings. Museums of Florence Nightingale and the Crimean War.

Cliveden

Taplow SL6 0JA
t (01628) 605069
w nationaltrust.org.uk
open House: Apr-Oct, Thu, Sun 1500-1730.
Garden: Apr-Oct, daily 1100-1800.
Nov-Dec, daily 1100-1600.
Woodland: Apr-Oct, daily 1100-1730. Nov-Feb, daily 1100-1600.
admission ££

Overlooking the Thames, the present house, built in 1851, was once the home of Lady Astor, and is situated in 375 acres of gardens, woodland and riverside walks.

Hell-Fire Caves

West Wycombe, High Wycombe HP14 3AH
t (01494) 533739 **w** hellfirecaves.co.uk
open Apr-Oct daily 1100-1730. Nov-Mar, Sat-Sun 1100-1730.
admission Adult: £5

The Caves, excavated in the 1750s, extend half a mile underground along passages leading down through the Banqueting Hall, and finally reaching the Inner Temple by the River Styx. Visit our tea room and gift shop with award-winning murals.

Map ref 2C2

Hughenden Manor

High Wycombe HP14 4LA
t (01494) 755573
w nationaltrust.org.uk
open House: Apr-Oct, Wed-Sun 1300-1700.
Dec, Sat-Sun 1200-1500.
Garden: Apr-Oct, Wed-Sun 1100-1700.
Dec, Sat-Sun 1100-1600. Park: Daily.
admission ££

Victorian home of Prime Minister and statesman Benjamin Disraeli from 1848 until his death in 1881. Most of his furniture, books and pictures remain in this, his private retreat.

Taplow Court

Berry Hill, Taplow SL6 0ER
t (01628) 591215
open May-Jul, Sun, Bank Hols 1400-1700.
admission Free

Set high above the Thames, affording spectacular views,Taplow Court was remodelled in the mid-19thC by William Burn. Tranquil gardens and grounds. Anglo-Saxon burial mound. Temporary exhibitions.

For key to symbols see inside back cover.

Waddesdon Manor

Waddesdon, Aylesbury HP18 0JH
t (01296) 653226 **w** waddesdon.org.uk
open Gardens: Apr-Dec, Wed-Sun, Bank Hols
1000-1700. House: Apr-Oct, Wed-Fri, Bank Hols
1200-1600, Sat-Sun 1100-1600.
admission £££

*A French Renaissance-style chateau housing the
Rothschild Collection of art treasures, wine cellars, two
licensed restaurants, gift and wine shops, an aviary and
spectacular gardens.*

West Wycombe Park

West Wycombe HP14 3AJ
t (01494) 513569 **w** nationaltrust.org.uk
open Grounds: Apr-Aug, Mon-Thu, Sun 1400-1800.
House: Jun-Aug, Mon-Thu, Sun 1400-1800.
admission ££

*Palladian house with frescoes and painted ceilings
fashioned for Sir Francis Dashwood in the mid 18thC.
Landscape and lake also laid out at the same time.*

OUTDOOR ACTIVITIES

Gulliver's Land

Livingstone Drive,
Newlands,
Milton Keynes MK15 0DT
t (01908) 609001 **w** gulliversfun.co.uk
open Apr-Sep, phone for details. Opening
times vary during the Christmas period.
admission Adult: £10.99

A magical land for families with children aged
two to 13 years of age. With 30 rides and
attractions it will entertain your child all day.
Visit one of our many shows or relax in one of
our many restaurants.

  Map ref 2C1

Stowe Landscape Gardens

The National Trust, Stowe Landscape
Gardens, Stowe MK18 5EH
t (01280) 822850 (01280) 818825
w nationaltrust.org.uk/stowegardens
open 1 Mar-4 Nov, Wed-Sun 1030-1730. 10
Nov-24 Feb 08, Sat-Sun 1030-1600. Gardens
closed 26 May.
admission Adult: £6

Discover Stowe, a garden full of mystery and
hidden meanings - one of Europe's most
beautiful and influential landscape gardens.
Perfect for a family picnic or for those seeking
peace and tranquillity, with walks and trails for
all to enjoy. Visit our website for news of events
throughout the year.

  Map ref 2C1

Temple of Ancient Virtue, Stowe Landscape Gardens

ENTERTAINMENT AND CULTURE

Buckinghamshire County Museum
Church Street, Aylesbury HP20 2QP
t (01296) 331441 **w** buckscc.gov.uk/museum
open All year, Mon-Sat, Bank Hols 1000-1700, Sun
1400-1700.
admission £
*Lively hands-on, innovative museum complex consisting
of county heritage displays, regional art gallery and
Roald Dahl Children's Gallery in lovely garden setting.*

Milton Keynes Museum
Stacey Hill Farm, Southern Way, Wolverton MK12 5EJ
t (01908) 316222 **w** mkmuseum.org.uk
open Apr-Oct, Wed-Sun, Bank Hols 1100-1630.
Nov-Mar, Sat-Sun, 1100-1630.
admission £
*Extensive display of agricultural and industrial
machinery, domestic, printing and photographic
artefacts tracing past 100 years of local north
Buckinghamshire life.*

The Roald Dahl Museum
81-83 High Street, Great Missenden HP16 0AL
t (01494) 892192 **w** roalddahlmuseum.org
open All year, Tue-Sun, Bank Hols 1000-1700.
admission £
*The Roald Dahl Museum and Story Centre is in Great
Missenden where Roald Dahl (1916-1990) lived and
wrote many of his well-loved books.*

Pitstone

East Sussex

Enjoy the fun of a special event or visit one of
the attractions listed for a great day out. For
more inspiring ideas go to **enjoyengland.com**.

5–27 May
Brighton Festival
Various venues, Brighton
(01273) 709709
brighton-festival.org.uk

17–19 May
The Great Escape
Various venues, Brighton
(020) 7691 4245
escapegreat.com

17 Jun
London to Brighton Bike Ride
Madeira Drive, Brighton
0845 070 8070
bhf.org.uk

4 Aug
Herstmonceaux Open Air Classical Concert
Herstmonceaux Castle
(01233) 860846
classicalprom.com

21 Dec
Burning The Clocks
Madeira Drive, Brighton
(01273) 571106
burningtheclocks.co.uk

FAMILY FUN

Bluebell Railway

Sheffield Park Station, TN22 3QL
t (01825) 720800
w bluebell-railway.co.uk
open Apr-Oct, daily. Nov-Mar, Sat-Sun.
admission Adult: £9.80

An 18-mile round trip through open countryside. Daily service from April to October and every weekend throughout the year. Large fleet of steam engines dating from 1870s to 1950s. Licensed restaurant at Sheffield Park Station.

Map ref 2D3

Brighton Marina
Brighton BN2 5UF
t (01273) 818504
w brightonmarinauk.co.uk
open Daily.
admission Free

A 2,000-berth yacht marina with outlet shopping, quayside bars and restaurants, leisure, fishing and sailing, offering something for all the family.

Brighton Pier
Madeira Drive, Brighton BN2 1TW
t (01273) 609361
w brightonpier.co.uk
open All year, Mon-Fri 1000-2200, Sat-Sun 1000-2300.
admission Free

A Victorian pier – one of Brighton's landmarks – with various food and drink outlets, fairground attractions, slot machines and Palace of Fun arcade.

Eastbourne Pier
Grand Parade, Eastbourne BN21 3EL
t (01323) 410466
w eastbournepier.com
open All year, Mon-Tue, Sun 0700-2300. Wed-Thu 0700-0200, Fri-Sat 0700-0400.
admission Free

A fine example of a Victorian pier, which opened in 1872 and now has an amusement centre, night club and a Victorian bar serving food. Boat trips from the pier.

Farm World
Great Knelle Farm, Whitebread Lane, Beckley TN31 6UB
t (01797) 260321
w farmworld-rye.co.uk
open Apr-Oct, Tue-Sat 1030-1700. School holidays, daily.
admission ££

Traditional 600-acre working farm with animals and tractor train. Dairy experience, hop picking, adventure playground, BMX bike hire and quad bikes.

The Flamingo Family Fun Park
The Stade, East Beach, Hastings TN34 3AR
t (01424) 715133
open Apr-Oct, daily 1000-1800. Nov-Mar, Sat-Sun 1100-1700.
admission Free

A family amusement park and entertainment centre offering rides for children, a rollercoaster, dodgems, boating lake and many other rides and amusements.

Fort Fun
Royal Parade, Eastbourne BN22 7LQ
t (01323) 642833
w fortfun.co.uk
open Fun Park: Apr-Oct, Sat-Sun 1000-1600. Adventureland: Daily 1000-1800.
admission Free

A children's fun park with runaway train, roller-coaster, go-karts, Concord jet ride and bat ride. Rockys Adventureland soft play area. Crazy golf.

Knockhatch Adventure Park
Hempstead Lane, Hailsham BN27 3PR
t (01323) 442051
w knockhatch.com
open See website for details.
admission ££

For all the family: raptors, reptiles, farm animals, various playgrounds, sky leap, boating, toboggan ride and much more. Extra charge: karting, laser game.

Middle Farm
Firle BN8 6LJ
t (01323) 811411
w middlefarm.com
open Daily 0930-1700.
admission Free

Family-owned and run, working open farm with large farm shop, National Collection of Cider And Perry, restaurant, craft and plant sales, play and picnic areas.

Paradise Park
Avis Road, Newhaven BN9 0DH
t (01273) 512123
w paradisepark.co.uk
open All year, Mon-Sun, Bank Hols 0900-1800.
admission ££

Exotic planthouses, museum of natural history, dinosaurs, gardens and Sussex History Trail. Garden centre and terrace cafe, miniature railway, golf and children's amusements.

Rye Heritage Centre

Strand Quay, Rye TN31 7AY
t (01797) 226696 **w** visitrye.co.uk
open Apr-Oct 1000-1700, last entry 1630.
Nov-Mar, check for shorter opening times.
admission Adult: £3

Home to Rye Town Model featuring the 'Story of Rye', a dramatic sound and light show taking you back through 700 years of Rye's fascinating history, and an exhibition of amusement machines dating from the last century, but which can still be enjoyed today. Adults £3.00, children £1.00, concessions £1.50.

Map ref 3B4

Seven Sisters Sheep Centre
Birling Manor Farm, East Dean BN20 0DG
t (01323) 423302
w sheepcentre.co.uk
open Apr-May, Mon-Fri 1400-1700, Sat-Sun 1000-1700.
Jun-Sep, Mon-Fri 1400-1700, Sat-Sun 1100-1700.
admission £
Visitors can see lambing, shearing, sheep milking, cheese making and spinning. There are young animals and over 40 breeds of British sheep.

Spring Barn Farm Park
Kingston Road, Lewes BN7 3ND
t (01273) 488450
w springbarnfarmpark.co.uk
open Apr-Sep, daily 1000-1730. Oct-Dec, Wed-Sun 1000-1730.
admission ££
Ideal venue for family fun days down on the farm. Watch 'piggies' teatime, help bottle feed newborn lambs, go to a 'pat-a-pet' session. Indoor and outdoor play areas.

NATURE AND WILDLIFE

Arlington Bluebell Walk & Farm Trail
Bates Green Farm, Tyehill Road,
Arlington BN26 6SH
t (01323) 485151
w bluebellwalk.co.uk
open Apr-May, daily 1000-1700.
admission £
Enjoy vistas of bluebells in 23 acres of ancient woodland. Walks and trails through three farms. Countryside exhibition. One walk is wheelchair friendly.

Ashdown Forest Llama Park
Wych Cross RH18 5JN
t (01825) 712040
w llamapark.co.uk
open Daily 1000-1700.
admission £
Llamas, alpacas. Picnic area, farm trail, museum. Coffee shop and shop selling 'llamarabilia' and alpaca knitwear. 'Walking with Llamas' – booking essential.

Bentley Wildfowl and Motor Museum
Bentley, Halland BN8 5AF
t (01825) 840573
w bentley.org.uk
open Apr-Oct, daily 1030-1730. Nov-Mar, Sat-Sun 1030-1600. House: Apr-Oct, daily 1200-1730.
admission ££
Over 1,000 wildfowl in parkland with lakes. The house contains antique furniture and wildfowl paintings. Motor museum with vintage cars. House, children's play facilities and woodland walk.

Bewl Water
Lamberhurst TN3 8JH
t (01892) 890661
w bewl.co.uk
open Apr-Oct, daily 1000-1800. Nov-Mar, daily 1000-1600.
admission £
Beautiful lake and country park within the Weald countryside. Watersports, fly fishing, walks and rides, boat trips, visitor centre, restaurant and conference facilities. Summer events.

Brighton Sea Life
Marine Parade, Brighton BN2 1TB
t (01273) 604234
w sealifeeurope.com
open Daily 1000-1700.
admission £££
A fun and educational day with over 150 species and 57 displays, including giant turtles, sharks, jelly fish, poison-arrow frogs, lion fish and sea snakes.

For key to symbols see inside back cover.

Drusillas Park

Alfriston BN26 5QS
t (01323) 874100 **w** drusillas.co.uk
open Apr-Oct, daily 1000-1700. Nov-Mar, daily 1000-1600.
admission £££

The best small zoo in England with animals in natural habitats. Playland is masses of fun for children from 2-12. Amazon Adventure.

Gardens and Grounds of Herstmonceux Castle

Herstmonceux BN27 1RN
t (01323) 833816 **w** herstmonceux-castle.com
open Apr-Sep, daily, 1000-1800. Oct, daily 1000-1700.
admission £

Visitors can explore the Elizabethan walled garden, flower gardens and nature trail surrounding the castle. Children can enjoy the woodland play area.

The Gardens of King John's Lodge

King John's Lodge, Sheepstreet Lane, Etchingham TN1 7AZ
t (01580) 819232 **w** kingjohnslodge.co.uk
open Apr-Oct, please phone for details.
admission £

Beautiful romantic five-acre garden. Wild and secret gardens. Borders, water features, parkland. Nursery. Formal garden surrounding historic house. Orchards surround medieval barn.

Merriments Gardens

Hawkhurst Road, Hurst Green TN19 7RA
t (01580) 860666 **w** merriments.co.uk
open All year, Mon-Sat 1000-1730, Sun 1030-1730.
admission £

A four-acre garden featuring herbaceous borders, unusual plants, colour-themed borders, and a hidden stream which links two large ponds, a bog garden and a rock garden.

Pashley Manor Gardens

Pashley Manor, Ticehurst TN5 7HE
t (01580) 200888 **w** pashleymanorgardens.com
open Apr-Sep, Tue-Thu, Sat, Bank Hols 1100-1700. Oct, Mon-Fri 1000-1600.
admission ££

Offers a blend of romantic landscaping, imaginative plantings and fine old trees, fountains, springs and large ponds. An English garden of a very individual character.

Rye Harbour Nature Reserve

Lime Kiln Cottage, Rye Harbour TN31 7TT
t (01797) 227784 **w** wildrye.info
open Reserve: Daily, dawn-dusk. Information Centre: Apr-Oct, daily 1000-1700. Oct-Mar, daily 1000-1600.
admission Free

Large coastal nature reserve with a vast array of wildlife. Network of footpaths leading to four birdwatching hides (three wheelchair accessible). Information centre.

Sheffield Park Garden

Sheffield Park TN22 3QX
t (01825) 790231 **w** nationaltrust.org.uk
open Apr, Jun-Sep, Tue-Sun 1030-1730. May, Oct-Nov, daily 1030-1730. Dec, Tue-Sun 1030-1600. Jan-Feb, Sat-Sun 1030-1600.
admission ££

Capability Brown-designed landscaped gardens and woodland of 120 acres with four lakes on different levels. Noted for its rhododendrons, azaleas, rare shrubs and trees.

A Smugglers Adventure at St Clements Caves

West Hill, Hastings TN34 3HY
t (01424) 422964
w discoverhastings.co.uk
open Apr-Oct, daily 1000-1730. Nov-Mar, daily 1100-1630.
admission ££

An extensive exhibition of 18thC smuggling, housed in 2,000 sq m of caves. Exhibition, museum, video theatre, extensive Adventure Walk incorporating dramatic special effects.

Underwater World, Hastings

Rock-a-Nore Road, Hastings TN34 3DW
t (01424) 718776
w discoverhastings.co.uk
open Apr-Oct, daily 1000-1700. Nov-Mar, daily 1100-1600.
admission ££

Display of marine life with hundreds of marine creatures including sharks, rays, crabs and starfish. There is also a tunnel and a sea life nursery for newly-born creatures.

HISTORIC ENGLAND

1066 Battle Abbey and Battlefield

High Street, Battle TN33 0AD
t (01424) 773792 **w** english-heritage.org.uk
open Apr-Sep, daily 1000-1800. Oct-Mar, daily 1000-1600.
admission ££

An abbey founded by William the Conqueror on the site of the Battle of Hastings. The church altar is on the spot where King Harold was killed.

Alfriston Clergy House

The Tye, Alfriston BN26 5TL
t (01323) 870001 **w** nationaltrust.org.uk
open Apr-Oct, Mon, Wed-Thu, Sat-Sun 1000-1700. Nov-Dec, Mon, Wed-Thu, Sat-Sun 1100-1600.
admission £

A beautiful thatched medieval hall house, the first building to be acquired by the National Trust in 1896. Pretty cottage garden with a charming gift shop.

Bateman's
Burwash TN19 7DS
t (01435) 882302 **w** nationaltrust.org.uk
open House: Apr-Oct, Mon-Wed, Sat-Sun 1100-1700.
Gardens: Apr-Oct, Mon-Wed, Sat-Sun 1100-1730.
Nov-Dec, Wed-Sun 1100-1600.
admission ££

A 17thC ironmaster's house which was the home of Rudyard Kipling between 1902 and 1935. His study and Rolls Royce can be seen. Garden with working watermill.

Bluebell Railway

Sheffield Park Station, TN22 3QL
t (01825) 720800
w bluebell-railway.co.uk
open Apr-Oct, daily. Nov-Mar, Sat-Sun.
admission Adult: £9.80

An 18-mile round trip through open countryside. Daily service from April to October and every weekend throughout the year. Large fleet of steam engines dating from 1870s to 1950s. Licensed restaurant at Sheffield Park Station.

Map ref 2D3

Bodiam Castle
Bodiam TN32 5UA
t (01580) 830436 **w** nationaltrust.org.uk
open Apr-Oct, daily 1030-1800. Nov-Jan, Sat-Sun 1030-1600. Feb, daily 1030-1800.
admission £
One of the most famous castles in Britain, Bodiam was built in 1385 as both a defence and a comfortable home. Wonderful views of the Rother Valley.

Firle Place
Firle BN8 6LP
t (01273) 858307 **w** firleplace.co.uk
open Jun-Sep, Wed-Thu, Sun, Bank Hols 1400-1615.
admission ££
A Tudor house with Georgian additions in a downland park setting. Important English and European Old Master paintings, fine furniture and notable Sevres porcelain.

Glynde Place
Glynde BN8 6SX
t (01273) 858224 **w** glyndeplace.com
open May-Aug, Wed, Sun, Bank Hols 1400-1700.
admission ££
A 16thC Sussex brick and flint house around a courtyard. Interior features include a panelled Long Gallery, old masters' portraits, furniture, embroidery and 18thC bronzes.

Great Dixter House and Gardens
Northiam TN31 6PH
t (01797) 252878 **w** greatdixter.co.uk
open House: Apr-Oct, Tue-Sun, Bank Hols 1400-1700.
Gardens: Apr-Oct, Tue-Sun, Bank Hols 1100-1700.
admission ££
An example of a 15thC manor house with antique furniture and needlework. Home of gardening writer Christopher Lloyd. The house is restored and the gardens were designed by Lutyens.

Hammerwood Park
Hammerwood RH19 3QE
t (01342) 850594 **w** mistral.co.uk/hammerwood
open Jun-Sep, Wed, Sat, Bank Hols 1400-1730.
admission ££
House built in 1792 by Latrobe, White House architect, and now being restored. The interior contains varied furniture, a copy of the Elgin marbles and musical instruments.

Hastings Castle and 1066 Story
West Hill, Hastings TN34 3HY
t (01424) 781112 **w** discoverhastings.co.uk
open Apr-Jul, daily 0900-1700. Aug-Sep, daily 1000-1730. Oct-Mar, daily 1000-1600.
admission £
Fragmentary remains of Norman Castle built on West Hill after William the Conqueror's victory at the Battle of Hastings. 1066 Story interpretation centre in siege tent.

Lamb House
West Street, Rye TN31 7ES
t (01797) 229542 **w** nationaltrust.org.uk
open Apr-Oct, Thu, Sat 1400-1800.
admission £
Early Georgian house and walled garden, home of writer Henry James and later of E F Benson, author of the Mapp and Lucia Tales. Exhibits include letters, pictures and furniture.

Lewes Castle and Barbican House Museum

Barbican House, 169 High Street,
Lewes BN7 1YE
t (01273) 486290 **w** sussexpast.co.uk
open All year, Mon 1100-1730, Tue-Sat 1000-1730, Sun, Bank Hols 1100-1730.
admission £
Historic display interpreting Lewes with indoor audiovisual programme and scale-model of the town c120 years ago. Norman castle remains. History of Lewes from Saxon times.

Lewes Priory
Southover, Lewes
t (01273) 471148 **w** lewespriory.org.uk
open Daily.
admission Free
The remains of a great Cluniac priory built from 1077 and destroyed on the orders of Henry VIII. There is a monument to the Battle of Lewes, a herb garden and display panels.

Michelham Priory

Upper Dicker BN27 3QS
t (01323) 844224 **w** sussexpast.co.uk
open Apr-Jul, Sep, Tue-Sun, Bank Hols 1030-1700. Aug, Tue-Sun, Bank Hols 1030-1730. Oct, Tue-Sun, Bank Hols 1030-1630.
admission ££

An Augustinian priory incorporated into a Tudor mansion. There are seven acres of moated gardens, a working watermill, an Elizabethan Great Barn, smithy and a rope museum.

Monks House

Rodmell BN7 3HF
t (01372) 453401 **w** nationaltrust.org.uk
open Apr-Oct, Wed, Sat 1400-1730.
admission £

Small converted farmhouse, home to Virginia Woolf and her husband Leonard from 1919 until his death in 1969. Furniture and personal items, garden and summerhouse.

Newhaven Fort

Fort Road, Newhaven BN9 9DS
t (01273) 517622 **w** newhavenfort.org.uk
open Apr-Oct, daily 1030-1800.
admission ££

A Victorian coastal fortress covering 10 acres and overlooking Seaford Bay. The fort has barrack rooms housing military and wartime displays and dioramas.

The Observatory Science Centre

Herstmonceux BN27 1RN
t (01323) 832731 **w** the-observatory.org
open Apr-Sep, daily 1000-1800. Oct-Dec, daily 1000-1700.
admission ££

The Science Centre, set in beautiful English countryside, has interactive exhibits and provides the opportunity to see old telescopes and learn about this historic site.

Pevensey Castle

High Street, Pevensey BN24 5LE
t (01323) 762604 **w** english-heritage.org.uk
open Apr-Sep, daily 1000-1800. Oct, Sat-Sun 1000-1600.
admission £

A Roman fortress built in 4thC as a defence against Saxon pirates, includes fine west gate. Norman castle built within Roman walls contains remains of unusual keep. Tudor gun.

Preston Manor

Preston Park, Brighton BN1 6SD
t (01273) 292770 **w** virtualmuseum.info
open Apr-Sep, Tue-Sat 1000-1700, Sun 1400-1700.
admission £

A delightful manor house with the interior of an Edwardian home containing ceramics, furniture, glass, clocks and silver. Servants' quarters and restored kitchen. Garden.

Royal Pavilion

Brighton BN1 1EE
t (01273) 290900
w royalpavilion.org.uk
open Apr-Sep, daily 0930-1745. Oct-Mar, daily 1000-1715.
admission ££

The Royal Pavilion is the magnificent former seaside residence of King George IV. It is decorated in Chinese taste and has an Indian exterior.

ENTERTAINMENT AND CULTURE

Anne of Cleves House

52 Southover High Street, Lewes BN7 1JA
t (01273) 474610
w sussexpast.co.uk
open Apr-Oct, Tue-Sat 1000-1700, Sun, Bank Hols 1100-1700. Nov-Mar, Tue-Sat 1000-1700.
admission £

The house given to Anne as part of her divorce settlement from Henry VIII in 1541. It now contains various items of historical interest from throughout Sussex.

Booth Museum of Natural History

194 Dyke Road, Brighton BN1 5AA
t (01273) 292777
w virtualmuseum.info
open All year, Mon-Sat 1000-1700, Sun 1400-1700.
admission Free

A comprehensive collection of British birds in re-creations of their natural environment. Galleries of skeletons, butterflies, Sussex geology and nature conservation, temporary exhibitions and a well-stocked shop.

Brighton Museum and Art Gallery

Royal Pavilion Gardens, Brighton BN1 1EE
t (01273) 290900
w virtualmuseum.info
open All year, Tue 1000-1900, Wed-Sat, 1000-1700, Sun, Bank Hols 1400-1700.
admission Free

Featuring state-of-the-art visitor facilities, Brighton Museum and Art Gallery houses collections of 20thC art and design, fashion, paintings, ceramics and world art.

Fishermen's Museum

Rock-a-Nore Road, Hastings TN34 3DW
t (01424) 461446
w hastingsfish.co.uk
open Daily, please phone for details.
admission Free

A former fishermen's church by the old net shops, now a museum on local fishing with ship models, nets, old photos and the Lugger 'Enterprise' which was built in 1912.

'How We Lived Then' Museum of Shops and Social History
20 Cornfield Terrace, Eastbourne BN21 4NS
t (01323) 737143
w how-we-lived-then.co.uk
open Daily, please phone for details.
admission £

One hundred years of social history (1850-1950) depicted by well over 100,000 exhibits displayed in street scenes of authentic old shops, room settings and displays.

The Redoubt Fortress
Royal Parade, Eastbourne BN21 7AQ
t (01323) 410300
w eastbournemuseums.co.uk
open Apr-Oct, Tue-Sun 1000-1700.
admission £

Fully-restored Napoleonic fortress, gun emplacements, battlements. Sussex Combined Services Museum. Collections of the Royal Sussex Regiment, Queen's Royal Irish Hussars.

Rye Heritage Centre
Strand Quay, Rye TN31 7AY
t (01797) 226696 **w** visitrye.co.uk
open Apr-Oct 1000-1700, last entry 1630.
Nov-Mar, check for shorter opening times.
admission Adult: £3

Home to Rye Town Model featuring the 'Story of Rye', a dramatic sound and light show taking you back through 700 years of Rye's fascinating history, and an exhibition of amusement machines dating from the last century, but which can still be enjoyed today. Adults £3.00, children £1.00, concessions £1.50.

Map ref 3B4

Rye Castle Museum
3 East Street, Rye TN31 7JY
t (01797) 226728
w ryemuseum.co.uk
open Apr-Oct, Mon-Thu 1030-1300, 1400-1700.
Nov-Mar, Sat-Sun 1030-1530.
admission £

A tower built as a defence to Rye in 1249, standing on high ground with rare views over Romney Marsh and to the sea. Topographical model of the area.

Yesterday's World
89-90 High Street, Battle TN33 0AQ
t (01424) 893938
w yesterdaysworld.co.uk
open Daily 0930-1730.
admission ££

Discover a magical journey through British history with over 100,000 nostalgic artefacts on display at one of the south's best loved family attractions.

FOOD AND DRINK

Barnsgate Manor Vineyard
Herons Ghyll TN22 4DB
t (01825) 713366
w barnsgate.co.uk
open All year, Mon-Sun, Bank Hols 1000-dusk.
admission Free

Magnificent views, vineyard walks, donkeys and llamas. Tearoom, restaurant. Gift shop selling 'Barnsgate' wines, gifts and beautiful alpaca knitwear.

Carr Taylor Wines Ltd
Wheel Lane, Westfield TN35 4SG
t (01424) 752501
w carr-taylor.co.uk
open Daily 1000-1700.
admission Free

A mature 37-acre vineyard with winery, wine-making machinery and wine-tasting rooms. Sample the vineyard's wine and England's first Methode Champenoise sparkling wine.

RELAXING AND PAMPERING

Beckhurst Glass The Glass Studio
The Pier, Eastbourne BN21 3EL
t 07050 055718
w pierglassstudio.co.uk
open Daily 1000-1800.
admission Free

Watch the complete process of glass models being made on marble bases, including birds in flight and animals. A large selection of art-silk flowers can also be seen.

Hampshire

FAMILY FUN

The Hawk Conservancy Trust

Sarson Lane, Weyhill, nr Andover SP11 8DY
t (01264) 773850
w hawk-conservancy.org
open Feb half-term to Oct half-term,
1030-1730. Phone for winter opening times.
admission Adult: £9

A national-award-winning family tourist
attraction, set in 22 acres of grounds both
woodland and wildflower meadow, and with
over 150 birds on display. Three flying displays
daily, including the spectacular Valley of the
Eagles at 1400. All visitors have the opportunity
to fly and hold a bird of prey.

Map ref 2C2

V voucher offer – see back section

Enjoy the fun of a special event or visit one of
the attractions listed for a great day out. For
more inspiring ideas go to **enjoyengland.com**.

2007
Year of Sculpture
Various venues, Winchester
hampshiresculpturetrust.org

23 Jun–8 Jul
Hampshire Food Festival
Venues across Hampshire
(01962) 845999
hampshirefare.co.uk

24–26 Jul
New Forest Show
The Showground, New Park, Brockenhurst
newforestshow.co.uk

14–23 Sep
Southampton Boat Show
Mayflower Park, Southampton
(01784) 472222
southamptonboatshow.com

30 Nov–2 Dec
Festival of Christmas
Portsmouth Historic Dockyard
flagship.org.uk

Intech Science and Discovery Centre
Telegraph Way,
Morn Hill,
Winchester SO21 1HX
t (01962) 863791
w intech.uk.com
open Daily 1000-1600.
admission ££
*Intech Science and Discovery Centre has been
set up to bring to life the worlds of science,
technology, engineering and mathematics for
every age group.*

Longdown Activity Farm

Deerleap Lane, Longdown, Ashurst SO40 7EH
t (023) 8029 3326 **w** longdownfarm.co.uk
open Apr-Oct, daily 1000-1700. Nov-Dec, Sat-Sun
1000-1700.
admission ££

*Hands-on activities every day – small animal handling,
bottle-feeding goat kids and calves, feeding ducks and
pigs. Indoor and outdoor play areas, tearoom and
excellent gift shop.*

Marwell Zoological Park

Colden Common, Winchester SO21 1JH
t (01962) 777407 **w** marwell.org.uk
open Daily from 1000.
admission Adult: £12.50

Set in a hundred acres of delightful Hampshire
countryside, Marwell is a relaxing and
fascinating zoological park at the heart of
wildlife conservation. New for 2007 is an
amazing Australian bush walk. Over 200
species of animals including giraffe
and rhino.

Map ref 2C3

Mid-Hants Railway PLC 'Watercress Line'

Alresford Station, Alresford SO24 9JG
t (01962) 733810 **w** watercressline.co.uk
open See website for details.
admission ££

*Ten miles of preserved steam railway running between
Alton and Alresford. Large and powerful steam
locomotives work hard to haul passengers over the
steeply inclined route.*

Off-road in the New Forest

Milestones, Hampshire's Living History Museum

Leisure Park, Churchill Way West,
Basingstoke RG21 6YR
t (01256) 477766 **w** milestones-museum.com
open Tue-Fri, Bank Holiday Mon 1000-1700.
Sat-Sun 1100-1700.
admission Adult: £7.25

Imagine an open-air museum inside a massive
modern building, a network of streets with
shops, a village green and even a pub. Dating
from Victorian times and the 1930s, it's fun,
with a surprise around every corner. Fully
accessible site with cafe, gift shop and free
parking.

Map ref 2C2

V *voucher offer – see back section*

Paultons Park

Ower SO51 6AL
t (023) 8081 4442
w paultonspark.co.uk
open See website for details.
admission ££££

*A great day out for all ages with over 50 attractions
included in price. Big and small rides, play areas, exotic
birds, lake and beautiful gardens.*

Whitchurch Silk Mill

28 Winchester Street, Whitchurch RG28 7AL
t (01256) 892065
w whitchurchsilkmill.org.uk
open All year, Tue-Sun, Bank Hols 1030-1700.
admission £

*Unique Georgian silk-weaving watermill, now a working
museum producing fine silk fabrics on Victorian
machinery. Riverside garden, tearoom for light meals,
silk gift shop.*

NATURE AND WILDLIFE

Blue Reef Aquarium
Clarence Esplanade, Southsea PO5 3PB
t (023) 9287 5222 **w** BlueReefAquarium.co.uk
open Apr-Oct, daily 1000-1700. Nov-Feb, daily
1000-1600. Mar, daily 1000-1700.
admission ££
*The aquarium is one of Portsmouth's newest venues.
Take a safari from the Solent to the tropical coral reef. A
memorable visit for all the family.*

Braxton Gardens
Lymore Lane, Milford-on-Sea SO41 0TX
t (01590) 642008
open Daily 1000-1700.
admission Free
*Beautiful gardens set around attractive Victorian farm
buildings. David Austin rose garden. Plant centre, gift
shop, tearoom and garden-design service..*

Exbury Gardens and Steam Railway
Exbury Estate Office, Exbury SO45 1AZ
t (023) 8089 1203 **w** exbury.co.uk.
open Apr-Nov, daily 1000-1730.
admission ££

*Over 200 acres of woodland garden, including the
Rothschild collection of rhododendrons, azaleas,
camellias and magnolias. Enjoy our 12.25-inch narrow-
gauge steam railway.*

Furzey Gardens
School Lane, Minstead SO43 7GL
t (023) 8081 2464 **w** furzey-gardens.org
open Gallery: Apr-Oct, daily 1000-1700. Gardens: Daily,
dawn-dusk.
admission £
*Eight acres of gardens. Gallery displaying local crafts and
paintings, many by local people. Old forest cottage.
Nursery shop. Children's play log houses, lake.*

Hidden Britain Tours

28 Chequers Road, Basingstoke RG21 7PU
t (01256) 814222
w hiddenbritaintours.co.uk
open Phone to arrange a tour.
admission Please phone for pricing details

Take a tour of the New Forest or visit the
landscape that inspired Jane Austen. Discover
the secrets of the county on the Hidden
Hampshire Tour. Why walk when you can ride
with a guide? A trip to remember. Forever.

Map ref 2C2

The Hawk Conservancy Trust

Sarson Lane, Weyhill, nr Andover SP11 8DY
t (01264) 773850
w hawk-conservancy.org
open Feb half-term to Oct half-term,
1030-1730. Phone for winter opening times.
admission Adult: £9

A national-award-winning family tourist
attraction, set in 22 acres of grounds both
woodland and wildflower meadow, and with
over 150 birds on display. Three flying displays
daily, including the spectacular Valley of the
Eagles at 1400. All visitors have the opportunity
to fly and hold a bird of prey.

Map ref 2C2

V *voucher offer – see back section*

Hinton Ampner Garden
Hinton Ampner, Bramdean SO24 0LA
t (01962) 771305 **w** nationaltrust.org.uk
open Garden: Apr-Oct, Mon-Wed, Sat-Sun 1100-1700.
House: Apr-Jul, Sep-Oct, Tue-Wed, Sun, Bank Hols
1300-1700. Aug, Tue-Wed, Sat-Sun, Bank Hols
1300-1700.
admission ££
*Splendid 20thC shrub garden offering delightful walks
and unexpected vistas. House contains a fine collection
of Regency furniture and Italian paintings.*

Houghton Lodge Gardens
Houghton SO20 6LQ
t (01264) 810502 **w** houghtonlodge.co.uk
open Apr-Oct, Mon-Tue, Thu-Sun 1000-1700.
admission £
Tranquil landscaped gardens (Grade II Listed house)
surround 18thC 'Cottage Ornee', overlooking River
Test. Walled garden with borders and fine trees. House
open by appointment.*

Itchen Valley Country Park
Allington Lane, West End, Eastleigh SO30 3HQ
t (023) 8046 6091 **w** eastley.gov.uk
open Apr-Sep, daily 0830-2100. Oct-Mar, daily 0830-1900.
admission Free
Itchen Valley Country Park is an unspoilt area of water meadows, ancient woodland and grazing pasture situated beside the River Itchen, between Eastleigh and Southampton.

Lepe Country Park
Lepe, Exbury SO45 1AD
t (023) 8089 9108 **w** hamps.gov.uk
open Daily 0730-dusk.
admission Free
Country park on the shores of the Solent – ideal place to picnic, watch sailboards, fish or swim. Also children's playground, wildlife and historic interest.

Marwell Zoological Park

Colden Common, Winchester SO21 1JH
t (01962) 777407 **w** marwell.org.uk
open Daily from 1000.
admission Adult: £12.50

Set in a hundred acres of delightful Hampshire countryside, Marwell is a relaxing and fascinating zoological park at the heart of wildlife conservation. New for 2007 is an amazing Australian bush walk. Over 200 species of animals including giraffe and rhino.

Map ref 2C3

New Forest Otter, Owl and Wildlife Conservation Park
Longdown, Ashurst SO40 4UH
t (023) 8029 2408 **w** ottersandowls.co.uk
open Apr-Oct, daily 1000-1730. Nov-Dec, Feb-Mar, daily 1000-dusk. Jan, Sat-Sun 1000-dusk.
admission ££
Situated within the New Forest heritage area – otter, owls and other native species can be seen in natural surroundings.

Quality counts

Look out for the Quality Assured Visitor Attraction sign. These attractions are assessed annually and meet the standards required to receive the quality marque.

enjoyEngland.com

QUALITY ASSURED
VISITOR
ATTRACTION

Queen Eleanor's Garden
Great Hall, The Castle, Winchester SO23 8PJ
t (01962) 846476
w hants.gov.uk/discover/places/great-hall.html
open Apr-Oct, daily 1000-1700. Nov-Mar, daily 1000-1600.
admission Free
A reconstruction of a 13thC garden at Winchester Castle named after Queen Eleanor. Also Great Hall with King Arthur's Round Table.

Queen Elizabeth Country Park
Gravel Hill, Horndean PO8 0QE
t (023) 9259 5040 **w** hants.gov.uk/countryside/qecp
open Park: Daily. Vistor Centre: Apr-Oct, Mar, daily 1000-1730. Nov-Feb, daily 1000-1630.
admission Free
Fourteen hundred acres of downlands and woodlands situated in south east Hampshire. Waymarked trails. Programme of events and activities. Visitor Centre, shop and cafe.

The Sir Harold Hillier Gardens
Jermyns Lane, Ampfield SO51 0QA
t (01794) 368787 **w** hilliergardens.org.uk
open Daily 1000-dusk.
admission ££
Established in 1953, this magnificent collection of over 42,000 trees and shrubs is one of the most important modern plant collections in the world.

Spinners
Boldre SO41 5QE
t (01590) 673347
open Gardens: Apr-Sep, Tue-Sat 1000-1700. Nursery: All year, 1000-1700.
admission £
Woodland garden with a wide selection of less common shrubs. Rhododendrons, azaleas, camellias interplanted with wide range of ground cover and choice shade plants. Also nursery.

Staunton Country Park
Middle Park Way, Havant PO9 5HB
t (023) 9245 3405 **w** hants.gov.uk/staunton
open Park: Daily. Visitor Centre: Daily 1000-1700.
admission £
Discover rainforest, a maze, friendly animals and 1000 acres of parkland with follies in the pleasure gardens created by Regency botanist Sir George Staunton.

West Green House Garden
West Green House, Thackham's Lane, West Green, Hartley Wintney RG27 8JB
t (01252) 845582 **w** westgreenhousegardens.co.uk
open Apr-Sep, Wed-Sun, Bank Hols 1100-1630.
admission £
Painstakingly restored Queen Anne house and 18thC gardens surrounded by a neo-classical park with lake, follies, monuments, a water feature and ornamental birdcages.

For key to symbols see inside back cover.

HISTORIC ENGLAND

Abbey of Our Lady and Saint John
Beech GU34 4AP
t (01420) 562145
open Daily.
admission Free

Alton Abbey is home for a community of Benedictine monks. The abbey church and conventual buildings, built of local flint, are to a design by Sir Charles Nicholson.

Breamore House

Breamore SP6 2DF
t (01725) 512233
w breamorehouse.com
open Apr, Tue, Sun 1400-1730. May-Sep, Tue-Thu, Sat-Sun, Bank Hols 1400-1730.
admission ££

An Elizabethan manor house dating from 1583, with a fine collection of works of art. Furniture, tapestries, needlework, paintings (mainly Dutch School 17thC and 18thC).

Broadlands
Romsey SO51 9ZD
t (01794) 505010
w broadlands.net
open Jun-Sep, Mon-Fri, Bank Hols 1300-1730.
admission ££

One of the finest examples of mid-Georgian architecture in England and home of the late Lord Mountbatten. Magnificent 18thC house and contents. Mountbatten exhibition.

Buckler's Hard
Beaulieu SO42 7XB
t (01590) 616203
w bucklershard.co.uk
open Apr-Sep, daily 1030-1700. Oct-Mar, daily 1100-1600.
admission ££

The Buckler's Hard Story reflects the history of the village. Displays in the historic cottages recreate 18thC life. Beaulieu River cruises are available to book.

Catholic Cathedral of St John
Edinburgh Road, Portsmouth PO1 3HG
t (023) 9282 6170
w portsmouthcatholiccathedral.org.uk
open Daily 0800-1730.
admission Free

A Victorian church with wooden vaulted ceiling. Restored in 2002. Awarded 'Best Restored Building in Portsmouth'. The Cathedral Discovery Centre offers a large range of books and religious items.

The Great Hall
The Castle, Winchester SO23 8PJ
t (01962) 846476
w hants.gov.uk/discover/places/great-hall.html
open Apr-Oct, daily 1000-1700. Nov-Feb, daily 1000-1600.
admission £

Great Hall featuring 'King Arthur's Round Table' and 13thC herb garden named after Queen Eleanor. The Round Table has hung here for over 600 years

Highclere Castle and Gardens
Highclere RG20 9RN
t (01635) 253210 **w** highclerecastle.co.uk
open Apr, Jul-Aug, Mon-Thu, Sun, Bank Hols 1100-1630.
admission ££

Highclere Castle is a splendid example of early Victorian architecture built in 1838-42. Home of the Earl of Carnarvon. Unique display of Egyptian antiquities.

Milestones, Hampshire's Living History Museum

Leisure Park, Churchill Way West, Basingstoke RG21 6YR
t (01256) 477766 **w** milestones-museum.com
open Tue-Fri, Bank Holiday Mon 1000-1700. Sat-Sun 1100-1700.
admission Adult: £7.25

Imagine an open-air museum inside a massive modern building, a network of streets with shops, a village green and even a pub. Dating from Victorian times and the 1930s, it's fun, with a surprise around every corner. Fully accessible site with cafe, gift shop and free parking.

Map ref 2C2

 voucher offer – see back section

Mottisfont Abbey Garden, House and Estate

Mottisfont SO51 0LP
t (01794) 340757
w nationaltrust.org.uk
open House: Apr-May, Sep-Oct, Mon-Wed, Sat-Sun, 1100-1700. Jun, daily 1100-1700. Jul, Mon-Thu, Sat-Sun 1100-1700. Garden: Apr-May, Sep-Oct, Mon-Wed, Sat-Sun 1100-1700. Jun, daily 1100-2030. Jul-Aug, Mon-Thu, Sat-Sun 1100-1700. Nov-Dec, Sat-Sun 1100-1600.
admission ££

With a tributary of the River Test flowing through, the garden, with its collection of old-fashioned roses, forms a superb setting for the 12thC priory.

Portchester Castle

Castle Street, Portchester PO16 9QW
t (023) 9237 8291
w english-heritage.org.uk
open Apr-Sep, daily 1000-1800. Oct-Mar, daily 1000-1600.
admission £

A Roman-Saxon shore fort with Norman additions. A near-perfect keep and Norman church within the walls. Spectacular views over the castle and Portsmouth.

Portsmouth Cathedral

High Street, Portsmouth PO1 2HH
t (023) 9282 3300
w portsmouthcathedral.org.uk
open Daily 0700-1900.
admission Free

Maritime cathedral with strong seafaring links. Tomb of unknown sailor from the Mary Rose. D-Day memorial window. The final stages of building were completed in 1991.

Portsmouth Historic Dockyard

The Visitor Centre, Victory Gate, HM Naval Base, Portsmouth PO1 3LJ
t (023) 9283 9766
w historicdockyard.co uk
open Apr-Oct, daily 1000-1800. Nov-Mar, daily 1000-1730.
admission Free

Discover the world famous historic ships, HMS Victory, the Mary Rose & HMS Warrior 1860 that have shaped British history at Portsmouth Historic Dockyard.

map ref 2C3
see ad on p381

Royal Armouries – Fort Nelson

Down End Road, Fareham PO17 6AN
t (01329) 233734
w royalarmouries.org
open Apr-Oct, Mon, Wed-Sun 1000-1700, Tue 1100-1700. Nov-Mar, Mon, Wed-Sun 1030-1600, Tue 1130-1600.
admission Free

Wonderfully restored Victorian fort, home to the Royal Armouries collection of big guns. Daily guided tours and dramatic performances with special events throughout year.

Spinnaker Tower

Gunwharf Quays, Portsmouth PO1 3TT
t (023) 9285 7520
w spinnakertower.co.uk
open All year, Mon-Fri, Sun 1000-1700, Sat 1000-2200.
admission ££

The Spinnaker Tower is a new national icon. It is a striking viewing tower on the south coast offering the public spectacular views from three platforms.

Stratfield Saye House

Stratfield Saye RG7 2BZ
t (01256) 882882
w stratfield-saye.co.uk
open July, Mon-Fri 1130-1700, Sat-Sun 1030-1700.
admission ££

Family home of the Dukes of Wellington since 1817. The house, the Wellington exhibition, the great Duke's funeral carriage, the grave of Copenhagen and state coach.

The Vyne

Vyne Road, Sherborne St John RG24 9HL
t (01256) 883858
w nationaltrust.org.uk
open House: Apr-Oct, Mon-Wed 1300-1700. Sat-Sun 1100-1700. Grounds: Apr-Oct, Mon-Wed, Sat-Sun 1100-1700. Feb, Sat-Sun 1100-1700.
admission ££

Original house dating back to Henry VIII's time. Extensively altered in mid 17thC. Tudor chapel, beautiful gardens and lake. Woodland walks.

Winchester Cathedral

The Close, Winchester SO23 9LS
t (01962) 857225
w winchester-cathedral.org.uk
open All year, Mon-Sat 0830-1800, Sun 0830-1730.
admission £

Magnificent medieval cathedral, soaring Gothic nave converted from Norman 12thC illuminated Winchester Bible, Jane Austen's tomb, library, gallery, crypt, chapels.

ENTERTAINMENT AND CULTURE

Artsway

Station Road, Sway SO41 6BA
t (01590) 682260
w artsway.org.uk
open All year, Tue-Sun 1100-1700.
admission Free

Contemporary visual arts centre in the New Forest. Craft cabinets and gallery shop, outdoor sculpture and community boules court. Gallery talks and events.

Breamore Countryside Museum

Breamore SP6 2DF
t (01725) 512468
w breamorehouse.com
open Apr, Tue, Sun 1300-1730. May-Sep, Tue-Thu,
Sat-Sun, Bank Hols 1300-1730.
admission ££

Farm buildings in a walled garden provide a fascinating insight into the days when a village was self-sufficient. Great British maze.

Charles Dickens Birthplace Museum

393 Old Commercial Road, Portsmouth PO1 4QL
t (023) 9282 7261
w charlesdickensbirthplace.co.uk
open Apr-Oct, daily 1000-1730.
admission ££

A small terraced house dating from 1805 where the famous novelist was born and lived for a short time. Restored and furnished to illustrate the middle-class taste of the time.

The D-Day Museum and Overlord Embroidery

Clarence Esplanade, Portsmouth PO5 3NT
t (023) 9282 7261
w ddaymuseum.co.uk
open Apr-Oct, daily 1000-1730.
admission ££

The magnificent 83m-long 'Overlord Embroidery' depicts the allied invasion of Normandy on 6 June1944, with sound guides available in four languages.

Explosion! Museum of Naval Firepower

Priddy's Hard, Gosport PO12 4LE
t (023) 9250 5600   **w** explosion.org.uk
open Apr-Oct, daily 1000-1730. Nov-Mar, Thu, Sat-Sun
1000-1600.
admission ££

The amazing story of naval firepower, from gunpowder to the Exocet, in an exciting new visitor experience for all the family on the shores of Portsmouth Harbour.

Gilbert White's House and The Oates Museum

High Street, Selborne GU34 3JH
t (01420) 511275   **w** gilbertwhiteshouse.org.uk
open Apr-May, Sep-Dec, Tue-Sun, Bank Hols
1100-1700. Jun-Aug, daily 1100-1700.
admission ££

Historic house and garden, home of Gilbert White, author of 'The Natural History of Selborne'. Exhibition on Frank Oates, explorer and Capt Laurence Oates of Antarctic fame.

The Gurkha Museum

Peninsula Barracks, Romsey Road,
Winchester SO23 8TS
t (01962) 842832   **w** thegurkhamuseum.co.uk
open All year, Mon-Sat 1000-1700, Sun 1200-1600.
admission £

History of Gurkhas service to the Crown 1815-1993. Militaria, badges, medals, figures and uniforms, plus interactive exhibits and sound and light displays.

Hidden Britain Tours

28 Chequers Road, Basingstoke RG21 7PU
t (01256) 814222
w hiddenbritaintours.co.uk
open Phone to arrange a tour.
admission Please phone for pricing details

Take a tour of the New Forest or visit the landscape that inspired Jane Austen. Discover the secrets of the county on the Hidden Hampshire Tour. Why walk when you can ride with a guide? A trip to remember. Forever.

Map ref 2C2

Museum of Army Flying
Middle Wallop SO20 8DY
t (01980) 674421 **w** flying-museum.org.uk
open Daily 1000-1630.
admission ££
Award-winning and unique collection of flying machines and displays depicting the role of army flying since the 1870s including the national collection of army assault gliders.

National Motor Museum Beaulieu
John Montagu Building, Beaulieu SO42 7ZN
t (01590) 612345 **w** beaulieu.co.uk
open Apr, daily 1000-1700. May-Sep, daily 1000-1800. Oct-Mar, daily 1000-1700.
admission £££
Motor museum with over 250 exhibits showing history of motoring from 1896. Also Palace House, Wheels Experience, Beaulieu Abbey ruins and a display of monastic life.

New Forest Museum
High Street, Lyndhurst SO43 7NY
t (023) 8028 3444 **w** newforestmuseum.org.uk
open Daily 1000-1700.
admission £
Museum covering the traditions, history and wildlife of the New Forest. Interactive displays, quizzes and changing exhibitions provide an extensive history of this area

Portsmouth City Museum and Record Office
Museum Road, Portsmouth PO1 2LJ
t (023) 9282 7261 **w** portsmouthmuseums.co.uk
open Apr-Sep, daily 1000-1730. Oct-Mar, daily 1000-1700.
admission Free
Museum containing displays of local history, furniture, decorative art and contemporary crafts. Story of Portsmouth exhibition. Regular temporary exhibitions. Records office.

Royal Marines Museum
Southsea PO4 9PX
t (023) 9281 9385 **w** royalmarinesmuseum.co.uk
open Apr-May, Sep-Mar, daily 1000-1630. Jun-Aug, daily 1000-1700.
admission £
History of Royal Marines 1664 to present day. Jungle and trench warfare sight and sound exhibitions. D-Day, Falklands' cinemas and supporting exhibitions.

Royal Navy Submarine Museum
Haslar Jetty Road, Gosport PO12 2AS
t (023) 9252 9217 **w** rnsubmus.co.uk
open Apr-Oct, daily 1000-1700. Nov-Mar, daily 1000-1630.
admission ££
Dive into the past and the future and explore the challenges of the deep! Discover all about submarines and the men who fought in them.

St Barbe Museum and Art Gallery
New Street, Lymington SO41 9BH
t (01590) 676969 **w** stbarbe-museum.org.uk
open All year, Mon-Sat 1000-1600.
admission £
The museum of the New Forest coast plus art galleries with high quality exhibitions Museum displays include boat building, smuggling, salt making and fishing.

Sammy Miller Museum (Transport) (Sammy Miller Museum Trust)
Bashley Cross Road, New Milton BH25 5SZ
t (01425) 620777 **w** sammymiller.co.uk
open Daily 1000-1630.
admission £
One of the world's largest collections of racing, trials and historic motorcycles, including many machines that are the only surviving examples in the world.

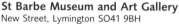

For key to symbols see inside back cover.

Southampton City Art Gallery

Civic Centre, Commercial Road, Southampton SO14 7LP
t (023) 8083 2277 **w** southampton.gov.uk/art
open All year, Tue-Sat 1000-1700, Sun 1300-1600.
admission Free

Major collection of British and European paintings from the 14th to 20thC with emphasis on 20thC British art. The gallery has a lively programme of workshops, lectures and other activities.

Southampton Maritime Museum

Wool House, Town Quay,
Southampton SO14 2AR
t (023) 8022 3941
w southampton.gov.uk/leisure/heritage
open All year, Tue-Fri 1000-1600, Sat 1000-1300
1400-1600, Sun 1300-1700.
admission Free

Medieval stone warehouse with timber roof. Exhibitions on the port of Southampton, ship models including ocean liners. A permanent exhibition on the RMS Titanic and Southampton.

Winchester City Museum

The Square, Winchester SO23 9ES
t (01962) 848269 **w** winchester.gov.uk
open Apr-Oct, Mon-Sat 1000-1700, Sun 1200-1700.
Nov-Mar, Tue-Sat 1000-1600, Sun 1200-1600.
admission Free

Tells story of Winchester, Roman town, and principal city of King Alfred, Anglo-Saxon and Norman England, through to modern times. Reconstructed Victorian shops.

RELAXING AND PAMPERING

Grayshott Pottery

School Road, Grayshott GU26 6LR
t (01428) 604404
w grayshottpottery.com
open Factory: All year, Mon-Fri 1100-1300, 1400-1600.
Gift Shop: All year, Mon-Sat 0900-1730, Sun, Bank Hols
1000-1600.
admission Free

A spacious gift shop offering every gift imaginable including Dartington crystal, jewellery, stationery, toiletries and toys. Visitors may watch the pottery being made using traditional methods and skills.

Gunwharf Quays

Gunwharf Quays Management Ltd,
Centre Management Suite, Gunwharf Quay,
Portsmouth PO1 3TZ
t (023) 9283 6700
w gunwharf-quays.com
open Daily.
admission Free

Gunwharf Quays is Europe's most innovative and exciting retail, restaurant and leisure destination as well as offering a year-round events programme of music, street theatre and seasonal festivals

The Great Hall, Winchester

Isle of Wight

Enjoy the fun of a special event or visit one of the attractions listed for a great day out. For more inspiring ideas go to **enjoyengland.com**.

Jun
Isle of Wight Festival
Seaclose Park, Newport
0870 532 1321
isleofwightfestival.com

4–11 Aug
Cowes Week
The Solent, Cowes
(01983) 295744
skandiacowesweek.co.uk

27 Aug–2 Sep
White Air Festival
Various venues across the island
whiteair.co.uk

7–9 Sep
Bestival Music Festival
Robin Hill Country Park, Newport
bestival.net

May 08
Isle of Wight Walking Festival
Various venues across the island
isleofwightwalkingfestival.co.uk

FAMILY FUN

Blackgang Chine Fantasy Park
Blackgang Chine, Chale PO38 2HN
t (01983) 730330 **w** blackgangchine.com
open Apr-Oct, daily 1000-dusk.
admission ££
Fantasy park with water and cliff-top gardens, dinosaur park, Frontierland, maze, Nurseryland, Smugglerland, Fantasyland, Rumpus Mansion, Water-Force and Cliffhanger. Also Sawmill exhibition.

The Model Village
The Old Vicarage, High Street, Godshill PO38 3HH
t (01983) 840270 **w** modelvillagegodshill.co.uk
open Apr-Jun, Sep-Oct, daily 1000-1700. Jul-Aug, daily 1000-1800.
admission £
Model village with 2,000+ 'in scale' conifers. Amble the streets to enjoy model houses, a railway, little people and planes. A must-see attraction for all.

The Needles Park
Alum Bay PO39 0JD
t 0870 458 0022 **w** theneedles.co.uk
open Apr-Oct, daily 1000-1700. Nov-Mar, daily 1000-1600.
admission Free
Home of the world-famous coloured sand cliffs. Ride the chairlift for spectacular views of the Needles Rocks and lighthouse. Watch craftsmen making glass and sweets.

NATURE AND WILDLIFE

Amazon World Zoo Park
Watery Lane, Newchurch PO36 0LX
t (01983) 867122 **w** amazonworld.co.uk
open Apr-Oct, daily 1000-1730. Nov-Mar, daily 1000-1500.
admission ££
Amazon World Zoo Park, the largest exotic-animal attraction on the island, recreating the story of the rainforest. Awarded top family attraction.

Butterfly World and Fountain World
Staplers Road, Wootton, Ryde PO33 4RW
t (01983) 883430 **w** butterfly-fountain-world.co.uk
open Apr-Oct, daily 1000-1730.
admission ££
Tropical indoor garden with butterflies from around the world. Fountain World has many fountains, water features and huge fish. Italian and Japanese gardens.

Admission is based on an adult price. Please check opening times and admission before travelling.

Isle of Wight Zoo, Home of the Tiger Sanctuary and Lemurland

Sandown PO36 8QB
t (01983) 403883 **w** isleofwightzoo.com
open Apr-Sep, daily 1000-1800. Oct, daily 1000-1600.
Nov, Sat-Sun 1000-1600.
admission ££

Isle of Wight Family Attraction of 2004, the zoo specialises in tigers, big cats and primates. Talks and tours throughout the day.

Mottistone Manor Garden
Mottistone PO30 4ED
t (01983) 741302 **w** nationaltrust.org.uk
open Apr-Oct, Mon-Thu, Sun 1100-1730.
admission £

A formal terraced garden noted for its colourful herbaceous borders, grassy terraces planted with fruit trees and its sea views.

Ventnor Botanic Garden and Visitor Centre
Undercliff Drive, Ventnor PO38 1UL
t (01983) 855397 **w** botanic.co.uk
open Gardens: Daily. Visitor Centre: Apr-Oct, Mar, daily 1000-1700. Nov-Feb, Sat-Sun 1000-1600.
admission Free

Twenty-two acres of world themed gardens with a visitor centre, gift shop, cafe, two semi-permanent exhibitions and a plant sales area.

HISTORIC ENGLAND

Appuldurcombe House and Isle of Wight Falconry Centre
Wroxall PO38 3EW
t (01983) 840188 **w** appuldurcombe.co.uk
open Apr-Sep, daily 1000-1600.
admission ££

Ruins of 18thC house and garden. Park landscaped by Capability Brown. Front of house re-roofed and windows reglazed. Home of Isle of Wight Owl and Falconry Centre.

Carisbrooke Castle
Castle Hill, Newport PO30 1XY
t (01983) 522107
w english-heritage.org.uk
open Apr-Oct, daily 1000-1700. Nov-Mar, daily 1000-1600.
admission ££

A splendid Norman castle, where Charles I was imprisoned. The governor's lodge houses the county museum. Wheelhouse with wheel operated by donkeys.

Needles Old Battery
West Highdown, Totland Bay PO39 0JH
t (01983) 754772
w nationaltrust.org.uk
open Apr-Jun, Sep-Oct, Mon-Thu, Sat-Sun 1030-1700. Jul-Aug, daily 1030-1700.
admission £

The threat of a French invasion prompted the 1862 construction of this spectacularly sited fort, still retaining its original gun barrels and a 65m tunnel.

Nunwell House
Coach Lane, Brading PO36 0JQ
t (01983) 407240
open Jul-Sep, Mon-Wed 1300-1700.
admission £

Nunwell with its historic connections with Charles I is set in beautiful gardens and parkland with channel views. House has Jacobean and Georgian wings. Family military collection.

Osborne House
York Avenue., East Cowes,
Isle of Wight PO32 6JX
t (01983) 200022
w english-heritage.org.uk
open Apr-Sep, daily 1000-1800. Oct, daily 1000-1600.
Nov-Mar, please phone for details.
admission ££

Queen Victoria and Prince Albert's seaside holiday home. Swiss Cottage where royal children learnt cooking and gardening. Victorian carriage rides. Award-winning gardens. New visitor centre with exhibition and shop.

Freshwater Bay

Saint Mildred's Church and Church Centre

Beatrice Avenue, Whippingham, East Cowes PO32 6LW
t (01983) 200107
w iowight/stmildreds
open May-Oct, Mon-Fri 1000-1600.
admission Free

Church designed by Prince Albert, place of worship when Queen Victoria stayed at Osborne House. Church and centre with displays of royal and local photographs and artefacts.

ENTERTAINMENT AND CULTURE

Cowes Maritime Museum

Beckford Road, Cowes PO31 7SG
t (01983) 823847
w iwight.com
open All year, Mon-Tue, Fri 0930-1730, Wed 1100-1900, Sat 0930-1630.
admission Free

The museum contains boats, paintings and models depicting the maritime history of Cowes and the Isle of Wight. Another collection of boats represents the modern yacht-building industry

Dinosaur Isle

Culver Parade, Sandown PO36 8QA
t (01983) 404344
w dinosaurisle.com
open Apr-Sep, daily 1000-1800. Oct, daily 1000-1700. Nov-Mar, daily 1000-1600.
admission £

In Britain's first purpose-built dinosaur attraction, walk back through fossilized time and meet life-sized replicas of dinosaurs, including an Animatronic Neovenator.

Lilliput Museum of Antique Dolls and Toys

High Street, Brading PO36 0DJ
t (01983) 407231
w lilliputmuseum.com
open Daily 1000-1700.
admission £

Over 2,000 antique dolls and toys dating from c2000 BC to c1945 housed in mainly 17thC buildings. BTA Award winner – nationally recognised museum.

Quay Arts

Sea Street, Newport Harbour, Newport PO30 5BD
t (01983) 822490
w quayarts.org
open All year, Mon, Wed-Sat 0930-1700, Tue, 0930-2000.
admission Free

Quay Arts is housed in an 18thC warehouse at Newport Harbour. There are three galleries, craft shop, dance studio, 134-seat theatre, cafe and bar.

Kent

Enjoy the fun of a special event or visit one of the attractions listed for a great day out. For more inspiring ideas go to **enjoyengland.com**.

16–24 Jun
Broadstairs Dickens Festival
(70th Anniversary)
Broadstairs
(01843) 861827
broadstairsdickensfestival.co.uk

8 Jul
Tour de France Stage 1
London to Canterbury
Various venues, Canterbury
(020) 7222 1234
tourdefrancelondon.com

13–15 Jul
Kent Show
Kent County Showground, Maidstone
(01622) 630975
kentshow.co.uk

19–21 Jul
Kent Beer Festival
Merton Farm, Canterbury
(01227) 463478
kentbeerfestival.co.uk

1–2 Sep
Faversham Hop Festival
Faversham
(01795) 585601
swale.gov.uk/hopfestival

For key to symbols see inside back cover.

FAMILY FUN

The Canterbury Tales
St Margaret's Street, Canterbury CT1 2TG
t (01227) 479227 **w** canterburytales.org.uk
open Apr-Jun, Sep-Oct, Mar, daily 1000-1700. Jul-Aug,
daily 0930-1700. Nov-Feb, daily 1000-1630.
admission ££

*An audiovisual recreation of life in medieval England.
Join Chaucer's pilgrims on their journey from the Tabard
Inn in London to St Thomas Becket's shrine at
Canterbury.*

Diggerland
Roman Way, Medway Valley Park, Strood ME2 2NU
t 0870 034 4437 **w** diggerland.com
open See website for details.
admission £££

*An adventure park where children of all ages can ride
and drive diggers and small dumpers. A huge variety of
equipment is available for a day of family fun.*

Farming World
Nash Court, Boughton, Faversham ME13 9SW
t (01227) 751144 **w** farming-world.com
open Apr-Oct, Mar, daily 0930-1730. Nov-Dec,
Wed-Sat 1000-1600.
admission ££

*An open farm with over 100 farm animals, pet area, rare
breeds, heavy horses, adventure playgrounds,
agricultural museum and farm trail. Hawking centre and
sensory garden.*

The Hop Farm Country Park

Paddock Wood TN12 6PY
t (01622) 872068 w thehopfarm.co.uk
admission Adult: £7.50

Set in 400 acres of unspoilt Kent countryside,
this once-working hop farm is one of Kent's
most popular attractions. The spectacular Oast
Village is home to an indoor and outdoor play
area, interactive museum, shire horses and an
animal farm, as well as hosting over 30 special
events throughout the year.

Map ref 3B4

V *voucher offer – see back section*

Penshurst Place and Gardens

Kent & East Sussex Railway

Tenterden Town Station, Tenterden TN30 6HE
t (01580) 765155
w kesr.org.uk
open See website for details.
admission £££

Full-size heritage railway. Restored Edwardian stations at Tenterden and Northiam, 14 steam engines, Victorian coaches and Pullman carriages. Museum. Children's play area.

Romney, Hythe and Dymchurch Railway

New Romney Station, New Romney TN28 8PL
t (01797) 362353
w rhdr.org.uk
open See website for details.
admission £££

The world's only main line in miniature. Fourteen miles of 15in gauge across Romney Marsh. Steam and diesel locomotives, engine sheds and a Toy and Model Museum.

South of England Rare Breeds Centre

Highlands Farm, Woodchurch TN26 3RJ
t (01233) 861493
w rarebreeds.org.uk
open Apr-Oct, daily 1030-1730. Nov-Mar, Tue-Sun 1030-1600.
admission ££

Large collection of rare farm breeds on a working farm with children's play activities. Home to the 'Tamworth Two'. Woodland walks.

NATURE AND WILDLIFE

Bedgebury National Pinetum

Park Lane, Goudhurst TN17 2SL
t (01580) 211044
w bedgeburypinetum.org.uk
open Daily 0800-1700.
admission £

A stunning, unique and internationally famous collection of conifers amidst beautifully landscaped lakes and avenues. Be amazed at the variety of colours, shapes and scents.

Beech Court Gardens

Beech Court, Canterbury Road, Challock TN25 4DJ
t (01233) 740735
w beechcourtgardens.co.uk
open Apr-Sep, Mon-Thu, Sat-Sun 1030-1730. Oct, Sat-Sun 1030-1730.
admission £

Informal woodland garden surrounding a medieval farmhouse. Fine collection of trees and shrubs, herbaceous borders and water garden. Meandering paths with surprising vistas.

Brogdale Horticultural Trust

Brogdale Road, Faversham ME13 8XZ
t (01795) 535286 **w** brogdale.org.uk
open Apr-Oct, daily 1000-1700. Nov-Feb, daily 1000-1630.
admission ££

The National Fruit Collection has 4,000 varieties of fruit in 150 acres: apples, pears, cherries, plums, currants, quinces, medlars. Plant centre, tearoom and gift shop.

Doddington Place Gardens

Doddington ME9 0BB
t (01795) 886101 **w** doddington-place-gardens.co.uk
open Apr-Jun, Sun 1400-1700, Bank Hols 1100-1700.
admission £

Ten acres of landscaped gardens with formal sunken garden, Edwardian rock garden, fine trees, woodland, rhododendrons, azaleas, clipped yews and extensive lawns.

Eagle Heights

Lullingstone Lane, Eynsford DA4 0JB
t (01322) 866466 **w** eagleheights.co.uk
open Apr-Oct, Mar, daily 1030-1700. Nov, Jan-Feb, Sat-Sun 1100-1600.
admission ££

Bird of prey centre housed undercover where visitors can see eagles, hawks, falcons, owls and vultures from all over the world. Reptile centre, play area and sandpit.

Emmetts Garden

Ide Hill TN14 6AY
t (01732) 868381 **w** nationaltrust.org.uk
open Apr-May, Tue-Sun 1100-1700. Jun, Wed-Sun 1100-1700. Jul-Oct, Wed, Sat-Sun 1100-1700.
admission ££

A shrub garden on a hillside with notable spring and autumn colours. Rare trees, shrubs and carpets of bluebells. Wonderful views over the Weald.

Goodnestone Park Gardens

Wingham CT3 1PL
t (01304) 840107 **w** goodnestoneparkgardens.co.uk
open Apr-Oct, Wed-Sat 1100-1700, Sun, Bank Hols 1200-1700.
admission £

A 14-acre garden with fine trees, a large collection of shrubs and old fashioned roses, walled garden, woodland garden, small arboretum and Jane Austen connections.

Great Comp Garden

Comp Lane, Platt, Borough Green TN15 8QS
t (01732) 886154 **w** greatcomp.co.uk
open Apr-Oct, daily 1100-1700.
admission £

A skilfully designed seven-acre garden with well-maintained lawns, a tree collection, shrubs, heathers, herbaceous plants, walls and terraces. Annual music festival.

Admission is based on an adult price. Please check opening times and admission before travelling.

Groombridge Place Gardens and Enchanted Forest

Groombridge Asset Management Ltd, Groombridge TN3 9QG
t (01892) 861444 **w** groombridge.co.uk
open Apr-Nov, daily 1000-1730.
admission ££

Winner of 'Best Tourism Experience' – Tourism Excellence Awards 2005. Gardens featuring traditional and 17thC walled gardens. In the ancient woodland of the Enchanted Forest there is mystery, innovation and excitement for all.

Howletts Wild Animal Park

Bekesbourne CT4 5EL
t (01227) 721286 **w** totallywild.net
open Apr-Sep, daily 1000-1800. Oct-Mar, daily 1000-1630.
admission £££

Set in 90 acres of mature parkland with gorillas, tigers, small cats, tapirs, wolves, bongo, African elephants and many endangered species.

Iden Croft Herbs & Walled Gardens

Frittenden Road, Staplehurst TN12 0DH
t (01580) 891432 **w** herbs-uk.com
open Apr-Sep, Mon-Sat 0900-1700, Sun, Bank Hols 1100-1700. Oct-Mar, Mon-Fri 0900-dusk.
admission £

Extensive aromatic herb gardens with walled garden and a variety of themed gardens demonstrating the beauty and use of herbs. National Collections of mentha and origanum.

Macfarlanes Butterfly Centre

A260 Canterbury Road, Swingfield, Dover CT15 7HX
t (01303) 844244 **w** macfarlanesgarden.co.uk
open Apr-Sep, daily 1000-1700.
admission £

A large purpose-built greenhouse with butterflies from all over the world flying free in landscaped tropical gardens. Life-cycle exhibits. Large tree, shrub and plant centre.

Marle Place Gardens and Gallery

Marle Place Road, Brenchley TN12 7HS
t (01892) 722304 **w** marleplace.co.uk
open Apr-Oct, Mon, Fri-Sun 1000-1700.
admission £

Romantic, peaceful, plantsman's gardens with topiary, unusual shrubs and plants, ponds, Edwardian rockery and Victorian gazebo. Walled scented garden and sculptures.

Mount Ephraim Gardens

Hernhill ME13 9TX
t (01227) 751496 **w** mountephraimgardens.co.uk
open Apr-Sep, Wed-Thu, Sat-Sun 1300-1800, Bank Hols 1100-1800.
admission £

Fine herbaceous border, daffodils, rose terraces, topiary and a small lake. New water garden. Woodland area, orchard walk, Japanese style rock garden.

The Pines Garden

Beach Road, St Margaret's Bay CT15 6DZ
t (01304) 851737 **w** baytrust.org.uk
open Daily 1000-1700.
admission Free

Six acres of tranquillity. Mature trees, lawns, specimen shrubs, spring bulbs, lake, waterfall, grass labyrinth and rockery. Oscar Nemon's statue of Sir Winston Churchill.

Port Lympne Wild Animal Park, Mansion and Gardens

Aldington Road, Lympne CT21 4PD
t (01303) 264647 **w** totallywild.net
open Apr-Sep, daily 1000-1800. Oct-Mar, daily 1000-1630.
admission £££

See many rare and endangered species in a natural environment and enjoy the African Safari Experience where animals roam free as if on the plains of Africa.

Scotney Castle Garden and Estate

Lamberhurst TN3 8JN
t (01892) 893868 **w** nationaltrust.org.uk
open Garden: Apr-Oct, Wed-Sun 1100-1730. Nov-Dec, Sat-Sun 1100-1600. Estate: Daily.
admission ££

Romantic gardens created around the ruins of a 14thC moated castle containing exhibitions. Gardens created by the Hussey family with shrubs, winding paths and superb views.

Sissinghurst Castle Garden

Sissinghurst TN17 2AB
t (01580) 710701 **w** nationaltrust.org.uk
open Apr-Oct, Mon-Tue, Fri-Sun 1100-1830.
admission ££

A garden created by Vita Sackville-West and Harold Nicolson around an Elizabethan mansion. A series of small enclosed compartments, intimate in scale and romantic in atmosphere.

Wildwood Trust

Wildwood, Herne Common, Herne Bay CT6 7LQ
t (01227) 712111 **w** wildwoodtrust.org
open Apr-Sep, daily 1000-1800. Oct-Mar, daily 1000-1700.
admission ££

Wildwood depicts wildlife and early man in a classic Kent setting. There are many different species of animals, special events and a play area.

Yalding Organic Gardens

Benover Road, Yalding ME18 6EX
t (01622) 814650 **w** hdra.org.uk
open Apr-Oct, Wed-Sun 1000-1700.
admission £

Five acres of stunning gardens – themed history displays, practical demonstrations of compost making and safe pest control. Cafe and shop.

HISTORIC ENGLAND

Bayham Abbey
Lamberhurst TN3 8DE
t (01892) 890381
w english-heritage.org.uk
open Apr-Sep, daily 1100-1700.
admission £   ⊓ ✗ ら

Impressive abbey ruins, founded in 1208 by Premonstratensian monks and dissolved by Wolsey in 1525. Ruins of church buildings and gatehouse, set in valley of River Teise.

Belmont House and Gardens
Belmont Park, Throwley ME13 0HH
t (01795) 890202
w belmont-house.org
open House: Apr-Sep, Sat-Sun, Bank Hols 1400-1700. Gardens: Daily 1000-dusk.
admission ££   ⊒ ✗ ⬛

A late-18thC country mansion designed by Samuel Wyatt, seat of the Harris family since 1801. Harris clock collection, mementos of connections with India. Gardens and pinetum.

Canterbury Cathedral
The Precincts, Canterbury CT1 2EH
t (01227) 762862
w canterbury-cathedral.org
open All year, Mon-Sat 0900-1700, Sun 1230-1400.
admission ££   ⊒ ⊓ ら

Founded in AD597, it is the Mother Church of Anglican Communion and has a Romanesque crypt, 12thC Gothic quire and 14thC nave. Site of Thomas Becket's murder in AD1170.

Chartwell
Mapleton Road, Westerham TN16 1PS
t (01732) 868381
w nationaltrust.org.uk
open Apr-Jun, Sep-Oct, Wed-Sun 1100-1700. Jul-Aug, Thu-Sun 1100-1700.
admission £££   ⊒ ⊓ ⬛

The home of Sir Winston Churchill with study, studio and museum rooms with gifts, uniforms and photos. Garden, Golden Rose walk, lakes and exhibition.

Deal Castle
Victoria Road, Deal CT14 7BA
t (01304) 372762
w english-heritage.org.uk
open Apr-Sep, Mon-Fri 1000-1800, Sat 1000-1700, Sun 1000-1800.
admission £   ⊒ ✗ ら

The largest of Henry VIII's coastal forts built c1540 with 119 gun positions. Tudor-rose shaped with outer moat. It also has a coastal-defence exhibition.

Dover Castle and Secret Wartime Tunnels

Dover Castle, Dover CT16 1HU
t (01304) 211067
w english-heritage.org.uk
open All year, Mon, Thu-Sun 1000-1600.
admission ££   ⊒ ⊓ ✗ ⬛

One of the most powerful medieval fortresses in Western Europe. St Mary-in-Castro Saxon church, Roman lighthouse, secret wartime tunnels, Henry II Great Keep.

The Friars
Aylesford Priory,
Aylesford ME20 7BX
t (01622) 717272
w thefriars.org.uk
open Apr-Sep, daily 1000-1700. Oct-Mar, daily 1000-1600.
admission Free   ⊒ ⊓ ✗ ⬛

A 13thC priory with 14thC cloisters and a shrine. Visitors can see sculpture and ceramics by contemporary artists. Medieval barns, pottery, upholstery workshops can be seen.

Godinton House and Gardens
Godinton Lane, Ashford TN23 3BP
t (01233) 620773
w godinton-house-gardens.co.uk
open Gardens: Apr-Oct, Mon, Thu-Sun 1400-1730. House: Apr-Oct, Fri-Sun 1400-1730.
admission ££   ⊒ ⊓ ✗ ⬛

The house dates back to 1390 and has exquisite carving and a fine collection of furniture and porcelain. The famous yew hedge encloses contrasting gardens, from formal to wild.

Hever Castle and Gardens
Hever TN8 7NG
t (01732) 865224
w hevercastle.co.uk
open Grounds: Apr-Nov, daily 1100-1800. Castle: Apr-Nov, daily 1200-1800.
admission ££   ⊒ ⊓ ⬛

A moated castle once the childhood home of Anne Boleyn. Restored by the Astor family, it contains furniture, paintings and panelling. Set in award-winning gardens.

Ightham Mote
Ivy Hatch TN15 0NT
t (01732) 811145
w nationaltrust.org.uk
open House: Apr-Oct, Mon, Wed-Fri, Sun 1030-1730. Garden: Apr-Oct, Mon, Wed-Fri, Sun 1000-1730. Estate: All year, dawn-dusk.
admission ££   ⊒ ⊓ ✗ ⬛

A medieval moated manor house with Great Hall, two chapels, 18thC drawing room and courtyard. Garden and woodland walk. Ongoing repair programme.

Knole
Sevenoaks TN15 0RP
t (01732) 462100
w nationaltrust.org.uk
open House: Apr-Oct, Wed-Sun, Bank Hols 1200-1600.
Garden: Apr-Oct, Wed, Bank Hols 1100-1600. Park:
Daily.
admission ££
One of England's 'Treasure Houses', dating from 1456. Important collections of portraits, silver, tapestries and unique 17thC Royal Stuart furniture. Set in deer park.

Leeds Castle and Gardens
Broomfield, Maidstone ME17 1PL
t (01622) 765400
w leeds-castle.com
open Gardens: Daily 1000-1700. Castle: Daily
1030-1600.
admission £££
A castle on two islands in a lake, dating from 9thC. Furniture, tapestries, art treasures, dog collar museum, gardens, duckery, aviaries, maze, grotto and vineyard.

Lullingstone Roman Villa
Lullingstone Lane, Eynsford DA4 0JA
t (01322) 863467
w english-heritage.org.uk
open Please phone for details.
admission £
The remains of an important villa built during the 1stC and occupied until early 5thC. It has been excavated and includes outstanding mosaic floors. Early Christian chapel.

Minster Abbey
Minster-in-Thanet CT12 4HF
t (01843) 821254
open Chapel: Daily. Tours: Please phone for details.
admission Free
Founded in 670, the Abbey was destroyed in 840 and restored in 1027. Two wings of the old building with Norman crypt contain the ruin of a church tower.

Penshurst Place and Gardens
Penshurst TN11 8DG
t (01892) 870307
w penshurstplace.com
open Gardens: Apr-Oct, daily 1030-1800. House:
Apr-Oct, daily 1200-1600.
admission ££
A medieval manor house with Baron's Hall, portraits, tapestries, armour, park, lake, venture playground, toy museum and with Tudor gardens. Gift shop.

Pleasant Promenades Guided Walking Tours

Royal Tunbridge Wells Tourist Information
Centre, The Old Fish Market, The Pantiles,
Royal Tunbridge Wells TN2 5TN
t (01892) 515675 **w** visittunbridgewells.com
open All year, Thu & Sat 1130-1230 (approx
finish time).
admission Adult: £3.50

Discover the 400-year history of the spa town
of Royal Tunbridge Wells on a guided stroll
through the Pantiles and the historic heart of
the town. Hear about the many famous visitors
- from Queen Anne to Samuel Pepys - who
made Tunbridge Wells the place to see and
be seen.

Map ref 3B4

V *voucher offer – see back section*

Quebec House
Quebec Square, Westerham TN16 1TD
t (01732) 868381 **w** nationaltrust.org.uk
open Apr-Oct, Wed-Sun, Bank Hols 1300-1630.
admission £
A mostly 17thC red brick gabled house and the boyhood home of General Wolfe. Four rooms on view contain family photographs and prints. Exhibition on Battle of Quebec.

enjoyEngland.com

A great attraction or activity can often make the perfect holiday.
Enjoyengland.com features a comprehensive list of every quality-assured
theme park, landmark, museum, national park and activity in England.

Restoration House

17-19 Crow Lane, Rochester ME1 1RF
t (01634) 848520 **w** restorationhouse.co.uk
open Jun-Sep, Thu-Fri 1000-1700.
admission ££

An historic city mansion with a unique atmosphere and links to Charles II, Pepys and Dickens. There are beautiful interiors and a classic English garden.

Richborough Roman Fort

Richborough CT13 9JW
t (01304) 612013 **w** english-heritage.org.uk
open Apr-Sep, daily 1000-1800.
admission £

The ruins of a Roman fort and the landing place of the invasion of AD43. Fortified in the 3rdC and then improved by the Saxons.

Rochester Cathedral

The Precinct, Rochester ME1 1SX
t (01634) 401301 **w** rochestercathedral.org
open All year, Mon-Fri 0700-1800, Sat-Sun 0700-1700.
admission £

Consecrated in AD604, the present building dates from 1080. A blend of Norman and Gothic architecture raised above a crypt with medieval wall paintings.

St Augustine's Abbey

Longport, Canterbury CT1 1TF
t (01227) 767345 **w** english-heritage.org.uk
open Apr-Jun, Wed-Sun 1000-1700. Jul-Aug, daily 1000-1800. Sep-Mar, Sun 1100-1700.
admission £

Now a World Heritage Site, this Benedictine Abbey was founded in AD598 by St Augustine. The remains include a Norman church and ruins of the 7thC church of St Pancras.

Smallhythe Place

Smallhythe, Tenterden TN30 7NG
t (01580) 762334 **w** nationaltrust.org.uk
open Apr-Oct, Mon-Wed, Sat-Sun 1100-1700.
admission £

A 16thC house, home of actress Dame Ellen Terry containing personal and theatrical mementoes. Cottage grounds include her rose garden, orchard, nuttery and the Barn Theatre.

Squerryes Court Manor House and Gardens

Westerham TN16 1SJ
t (01959) 562345
w squerryes.co.uk
open Apr-Sep, Wed-Thu, Sun, Bank Hols 1130-1630.
admission ££

Beautiful manor house, built 1681 containing tapestries, Old Master paintings, porcelain, furniture and items relating to General Wolfe. Gardens, lake, walks, and formal garden.

Stoneacre

Otham ME15 8RS
t (01622) 862871
w nationaltrust.org.uk
open Apr-Sep, Sat 1100-1800.
admission £

A small, attractive half-timbered manor house built mainly in the late 15thC. Visitors can see the Great Hall, crownpost and the newly-restored cottage-style garden.

Tonbridge Castle

Castle Street, Tonbridge TN9 1BG
t (01732) 770929
w tonbridgecastle.org
open Apr-Sep, Mon-Fri 0900-1700, Sat 0900-1700, Sun 1030-1700. Oct-Mar, Mon-Fri 0900-1700, Sat 0900-1600, Sun 1030-1600.
admission ££

The remains of a Norman motte-and-bailey castle in grounds by the River Medway. A 13thC gatehouse with models, scenes and audiovisual effects depicts life at that time.

Walmer Castle and Gardens

Kingsdown Road, Walmer CT14 7LJ
t (01304) 364288
w english-heritage.org.uk
open Apr-Sep, Mon-Fri 1000-1800, Sat 1000-1600, Sun 1000-1800. Oct, Wed-Sun 1000-1600. Mar, Wed-Sun 1000-1600.
admission ££

Walmer Castle is Tudor rose-shaped with a central tower and moat. It is the official residence of the Lord Warden of the Cinque Ports and contains contemporary Gardens.

Harvest time, Tenterden Vineyard

Admission is based on an adult price. Please check opening times and admission before travelling.

OUTDOOR ACTIVITIES

Pleasant Promenades Guided Walking Tours

Royal Tunbridge Wells Tourist Information Centre, The Old Fish Market, The Pantiles, Royal Tunbridge Wells TN2 5TN
t (01892) 515675 **w** visittunbridgewells.com
open All year, Thu & Sat 1130-1230 (approx finish time).
admission Adult: £3.50

Discover the 400-year history of the spa town of Royal Tunbridge Wells on a guided stroll through the Pantiles and the historic heart of the town. Hear about the many famous visitors - from Queen Anne to Samuel Pepys - who made Tunbridge Wells the place to see and be seen.

                    Map ref 3B4

v voucher offer – see back section

The choice is yours

Whether it's indoor or outdoor fun you're after, a relaxing treat or something a little more cultural, this guide will help you find the perfect solution.

ENTERTAINMENT AND CULTURE

C M Booth Collection of Historic Vehicles
Falstaff Antiques, 63-67 High Street, Rolvenden TN17 4LP
t (01580) 241234
w morganmuseum.org.uk
open All year, Mon-Sat 1000-1730.
admission £
The display includes a unique collection of Morgan cars dating from 1913 to 1935, a 1904 Humber Tri-car, and other historic cars, motorcycles and automobilia.

Canterbury Roman Museum
Butchery Lane, Canterbury CT1 2JR
t (01227) 785575
w canterbury-museum.co.uk
open Apr-May, Nov-Mar, Mon-Sat 1000-1700. Jun-Oct, Mon-Sat 1000-1700, Sun 1330-1700.
admission £
A museum set around the preserved remains of a Roman town house with fine mosaics, hands-on area and computer-generated reconstruction images, market place and kitchen.

Canterbury Royal Museum, Art Gallery & Buffs Regimental Museum
18 High Street, Canterbury CT1 2RA
t (01227) 452747
w canterbury-artgallery.co.uk
open All year, Mon-Sat 1000-1700.
admission Free
Canterbury's art museum displaying fine arts, rare porcelain and antiques. Art gallery for major exhibitions. Adjoining is the museum of the local regiment, The Buffs.

Dickens House Museum
2 Victoria Parade, Broadstairs CT10 1QS
t (01843) 863453
w dickenshouse.co.uk
open Apr-Oct, daily 1030-1600.
admission £
The model for Betsey Trotwood's house in 'David Copperfield', it is now a museum of Dickens' letters and possessions, Victorian costumes and other items.

Finchcocks
Goudhurst TN17 1HH
t (01580) 211702
w finchcocks.co.uk
open Apr-Jul, Sep, Sun 1400-1800. Aug, Wed-Thu, Sun 1400-1800.
admission ££
A fine early-Georgian house with gardens set in parkland and housing a remarkable collection of historical keyboard instruments in full playing order. Restored garden.

The Historic Dockyard Chatham

Dock Road, Chatham ME4 4TZ
t (01634) 823800
w chdt.org.uk
open Apr-Oct, daily 1000-1800. Nov, Sat-Sun 1000-1600.
admission £££

Maritime heritage site with stunning architecture and displays including Britain's last World War II destroyer and a spy submarine. RNLI exhibition and 18thC adventure.

The Hop Farm Country Park

Paddock Wood TN12 6PY
t (01622) 872068 w thehopfarm.co.uk
admission Adult: £7.50

Set in 400 acres of unspoilt Kent countryside, this once-working hop farm is one of Kent's most popular attractions. The spectacular Oast Village is home to an indoor and outdoor play area, interactive museum, shire horses and an animal farm, as well as hosting over 30 special events throughout the year.

                                         Map ref 3B4

ⓥ *voucher offer – see back section*

Maidstone Museum and Bentlif Art Gallery
St Faith's Street,
Maidstone ME14 1LH
t (01622) 602838
w museum.maidstone.gov.uk
open All year, Mon-Sat 1000-1715, Sun 1100-1600.
admission Free

A museum with many fine collections, housed in an Elizabethan manor house. Galleries with displays of costumes and natural history.

Maison Dieu
Town Hall, Biggin Street, Dover CT16 1DL
t (01304) 201200 w leisureforce.co.uk
open All year, Mon-Fri 0900-1700, Sat 1000-1700.
admission Free

Once a pilgrim's hostel, dating from 1203, the magnificent interior features stained glass windows, an armoury and paintings of Lord Wardens of Cinque Ports.

Museum of Kent Life
Cobtree, Lock Lane, Sandling ME14 3AU
t (01622) 763936 w museum-kentlife.co.uk
open Apr-Nov, Feb-Mar, daily 1000-1700.
admission ££

Kent's award-winning open-air museum is home to a collection of historic buildings which house both static and interactive exhibitions. Livestock centre and gardens.

Powell Cotton Museum, Quex House and Gardens

Quex Park, Birchington CT7 0BH
t (01843) 842168 w powell-cottonmuseum.co.uk
open Museum and Gardens: Apr-Oct, Mon-Thu, Sun, Bank Hols 1100-1700. Nov-Mar, Sun 1300-1530. House: Mar-Oct, Mon-Thu, Sun, Bank Hols 1400-1630.
admission £

A museum with ethnographic collections, dioramas of African and Asian animal displays, weapons, archaeology and Chinese porcelain. Regency house, gardens and a restaurant.

Royal Engineers Museum
Prince Arthur Road, Gillingham ME4 4UG
t (01634) 822839 w royalengineers.org.uk
open All year, Tue-Fri 0900-1700, Sat-Sun, Bank Hols 1130-1700.
admission ££

There is something for all the family. Zulu War items, Boer War, World Wars I and II, planes, trains, tanks, bridges, bombs, 25 galleries.

St Margarets Museum
Beach Road, St Margaret's Bay CT15 6DZ
t (01304) 851737 w baytrust.org.uk
open May-Sep, Wed-Sun, Bank Hols 1400-1700.
admission Free

A museum with items of local and marine interest, covering the World War I and World War II periods. Figureheads and temporary exhibitions.

Tunbridge Wells Museum and Art Gallery
Civic Centre, Mount Pleasant,
Royal Tunbridge Wells TN1 1JN
t (01892) 554171 w tunbridgewells.gov.uk/museum
open All year, Mon-Sat 0930-1700, Sun 1000-1600.
admission Free

Enjoy our wonderful collections, share the special story of Tunbridge Wells, visit our major exhibitions and take part in activities for everyone.

Whitstable Museum and Gallery

Oxford Street, Whitstable CT5 1DB
t (01227) 276998 **w** whitstable-museum.co.uk
open Apr-Jun, Sep-Mar, Mon-Sat 1000-1600. Jul-Aug,
Mon-Sat 1000-1600, Sun 1300-1600.
admission Free

A coastal museum exploring the sea-faring traditions of
the town with special features on divers, shipbuilders
and oyster-fishers. Gallery with regularly changing
exhibitions.

FOOD AND DRINK

Biddenden Vineyards and Cider Works

Little Whatmans, Gribble Bridge Lane,
Biddenden TN27 8DF
t (01580) 291726 **w** biddendenvineyards.com
open All year, Mon-Sat 1000-1700, Sun 1100-1700.
admission Free

Kent's oldest commercial vineyard with 22 acres of vines
to walk through. Sample English wines and Kentish
ciders and apple juice.

Elham Valley Vineyards

Breach, Barham CT4 6LN
t (01227) 831266
open All year, Tue-Fri 1030-1600, Sat-Sun 1100-1630.
admission Free

Picturesque vineyard in an Area of Outstanding Natural
Beauty. Tours and wine tastings, cream teas and light
lunches, a craft shop and a working pottery.

Shepherd Neame Brewery Tours

17 Court Street, Faversham ME13 7AX
t (01795) 542016 **w** shepherd-neame.co.uk
open Daily. Please phone for details.
admission ££

Visit Shepherd Neame and tour Britain's oldest brewery.
See how beer is made, from barley to bottle and sample
the company's acclaimed ales and famous lagers.

RELAXING AND PAMPERING

Apple Craft Centre

Macknade, Selling Road, Faversham ME13 8XF
t (01795) 590504
open Daily 0930-1730.
admission Free

A craft centre housed in a quadruple square oast house.
Coffee shop and restaurant on first floor. Various
exhibitions throughout the year.

McArthurGlen Designer Outlet Ashford

Kimberley Way, Ashford TN24 0SD
t (01233) 895900 **w** mcarthurglen.com/ashford
open All year, Mon-Fri 1000-2000, Sat 1000-1900, Sun
1000-1700, Bank Hols 1000-1800.
admission Free

One of Europe's most spectacular shopping destinations
with over 70 stores offering up to 50% discount on
famous named brands.

Kingsgate Bay

London

Enjoy the fun of a special event or visit one of the attractions listed for a great day out. For more inspiring ideas go to **enjoyengland.com**.

22–26 May
Chelsea Flower Show
Royal Hospital, SW3
(020) 7649 1885
rhs.org.uk

13 Jul–8 Sep
The Proms
Royal Albert Hall, SW7
(020) 7765 5575
bbc.co.uk/proms

26–27 Aug
Notting Hill Carnival
Ladbroke Grove area, W11
(020) 8964 0544

Nov
Tutankhamen and the Golden Age of the Pharaohs
The O², Greenwich
kingtut.org

Nov
Diwali
Trafalgar Square, SW1
london.gov.uk

FAMILY FUN

Battersea Park Children's Zoo

Battersea Park, London SW11 4NJ
t (020) 7924 5826
w batterseaparkzoo.co.uk
open Summer: 1000-17.30.
Winter: 1000-1630.
admission Adult: £5.95

Battersea Park Children's Zoo, found in the heart of South London, offers an exciting animal experience that combines a zoo, animal encounters, play area and relaxing cafe. Come and pat a goat, talk to a monkey or come face to face with a meerkat.

Map ref 6B2

BBC Television Centre Tours

BBC Television Centre,
Wood Lane,
London W12 7RJ
t 0870 603 0304
w bbc.co.uk/tours
open All year, Mon-Sat, please phone for details.
admission ££

The general tour includes studios, news centre, dressing rooms, interactive studio and the Blue Peter garden. The CBBC Tour is suitable for 7-12 year olds.

Admission is based on an adult price. Please check opening times and admission before travelling.

British Airways London Eye

Riverside Building, County Hall,
Westminster Bridge Road, London SE1 7PB
t 0870 500 0600 **w** ba-londoneye.com
open June-Sep, daily 1000-2100. Oct-May, daily
1000-2000.
admission £££

*The London Eye is recognised worldwide. At 135m, it is
the world's tallest observation wheel, giving stunning
panoramic views of up to 40km/25 miles on a clear day.*

Chessington World of Adventures

Leatherhead Road, Chessington KT9 2NE
t 0870 444 7777 **w** chessington.com
open See website for details.
admission ££££

*Family fun, great rides and attractions, excellent-value
price options, queue-busting family day-planner tickets,
themed land especially for mini-sized adventurers.*

Houses of Parliament Summer Opening

Parliament Square, Westminster, London SW1A 0AA
t 0870 906 3773 **w** parliament.uk
open Aug, Mon-Tue, Fri-Sat 0915-1630. Sep, Mon,
Fri-Sat 0915-1630.
admission £££

*A fully guided tour of the Palace of Westminster
including the Chamber of the House of Lords, House of
Commons and Westminster Hall.*

Kentish Town City Farm

1 Cressfield Close, London NW5 4BN
t (020) 7916 5421 **w** ktcityfarm.org.uk
open Daily 0900-1700.
admission Free

*A small city farm with a wide range of livestock, poultry
and horses. Suitable for people of all ages and abilities.
Pony rides on Saturday and Sunday, 1330-1430.*

The London Dungeon

28-34 Tooley Street, London SE1 2SZ
t (020) 7403 7221 **w** thedungeons.com
open Daily 1030-1700.
admission ££££

*Re-enact the blood and guts, torture and terror of some
of the most gruesome events in British history. It's so
much fun it's frightening!*

Madame Tussauds and the London Planetarium

Marylebone Road, London NW1 5LR
t 0870 400 3000 **w** madame-tussauds.com
open Daily 0900-1800.
admission ££££

*The interactive attraction where guests come face to
face with A-list stars and icons, in life-like wax figure
form, and get a chance to participate in the things that
famous people do.*

Museum of Rugby and Twickenham Stadium Tours

Rugby Road, Twickenham TW1 1DZ
t 0870 405 2001 **w** rfu.com/microsites/museum
open All year, Tue-Sat 1000-1700, Sun 1100-1700.
admission ££

*Combine a fascinating behind-the-scenes guided tour of
the world's most famous rugby stadium with a visit to
The Museum of Rugby. See inside the England dressing
room and players' tunnel.*

Royal Observatory Greenwich

Greenwich Park, London SE10 9NF
t (020) 8858 4422 **w** nmm.ac.uk
open Daily 1000-1700.
admission Free

*Stand on the Greenwich meridian line, longitude zero,
which divides east and west. Watch the time ball fall at 1
o'clock. Explore the history of time and astronomy in this
charming Wren building.*

NATURE AND WILDLIFE

Battersea Dogs Home

4 Battersea Park Road, London SW8 4AA
t (020) 7622 3626 **w** dogshome.org
open Daily 1030-1600.
admission Free

*The world's oldest home for lost and stray dogs. This
internationally famous dog and cat home has about 400
dogs on any one day, of which about 200 are available
for sale.*

View towards Big Ben and the Houses of Parliament from the South Bank

Battersea Park Children's Zoo

Battersea Park, London SW11 4NJ
t (020) 7924 5826
w batterseaparkzoo.co.uk
open Summer: 1000-17.30.
Winter: 1000-1630.
admission Adult: £5.95

Battersea Park Children's Zoo, found in the heart of South London, offers an exciting animal experience that combines a zoo, animal encounters, play area and relaxing cafe. Come and pat a goat, talk to a monkey or come face to face with a meerkat.

 Map ref 6B2

Capel Manor College & Gardens

Bullsmoor Lane, Enfield EN1 4RQ
t 08456 122 122 **w** capel.ac.uk
open Mar-Oct 1000-1800, last entry 1630.
Nov-Feb, weekdays 1000-1730, last entry 1600.
admission Adult: £4

Thirty acres of beautiful themed gardens including a Japanese Garden, Italianate Maze, Gardening Which? Trial Gardens and Kim Wilde's Jungle Gym Garden, plus our animal corner, await you. Find out about the shows and events running throughout the year, from the spectacular Spring Gardening Show to musical delights and classic motors.

 Map ref 6C1

 v *voucher offer – see back section*

Shri Swaminarayan Mandir Temple, Neasden

For key to symbols see inside back cover.

Chelsea Physic Garden

Swan Walk, (off Royal Hospital Road),
London SW3 4HS
t (020) 7352 5646
w chelseaphysicgarden.co.uk
open Apr-Oct, Wed 1200-dusk, Thu-Fri 1200-1700, Sun 1200-1800. Last entry 30 mins before closing.
admission Adult: £7

London's oldest botanic garden and best-kept secret - a magical 300-year-old oasis in the heart of the capital. Discover the myriad uses of plants via free guided tours with entertaining guides, enjoy delicious refreshments at the garden's renowned tearoom, and browse the eclectic selection of garden-related gifts in the shop.

                 Map ref 7B2

v *voucher offer – see back section*

Chislehurst Caves
Old Hill, Chislehurst BR7 5NB
t (020) 8467 3264 w chislehurstcaves.co.uk
open All year, Wed-Sun 1000-1600.
admission £

A 45-minute lamplit guided tour through the darkness of these unique manmade caves. Hear about Druids, Romans, Saxons, World War II and more.

Quality counts

Look out for the Quality Assured Visitor Attraction sign. These attractions are assessed annually and meet the standards required to receive the quality marque.

Greenwich Park
London SE10 8QY
t (020) 8858 2608 w royalparks.org.uk
open Apr, Sep, 0600-2000. May, Aug, 0600-2100. Jun-Jul, 0600-2130. Oct, Mar, 0600-1900. Nov-Feb, 0600-1800.
admission Free

The oldest Royal Park, created in 1433. The Royal Observatory is in the centre of the park. Also deer enclosure, formal gardens, tree-lined avenues, boating lake, children's playground and sports facilities.

Hyde Park
London W2 2UH
t (020) 7262 5484 w royalparks.gov.uk
open Daily, 0500-2330.
admission Free

The park is famous for boating and swimming in its lake, The Serpentine, and its riding track, Rotten Row, was the first public road to be lit at night.

Kew Gardens (Royal Botanic Gardens)
Kew, Richmond TW9 3AB
t (020) 8332 5655 w kew.org
open Apr-Aug, daily 0930-1830. Sep-Oct, daily 0930-1800. Nov-Jan, daily 0930-1615. Feb-Mar, daily 0930-1730.
admission £££

A World Heritage Site with stunning vistas, magnificent glasshouses and beautiful landscapes beside the River Thames. It represents nearly 250 years of historical gardens, and is home to over 30,000 types of plant.

Lee Valley Nature Reserve – The Waterworks and Golf Centre
Lammas Road, Leyton, London E10 7NU
t (020) 8988 7566 w leevalleypark.org.uk
open Apr-Oct, daily 0830-2100. Nov-Mar, daily 0830-dusk.
admission Free

A visitor centre with interactive display about The Waterworks site and nature reserve. Eighteen-hole pay and play golf course.

London Aquarium
County Hall, Riverside Building, London SE1 7PB
t (020) 7967 8000 w londonaquarium.co.uk
open Daily 1000-1800.
admission £££

The only place in the capital where visitors can see sharks and deadly stone fish. Over 350 species from every major environment across the globe, plus daily talks, dives and feeds.

London Butterfly House
Syon Park, Brentford TW8 8JF
t (020) 8560 0378 w butterflies.org.uk
open Apr-Oct, daily 1000-1700. Nov-Mar, daily 1000-1530.
admission ££

Free-flying butterflies in exotic jungle setting. Giant spiders, leaf-cutting ants, locusts and many other small insects, tropical trees and shrubs.

London Wetland Centre

Queen Elizabeth's Walk, Barnes,
London SW13 9WT
t (020) 8409 4400 w wwt.org.uk
open Apr-Oct, daily 0930-1800. Nov-Mar, daily
0930-1700.
admission ££
A unique wildlife visitor attraction just 25 minutes from central London. Run by the Wildfowl and Wetlands Trust (WWT), it is acclaimed as the best urban site in Europe to watch wildlife.

London Zoo
Regent's Park, London NW1 4RY
t (020) 7722 3333 w londonzoo.co.uk
open Mar-Oct, daily 1000-1730. Nov-Feb 1000-1600.
admission £££
Come face to face with the hairiest and scariest animals on the planet, right in the heart of London. Also talks, animal displays, walk-through enclosures, historic buildings and beautiful gardens.

Morden Hall Park (National Trust)
Morden Hall Road, Morden SM4 5JD
t (020) 8545 6850 w nationaltrust.org.uk
open Daily 0800-1800.
admission Free
A green oasis in the heart of South West London. A former deer park with a network of waterways including meadow, wetland and woodland habitats. Spectacular rose garden.

Myddelton House Gardens
Bulls Cross, Enfield EN2 9HG
t (01992) 717711 w leevalleypark.org.uk
open Apr-Sep, Mon-Fri 1000-1630, Sun 1200-1600,
Bank Hols 1200-1600. Oct-Mar, Mon-Fri 1000-1500.
admission £
Gardens created by E A Bowles (1865-1954) featuring many unusual plants. Includes national collection of award-winning Bearded Iris.

Regent's Park
London NW1 4NR
t (020) 7486 7905 w royalparks.gov.uk
open Daily 0600-dusk.
admission Free
The park houses a private residential estate, parkland, Queen Mary's Gardens and the Rose Gardens, a lake, a heronry and waterfowl collection.

Richmond Park
Richmond TW10 5HS
t (020) 8940 0654 w royalparks.gov.uk
open Apr-Sep, daily 0700-dusk. Oct-Mar, daily
0730-dusk.
admission Free
The largest open space in London and a heritage landscape of national importance. It is home to herds of fallow and red deer that have been roaming the park since 1637.

Royal Mews
Buckingham Palace, London SW1A 1AA
t (020) 7766 7302 w royalcollection.org.uk
open Apr-Oct, Mon-Thu 1100-1600.
admission ££
This is a working establishment, and the number of horses and carriages on show may vary from time to time. Opening times are subject to change at short notice.

St James's Park
London SW1A 2BJ
t (020) 7930 1793 w royalparks.gov.uk
open Daily 0500-2330.
admission Free
The park is famous for its views, waterfowl and flower displays and reflects the English Picturesque style of landscaping which was prominent in the 19th century.

HISTORIC ENGLAND

2 Willow Road
London NW3 1TH
t (020) 7435 6166 w nationaltrust.org.uk
open Apr-Oct, Thu-Sat 1200-1700. Nov, Mar
1200-1700.
admission £
Designed and built by Erno Goldfinger in 1939, it is one of Britain's most important examples of Modernist architecture and is filled with furniture also designed by Goldfinger.

All Souls Church, Langham Place
2 All Souls Place, London W1B 3DA
t (020) 7580 3522 w allsouls.org
open All year, Mon-Fri 0930-1800, Sun 0800-2000.
admission Free
Designed by John Nash and built in 1824 as the pivot point of his plan for Regent Street. Painting on east wall, 'Behold The Man' by Westall, was presented by George IV.

Buckingham Palace
London SW1A 1AA
t (020) 7766 7300 w royalcollection.org.uk
open Aug-Sep, daily 0945-1545.
admission £££
The official London residence of the Queen. Its 19 state rooms are lavishly furnished with some of the finest treasures from the Royal Collection.

Buddhapadipa Temple (Thai Temple)
14 Calonne Road, Wimbledon, London SW19 5HJ
t (020) 8946 1357 w buddhapadipa.org
open All year, Sat-Sun 0900-1800.
admission Free
A temple building in Thai architectural style featuring mural paintings and gardens. The original house is now the monks' residence.

Carlyle's House
24 Cheyne Row, London SW3 5HL
t (020) 7352 7087 **w** nationaltrust.org.uk
open Apr-Oct, Wed-Fri 1400-1700, Sat-Sun 1100-1700.
admission £
*This Queen Anne house was the home of historian,
social writer and ethical thinker Thomas Carlyle and his
wife Jane. The furniture, pictures, portraits and books
are all still in place.*

Central Hall Westminster
Storey's Gate, London SW1H 9NH
t (020) 7222 8010 **w** c-h-w.com
open All year, Mon-Fri 0800-1800, Sat-Sun 0900-1800.
admission Free
*Take a guided tour at this unique, historic Edwardian
building, see the Great Hall with its magnificent organ
and the superb view from the balcony.*

Chelsea Physic Garden
Swan Walk, (off Royal Hospital Road),
London SW3 4HS
t (020) 7352 5646
w chelseaphysicgarden.co.uk
open Apr-Oct, Wed 1200-dusk, Thu-Fri 1200-
1700, Sun 1200-1800. Last entry 30 mins
before closing.
admission Adult: £7

London's oldest botanic garden and best-kept
secret - a magical 300-year-old oasis in the
heart of the capital. Discover the myriad uses of
plants via free guided tours with entertaining
guides, enjoy delicious refreshments at the
garden's renowned tearoom, and browse the
eclectic selection of garden-related
gifts in the shop.

Map ref 7B2

 voucher offer – see back section

Chapel Royal of St Peter Ad Vincula
Tower of London, London EC3N 4AB
t (020) 7488 5689 **w** hrp.org.uk
open All year, Sun 0915-1200.
admission Free
*The Tudor burial place of Queen Anne Boleyn, Queen
Catherine Howard and Sir Thomas More.*

Chiswick House
Burlington Lane, London W4 2RP
t (020) 8995 0508 **w** english-heritage.org.uk
open Apr-Oct, Wed-Fri 1000-1700, Sat 1000-1400, Sun,
Bank Hols 1000-1700.
admission £
*The celebrated villa of Lord Burlington with impressive
grounds featuring Italianate garden with statues,
temples, obelisks and urns.*

Church of St Anne's Limehouse
Commercial Road, London E14 7HP
t (020) 7987 1502
open All year, Sun 1000-1300.
admission Free
*A 1730 Hawksmoor masterpiece, with the exterior fully
restored. On display is the Gray and Davison organ
which won the gold medal at the Great Exhibition of
1851.*

Crofton Roman Villa
Crofton Road, Orpington BR6 8AF
t (020) 8460 1442
open Apr-Oct, Wed, Fri 1000-1700, Sun 1400-1700.
admission £
*Remains of a Roman villa house dating from AD140
within a modern building, with graphic displays, models,
touch table of Roman artefacts and activities for
children.*

Eltham Palace
Court Yard, London SE9 5QE
t (020) 8294 2548 **w** english-heritage.org.uk
open Apr-Oct, Mon-Wed, Sun 1000-1700. Nov-Dec,
Mon-Wed, Sun 1000-1600. Feb-Mar, Mon-Wed, Sun
1000-1600.
admission ££
*A spectacular fusion of 1930s Art Deco villa and
magnificent 15thC Great Hall. Surrounded by period
gardens.*

Fenton House
Hampstead Grove, London NW3 6SP
t (020) 7435 3471 **w** nationaltrust.org.uk
open Apr-Oct, Wed-Fri 1400-1700,
Sat-Sun 1100-1700.
admission ££
*A delightful 17thC merchant's house set among the
winding streets of old Hampstead. The charming interior
houses outstanding collections of Oriental and European
porcelain, needlework, furniture and early keyboard
instruments.*

Hall Place and Gardens
Hall Plac, Bourne Road, Bexley DA5 1PQ
t (01322) 526574
w hallplaceandgardens.com
open House: Apr-Oct, Mon-Sat 1000-1700, Sun, Bank
Hols 1100-1700. Nov-Mar, Tue-Sat 1000-1615. Gardens:
Daily, 0800-dusk.
admission Free
*Tudor house and award-winning gardens built for the
Lord Mayor of London in the reign of Henry VIII in 1537.*

Ham House
Ham Street, Ham, Richmond TW10 7RS
t (020) 8940 1950
w nationaltrust.org.uk
open House: Apr-Oct, Mon-Wed, Sat-Sun 1300-1700.
Garden: All year, Mon-Wed, Sat-Sun 1100-1800.
admission ££
*The most complete survivor of 17thC fashion and
power. Built in 1610 and enlarged in the 1670s, it was at
the heart of Restoration court life and intrigue.
Significant formal garden.*

Hampton Court Palace
Surrey KT8 9AU
t 0870 752 7777
w hrp.org.uk
open Apr-Oct, daily 1000-1800. Nov-Mar, daily
1000-1630.
admission £££
*Explore Henry VIII's state apartments, where history is
brought to life with costumed guides. See the historic
royal gardens and the world-famous maze – the oldest-
surviving hedge maze still in use.*

Hindu Temple (Shri Swaminarayan Mandir)
105/115 Brentfield Road, Neasden, London NW10 8JP
t (020) 8965 2651
w mandir.org
open Daily 0900-1800.
admission Free
*The first traditional Hindu Mandir in Europe, carved and
constructed entirely according to the ancient
Shipsashtras (treatise on temple architecture). Also
Hinduism exhibition.*

Historic Royal Palaces
w hrp.org.uk
see maps 6 and 7
see ad on p33

HMS Belfast
Morgan's Lane, Tooley Street, London SE1 2JH
t (020) 7940 6300
w iwm.org.uk
open Mar-Oct, daily 1000-1800. Nov-Feb, daily
1000-1700.
admission ££
*Launched 1938, HMS Belfast served throughout WWII,
playing a leading part in the destruction of the German
battle cruiser Scharnhorst and in the Normandy
Landings. She is a reminder of Britain's naval heritage.*

Jewel Tower
Abingdon Street, Westminster,
London SW1P 3JY
t (020) 7222 2219
w english-heritage.org.uk
open Apr-Oct, daily 1000-1700. Nov-Mar, daily
1000-1600.
admission £
*One of only two original surviving buildings of
the Palace of Westminster. Home today to
'Parliament Past and Present' – a fascinating
account of the House of Lords and the House of
Commons.*

Kensington Palace State Apartments
Kensington Gardens,
London W8 4PX
t 0870 751 5170
w hrp.org.uk
open Mar-Oct, daily 1000-1800. Nov-Feb, daily
1000-1700.
admission £££
*Home to the Royal Ceremonial Dress
Collection, which includes some of Queen
Elizabeth II's dresses worn throughout her
reign, as well as 14 of Diana, Princess of Wales'
evening dresses.*

Kenwood House
Hampstead Lane, London NW3 7JR
t (020) 8348 1286
w english-heritage.org.uk
open Apr-Oct, daily 1100-1700. Nov-Mar, daily
1100-1600.
admission Free
*A beautiful 18thC villa with fine interiors and a
world-class collection of paintings. Also fabulous
landscaped gardens and an award-winning
restaurant.*

Lauderdale House
Waterlow Park, Highgate Hill, London N6 5HG
t (020) 8348 8716
w lauderdale.org.uk
open All year, Tue-Fri 1100-1600, Sat 1330-1700, Sun
1200-1700.
admission Free
*An old manor house built in 1582, situated in Waterlow
Park. Community arts centre with a variety of concerts,
children's shows, crafts and antiques fairs throughout
the year.*

London's Roman Amphitheatre
Guildhall Art Gallery, Guildhall Yard, London EC2P 2EJ
t (020) 7332 3700
w guildhall-art-gallery.org.uk
open All year, Mon-Sat 1000-1700, Sun 1200-1600.
admission £
*Visit this unique Roman amphitheatre and see evocative
light and sound effects which bring the age of gladiators
alive.*

Lord's Tour

Lord's Ground,
London NW8 8QN
t (020) 7616 8595 (020) 7616 8596
w lords.org.uk
open Apr-Sep 1000, 1200 & 1400,
Oct-Mar 1200 & 1400.
admission Adult: £10

Guided tours of the world-famous home of cricket that can be tailored to meet your needs. Includes visit to pavilion, MCC Museum, media centre and other places of interest.

                                    Map ref 7A3

Marble Hill House
Richmond Road, Twickenham TW1 2NL
t (020) 8892 5115 **w** english-heritage.org.uk
open Apr-Oct, Sat 1000-1400, Sun 1000-1700.
admission £
A Palladian villa built for Henrietta Howard, mistress of King George II, set in 66 acres of parkland. The villa's intimate interiors give you a fascinating glimpse into Henrietta's lifestyle.

Museum of Fulham Palace
Bishops Avenue, London SW6 6EA
t (020) 7736 3233 **w** fulhampalace.org
open All year, Mon-Tue 1200-1600, Sat 1100-1400, Sun 1130-1530.
admission Free
A historic building. Highlights include Tudor courtyard, 18thC walled garden, botanical collection and Museum of Fulham Palace. Tours include the Great Hall and Chapel.

Old Palace, Croydon
Old Palace Road, Croydon CR0 1AX
t (020) 8256 1891 **w** friendsofoldpalace.org
open See website for details.
admission ££
Fifteenth-century Great Hall, Great Chamber and chapel, Long Gallery, 13thC undercroft and the bedroom of Queen Elizabeth I. Now a girls' school. Guided tours as announced.

Old Royal Naval College
Cutty Sark Gardens, Greenwich, London SE10 9LW
t (020) 8269 4791 **w** oldroyalnavalcollege.org
open Daily 1000-1700.
admission Free
In the heart of maritime Greenwich, the college is the site of the Greenwich Royal Hospital for Seamen, built to the designs of Christopher Wren, which later became the Royal Naval College.

Osterley Park House (National Trust)
Jersey Road, Isleworth TW7 4RB
t (020) 8232 5050
w nationaltrust.org.uk
open Apr-Oct, Wed-Sun 1300-1630.
admission ££
In 1761, the founders of Child's Bank commissioned Robert Adam to transform a crumbling Tudor mansion into an elegant neo-Classical villa. The spectacular interiors contain one of Britain's most complete examples of Adam's work.

Queen's House
Romney Road, London SE10 9NF
t (020) 8858 4422
w nmm.ac.uk
open Daily 1000-1700.
admission Free
The first Palladian-style house in England designed by Inigo Jones for the Stuart queens Anne of Denmark and Henrietta Maria. The elegant interiors display portraits/paintings of Greenwich and its naval history.

Rainham Hall
The Broadway, Rainham RM13 9YN
t (020) 7799 4552
w nationaltrust.org.uk
open Apr-Oct, Sat, Bank Hols 1400-1700.
admission £
An attractive red-brick house, built in 1729, with stone dressing on symmetrical pattern. Exterior – brickwork and iron gates. Interior – trompe l'oeil paintwork.

Royal Albert Hall

Kensington Gore,
London SW7 2AP
t (020) 7589 8212 **w** royalalberthall.com
open Daily tours Fri-Tue subject to availability.
admission Adult: £7.50

Join our entertaining guides for a journey through the history of the Royal Albert Hall, one of the most famous entertainment venues in the world. Six tours, lasting for around an hour and conducted in English, daily from Friday to Tuesday.

                                    Map ref 7B3

Royal Hospital Chelsea
Royal Hospital Road, Chelsea, London SW3 4SR
t (020) 7881 5204
open All year, Mon-Sat 1000-1200, 1400-1600.
admission Free
Home of the Chelsea Pensioners, built by Sir Christopher Wren between 1682 and 1690. The chapel, Great Hall, Figure Court and museum are of particular interest.

St Clement Danes Church
Strand, London WC2R 1DH
t (020) 7242 8282
open Daily 0900-1600.
admission Free
This is the 'Oranges and Lemons' church, and features include a Grinling Gibbons pulpit and Samuel Johnson statue. Central church of Royal Air Force with Books of Remembrance.

St George's Church Hanover Square
St George Street, London W1S 1FX
t (020) 7629 0874
w stgeorgeshanoversquare.org
open All year, Mon-Fri 0800-1600, Sun 0800-1200.
admission Free
Classical church building designed by John James and consecrated in 1725. Early-16thC Flemish stained glass from Antwerp. 'Last Supper' painted by William Kent.

St Giles Church Cripplegate
Fore Street, London EC2Y 8DA
t (020) 7638 1997
w stgilescripplegate.com
open All year, Mon-Fri 1100-1600, Sun 0800-1630.
admission Free
A church of great historical and architectural interest. Roman wall in churchyard. John Milton is buried here, and Oliver Cromwell married here. Recitals held.

St James's Church Piccadilly
197 Piccadilly, London W1J 9LL
t (020) 7734 4511
w st-james-piccadilly.org
open Daily 0800-1830.
admission Free
The church, designed by Sir Christopher Wren, opened in 1684. Regular concerts, services and lectures. Market Wednesday to Saturday. Antiques market on Tuesday.

St Margaret's Church
Parliament Square, London SW1P 3JX
t (020) 7654 4840
w westminster-abbey.org
open All year, Mon-Fri 0930-1545, Sat 0930-1345, Sun 1400-1700.
admission Free
A fine 16thC building with notable medieval and modern stained glass. The burial place of Sir Walter Raleigh and parish church of the House of Commons.

St Martin-in-the-Fields Church
Trafalgar Square, London WC2N 4JJ
t (020) 7766 1100
w smitf.org
open From Oct, daily 0900-1800.
admission Free
One of London's best-loved churches, with a superb arts venue, holding more than 350 concerts every year. The18thC crypt houses a cafe, a shop and the London Brass Rubbing Centre.

St Mary Le Bow Church
Cheapside, London EC2V 6AU
t (020) 7248 5139
w stmarylebow.co.uk
open All year, Mon 0815-1745, Tue 0730-1745, Wed 0815-1745, Thu 0815-1805, Fri 0815-1305.
admission Free
Rebuilt by Christopher Wren after the Great Fire of London. Home to the Bow Bells. The Norman crypt with its chapel is the oldest parochial building still in use in London.

St Paul's Cathedral
St Paul's Churchyard, London EC4M 8AD
t (020) 7246 8357
w stpauls.co.uk
open All year, Mon-Sat 0830-1600.
admission ££
The cathedral was designed by Sir Christopher Wren and was built between 1675 and 1710 after its predecessor was destroyed in the Great Fire of London.

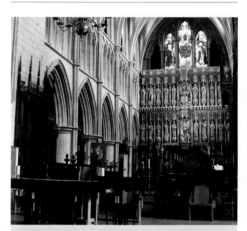

Southwark Cathedral

London Bridge, London SE1 9DA
t (020) 7367 6700 (020) 7367 6734
w southwark.anglican.org/cathedral
admission Adult: £4

London's oldest Gothic church building with links to William Shakespeare and US-university benefactor John Harvard. The churchyard gardens contain a memorial to Mahomet Weyonomon of the Mohegan tribe. Gardens have Shakespearian and Biblical planting. There is a shop and self-assisted refectory/restaurant. Audio tour narrated by local actors.

Map ref 7B1

 voucher offer – see back section

Somerset House
Strand, London WC2R 1LA
t (020) 7845 4670
w somerset-house.org.uk
open Daily 1000-1800.
admission £
A place for enjoyment, refreshment, arts and learning. This magnificent 18thC building houses the celebrated collections of the Courtauld Institute of Art Gallery, the Gilbert Collection and the Hermitage Rooms.

Sutton House (National Trust)
2-4 Homerton High Street, London E9 6JQ
t (020) 8986 2264
w nationaltrust.org.uk
open Feb-Dec, Thu-Sun 1230-1630.
admission £
Built in 1535, the house became home to successive merchants, Huguenot silk weavers, Victorian schoolmistresses and Edwardian clergy, and, although altered over the years, remains an essentially Tudor house.

Syon House
Syon Park, Brentford TW8 8JF
t (020) 8560 0881
w syonpark.co.uk
open House: Apr-Oct, Wed-Thu. Sun, Bank Hols 1100-1700. Gardens: Mar-Oct, daily 1030-1700. Nov-Feb, Sat-Sun 1030-1600.
admission ££
The house is set within 200 acres of Capability Brown-landscaped parkland and contains some of Robert Adam's finest interiors. The gardens incorporate the spectacular Great Conservatory and over 200 species of trees.

Thames Barrier Information and Learning Centre
1 Unity Way, Woolwich, London SE18 5NJ
t (020) 8305 4188
w environment-agency.gov.uk
open Apr-Sep, daily 1030-1630. Oct-Mar, daily 1030-1530.
admission £
An exhibition with ten-minute video and a working scale model. Also riverside walkways, children's play area, Thames Barrier Cafe and Learning Centre. School packages available.

Tower of London
Tower Hill, London EC3N 4AB
t 0870 756 6060
w hrp.org.uk
open Mar-Oct, Mon, 1000-1800, Tue-Sat 0900-1800, Sun 1000-1800. Nov-Feb, Mon 1000-1700, Tue-Sat 0900-1700, Sun 1000-1700.
admission ££££
The tower is a fortress, palace, prison, arsenal and garrison. It is one of the most famous fortified buildings in the world and houses the Crown Jewels, armouries, Yeoman Warders and ravens.

Wellington Arch
Hyde Park Corner,
London W1J 7JZ
t (020) 7930 2726
w english-heritage.org.uk
open Apr-Oct, Wed-Sun 1000-1700. Nov-Mar, Wed-Sun 1000-1600.
admission £
Come inside this famous landmark. Recently opened to visitors, this splendid triumphal arch at Hyde Park Corner was originally designed as a grand approach to Buckingham Palace.

Westminster Abbey
Parliament Square,
London SW1P 3PA
t (020) 7222 5152
w westminster-abbey.org
open See website for details.
admission ££
One of Britain's finest Gothic buildings. Scene of the coronation, marriage and burial of British monarchs. Nave and cloisters, royal chapels and Undercroft Museum.

Westminster Cathedral
Victoria Street,
London SW1P 1QW
t (020) 7798 9055
w westminstercathedral.org.uk
open All year, Mon-Fri 0700-1900, Sat-Sun 0800-1900.
admission ££
England's principal Roman Catholic cathedral completed in 1903. Brick built in Byzantine style with interior marbles, mosaics and famous 'Stations of the Cross' by Eric Gill.

Winston Churchill's Britain at War Experience

Churchill House, 64/66 Tooley Street, London Bridge SE1 2TF
t (020) 7403 3171 **w** britainatwar.co.uk
open Apr-Sep 1000-1800, last entry 1700. Oct-Mar 1000-1700, last entry 1600 (excl 24-26 Dec).
admission Adult: £9.50

A museum of civilian life in WWII. Film footage, rationing, evacuation, women at war, weddings, bomb disposal, shelters. Children can try on gas-masks and uniforms. Walk through the London Blitz. See it! Feel it! Breathe it!

 Map ref 7B1

OUTDOOR ACTIVITIES

London Ducktours
Chichley Street, London SE1 8PJ
t (020) 7928 3132
w londonducktours.co.uk
open Daily 1030-1600.
admission ££££
Take a unique sightseeing tour of London in an amphibious vehicle around the streets and onto the River Thames.

ENTERTAINMENT AND CULTURE

Alexander Fleming Laboratory Museum
St Mary's Hospital, Praed Street, London W2 1NY
t (020) 7886 6528
open All year, Mon-Thu 1000-1300.
admission £
The laboratory in which Alexander Fleming discovered penicillin with bacteriology laboratory equipment, penicillin artefacts and photographs of Fleming.

Apsley House
149 Piccadilly, Hyde Park Corner, London W1J 7NT
t (020) 7499 5676
w english-heritage.org.uk
open Apr-Oct, Tue-Sun 1000-1700. Nov-Mar, Tue-Sun 1000-1600.
admission ££
The former residence of the first Duke of Wellington. This great 18thC town house pays homage to the Duke's dazzling military career, which culminated in his victory at Waterloo in 1815.

Bank of England Museum
Bartholomew Lane, London EC2R 8AH
t (020) 7601 5545
w bankofengland.co.uk/museum
open All year, Mon-Fri 1000-1700.
admission Free
The museum tells the story of the bank from its foundation in 1694 to its role in today's economy. Interactive programmes with graphics and video help explain its many roles.

Barbican Art Gallery
Level 3, Barbican Centre, Silk Street, London EC2Y 8DS
t 0845 120 7500
w barbican.org.uk
open See website for details.
admission ££
The gallery has a changing programme of major photography, fine art and design exhibitions.

Bramah Museum of Tea & Coffee
40 Southwark Street, London SE1 1UN
t (020) 7403 5650
w teaandcoffeemuseum.com
open Daily 1000-1800.
admission £
This museum tells the 400-year-old social and commercial history of two of the world's most famous drinks – in ceramics, metal and graphic arts.

British Library
96 Euston Road, London NW1 2DB
t (020) 7412 7332
w bl.uk
open All year, Mon 0930-1800, Tue 0930-2000, Wed-Fri 0930-1800, Sat 0930-1700, Sun, Bank Hols 1100-1700.
admission Free
The library houses the world's greatest treasure house of books, manuscripts, maps, stamps and sound recordings. It has galleries, a public-events programme, bookshop and guided tours.

British Museum
Great Russell Street, London WC1B 3DG
t (020) 7323 8299
w thebritishmuseum.ac.uk
open All year, Mon-Wed, 1000-1730, Thu-Fri 1000-2030, Sat-Sun 1000-1730.
admission Free
A permanent display and special exhibitions of works of man from prehistory to the present day, together with displays of antiquities from around the world.

Brunel Museum
Railway Avenue, Rotherhithe, London SE16 4LF
t (020) 7231 3840
w brunel-museum.org.uk
open Daily 1000-1700.
admission £
Isambard Kingdom Brunel's first project with his father, a scheduled ancient monument and international landmark site, now a museum. The oldest section of the London tube.

Churchill Museum and Cabinet War Rooms

Clive Steps, King Charles Street, London SW1A 2AQ
t (020) 7930 6961
w iwm.org.uk
open Daily 0930-1800.
admission £££
Visit the secret underground rooms, untouched since 1945, from which Sir Winston Churchill ran Britain's contribution to WWII. Also visit the new, award-winning Churchill Museum.

For key to symbols see inside back cover.

Capel Manor College & Gardens

Bullsmoor Lane, Enfield EN1 4RQ
t 08456 122 122 **w** capel.ac.uk
open Mar-Oct 1000-1800, last entry 1630.
Nov-Feb, weekdays 1000-1730, last entry
1600.
admission Adult: £4

Thirty acres of beautiful themed gardens
including a Japanese Garden, Italianate Maze,
Gardening Which? Trial Gardens and Kim
Wilde's Jungle Gym Garden, plus our animal
corner, await you. Find out about the shows
and events running throughout the year, from
the spectacular Spring Gardening Show to
musical delights and classic motors.

                    Map ref 6C1

V *voucher offer – see back section*

Courtauld Institute Gallery
Courtauld Institute of Art, Somerset House, Strand,
London WC2R 0RN
t (020) 7848 2526 **w** courtauld.ac.uk/gallery
open Daily 1000-1800.
admission £
*The finest collection of Impressionist paintings in Britain,
as well as masterpieces by Botticelli, Tiepolo, Rubens
and Goya, housed in one of the most beautiful 18thC
buildings in London.*

Design Museum
Shad Thames, London SE1 2YD
t 0870 833 9955 **w** designmuseum.org
open Daily 1000-1745.
admission ££
*The world's leading museum of design, fashion and
architecture. Concerned as much with the future as the
past, its changing programme captures the excitement
of design's evolution through the 20th and 21st
centuries.*

Down House – Home of Charles Darwin

Luxted Road, Downe, Orpington BR6 7JT
t (01689) 859119 **w** english-heritage.org.uk
open Apr-Jun, Wed-Sun 1100-1700. Jul-Aug, daily
1100-1700. Sep-Oct, Wed-Sun 1100-1700. Nov-Dec,
Mar, Wed-Sun 1100-1600.
admission ££
*The family home and workplace of Charles Darwin.
Learn about mankind and its origins through interactive
displays, and visit the grounds which inspired the
genius.*

Dulwich Picture Gallery
Gallery Road, London SE21 7AD
t (020) 8693 5254 **w** dulwichpicturegallery.org.uk
open All year, Tue-Fri 1000-1700, Sat-Sun, Bank Hols
1100-1700.
admission £
*Described as 'the most beautiful small art gallery in the
world', with its outstanding collection of Old Master
paintings and lovely setting in Dulwich village.*

Estorick Collection of Modern Italian Art
39a Canonbury Square, London N1 2AN
t (020) 7704 9522 **w** estorickcollection.com
open All year, Wed-Sat 1100-1800, Sun 1200-1700.
admission £
*A world-famous collection of Italian Futurists, together
with work by Modigliani, Morandi and others in a
beautiful Georgian house. Also temporary exhibitions,
events, library and shop.*

Florence Nightingale Museum
St Thomas Hospital, 2 Lambeth Palace Road,
London SE1 7EW
t (020) 7620 0374 **w** florence-nightingale.co.uk
open All year, Mon-Fri 1000-1700, Sat-Sun, Bank Hols
1000-1630.
admission ££
*Florence Nightingale is famous for her influence on
modern nursing. Come and discover the woman behind
the legend.*

Forty Hall Museum and Gardens
Forty Hill, Enfield EN2 9HA
t (020) 8363 8196 **w** enfield.gov.uk/fortyhall
open All year, Wed-Sun 1100-1600.
admission Free
*A Grade I Listed historic building housing local museum
displays of 17thC and 18thC furniture and pictures. Set
in parkland.*

Foundling Museum
40 Brunswick Square, London WC1N 1AZ
t (020) 7841 3600
w foundlingmuseum.org.uk
open All year, Tue-Sat 1000-1800, Sun 1200-1800.
admission £
The museum tells the story of the abandoned children cared for in the Foundling Hospital. It houses the hospital's art collection, donated by artists including Hogarth, Reynolds and Gainsborough.

Freud Museum
20 Maresfield Gardens, London NW3 5SX
t (020) 7435 2002
w freud.org.uk
open All year, Wed-Sun 1200-1700.
admission £
The library and study of Sigmund Freud's London home. Includes Freud's antiquity collection, library and furniture. Also exhibitions and videos.

Geffrye Museum
136 Kingsland Road, London E2 8EA
t (020) 7739 9893
w geffrye-museum.org.uk
open All year, Tue-Sat 1000-1700, Sun, Bank Hols 1200-1700.
admission Free
The museum depicts the quintessential style of English middle-class living rooms from 1600 to the present day through a series of period rooms.

Greenwich Heritage Centre
Building 41, Artillery Square,
Royal Arsenal, Woolwich, London SE18 4DX
t (020) 8854 2452
w greenwich.gov.uk
open All year, Tue-Sat 0900-1700.
admission Free
A local-history museum with displays of archaeology, natural history and geology. Also temporary exhibitions, schools service, sales point and Saturday club.

Guildhall Art Gallery
Guildhall Yard, London EC2P 2EJ
t (020) 7332 1632
w guildhall-art-gallery.org.uk
open All year, Mon-Sat 1000-1700, Sun 1200-1600.
admission £
The Corporation of London's collection of 17thC-20thC works of art including works by Constable, Landseer, Rossetti, Tissot and Millais, among many others.

Hayward Gallery
Belvedere Road, London SE1 8XZ
t 0870 169 1000
w hayward.org.uk
open Daily 1000-1800.
admission £
As part of London's South Bank, this famous international gallery shows four major exhibitions annually. There are no permanent collections.

Hermitage Rooms
Somerset House, Strand, London WC2R 1LA
t (020) 7845 4630
w hermitagerooms.org.uk
open See website for details.
admission £
Changing exhibitions from the collection of the State Hermitage Museum in St Petersburg, one of the four greatest museums in the world.

Historic Royal Palaces
w hrp.org.uk
see maps 6 and 7
see ad on p33

Horniman Museum and Gardens
100 London Road, London SE23 3PQ
t (020) 8699 1872
w horniman.ac.uk
open Daily 1030-1730.
admission Free
The museum consists of six permanent exhibitions. The Living Waters Aquarium, Natural History and African Worlds. Set in Arts and Crafts building.

Imperial War Museum
Lambeth Road, London SE1 6HZ
t (020) 7416 5320
w iwm.org.uk
open Daily 1000-1800.
admission Free
This award-winning museum tells the story of conflict involving Britain and the Commonwealth since 1914. See thousands of imaginatively displayed exhibits, from art to aircraft and utility clothes to U-boats.

Kew Bridge Steam Museum
Green Dragon Lane, Brentford TW8 0EN
t (020) 8568 4757
w kbsm.org
open All year, Tue-Sun, Bank Hols 1100-1700.
admission ££
A Victorian waterworks plus steam railway, 'Water for Life' gallery and waterwheel. Also a tea room, shop and car park.

London Motorcycle Museum
Ravenor Farm, 29 Oldfield Lane South,
Greenford UB6 9LB
t (020) 8575 6644
w london-motorcycle-museum.org
open All year, Sat-Sun, Bank Hols 1000-1630.
admission £
The museum is the focal point for the serious biker or anyone with an interest in biking. The collection is currently dedicated to Britbikes.

Admission is based on an adult price. Please check opening times and admission before travelling.

Lord's Tour

Lord's Ground,
London NW8 8QN
t (020) 7616 8595 (020) 7616 8596
w lords.org.uk
open Apr-Sep 1000, 1200 & 1400,
Oct-Mar 1200 & 1400.
admission Adult: £10

Guided tours of the world-famous home of
cricket that can be tailored to meet your needs.
Includes visit to pavilion, MCC Museum, media
centre and other places of interest.

Map ref 7A3

Museum in Docklands
1 Warehouse, West India Quay, Hertsmere Road,
London E14 4AL
t 0870 444 3857
w museumindocklands.org.uk
open Daily 1000-1800.
admission £

*The story of London's river, port and people from
Roman to modern times. Artefacts, paintings, engravings
and photographs from the collections at the Museum of
London and the Port of London Authority.*

Museum of Childhood at Bethnal Green
Cambridge Heath Road, London E2 9PA
t (020) 8983 5200
w museumofchildhood.org.uk
open Daily 1000-1745.
admission Free

*Part of the V&A museum, housing a world-famous
collection of dolls and dolls' houses, games, puppets,
toys, children's costume and furniture.*

The Museum of Domestic Design and Architecture
Middlesex University, Cat Hill, Barnet EN4 8HT
t (020) 8411 5244
w moda.mdx.ac.uk
open All year, Tue-Sat 1000-1700, Sun 1400-1700.
admission Free

*A place of inspiration and enjoyment for visitors of all
ages who are interested in the history of design for the
home.*

Museum of Garden History
Lambeth Palace Road, London SE1 7LB
t (020) 7401 8865
w museumgardenhistory.org
open Daily 1030-1700.
admission £

*The museum provides an insight into the development
of gardening in the UK, with reproduction 17thC knot
garden and collection of historic garden tools, ephemera
and curiosities.*

Museum of London
150 London Wall, London EC2Y 5HN
t 0870 444 3852 **w** museumoflondon.org.uk
open All year, Mon-Sat 1000-1750, Sun 1200-1750.
admission Free

*The world's largest urban-history museum. The
permanent galleries tell the story of London from
prehistoric times to the present.*

Museum of the Order of St John
St John's Gate, St John's Lane,
London EC1M 4DA
t (020) 7324 4070 **w** sja.org.uk/museum
open All year, Mon-Fri 1000-1700, Sat 1000-1600.
admission Free

*A 16thC gatehouse with a 12thC crypt containing
treasures of the Knights of St John and the social history
collections of St John Ambulance.*

National Gallery
Trafalgar Square, London WC2N 5DN
t (020) 7747 2888 **w** nationalgallery.org.uk
open All year, Mon-Tue, 1000-1800, Wed 1000-2100,
Thu-Sun 1000-1800.
admission Free

*The gallery houses one of the greatest collections of
European paintings in the world. A permanent collection
spans the period 1250-1900 and comprises over 2,300
Western European paintings by many world-famous
artists.*

National Maritime Museum
Romney Road, London SE10 9NF
t (020) 8858 4422 **w** nmm.ac.uk
open Daily 1000-1700.
admission Free

*Britain's seafaring history housed in an impressive
modern museum. Themes include exploration, Nelson,
trade and empire, passenger shipping, luxury liners,
maritime London, costume, the sea, the future and
environmental issues.*

National Portrait Gallery
St Martin's Place, London WC2H 0HE
t (020) 7306 0055 **w** npg.org.uk
open All year, Mon-Wed, 1000-1800, Thu-Fri
1000-2100, Sat-Sun 1000-1800.
admission Free

*With the world's largest collection of portraits, the
National Portrait Gallery is the essential guide to 400
years of Britain's greatest movers and shakers.*

Natural History Museum
Cromwell Road, London SW7 5BD
t (020) 7942 5000 **w** nhm.ac.uk
open Daily 1000-1750.
admission Free

*The museum reveals how the jigsaw of life fits together.
Animal, vegetable or mineral, the best of our planet's
most amazing treasures are here for you to see.*

Old Operating Theatre, Museum and Herb Garret
9a St Thomas' Street, London SE1 9RY
t (020) 7188 2679 **w** thegarret.org.uk
open Daily 1030-1700.
admission ££

This restored 1821 women's operating theatre is the only 19thC operating theatre in England. Exhibits tell the story of surgery and herbal medicine.

Queen's Gallery Buckingham Palace
Buckingham Palace Road, London SW1A 1AA
t (020) 7766 7301 **w** royalcollection.org.uk
open Apr-Jan, daily 1000-1730.
admission ££

The gallery provides a showcase for displays from the Royal Collection, ranging from paintings, prints, drawings and watercolours to decorative art such as furniture, porcelain, miniatures, enamels and jewellery.

Royal Air Force Museum Hendon
Grahame Park Way, Hendon, London NW9 5LL
t (020) 8205 2266 **w** rafmuseum.org
open All year, Mon-Fri 1030-1630, Sat-Sun 1000-1800.
admission Free

Take off to the Royal Air Force Museum and fly past the history of aviation with an exciting display of suspended aircraft, touch-screen technology, simulator rides, hands-on section and film shows.

Royal Albert Hall
Kensington Gore,
London SW7 2AP
t (020) 7589 8212 **w** royalalberthall.com
open Daily tours Fri-Tue subject to availability.
admission Adult: £7.50

Join our entertaining guides for a journey through the history of the Royal Albert Hall, one of the most famous entertainment venues in the world. Six tours, lasting for around an hour and conducted in English, daily from Friday to Tuesday.

Map ref 7B3

Royal London Hospital Archives and Museum

St Philips Church, Newark Street, Whitechapel, London E1 2AA
t (020) 7377 7608 **w** brlcf.org.uk
open Museum: All year, Mon-Fri 1000-1630. Archives: By appointment only.
admission ££

Archives and museum housed in the crypt of a fine 19thC Gothic church where the story of the Royal London Hospital (founded 1740) is told.

Science Museum
Exhibition Road, London SW7 2DD
t 0870 870 4868
w sciencemuseum.org.uk
open Daily 1000-1800.
admission Free

The museum – the largest of its kind in the world – offers an IMAX cinema, simulators, special exhibitions and amazing permanent collections.

Shakespeare's Globe Exhibition and Tour
New Globe Walk, Bankside, London SE1 9DT
t (020) 7902 1500
w shakespeares-globe.org
open May-Sep, Mon-Sat 0900-1200, 1230-1700, Sun 0900-1130, 1200-1700. Oct-Apr, daily 1000-1700.
admission ££

Shakespeare's Globe Exhibition and Theatre Tour offer a fascinating introduction to the Globe Theatre and life in Shakespeare's London.

Sir John Soane's Museum
13 Lincoln's Inn Fields, London WC2A 3BP
t (020) 7405 2107
w soane.org
open All year, Tue-Sat 1000-1700.
admission Free

The former residence of Sir John Soane, architect of the Bank of England. Architectural drawings, antiquities, paintings and Egyptian sarcophagus of Seti I.

South London Gallery
65 Peckham Road, London SE5 8UH
t (020) 7703 6120
w southlondongallery.org
open All year, Tue-Sun 1200-1800.
admission Free

One of London's most important contemporary art exhibition spaces, having shown artists such as Gilbert and George, Tracey Emin, Mark Quinn and Julian Schnabel.

Tate Britain
Millbank, London SW1P 4RG
t (020) 7887 8888
w tate.org.uk
open Daily 1000-1750.
admission Free

Tate Britain presents the world's greatest collection of British art in a dynamic series of new displays and exhibitions.

Tate Modern
Bankside, London SE1 9TG
t (020) 7887 8008
w tate.org.uk
open All year, Mon-Thu 1000-1800, Fri-Sat 1000-2200, Sun 1000-1800.
admission Free

Tate Modern is the UK's largest modern art gallery presenting masterpieces by Dali, Picasso, Warhol and Matisse. Catch one of the excellent exhibitions that are presented throughout the year.

For key to symbols see inside back cover.

Tower Bridge Exhibition
Tower Bridge, London SE1 2UP
t (020) 7403 3761 **w** towerbridge.org.uk
open Apr-Sep, daily 1000-1830. Oct-Mar, daily
0930-1800.
admission ££

*Here, you will travel up to the high-level walkways,
located 140ft above the Thames, and witness stunning
panoramic views of London before visiting the Victorian
engine rooms.*

Victoria and Albert Museum
Cromwell Road, London SW7 2RL
t (020) 7942 2000 **w** vam.ac.uk
open All year, Mon-Thu, 1000-1745, Fri 1000-2200,
Sat-Sun 1000-1745.
admission Free

*One of the world's leading museums of art and design
and home to 3,000 years' worth of amazing artefacts
from many of the world's richest cultures.*

Vinopolis – London's Wine Tasting Visitor Attraction
1 Bank End, London SE1 9BU
t 0870 241 4040 **w** vinopolis.co.uk
open All year, Mon 1200-2100, Wed 1200-1800,
Thu-Sat 1200-2100, Sun 1200-1800.
admission ££££

*Take a tour through the world's wine regions at
Vinopolis and stimulate your senses at the tasting tables.
Five wine tastings and a cocktail are included in the
admission price.*

Wallace Collection
Hertford House, Manchester Square, London W1U 3BN
t (020) 7563 9551 **w** wallacecollection.org
open Daily 1000-1700.
admission Free

*A national museum displaying superb works of art in a
historic London town house. Collections of French
18thC paintings, furniture and porcelain together with
paintings by Titian, Canaletto, Rembrandt and
Gainsborough.*

White Cube
48 Hoxton Square, London N1 6PB
t (020) 7930 5373 **w** whitecube.com
open All year, Tue-Sat 1000-1800.
admission Free

*The gallery, showing a wide variety of contemporary art,
is housed in a 1920s industrial building in Hoxton
Square, home to a large community of artists.*

Wimbledon Lawn Tennis Museum & Tour
All England Lawn Tennis & Croquet Club,
Church Road, London SW19 5AE
t (020) 8946 6131 **w** wimbledon.org/museum
open Daily 1030-1700.
admission £££

*A fantastic collection of memorabilia dating from 1555,
including championship trophies. Art gallery,
220-degree cinema and special exhibitions, reflecting
the game and championships of today.*

FOOD AND DRINK

Southwark Cathedral

London Bridge, London SE1 9DA
t (020) 7367 6700 (020) 7367 6734
w southwark.anglican.org/cathedral
admission Adult: £4

London's oldest Gothic church building with
links to William Shakespeare and US-university
benefactor John Harvard. The churchyard
gardens contain a memorial to Mahomet
Weyonomon of the Mohegan tribe. Gardens
have Shakespearian and Biblical planting. There
is a shop and self-assisted refectory/restaurant.
Audio tour narrated by local actors.

Map ref 7B1

V *voucher offer – see back section*

RELAXING AND PAMPERING

Camden Lock
Camden Lock Place, Chalk Farm Road,
London NW1 8AF
t (020) 7485 7963 **w** camdenlockmarket.com
open Daily 1000-1800.
admission Free

*Camden Lock is open seven days a week with craft
workshops, stalls, shops, cafes, restaurants and bars.
One of London's best-known and busiest markets.*

Oxfordshire

Enjoy the fun of a special event or visit one of the attractions listed for a great day out. For more inspiring ideas go to **enjoyengland.com**.

Jan–Dec
Oxfordshire 2007
Venues across the county
(01865) 815525
oxfordshire2007.com

4–8 Jul
Henley Royal Regatta
Henley-on-Thames
(01491) 572153
hrr.co.uk

6–9 Sep
Blenheim International Horse Trials
Blenheim Palace, Woodstock
0870 060 2080
blenheimpalace.com

10 Nov–9 Dec
Christmas at Blenheim
Blenheim Palace, Woodstock
0870 060 2080
blenheimpalace.com

May 08
Henley Food Festival
Various venues, Henley-on-Thames
henleyfoodfestival.co.uk

FAMILY FUN

Didcot Railway Centre
Great Western Society, Didcot OX11 7NJ
t (01235) 817200
w didcotrailwaycentre.org.uk
open All year, Sat-Sun 1000-1700. Mon-Fri see website for details.
admission ££
A living museum recreating the golden age of the Great Western Railway. Steam locomotives and trains, Brunel's broad-gauge railway, engine shed and small-relics museum.

Oxfordshire Cotswolds
t (01993) 704645
w oxfordshirecotswolds.org
map ref 2C1
see ad on p413

NATURE AND WILDLIFE

Cotswold Wildlife Park
Bradwell Grove, Burford OX18 4JW
t (01993) 823006
w cotswoldwildlifepark.co.uk
open Daily 1000-dusk.
admission ££
A wildlife park in 200 acres of gardens and woodland. A variety of animals from all over the world. Narrow-gauge railway and landscaped picnicking areas.

Harcourt Arboretum
Nuneham Courtenay OX44 9PX
t (01865) 343501
w botanic-garden.ox.ac.uk
open Apr, Sep-Oct, Mar, daily 0900-1700. May-Aug, daily 0900-1800. Jan-Feb, Nov-Dec, daily 0900-1730.
admission £
Eighty acres of trees, shrubs, woodland, meadow and pond. Many trees over 200 years old. Highlights include Japanese Acers, a bluebell woodland and wild-flower meadows.

The choice is yours

Whether it's indoor or outdoor fun you're after, a relaxing treat or something a little more cultural, this guide will help you find the perfect solution.

University of Oxford Botanic Garden

Rose Lane, Oxford OX1 4AZ
t (01865) 286690
w botanic-garden.ox.ac.uk
open Apr-Nov, daily 1000-1700. Dec-Mar, Mon-Fri 1000-1630.
admission Free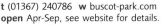

Over 6,000 species of plants in garden, glasshouses, rock and water gardens, housed within the oldest botanic garden in Britain.

The Warburg Reserve

Bix Bottom, Henley-on-Thames RG9 6BL
t (01491) 642001 **w** bbowt.org.uk
open Daily 0900-1700.
admission Free

A beautiful Chiltern valley with woodland, downland and abundant wildlife. There is a small visitor centre and glorious nature trail.

Waterperry Gardens Limited

Waterperry OX33 1JZ
t (01844) 339254 **w** waterperrygardens.co.uk
open Apr-Oct, daily 0900-1730. Nov-Feb, daily 1000-1700.
admission £

Ornamental gardens covering six acres of the 83-acre 18thC Waterperry House estate. A Saxon village church, garden shop teashop, art and craft gallery are found within the grounds.

HISTORIC ENGLAND

Blenheim Palace

Woodstock OX20 1PX
t (01993) 811091 **w** blenheimpalace.com
open Palace: Apr-Oct, Feb-Mar, daily 1030-1730. Nov-Dec, Wed-Sun 1030-1730. Park: Apr-Oct, Feb-Mar, daily 0900-dusk. Nov-Dec, Wed-Sun 0900-dusk.
admission £££

The birthplace of Sir Winston Churchill, set in the Oxfordshire Cotswolds. Superb collection of tapestries, paintings, porcelain and furniture. Beautiful Capability Brown parkland, lakes, fountains and formal gardens.

map ref 2C1

see ad on p14

Buscot Park

Buscot SN7 8BU
t (01367) 240786 **w** buscot-park.com
open Apr-Sep, see website for details.
admission ££

An 18thC Palladian-style house with park and water garden. Home of the Faringdon collection of paintings and furniture. The park is landscaped with extensive water gardens.

Christ Church
St Aldate's, Oxford OX1 1DP
t (01865) 276492 **w** chch.ox.ac.uk
open All year, Mon-Sat 0900-1700, Sun 1300-1700.
admission £
The largest college in Oxford with a cathedral within its walls. The home of Lewis Carroll and Alice in Wonderland.

Kelmscott Manor
Kelmscott GL7 3HJ
t (01367) 252486 **w** kelmscottmanor.co.uk
open See website for details.
admission ££
The country home of William Morris 1871-1896. The house contains a collection of the works of Morris and his associates, including furniture, textiles, carpets and ceramics.

Mapledurham House
The Estate Office, Mapledurham RG4 7TR
t (0118) 972 3350 **w** mapledurham.co.uk
open Apr-Sep, Sat-Sun, Bank Hols 1400-1700.
admission ££
An Elizabethan manor house alongside the River Thames, containing paintings, oak staircases, and moulded ceilings. Home to the Blount family for over 500 years.

The Oxford Story
6 Broad Street, Oxford OX1 3AJ
t (01865) 728822 **w** oxfordstory.co.uk
open Apr-Jun, Sep-Mar, Mon-Sat 1000-1630, Sun 1100-1630. Jul-Aug, daily 0930-1700.
admission ££
Take your seat on our amazing 'dark' ride and journey through scenes from 900 years of university history, complete with sights, sounds and smells!

Oxfordshire Cotswolds
t (01993) 704645 **w** oxfordshirecotswolds.org
map ref 2C1
see ad on p413

ENTERTAINMENT AND CULTURE

Ashmolean Museum (of Art and Archaeology)
Beaumont Street, Oxford OX1 2PH
t (01865) 278000 **w** ashmolean.org
open All year, Tue-Sat, Bank Hols 1000-1700, Sun 1200-1700.
admission Free
Collection of art and archaeology, from ancient Egypt to the 20th century. Paintings, sculpture, ceramics, silver, glass and coins, plus art from the Far East.

Banbury Museum
Spiceball Park Road,
(Entrance in Castle Quay Shopping Centre),
Banbury OX16 2PQ
t (01295) 259855
w cherwell-dc.gov.uk/banburymuseum
open All year, Mon-Sat 0930-1700, Sun, Bank Hols 1030-1630.
admission Free
The museum galleries tell the story of Banbury. The displays illustrate the English Civil War and Victorian Banbury. Costume display dating back to the 17th century. Interactive displays.

Bodleian Library
Broad Street, Oxford OX1 3BG
t (01865) 277224
w bodley.ox.ac.uk
open All year, Mon-Sat 0900-1700. Tours: Mon-Sat 1030, 1130, 1400, 1500.
admission ££
The main research library of the University of Oxford. Fifteenth-century Divinity School, historic Old Schools Quadrangle, Exhibition Room and Tower of the Five Orders.

Christ Church Picture Gallery
Canterbury Quadrangle, Christ Church,
Oxford OX1 1DP
t (01865) 276172
w chch.ox.ac.uk
open Apr, Oct-Mar, Mon-Sat 1030-1300, 1400-1630, Sun 1400-1630. May-Sep, Mon-Sat 1030-1700, Sun 1400-1700.
admission £
The gallery, designed in 1968 by Powell and Moya, holds 300 paintings and 2,000 drawings by famous Old Masters Van Dyck, Leonardo, Michelangelo and Rubens.

Dorchester Abbey Museum
Dorchester Abbey, Dorchester on Thames OX10 7HZ
t (01865) 340054
w dorchester-abbey.org.uk
open Abbey: Daily 0800-1800. Museum: Apr-Sep, daily 1400-1700.
admission Free
The abbey, together with the displays managed by the Abbey Museum, illustrates the history of Dorchester-on-Thames and its environs. Cloister Gallery, Abbey Guest House.

Modern Art Oxford
30 Pembroke Street, Oxford OX1 1BP
t (01865) 722733
w modernartoxford.org.uk
open All year, Tue-Sat 1000-1700, Sun 1200-1700.
admission Free
Centre for modern and contemporary visual art with a constantly changing exhibition programme. We are the South East's leading centre for modern and contemporary art.

For key to symbols see inside back cover.

Museum of Oxford
St Aldates, Oxford OX1 1DZ
t (01865) 252761
w museumofoxford.org.uk
open All year, Tue-Fri 1000-1700, Sat-Sun 1200-1700.
admission Free

History of Oxford with graphics/models, reconstructed period rooms, Elizabethan inn parlour, 18thC student's room, and 19thC Jericho kitchen. Town Seal 1191 and exhibitions.

Museum of the History of Science
Broad Street, Oxford OX1 3AZ
t (01865) 277280
w mhs.ox.ac.uk/
open All year, Tue-Sat 1200-1600, Sun 1400-1700.
admission Free

Displays include scientific instruments, fine Islamic and European astrolabes, early chemical apparatus, a fine collection of clocks, medical instruments, original penicillin apparatus.

Oxford University Museum of Natural History
Parks Road, Oxford OX1 3PW
t (01865) 272950
w oum.ox.ac.uk
open Daily 1200-1700.
admission Free

Fascinating Victorian-Gothic building with displays of animals, insects, birds, fossils, dinosaurs, gemstones, the remains of Alice's dodo and a working observation beehive.

Pitt Rivers Museum
Parks Road, Oxford OX1 3PP
t (01865) 270927 **w** prm.ox.ac.uk
open Daily 1200-1630.
admission Free

Outstanding anthropological collections from many cultures around the world, past and present, displayed in original period setting providing insights into human skills.

River & Rowing Museum
Mill Meadows, Henley-on-Thames RG9 1BF
t (01491) 415600 **w** rrm.co.uk
open May-Aug, daily 1000-1730. Sep-Apr, daily 1000-1700.
admission £

A unique, award-winning museum with galleries dedicated to rowing, the River Thames and the town of Henley. Special exhibitions run throughout the year.

RELAXING AND PAMPERING

Bicester Village Outlet Shopping
50 Pingle Drive, Oxford Road, Bicester OX26 6WD
t (01869) 369055 **w** bicestervillage.com
open All year, Mon-Fri, Sun 1000-1800, Sat 0930-1900, Bank Hols 1000-1900.
admission Free

Outlet shopping centre with over 100 stores selling famous brands at much-reduced prices. Only one hour by train from London Marylebone or Birmingham Moor Street.

Stanton Harcourt

Surrey

Enjoy the fun of a special event or visit one of the attractions listed for a great day out. For more inspiring ideas go to **enjoyengland.com**.

28 May
Surrey County Show
Stoke Park, Guildford
(01483) 890810
surreycountyshow.co.uk

1–2 Jun
Vodafone Derby
Epsom Downs Racecourse, Epsom
(01372) 470047
epsomderby.co.uk

3–8 Jul
Hampton Court Palace Flower Show
Hampton Court, East Molesey
(020) 7649 1885
rhs.org.uk/hamptoncourt

13–15 Jul
Guilfest
Stoke Park, Guildford
(01483) 454159
guilfest.co.uk

Oct
Guildford Book Festival
Various venues, Guildford
(01483) 444334
guildfordbookfestival.co.uk

FAMILY FUN

Bird World

Holt Pound, Farnham GU10 4LD
t (01420) 22140 **w** birdworld.co.uk
open 1 Jan-24 Mar, 29 Oct-31 Dec 1000-1630. 25 Mar-28 Oct 1000-1800.
admission Adult: £10.95

Bird-park and gardens covering 26 acres. Admission includes Underwater World and Jenny Wren children's farm. Path to adjacent Forest Lodge Garden Centre. Puddleducks restaurant serves hot meals and snacks. Kiosks in the park serve drinks and snacks. Penguin feeding twice daily, and children can meet the animals at animal encounter sessions.

Map ref 2C2

v *voucher offer – see back section*

Burpham Court Farm Park
Clay Lane, Jacobswell GU4 7NA
t (01483) 576089 **w** burphamcourtfarm.com
open Daily 1000-dusk.
admission £
Farm centre for endangered breeds: cattle, sheep, pigs, goats and poultry. Nature trail, animal feeding and 'help the farmer'. Educational visits, parties and angling.

Travel update

Get the latest travel information – just dial the RAC on 1740 from your mobile phone.

Admission is based on an adult price. Please check opening times and admission before travelling.

Farncombe Boat House

Catteshall Lock, Godalming GU7 1NH
t (01483) 421306
w farncombeboats.co.uk
open Easter-31 Oct 0900-1730.
admission Please phone for full pricing details

Idyllic setting on National Trust River Wey. Rowing boats, punts and canoes for hire by the hour. Purpose-built day narrowboats especially suitable for family outings or business entertainment. Short breaks or longer narrowboat holidays. Riverside bistro is open all year.

                    Map ref 2D2

Godstone Farm

Tilburstow Hill Road, Godstone RH9 8LX
t (01883) 742546 **w** godstonefarm.co.uk
open Apr-Oct, daily 1000-1800. Nov-Mar, daily 1000-1700.
admission £

A popular children's farm set in South East England's attractive scenery with friendly animals (some to climb in with) and enormous play areas inside and out.

Guildford Boat House

Millbrook, Guildford GU1 3XJ
t (01483) 504494
w guildfordboats.co.uk
open Easter-Oct 0900-1730. Narrowboats all year.
admission Please phone for full pricing details

Enjoy one of the prettiest stretches of River Wey in Guildford. River trips for individuals and groups onboard two purpose-built boats. Choice of menus. Rowing boats for hire. Short breaks or weekly holidays on brightly painted narrow boats.

Map ref 2D2

Thorpe Park

Staines Road, Chertsey KT16 8PN
t 0870 444 4466 **w** thorpepark.com
open See website for details.
admission ££££

Get ready for thrill overload as Slammer joins the adrenaline-charged line-up at Thorpe Park. Experience Nemesis Inferno and Colossus, amongst others.

NATURE AND WILDLIFE

Bird World

Holt Pound, Farnham GU10 4LD
t (01420) 22140 **w** birdworld.co.uk
open 1 Jan-24 Mar, 29 Oct-31 Dec 1000-1630. 25 Mar-28 Oct 1000-1800.
admission Adult: £10.95

Bird-park and gardens covering 26 acres. Admission includes Underwater World and Jenny Wren children's farm. Path to adjacent Forest Lodge Garden Centre. Puddleducks restaurant serves hot meals and snacks. Kiosks in the park serve drinks and snacks. Penguin feeding twice daily, and children can meet the animals at animal encounter sessions.

                    Map ref 2C2

V *voucher offer – see back section*

British Wildlife Centre

Newchapel,
Lingfield RH7 6LF
t (01342) 834658
w britishwildlifecentre.co.uk
open Apr-Oct, Sat-Sun, Bank Hols 1000-1700. Open daily in school holidays.
admission ££

A peaceful, relaxing place to see and learn about Britain's fascinating native wildlife, from tiny harvest mice to magnificent red deer.

Busbridge Lakes Ornamental Waterfowl and Gardens
Hambledon Road, Godalming GU8 4AY
t (01483) 421955 **w** busbridgelakes.co.uk
open See website for details.
admission £

Visitors to Busbridge Lakes can see over 1,000 birds – mainly ornamental waterfowl, pheasants and parkland birds. Within the 40 acres are three lakes, rare trees and nature trails.

Claremont Landscape Garden
Portsmouth Road, Esher KT10 9JG
t (01372) 467806 **w** nationaltrust.org.uk
open Apr-Oct, daily 1000-1800. Nov-Mar, Tue-Sun 1000-1700.
admission ££

One of the earliest-surviving English landscape gardens by Vanbourgh and Bridgeman. Lake, island, view points and avenues with pavilion grotto and turf amphitheatre.

Devils Punch Bowl Country Park & Cafe
London Road, Hindhead GU26 6AB
t (01428) 608771 **w** nationaltrust.org.uk
open Commons: Daily. Café: Apr-Oct, daily 0900-1700. Nov-Feb, daily 0900-1600.
admission Free

Enjoy the stunning scenery of the Devil's Punch Bowl and Hindhead Commons from the viewpoint 50m from the Devil's Punch Bowl cafe.

Gatton Park
Reigate RH2 0TW
t (01737) 649068 **w** gattonpark.com
open See website for details.
admission Free

Gatton Park is a spectacular, historic park landscaped by 'Capability' Brown situated at the foot of the North Downs. Enjoy lost gardens, lakes, woodland in stunning setting.

Loseley Park

Estate Offices, Loseley Park, Guildford GU3 1HS
t (01483) 405112 **w** loseley-park.com
open Gardens/grounds: May-Sep, Tue-Sun, Bank Holiday Mon 1100-1700. House: May-Aug, Tue-Thu, Sun, 1300-1700, Bank Holiday Mon 1200-1700.
admission Adult: £7

Steeped in history and home of the More-Molyneux family for nearly 500 years, Loseley House is surrounded by glorious countryside and boasts one of the most beautiful gardens in the country. '...an amazing treasure of a house, a quiet, uncommercial treat, so personal'. Tourism South East ExSEllence award winner 2006.

Map ref 2D2

 voucher offer – see back section

View across to Surrey Hills from Leith Hill

For key to symbols see inside back cover.

Painshill Park

Portsmouth Road,
Cobham KT11 1JE
t (01932) 868113 **w** painshill.co.uk
open Mar-Oct 1030-1800, last entry 1630.
Nov-Feb 1030-1600 (or dusk), last entry 1500.
admission Adult: £6.60

Painshill Park is one of the most important
18thC parks in Europe with 160 acres of
authentically restored park, with folly buildings
and 18thC plantings. American Roots
exhibition (NCCPG award), family events,
children's trails, full educational programme,
talks - something for everyone. Tea room and
gift shop.

    Map ref 2D2

 voucher offer – see back section

RHS Garden Wisley

Wisley GU23 6QB
t (01483) 224234 **w** rhs.org.uk
open Apr-Oct, Mar, Mon-Fri 1000-1800, Sat-Sun
0900-1800. Nov-Feb, Mon-Fri 1000-1630, Sat-Sun
0900-1430.
admission ££
*Stretching over 240 acres of glorious garden, Wisley
demonstrates the best in British gardening practices,
whatever the season. Plant centre, gift shop and
restaurant.*

enjoy**England**.com

A great attraction or activity can
often make the perfect holiday.
Enjoyengland.com features a
comprehensive list of every
quality-assured theme park, landmark,
museum, national park and activity
in England.

The Savill Garden, Windsor Great Park

Wick Lane, Englefield Green, Windsor TW20 0UU
t (01753) 847518
w theroyallandscape.co.uk
open Apr-Oct, Mar, daily 1000-1800. Nov-Feb, daily
1000-1630.
admission £
*Woodland garden with adjoining formal rose gardens
and herbaceous borders, offering much of great interest
and beauty at all seasons. Plant centre, gift shop,
restaurant.*

Winkworth Arboretum

The National Trust, Hascombe Road,
Hascombe GU8 4AD
t (01483) 208477
w nationaltrust.org.uk
open All year, dawn-dusk.
admission £
*One hundred acres of hillside planted with rare trees
and shrubs. Good views, lakes, newly-restored
boathouse, azaleas, bluebells, wild spring flowers and
autumn colours.*

HISTORIC ENGLAND

Clandon Park

West Clandon GU4 7RQ
t (01483) 222482
w nationaltrust.org.uk
open House: Apr-Oct, Tue-Thu, Sun 1100-1630.
Garden: Apr-Oct, Tue-Thu, Sun 1100-1700. Museum:
Apr-Oct, Tue-Thu, Sun 1200-1700.
admission ££
*A Palladian-style house built for Lord Onslow c1730.
Marble hall, Gubbay collection of furniture, needlework
and porcelain, Royal Surrey Regiment Museum, parterre
in garden.*

Dapdune Wharf

Wharf Road, Guildford GU1 4RR
t (01483) 561389
w nationaltrust.org.uk
open Apr-Oct, Mon, Thu-Sun 1100-1700.
admission £
*The home of 'Reliance', a restored Wey barge, as well as
an interactive exhibition which tells the story of the
waterway and those who lived and worked on it.*

Guildford Cathedral

Stag Hill, Guildford GU2 7UP
t (01483) 547860
w guildford-cathedral.org
open Daily 0830-1730. Tours: Daily 0940-1600.
admission Free
*New Anglican cathedral, the foundation stone of which
was laid in 1936. Notable sandstone interior and marble
floors. Restaurant and shops.*

Hatchlands Park

East Clandon GU4 7RT
t (01483) 222482 **w** nationaltrust.org.uk
open Park: Apr-Oct, daily 1100-1800. House: Apr-Jul,
Sep-Oct, Tue-Thu, Sun 1400-1730. Aug, Tue-Fri, Sun
1400-1730.
admission ££

*Built in 1758 and set in a Repton park, Hatchlands has
splendid interiors by Robert Adam and houses the
Cobbe collection of keyboard musical instruments. Jekyll
Garden.*

Loseley Park

Estate Offices, Loseley Park,
Guildford GU3 1HS
t (01483) 405112 **w** loseley-park.com
open Gardens/grounds: May-Sep, Tue-Sun,
Bank Holiday Mon 1100-1700. House: May-
Aug, Tue-Thu, Sun, 1300-1700, Bank Holiday
Mon 1200-1700.
admission Adult: £7

Steeped in history and home of the More-
Molyneux family for nearly 500 years, Loseley
House is surrounded by glorious countryside
and boasts one of the most beautiful gardens in
the country. '...an amazing treasure of a house,
a quiet, uncommercial treat, so personal'.
Tourism South East ExSEllence award winner
2006.

Map ref 2D2

V *voucher offer – see back section*

Painshill Park

Portsmouth Road,
Cobham KT11 1JE
t (01932) 868113 **w** painshill.co.uk
open Mar-Oct 1030-1800, last entry 1630.
Nov-Feb 1030-1600 (or dusk), last entry 1500.
admission Adult: £6.60

Painshill Park is one of the most important
18thC parks in Europe with 160 acres of
authentically restored park, with folly buildings
and 18thC plantings. American Roots
exhibition (NCCPG award), family events,
children's trails, full educational programme,
talks - something for everyone. Tea room and
gift shop.

Map ref 2D2

V *voucher offer – see back section*

Polesden Lacey

Great Bookham RH5 6BD
t (01372) 458203 **w** nationaltrust.org.uk
open House: Apr-Oct, Wed-Sun 1100-1700. Gardens:
Apr-Oct, daily 1100-1700. Nov-Feb, daily 1100-1600.
admission ££

*A Regency villa, re-modelled after 1906 with collections
of paintings, porcelain, tapestries and furniture. Walled
rose garden, extensive grounds with landscape walks
and woodland.*

Titsey Place and Gardens

Titsey Place, Oxted RH8 0SD
t (01273) 407056 **w** titsey.org
open May-Sep, Wed, Sun, Bank Hols 1300-1700.
admission £

*A guided tour of Titsey Place includes the library, old
servants' hall, dining room and drawing room. The
gardens comprise 10 acres of formal gardens and a
walled garden.*

Quality counts

Look out for the Quality Assured
Visitor Attraction sign. These
attractions are assessed annually
and meet the standards required
to receive the quality marque.

 # OUTDOOR ACTIVITIES

Farncombe Boat House

Catteshall Lock, Godalming GU7 1NH
t (01483) 421306
w farncombeboats.co.uk
open Easter-31 Oct 0900-1730.
admission Please phone for full pricing details

Idyllic setting on National Trust River Wey. Rowing boats, punts and canoes for hire by the hour. Purpose-built day narrowboats especially suitable for family outings or business entertainment. Short breaks or longer narrowboat holidays. Riverside bistro is open all year.

                    Map ref 2D2

Godalming Packetboat Company
The Wharf, River Wey,
Godalming GU7 3NP
t (01483) 414938
w horseboat.org.uk
open Apr-Sep, daily. Please phone for details.
admission ££

Unusual river trips along the River Wey on the traditional horse-drawn narrow boat 'Iona'. Trips last approximately two hours and include passing through a lock.

Guildford Boat House

Millbrook, Guildford GU1 3XJ
t (01483) 504494
w guildfordboats.co.uk
open Easter-Oct 0900-1730. Narrowboats all year.
admission Please phone for full pricing details

Enjoy one of the prettiest stretches of River Wey in Guildford. River trips for individuals and groups onboard two purpose-built boats. Choice of menus. Rowing boats for hire. Short breaks or weekly holidays on brightly painted narrow boats.

                                    Map ref 2D2

 # ENTERTAINMENT AND CULTURE

Guildford House Gallery
155 High Street, Guildford GU1 3AJ
t (01483) 444740 **w** guildford.gov.uk
open All year, Tue-Sat 1000-1645.
admission Free

An exhibition gallery in a restored 17thC house of architectural interest. Temporary exhibitions and selections from the Borough's art collection.

Guildford Museum
Castle Arch, Quarry Street, Guildford GU1 3SX
t (01483) 444750 **w** guildfordmuseum.co.uk
open All year, Mon-Sat 1100-1700.
admission Free

A 17thC house with collections of local history, needlework collection, Wealden ironwork and items relating to Lewis Carroll. Gallery displaying Surrey archaeology.

 # FOOD AND DRINK

Denbies Wine Estate
London Road, Dorking RH5 6AA
t (01306) 876616 **w** denbiesvineyard.co.uk
open Apr-Dec, Mon-Sat 1000-1730, Sun 1130-1730. Jan-Mar, Mon-Fri 1000-1700, Sat 1000-1730, Sun 1130-1730. Tours: All year, Mon-Sat 1100-1600, Sun 1200-1600.
admission ££

England's largest vineyard, set in 265 acres. The visitor centre offers a range of facilities including tours, shopping, restaurants, picture gallery and much more.

Fun at Painshill Park, Cobham

West Sussex

Enjoy the fun of a special event or visit one of the attractions listed for a great day out. For more inspiring ideas go to **enjoyengland.com**.

22–24 Jun
Goodwood Festival of Speed
Goodwood Park, Chichester
(01243) 755055
goodwood.co.uk

25–29 Jul
Longines Royal International Horse Show
All England Jumping Course, Hickstead,
Haywards Heath
(01273) 834315
hickstead.co.uk

31 Jul–4 Aug
Glorious Goodwood
Goodwood Racecourse, Chichester
0800 018 8191
goodwood.co.uk

1–2 Sep
International Bognor Birdman
Seafront and pier, Bognor Regis
sussexbythesea.com

26 Dec–1 Jan 08
A Sussex Christmas
Town Lane, Singleton, Chichester
wealddown.co.uk

FAMILY FUN

Butlins
Upper Bognor Road, Bognor Regis PO21 1JJ
t (01243) 822445 **w** butlins.co.uk
open Please phone for details.
admission £££
Experience all the best elements of a Butlins holiday in a day including a subtropical waterworld, funfair and non-stop entertainment in the Skyline Pavilion.

Fishers Farm Park
Fishers Farm, Newpound Lane,
Wisborough Green RH14 0EG
t (01403) 700063 **w** fishersfarmpark.co.uk
open Daily 1000-1700.
admission ££
Farm park with shire horses, Shetland ponies, ducks, sheep and goats. There are adventure play areas, play barns, a paddling pool and tractor rides.

Harbour Park
Seafront, Littlehampton BN17 5LL
t (01903) 721200
w harbourpark.com
open All year, phone for details.
admission Free

Harbour Park is an all-weather theme park including dodgems, log flume, adventure golf and an indoor skating rink. Have a meal in the Galley Restaurant or the coffee bar. Enjoy sandy beaches and grass picnic areas. All the makings for a fun-filled day out for the whole family.

Map ref 2D3

  voucher offer – see back section

Tulleys Farm
Turners Hill, Crawley RH10 4PE
t (01342) 718472 **w** tulleysfarm.com
open Daily 0900-1700.
admission £

A farm with pick-your-own fruit and vegetables. A seven-acre maize maze puzzle will entertain all the family. Tearoom, farm shop, children's play area and pets corner.

Washbrooks Farm Centre
Washbrooks Farm, Brighton Road,
Hurstpierpoint BN6 9EF
t (01273) 832201 **w** washbrooks.co.uk
open Daily 0930-1700.
admission £

Pigs, cows, horses, ponies, donkeys, sheep, goats, poultry and rabbits, usually with their young, may be seen and touched. Adventure playground and tractor rides.

Weald & Downland Open Air Museum

Singleton, Chichester PO18 0EU
t (01243) 811348
w wealddown.co.uk
open All year. Phone or see website for details.
admission Adult: £8.25

Over 45 rescued historic buildings rebuilt in a beautiful 50-acre setting, bringing to life the homes, farms and workplaces of the South East over the past 500 years. Watch the Shire horses at work; visit the medieval farmstead, working Tudor kitchen and 17thC watermill; or relax with a picnic by the lakeside.

Map ref 2C3

 voucher offer – see back section

NATURE AND WILDLIFE

Arundel Wildfowl and Wetlands Centre
Mill Road, Arundel BN18 9PB
t (01903) 883355
w wwt.org.uk
open Daily 0930-1700.
admission ££

Have a fantastic day out, feeding and learning about wetland birds and wildlife. Set in over 60 acres of ponds, lakes and reed beds.

Borde Hill Garden
Balcombe Road, Haywards Heath RH16 1XP
t (01444) 450326
w bordehill.co.uk
open Apr-Oct, daily 1000-1800.
admission ££

Spring is heralded by magnificent magnolias, rhododendrons and azaleas, blending into summer with fragrant roses and herbaceous plants, followed by the rich colours of autumn.

Denmans Garden
Denmans Lane, Fontwell BN18 0SU
t (01243) 542808
w denmans-garden.co.uk
open Apr-Sep, daily 0900-1700. Nov-Mar, daily 0900-dusk.
admission £

A beautiful four-acre garden designed for year-round interest through use of form, colour and texture. Beautiful plant centre, fully licensed Garden Cafe (Les Routiers approved).

Earnley Butterflies and Gardens
133 Almodington Lane, Earnley PO20 7JR
t (01243) 512637
w earnleybutterfliesandgardens.co.uk
open Apr-Oct, daily 1000-1800.
admission ££

A tropical-butterfly house, covered theme gardens, exotic-bird garden, children's play area, small-animal farm and crazy golf. Rejectamenta museum. Noah's Ark rescue centre.

High Beeches Woodland & Water Gardens
Handcross RH17 6HQ
t (01444) 400589
w highbeeches.com
open Mar-Oct, Mon-Tue, Thu-Sun 1300-1700.
admission ££

Twenty-five acres of peaceful, landscaped woodland and water gardens with many rare plants, wildflower meadow, spring bulbs and glorious autumn colour.

Highdown Gardens
Littlehampton Road, Highdown, Worthing BN12 6PE
t (01903) 221112 **w** worthing.gov.uk
open Apr-Sep, daily 1000-1800. Oct-Nov, Mon-Fri
1000-1630. Dec-Jan, Mon-Fri 1000-1600. Feb-Mar,
1000-1630.
admission Free
A nine-acre chalk pit garden on a southern slope. Rock plants and flowering shrubs thriving on lime soil, rose garden and spring bulb collection including naturalised daffodils.

Holly Gate Cactus Nursery and Garden
Billingshurst Road, Ashington RH20 3BB
t (01903) 892930 **w** hollygatecactus.co.uk
open Daily 0900-1700.
admission £
A famous collection of over 20,000 rare cactus and succulent plants from around the world landscaped in 10,000sq ft of glasshouses.

Huxleys Experience
Hilliers Garden Centre, Brighton Road,
Horsham RH13 6QD
t (01403) 273458 **w** flyingfalcons.co.uk
open Apr-Oct, Mar, Mon, Wed-Sun 1100-1700.
Nov-Feb, Sun 1100-1630.
admission £
A large collection of birds of prey housed in aviaries typical of their natural habitat set in a landscaped garden. Flying demonstrations.

Leonardslee Lakes and Gardens
Lower Beeding RH13 6PP
t (01403) 891212 **w** leonardslee.com
open Apr-Oct, daily 0930-1800.
admission ££
Rhododendrons and azaleas in 240-acre valley with seven lakes. Rock garden, bonsai, wallabies and wildfowl. Victorian motor cars and 1/12th scale country estate of 100 years ago.

Nymans Garden
Handcross RH17 6EB
t (01444) 400321 **w** nationaltrust.org.uk
open Mar-Dec, Wed-Sun 1100-1800.
admission ££
A large romantic garden around the ruins of an old house with good views. Outstanding international collection of rare trees, shrubs and plants.

Pulborough Brooks RSPB Nature Reserve
Wiggonholt, Pulborough RH20 2EL
t (01798) 875851 **w** rspb.org.uk
open Daily, dawn-dusk.
admission £
An extensive RSPB nature reserve with nature trails, scenic views and viewing hides. Upperton's Barn visitor centre has information displays.

Tilgate Park and Nature Centre
Tilgate Park, Crawley RH10 5PQ
t (01293) 521168
w crawley.gov.uk
open Park: Daily. Nature Centre: Apr-Oct, daily
1000-1800. Nov-Mar, daily 1000-1600.
admission £
Beautiful parkland surrounds the Nature Centre with its rare animals, ornamental walled garden, Shire stables and craft units. A public golf centre adjoins.

Wakehurst Place Gardens
Ardingly RH17 6TN
t (01444) 894066
w kew.org
open Mar-Oct, daily 1000-1800. Nov-Feb, daily
1000-1630.
admission ££
Extensive estate gardens administered by Royal Botanic Gardens, Kew and has a series of lakes, ponds and an important collection of exotic trees, plants and shrubs.

West Dean Gardens
West Dean PO18 0QZ
t (01243) 818210
w westdean.org.uk
open Mar-Oct, 1030-1700. Nov-Feb, Wed-Sun
1030-1600.
admission ££
Highlights of this award-winning garden include a beautifully restored walled kitchen garden with Victorian glasshouses, extensive formal gardens, arboretum, pergola.

HISTORIC ENGLAND

Arundel Castle
Arundel BN18 9AB
t (01903) 883136
w arundelcastle.org
open Mar-Oct, Tue-Sun 1100-1630.
admission ££
Fortified castle and stately home since 1067. Fine works of art. Medieval keep. Fitzalan chapel. Grounds, kitchen and flower gardens. Special-events programme.

Bignor Roman Villa
Bignor RH20 1PH
t (01798) 869259
open Mar-Apr, Tue-Sun 1000-1700. May, daily
1000-1700. June-Sep, daily 1000-1800. Oct, daily
1000-1700.
admission £
The remains of a large villa containing some of the finest mosaic pavements outside Italy, including a 24m corridor mosaic, underfloor heating system and Roman artefacts.

Admission is based on an adult price. Please check opening times and admission before travelling.

Chichester Cathedral

West Street, Chichester PO19 1PX
t (01243) 782595 **w** chichestercathedral.org.uk
open Apr-Oct, daily 0715-1900. Nov-Mar,daily
0715-1800.
admission Free

Mainly Norman architecture. Detached bell tower,
Sutherland painting, Chagall window, Skelton font,
modern tapestries. Site of the Shrine of St Richard.
Romanesque stone carvings.

Chichester, St John the Evangelist Chapel

St. Johns Street, Chichester PO19 1UR
t (020) 7213 0660 **w** visitchurches.org.uk
open Daily 1000-1600.
admission Free

A rare and almost unchanged example of an evangelical
preaching house. The layout of the interior reflects the
importance laid on sermons and reading from scripture.

Fishbourne Roman Palace

Salthill Road, Fishbourne PO19 3QR
t (01243) 785859 **w** sussexpast.co.uk
open Mar-Jul, daily 1000-1700. Aug, daily 1000-1800.
Sep-Oct, daily 1000-1700. Nov, daily 1000-1600. Jan,
Sat-Sun 1000-1600. Feb, daily 1000-1600.
admission ££

Remains of the largest Roman residence in Britain. AV
presentation, beautiful mosaics, Roman gardens,
hypocaust, new Collections Discovery Centre and
Museum of Finds.

Goodwood House

Goodwood, Chichester PO18 0PX
t (01243) 755000 **w** goodwood.co.uk
open 25 Mar-9 Oct, Sun-Mon 1300-1700. 5-30
Aug, Sun-Thu 1300-1700. Last entry 1600.
Closed for occasional event days - phone
(01243) 755040 before visiting.
admission Adult: £8

Goodwood House is the Regency home of the
Dukes of Richmond. Collections include
significant paintings by George Stubbs and
Canaletto, unique Sevres porcelain, fine French
furniture and beautiful tapestries.

    Map ref 2C3

Lancing College Chapel

Lancing College, Lancing BN15 0RW
t (01273) 452213 **w** lancingcollege.co.uk
open All year, Mon-Sat 1000-1600, Sun 1200-1600.
admission Free

Lancing College Chapel was built in 13thC Gothic style
from 1868 and dedicated in 1911. The 32ft rose window
is one of the largest in England.

Parham House and Gardens

Parham Park, Storrington RH20 4HS
t (01903) 744888
open Apr-Jul, Sep, Wed-Thu, Sun, Bank Hols
1200-1700. Aug, Tue-Fri, Sun, Bank Hols 1200-1700.
admission ££

An Elizabethan house set in a deer park with great hall,
great parlour, saloon and long gallery. Displays include
portraits, needlework, tapestries. Also gardens and a
maze.

Petworth House and Park

Petworth GU28 0AE
t (01798) 342207
w nationaltrust.org.uk/petworth
open House: Apr-Oct, Mon-Wed, Sat-Sun 1100-1700.
Park: Daily 0800-dusk.
admission ££

A late 17thC mansion set in 'Capability' Brown
landscaped park. The house is noted for its paintings,
Gibbons carvings and fine collection of furniture and
sculpture.

Priest House

North Lane, West Hoathly RH19 4PP
t (01342) 810479 **w** sussexpast.co.uk
open Mar-Oct, Tue-Sun 1030-1730.
admission £

Set in the surroundings of a traditional cottage garden,
The Priest House is an early 15thC timber-framed hall-
house which contains displays of domestic furniture and
equipment.

St Mary's House and Gardens

Bramber BN44 3WE
t (01903) 816205 **w** stmarysbramber.co.uk
open Apr-Oct, daily 1000-1800.
admission ££

A medieval timber-framed Grade I house with rare
16thC wall-leather, fine panelled rooms and a unique
painted room. Five acres of beautiful gardens including
topiary.

Friendly help and advice

Tourist Information Centres offer suggestions of places
to visit and things to do as well as friendly help with
accommodation and holiday ideas. To find the one
nearest to you text TIC LOCATE to 64118.

Standen

West Hoathly Road,
East Grinstead RH19 4NE
t (01342) 323029
w nationaltrust.org.uk
open Apr-Jul, Wed-Sun 1100-1630.
Aug, Mon, Wed-Sun 1100-1630. Sep-Oct,
Wed-Sun 1100-1630. Nov-Dec, Mar, Sat-Sun
1100-1500.
admission ££

A large family house built in 1894, designed by Philip Webb, which remains unchanged with its Morris textiles and wallpapers. Fine views from the hillside gardens.

Stansted Park

Rowland's Castle PO9 6DX
t (023) 9241 2265
w stanstedpark.co.uk
open House: Apr-Jun, Mon, Sun 1300-1700.
Jul-Aug, Mon-Wed, Sun 1300-1700. Gardens: Daily
0900-1700.
admission ££

A beautiful house with ancient chapel, walled gardens and arboretum surrounded by parkland and forest. The house contains the Bessborough collection of paintings and family furnishings.

Uppark

South Harting,
Petersfield GU31 5QR
t (01730) 825857
w nationaltrust.org.uk
open Apr-Oct, Mon-Thu, Sun 1230-1630.
admission ££

Extensive exhibition shows the exciting work which restored this beautiful house and its treasures. Rescued paintings, ceramics and famous dolls' house. Nostalgic servants' rooms.

Weald & Downland Open Air Museum

Singleton, Chichester PO18 0EU
t (01243) 811348
w wealddown.co.uk
open All year. Phone or see website for details.
admission Adult: £8.25

Over 45 rescued historic buildings rebuilt in a beautiful 50-acre setting, bringing to life the homes, farms and workplaces of the South East over the past 500 years. Watch the Shire horses at work; visit the medieval farmstead, working Tudor kitchen and 17thC watermill; or relax with a picnic by the lakeside.

Map ref 2C3

v *voucher offer – see back section*

View over the West Sussex South Downs

For key to symbols see inside back cover.

OUTDOOR ACTIVITIES

Harbour Park

Seafront, Littlehampton BN17 5LL
t (01903) 721200
w harbourpark.com
open All year, phone for details.
admission Free

Harbour Park is an all-weather theme park including dodgems, log flume, adventure golf and an indoor skating rink. Have a meal in the Galley Restaurant or the coffee bar. Enjoy sandy beaches and grass picnic areas. All the makings for a fun-filled day out for the whole family.

Map ref 2D3

V voucher offer – see back section

ENTERTAINMENT AND CULTURE

Amberley Working Museum
Houghton Bridge, Amberley BN18 9LT
t (01798) 831370
w amberleymuseum.co.uk
open Mar-Oct, Wed-Sun, Bank Hols 1000-1730.
admission ££

Open-air industrial history centre in South Downs chalk quarry. Working craftsmen, narrow-gauge railway, early buses, working machines and other exhibits. Nature trail/visitor centre.

Goodwood Racecourse
Goodwood PO18 0PS
t (01243) 755022 **w** goodwood.co.uk
open See website for details.
admission £££

One of the most beautiful racecourses in the world. Many events are held here. Goodwood House provides a stunning setting for one of the most significant private art collections in the country.

Marlipins Museum

High Street, Shoreham-by-Sea BN43 5DA
t (01273) 462994 **w** sussexpast.co.uk
open May-Oct, Tue-Sat 1030-1630.
admission £

Twelfth-century secular building with architectural features housing museum of the history of Shoreham as a port. Maritime paintings, models. Occasional special exhibitions.

Tangmere Military Aviation Museum
Tangmere PO20 6ES
t (01243) 775223 **w** tangmere-museum.org.uk
open Mar-Oct, daily 1000-1730. Nov, Feb, daily 1000-1630.
admission £

A famous Battle of Britain airfield and now a museum with aircraft, photos, displays, working models and a Spitfire simulator, recalling the history of military flying.

Worthing Museum and Art Gallery
Chapel Road, Worthing BN11 1HP
t (01903) 221140 **w** worthing.gov.uk
open All year, Tue-Sat 1000-1700.
admission Free

Varied collections including art, costume, toys, archaeology and local history. Exciting programme of temporary exhibitions in three galleries and a sculpture garden throughout the year.

View across the River Arun towards Arundel Castle

Beaches in
South East England

Beaches with have been awarded the prestigious Blue Flag award. For more information, visit **blueflag.org.uk**

A resort beach actively encourages visitors and is normally near a town with recreational facilities.

A rural beach has limited facilities, is generally more remote than a resort beach and will not be actively managed.

Ramsgate Marina

Eastbourne Beach

East Sussex

Bexhill-on-Sea Beach
t (01424) 787924
Access Bexhill is the nearest town and railway station. Accessible by road via the A259. Links to London via the A259, A21 and A22.

Birling Gap
t (01323) 897426
Access There is a local bus service from Brighton, but if you want to access it by car you need to get onto the A259 and head for Birling Gap.

Camber Sands
t (01797) 225207
Access Off the main A259 coast road via the C24. The nearest town is Rye, which has rail links to Ashford and Hastings. A bus service operates from Rye to the beach. Sustrans have recently completed a new cycle trail between Rye and Camber, which is being extended.

Cooden Beach
t (01424) 787924
Access Cooden Beach station is adjacent to the beach. Regular train services operate to Eastbourne, Lewes and London. Road access is via the main A259/A27 coast road. UC7106 links Normans Bay to Cooden Beach and Bexhill. The Sustrans south coast cycle route also passes through.

Eastbourne Beach - Pier to Wish Tower
t (01323) 412290
Access Eastbourne is easily accessible by both road and rail. There are twice hourly services to London Victoria and the M25 is 50 minutes' drive from the town centre. The main roads are the A27/A23 and the A22. All parts of the enlarged south east region can be reached within easy travelling time.

Holywell Beach
t (01323) 412290
Access Eastbourne is easily accessible by both road and rail. There are twice hourly services to London Victoria and the M25 is 50 minutes' drive from the town centre. The main roads are the A27/A23 and the A22.

Normans Bay Beach
t (01424) 787500
Access Normans Bay station is adjacent to the beach. Regular train services operate to Eastbourne, Lewes and London. Road access is via the A259/A27 coast road. UC7106 links Normans Bay to Cooden Beach and Bexhill. South coast cycle route two (SUSTRANS) passes the beach.

Pelham Beach
t (01424) 781138
Access Accessible via the A259 along the coast and the A21 direct from London. Rail links with all major London stations and Ashford International with links to Europe. Well signposted from all Hastings main routes and five minutes' walk from Hastings Station.

Pevensey Bay Beach
t (09067) 112212
Access In peak season, trains run from Pevensey Bay to the centre of town. By car you can access the bay from the A27 then joining the A259. Alternatively taking the A259 from Eastbourne.

Seaford Bay
t (01323) 897426
Access The nearest town is Seaford. Access/public transport via the A259 south coast road. Railway station (Seaford) close by. Newhaven car/passenger ferry (Transmanche Ferries). Bus routes 12, 12A from Brighton and Eastbourne.

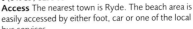

Winchelsea Beach
t (01797) 225207
Access The nearest town is Rye, which has rail links to Ashford and Hastings. A bus service is operated from Rye to Winchelsea. Accessible via the A259 coast road via the C92.

Hampshire
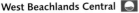

Eastoke Beach
t (023) 9246 3297
Access Located on the south coast of Hayling Island's southern shore. Can be reached by road, bus, train or the Hayling Billy five-mile cycle/walk route to Hayling Island. Ferry from Eastney (Portsmouth) to Hayling.

West Beachlands Central
t (023) 9246 3297
Access Located to the western end of Hayling Island's southern shore. Signposted from the A27 after Chichester. Havant Station connects with the bus station to Hayling beach. The 'Hayling Billy' cycle route also connects the station to the beaches.

West Beachlands West
t (023) 9246 3297
Access Located to the western end of Hayling Island's southern shore. Signposted from the A27 after Chichester. Havant station connects with the bus station to Hayling beach. The 'Hayling Billy' cycle route also connects the station to the beaches.

Isle of Wight

Colwell Bay
t (01481) 717200
Access Colwell Bay can be accessed by foot, car or local public transport.

East Cowes Beach
t (01983) 823368
Access The beach is easily accessed by car, foot or local transport such as the floating bridge. The local shops are within a short walking distance.

Gurnard Beach
t (01983) 823368
Access The beach is located to the north of Gurnard and is on the route to Cowes. It is serviced by local buses and is accessible by foot.

Ryde Beach
Access The beach is situated to the north of Ryde town centre, which is accessible by foot, public transport or the Ryde Dotto Train.

Sandown Beach
t (01983) 823368
Access Sandown Esplanade and foreshore is an integral part of the town, which is serviced by public transport or the local dotto train. Ample parking is available if using own transport.

Seagrove Beach
t (01983) 823368
Access The bay is mainly accessible by foot, as parking is limited. A local bus service can take you to or from nearby Nettlestone or Seaview, with a short walk to the beach.

Shanklin Beach
t (01983) 823368
Access Shanklin Town and Old Village is the nearest town to the beach, which can be accessed by public transport or a leisure ride on the dotto train.

Springvale Beach
t (01983) 823368
Access The nearest town is Ryde. The beach area is easily accessed by either foot, car or one of the local bus services.

St Helens Beach
t (01983) 823368
Access Public transport is available to the village, giving a fifteen- to twenty-minute walk to the beach. St Helens is a short walk away.

Totland Beach
t (01983) 823368
Access The beach can be accessed from town by foot or by car via a narrow road which passes through low-lying cliffs.

Ventnor

Ventnor Beach
t (01983) 823368
Access Ventnor town lies high above the beach and esplanade. Both locations are easily accessible by car, foot or public transport.

West Cowes Beach
t (01983) 823368
Access The beach is situated to the west of Cowes town centre and is easily accessible by car, foot or local transport.

Yaverland Beach
t (01983) 823368
Access Yaverland is readily accessible by car or foot. There is ample parking and Sandown town centre is only 1.5km away.

Kent

Beach Street, Sheerness
t (01795) 667 7015
Access Follow the A29 signposted to the docks. Turn left into Millennium Way, take the first left into Victory Street and across the junction to Beach Street.

Botany Bay
t (01843) 577274
Access Broadstairs is the nearest town. Accessible via the A299 and A253.

Herne Bay Central Beach
t (01227) 266719
Access The beach is located at the entrance to the Thames Estuary on the north Kent coast. The nearest town is Herne Bay which has easy access from the A299/M2 coast route. In addition the A291 provides a direct route to Canterbury. The bus station has services to and from the beach.

Botany Bay

Herne Bay West Beach
t (01227) 266719
Access The beach is located at the entrance to the Thames Estuary on the north Kent coast. The nearest town is Herne Bay which has easy access from the A299/M2 coast route. In addition the A291 provides a direct route to Canterbury. The bus station has services to and from the beach.

Joss Bay
t (01843) 577274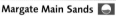
Access The nearest town is Broadstairs. Access routes via the A299 or A253. Accessible via South Eastern Trains.

Leysdown Beach
Access The nearest town is Sheerness. Take the A249 to the Isle of Sheppey, B2231 to Leysdown and the first roundabout. The seafront is the first left into Leysdown.

Margate Main Sands
t (01843) 577274
Access Margate is the closest town. Accessible via the A299 and A28. Also by South Eastern Trains.

Minnis Bay
t (01843) 577274
Access The nearest town is Birchington. Accessible via the A299, A28 and South Eastern Trains.

Minster Leas Beach
t (01795) 534542
Access Access is via the A249 into the Isle of Sheppey. Take left exit at first roundabout, third exit at following roundabout. Follow the B2008, Minster Road, then take first exit at mini-roundabout to the beach. Buses available from the bus station in Sheerness.

Ramsgate Main Sands
t (01843) 577274
Access Ramsgate accessible via the A299, A253 or B2050.

Reculver Beach
t (01227) 266719
Access The beach is located close to the main resort of Herne Bay, on the North Kent coast, which has easy access from the A299/M2 coast route. The A291 provides a direct route to Canterbury. Herne Bay is served by a mainline railway station from London (90 minutes).

St Mildred's Bay
t (01843) 577274
Access Accessible via the A299 from Margate and the A28 from the south east.

Tankerton Beach
t (01227) 266719
Access This beach is located at the entrance to the Thames Estuary on the North Kent coast. The nearest town is Whitstable which has easy access from the A299/M2 coast route. In addition, the A290 provides a direct route to Canterbury.

Viking Bay, Broadstairs
t (01843) 577274
Access Broadstairs is the nearest town. Accessible via the A299 and A253.

Walpole Bay, Margate
t (01843) 577274
Access Accessible via the A299 and A28.

West Bay, Westgate
Access The nearest town is Westgate. Accessible from the A200 and A28.

Westbrook Bay
t (01843) 577274
Access Margate is the nearest town. Accessible via the A299 and A28.

West Sussex

Bognor Regis Beach (east of the Pier)
t (01243) 823140
Access Accessible by bus, coach or car from London or from east and west via the A29. Town centre adjacent to beach. By train to Bognor Regis station. Beach is a ten-minute walk south through shopping precinct.

Littlehampton Coastguards Beach
t (01903) 721866
Access Take the A24 from London, then A259 from the east or west. By train to Littlehampton, beach is about 10-15 minutes' walk via the town and new riverside walkway by the sea visitor centre.

West Wittering Beach
t (01243) 514143
Access The nearest town is Chichester. Buses run to West Wittering from Chichester bus station to Old House at Home public house, every 30 minutes. From the A27 Chichester by-pass head south along the A286 towards the Witterings.

Worthing Town Beach
t (01903) 238977
Access Worthing is the nearest town with direct access from coast road.

Margate Main Sands

Places to stay in
South East England

Accommodation in this section is listed alphabetically by place name (shown in the blue bands), establishment category and establishment name.

All the place names can be found on the maps at the front of this guide – use the map references to locate them.

Accommodation symbols
Symbols give useful information about services and facilities. A key to these symbols can be found on the inside back-cover flap. Keep it open for easy reference.

AMERSHAM, Buckinghamshire Map ref 2D1   **SELF CATERING**

★★★★
SELF CATERING

Units   **1**
Sleeps   **8**
Low season per wk
£1,000.00
High season per wk
£1,000.00–£1,400.00

Chiltern Cottages, Amersham

contact Mr Stephen Hinds, Chiltern Cottages, Hill Farm Lane, Chalfont St Giles HP8 4NT
t (01494) 874826   **e** bookings@chilterncottages.org   **w** chilterncottages.org

open All year
payment Cash/cheques

This fine 15thC residence, in the heart of Amersham old town, boasts a large dining room with 16thC wall paintings, a fully equipped kitchen, comfortable, high-quality living room and a four-poster bed in the master bedroom. Free car parking. Approximately one mile from London Underground station.

⊕ Head for Amersham Old Town and the Old Town Centre. The Old House is about 250m after the marketplace (in the centre of the road).

♥ Short-break bookings permitted 2 months before start date. Price: weekly rate less 10% per day not used.

Children 🐕 🎱 🛝 🖧   Unit 🛏 📺 🗑 📠 🔔 🍽 🔌 🗕 🎮 ✿
General **P** 🛉 **S**   Leisure **P**   Shop < 0.5 miles   Pub < 0.5 miles

---

ASHFORD, Kent Map ref 3B4   **SELF CATERING**

★★★
SELF CATERING

Units   **6**
Sleeps   **1–4**
Low season per wk
£255.00–£460.00
High season per wk
£460.00–£645.00

Eversleigh Woodland Lodges, Ashford

contact Mrs Christine Drury, Eversleigh Woodland Lodges, Hornash Lane, Shadoxhurst, Ashford TN26 1HX
t (01233) 733248   **f** (01233) 733248   **e** enquiries@eversleighlodges.co.uk   **w** eversleighlodges.co.uk

Spacious, detached lodges in woodland setting. One double, one twin. Heated indoor swimming pool, games room, gymnasium, solarium, gardens. Easy access south coast, London, Canterbury, Channel ports and tunnel.

open All year
payment Credit/debit cards, cash/cheques

Children 🐕 🎱 🛝 ⚥   Unit 🛏 📺 🗑 📠 🗕 ✿
General 🛉 🖥 **S**   Leisure 🎿 🎣   Shop 2 miles   Pub 1.5 miles

---

Rest assured
All accommodation in this guide has been rated, or is awaiting assessment, by a professional assessor.

BIRCHINGTON, Kent Map ref 3C3 — CAMPING & CARAVANNING

★★★★★
HOLIDAY, TOURING
& CAMPING PARK
🚐(100) £12.00–£20.00
🚍(100) £12.00–£20.00
⛺ (100) £12.00–£20.00
300 touring pitches

Two Chimneys Holiday Park
Shottendane Road, Birchington CT7 0HD t (01843) 841068 f (01843) 848099
e info@twochimneys.co.uk w twochimneys.co.uk

payment Credit/debit cards, cash/cheques

A friendly, family-run country site near sandy beaches. Spacious, level pitches. Modern wc/shower and laundry facilities including disabled. Children's play and ball-games areas. Open Easter to 31 October.

⊕ A2 then A28 to Birchington. Turn right into Park Lane, bear left into Manston Road, left at crossroads (B2049), site on right.

General 🖳P🔌🗘🍴🍵🍃⊙🍴🗄🌡🐾☼ Leisure 🎣🍴🔴🎢🎾⛵🏌

BOGNOR REGIS, West Sussex Map ref 2C3 — HOTEL

★★
HOTEL
B&B per room per night
s £50.00–£60.00
d £59.00–£75.00
HB per person per night
£41.00–£64.50

Beachcroft Hotel
Clyde Road, Felpham, Bognor Regis PO22 7AH t (01243) 827142 f (01243) 863500
e reservations@beachcroft-hotel.co.uk w beachcroft-hotel.co.uk

open All year
bedrooms 16 double, 12 twin, 2 single, 4 family
bathrooms All en suite
payment Credit/debit cards, cash/cheques

Family owned and managed, on seafront in Felpham village, within 0.5 miles of restaurants, shops, pubs, tennis, putting. Bognor Regis one mile. En suite bedrooms with telephone, TV, hospitality tray. Renowned restaurant, indoor heated pool and beauty spa. Within ten miles of Chichester Cathedral and theatre, Arundel Castle and Goodwood horse-racing. Seven golf courses.

♥ Discounts available for 2 or more nights' B&B or HB on various dates throughout the year.

Children 🐥🏊🎣📞🎢🖋🖼 Room 🛏🍵📺🛁🍵🦶 General P🍴🍴🛎♿ Leisure 🎣⛵▶

BRIGHTON & HOVE, East Sussex Map ref 2D3 — GUEST ACCOMMODATION

★★★★
GUEST ACCOMMODATION
B&B per room per night
s £36.00–£65.00
d £55.00–£120.00

Ambassador Hotel
23 New Steine, Marine Parade, Brighton BN2 1PD t (01273) 676869 f (01273) 689988
e info@ambassadorbrighton.co.uk w ambassadorbrighton.co.uk

open All year
bedrooms 8 double, 7 single, 9 family
bathrooms All en suite
payment Credit/debit cards, cash/cheques, euros

Centrally located in Georgian garden square overlooking the sea, 24-hour reception and security, residents' bar. Our breakfast menu and bar offer local Sussex farm and organic produce. Gold Award Green Tourism Scheme member. A few minutes' walk to Brighton Centre, Dome, theatres, restaurants, nightlife, Royal Pavilion etc; racecourse nearby.

⊕ Follow A23 to roundabout opposite Brighton Pier, take 1st left into Marine Parade. After 2 minutes you will see New Steine on your left.

♥ Mid-week breaks Sun-Thu £35pppn Nov-May and £40pppn Jun-Oct, min 2 nights.

Children 🐥🏊🎣🖋 Room 🛏🍵📺🛁 General 🍴🍴🍴🖼♿☼🐾 Leisure 🍴🚲📷

BRIGHTON & HOVE, East Sussex Map ref 2D3　　　　　　　　　　**SELF CATERING**

Kilcolgan Bungalow, Rottingdean, Brighton

★★★★★
SELF CATERING

Units　**1**
Sleeps　**2–6**

Low season per wk
£500.00–£650.00

High season per wk
£700.00–£850.00

contact Mr J C St George, 22 Baches Street, London N1 6DL
t (020) 7250 3678　**f** (020) 7250 1955　**e** jc.stgeorge@virgin.net　**w** holidaybungalowsbrightonuk.com

open All year
payment Cash/cheques, euros

Welcome to excellence in self-catering accommodation. Exceptional, detached, three-bedroomed bungalow comprehensively equipped, with emphasis on comfort. Secluded, landscaped garden overlooking farmland. Garage parking for two vehicles. Accessible to the disabled. Rottingdean is a delightful seaside village with seafront and promenade, four miles from Brighton. Ideal, quiet retreat. Pets by arrangement (small charge).

⊕ *Left at Brighton Pier onto A259 towards Newhaven. At Rottingdean traffic lights, left onto High Street. Bear right around Kipling gardens, then left into Dean Court Road.*

♥ *Short breaks (min 3 nights) possible during low season (excl Christmas and New Year). Terms on request.*

Children 🛏 🖽 ⚥　Unit 🖳 TV 🖵 🖾 🖴 🔲 🍽 🍷 🔌 🍳 ⚙　General P ✂ Ⓢ 🐾　Leisure Ụ ►　Shop 0.75 miles　Pub 0.75 miles

BROADSTAIRS, Kent Map ref 3C3　　　　　　　　　　　　　　**SELF CATERING**

Fisherman's Cottage, Broadstairs

★★★★
SELF CATERING

Units　**1**
Sleeps　**2–6**

Low season per wk
£320.00–£450.00

High season per wk
£480.00–£630.00

contact Ms Linda Spillane, 33 St James' Drive, Wandsworth, London SW17 7RN
t (020) 8672 4150　**e** linda.spillane@virgin.net　**w** fishermanscottagebroadstairs.co.uk

open All year
payment Cash/cheques

Delightfully converted, four-storey, Grade II Listed flint cottage in Broadstairs conservation area. One minute to harbour and beach. The cottage has three bedrooms, a well-equipped kitchen and spacious living areas. The floors are linked by a wooden spiral staircase – see virtual tour on our website.

⊕ *From Broadstairs town centre follow directions to the harbour, continuing on Harbour Street. Fisherman's Cottage is on the left after 100m, behind the cafe.*

Children 🛏 ⚥　Unit 🖳 TV 🖵 🖾 🔲 🍽 🍷 🔌 🍳 ⚙　General ✂

CANTERBURY, Kent Map ref 3B3　　　　　　　　　　　　　　**SELF CATERING**

Canterbury Self-catering, Canterbury

★★★★
SELF CATERING

Units　**1**
Sleeps　**8**

Low season per wk
£400.00–£500.00

High season per wk
£500.00–£550.00

contact Mrs Kathryn Nevell, Canterbury Holiday Lets, 4 Harbledown Park, Harbledown, Canterbury CT2 8NR
t (01227) 763308 & 07941 969110　**e** rnevell@aol.com　**w** canterburyselfcatering.com

Five-bedroomed, detached, well-equipped accommodation. Sports facilities and woodland walks. Half a mile to nature reserve, 1.5 miles from city centre. Excellent value for money. Use of outdoor swimming pool by private arrangement.

payment Credit/debit cards, cash/cheques

Children 🛏 🖽 ⚥ 🗒 ⛰　Unit 🖳 TV 🖵 🖾 🔲 🍽 🍷 🔌 🍳 ⚙　General P ✂　Leisure ❍ 🚲 🏊　Shop < 0.5 miles　Pub < 0.5 miles

Take a break

Look out for special promotions and themed breaks. This could be your chance to indulge an interest, find a new one, or just relax and enjoy exceptional value! Offers are highlighted in colour (and are subject to availability).

CHICHESTER, West Sussex Map ref 2C3 — SELF CATERING

★★★★
SELF CATERING

Units **1**
Sleeps **1–6**
Low season per wk
£385.00–£555.00
High season per wk
£555.00–£645.00

Cornerstones, Chichester

contact Mrs Higgins, Goodwood Gardens, Chichester PO20 1SP
t (01243) 839096 **e** v.r.higgins@dsl.pipex.com **w** cornercottages.com

open All year
payment Cash/cheques

Sussex-style house. Two bedrooms upstairs, one downstairs. Bathroom. Separate shower room. Equipped to high standard. Double garage. Enclosed gardens. Village between Chichester and coast. Easy walks to pub/restaurant, post office/shop, church and Pagham nature reserve. Five-minute drive to Chichester. Ten minutes to Goodwood Racecourse.

⊕ A27 Chichester bypass. Roundabout with A259 Bognor take minor road (Pagham and Runcton). Next mini-roundabout left (Pagham). After 0.25 miles right into Brookside Lane, right into Brookside Close.

♥ Short breaks available Oct-May. Reduced rates for couples Oct-May.

Children 🛝 🎱 ♿ 📷 Unit 🛏 📺 🎮 ♨ 🍽 💻 🔒 🍴 🧺 🛁 🍳 💧 ❄
General **P** ♿ Shop 0.5 miles Pub < 0.5 miles

DEAL, Kent Map ref 3C4 — GUEST ACCOMMODATION

◆◆◆◆
GUEST ACCOMMODATION

B&B per room per night
s £45.00–£50.00
d £60.00–£70.00

Ilex Cottage

Temple Way, Worth, Deal CT14 0DA **t** (01304) 617026 **f** (01304) 620890 **e** info@ilexcottage.com
w ilexcottage.com

Renovated 1736 house with lovely conservatory and country views. Secluded yet convenient village location north of Deal. Sandwich five minutes, Canterbury, Dover and Ramsgate 25 minutes.

open All year
bedrooms 1 double, 2 twin
bathrooms All en suite
payment Credit/debit cards, cash/cheques

Children 🛝 🎱 ♿ 🌙 ✏ Room 🍴 📺 ♨ 🍳 General **P** ♿ 🎱 ❄ 🔥 Leisure ⚡ ひ ♪ ► 🚴 🏊

DOVER, Kent Map ref 3C4 — GUEST ACCOMMODATION

★★★★
GUEST HOUSE

B&B per room per night
s £27.00–£30.00
d £42.00–£50.00

Maison Dieu Guest House

89 Maison Dieu Road, Dover CT16 1RU **t** (01304) 204033 **f** (01304) 242816
e info@maisondieu.co.uk **w** maisondieu.com

open All year
bedrooms 1 double, 1 twin, 2 single, 3 family
bathrooms 4 en suite, 1 private
payment Credit/debit cards, cash/cheques

Welcoming, convenient and comfortable – open all year (including Christmas and New Year). Maison Dieu Guest House is central, with forecourt parking, and is minutes from Dover Castle, White Cliffs, Dover Museum, Roman Painted House, ferry/cruise terminals, bus/train stations, local restaurants and amenities. For business, stop-over or short break.

⊕ A20/Townhall Street, turn into York Street, at roundabout take 2nd exit (Priory Road). At traffic signals turn right (Ladywell). At traffic signals turn right (Maison Dieu Road).

Children 🛝 🎱 ♿ Room 📺 ♨ 🍳 General **P** ♿ 🍽 Leisure ひ ♪ 🏊

It's all quality-assessed accommodation

Our commitment to quality involves wide-ranging accommodation assessment. Ratings and awards were correct at the time of going to press but may change following a new assessment. Please check at the time of booking.

EAST MOLESEY, Surrey Map ref 2D2 — SELF CATERING

★★★★
SELF CATERING

Units **1**
Sleeps **6**

Low season per wk
£1,000.00
High season per wk
£1,000.00

Wisteria Cottage, East Molesey

contact Jenny Bailey, 11 Riverside Avenue, East Molesey KT8 0AE
t (020) 8339 1278 **f** (020) 8339 1278 **e** jenny@riversiderentals.co.uk **w** riversiderentals.co.uk

Newly renovated cottage with three double bedrooms, two bathrooms and beautiful private gardens backing on to river. Eight minutes' walk to Hampton Court Palace, 35 minutes' direct train journey to London.

open All year
payment Credit/debit cards, cash/cheques

Children 🛏 🍴 🔥 Unit 📺 🖥 💻 🍳 🛎 🔌 🎿 General **P** 🔆 **S** Leisure 🎣 🥾 ⛳ Shop < 0.5 miles Pub < 0.5 miles

EASTBOURNE, East Sussex Map ref 3B4 — CAMPING & CARAVANNING

★★★★
TOURING &
CAMPING PARK

🚐 (60) £11.00–£16.00
🚐 (60) £11.00–£16.00
⛺ (60) £11.00–£16.00
60 touring pitches

Fairfields Farm Caravan & Camping Park

Eastbourne Road, Westham, Pevensey BN24 5NG **t** (01323) 763165 **f** (01323) 469175
e enquiries@fairfieldsfarm.com **w** fairfieldsfarm.com

payment Credit/debit cards, cash/cheques

A quiet country touring site on a working farm. Close to the beautiful seaside resort of Eastbourne, and a good base from which to explore the diverse scenery and attractions of south east England. Open April to October.

⊕ *Signposted off A27 Pevensey roundabout. Straight through Pevensey and Westham villages towards castle. Then B2191 (left) to Eastbourne east, over level crossing on the left.*

♥ *Special low season, mid-week offer: 3 nights for the price of 2. Contact us for more details.*

General 🔌 **P** 🔦 👕 🍳 👣 ⊙ 📷 🛎 🐕 ⚡ ☀ Leisure 🎣 🚲

FAREHAM, Hampshire Map ref 2C3 — HOTEL

★★
SMALL HOTEL

B&B per room per night
s **£55.00**
d **£78.00–£80.00**

Upland Park Hotel & Conference Centre

Garrison Hill (A32), Droxford, Southampton SO32 3QL **t** (01489) 878507 **f** (01489) 877853
e reservations@uplandparkhotel.co.uk **w** uplandparkhotel.co.uk

open All year except Christmas
bedrooms 14 double, 2 twin, 2 family, 1 suite
bathrooms All en suite
payment Credit/debit cards, cash/cheques

Family-run hotel set in ten acres of landscaped gardens in the Meon Valley, with a private lake adjoining the Meon river. Well situated for touring Southern England – only six miles from the M27 and at the foot of South Downs Way. Welcoming staff and award-winning restaurant.

⊕ *On A32 between Alton and Fareham. Six miles off jct 10 of the M27 westbound.*

♥ *Thu jazz evenings; DB&B package available.*

Children 🛏 🍴 🔥 ✏ 💻 Room 🛏 📞 📺 ☕ 🍽 🔌 General **P** 🍴 🍽 🔌 ☀ 🐕 Leisure ⚡ 🎣 🥾

enjoy**England**.com

Big city buzz or peaceful panoramas? Take a fresh look at England and you may be surprised at what's right on your doorstep. Explore the diversity online at enjoyengland.com.

FINDON, West Sussex Map ref 2D3 | GUEST ACCOMMODATION

◆◆◆◆

GUEST ACCOMMODATION

B&B per room per night
s £60.00–£65.00
d £80.00–£90.00
Evening meal per person
£10.00–£15.00

John Henry's Inn

The Forge, Nepcote Lane, Findon, Worthing BN14 0SE **t** (01903) 877277 **f** (01903) 877178
e enquiries@john-henrys.com **w** john-henrys.com

open All year
bedrooms 3 double, 2 family, 1 suite
bathrooms All en suite
payment Credit/debit cards, cash/cheques, euros

In the heart of the village, John Henry's Inn has luxury en suite rooms, most with vaulted ceilings, including a suite with washer/dryer, satellite TV/DVD and air-conditioning. Fully licensed bar and restaurant. Open to non-residents. Ideally situated for Goodwood, Arundel, Chichester and Brighton. Wireless Internet.

⊕ *At roundabout on junction of A24 and A280 take Findon direction. Down hill to crossroad. Straight on for 350yds. Establishment is on left and ahead in fork of the lanes.*

Children 🛝 🎱 🏃 ✏ CM Room 🛏 📺 ☕ 🍳 General P 🍴 ✗ ✿ 🐾 Leisure ❀ ∪ ♪ ▶ 🚲 🏤

GATWICK, West Sussex Map ref 2D2 | GUEST ACCOMMODATION

★★★★
GUEST HOUSE
SILVER AWARD

B&B per room per night
s £45.00–£50.00
d £58.00–£63.00

The Lawn Guest House

30 Massetts Road, Horley RH6 7DF **t** (01293) 775751 **f** (01293) 821803
e info@lawnguesthouse.co.uk **w** lawnguesthouse.co.uk

open All year
bedrooms 3 double, 3 twin, 6 family
bathrooms All en suite
payment Credit/debit cards, cash/cheques, euros

Imposing Victorian house in pretty gardens. Five minutes Gatwick. Two minutes' walk Horley. Station 300yds. London 40 minutes. Bedrooms all en suite. Full English breakfast and continental for early departures. Guests' ice machine. On-line residents' computer for emails. Overnight/long-term parking. Airport transfers by arrangement.

⊕ *M23 jct 9 (Gatwick). 1st 2 roundabouts A23 (Redhill). 3rd roundabout, Esso petrol station on left – 3rd exit. 300yds right, Massetts Road. Property 500yds on left.*

Children 🛝 🎱 🏃 ✏ Room 📞 📺 ☕ 🍳 General P ✂ 🛏 ✿ 🐾 Leisure ▶

GILLINGHAM, Kent Map ref 3B3 | GUEST ACCOMMODATION

★★★
GUEST ACCOMMODATION

B&B per room per night
s £42.00–£44.00
d £50.00–£52.00
Evening meal per person
£5.00–£25.00

King Charles Hotel

Brompton Road, Gillingham ME7 5QT **t** (01634) 830303 **f** (01634) 829430
e enquiries@kingcharleshotel.co.uk **w** kingcharleshotel.co.uk

open All year
bedrooms 30 double, 30 twin, 10 single, 26 family, 2 suites
bathrooms All en suite
payment Credit/debit cards, cash/cheques, euros

A privately owned, modern hotel with a cosy restaurant and first-class conference and banqueting facilities. All bedrooms have en suite bathroom, tea-/coffee-making facilities, hairdryer, telephone and TV. We are ideal as a base for exploring South East England and London, and we offer extremely competitive group rates.

⊕ *M2 jct 4 to Gillingham/Medway Tunnel. Turn left to Brompton before tunnel. We are on left.*

Children 🛝 🎱 🏃 ✏ CM Room 🛏 📞 📺 ☕ 🍳 General P 🍴 ✗ 🎱 🛏 ⊡ ✿ 🐾 Leisure ❀ ♪ ▶ 🚲 🏤

HAILSHAM, East Sussex Map ref 2D3 | **SELF CATERING**

★★★–★★★★★
SELF CATERING

Units **5**
Sleeps **4–11**
Low season per wk
Min £385.00
High season per wk
Max £1,586.00

Pekes, Chiddingly

contact Ms Eva Morris, 124 Elm Park Mansions, Park Walk, London SW10 0AR
t (020) 7352 8088 **f** (020) 7352 8125 **e** pekes.afa@virgin.net **w** pekesmanor.com

open All year
payment Cash/cheques

Spacious oast house, cottages and wing of Tudor manor in extensive grounds. Hard tennis court, indoor heated pool, sauna, jacuzzi, badminton. Children and pets welcome. Prices shown are for the cottages; oast house is £1,220.00-£1,586.00.

⊕ *Directions given at time of booking.*

♥ *Off-peak and short breaks available (excl school holidays). Cottages £235-£650, oast house £825-£1,045.*

Children ⏰ 🛏 🎎 Unit 🔲 TV 📶 🍴 🔲 🔲 🔲 🔊 🔲 🔲 🔲 ❄
General P S 🔥 Leisure 🔍 🔍 ∪ ⛳ Shop 1.25 miles Pub 1.25 miles

HOLLINGBOURNE, Kent Map ref 3B3 | **SELF CATERING**

★★★★★
SELF CATERING

Units **1**
Sleeps **7**
Low season per wk
£625.00-£795.00
High season per wk
£850.00-£1,195.00

Well Cottage, Hollingbourne

contact Mr & Mrs Paul & Angela Dixon, North Downs Country Cottages, The Courtyard, Hollingbourne House, Hollingbourne, Maidstone ME17 1QJ
t (01622) 880991 **f** (01622) 880991 **e** info@wellcottagekent.co.uk **w** wellcottagekent.co.uk

open All year
payment Credit/debit cards, cash/cheques

Situated on top of the North Downs, an Area of Outstanding Natural Beauty, Well Cottage is Grade II Listed and restored to the highest standards. Large farmhouse kitchen/diner, characterful lounge with wood-burning stove, atmospheric dining room, two double bedrooms with en suites, a twin and single bedroom and family bathroom.

⊕ *M20 jct 8, follow A20 towards Lenham, at roundabout turn left. Go through Hollingbourne, up Hollingbourne Hill. On brow turn right into Hollingbourne House, take left fork to cottage.*

♥ *Short breaks available all year (excl Christmas and New Year).*

Children ⏰ 🛏 🎎 🖼 Unit 🔲 TV 📶 🍴 🔲 🔲 🔲 🔊 🔲 🔲 🔲 ❄
General P ✂ S Leisure ∪ 🎣 ⛳ 🚣 Shop 1.5 miles Pub 0.5 miles

HOVE

See under Brighton & Hove

ISLE OF WIGHT

See under Sandown, Shanklin, Ventnor

LONDON W1 | **GUEST ACCOMMODATION**

B&B per room per night
s £49.00-£68.00
d £75.00-£95.00
Evening meal per person
£15.00-£25.00

Bentinck House Hotel

20 Bentinck Street, London W1U 2EU **t** (020) 7935 9141 **f** (020) 7224 5903
e reception@bentinck-househotel.co.uk **w** bentinck-househotel.co.uk

Family-run budget hotel in the heart of London's fashionable West End, close to Bond Street Underground and Oxford Street. Comfortable rooms with colour TV, direct-dial telephone, room service, fax and Internet facilities.

open All year
bedrooms 2 double, 2 twin, 8 single, 5 family
bathrooms 12 en suite
payment Credit/debit cards, cash/cheques, euros

Children ⏰ 🛏 🎎 ✏ Room 🛏 📞 TV General ✗ 🛏 🐾

Check it out

Please check prices, quality ratings and other details when you book.

LONDON W2

★★★
GUEST ACCOMMODATION

B&B per room per night
s £39.00–£60.00
d £70.00–£80.00

Barry House Hotel

12 Sussex Place, London W2 2TP t (020) 7723 7340 f (020) 7723 9775 e hotel@barryhouse.co.uk
w barryhouse.co.uk

open All year
bedrooms 4 double, 6 twin, 4 single, 4 family
bathrooms 14 en suite, 1 private
payment Credit/debit cards, cash/cheques

The family-run Barry House offers warm hospitality in a Victorian townhouse. Comfortable en suite rooms with English breakfast served each morning. Located close to the West End. Paddington Station and Hyde Park are just three minutes' walk away.

⊕ *From A40 take Paddington exit and follow the road, then turn left into Sussex Gardens, then 1st right into Sussex Place.*

♥ *Stay 7 nights, get 1 night free.*

Children 🐾 🎱 ✏ Room 🛗 📞 📺 🧺 🍵 General 🏛 Leisure ∪

LONDON W2

★★★
GUEST ACCOMMODATION

B&B per room per night
s £50.00–£60.00
d £60.00–£80.00

Rhodes House Hotel

195 Sussex Gardens, London W2 2RJ t (020) 7262 5617 f (020) 7723 4054
e chris@rhodeshotel.com w rhodeshotel.com

open All year
bedrooms 3 double, 3 twin, 3 single, 9 family
bathrooms All en suite
payment Credit/debit cards, cash/cheques, euros

All rooms with private facilities, secondary glazing, free internet access, voice mail, air-conditioning, satellite TV and DVD, telephone, refrigerator, hairdryer and tea-/coffee-making facilities. Room with jacuzzi and balcony. Friendly atmosphere. Families especially welcome. Excellent transport for sightseeing and shopping.

⊕ *Follow A40 and sign into Paddington. Follow Westbourne terrace. At roundabout joining Sussex Gardens, left. Hotel is on other side of the road on 1st block.*

Children 🐾 🎱 🏃 ✏ Room 🛗 📞 📺 🧺 🍵 General P 🏛

Walkers and cyclists
welcome

Look out for quality-assessed accommodation displaying the Walkers Welcome and Cyclists Welcome signs.

Participants in these schemes actively encourage and support walking and cycling. In addition to special meal arrangements and helpful information, they'll provide a water supply to wash off the mud, an area for drying wet clothing and footwear, maps and books to look up cycling and walking routes and even an emergency puncture-repair kit! Bikes can also be locked up securely undercover.

The standards for the schemes have been developed in partnership with the tourist boards in Northern Ireland, Scotland and Wales, so wherever you're travelling in the UK you'll receive the same welcome.

CYCLISTS WELCOME
WALKERS WELCOME

LONDON W8 | HOTEL

London Lodge Hotel

★★★
TOWN HOUSE HOTEL

B&B per room per night
s £96.00–£137.00
d £126.00–£201.00
HB per person per night
£61.00–£148.00

134-136 Lexham Gardens, London W8 6JE t (020) 7244 8444 f (020) 7373 6661
e info@londonlodgehotel.com w londonlodgehotel.com

open All year
bedrooms 12 double, 8 twin, 7 single, 1 family
bathrooms All en suite
payment Credit/debit cards, cash/cheques

Beautifully refurbished townhouse hotel, ideally situated in a quiet street in the heart of Kensington. Perfectly placed for business, shopping and seeing London. All rooms individually designed and air-conditioned. Satellite TV, PC modem lines, wireless Internet, mini-bar. Executive rooms have whirlpool bath and private safe. Car parking available, bookings essential.

⊕ *Underground: straight down Earls Court Road over Cromwell Road crossing, 1st on right. Road: from A4, 1st left after crossroads, between Cromwell Road and Earls Court Road.*

♥ *Double rooms at £99 per room per night including breakfast, min 2 nights. Other offers available – please enquire.*

Children 🛝 🏠 🎠 🛶 ✏ 📷 Room 🛏 ☎ 📺 🚭 🧺 🍴 ⊛ General P ✂ 🍽 🎱 🅿 🔊

ROCHESTER, Kent Map ref 3B3 | SELF CATERING

Stable Cottages, Rochester

★★★★
SELF CATERING

Units   6
Sleeps   5–8

Low season per wk
£250.00–£450.00
High season per wk
£400.00–£600.00

contact Mrs Debbie Symonds, Stable Cottages, Fenn Croft, Newland Farm Road, St Mary Hoo, Rochester ME3 8QS
t (01634) 272439 & 07802 662702 f (01634) 272205 e stablecottages@btinternet.com
w stable-cottages.com

open All year
payment Cash/cheques

These luxury, oak-beamed cottages are set in 20 acres of secluded farmland close to RSPB reserve with panoramic views of the Thames. Access to motorways and ports. London/Canterbury 45 minutes. Perfect base for walking, bird-watching, sightseeing or just getting away from it all. Warm welcome. Family run. Indoor pool.

⊕ *From M2 jct 1, follow A228 towards Grain, turn off towards Allhallows. 1st left, follow lane to end, bear right at pond and follow track to end.*

♥ *Short breaks and split weeks available.*

Children 🛝 🏠 🎠 🏠 ⛰ Unit 🍴 📺 📧 💻 📀 🧺 🍳 💿 ❄
General P Ⓟ Ⓢ 🐕 Leisure 🏊 🎣 Shop 3 miles Pub 1 mile

Official tourist board guide **Days Out For All**

RUCKINGE, Kent Map ref 3B4 · SELF CATERING

★★★
SELF CATERING

Units **1**
Sleeps **1–7**
Low season per wk
£295.00–£375.00
High season per wk
£400.00–£525.00

The Old Post Office, Ashford

contact Mr Chris Cook, 121 The Drive, Beckenham BR3 1EF
t (020) 8655 4466 **f** (020) 8656 7755 **e** c.cook@btinternet.com **w** ruckinge.info

open All year
payment Credit/debit cards, cash/cheques

A comprehensively equipped large house, very suitable for two families holidaying together. Four bedrooms, two kitchens, two bathrooms, a huge garden from which public footpaths lead off, canal walks 100yds. Full central heating, digital TV and many books and guides. Website has pictures of all the rooms.

⊕ *M20 jct 10, south on A2070 (Brenzett). After 4 miles onto B2067 through Ham Street. Property on left after 1.5 miles – follow Ruckinge direction signs.*

♥ *Short breaks Sep-Jun.*

Children 🐕 🛏 🎠 ⚠ Unit 🖳 📺 🎦 📺 📠 🎛 📼 🎚 🎛 🔌 ✿
General **P** Ⓢ 🐾 Leisure ♪ Shop 1.5 miles Pub < 0.5 miles

SANDOWN, Isle of Wight Map ref 2C3 · GUEST ACCOMMODATION

★★★★
GUEST HOUSE

B&B per room per night
s £29.00–£36.00
d £58.00–£72.00
Evening meal per person
£15.00–£25.00

Rooftree Hotel

26 Broadway, Sandown PO36 9BY **t** (01983) 403175 **f** (01983) 403175 **w** rooftree-hotel.co.uk

Rooftree is a friendly, family-run hotel set in its own grounds. Children are welcome (toys available). English and Japanese alternative menu. Free dance lessons. We welcome you to our hotel.

open All year
bedrooms 6 double, 1 twin, 2 family
bathrooms All en suite
payment Credit/debit cards, cash/cheques

Children 🐕 🛏 🎠 🐾 ✐ CM Room 🛁 📺 ♿ 🍵 General **P** 🍴 ♟ ✗ 🏮 ⚿ ✿

SHANKLIN, Isle of Wight Map ref 2C3 · HOTEL

★★
HOTEL

B&B per room per night
s £30.00–£50.00
d £60.00–£100.00
HB per person per night
£40.00–£60.00

Orchardcroft Hotel

Victoria Avenue, Shanklin PO37 6LT **t** (01983) 862133 **f** (01983) 862133

open All year
bedrooms 7 double, 4 twin, 2 single, 3 family
bathrooms All en suite
payment Credit/debit cards, cash/cheques, euros

This elegant but friendly hotel has a private leisure complex, secluded gardens, and a reputation for good food and service. 'A very family-friendly hotel who do all they can to ensure a pleasant stay. Friendly staff, good food and wonderful pool and games facilities' – Hazel and Darren, London.

⊕ *Situated on Victoria Avenue, the main road into Shanklin from Godshill.*

♥ *Excellent-value, ferry-inclusive breaks available Oct-May. Christmas and New Year packages. Discounts on ferry prices all year.*

Children 🐕 🛏 🎠 🐾 ⚘ ⚠ ✐ CM 🎥 Room 🛁 📺 ♿ 🍵 ⚲ General **P** ♟ 🏮 ⚿ ✿ 🐾
Leisure 🦅 ♨ ∪ ♪ ▶ 🚲 🎣

Check the maps

Colour maps at the front pinpoint all the places you will find accommodation entries in the regional sections. Pick your location and then refer to the place index at the back to find the page number.

SHANKLIN, Isle of Wight Map ref 2C3 · SELF CATERING

★★★
SELF CATERING

Units **7**
Sleeps **2–6**

Low season per wk
£190.00–£320.00
High season per wk
£425.00–£710.00

Lyon Court, Shanklin

contact Mrs Sandra Humphreys, Lyon Court, Westhill Road, Shanklin PO37 6PZ
t (01983) 865861 e info@lyoncourtshanklin.co.uk w lyoncourtshanklin.co.uk

open All year
payment Cash/cheques

Charming Victorian country house with self-catering apartments. Delightful gardens, heated outdoor swimming pool and spa pool, garden sauna, children's play area. Situated on the edge of the downs, near Shanklin Old Village and beaches. Easy access to Shanklin Down, Worsley Trail and Coastal path. Good bus and rail links.

⊕ From Newport follow the A3020 to Shanklin. Half a mile after entering Shanklin, turn right into Westhill Road. Lyon Court is 2nd property on the left.

♥ Short breaks available Oct–May.

Children 🛇 🎠 🔥 🗓 /🛝 Unit 🏠 📺 ▣ ▣ 🔌 🎍 ✿
General 🔘 🆂 Leisure ⚡ Shop 0.5 miles Pub 0.5 miles

THURNHAM, Kent Map ref 3B3 · GUEST ACCOMMODATION

◆◆◆◆
GUEST ACCOMMODATION
SILVER AWARD

B&B per room per night
s £60.00–£70.00
d £75.00–£85.00
Evening meal per person
£7.00–£15.00

Black Horse Inn

Pilgrims Way, Thurnham, Maidstone ME14 3LD t (01622) 737185 f (01622) 739170
e info@wellieboot.net w wellieboot.net

Kentish country pub with award-winning restaurant in the heart of the North Downs. Beautiful gardens with fountains and ponds. Alfresco terrace dining. Fantastic walking area.

open All year
bedrooms 6 double, 3 twin, 2 family
bathrooms All en suite
payment Credit/debit cards, cash/cheques

Children 🛇 🎠 🔥 /🛝 ✎ 🖾 🗓 Room 🛁 📺 🔥 🔌 General 🅿 🍽 ✕ 🎦 ✿ 🐴 Leisure ∪ ⚓ ▸ 🚴 🚣

VENTNOR, Isle of Wight Map ref 2C3 · SELF CATERING

★★★★
SELF CATERING

Units **1**
Sleeps **2–8**

Low season per wk
£500.00–£750.00
High season per wk
£800.00–£1,000.00

Garden House, Ventnor

contact Mr Philip Barton, 67 Strode Road, London SW6 6BL
t (01983) 854451 & 07887 848146 e philip@peoplesense.co.uk
w holidaylets.net/prop_detail.asp?id=13874

open All year
payment Cash/cheques

Comfortable and spacious family house with pretty, secluded garden, children's playhouse, barbecue and outside eating area. Garden House provides a perfect holiday setting for families and walkers. A few minutes' walk from pretty beaches, the stunning South Wight Coastal Path, Bonchurch village and the quiet Victorian resort of Ventnor.

⊕ At the junction of the A3055 and B3327 in Ventnor, turn left into St Boniface Road towards Bonchurch. Garden House is directly opposite Maples Drive.

♥ Long weekends and short breaks (ideal for families and walkers) available off-peak.

Children 🛇 🗓 /🛝 Unit 🏠 📺 🔥 ▣ 🖾 ▣ 🔒 🗓 🖽 🖲 🔌 ✿
General 🆂 Shop 0.5 miles Pub 0.5 miles

Check it out

Information on accommodation listed in this guide has been supplied by proprietors. As changes may occur you should remember to check all relevant details at the time of booking.

WALTON ON THE HILL, Surrey Map ref 2D2 — SELF CATERING

★★★★★
SELF CATERING

Far End, Walton on the Hill

contact Jacquelyn Beesley, Streele Farm, Dewlands Hill, Crowborough TN6 3RU
t (01892) 852579 **e** stay@compasscottages.co.uk **w** compasscottages.co.uk

Units **1**
Sleeps **20**
Low season per wk
£2,900.00–£3,200.00
High season per wk
£3,900.00–£4,500.00

open All year
payment Cash/cheques, euros

Beautiful Edwardian mansion with many original period features. Luxury accommodation including eight double bedrooms (three master suites), six bathrooms, huge oak-panelled dining room, two surround-sound TV rooms, pool table, play room, gas barbecue. Ideal for family reunions, group holidays and celebrations. Pubs, restaurants, shops, golf, horse-riding, London and south-east attractions within easy reach.

⊕ M25 jct 8. A217 (Sutton). Left onto B2032 (Walton on the Hill). At T-junction, left (Dorking Road). After one mile, right (Deans Lane), past golf course, next left.

♥ 3-night weekend and 4-night mid-week breaks available year round from £2,000.

Children ⛄ ▦ ⛶ /⋀ Unit ▦ TV ▦ ⊡ ▨ ▣ ♨ ⊡ ⏱ ⊡ ♨ ۞ ✿
General **P** ⅍ ⊡ S ★ Leisure ☀ ∪ ♪ ▶ ⚲ ⚓ Shop < 0.5 miles Pub < 0.5 miles

WINDSOR, Berkshire Map ref 2D2 — HOTEL

★★★★
HOTEL
SILVER AWARD

Runnymede Hotel & Spa

Windsor Road, Egham TW20 0AG **t** (01784) 436171 **f** (01784) 436340
e info@runnymedehotel.com **w** runnymedehotel.com

B&B per room per night
s £96.00–£247.95
d £158.00–£314.90
HB per person per night
£102.00–£114.50

open All year
bedrooms 97 double, 80 single, 3 suites
bathrooms All en suite
payment Credit/debit cards, cash/cheques

Delightfully situated overlooking the Thames at Bell-Weir Lock, a privately owned, modern hotel set in 12 acres of landscaped gardens. Extensive state-of-the-art spa and beauty facilities including 18m indoor pool and five outdoor tennis courts. Ideally located for the wealth of tourist attractions in the area. On A308, off M25 jct 13. Prices quoted are weekend rates.

♥ Please call for details of health breaks, Legoland packages and other special promotions.

Children ⛄ ▦ ♟ ◀ /⋀ ✎ ▣ Room ☎ TV ♨ ♨ ᵏ ⊜ General **P** ♟ ⋈ ⊡ ✿ Leisure ⌕ ☿ ♪ ▶

Further
information

Ilkley, North Yorkshire

Enjoy England **Quality Rose assessment schemes**

When you're looking for a place to stay, you need a rating system you can trust. Enjoy England ratings are your clear guide to what to expect, in an easy-to-understand form.

Enjoy England professional assessors pay unannounced visits to establishments that are new to the rating scheme and stay overnight where appropriate. Once in the scheme establishments receive an annual pre-arranged day visit, with an overnight stay generally every other year for hotel and B&B guest accommodation. On these occasions the assessors book in anonymously, and test all the facilities and services.

Based on internationally recognised star ratings, the system puts great emphasis on quality, and reflects exactly what consumers are looking for. Ratings are awarded from one to five stars – the more stars, the higher the quality and the greater the range of facilities and services provided – and are the sign of quality assurance, giving you the confidence to book the accommodation that meets your expectations.

Look out, too, for Enjoy England Gold and Silver Awards, which are awarded to hotels and guest accommodation achieving the highest levels of quality within their star rating. While the overall rating is based on a combination of facilities and quality, the Gold and Silver Awards are based solely on quality.

Hotels

All hotels that are awarded a star rating will meet the minimum standards – so you can be confident that you will find the basic services that you would expect, such as:

- All bedrooms with an en suite or private bathroom
- A designated reception facility and staff members who will be available during the day and evening (24hrs in case of an emergency)
- A licence to serve alcohol (unless a temperance hotel)
- Access to the hotel at all times for registered guests

- Dinner available at least five days a week (with the exception of a Town House Hotel or Metro Hotel)
- All statutory obligations will be met.

Hotels have to provide certain additional facilities and services at the higher star levels, some of which may be important to you:

TWO-STAR hotels must provide:
- Dinner seven nights a week.

THREE-STAR hotels must provide:
- All en suite bedrooms (ie no private bathrooms)
- Direct dial phones in all rooms
- Room service during core hours
- A permanently staffed reception.

FOUR-STAR hotels must provide:
- 24-hour room service
- 50% of all en suites with bath **and** shower.

FIVE-STAR hotels must provide:
- Some permanent suites
- Enhanced services, such as concierge.

Sometimes a hotel with a lower star rating has exceptional bedrooms and bathrooms and offers its guests a very special welcome, but cannot achieve a higher rating because, for example, it does not offer dinner every evening (two star), room service (three star) or does not have the minimum 50% of bathrooms with bath and shower (four star).

Quality
The availability of additional services alone is not enough for an establishment to achieve a higher star rating. Hotels have to meet exacting standards for quality in critical areas. Consumer research has shown the critical areas to be: cleanliness, bedrooms, bathrooms, hospitality and service, and food.

Guest accommodation

All guest accommodation that is awarded a star rating will meet the minimum standards – so you can be confident that you will find the basic services that you would expect, such as:

- A clear explanation of booking charges, services offered and cancellation terms
- A full cooked breakfast or substantial continental breakfast
- At least one bathroom or shower room for every six guests
- For a stay of more than one night, rooms cleaned and beds made daily
- Printed advice on how to summon emergency assistance at night
- All statutory obligations will be met.

TWO-STAR accommodation provides all of the above but the rating reflects a higher quality of services and facilities than one-star accommodation.

Proprietors of guest accommodation have to provide certain additional facilities and services at the higher star levels, some of which may be important to you:

THREE-STAR accommodation must provide:
- Private bathroom/shower room (cannot be shared with the owners)
- Bedrooms must have a washbasin if not en suite.

FOUR-STAR accommodation must provide:
- 50% of bedrooms en suite or with private bathroom.

FIVE-STAR accommodation must provide:
- All bedrooms with en suite or private bathroom.

Sometimes guest accommodation has exceptional bedrooms and bathrooms and offers visitors a very special welcome, but cannot achieve a higher star rating because, for example, there are no en suite bedrooms, or it is difficult to put washbasins in the bedrooms (three star). This is sometimes the case with period properties.

Quality
The availability of additional facilities alone is not enough for an establishment to achieve a higher star rating. Guest accommodation has to meet exacting standards for quality in critical areas. Consumer research has shown the critical areas to be: cleanliness, bedrooms, bathrooms, hospitality and food.

Self-catering accommodation

All self-catering accommodation that is awarded a star rating will meet the minimum standards – so you can be confident that you will find the basic services that you would expect, such as:

- Clear information prior to booking on all aspects of the accommodation including location, facilities, prices, deposit, policies on smoking, children etc
- No shared facilities, with the exception of a laundry room in multi-unit sites
- All appliances and furnishings will meet product safety standards for self-catering accommodation, particularly regarding fire safety
- At least one smoke alarm in the unit and a fire blanket in the kitchen
- Clear information on emergency procedures, including who to contact
- Contact details for the local doctor, dentist etc
- All statutory obligations will be met including an annual gas check and public liability insurance.

Certain additional facilities and services are required at the higher star levels, some of which may be important to you:

TWO-STAR accommodation must provide:
- Single beds of 3ft width and double beds of 4ft 6in.

THREE-STAR accommodation must provide:
- Bed linen (with or without additional charge).

FOUR-STAR accommodation must provide:
- All sleeping space in bedrooms, unless a studio (bed settees can not be advertised)
- Bed linen included in the hire charge.

FIVE-STAR accommodation must provide:
- At least two of the following items: tumble-dryer, telephone, Hi-Fi, video, DVD.

Some self-catering establishments offer a choice of accommodation units that may have different star ratings. In this case, the entry shows the range available.

Quality
The availability of additional facilities, such as a dishwasher or DVD, is not enough to achieve a higher star rating. Self-catering accommodation with a lower star rating may offer some or all of the above, but to achieve the higher star ratings, the overall quality score has to be reached and exacting standards have to be met in critical areas. Consumer research has shown these to be: cleanliness, bedrooms, bathrooms, kitchens and public areas.

The British Graded
Holiday Parks Scheme

When you're looking for a place to stay, you need a rating system you can trust. The British Graded Holiday Parks Scheme, operated jointly by the national tourist boards for England, Scotland, Wales and Northern Ireland, was devised in association with the British Holiday and Home Parks Association and the National Caravan Council. It gives you a clear guide of what to expect in an easy-to-understand form.

The process to arrive at a star rating is very thorough to ensure that when you make a booking you can be confident it will meet your expectations. Professional assessors visit parks annually and take into account over 50 separate aspects, from landscaping and layout to maintenance, customer care and, most importantly, cleanliness.

Strict guidelines are in place to ensure that every park is assessed to the same criteria. A random check is made of a sample of accommodation provided for hire (caravans, chalets etc) but the quality of the accommodation itself is not included in the grading assessment.

In addition to The British Graded Holiday Parks Scheme, VisitBritain operates a rating scheme for Holiday Villages. The assessor stays on the site overnight and grades the overall quality of the visitor experience, including accommodation, facilities, cleanliness, service and food.

So you can rest assured that when you choose a star-rated park or holiday village you won't be disappointed.

Star ratings

Parks are required to meet progressively higher standards of quality as they move up the scale from one to five stars:

ONE STAR Acceptable
To achieve this grade, the park must be clean with good standards of maintenance and customer care.

TWO STAR Good
All the above points plus an improved level of landscaping, lighting, refuse disposal and maintenance. May be less expensive than more highly rated parks.

THREE STAR Very good
Most parks fall within this category; three stars represent the industry standard. The range of facilities provided may vary from park to park, but they will be of a very good standard and will be well maintained.

FOUR STAR Excellent
You can expect careful attention to detail in the provision of all services and facilities. Four-star parks rank among the industry's best.

FIVE STAR Exceptional
Highest levels of customer care will be provided. All facilities will be maintained in pristine condition in attractive surroundings.

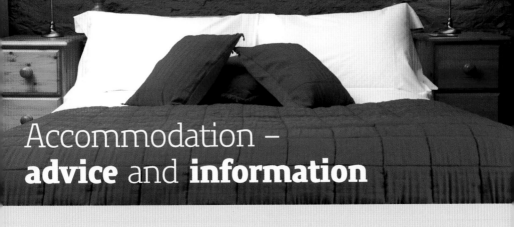

Accommodation – advice and information

Making a booking

When enquiring about accommodation, make sure you check prices, the quality rating and other important details. You will also need to state your requirements clearly and precisely, for example:

- Arrival and departure dates, with acceptable alternatives if appropriate
- The type of accommodation you need – for example, room with twin beds, en suite bathroom
- The terms you want – for example, room only, bed and breakfast
- The age of any children with you, whether you want them to share your room or be next door, and any other requirements, such as a cot
- Any particular requirements you may have, such as a special diet, ground-floor room.

Confirmation

Misunderstandings can easily happen over the telephone, so do request a written confirmation, together with details of any terms and conditions.

Deposits

If you make a hotel or guest accommodation reservation weeks or months in advance, you will probably be asked for a deposit, which will then be deducted from the final bill when you leave. The amount will vary from establishment to establishment and could be payment in full at peak times.

Proprietors of self-catering accommodation will normally ask you to pay a deposit immediately, and then to pay the full balance before your holiday date. This safeguards the proprietor in case you decide to cancel at a late stage or simply do not turn up. He or she may have turned down other bookings on the strength of yours and may find it hard to re-let if you cancel.

In the case of camping and caravan parks the full charge often has to be paid in advance. This may be in two instalments – a deposit at the time of booking and the balance by, say, two weeks before the start of the booked period.

Payment on arrival

Some establishments, especially large hotels in big towns, ask you to pay for your room on arrival if you have not booked it in advance. This is especially likely to happen if you arrive late and have little or no luggage.

If you are asked to pay on arrival, it is a good idea to see your room first, to make sure it meets your requirements.

Cancellations

Legal contract

When you accept accommodation that is offered to you, by telephone or in writing, you enter a legally binding contract with the proprietor. This means that if you cancel your booking, fail to take up the accommodation or leave early, the proprietor may be entitled to compensation if he or she cannot re-let for all or a good part of the booked period. You will probably forfeit any deposit you have paid, and may well be asked for an additional payment.

At the time of booking you should be advised of what charges would be made in the event of cancelling the accommodation or leaving early. If this is not mentioned you should ask so that future disputes can be avoided. The proprietor cannot make a claim until after the booked period, and during that time he or she should make every effort to re-let the accommodation. If there is a dispute it is sensible for both sides to seek legal advice on the matter. If you do have to change your travel plans, it is in your own interests to let the proprietor know in writing as soon as possible, to give them a chance to re-let your accommodation.

And remember, if you book by telephone and are asked for your credit card number, you should check whether the proprietor intends charging your credit card account should you later cancel your reservation. A proprietor should not be able to charge your credit card account with a cancellation fee unless he or she has made this clear at the time of your booking and you have agreed. However, to avoid later disputes, we suggest you check whether this is the intention.

Insurance

A travel or holiday insurance policy will safeguard you if you have to cancel or change your holiday plans. You can arrange a policy quite cheaply through your insurance company or travel agent. Some hotels also offer their own insurance schemes and many self-catering agencies insist their customers take out a policy when they book their holidays.

Arrival time

If you know you will be arriving late in the evening, it is a good idea to say so when you book. If you are delayed on your way, a telephone call to say that you will be late would be appreciated.

It is particularily important to liaise with the owner of self-catering accommodation about key collection as he or she will not necessarily be on site.

Service charges and tipping

These days many places levy service charges automatically. If they do, they must clearly say so in their offer of accommodation, at the time of booking. The service charge then becomes part of the legal contract when you accept the offer of accommodation.

If a service charge is levied automatically, there is no need to tip the staff, unless they provide some exceptional service. The usual tip for meals is 10% of the total bill.

Telephone charges

Establishments can set their own charges for telephone calls made through their switchboard or from direct-dial telephones in bedrooms. These charges are often much higher than telephone companies' standard charges (to defray the cost of providing the service).

Comparing costs

It is a condition of Enjoy England's Quality Rose assessment scheme that an establishment's unit charges are on display by the telephones or with the room information. It is not always easy to compare these charges with standard rates, so before using a telephone for long-distance calls, you may decide to ask how the charges compare.

Security of valuables

You can deposit your valuables with the proprietor or manager during your stay, and we recommend you do this as a sensible precaution. Make sure you obtain a receipt for them. Some places do not accept articles for safe custody, and in that case it is wisest to keep your valuables with you.

Disclaimer

Some proprietors put up a notice that disclaims liability for property brought on to their premises by a guest. In fact, they can only restrict their liability to a minimum laid down by law (The Hotel Proprietors Act 1956). Under that Act, a proprietor is liable for the value of the loss or damage to any property (except a car or its contents) of a guest who has engaged overnight accommodation, but if the proprietor has the notice on display as prescribed under that Act, liability is limited to £50 for one article and a total of £100 for any one guest. The notice must be prominently displayed in the reception area or main entrance. These limits do not apply to valuables you have deposited with the proprietor for safekeeping, or to property lost through the default, neglect or wilful act of the proprietor or his staff.

Bringing pets to England

Dogs, cats, ferrets and some other pet mammals can be brought into the UK from certain countries without having to undertake six months' quarantine on arrival provided they meet all the rules of the Pet Travel Scheme (PETS).

For full details, visit the PETS website at
w defra.gov.uk/animalh/quarantine/index.htm or contact the PETS Helpline
t +44 (0)870 241 1710
e quarantine@defra.gsi.gov.uk
Ask for fact sheets which cover dogs and cats, ferrets or domestic rabbits and rodents.

Comments and complaints

The law

Places that offer accommodation have legal and statutory responsibilities to their customers, such as providing information about prices, providing adequate fire precautions and safeguarding valuables. Like other businesses, they must also abide by the Trades Description Acts 1968 and 1972 when they describe their accommodation and facilities. All the places featured in this guide have declared that they do fulfil all applicable statutory obligations.

Information

The proprietors themselves supply the descriptions of their establishments and other information for the entries, (except Enjoy England ratings and awards). VisitBritain cannot guarantee the accuracy of information in this guide, and accepts no responsibility for any error or misrepresentation. All liability for loss, disappointment, negligence or other damage caused by reliance on the information contained in this guide, or in the event of bankruptcy or liquidation or cessation of trade of any company, individual or firm mentioned, is hereby excluded. We strongly recommend that you carefully check prices and other details when you book your accommodation.

Quality Rose signage

All establishments/parks displaying a Quality Rose sign have to hold current membership of an Enjoy England Quality Rose assessment scheme or The British Graded Holiday Parks Scheme. When an establishment is sold the existing rating cannot be automatically transferred to the new owner.

Problems

Of course, we hope you will not have cause for complaint, but problems do occur from time to time. If you are dissatisfied with anything, make your complaint to the management immediately. Then the management can take action at once to investigate the matter and put things right. The longer you leave a complaint, the harder it is to deal with it effectively.

In certain circumstances, VisitBritain may look into complaints. However, VisitBritain has no statutory control over establishments or their methods of operating. VisitBritain cannot become involved in legal or contractual matters, nor can they get involved in seeking financial recompense.

If you do have problems that have not been resolved by the proprietor and which you would like to bring to our attention, please write to: Quality in Tourism, Farncombe House, Broadway, Worcestershire WR12 7LJ.

Quality
visitor attractions

Enjoy England operates a Visitor Attraction Quality Assurance Service.

Participating attractions are visited annually by trained, impartial assessors who look at all aspects of the visit, from initial telephone enquiries to departure, customer service to catering, as well as all facilities and activities.

Only those attractions which have been assessed by Enjoy England and meet the standard receive the quality marque, your sign of a Quality Assured Visitor Attraction.

Look out for the quality marque and visit with confidence.

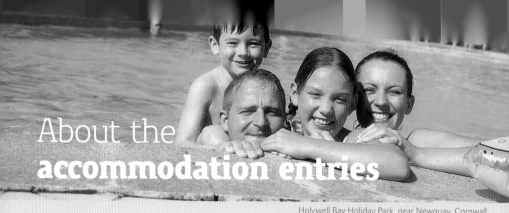

About the
accommodation entries

Entries

All the establishments/parks featured in this guide have been assessed or have applied for assessment under an Enjoy England's Quality Rose assessment scheme or The British Graded Holiday Parks Scheme. Guest accommodation showing a diamond rating is awaiting re-assessment under the new common standards star-rating scheme.

Proprietors have paid to have their establishment/ park featured in either a standard entry (includes description, facilities and prices) or enhanced entry (photograph and extended details).

Locations

Places to stay are generally listed under the town, city or village where they are located. If a place is in a small village, you may find it listed under a nearby town (providing it is within a seven-mile radius).

Place names are listed alphabetically within each regional section of the guide, along with the ceremonial county they are in and their map reference.

Complete addresses for self-catering properties are not given and the town(s) listed may be a distance from the actual establishment. Please check the precise location at the time of booking.

Map references

These refer to the colour location maps at the front of the guide. The first figure shown is the map number, the following letter and figure indicate the grid reference on the map. Some entries were included just before the guide went to press, so they do not appear on the maps.

Addresses

County names, which appear in the place headings, are not repeated in the entries. When you are writing, you should of course make sure you use the full address and postcode.

Telephone numbers

Telephone numbers are listed below the accommodation address for each entry. Area codes are shown in brackets.

Prices

The prices shown are only a general guide; they were supplied to us by proprietors in summer 2006. Remember, changes may occur after the guide goes to press, so we strongly advise you to check prices when you book your accommodation.

Prices are shown in pounds sterling and include VAT where applicable. Some places also include a service charge in their standard tariff, so check this when you book.

Bed and breakfast: the prices shown are per room for overnight accommodation with breakfast. The double room price is for two people. (If a double room is occupied by one person there is sometimes a reduction in price.)

Half board: the prices shown are per person per night for room, evening meal and breakfast. These prices are usually based on two people sharing a room.

Evening meal: the prices shown are per person per night.

Some places only provide a continental breakfast in the set price, and you may have to pay extra if you want a full English breakfast.

According to the law, establishments with at least four bedrooms or eight beds must display their overnight accommodation charges in the reception area or entrance. In your own interests, do make sure you check prices and what they include.

Self catering: prices shown are per unit per week and include VAT.

Camping: Touring pitches are based on the minimum and maximum charges for one night for two persons, car and either caravan or tent. (Some parks may charge separately for car, caravan or tent, and for each person and there may be an extra charge for caravan awnings.) Minimum and maximum prices for caravan holiday homes are given per week.

Children's rates

You will find that many places charge a reduced rate for children, especially if they share a room with their parents. Some places charge the full rate, however, when a child occupies a room which might otherwise have been let to an adult. The upper age limit for reductions for children varies from one hotel to another, so check this when you book.

Seasonal packages and special promotions

Prices often vary through the year and may be significantly lower outside peak holiday weeks. Many places offer special package rates – fully inclusive weekend breaks, for example – in the autumn, winter and spring. A number of establishments taking an enhanced entry have included any special offers, themed breaks etc that are available.

You can get details of other bargain packages that may be available from the establishments themselves, regional tourism organisations or your local Tourist Information Centre (TIC). Your local travel agent may also have information and can help you make reservations.

Bathrooms (hotels and guest accommodation)

Each accommodation entry shows you the number of en suite and private bathrooms available. En suite bathroom means the bath or shower and wc are contained behind the main door of the bedroom. Private bathroom means a bath or shower and wc solely for the occupants of one bedroom, on the same floor, reasonably close and with a key provided. If the availability of a bath, rather than a shower, is important to you, remember to check when you book.

Meals (hotels and guest accommodation)

It is advisable to check availability of meals and set times when making your reservation. Some smaller places may ask you at breakfast whether you want an evening meal. The prices shown in each entry are for bed and breakfast or half board, but many places also offer lunch.

Chalets/villas for hire (camping and caravan parks)

Where a site has chalets or villas for hire this is indicated by this symbol ◪. Please note that this type of accommodation is not necessarily included within the official quality rating for the park and it is advisable that you contact the proprietor directly if you require further information.

Opening period

If an entry does not indicate an opening period, please check directly with the establishment.

Symbols

The at-a-glance symbols included at the end of each entry show many of the services and facilities available at each establishment. You will find the key to these symbols on the back-cover flap – open it out and check the meanings as you go.

Smoking

Many places provide no-smoking areas – from no-smoking bedrooms and lounges to no-smoking sections of the restaurant. Some places prefer not to accommodate smokers, and in such cases the descriptions or symbols in each entry make this clear.

Alcoholic drinks

All hotels (except temperance hotels) hold an alcohol licence. Some guest accommodation may also be licensed, however, the licence may be restricted – to diners only, for example. If a bar is available this is shown by the ♟ symbol.

Pets

Many places accept guests with dogs, but we do advise that you check this when you book, and ask if there are any extra charges or rules about exactly where your pet is allowed. The acceptance of dogs is not always extended to cats and it is strongly advised that pet owners contact the establishment well in advance. Some establishments do not accept pets at all. Pets are welcome by arrangement where you see this symbol ↑.

The quarantine laws have changed in England, and dogs, cats and ferrets are able to come into Britain from over 50 countries. For details of the Pet Travel Scheme (PETS) please turn to page 448.

Payment accepted

The types of payment accepted by an establishment are listed in the payment accepted section. If you plan to pay by card, check that the establishment will take your particular card before you book. Some proprietors will charge you a higher rate if you pay by credit card rather than cash or cheque. The difference is to cover the percentage paid by the proprietor to the credit card company. When you book by telephone, you may be asked for your credit card number as confirmation. But remember, the proprietor may then charge your credit card account if you cancel your booking. See under Cancellations on page 447.

Awaiting confirmation of rating

At the time of going to press some establishments/parks featured in this guide had not yet been assessed for their rating for the year 2007 and so their new rating could not be included. Rating Applied For indicates this.

Getting around
England

England is a country of perfect proportions – big enough to find a new place to discover, yet small enough to guarantee it's within easy reach. Getting from A to B can be easier than you think...

Planning your journey

Make transportdirect.info your first portal of call! It's the ultimate journey-planning tool to help you find the best way from your home to your destination by car or public transport. Decide on the quickest way to travel by comparing end-to-end journey times and routes. You can even buy train and coach tickets and find out about flights from a selection of airports.

With so many low-cost domestic flights, flying really is an option. Just imagine, you could finish work in Bishop's Stortford and be in Newquay just three hours later for a fun-packed weekend!

You can island hop too, to the Isle of Wight or the Isles of Scilly for a relaxing break. No worries.

If you're travelling by car and want an idea of distances check out the mileage chart overleaf. Or let the train take the strain – the National Rail network is also shown overleaf.

Think green

If you'd rather leave your car behind and travel by 'green transport' when visiting some of the attractions highlighted in this guide you'll be helping to reduce congestion and pollution as well as supporting conservation charities in their commitment to green travel.

The National Trust encourages visits made by non-car travellers. It offers admission discounts or a voucher for the tearoom at a selection of its properties if you arrive on foot, cycle or public transport. (You'll need to produce a valid bus or train ticket if travelling by public transport.)

More information about The National Trust's work to encourage car-free days out can be found at nationaltrust.org.uk. Refer to the section entitled Information for Visitors.

To help you on your way you'll find a list of useful contacts at the end of this section.

In which region
is the county I wish to visit?

If you know what county you wish to visit you'll find it in the regional section shown below.

county	region	county	region
Bedfordshire	Central England	Leicestershire	Central England
Berkshire	South East England	Lincolnshire	Central England
Bristol	South West England	London	South East England
Buckinghamshire	South East England	Merseyside	Northern England
Cambridgeshire	Central England	Norfolk	Central England
Cheshire	Northern England	Northamptonshire	Central England
Cornwall	South West England	Northumberland	Northern England
County Durham	Northern England	Nottinghamshire	Central England
Cumbria	Northern England	Oxfordshire	South East England
Derbyshire	Central England	Rutland	Central England
Devon	South West England	Shropshire	Central England
Dorset	South West England	Somerset	South West England
East Sussex	South East England	Staffordshire	Central England
Essex	Central England	Suffolk	Central England
Gloucestershire	South West England	Surrey	South East England
Greater Manchester	Northern England	Tees Valley	Northern England
Hampshire	South East England	Tyne and Wear	Northern England
Herefordshire	Central England	Warwickshire	Central England
Hertfordshire	Central England	West Midlands	Central England
Isle of Wight	South East England	West Sussex	South East England
Isles of Scilly	South West England	Yorkshire	Northern England
Kent	South East England	Wiltshire	South West England
Lancashire	Northern England	Worcestershire	Central England

To help readers we do not refer to unitary authorities in this guide.

By **car** and by **train**

Distance chart

The distances between towns on the chart below are given to the nearest mile, and are measured along routes based on the quickest travelling time, making maximum use of motorways or dual-carriageway roads. The chart is based upon information supplied by the Automobile Association.

To calculate the distance in kilometres multiply the mileage by 1.6

For example: Brighton to Dover
82 miles x 1.6 = 131.2 kilometres

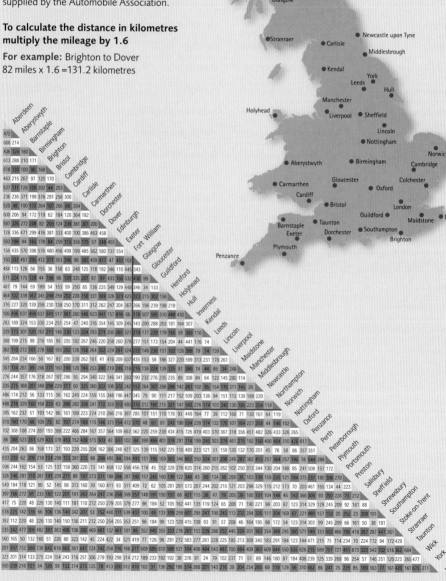

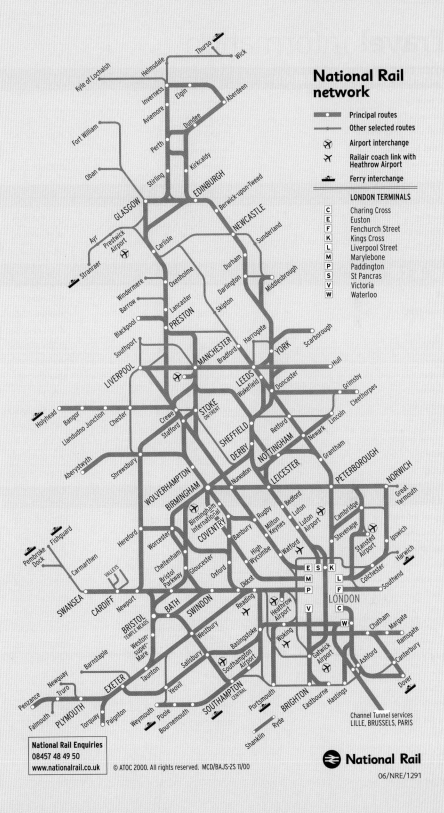

National Rail network

— Principal routes
— Other selected routes
✈ Airport interchange
✈ Railair coach link with Heathrow Airport
⛴ Ferry interchange

LONDON TERMINALS

C Charing Cross
E Euston
F Fenchurch Street
K Kings Cross
L Liverpool Street
M Marylebone
P Paddington
S St Pancras
V Victoria
W Waterloo

Channel Tunnel services
LILLE, BRUSSELS, PARIS

National Rail Enquiries
08457 48 49 50
www.nationalrail.co.uk
© ATOC 2000. All rights reserved. MCD/BAJS-2S 11/00

National Rail

06/NRE/1291

Travel information

general travel information

Streetmap	streetmap.co.uk	
Transport Direct	transportdirect.info	
Transport for London	tfl.gov.uk	(020) 7222 5600
Travel Services	departures-arrivals.com	
Traveline	traveline.org.uk	0870 608 2608

bus & coach

Megabus	megabus.com	0901 331 0031
National Express	nationalexpress.com	0870 580 8080
WA Shearings	washearings.com	(01942) 824824

car & car hire

AA	theaa.com	0870 600 0371
Green Flag	greenflag.co.uk	0845 246 1557
RAC	rac.co.uk	0870 572 2722
Alamo	alamo.co.uk	0870 400 4562
Avis	avis.co.uk	0870 010 0287
Budget	budget.co.uk	0844 581 2231
Easycar	easycar.com	0906 333 3333
Enterprise	enterprise.com	0870 350 3000*
Hertz	hertz.co.uk	0870 844 8844*
Holiday Autos	holidayautos.co.uk	
National	nationalcar.co.uk	0870 400 4581
Thrifty	thrifty.co.uk	(01494) 751500*

air

Airport information	a2btravel.com/airports	0870 888 1710
Air Southwest	airsouthwest.com	0870 043 4553
Blue Islands (Channel Islands)	blueislands.com	(01481) 727567
BMI	flybmi.com	0870 607 0555
BMI Baby	bmibaby.com	0871 224 0224
BNWA (Isle of Man to Blackpool)	flybnwa.co.uk	0800 083 7783
British Airways	ba.com	0870 850 9850
British International (Isles of Scilly to Penzance)	islesofscillyhelicopter.com	(01736) 363871
Eastern Airways	easternairways.com	0870 366 9100
Easyjet	easyjet.com	0871 244 2366
Flybe	flybe.com	0871 700 0535
Jet2.com	jet2.com	0871 226 1737
Ryanair	ryanair.com	0871 246 0000
Skybus (Isles of Scilly)	islesofscilly-travel.com	0845 710 5555
VLM	flyvlm.com	0871 666 5050

train

National Rail Enquiries	nationalrail.co.uk	0845 748 4950
The Trainline	trainline.co.uk	
UK train operating companies	rail.co.uk	
Arriva Trains	arriva.co.uk	0845 748 4950
c2c	c2c-online.co.uk	0845 601 4873*
Central Trains	centraltrains.co.uk	(0121) 634 2040
Chiltern Railways	chilternrailways.co.uk	0845 600 5165
First Capital Connect	firstcapitalconnect.co.uk	0845 748 4950
First Great Western	firstgreatwestern.co.uk	0845 700 0125*
Gatwick Express	gatwickexpress.co.uk	0845 850 1530
GNER	gner.co.uk	0845 722 5333
Heathrow Express	heathrowexpress.com	0845 600 1515
Hull Trains	hulltrains.co.uk	0845 071 0222
Island Line	island-line.co.uk	0845 748 4950
Merseyrail	merseyrail.org	0845 748 4950
Midland Mainline	midlandmainline.com	0845 712 5678
Northern Rail	northernrail.org	0845 748 4950
One Railway	onerailway.com	0845 600 7245
Silverlink	silverlink-trains.com	0845 601 4868
South Eastern Trains	southeasternrailway.co.uk	0845 748 4950
South West Trains	southwesttrains.co.uk	0845 600 0650
Southern	southernrailway.com	0845 127 2920
Stansted Express	stanstedexpress.com	0845 600 7245
Transpennine Express	tpexpress.co.uk	0845 748 4950
Virgin Trains	virgintrains.co.uk	0870 789 1234

ferry

Ferry information	sailanddrive.com	
Condor Ferries (Channel Islands)	condorferries.co.uk	0870 243 5140*
Steam Packet Company (Isle of Man)	steam-packet.com	0870 552 3523
Isles of Scilly Travel	islesofscilly-travel.co.uk	0845 710 5555
Red Funnel (Isle of Wight)	redfunnel.co.uk	0870 444 8898
Wight Link (Isle of Wight)	wightlink.co.uk	0870 582 7744

Phone numbers listed are for general enquiries unless otherwise stated.

* Booking line only

National cycle network

Sections of the National Cycle Network are shown on the maps in this guide. The numbers on the maps will appear on the signs along your route ▣ . Here are some tips about finding and using a route.

- **Research and plan your route online**
  Log on to **sustrans.org.uk** and clink on 'Get cycling' to find information about routes in this guide or other routes you want to use.

- **Order a route map**
  Useful, easy-to-use maps of many of the most popular routes of the National Cycle Network are available from Sustrans, the charity behind the Network. These can be purchased online or by mail order – visit sustransshop.co.uk or call 0845 113 0065.

- **Order Cycling in the UK**
  The official guide to the National Cycle Network gives details of rides all over the UK, detailing 148 routes and profiles of 43 days rides on traffic-free paths and quiet roads. Perfect for those new to cycling or with young families.

ROUTE NUMBER	ROUTE/MAP NAME	START/END OF ROUTE
South West		
3	The West Country Way	Bath & Bristol – Padstow
3 & 32	The Cornish Way	Bude – Land's End
South East		
5	West Midlands	Oxford – Derby via Birmingham
1, 2 & 18	Garden of England	Dover – London – Hastings
East of England		
1	East of England pack	Harwich – Fakenham – Hull
Heart of England		
5 & 54	West Midlands	Oxford – Derby via Birmingham
North East England		
1	Coast & Castles	Newcastle upon Tyne – Berwick-upon-Tweed – Edinburgh
10	Reivers	Tyne – Kielder – Cumbria
68	Pennine Cycleway (North)	Appleby-in-Westmorland or Penrith – Berwick-upon-Tweed
7, 14 & 71	C2C – Sea to Sea	Whitehaven/Workington – Sunderland or Newcastle upon Tyne
72	Hadrian's Cycleway	Ravenglass to Tynemouth/South Shields
Yorkshire and North West England		
62 & 65	Trans Pennine Trail Pack	Yorkshire – North Sea
		Irish Sea – Yorkshire
		Derbyshire – Yorkshire

To order any of the above maps call Sustrans **0845 113 0065** or visit **sustransshop.co.uk**.

Places to visit index by
attraction name

All places to visit featured in this guide are listed below. Places in colour have a detailed entry.

Index by attraction name

Places to visit in colour have a detailed entry in this guide.

Index by attraction name

Places to visit in colour have a detailed entry in this guide.

d continued

e

f

	page

g

	page

Places to visit in colour have a detailed entry in this guide.

Places to visit in colour have a detailed entry in this guide.

Places to visit in colour have a detailed entry in this guide.

m continued

m continued page

n page

Places to visit in colour have a detailed entry in this guide.

Places to visit in colour have a detailed entry in this guide.

Places to visit in colour have a detailed entry in this guide.

Places to visit in colour have a detailed entry in this guide.

Places to visit in colour have a detailed entry in this guide.

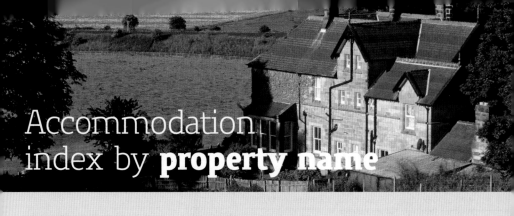

Accommodation index by **property name**

All accommodation featured in this guide is listed below.

Establishments listed here have a detailed entry in this guide.

Accommodation index by **place name**

The following places all have accommodation in this guide. If the place where you wish to stay is not shown, the location maps (starting on page 20) will help you to find somewhere to stay in the area.

Turn to the pages indicated for detailed accommodation entries in these places.

SPECIAL OFFER VOUCHER

One child free with a full paying adult

Alnwick Castle
Alnwick NE66 1NQ

SPECIAL OFFER VOUCHER

Free child entry

Bekonscot Model Village & Railway
Beaconsfield HP9 2PL

SPECIAL OFFER VOUCHER

One child free with every three people

Apple Jacks Farm
Appleton Thorn

SPECIAL OFFER VOUCHER

One child free with every paying adult

The Big Sheep
nr Bideford EX39 5AP

SPECIAL OFFER VOUCHER

Free admission for one child

Bedford Butterfly Park
Wilden, Bedford MK44 2PX

SPECIAL OFFER VOUCHER

One person free with one full paying

Birdworld
Farnham GU10 4LD

VisitBritain Official Guides
Terms & Conditions for Attraction voucher

1. One child free when accompanied by a full paying adult. One voucher per family.
2. Each voucher entitles the holder to the discount specified by the selected attraction.
3. Valid for use until 31/10/2008 (unless otherwise specified, or if attraction season finishes prior to this). Vouchers are subject to the terms, conditions and restrictions of the selected attraction.
4. One voucher per party will be accepted and cannot be used in conjunction with any other offer. Photocopies will not be accepted.
5. All attractions offering a discount have confirmed their willingness to participate. All information is subject to change without notice and should any attraction close or decline to accept a voucher for any reason, VisitBritain is not liable and cannot be held responsible.
6. VisitBritain shall not accept liability for any loss, accident or injury that may occur at a participating attraction and any dispute must be settled direct with the attraction concerned.
7. There is no cash alternative in lieu of tickets or listed savings.
8. You are advised to check all relevant information with your chosen attraction before commencing your journey.

VisitBritain Official Guides
Terms & Conditions for Attraction voucher

1. Not to be used in conjunction with other offers. Not valid on public holidays. Applies to normal daily castle admission only.
2. Each voucher entitles the holder to the discount specified by the selected attraction.
3. Valid for use until 31/10/2008 (unless otherwise specified, or if attraction season finishes prior to this). Vouchers are subject to the terms, conditions and restrictions of the selected attraction.
4. One voucher per party will be accepted and cannot be used in conjunction with any other offer. Photocopies will not be accepted.
5. All attractions offering a discount have confirmed their willingness to participate. All information is subject to change without notice and should any attraction close or decline to accept a voucher for any reason, VisitBritain is not liable and cannot be held responsible.
6. VisitBritain shall not accept liability for any loss, accident or injury that may occur at a participating attraction and any dispute must be settled direct with the attraction concerned.
7. There is no cash alternative in lieu of tickets or listed savings.
8. You are advised to check all relevant information with your chosen attraction before commencing your journey.

VisitBritain Official Guides
Terms & Conditions for Attraction voucher

1. Not to be used in conjunction with any other offer.
2. Each voucher entitles the holder to the discount specified by the selected attraction.
3. Valid for use until 31/10/2008 (unless otherwise specified, or if attraction season finishes prior to this). Vouchers are subject to the terms, conditions and restrictions of the selected attraction.
4. One voucher per party will be accepted and cannot be used in conjunction with any other offer. Photocopies will not be accepted.
5. All attractions offering a discount have confirmed their willingness to participate. All information is subject to change without notice and should any attraction close or decline to accept a voucher for any reason, VisitBritain is not liable and cannot be held responsible.
6. VisitBritain shall not accept liability for any loss, accident or injury that may occur at a participating attraction and any dispute must be settled direct with the attraction concerned.
7. There is no cash alternative in lieu of tickets or listed savings.
8. You are advised to check all relevant information with your chosen attraction before commencing your journey.

VisitBritain Official Guides
Terms & Conditions for Attraction voucher

1. Not valid with any offer. Not exchangeable for monies. Weekdays only. Valid until 10 November 2007.
2. Each voucher entitles the holder to the discount specified by the selected attraction.
3. Valid for use until 31/10/2008 (unless otherwise specified, or if attraction season finishes prior to this). Vouchers are subject to the terms, conditions and restrictions of the selected attraction.
4. One voucher per party will be accepted and cannot be used in conjunction with any other offer. Photocopies will not be accepted.
5. All attractions offering a discount have confirmed their willingness to participate. All information is subject to change without notice and should any attraction close or decline to accept a voucher for any reason, VisitBritain is not liable and cannot be held responsible.
6. VisitBritain shall not accept liability for any loss, accident or injury that may occur at a participating attraction and any dispute must be settled direct with the attraction concerned.
7. There is no cash alternative in lieu of tickets or listed savings.
8. You are advised to check all relevant information with your chosen attraction before commencing your journey.

VisitBritain Official Guides
Terms & Conditions for Attraction voucher

1. Not valid on Bank Holidays. Not valid for groups. Cheapest person goes free.
2. Each voucher entitles the holder to the discount specified by the selected attraction.
3. Valid for use until 31/10/2008 (unless otherwise specified, or if attraction season finishes prior to this). Vouchers are subject to the terms, conditions and restrictions of the selected attraction.
4. One voucher per party will be accepted and cannot be used in conjunction with any other offer. Photocopies will not be accepted.
5. All attractions offering a discount have confirmed their willingness to participate. All information is subject to change without notice and should any attraction close or decline to accept a voucher for any reason, VisitBritain is not liable and cannot be held responsible.
6. VisitBritain shall not accept liability for any loss, accident or injury that may occur at a participating attraction and any dispute must be settled direct with the attraction concerned.
7. There is no cash alternative in lieu of tickets or listed savings.
8. You are advised to check all relevant information with your chosen attraction before commencing your journey.

VisitBritain Official Guides
Terms & Conditions for Attraction voucher

1. Each voucher entitles the holder to the discount specified by the selected attraction.
2. Valid for use until 31/10/2008 (unless otherwise specified, or if attraction season finishes prior to this). Vouchers are subject to the terms, conditions and restrictions of the selected attraction.
3. One voucher per party will be accepted and cannot be used in conjunction with any other offer. Photocopies will not be accepted.
4. All attractions offering a discount have confirmed their willingness to participate. All information is subject to change without notice and should any attraction close or decline to accept a voucher for any reason, VisitBritain is not liable and cannot be held responsible.
5. VisitBritain shall not accept liability for any loss, accident or injury that may occur at a participating attraction and any dispute must be settled direct with the attraction concerned.
6. There is no cash alternative in lieu of tickets or listed savings.
7. You are advised to check all relevant information with your chosen attraction before commencing your journey.

SPECIAL OFFER VOUCHER

One free concession with a full paying adult

The Birmingham Botanical Gardens & Glasshouses
Birmingham B15 3TR

SPECIAL OFFER VOUCHER

Two for the price of one

Darlington Railway and Museum
Darlington DL3 6ST

SPECIAL OFFER VOUCHER

Two for the price of one

Capel Manor College & Gardens
Enfield EN1 4RQ

SPECIAL OFFER VOUCHER

Child goes free with a full paying adult

DIG
York YO1 8NN

SPECIAL OFFER VOUCHER

Two adult tickets for the price of one

Chelsea Physic Garden
London SW3 4HS

SPECIAL OFFER VOUCHER

Two for the price of one

Eastbury Manor House
Barking IG11 9SN

VisitBritain Official Guides
Terms & Conditions for Attraction voucher

1 Offer applies to normal museum opening days, but not to the museum's special event days.

2 Each voucher entitles the holder to the discount specified by the selected attraction.

3 Valid for use until 31/10/2008 (unless otherwise specified, or if attraction season finishes prior to this). Vouchers are subject to the terms, conditions and restrictions of the selected attraction.

4 One voucher per party will be accepted and cannot be used in conjunction with any other offer. Photocopies will not be accepted.

5 All attractions offering a discount have confirmed their willingness to participate. All information is subject to change without notice and should any attraction close or decline to accept a voucher for any reason, VisitBritain is not liable and cannot be held responsible.

6 VisitBritain shall not accept liability for any loss, accident or injury that may occur at a participating attraction and any dispute must be settled direct with the attraction concerned.

7 There is no cash alternative in lieu of tickets or listed savings.

8 You are advised to check all relevant information with your chosen attraction before commencing your journey.

VisitBritain Official Guides
Terms & Conditions for Attraction voucher

1 Excluding special events where tickets are required.

2 Each voucher entitles the holder to the discount specified by the selected attraction.

3 Valid for use until 31/10/2008 (unless otherwise specified, or if attraction season finishes prior to this). Vouchers are subject to the terms, conditions and restrictions of the selected attraction.

4 One voucher per party will be accepted and cannot be used in conjunction with any other offer. Photocopies will not be accepted.

5 All attractions offering a discount have confirmed their willingness to participate. All information is subject to change without notice and should any attraction close or decline to accept a voucher for any reason, VisitBritain is not liable and cannot be held responsible.

6 VisitBritain shall not accept liability for any loss, accident or injury that may occur at a participating attraction and any dispute must be settled direct with the attraction concerned.

7 There is no cash alternative in lieu of tickets or listed savings.

8 You are advised to check all relevant information with your chosen attraction before commencing your journey.

VisitBritain Official Guides
Terms & Conditions for Attraction voucher

1 Offer not valid when pre-booking, during half term holidays or for the Viking Festival (14-18 February 2007). Not valid in conjunction with any other offer and not exchangeable for cash.

2 Each voucher entitles the holder to the discount specified by the selected attraction.

3 Valid for use until 31/10/2008 (unless otherwise specified, or if attraction season finishes prior to this). Vouchers are subject to the terms, conditions and restrictions of the selected attraction.

4 One voucher per party will be accepted and cannot be used in conjunction with any other offer. Photocopies will not be accepted.

5 All attractions offering a discount have confirmed their willingness to participate. All information is subject to change without notice and should any attraction close or decline to accept a voucher for any reason, VisitBritain is not liable and cannot be held responsible.

6 VisitBritain shall not accept liability for any loss, accident or injury that may occur at a participating attraction and any dispute must be settled direct with the attraction concerned.

7 There is no cash alternative in lieu of tickets or listed savings.

8 You are advised to check all relevant information with your chosen attraction before commencing your journey.

VisitBritain Official Guides
Terms & Conditions for Attraction voucher

1 One person goes free when accompanied by a full paying adult. Not valid at musical or theatrical events.

2 Each voucher entitles the holder to the discount specified by the selected attraction.

3 Valid for use until 31/10/2008 (unless otherwise specified, or if attraction season finishes prior to this). Vouchers are subject to the terms, conditions and restrictions of the selected attraction.

4 One voucher per party will be accepted and cannot be used in conjunction with any other offer. Photocopies will not be accepted.

5 All attractions offering a discount have confirmed their willingness to participate. All information is subject to change without notice and should any attraction close or decline to accept a voucher for any reason, VisitBritain is not liable and cannot be held responsible.

6 VisitBritain shall not accept liability for any loss, accident or injury that may occur at a participating attraction and any dispute must be settled direct with the attraction concerned.

7 There is no cash alternative in lieu of tickets or listed savings.

8 You are advised to check all relevant information with your chosen attraction before commencing your journey.

VisitBritain Official Guides
Terms & Conditions for Attraction voucher

1 Valid on adult admission for family days on the first Saturday of each month only.

2 Each voucher entitles the holder to the discount specified by the selected attraction.

3 Valid for use until 31/10/2008 (unless otherwise specified, or if attraction season finishes prior to this). Vouchers are subject to the terms, conditions and restrictions of the selected attraction.

4 One voucher per party will be accepted and cannot be used in conjunction with any other offer. Photocopies will not be accepted.

5 All attractions offering a discount have confirmed their willingness to participate. All information is subject to change without notice and should any attraction close or decline to accept a voucher for any reason, VisitBritain is not liable and cannot be held responsible.

6 VisitBritain shall not accept liability for any loss, accident or injury that may occur at a participating attraction and any dispute must be settled direct with the attraction concerned.

7 There is no cash alternative in lieu of tickets or listed savings.

8 You are advised to check all relevant information with your chosen attraction before commencing your journey.

VisitBritain Official Guides
Terms & Conditions for Attraction voucher

1 Not valid at Summer Fair (Sunday 24 June 2007) or in conjunction with any other offer.

2 Each voucher entitles the holder to the discount specified by the selected attraction.

3 Valid for use until 31/10/2008 (unless otherwise specified, or if attraction season finishes prior to this). Vouchers are subject to the terms, conditions and restrictions of the selected attraction.

4 One voucher per party will be accepted and cannot be used in conjunction with any other offer. Photocopies will not be accepted.

5 All attractions offering a discount have confirmed their willingness to participate. All information is subject to change without notice and should any attraction close or decline to accept a voucher for any reason, VisitBritain is not liable and cannot be held responsible.

6 VisitBritain shall not accept liability for any loss, accident or injury that may occur at a participating attraction and any dispute must be settled direct with the attraction concerned.

7 There is no cash alternative in lieu of tickets or listed savings.

8 You are advised to check all relevant information with your chosen attraction before commencing your journey.

SPECIAL OFFER VOUCHER

Two for the price of one

Easton Farm Park
Easton, Woodbridge IP13 0EQ

SPECIAL OFFER VOUCHER

Two for one on the skating rink

Harbour Park
Littlehampton BN17 5LL

SPECIAL OFFER VOUCHER

15% discount

Farncombe Estate Centre
Broadway WR12 7LJ

SPECIAL OFFER VOUCHER

£1 off child's admission ticket

The Hawk Conservancy Trust
nr Andover SP11 8DY

SPECIAL OFFER VOUCHER

One child free with full paying adult

Glastonbury Abbey
Glastonbury BA6 9EL

SPECIAL OFFER VOUCHER

One child free with a full paying adult

The Hop Farm Country Park
Paddock Wood TN12 6PY

VisitBritain Official Guides
Terms & Conditions for Attraction voucher

1 Not valid with any other offers.

2 Each voucher entitles the holder to the discount specified by the selected attraction.

3 Valid for use until 31/10/2008 (unless otherwise specified, or if attraction season finishes prior to this). Vouchers are subject to the terms, conditions and restrictions of the selected attraction.

4 One voucher per party will be accepted and cannot be used in conjunction with any other offer. Photocopies will not be accepted.

5 All attractions offering a discount have confirmed their willingness to participate. All information is subject to change without notice and should any attraction close or decline to accept a voucher for any reason, VisitBritain is not liable and cannot be held responsible.

6 VisitBritain shall not accept liability for any loss, accident or injury that may occur at a participating attraction and any dispute must be settled direct with the attraction concerned.

7 There is no cash alternative in lieu of tickets or listed savings.

8 You are advised to check all relevant information with your chosen attraction before commencing your journey.

VisitBritain Official Guides
Terms & Conditions for Attraction voucher

1 One child free with a full paying adult during 2007. Not to be used in conjunction with any other offer.

2 Each voucher entitles the holder to the discount specified by the selected attraction.

3 Valid for use until 31/10/2008 (unless otherwise specified, or if attraction season finishes prior to this). Vouchers are subject to the terms, conditions and restrictions of the selected attraction.

4 One voucher per party will be accepted and cannot be used in conjunction with any other offer. Photocopies will not be accepted.

5 All attractions offering a discount have confirmed their willingness to participate. All information is subject to change without notice and should any attraction close or decline to accept a voucher for any reason, VisitBritain is not liable and cannot be held responsible.

6 VisitBritain shall not accept liability for any loss, accident or injury that may occur at a participating attraction and any dispute must be settled direct with the attraction concerned.

7 There is no cash alternative in lieu of tickets or listed savings.

8 You are advised to check all relevant information with your chosen attraction before commencing your journey.

VisitBritain Official Guides
Terms & Conditions for Attraction voucher

1 Child must be accompanied by a full paying adult. Not valid with a family ticket.

2 Each voucher entitles the holder to the discount specified by the selected attraction.

3 Valid for use until 31/10/2008 (unless otherwise specified, or if attraction season finishes prior to this). Vouchers are subject to the terms, conditions and restrictions of the selected attraction.

4 One voucher per party will be accepted and cannot be used in conjunction with any other offer. Photocopies will not be accepted.

5 All attractions offering a discount have confirmed their willingness to participate. All information is subject to change without notice and should any attraction close or decline to accept a voucher for any reason, VisitBritain is not liable and cannot be held responsible.

6 VisitBritain shall not accept liability for any loss, accident or injury that may occur at a participating attraction and any dispute must be settled direct with the attraction concerned.

7 There is no cash alternative in lieu of tickets or listed savings.

8 You are advised to check all relevant information with your chosen attraction before commencing your journey.

VisitBritain Official Guides
Terms & Conditions for Attraction voucher

1 Terms and conditions apply. See brochure.

2 Each voucher entitles the holder to the discount specified by the selected attraction.

3 Valid for use until 31/10/2008 (unless otherwise specified, or if attraction season finishes prior to this). Vouchers are subject to the terms, conditions and restrictions of the selected attraction.

4 One voucher per party will be accepted and cannot be used in conjunction with any other offer. Photocopies will not be accepted.

5 All attractions offering a discount have confirmed their willingness to participate. All information is subject to change without notice and should any attraction close or decline to accept a voucher for any reason, VisitBritain is not liable and cannot be held responsible.

6 VisitBritain shall not accept liability for any loss, accident or injury that may occur at a participating attraction and any dispute must be settled direct with the attraction concerned.

7 There is no cash alternative in lieu of tickets or listed savings.

8 You are advised to check all relevant information with your chosen attraction before commencing your journey.

VisitBritain Official Guides
Terms & Conditions for Attraction voucher

1 Excludes KM War and Peace show 18-22 July 2007.

2 Each voucher entitles the holder to the discount specified by the selected attraction.

3 Valid for use until 31/10/2008 (unless otherwise specified, or if attraction season finishes prior to this). Vouchers are subject to the terms, conditions and restrictions of the selected attraction.

4 One voucher per party will be accepted and cannot be used in conjunction with any other offer. Photocopies will not be accepted.

5 All attractions offering a discount have confirmed their willingness to participate. All information is subject to change without notice and should any attraction close or decline to accept a voucher for any reason, VisitBritain is not liable and cannot be held responsible.

6 VisitBritain shall not accept liability for any loss, accident or injury that may occur at a participating attraction and any dispute must be settled direct with the attraction concerned.

7 There is no cash alternative in lieu of tickets or listed savings.

8 You are advised to check all relevant information with your chosen attraction before commencing your journey.

VisitBritain Official Guides
Terms & Conditions for Attraction voucher

1 Not valid in August. Not valid in conjunction with any other offer.

2 Each voucher entitles the holder to the discount specified by the selected attraction.

3 Valid for use until 31/10/2008 (unless otherwise specified, or if attraction season finishes prior to this). Vouchers are subject to the terms, conditions and restrictions of the selected attraction.

4 One voucher per party will be accepted and cannot be used in conjunction with any other offer. Photocopies will not be accepted.

5 All attractions offering a discount have confirmed their willingness to participate. All information is subject to change without notice and should any attraction close or decline to accept a voucher for any reason, VisitBritain is not liable and cannot be held responsible.

6 VisitBritain shall not accept liability for any loss, accident or injury that may occur at a participating attraction and any dispute must be settled direct with the attraction concerned.

7 There is no cash alternative in lieu of tickets or listed savings.

8 You are advised to check all relevant information with your chosen attraction before commencing your journey.

SPECIAL OFFER VOUCHER

Child goes free with a full paying adult

JORVIK Viking Centre
York YO1 9WT

SPECIAL OFFER VOUCHER

Two for the price of one

Lulworth Castle & Park
Wareham BH20 5QS

SPECIAL OFFER VOUCHER

Special rates for parties over ten persons

The Laurel and Hardy Museum
Ulverston LA12 7BH

SPECIAL OFFER VOUCHER

One child free with two full paying adults

Making It! Discovery Centre
Mansfield NG18 1AH

SPECIAL OFFER VOUCHER

Two for the price of one

Loseley Park
Guildford GU3 1HS

SPECIAL OFFER VOUCHER

Two for the price of one

Milestones, Hampshire's Living History Museum
Basingstoke RG21 6YR

VisitBritain Official Guides
Terms & Conditions for Attraction voucher

1 Lowest entry price free. Valid 1 April 2007 to 31 March 2008. Not valid for special events or with any other offer.

2 Each voucher entitles the holder to the discount specified by the selected attraction.

3 Valid for use until 31/10/2008 (unless otherwise specified, or if attraction season finishes prior to this). Vouchers are subject to the terms, conditions and restrictions of the selected attraction.

4 One voucher per party will be accepted and cannot be used in conjunction with any other offer. Photocopies will not be accepted.

5 All attractions offering a discount have confirmed their willingness to participate. All information is subject to change without notice and should any attraction close or decline to accept a voucher for any reason, VisitBritain is not liable and cannot be held responsible.

6 VisitBritain shall not accept liability for any loss, accident or injury that may occur at a participating attraction and any dispute must be settled direct with the attraction concerned.

7 There is no cash alternative in lieu of tickets or listed savings.

8 You are advised to check all relevant information with your chosen attraction before commencing your journey.

VisitBritain Official Guides
Terms & Conditions for Attraction voucher

1 Offer not valid when pre-booking, during half term holidays or for the Viking Festival (14-18 February 2007). Not valid in conjunction with any other offer and not exchangeable for cash.

2 Each voucher entitles the holder to the discount specified by the selected attraction.

3 Valid for use until 31/10/2008 (unless otherwise specified, or if attraction season finishes prior to this). Vouchers are subject to the terms, conditions and restrictions of the selected attraction.

4 One voucher per party will be accepted and cannot be used in conjunction with any other offer. Photocopies will not be accepted.

5 All attractions offering a discount have confirmed their willingness to participate. All information is subject to change without notice and should any attraction close or decline to accept a voucher for any reason, VisitBritain is not liable and cannot be held responsible.

6 VisitBritain shall not accept liability for any loss, accident or injury that may occur at a participating attraction and any dispute must be settled direct with the attraction concerned.

7 There is no cash alternative in lieu of tickets or listed savings.

8 You are advised to check all relevant information with your chosen attraction before commencing your journey.

VisitBritain Official Guides
Terms & Conditions for Attraction voucher

1 Nottinghamshire school holidays only.

2 Each voucher entitles the holder to the discount specified by the selected attraction.

3 Valid for use until 31/10/2008 (unless otherwise specified, or if attraction season finishes prior to this). Vouchers are subject to the terms, conditions and restrictions of the selected attraction.

4 One voucher per party will be accepted and cannot be used in conjunction with any other offer. Photocopies will not be accepted.

5 All attractions offering a discount have confirmed their willingness to participate. All information is subject to change without notice and should any attraction close or decline to accept a voucher for any reason, VisitBritain is not liable and cannot be held responsible.

6 VisitBritain shall not accept liability for any loss, accident or injury that may occur at a participating attraction and any dispute must be settled direct with the attraction concerned.

7 There is no cash alternative in lieu of tickets or listed savings.

8 You are advised to check all relevant information with your chosen attraction before commencing your journey.

VisitBritain Official Guides
Terms & Conditions for Attraction voucher

1 Each voucher entitles the holder to the discount specified by the selected attraction.

2 Valid for use until 31/10/2008 (unless otherwise specified, or if attraction season finishes prior to this). Vouchers are subject to the terms, conditions and restrictions of the selected attraction.

3 One voucher per party will be accepted and cannot be used in conjunction with any other offer. Photocopies will not be accepted.

4 All attractions offering a discount have confirmed their willingness to participate. All information is subject to change without notice and should any attraction close or decline to accept a voucher for any reason, VisitBritain is not liable and cannot be held responsible.

5 VisitBritain shall not accept liability for any loss, accident or injury that may occur at a participating attraction and any dispute must be settled direct with the attraction concerned.

6 There is no cash alternative in lieu of tickets or listed savings.

7 You are advised to check all relevant information with your chosen attraction before commencing your journey.

VisitBritain Official Guides
Terms & Conditions for Attraction voucher

1 One adult/concession free with full paying adult. Not valid for special events. Daytime admission only. Expires 31 December 2007.

2 Each voucher entitles the holder to the discount specified by the selected attraction.

3 Valid for use until 31/10/2008 (unless otherwise specified, or if attraction season finishes prior to this). Vouchers are subject to the terms, conditions and restrictions of the selected attraction.

4 One voucher per party will be accepted and cannot be used in conjunction with any other offer. Photocopies will not be accepted.

5 All attractions offering a discount have confirmed their willingness to participate. All information is subject to change without notice and should any attraction close or decline to accept a voucher for any reason, VisitBritain is not liable and cannot be held responsible.

6 VisitBritain shall not accept liability for any loss, accident or injury that may occur at a participating attraction and any dispute must be settled direct with the attraction concerned.

7 There is no cash alternative in lieu of tickets or listed savings.

8 You are advised to check all relevant information with your chosen attraction before commencing your journey.

VisitBritain Official Guides
Terms & Conditions for Attraction voucher

1 Valid for entry into the house and gardens from May to August.

2 Each voucher entitles the holder to the discount specified by the selected attraction.

3 Valid for use until 31/10/2008 (unless otherwise specified, or if attraction season finishes prior to this). Vouchers are subject to the terms, conditions and restrictions of the selected attraction.

4 One voucher per party will be accepted and cannot be used in conjunction with any other offer. Photocopies will not be accepted.

5 All attractions offering a discount have confirmed their willingness to participate. All information is subject to change without notice and should any attraction close or decline to accept a voucher for any reason, VisitBritain is not liable and cannot be held responsible.

6 VisitBritain shall not accept liability for any loss, accident or injury that may occur at a participating attraction and any dispute must be settled direct with the attraction concerned.

7 There is no cash alternative in lieu of tickets or listed savings.

8 You are advised to check all relevant information with your chosen attraction before commencing your journey.

SPECIAL OFFER VOUCHER

Guided tours: two for the price of one

Moggerhanger Park
Moggerhanger MK44 3RW

SPECIAL OFFER VOUCHER

Two for the price of one

National Wildflower Centre
Knowsley L16 3NA

SPECIAL OFFER VOUCHER

Two for the price of one

Muncaster
Ravenglass CA18 1RQ

SPECIAL OFFER VOUCHER

One child travels free with full paying adult

Nene Valley Railway
Peterborough PE8 6LR

SPECIAL OFFER VOUCHER

Two for the price of one

National Maritime Museum Cornwall
Falmouth TR11 3QY

SPECIAL OFFER VOUCHER

£1 off per person (up to six people)

Newquay Zoo
Newquay TR7 2LZ

VisitBritain Official Guides
Terms & Conditions for Attraction voucher

1 Voucher valid 1 March to 1 September.

2 Each voucher entitles the holder to the discount specified by the selected attraction.

3 Valid for use until 31/10/2008 (unless otherwise specified, or if attraction season finishes prior to this). Vouchers are subject to the terms, conditions and restrictions of the selected attraction.

4 One voucher per party will be accepted and cannot be used in conjunction with any other offer. Photocopies will not be accepted.

5 All attractions offering a discount have confirmed their willingness to participate. All information is subject to change without notice and should any attraction close or decline to accept a voucher for any reason, VisitBritain is not liable and cannot be held responsible.

6 VisitBritain shall not accept liability for any loss, accident or injury that may occur at a participating attraction and any dispute must be settled direct with the attraction concerned.

7 There is no cash alternative in lieu of tickets or listed savings.

8 You are advised to check all relevant information with your chosen attraction before commencing your journey.

VisitBritain Official Guides
Terms & Conditions for Attraction voucher

1 Valid 16 June to 9 September.

2 Each voucher entitles the holder to the discount specified by the selected attraction.

3 Valid for use until 31/10/2008 (unless otherwise specified, or if attraction season finishes prior to this). Vouchers are subject to the terms, conditions and restrictions of the selected attraction.

4 One voucher per party will be accepted and cannot be used in conjunction with any other offer. Photocopies will not be accepted.

5 All attractions offering a discount have confirmed their willingness to participate. All information is subject to change without notice and should any attraction close or decline to accept a voucher for any reason, VisitBritain is not liable and cannot be held responsible.

6 VisitBritain shall not accept liability for any loss, accident or injury that may occur at a participating attraction and any dispute must be settled direct with the attraction concerned.

7 There is no cash alternative in lieu of tickets or listed savings.

8 You are advised to check all relevant information with your chosen attraction before commencing your journey.

VisitBritain Official Guides
Terms & Conditions for Attraction voucher

1 Not valid for special events or Santa Specials.

2 Each voucher entitles the holder to the discount specified by the selected attraction.

3 Valid for use until 31/10/2008 (unless otherwise specified, or if attraction season finishes prior to this). Vouchers are subject to the terms, conditions and restrictions of the selected attraction.

4 One voucher per party will be accepted and cannot be used in conjunction with any other offer. Photocopies will not be accepted.

5 All attractions offering a discount have confirmed their willingness to participate. All information is subject to change without notice and should any attraction close or decline to accept a voucher for any reason, VisitBritain is not liable and cannot be held responsible.

6 VisitBritain shall not accept liability for any loss, accident or injury that may occur at a participating attraction and any dispute must be settled direct with the attraction concerned.

7 There is no cash alternative in lieu of tickets or listed savings.

8 You are advised to check all relevant information with your chosen attraction before commencing your journey.

VisitBritain Official Guides
Terms & Conditions for Attraction voucher

1 11 February to 4 November only.

2 Each voucher entitles the holder to the discount specified by the selected attraction.

3 Valid for use until 31/10/2008 (unless otherwise specified, or if attraction season finishes prior to this). Vouchers are subject to the terms, conditions and restrictions of the selected attraction.

4 One voucher per party will be accepted and cannot be used in conjunction with any other offer. Photocopies will not be accepted.

5 All attractions offering a discount have confirmed their willingness to participate. All information is subject to change without notice and should any attraction close or decline to accept a voucher for any reason, VisitBritain is not liable and cannot be held responsible.

6 VisitBritain shall not accept liability for any loss, accident or injury that may occur at a participating attraction and any dispute must be settled direct with the attraction concerned.

7 There is no cash alternative in lieu of tickets or listed savings.

8 You are advised to check all relevant information with your chosen attraction before commencing your journey.

VisitBritain Official Guides
Terms & Conditions for Attraction voucher

1 Cannot be used in conjunction with any other offer, including the family ticket.

2 Each voucher entitles the holder to the discount specified by the selected attraction.

3 Valid for use until 31/10/2008 (unless otherwise specified, or if attraction season finishes prior to this). Vouchers are subject to the terms, conditions and restrictions of the selected attraction.

4 One voucher per party will be accepted and cannot be used in conjunction with any other offer. Photocopies will not be accepted.

5 All attractions offering a discount have confirmed their willingness to participate. All information is subject to change without notice and should any attraction close or decline to accept a voucher for any reason, VisitBritain is not liable and cannot be held responsible.

6 VisitBritain shall not accept liability for any loss, accident or injury that may occur at a participating attraction and any dispute must be settled direct with the attraction concerned.

7 There is no cash alternative in lieu of tickets or listed savings.

8 You are advised to check all relevant information with your chosen attraction before commencing your journey.

VisitBritain Official Guides
Terms & Conditions for Attraction voucher

1 One voucher valid per entry.

2 Each voucher entitles the holder to the discount specified by the selected attraction.

3 Valid for use until 31/10/2008 (unless otherwise specified, or if attraction season finishes prior to this). Vouchers are subject to the terms, conditions and restrictions of the selected attraction.

4 One voucher per party will be accepted and cannot be used in conjunction with any other offer. Photocopies will not be accepted.

5 All attractions offering a discount have confirmed their willingness to participate. All information is subject to change without notice and should any attraction close or decline to accept a voucher for any reason, VisitBritain is not liable and cannot be held responsible.

6 VisitBritain shall not accept liability for any loss, accident or injury that may occur at a participating attraction and any dispute must be settled direct with the attraction concerned.

7 There is no cash alternative in lieu of tickets or listed savings.

8 You are advised to check all relevant information with your chosen attraction before commencing your journey.

SPECIAL OFFER VOUCHER
Two for the price of one
Oliver Cromwell's House
Ely CB7 4HF

SPECIAL OFFER VOUCHER
Three wristbands for the price of two
Pleasure Beach, Blackpool
Blackpool FY4 1EZ

SPECIAL OFFER VOUCHER
£1 voucher for Painshill tea room
Painshill Park
Cobham KT11 1JE

SPECIAL OFFER VOUCHER
Two for the price of one
The Raptor Foundation
Woodhurst PE28 3BT

SPECIAL OFFER VOUCHER
Two for the price of one
Pleasant Promenades - Guided Walking Tours
Royal Tunbridge Wells TN2 5TN

SPECIAL OFFER VOUCHER
10% off adult, child or family ticket
Roman Baths
Bath BA1 1LZ

VisitBritain Official Guides
Terms & Conditions for Attraction voucher

1 Valid until 4 November 2007. Excludes Saturdays during Blackpool Illuminations. Height restrictions apply. Ref 7004.

2 Each voucher entitles the holder to the discount specified by the selected attraction.

3 Valid for use until 31/10/2008 (unless otherwise specified, or if attraction season finishes prior to this). Vouchers are subject to the terms, conditions and restrictions of the selected attraction.

4 One voucher per party will be accepted and cannot be used in conjunction with any other offer. Photocopies will not be accepted.

5 All attractions offering a discount have confirmed their willingness to participate. All information is subject to change without notice and should any attraction close or decline to accept a voucher for any reason, VisitBritain is not liable and cannot be held responsible.

6 VisitBritain shall not accept liability for any loss, accident or injury that may occur at a participating attraction and any dispute must be settled direct with the attraction concerned.

7 There is no cash alternative in lieu of tickets or listed savings.

8 You are advised to check all relevant information with your chosen attraction before commencing your journey.

VisitBritain Official Guides
Terms & Conditions for Attraction voucher

1 Each voucher entitles the holder to the discount specified by the selected attraction.

2 Valid for use until 31/10/2008 (unless otherwise specified, or if attraction season finishes prior to this). Vouchers are subject to the terms, conditions and restrictions of the selected attraction.

3 One voucher per party will be accepted and cannot be used in conjunction with any other offer. Photocopies will not be accepted.

4 All attractions offering a discount have confirmed their willingness to participate. All information is subject to change without notice and should any attraction close or decline to accept a voucher for any reason, VisitBritain is not liable and cannot be held responsible.

5 VisitBritain shall not accept liability for any loss, accident or injury that may occur at a participating attraction and any dispute must be settled direct with the attraction concerned.

6 There is no cash alternative in lieu of tickets or listed savings.

7 You are advised to check all relevant information with your chosen attraction before commencing your journey.

VisitBritain Official Guides
Terms & Conditions for Attraction voucher

1 One voucher per family.

2 Each voucher entitles the holder to the discount specified by the selected attraction.

3 Valid for use until 31/10/2008 (unless otherwise specified, or if attraction season finishes prior to this). Vouchers are subject to the terms, conditions and restrictions of the selected attraction.

4 One voucher per party will be accepted and cannot be used in conjunction with any other offer. Photocopies will not be accepted.

5 All attractions offering a discount have confirmed their willingness to participate. All information is subject to change without notice and should any attraction close or decline to accept a voucher for any reason, VisitBritain is not liable and cannot be held responsible.

6 VisitBritain shall not accept liability for any loss, accident or injury that may occur at a participating attraction and any dispute must be settled direct with the attraction concerned.

7 There is no cash alternative in lieu of tickets or listed savings.

8 You are advised to check all relevant information with your chosen attraction before commencing your journey.

VisitBritain Official Guides
Terms & Conditions for Attraction voucher

1 Valid on production of this voucher. Excludes alcohol. Not to be used in conjunction with any other offer.

2 Each voucher entitles the holder to the discount specified by the selected attraction.

3 Valid for use until 31/10/2008 (unless otherwise specified, or if attraction season finishes prior to this). Vouchers are subject to the terms, conditions and restrictions of the selected attraction.

4 One voucher per party will be accepted and cannot be used in conjunction with any other offer. Photocopies will not be accepted.

5 All attractions offering a discount have confirmed their willingness to participate. All information is subject to change without notice and should any attraction close or decline to accept a voucher for any reason, VisitBritain is not liable and cannot be held responsible.

6 VisitBritain shall not accept liability for any loss, accident or injury that may occur at a participating attraction and any dispute must be settled direct with the attraction concerned.

7 There is no cash alternative in lieu of tickets or listed savings.

8 You are advised to check all relevant information with your chosen attraction before commencing your journey.

VisitBritain Official Guides
Terms & Conditions for Attraction voucher

1 Not valid for joint ticket with Museum of Costume.

2 Each voucher entitles the holder to the discount specified by the selected attraction.

3 Valid for use until 31/10/2008 (unless otherwise specified, or if attraction season finishes prior to this). Vouchers are subject to the terms, conditions and restrictions of the selected attraction.

4 One voucher per party will be accepted and cannot be used in conjunction with any other offer. Photocopies will not be accepted.

5 All attractions offering a discount have confirmed their willingness to participate. All information is subject to change without notice and should any attraction close or decline to accept a voucher for any reason, VisitBritain is not liable and cannot be held responsible.

6 VisitBritain shall not accept liability for any loss, accident or injury that may occur at a participating attraction and any dispute must be settled direct with the attraction concerned.

7 There is no cash alternative in lieu of tickets or listed savings.

8 You are advised to check all relevant information with your chosen attraction before commencing your journey.

VisitBritain Official Guides
Terms & Conditions for Attraction voucher

1 Each voucher entitles the holder to the discount specified by the selected attraction.

2 Valid for use until 31/10/2008 (unless otherwise specified, or if attraction season finishes prior to this). Vouchers are subject to the terms, conditions and restrictions of the selected attraction.

3 One voucher per party will be accepted and cannot be used in conjunction with any other offer. Photocopies will not be accepted.

4 All attractions offering a discount have confirmed their willingness to participate. All information is subject to change without notice and should any attraction close or decline to accept a voucher for any reason, VisitBritain is not liable and cannot be held responsible.

5 VisitBritain shall not accept liability for any loss, accident or injury that may occur at a participating attraction and any dispute must be settled direct with the attraction concerned.

6 There is no cash alternative in lieu of tickets or listed savings.

7 You are advised to check all relevant information with your chosen attraction before commencing your journey.

SPECIAL OFFER VOUCHER

One child free with full paying adult/OAP

Sacrewell Farm & Country Centre
Peterborough PE8 6HJ

SPECIAL OFFER VOUCHER

Two for the price of one – full adult ticket

Skipton Castle
Skipton BD23 1AW

SPECIAL OFFER VOUCHER

Free Close Guide

Salisbury Cathedral
Salisbury SP1 2EJ

SPECIAL OFFER VOUCHER

10% discount available in refectory/restaurant

Southwark Cathedral
London SE1 9DA

SPECIAL OFFER VOUCHER

Two for the price of one

The Shakespeare Houses
Stratford-upon-Avon CV37 6QW

SPECIAL OFFER VOUCHER

Two for the price of one

Thackray Museum
Leeds LS9 7LN

VisitBritain Official Guides
Terms & Conditions for Attraction voucher

1 Offer not valid over Bank Holidays or for special events. Voucher valid until 31 December 2007.

2 Each voucher entitles the holder to the discount specified by the selected attraction.

3 Valid for use until 31/10/2008 (unless otherwise specified, or if attraction season finishes prior to this). Vouchers are subject to the terms, conditions and restrictions of the selected attraction.

4 One voucher per party will be accepted and cannot be used in conjunction with any other offer. Photocopies will not be accepted.

5 All attractions offering a discount have confirmed their willingness to participate. All information is subject to change without notice and should any attraction close or decline to accept a voucher for any reason, VisitBritain is not liable and cannot be held responsible.

6 VisitBritain shall not accept liability for any loss, accident or injury that may occur at a participating attraction and any dispute must be settled direct with the attraction concerned.

7 There is no cash alternative in lieu of tickets or listed savings.

8 You are advised to check all relevant information with your chosen attraction before commencing your journey.

VisitBritain Official Guides
Terms & Conditions for Attraction voucher

1 One child free per voucher. No photocopies. Extra charges may apply for special events.

2 Each voucher entitles the holder to the discount specified by the selected attraction.

3 Valid for use until 31/10/2008 (unless otherwise specified, or if attraction season finishes prior to this). Vouchers are subject to the terms, conditions and restrictions of the selected attraction.

4 One voucher per party will be accepted and cannot be used in conjunction with any other offer. Photocopies will not be accepted.

5 All attractions offering a discount have confirmed their willingness to participate. All information is subject to change without notice and should any attraction close or decline to accept a voucher for any reason, VisitBritain is not liable and cannot be held responsible.

6 VisitBritain shall not accept liability for any loss, accident or injury that may occur at a participating attraction and any dispute must be settled direct with the attraction concerned.

7 There is no cash alternative in lieu of tickets or listed savings.

8 You are advised to check all relevant information with your chosen attraction before commencing your journey.

VisitBritain Official Guides
Terms & Conditions for Attraction voucher

1 Each voucher entitles the holder to the discount specified by the selected attraction.

2 Valid for use until 31/10/2008 (unless otherwise specified, or if attraction season finishes prior to this). Vouchers are subject to the terms, conditions and restrictions of the selected attraction.

3 One voucher per party will be accepted and cannot be used in conjunction with any other offer. Photocopies will not be accepted.

4 All attractions offering a discount have confirmed their willingness to participate. All information is subject to change without notice and should any attraction close or decline to accept a voucher for any reason, VisitBritain is not liable and cannot be held responsible.

5 VisitBritain shall not accept liability for any loss, accident or injury that may occur at a participating attraction and any dispute must be settled direct with the attraction concerned.

6 There is no cash alternative in lieu of tickets or listed savings.

7 You are advised to check all relevant information with your chosen attraction before commencing your journey.

VisitBritain Official Guides
Terms & Conditions for Attraction voucher

1 Valid until 31 December 2007. Subject to availability when voucher presented in person at donation desk.

2 Each voucher entitles the holder to the discount specified by the selected attraction.

3 Valid for use until 31/10/2008 (unless otherwise specified, or if attraction season finishes prior to this). Vouchers are subject to the terms, conditions and restrictions of the selected attraction.

4 One voucher per party will be accepted and cannot be used in conjunction with any other offer. Photocopies will not be accepted.

5 All attractions offering a discount have confirmed their willingness to participate. All information is subject to change without notice and should any attraction close or decline to accept a voucher for any reason, VisitBritain is not liable and cannot be held responsible.

6 VisitBritain shall not accept liability for any loss, accident or injury that may occur at a participating attraction and any dispute must be settled direct with the attraction concerned.

7 There is no cash alternative in lieu of tickets or listed savings.

8 You are advised to check all relevant information with your chosen attraction before commencing your journey.

VisitBritain Official Guides
Terms & Conditions for Attraction voucher

1 Buy one full price adult ticket and get another ticket of up to the same value free.

2 Each voucher entitles the holder to the discount specified by the selected attraction.

3 Valid for use until 31/10/2008 (unless otherwise specified, or if attraction season finishes prior to this). Vouchers are subject to the terms, conditions and restrictions of the selected attraction.

4 One voucher per party will be accepted and cannot be used in conjunction with any other offer. Photocopies will not be accepted.

5 All attractions offering a discount have confirmed their willingness to participate. All information is subject to change without notice and should any attraction close or decline to accept a voucher for any reason, VisitBritain is not liable and cannot be held responsible.

6 VisitBritain shall not accept liability for any loss, accident or injury that may occur at a participating attraction and any dispute must be settled direct with the attraction concerned.

7 There is no cash alternative in lieu of tickets or listed savings.

8 You are advised to check all relevant information with your chosen attraction before commencing your journey.

VisitBritain Official Guides
Terms & Conditions for Attraction voucher

1 Two for the price of one for a single house ticket to any one of the five Shakespeare Houses.

2 Each voucher entitles the holder to the discount specified by the selected attraction.

3 Valid for use until 31/10/2008 (unless otherwise specified, or if attraction season finishes prior to this). Vouchers are subject to the terms, conditions and restrictions of the selected attraction.

4 One voucher per party will be accepted and cannot be used in conjunction with any other offer. Photocopies will not be accepted.

5 All attractions offering a discount have confirmed their willingness to participate. All information is subject to change without notice and should any attraction close or decline to accept a voucher for any reason, VisitBritain is not liable and cannot be held responsible.

6 VisitBritain shall not accept liability for any loss, accident or injury that may occur at a participating attraction and any dispute must be settled direct with the attraction concerned.

7 There is no cash alternative in lieu of tickets or listed savings.

8 You are advised to check all relevant information with your chosen attraction before commencing your journey.

SPECIAL OFFER VOUCHER

One child free with every full paying adult

Weald & Downland Open Air Museum
Chichester PO18 0EU

SPECIAL OFFER VOUCHER

One child goes free

Wildfowl & Wetlands Trust
Slimbridge GL2 7BT

SPECIAL OFFER VOUCHER

£1 off purchased ticket (Max value £6)

West Somerset Railway
Minehead TA24 5BG

SPECIAL OFFER VOUCHER

Two for the price of one

World of Glass
St Helens WA10 1BX

South Shields Museum & Art Gallery

Special offer vouchers

VisitBritain Official Guides
Terms & Conditions for Attraction voucher

1 Not to be used with any other offer. No cash alternative. Photocopied vouchers not accepted. Voucher not for re-sale. Valid until 31 December 2007.

2 Each voucher entitles the holder to the discount specified by the selected attraction.

3 Valid for use until 31/10/2008 (unless otherwise specified, or if attraction season finishes prior to this). Vouchers are subject to the terms, conditions and restrictions of the selected attraction.

4 One voucher per party will be accepted and cannot be used in conjunction with any other offer. Photocopies will not be accepted.

5 All attractions offering a discount have confirmed their willingness to participate. All information is subject to change without notice and should any attraction close or decline to accept a voucher for any reason, VisitBritain is not liable and cannot be held responsible.

6 VisitBritain shall not accept liability for any loss, accident or injury that may occur at a participating attraction and any dispute must be settled direct with the attraction concerned.

7 There is no cash alternative in lieu of tickets or listed savings.

8 You are advised to check all relevant information with your chosen attraction before commencing your journey.

VisitBritain Official Guides
Terms & Conditions for Attraction voucher

1 Not valid for group bookings. No cash alternative. Not to be used with any offer.

2 Each voucher entitles the holder to the discount specified by the selected attraction.

3 Valid for use until 31/10/2008 (unless otherwise specified, or if attraction season finishes prior to this). Vouchers are subject to the terms, conditions and restrictions of the selected attraction.

4 One voucher per party will be accepted and cannot be used in conjunction with any other offer. Photocopies will not be accepted.

5 All attractions offering a discount have confirmed their willingness to participate. All information is subject to change without notice and should any attraction close or decline to accept a voucher for any reason, VisitBritain is not liable and cannot be held responsible.

6 VisitBritain shall not accept liability for any loss, accident or injury that may occur at a participating attraction and any dispute must be settled direct with the attraction concerned.

7 There is no cash alternative in lieu of tickets or listed savings.

8 You are advised to check all relevant information with your chosen attraction before commencing your journey.

VisitBritain Official Guides
Terms & Conditions for Attraction voucher

1 Valid until 31 December 2007. Not to be used in conjunction with any other offers.

2 Each voucher entitles the holder to the discount specified by the selected attraction.

3 Valid for use until 31/10/2008 (unless otherwise specified, or if attraction season finishes prior to this). Vouchers are subject to the terms, conditions and restrictions of the selected attraction.

4 One voucher per party will be accepted and cannot be used in conjunction with any other offer. Photocopies will not be accepted.

5 All attractions offering a discount have confirmed their willingness to participate. All information is subject to change without notice and should any attraction close or decline to accept a voucher for any reason, VisitBritain is not liable and cannot be held responsible.

6 VisitBritain shall not accept liability for any loss, accident or injury that may occur at a participating attraction and any dispute must be settled direct with the attraction concerned.

7 There is no cash alternative in lieu of tickets or listed savings.

8 You are advised to check all relevant information with your chosen attraction before commencing your journey.

VisitBritain Official Guides
Terms & Conditions for Attraction voucher

1 Not valid during special events or galas, shown as 'brown' dates on the WSR timetable.

2 Each voucher entitles the holder to the discount specified by the selected attraction.

3 Valid for use until 31/10/2008 (unless otherwise specified, or if attraction season finishes prior to this). Vouchers are subject to the terms, conditions and restrictions of the selected attraction.

4 One voucher per party will be accepted and cannot be used in conjunction with any other offer. Photocopies will not be accepted.

5 All attractions offering a discount have confirmed their willingness to participate. All information is subject to change without notice and should any attraction close or decline to accept a voucher for any reason, VisitBritain is not liable and cannot be held responsible.

6 VisitBritain shall not accept liability for any loss, accident or injury that may occur at a participating attraction and any dispute must be settled direct with the attraction concerned.

7 There is no cash alternative in lieu of tickets or listed savings.

8 You are advised to check all relevant information with your chosen attraction before commencing your journey.

Log on to **enjoyengland.com** to find a break that matches your mood. **experience** scenes that inspire and traditions that baffle. **discover** the world's most inventive cultural entertainment and most stimulating attractions. **explore** vibrant cities and rugged peaks. **relax** in a country pub or on a sandy beach.

 enjoyEngland.com

win
a full set of official
tourist board guides

Keep in touch and WIN a full set of 2007 official tourist board accommodation guides

VisitBritain would be delighted to hear what you think of this guide. Please complete the short questionnaire overleaf and send it back to us.

Questionnaires will be entered into a monthly draw to win a full set of 2007 official accommodation guides.

Title   First name

Surname

Address

Town/City   County

Postcode   Country

Mobile   Telephone

E-mail

Which age group are you in?
16-24 ❑   25-34 ❑   35-44 ❑   45-54 ❑   55-64 ❑   65+ ❑

When do you normally buy attraction guides? (please tick one box)
❑ Easter holidays
❑ Before main summer season, ie May
❑ Christmas/end of the year
❑ Anytime – planning a special occasion
❑ Anytime – planning a spontaneous occasion
❑ Anytime – planning a holiday
❑ Spontaneously purchased

How often do you buy attraction guides? (please tick one box)
❑ Every year
❑ Every 2 years
❑ Every 3 years
❑ Every 4 years
❑ Every 5 years
❑ Single purchase, ie I do not replace guide

Do you regularly use any other attraction guides? If yes, which ones?

What do you find useful about this official tourist board guide?

Is there any other information you would like to see added to this guide?

Would you like to be contacted by VisitBritain in future with news, ideas and special offers? Yes ❑ No ❑
Would you like to be contacted by VisitBritain's carefully chosen partners with news of more offers? Yes ❑ No ❑

Please complete, put in an envelope and return Freepost (no stamp required) **to:**

VisitBritain Commercial Publishing, Freepost RLXU–XLYY–UKLB
Thames Tower, Blacks Road, London W6 9EL

CUT ALONG LINE

enjoyEngland ™

Published by: VisitBritain, Thames Tower, Blacks Road, London W6 9EL
in partnership with England's tourism industry.
enjoyengland.com
Publishing Manager: Tess Lugos
Production Manager: Iris Buckley
Compilation, design, copywriting, production and advertisement sales:
Jackson Lowe, 3 St Andrews Place, Southover Road, Lewes,
East Sussex BN7 1UP
t (01273) 487487 jacksonlowe.com
Typesetting: Marlinzo Services, Somerset and Jackson Lowe
Maps: Based on digital map data © ESR Cartography, 2006
Printing and binding: Emirates Printing Press, Dubai, United Arab Emirates
Cover design: Jackson Lowe

Front cover: Oceanarium Bournemouth (oceanarium.co.uk)

Photography credits: Alton Towers; Bournemouth Oceanarium;
britainonview.com/Daniel Bosworth/Angus Bremner/Martin Brent/
brightononview/Rod Edwards/Adrian Houston/James McCormick/
McCormick-McAdam/Pawel Libera/Tony Pleavin/Grant Pritchard/
Ian Shaw; Caravan Club; Matt Cardy; Dorset County Council; East
Midlands Development Agency; Richard Foster rfoster@hop-skip-jump.com;
Killhope: The North of England Lead Mining Museum; Longleat
Enterprises Ltd; NTPL/Rob Judges; One NorthEast Tourism; Joan Russell;
Tyne & Wear Museums; Visit Southport/Chris Horan

© British Tourist Authority (trading as VisitBritain) 2007
ISBN 978-0-7095-8336-3

A VisitBritain Publishing guide

Key to attractions

Attractions are listed under the following categories within each county.

 Family fun

This category encompasses everything for thrills and spills all day long: theme parks, safari parks, farms, beaches, pools, adventure playgrounds, football stadium tours, railways, science centres – anything with the kids at heart!

 Nature and wildlife

Look out for this symbol if you enjoy the wide-open spaces of National Parks, country parks, forests and lakes, or the tranquillity of nature trails and formal gardens. The category also includes all sorts of animal attractions and nature reserves.

 Historic England

Brush up on your history with a visit to some of England's great historical sites. Choose from castles, cathedrals, palaces, ships and houses, to name but a few.

 Outdoor activities

For plenty of fresh air, this category is where you will find boat trips, ballooning and sporting activities.

 Entertainment and culture

This category includes arts centres, galleries and museums, as well as great entertainment venues, such as theatres, racecourses and ski slopes.

 Food and drink

Browse this category for a choice of eateries. It also includes pubs and vineyards for a pint of the local ale or a spot of wine tasting.

 Relaxing and pampering

This is the category for chilling out. Treat yourself at a spa or satisfy the shopaholic in you by browsing a selection of shopping centres, markets and craft centres.

 Look out, too, for the Quality Assured Visitor Attraction sign. This indicates that the attraction is assessed annually and meets the standards required to receive the quality marque. So rest assured, you'll have a great time.

Turn to the maps at the front of the guide to find the location of those attractions displaying a map reference.

The index on page 459 will help you to locate specific attractions with ease. For more great ideas for places to visit contact a local Tourist Information Centre or log on to **enjoyengland.com**.

Please note, as changes often occur after press date, it is advisable to confirm opening times and admission prices before travelling.

KEY TO ATTRACTIONS

Cafe/restaurant	☕
Picnic area	🛆
No dogs except service dogs	✕
Partial disabled access	♿
Full disabled access	♿

Where prices aren't specified, use the following guide for an adult admission:

£	up to £5
££	between £5 and £10
£££	between £10 and £15
££££	more than £15